THE TELECOMS TRADE WAR

The Telecoms Trade War

The United States, The European Union and the World Trade Organisation

by

MARK NAFTEL

Partner, Norton Rose, London

&

LAWRENCE J. SPIWAK

President, Phoenix Center for Advanced Legal and
Economic Public Policy Studies, Washington D.C.

Foreword by

Professor Lucien Rapp
University of Toulouse, France
Partner, Serra, Michaud et Associés, Paris

·HART·
PUBLISHING

OXFORD – PORTLAND OREGON
2000

Hart Publishing
Oxford and Portland, Oregon

Published in North America (US and Canada) by
Hart Publishing c/o
International Specialized Book Services
5804 NE Hassalo Street
Portland, Oregon
97213-3644
USA

Distributed in the Netherlands, Belgium and Luxembourg by
Intersentia, Churchillaan 108
B2900 Schoten
Antwerpen
Belgium

Hart Publishing Ltd is a specialist legal publisher based in Oxford, England.
To order further copies of this book or to request a list of other
publications please write to:

Hart Publishing Ltd, Salter's Boatyard, Folly Bridge,
Abingdon Road, Oxford OX1 4LB
Telephone: +44 (0)1865 245533 or Fax: (0)1865 794882
e-mail: mail@hartpub.co.uk
WEBSITE: http//www.hartpub.co.uk

British Library Cataloguing in Publication Data
Data Available
ISBN 1–84113–014–1 (hardback)

Typeset by Hope Services (Abingdon) Ltd.
Printed and bound in Great Britain on acid-free paper by
Biddles Ltd, www.biddles.co.uk

To our wives for their unconditional love and support,
and to our children, who must live tomorrow
in the world we create today.

"Those who love both laws and sausages
shall inquire how neither are made."

Otto Von Bismark

". . . it is always from a minority acting in ways different from what the
majority would prescribe that the majority in the end learns to do better."

F. A. Hayek

Foreword

THE TELECOMS TRADE WAR by Mark Naftel and Lawrence J. Spiwak is a truly revolutionary—and indeed unique—book. Rather than attempt to provide yet another hornbook on US and European telecoms law, the authors instead contribute to the public dialectic by seeking to expose the recent "cynical" attempts to substitute political trade policies for sound legal and economic telecommunications policy. Since both authors bring to this work of great scope a convinced obstinacy of demonstration and a real intelligence of all political, legal, economical and industrial matters relating to international telecommunications, their work demands respect. I sincerely recommend this book to all governments, regulators, competent international organisations officials, and also all concerned citizens who should not remain strangers to this important subject.

With restructuring and liberalisation of telecommunications markets during the past few years, it should be considered whether commercial conflicts among nations have disappeared and been replaced by competition among companies. Does the World Trade Organisation Agreement on Basic Telecommunications, effective from February 1998, appear, despite its insufficiencies, as a peace treaty concluded to permit the development of wide open relationships among the signatories? Are telecommunications markets really now free and competitive on an international basis?

Moreover, how does this growing trade war impact the growth of the Internet? The Internet explores obviously new spaces of liberty, but poses, crucially, the question of how to organise the conditions of its usage so that it does not constrain liberty itself. What difference exists between the prehistoric man setting up new tools for hunting or for war and the show given nowadays by our societies, confronted by the excesses of the Internet—from spamming to misuse of personal data, violations of intellectual property rights and so forth? Apparently none. So, where is progress?

The question could remain philosophical if it has not been already influencing social and international relations. This raises the question of whether and how we should regulate the Internet.

This question is where the debate takes an international dimension—in the absence of international conventions, nations create their own policy on the basis of national sovereignty, and this in turn remains the legal basis of international law and society.

This goes beyond telecommunications networks. Already we see circulation of black lists, denouncing States whose regulation is obviously insufficient, just as the worst times in history when informing was considered as proper. But how different could it be, considering there are no adapted rules in this area?

It is precisely these assertions, very generally expanded, that Naftel and Spiwak strongly challenge. In other words, Naftel and Spiwak convincingly illustrate that the market is neither free nor competitive—it is perverted by an approach denounced by the authors as "neo-mercantilism" in the meaning given by Adam Smith. The necessary protection of consumers is neglected by this neo-mercantilist policy.

The work of Naftel and Spiwak reminds us all that fundamental questions still need to be answered regarding telecommunications restructuring and competition.[1] What is competition in the domain of telecommunications? The fundamental scope of any restructuring policy in this sector of activity, being primordial in the economic order, must search for the erosion of the beneficiary margins or monopoly rents. Prices will thereby align with costs and permit the maximum circulation of the technical improvements. It stakes out the widest, domestic or international, opening of the market.

As the authors amply demonstrate and prove through many examples in this book, however, the on-going "telecoms trade war" turns these first principles on their collective head. Neo-mercantilism leads to statutory policies essentially marked by the protection of national interests. Market openings imply accessibility from the outside. National regulation today produces entry barriers— technical barriers to the intra-operability of infrastructures by a restrictive interconnection plan, economic barriers by a dissuasive system of settlement rates, exclusively made for the protection of the State's sovereign interests, legal barriers by a regulation of foreign investments, all the more inadequate since the telecommunications systems tend to become general and therefore, ignore frontiers.

Naftel and Spiwak make their points through comparing US and EU policies and mistakes. This is one of the virtues of the work, in addition to the mastery of the subject matter the authors demonstrate. The analysis escapes being too "American centric," and is placed somewhere in the Atlantic Ocean, half way between the political turbulences of the old and the new continent. By attempting to find uniform examples and principles, for example by reviewing EU and US approaches in similar areas, the authors contribute an innovative and significant perspective to the public dialectic.[2]

The first three sections of the book set the stage of the telecoms trade war in painstaking detail. To drive their points home, the fourth section of the book

---

[1] The method employed should be the same as the primordial questions marked out by the masterpiece of Siéyès' "What is Third Estate?" written on the eve of the French Revolution (1789). The immediate questions were: "1. What is Third Estate? Everything. 2. What role has it been playing in the economic order until now? None. 3. What is it asking for? Becoming something."

[2] Emmanuel Kohnstamm, vice-president of Time Warner Inc. in Brussels, perhaps gave the best characterisation of the traditional differences which separate the European people from their North-American counterparts in the approach of the legal problem of State and liberty: "In Europe, people don't trust companies, they trust government; in the US, it's the opposite way around: Citizens must be protected from actions of the government." Stephen Baker et al., "Europe's Privacy Cops", *Business Week*, 2 Nov. 1998 at 21.

provides a series of case studies illustrating policies that are so outlandish that neophytes would believe to be fiction, rather than accepting them as a tragic reality. Given my personal significant background in the satellite industry, I found the authors' exegesis on the FCC's international spectrum policies particularly compelling. Indeed, after reading Naftel and Spiwak's case study, how could we not be astonished by the difficulties encountered by all the operators of the satellite systems (Iridium, ICO and in a lesser level, Skybridge or Teledesic)? Beyond the costs of purchasing frequency rights through auction and actually deploying their satellites and services, the operators had to contend with regulatory barriers and interference, to the extent of incurring re-location costs for other operators. This is in addition to burdens such as limiting "foreign" ownership to 20 per cent, extraordinary licensing costs and so forth. Unfortunately, the same mistakes seem to be occurring with the grant of third generation mobile licenses in the United States and Europe.

In addressing such problems, Naftel and Spiwak's work is infused both with an energy of conviction yet a sadness at the present state of affairs. Although the current wind of "political cynicism" may try to drown out the authors' impassioned cry, all of is must strain to listen and accept their message. Although it is not too late to pay attention, this may be our last chance to affect meaningfully the emerging market structure of the telecoms industry and to maximise consumer welfare. I sincerely hope that many will be convinced and join their cause before the current "telecoms trade war" ruins any chance of progress towards peace.

Lucien Rapp
Professor of Public Law, University of Toulouse (France).
Partner, Serra, Michaud et Associés, Paris.

Preface

Given the lightning pace of change in the the telecoms industry, writing a book on the current status of the relevant laws and regulation is virtually an impossible (and, moreover, probably useless) task. Indeed, given personal experience, we are confident that some major regulatory initiative from either Washington or Brussels will no doubt come out just after we have submitted this manuscript for publication and before the ink is dry on the first print edition of this book.

For this reason, we decided not to write a strict hornbook of international telecoms law and regulation. Rather, we decided to take an alternative approach to this topic, and instead explore the respective efforts of the United States (US) and the European Union (EU) to implement the World Trade Organisation (WTO) Basic Agreement on Telecommunications Services, and how these initiatives to open up local markets affect markets for international telecoms services. As such, because economic theory is not bound by geographic borders, we will switch, as appropriate, between US and EU law as circumstances merit.

As we researched and wrote this book, we hoped to be able to tell our readers an uplifting story on about how the world was marching over the "bridge to the 21st Century" and into the "information society." Instead, we discovered two disturbing trends in recent telecoms regulation and competition law enforcement: (1) a growing telecoms trade war that is dangerously close to spinning out of hand; and (2), given the first point, a growing politicisation of, and cynicism towards, the regulatory process generally. Under both scenarios, therefore, we find that many regulatory initiatives post-WTO harm—rather than appropriately maximise—consumer welfare.

To explore these issues in detail, this book is divided into four parts.

In Part I, we set forth the analytical framework we use to analyse the growing telecoms trade war specifically and growing cynicism of the regulatory process generally.

In chapter 1, "Telecoms Policy for a New Millennium," we explore the growing telecoms trade war and show that trade has no place in regulatory decision-making. Moreover, we show that many policy-makers have no real desire to promote tangible competition. Instead, they are more interested in creating "fair, competition-type outcomes accompanied by the benevolent use of 'market-friendly regulation.'" As such, because many policy-makers perceive erroneously competition as a "zero-sum game" (i.e., the discredited notion that one firm can be made better off only if another firm can be made worse off), there is little opportunity or incentive to maximise consumer welfare.

In chapter 2, given the analysis in chapter 1, we ask the basic question: Why restructure in the first instance? Is it really to maximise consumer welfare, or are we just interested in reallocating rents from one party to another? As we explain, if the ostensible goal of restructuring is to move from a market characterised by monopoly (i.e., one firm) to a market characterised by competition (i.e., many firms), then policy-makers must affirmatively and aggressively promote new facilities-based entry. To help illustrate this point, we set forth the "Entry Condition" as an analytical framework to help determine whether, given a particular set of circumstances, new firms will find it profitable to enter and competition to occur. As we see once again, however, many regulators have been averse to promoting new entry to the detriment of consumer welfare.

In chapter 3, we set forth what we believe to be the appropriate analytical framework to assess the expanding restructuring process. Indeed, we try to go beyond the rhetoric and—in this era of convergence—explore how we should think about the market given the current technological developments. Among other things, we recommend that policy-makers should not only take a static review of the market as they currently find it but, as telecoms is an industry characterised by rapid technological change, also undertake a dynamic approach. Moreover, given such potential for change, we also caution against the use of overly broad—and, more importantly, overly narrow—market definitions and, *a fortiori*, exaggerations of the relevance of the Herfindahl-Hirschman Index (HHI) as a measure of market power. Finally, we outline what we believe is the appropriate role of regulation and competition law in this process, and examine the various tools government has at its disposal to make this restructuring process a success.

In chapter 4, "Evaluating Competition in a Post-WTO World," we return to first principles and examine some of the salient economic characteristics of various telecommunications markets using the Structure-Conduct-Performance ("SCP") paradigm of industrial organisation economics as an analytical "checklist." In so doing, we can attempt to glean an accurate picture of where these markets are currently and are likely to go in the future.

Section I of this book concludes with chapter 5, in which we explore the specific provisions of the WTO and the Basic Agreement on Telecommunications Services and, in particular, how the "telecoms trade war" fits into the larger trade skirmishes now raging among the community of nations. In addition, given many people's misconception of how the WTO process actually works, we briefly examine what the WTO does and, just as importantly, what it does not. Finally, in light of the specific provisions of the WTO, we seek to explore exactly what policy goals the WTO intended originally to achieve and the resulting market structure it hopes to produce.

From this analytical predicate, parts II and III of this book examine the respective efforts of the US and the EU to implement the WTO and promote international telecommunications competition.

Part II examines US efforts to promote both domestic and international telecoms competition. Chapter 6 begins with an analysis of the Federal Communications Commission's (FCC's) *International Carrier Paradigm*, which was nothing more that the FCC's introduction of its domestic *"Competitive Carrier"* paradigm to the international market. This decision marks the first clear statement by the FCC that, with proper regulatory incentives and constraints, it was possible to promote competition for international service—in addition to domestic long-distance service. Despite this constructive start, however, this Chapter concludes with an analysis of the FCC's *"Effective Competitive Opportunities"* analysis for international service applications. Although the FCC claimed that this policy would both promote entry by US carriers on the foreign end and also promote foreign entry into the US market, in reality this decision marked the debut of naked (of course, relative to the commonly accepted, historically implicit) trade concerns—rather than consumer concerns—as the top priority for FCC international policies.

In chapters 7 and 8, we discuss probably the most contentious battle in the growing telecoms trade war—the FCC's unilateral decision to impose settlement rate benchmarks on the rest of the international community. Claiming that such "competitive safeguards" were necessary because it did not trust the rest of the WTO community to meaningfully enforce their respective Member Commitments, the next two chapters show that both the FCC's economic rational behind these actions and the legal justification upholding the FCC's orders were at best flimsy. We also show the naked politicisation of the American legal system by demonstrating that the judicial decision upholding the FCC's action not only ignored numerous areas of well-settled jurisprudence, but also lacked the professional courtesy of even citing the International Telecommunication Union's charter and name correctly.

In chapter 9, which we call "Do as I Say, Not as I Do", we examine the FCC's efforts to promote local competition in US markets. As we show in this chapter, the FCC's actions since the passage of the US Telecommunications Act of 1996 reveal that it has absolutely no vision of an efficient, long-term industry market structure. Instead, all we see is a cynical regulatory *quid pro quo* between incumbents and new entrants, leaving the maximisation of consumer welfare out of the question entirely. To facilitate this analysis, we explore in this chapter the underlying theory of unbundling, and examine how the FCC has perverted this theory to such a significant degree as to make tangible facilities-based competition a far-off ephemeral dream. To further give some context to the FCC's recent actions, we also compare the FCC's actions today to the FCC's successful efforts to restructure the US long-distance markets in the early 1980's.

In part III, we cross the Atlantic and examine whether EU telecommunications policies have promoted competition. This part III begins with chapter 10, where we look at the foundations and institutions of the EU, as well as its important competition policy. Telecommunications competition in Europe happened largely through application of EU competition law to the sector so a thorough understanding of EU law and policy—particularly regarding findings of dominance and the curious EU essential facilities doctrine—is necessary for an appreciation of how the EU arrived at where it is today regarding telecommunications competition and regulation.

In chapter 11, we look at the EU's first efforts towards promotion of telecommunications competition, beginning with a judicial examination of competition, continuing through the European Commission's seminal *Telecommunications Green Paper*, and the first wave of Directives mandating competition in telecommunications equipment and services.

In chapter 12, we examine how well the EU framework is working. Real-life examples are closely examined in: the European Commission's efforts to bring down international calling prices through the promotion of international interconnection, the European Commission's and the European Court of Justice's application and interpretation of the concept of "special and exclusive rights"; the EU's Telecommunications Access Notice and finally the European Commission's on-going efforts to force incumbent telecommunications operators to unbundle local loops for competitor use.

In chapter 13, we look at the EU's approach to the Internet, contrasting the EU's Information Society outlook with the US-styled Information Superhighway. Europe lags behind the US in terms of Internet penetration and use, a matter of great concern to Europe's political leaders. What, if anything, governments can or should do about this situation is problematic, but policies designed to promote Internet penetration are coming to the fore in the EU nevertheless. This chapter examines the EU's Internet policies to date, specifically regarding possible regulation of Internet telephony, data protection (an area where the EU leads the world), and e-commerce initiatives.

In chapter 14, we examine the future of EU telecommunications regulation as expressed in the 1999 Telecommunications Review. This policy document makes many of the right noises in favour of consumer welfare, but the proof will be in what actually emerges from the political process over the following months.

In part IV, we examine various "hot spots" of contention in the growing "Telecoms Trade War," such as universal service, cable landing petitions, international spectrum issues, and regulatory and competition law authority review of international mergers, acquisitions and joint ventures.

In chapter 15, we compare and contrast the United States' and the European Union's approach to universal service, an area where the worst regulatory cynicism on the part of US officials may be observed. The actions of US regulators in imposing a huge tax in the name of universal service, in the form of the so-called e-rate, on all US interstate telecommunications providers, constitutes a huge dead-weight loss on the market. This is an expense that must be paid by all market participants and therefore consumers, all for the sake of a few politicians to score points by having their pictures taken with "kids 'n computers." More importunately, however, we also show that the improper politicisation of US universal service policies significantly deter new entry, thus rendering the entire process of universal service a self-defeating exercise. In contrast, the EU understands what universal service is all about, and has taken effective steps to reduce its application to what is essential. The result is that only one EU nation, France, even has a universal service fund today. This is a chance for the EU to steal a march on the US, whose telecommunications markets are now weighed down with an expensive universal service tax that in reality has nothing to do with universal service.

In chapter 16, we examine US international satellite spectrum policies. This chapter seeks to address a very simple and direct question: if the community of nations has made a collective decision that a vibrant global commercial satellite market is in the public interest, then why is the US, via the FCC, threatening to kill this industry (including America's own significant private space industry) by forcing new entrants into international satellite markets to pay spectrum relocation fees just as new entrants had to pay in the US domestic PCS context. Such a "cookie-cutter" approach to spectrum management is *per se* arbitrary and capricious, however, because what is good for the US domestic wireless industry is *not a fortiori* good for the international commercial satellite industry as well. While it is true that there are certain valuable lessons that can be learned from the US domestic experience and applied to the international market, because the domestic and international markets (as the FCC often readily admits) have very different structural economic characteristics, these markets therefore do not warrant homogeneous regulatory treatment.

In chapter 17, we examine how something as seemingly innocuous and ministerial as undersea cable landing petitions can become a major battleground in the growing telecoms trade war. Among other case studies, we examine the recent case of the Japan US Cable Consortium's petition to land a cable upon US shores. This case represents a textbook example of regulatory cynicism, not because of the merits of the case, but because it represents the epitome of how political connections and the "revolving door" are becoming more important than the law, economic theory, or even the facts.

In chapter 18, we examine how international mergers and acquisitions have become favourite forums to advance trade concerns. It appears impossible for enforcement officials in both the US and the EU to avoid the temptation to regulate through merger review. Given the incredible number of recent mergers in the telecommunications industry, enforcement officials are like children in a candy store. Although some mergers may alter market conditions so as to call for restructuring mergers or radical regulatory remedies, often enforcement officials engage in the worst forms of mercantilist aggression against foreign interests. This chapter gives a detailed look at how recent significant attempts at global, multi-national mergers in the telecommunications industry have fared under multi-jurisdictional review.

We realise that some readers may meet our analysis with incredulity. Readers should note, however, that the criticisms levelled in this book are not intended to be partisan in any way. Instead, we are just trying to report accurately recent developments as they occurred.

In a similar vein, nothing contained in this book should be read to mean that we think all people working in government service are regulatory megalomaniacs who could care less about the outcome of their actions. Both of us have had the privilege of working closely with regulatory staffers during the events described in this book (in fact, one of us worked for over five years in the FCC's now defunct Competition Division) and we know of many people in government who are trying to do the right thing in the face of intense political pressure.

In sum, given the huge societal implications raised by telecommunications restructuring, any discussion of these complex issues must be approached with the solemnity and seriousness they deserve. Indeed, the issues we talk about in this book literally affect the lives of *billions* of people around the globe and, therefore, cannot be taken lightly by any of the stakeholders in the debate. For these reasons, we intend this book to be provocative, because we do not like what we see. Certainly, we do not believe our story to be a pleasant tale, but we do believe it to be an accurate one. We hope that in exposing this growing cynicism, policy-makers will return to their prime directive and original mandate— *the maximisation of consumer welfare.*

Contents

PART II: US EFFORTS TO PROMOTE TELECOMS COMPETITION

Acknowledgements

We hope that readers will find this book both educational and enlightening. Given the provocative nature of our book, however, it is important at the outset for us to disclaim that the views expressed herein are ours exclusively, and do not represent the views of either: (a) the Phoenix Center, its adjunct fellows, or any of its individual editorial advisory board members; (b) Norton Rose and any of its partners and staff; or (c) any of our respective clients.

This being said, we nonetheless received invaluable insights and suggestions from a wide variety of friends and colleagues in the process of writing this book. As such, we thank from the bottom of our collective hearts: Bernard Amory, Bob Berger, Richard Cawley, Kevin Coates, Fran Coleman, Richard Dammery, Jerry Duvall, Jim Earl, Jade Eaton, Dan Fling, George Ford, Gitte Forsberg, David Graham, Jason Hoida, Flemming Dehn Jespersen, Valentine Korah, Tom Koutsky, Jeff Lanning, Scott Marcus, Barry Mendelsohn, Doug Metcalfe, Kent Nakamura, Kent Nilsson, Rick Oliver, Sam Paltridge, Lucien Rapp, Patrick Rey, Alan Silverstein, Hal Varian and Glen Woroch. All of their respective contributions made the drafting process a far more focused and effective effort.

Finally, and most significantly of all, we again want to thank our wives and kids for putting up with us during the writing process.

JMN & LJS

Table of Abbreviations

SMATV	Single Mast Antenna TV
TELRIC	Total Service Long Run Incremental Cost
TRIPS	(Agreement on Trade-Related Aspects of Intellectual Property Rights)
UMTS	Universal Mobile Telecommunications System
UNEs	Unbundled Network Elements
USO	Universal Service Obligation
WATS	Wide Area Telecommunications Service
WTO	World Trade Organisation
xDSL	Generic Digital Subscriber Line Service

PART I

ANALYTICAL AND LEGAL FRAMEWORK

1

Telecoms Policy for the New Millennium

I. INTRODUCTION

IF ONE WERE to believe the politicians and pundits in the trade press, as a result of the 1997 World Trade Agreement on Basic Telecommunications Services, the world is ostensibly is in midst of a "telecoms revolution." This may be true. Unfortunately, however, the actions of many regulators and competition law enforcement agencies more accurately reveal not a telecoms "revolution" but instead a growing telecoms *trade war* that is dangerously close to spiralling out of hand.

That is to say, over the last several years, people have realised around the globe that it is, in fact, possible to have competition in the telecoms industry and, with such competition, maximise consumer welfare on a wide variety of levels. What we show in this book, however, is that this basic idea has become, in many instances, so perverted by naked cynicism and political narcissism as to make the maximisation of consumer welfare an almost Quixotic ideal. In our view, despite the appearance of "short-term" achievements,[1] it is actually the heretofore unimaginable cynical and cavalier approach to towards the regulatory process and competition law enforcement—and its concurrent adverse effect on market structure—which harms consumer welfare in the long-run. Moreover, this growing mercantile "Telecoms Trade War" spills over onto other areas of international trade, damaging consumer welfare even further.

Accordingly, the criticisms levelled in this book should not be taken to mean that we are somehow against lowering settlement rates or opening up markets. That argument simply is not true, and to defend these regulators' actions against our analysis in such a way would be just another typical and cheap *ad hominem* attack. As explained passim, we are dismayed by the huge degree of the blatant politicisation of the process and the removal of any form

---

[1] For example, the United States claims that as the result of its aggressive international telecoms policies, international calling rates have fallen dramatically. While rates have indeed fallen over the last several years, can the FCC really claim primary credit? No. On one hand, restructuring initiatives were already well underway in many parts of Europe and elsewhere (e.g., the UK, New Zealand) well before the FCC started to proscribe settlement rate benchmarks for US carriers. Similarly, with the WTO, other Member Countries are starting to follow suit. On the other hand, telecoms is a declining cost industry and, as such, a monopolist will still lower its price *sua sponte* if its underlying costs decrease. As such the real question posited by this book is whether the FCC's policies will lead to sustained competition in the long run.

of analytical foundation from policy decision-making, because in the absence of such a foundation, policy-making is now conducted in an environment akin to "Alice through the Looking-Glass." Given such a cynical environment, there is no constituency (or even ability) for discussing these issues rationally by applying the law and economic theory to the facts. Instead, it is far easier just to engage in "litigation by Rolodex."

This is not to say that politics never play a role in the process and to argue otherwise is both naïve and unrealistic. One theme that is constant around the world is that consumers consider the telecoms business—unlike the wheat market or car industry—to a higher degree, and politicians around the world respond as such. However, if we truly want to maximise consumer welfare in the long run, then we must not sacrifice sustainable competition just to give the appearance of immediate competition in the present. Remember, when everyone is just reselling the exact same service from the exact same provider, "choices" are just not the same as "competition." If we really want restructuring to work therefore, then policy-makers will have to show both leadership and political will in the on-going public policy debate.[2]

II. WHY REGULATION AND TRADE POLICY JUST DON'T MIX

Over 200 years ago, Adam Smith, in his classic treatise *The Wealth of Nations*, powerfully demonstrated that whenever government attempts to co-ordinate the efforts of entrepreneurs, such policies almost invariably discourage economic growth and reduce economic well-being. Smith called this system "mercantilism."[3] Over the last eight years, however, many governments have improperly introduced trade considerations into both competition law enforcement and regulatory rulemakings and adjudications as a legitimate public interest factor.[4] By improperly attempting to reintroduce mercantilism under a new guise of "fair trade" in the "global economy", all that has been accom-

---

[2] See, e.g., Kevin J. Delaney, "France Government Withdraws an Amendment on Local Calls", *Wall Street Journal* 27 April 2000 (reporting that the French government withdrew a legislative amendment that would have opened France Telecom to new competition via unbundling following a request by Communist Party leaders).

[3] See James C. Miller et al., "Industrial Policy: Reindustrialization Through Competition or Co-ordinated Action?" (1984) 2 *Yale J. on Reg.* 1 at 5.

According to Adam Smith, mercantilism "retards, instead of accelerating, the progress of the society towards real wealth and greatness; and diminishes, instead of increasing, the real value of the annual produce of its land and labour" for two basic reasons: a tendency of special interests to turn government programs to their own narrow advantages, and a tendency of joint business efforts to result in collusion to reduce output and raise prices, especially when government willingly permits such collusion. As such, although "the law cannot hinder people of the same trade from sometimes assembling together, it ought to do nothing to facilitate such assemblies; much less to render them necessary." (Citations omitted.) It would seem, therefore, that "FCC" should not stand for "Facilitating Cartels and Collusion."

[4] See Catherine Yang, "Commentary: When Protectionism Wears Camouflage", *Business Week*, 2 June 1997, at 60.

plished is the re-baptism of Smith's original concept of mercantilism into the new, but equally flawed, "neo-mercantilism."[5] Yet, as trade concerns become an acceptable factor in competition law and regulatory lexicon, not one proponent of "neo-mercantilism" school has bothered to demonstrate what economic conditions have actually changed since Smith was alive that would merit a departure from his work.[6]

As a general proposition, it is very important to recognise that competition law and trade policy seek to promote *very* different goals. Antitrust and competition law policy appropriately focuses on *consumers*, not competitors. Trade policy, on the other hand, by its very definition, seeks to promote *competitors* (i.e., competitors of the "domestic" sort). Thus, while competition law is certainly one of a number of policies affecting international trade, the various national trade policies (which are very often not even in harmony with each other) may at times be in tension with competition law policies.[7]

This reasoning should apply equally to economic regulatory paradigms. For example, in the case of the United States, the US Supreme Court holds that administrative agencies responsible for economic regulation must

> "make findings related to the pertinent antitrust policies, draw conclusions from the findings, and weigh these conclusions along with other important public interest considerations."[8]

When the case law and economic literature are reviewed, these "other public interest considerations" should be limited to identifying and eliminating "policy-relevant" barriers to entry. Thus, because economic regulators also have responsibility for maximising consumer welfare, and therefore these regulators—just as under antitrust jurisprudence—are similarly "not at liberty to subordinate the public interest to the interest of equalising competition among competitors,"[9] trade considerations correspondingly should not be a legitimate "public interest factor" in regulatory decision-making. Unfortunately, research reveals that both competition law enforcement agencies and economic regulators on both sides of the Atlantic often lately are ignoring this basic principle.[10]

[5] See, e.g., Miller, *supra* n. 3 (doctrine of "neo-mercantilism" can be characterised as the principle that "in a world of monopolies, the nation with the biggest and strongest industries and firms can reign supreme and recoup for the mother country the supra-competitive profits earned from abroad").

[6] See Paul Magnusson, "Getting a Grip on Trade Sanctions", *Business Week*, 17 Nov. 1997, at 115. Magnusson reports that in the past four years, President Clinton has signed 62 laws and executive actions targeting 35 countries. These numbers account "for more than half the sanctions imposed [by the US] *in the past 80 years*." Moreover, Magnusson reported that the direct cost to US exporters in lost sales in 1995 alone was as high as $20 billion, an estimated 250,000 US jobs disappeared and "*no one can measure the damage to relations with angry allies.*" (Emphasis supplied.)

[7] See Antitrust Law Developments (Fourth) 991 (American Bar Association, 1997).

[8] See, e.g., *Gulf States Utilities Company* v. *FPC*, 411 U.S. 747, 755–62 (1973); see also *United States* v. *FCC*, 652 F.2d 72, 81–82 (D.C. Cir. 1980) (en banc) (quoting *Northern Natural Gas Co.* v. *FPC*, 399 F.2d 953, 961 (D.C. Cir. 1968)).

[9] See *SBC Communications* v. *FCC*, 56 F.3d 1484 (D.C. Cir. 1995).

[10] As noted in n. 3 *supra*, the rise of neo-mercantilism is clearly originating from the Executive Branch of the U.S. Government. See generally Clay Chandler, "Will the [National Economic

Many people nonetheless respond that there is absolutely no reason to be concerned about this recent "neo-mercantilist" influence on antitrust and "public interest" adjudications. They are wrong.

For example, once trade concerns enter regulatory decision-making, a "reciprocity" approach actually *creates*—rather than eliminates—significant barriers to entry for both new foreign firms into domestic telecommunications markets *and* domestic firms into foreign markets. Specifically, by adopting an aggressive "my country first" approach, both foreign governments and carriers will probably have a (if not exacerbating an existing) substantial *disincentive* to engage in good faith negotiations with domestic carriers to enter their home markets (which, paradoxically, is supposed to be the whole goal of such an approach in the first place).[11]

For example, take the case of international interconnection rates which, to state it politely, still remain high in many parts of the world. In many of these countries, however, regulators nonetheless want to do the proverbial "right thing" and lower these rates (because they know that their constituents would benefit from such an action). Yet, just when these regulators are building sufficient internal political consensus to lower interconnection rates, the FCC aggressively orders the international telecoms community to comply with *its* settlement rate benchmarks or be prohibited from delivering traffic to the US. In so doing, the FCC's aggressive actions have obliterated any internal political consensus to lower rates, because fighting the "Great Satan's" aggressive and mercantile policies has transformed the debate into a matter of national pride rather than an examination of sound economic principles.

Moreover, international commerce, by its very definition, raises far more

Council] Continue to be Clinton's Neglected Child?", *Washington Post*, 9 Nov. 1996, at H01, reporting that President Clinton often rewarded advisors seeking to circumvent the NEC and the specific advice of his chief economist, Laura D'Andrea-Tyson—e.g., when USTR Ambassador Mickey Kantor pushed Clinton directly to take a much tougher line with Japan in a dispute over auto exports. Just to refresh everyone's collective memory, this was the dispute where, at Detroit's urging, the US threatened to slap a 100 per cent tariff on all Japanese luxury cars—thus potentially throwing thousands of Americans who work at Lexus and Infinity dealerships out of jobs—if Japan did not permit Detroit to sell its cars in Tokyo. As this passion play was carried out, however, all of the Mercedes, Porche, BMW, Saab, Volvo, Jaguar, et al. dealerships were standing in the wings, chuckling at the notion that Detroit manufacturers actually believed that only they would gain US market share if the U.S. government removed their Japanese rivals from the market. See also Bob Woodward & Ann Devroy, "An Unusual Meeting of Chief Executives", *Washington Post*, 21 Aug. 1997, at A01 (reporting that when Tyson, fearing a trade war between Washington and Tokyo, objected to private, one-on-one meeting between President Clinton and Federal Express Chairman Fred Smith (who, along with Fed Ex, coincidentally just donated $275,000 to the Democratic National Committee) to discuss Fed Ex's trade concerns with Japan, D'Andrea-Tyson's objections were specifically overridden by former Clinton Chief of Staff and close personal friend Thomas "Mack" McLarty).

[11] See Miller, *supra* n. 3; see also Albert P. Halprin, "Two Steps Backward on Open Markets", *New York Times*, 20 July 1997, at F13 (FCC simply "wants to keep its ability to treat foreign carriers worse than its own domestic carriers—though this is exactly what the United States and 68 countries in Geneva promised not to do"—and a policy that will "delay other nations' entry into our market by months, if not years, while allowing identical investments by U.S. carriers to proceed immediately. *Free trade delayed is free trade denied.*" (emphasis in original and supplied)).

investment risks than domestic commerce does (e.g., through different or ineffective legal systems, political graft and retroactive or *post-hoc* "windfall" taxes). In order to reflect this risk, the prices for international goods that require the investment of substantial sunk costs are usually higher. An aggressive trade approach, therefore, merely exacerbates the possibility that a foreign country may, in an act of trade retaliation, "nationalise" a firm's sunk assets—often without adequate compensation.[12] This "uncertainty" can raise prices for consumers in two ways. first, the greater the risk, the higher a firm's cost of capital becomes; as a firm's cost of capital becomes higher, end-user prices for consumers increase. Second, as risk increases, a firm will have a greater incentive to *raise* its prices to ensure that it can recover its costs in the shortest time possible.[13]

More importantly, however, it is quite unclear how lower prices and new products and services—even if provided by foreign firms—are actually *bad* for domestic consumers.[14] Indeed, as former United States Federal Trade Commissioner Jim Miller noted well over ten years ago, in order for a dominant foreign firm to successfully lever its dominant foreign position to predate and take over the domestic industry, the targeted industry must be able to recoup its losses either by driving out its rivals in the domestic market and then charging consumers supra-competitive prices or by capturing monopoly rents from its home market. According to Miller,

> "to succeed just in the mother country is not enough. In fact, that would be counterproductive, since the losers would be that nation's own consumers and taxpayers, who must pay higher prices and underwrite the subsidies."

Moreover, if the attempted predation fails, the gainers would be "the consumers, the public, in those other nations, including the United States, whose industries have been targeted" because consumers would get the "benefits of lower prices."[15] As such, Miller argues,

---

[12] For example, take the hypothetical case (although loosely based on truth) where a foreign country, after nationalising substantial sunk assets, simply informed its investors that while it is a poor country (and therefore has no money to compensate its investors with), it nonetheless wanted to compensate its investors with its leading export: canned corned-beef. As such, the country provided its investors with a large container ship filled to the brim with canned corn beef that the investors were supposed to sell on the open market for whatever amount they could get.

[13] See Miller et al., *supra* n. 3. Moreover, retaliation can lead to violence as well. After all, it really is rather difficult to have a true "trade war" unless some kind of violence is actually involved. See, e.g., Paul Bluestein, "U.S. Plans to Ban Ships, Pushed Japan to Act", *Washington Post*, 19 Oct. 1997, at AO1 (Clinton Administration calls out the U.S. Coast Guard to enforce reciprocity policies against Japan in harbour dispute).

[14] See Robert Eisner, "A Free Trade Primer", *Wall Street Journal*, 13 Oct. 1997, at A22; James K. Glassman, "Consumers First", *Washington Post*, 24 Oct. 1997, at A21 ("If we make it easy for Italy to export inexpensive shoes to us, the U.S. shoemakers may have to find work in other fields. But, meanwhile, the 260 million Americans who wear shoes everyday get a bargain. The money they save can be used to buy other things and start businesses, such as software, in which Americans have a clear advantage").

[15] See Miller, *supra* n. 3 (citations omitted).

"*Why kick Santa Claus in the fact?* If other countries foolishly subsidise US consumers . . . why should we object? It could only be a distortion of our economy if they had any chance to achieve monopoly power to recoup the subsidies we would now be enjoying."[16]

Yet, according to the FCC's own words, this recoupment is not to happen anytime soon in US telecommunications markets.[17]

Finally, a naked reciprocity approach ignores basic concepts of international comity. At the end of the day, no one would disagree that open markets are the best way to maximise consumer welfare. Yet there are numerous countries that are, to state it politely, a bit recalcitrant to open their markets. So long as these foreign incumbents' monopoly power remains unchecked, therefore, they can engage in "whipsawing" (i.e., play competing foreign carriers off against each other to drive up the interconnection rate) and other numerous price and non-price discrimination strategies against or among another country's carriers.

Unfortunately, in these situations, basic international law is pretty clear about enforcement options: barring evidence that one country is using its territory to stage a military attack against another, a country may not interfere in the internal domestic affairs of another.[18] Thus, the best way to mitigate unilateral, strategic anticompetitive conduct for IMTS service is to convince the recalcitrant country to establish, *inter alia*, standard, cost-based interconnection rates and—especially as IMTS market structure rapidly moves away from a "half circuit" toward a "full circuit" world between country-pairs—termination rates, along with transparent regulation to mitigate against non-price discrimination. This is precisely what the hard-fought WTO agreement (mainly at US insistence) achieves. As such, from an economic point of view, if there are standard cost-based interconnection rates and other adequate regulatory safeguards in the foreign destination market, whether or not the originating country's carrier has the ability to set up a rival network in the destination country should be

---

[16] *Ibid.*, (emphasis supplied).

[17] See *Access Charge Reform*, CC Docket No. 96–262, *First Report & Order*, 62 Fed. Reg. 31,040 (6 June 1977), FCC Rcd., FCC 97–158, 275–82 (16 May 1997) (structure of U.S. domestic market makes recoupment unlikely); Market Entry and Regulation of Foreign-affiliated Entities, *Report and Order*, 11 FCCR 3873, 1 Comm. Reg. (P & F) 459 (1995) [hereinafter ECO Order] at 69–70 (because of both the bi-lateral nature of negotiations and the competitive pressures of the international market, it is still highly unlikely that a dominant foreign firm can "set the 'input' accounting rate level unilaterally"; as such, "[e]ven assuming *arguendo* that a dominant foreign carrier can unilaterally set an accounting rate" the structure of the IMTS market nevertheless indicates that "above-cost accounting rates on particular routes where a carrier has an affiliate on the foreign end [*cannot*] realistically jeopardise the ability of unaffiliated carriers to compete on those routes or in the US international services market as a whole. *Additionally, we believe the possibility of such harm is outweighed by the benefits of additional price and service competition that will result from further U.S. market entry*" (emphasis supplied).

[18] See UN Charter art. 2, 7; see also US Department of Justice and Federal Trade Commission, *Antitrust Enforcement Guidelines for International Operations* § 3.2 & n.73 (1995) (both the DOJ and the FTC must consider the legitimate interests of other nations); *Timberlane Lumber Co.* v. *Bank of America*, 549 F.2d 597 (9th Cir. 1976).

irrelevant to the question of whether a foreign firm can successfully engage in strategic conduct for domestically-originated traffic on that country-route.[19]

In sum, trade is, and will always continue to be, an important foreign policy priority and legitimate national interest. Yet when trade policies—especially those policies espousing naked mercantilism—are improperly cast in the guise of promoting "antitrust policies" or "public interest benefits," such policies will contribute to achieving neither (1) competition law's goal of maximising long-term consumer welfare with lower prices and more choices nor (2) trade policies' goal of helping domestic firms expand overseas. Rather, this approach will promote the opposite result. Accordingly, because trade goals are generally inapposite to the goals of competition law and economic regulation, trade policy is best left for those agencies or departments responsible for implementing these objectives—not with antitrust enforcement or independent regulatory agencies responsible for protecting and promoting static and dynamic economic efficiencies and the maximisation of consumer (not individual competitors') welfare.

III. THE GROWING REGULATORY CYNICISM HAS NO PLACE IN POLICY-MAKING

Nearly fifty years ago, US Supreme Court Justice Felix Frankfurter warned that the term "competition" may not be viewed in an "abstract, sterile way."[20] Unfortunately, it nonetheless appears that over the last eight years, both competition law enforcement and major public policy regulatory initiatives on both sides of the Atlantic have ignored Frankfurter's caveat by recasting the end-goal of "competition" (which, through rivalry, attempts to maximise consumer welfare by producing dynamic and static economic efficiencies) as something more akin to "fair, competition-like outcomes accompanied by the benevolent use of 'market-friendly' regulation." In other words, competition is a zero-sum game, where one firm can be made better off only if another firm is made worse off.[21]

As discussed more fully in this book, the WTO Agreement on Basic Telecoms Services is supposed to open markets, promote competition, and facilitate deregulation. Yet the means to this end—i.e., the concepts of "antitrust," the "public interest," and "competition policy"—appear no longer to have any

[19] *Cf.* Doug Galbi, *Model-Based Price Standards for Terminating International Traffic*, (FCC Staff Paper, Room Document No. 10), OECD Ad Hoc Meeting on International Telecommunications Charging Practices and Procedures, 17 Sept. 1997, (proposing a model that any country can use to compute economically relevant price standards for termination by its international correspondents).

[20] *FCC v. RCA Communications Inc.*, 346 US 86, 93–95 (1953).

[21] See Thomas W. Hazlett & George S. Ford, "The Fallacy of Regulatory Symmetry: An Economic Analysis of the 'Level Playing Field' ", in *Cable TV Franchising Statutes* (unpublished, 1997) (citing Harold Demsetz, "Information and Efficiency: Another Viewpoint", *J.L. & Econ.*, Apr. 1969, at 1–22) (notion of "fair, competition-like outcomes" is ridiculous because regulators will never "choose 'efficient' prices, outputs, and quality costlessly and with perfect information"); see also Paul McNulty, "Economic Theory and the Meaning of Competition", (1968) 82 *Q.J. Econ.* 639–56.

nexus to their original core purpose: the maximisation of consumer welfare.[22] In the absence of such a nexus, therefore, current policy goals have been described as the theory of "neo-competition."[23] The phrase "neo-competition" was deliberately chosen by blatantly disregarding (or, to use current parlance, "re-inventing" or "moving beyond") basic economic first principles. It is very unlikely that many telecoms policies post-WTO will produce, and accordingly permit consumers to enjoy, the economic benefits associated with good market performance—i.e., declining prices and additional new services and products.

Tragically, by introducing such *de rigueur* intellectual buzzwords like "convergence" and "choices" into the public dialectic, without any analytical foundation these policies have reduced the concept of "competition" to nothing more than an effective "smoke screen" to advance flawed economic theories that were soundly discredited the first time they were run up the flagpole. As discussed in varying degrees below, these failed economic theories include, *inter alia*, the discredited notions that: (1) until "perfect" competition is achieved, continued stringent regulation is necessary; (2) government can actually draft regulation that "mimics" competition or produces a "workably competitive market"; (3) by protecting competitors, we *a fortiori* protect "competition" (*aka* "competition without change"); (4) increased concentration can actually lead to more rivalry (i.e., with fewer firms in the market, the easier it is to regulate them); and (5) mercantilism actually promotes consumer welfare.

What is particularly disturbing, however, is that this approach appears to ignore the basic precept that those in a position to either influence or outright determine public policies or legal precedent owe a fiduciary duty to society as a whole, and not just to themselves. Thus, as the neo-competition doctrine—and its close sister, the neo-mercantilism doctrine—become increasingly entrenched in antitrust jurisprudence and in the rationales behind the current efforts to "restructure" the international telecoms market, it is high time to examine closely the merits of this neo-competition approach before all of the eggs are completely scrambled.

There are perhaps several plausible reasons why the neo-competition movement has been neither noticed explicitly nor discredited before. first, depending on the scope and ubiquity of regulatory oversight into a particular industry, a regulated entity has very little incentive to publicly protest neo-competition

---

[22] See James K. Glassman, "Consumers First", *Washington Post*, 24 Oct. 1997, at A21 (noting that Adam Smith concluded over 200 years ago: "Consumption is the sole end and purpose of all production, and the interests of producers ought to be attended to, only insofar as it may be necessary for promoting that of the consumer.").

[23] Lawrence J. Spiwak, "Antitrust, the 'Public Interest' and Competition Policy: The Search for Meaningful Definitions in a Sea of Analytical Rhetoric", *Antitrust Report* (Matthew Bender, 1997) (http://www.phoenix-center.org/library/neo_comp.doc).

[24] See Frank Easterbrook, "The Court and the Economic System", (1986) 98 *Harvard Law Review* 4, 39 ("[A]n agency with the power to deny . . . or to delay the grant of [an] application . . . only if the regulated firm agrees to conditions . . . is a potent way to *greatly increase the span of the agency's control*" (emphasis supplied)).

policies if the firm is, at the same time, wholly dependent on these same regulators for its corporate and financial existence.[24] Moreover, the antitrust/regulatory legal establishment in Washington and Brussels also has very little incentive to jeopardise their hard-won personal relationships and inside access with friends who have yet to exit through the revolving door. The problem with this approach, however, is that a sustained "go along/get along" strategy will not help a regulated firm's long-term bottom line and is, instead, more likely to result in nothing more than a shattered corporate shell.

Second, because regulated entities are extremely reluctant to draw public attention to their plight (lest they further incur the wrath of their omnipotent regulators), no one in the general public has any actual knowledge of, or real incentive to learn about, the unfolding societal and economic events around them. Thus, the promise of "competition without change" is a very enticing narcotic for both those specific individuals with an insatiable political narcissism and our society's generic natural desire for some sort of utopian paradise.[25]

As with all ideas built on shaky ground, however, it is unclear how long such policies can sustain themselves when consumers are nonetheless starting to recognise (and complain loudly) that neither deregulation nor competition is actually occurring in a form that would square with the basic purpose of regulation—i.e., that economic regulation is designed to be a *substitute for*, and *not a complement of*, competitive rivalry.[26] Quite to the contrary, because consumers continue to observe the daily promulgation of *more* regulation (both *sua sponte* from the regulator and by express legislative mandate) and a demonstrable proclivity in telecommunications industry re-concentration, they are starting to question seriously whether policies which take a "neo-competition" approach will actually succeed in concurrently promoting competition and reducing the need for stringent regulation.[27]

---

[25] Cf. George Orwell, *Animal Farm* (1945) (because the animal residents of the farm were promised, and always continued to believe in, a great utopian society—i.e., "four legs good, two legs bad"—everyone refused to accept and recognise the increasing amount of adverse developments occurring around them; the end result, of course, was not a utopian paradise, but was instead nothing more than a farm run by pigs).

[26] As discussed more fully below, however, this Book distinguishes between "economic" regulation (i.e., price, structural, and conduct regulation) and residual "public interest" regulation, which seeks to promote societal policies unrelated to competitive conduct.

[27] See, e.g., *Communications Daily*, 27 Aug. 1997, reporting that FCC's "pro-competitive actions," such as access charge reform, number portability, and universal service revisions, "could delay competition rather than speed it." In particular, the article reported that "at least" four FCC goals would "backfire": (1) lower long distance rates would be offset by increased subscriber line charges; (2) reductions in access charges to long distance companies would be offset by higher costs from "dramatic expansion" of universal service fund to cover such things as school and library wiring; (3) universal service goals would be "undermined by the FCC's failure to set cost-recovery mechanisms for high-cost service areas"; and (4) local phone companies could be unable to maintain network infrastructure properly because of cost drains resulting from "unfunded FCC mandates" to provide local number portability, make rate reductions, and offer interconnection. According to the article, the FCC's basic assumptions that "competition can be stimulated by regulatory decree" may be incorrect and, as such, "may have the unintended effect of suppressing competition and defeating the intent of the Telecom Act."

Rather than to re-examine the merits of the "neo-competition" approach and to correct the problems at hand, however, the frequent response to such criticism is that present restructuring policies are strictly designed to manage the "transition to competition."[28] Yet, as no one to date (private or public sector) has articulated a clear vision of long-term industry structure and performance (aside from apparently satisfying consumers' alleged desire for "one-stop-shopping" from a few dominant, vertically integrated firms[29] and the wiring of the schools of America and Europe[30]), this so-called "transition period" to competition may be a very long time to endure.[31]

[28] See, e.g., Paul Farhi, "Telephone Market Probes Planned: FCC, Senate Ask Why Competition Is on Hold", *Washington Post*, 16 July 1997, at C11. It should also be noted that another popular defence is the argument that consumers would be enjoying the benefits of competition if only the courts would accord regulatory agencies the unfettered discretion they deserve. See, e.g., Testimony of Reed E. Hundt, Chairman, Federal Communications Commission on the 1996 Telecommunications Act: An Anti-Trust Perspective, before the Subcommittee on Antitrust Business Rights and Competition, Committee on the Judiciary, U.S. Senate (17 Sept. 1997). According to Hundt, the prevalent "legal fog" of litigation that "surrounds every significant FCC decision immediately upon adoption" is significantly slowing "the pace of competition in the telecommunications industry." Congress, however, can help fix these problems by, *inter alia*, "re-affirm[ing] the deference courts should give to the FCC's expert judgement, as articulated by the Supreme Court in the *Chevron* case." Unfortunately, once again neo-competition proponents tragically miss the point: while it is true that courts must give great deference to an administration agencies' expertise, this expertise does not, nor should it ever, grant an administrative agency absolute immunity from review. See, e.g., *MCI* v. *AT&T*, 512 US 218, 229 (1994) ("an agency's interpretation of a statute is not entitled to deference when it goes beyond the meaning the statute can bear").

[29] See Michael J. Mandel et al., "A Pack of 800 lbs Gorillas: The Number of Major Corporate Players Is Shrinking. Is that Bad?", *Business Week*, 3 Feb. 1997; John Greenwald et al., "Hung Up on Competition", *Time*, 21 July 1997, at 50; see also Zaiba Nanji & Kirk Parsons, "So Many Choices", *Telephony*, 14 July 1997.

[30] See Jerry Hausman, "Taxation by Telecommunications Regulation", in *Tax Policy and the Economy* (1998) (calculating that the efficiency loss to society of policy to raise $2.25 billion per year to fund an Internet subsidy to schools and libraries to be approximately $1.25 per dollar raised, or a total of approximately $2.36 billion per year (in addition to the $2.25 billion per year of tax revenue)); Robert J. Samuelson, "Telephone Straddle", *Washington Post*, 14 May 1997, at A21 (FCC, at the behest of Congress, "perpetuated a baffling system of . . . subsidies—and created a huge new one to connect every school to the Internet" which will "prop up phone rates [and] prolong regulation." Moreover, because this program "is mostly a way to subsidise photo ops for politicians who like to be seen with children and computers . . . it's a lousy idea . . . because computers won't teach children how to read, write and think."); Michael Schrage, "Just Say No Net in Schools", *Hotwired*, 19 Feb. 1997 (notion of wiring the schools is "pathetic" because the idea is "just the latest technology that desperate educators, unhappy parents, and pandering politicians have tacked onto in hopes of avoiding the real problems confronting the schools").

[31] Actually, this point is a bit disingenuous. Given the huge amount of money at stake, coupled with the corresponding amount of legislative and regulatory capture behind the 1996 Act to get or protect a chunk of this money, it is very obvious that a lot of people did a lot of thinking about what long-term market structure should look like. The only problem with this process, however, is that consumer welfare was clearly at the bottom of everyone's priority list. Indeed, Scott Cleland, Director of Legg Mason's "Precursor Group," observed that the "political reality" behind the 1996 Act was that "the Bells and the local telcos were the driving force behind getting this legislation done" and that the politicians and regulators simply served as "natural accomplices" in spin that legislation was a "fair balance" rather than "admit they chose winners and losers, even though they did. . . . [However,] the cold reality is that the Bells WON and the long distance industry LOST" (emphasis in original.) Perhaps *Time* magazine summed it up the best: "if you were a local phone company with 100 per cent of the market, how helpful would you be in allowing a competitor into the area? Exactly." John Greenwald et al., *supra* n. 29.

In fact, a close look at the various economic restructuring paradigms proposed on both sides of the Atlantic over the last eight years often indicates that cynical, political *ad hoc* approach has become an acceptable substitute for sound legal and economic analysis in public-policy decision-making.[32] By doing so, government is now free to intervene into the market—via regulation or antitrust—and to reallocate wealth from one sector to another, without having to provide any rational nexus to the maximisation of overall consumer welfare.[33] What is more incredulous, however, is that no one has asked whether the "beneficiaries" of this "reallocation" are worthy of (or even want) this newfound wealth.[34] Given the foregoing, perhaps the only logical explanation for such an active policy of wealth reallocation is that once government can dislodge these nuggets of wealth from those who hold it currently, it will *a fortiori* be far easier for government to reappropriate this wealth at some later time.[35]

As this approach probably is not our society's most desired end-goal, this book seeks to remind people once again that, given the enormous economic and societal costs incurred whenever government decides to undertake a fundamental "restructuring" of major sectors of the economy, it is crucial for all of us to think (and openly and vigorously debate) today about what kind of a world we want to live in tomorrow.[36] As such, this book tries to move beyond the daily disputes and instead toward the fundamental, yet unanswered, issue confronting us all: *What is our real purpose behind this whole restructuring*

---

[32] See *Jacobellis* v. *Ohio*, 378 U.S. 184, 197 (1964) (Stewart, J., concurring) (while it is impossible to define "obscenity," "*I know it when I see it*" (emphasis supplied)). Thus, if government continues to intervene in the market without providing any legal or economic analysis to justify its actions, then the terms "market power," "dominant," or "anticompetitive" will essentially boil down to nothing more than the intellectual equivalent of "I don't like you." See *TV Communications Network Inc.* v. *Turner Network Television Inc.*, 964 F.2d 1022, 1026 (10th Cir.), *cert. denied*, 113 S. Ct. 601 (1992); see also *Hawaiian Telephone* v. *FCC*, 498 F.2d 771, 776–77 (D.C. Cir. 1974) (FCC "cannot merely assert the benefits of competition in an abstract, sterile way").

[33] See Samuelson, *supra* n. 30 (for Congress in the 1996 Act to order the FCC "[t]o do all this in the name of 'deregulation' is odd" because "Congress and the FCC praise deregulation and practice regulation"; moreover, "States, which control local rates, also like regulation"); see also James A. Miller III, "Reindustrialization Through the Free Market", 53 *Antitrust L.J.* 121, 124–25 (1984) (when government takes "an activist," collaborative approach to work with industry in order to promote "competition," it is virtually impossible to avoid the inevitable conclusion that the outcome of such policies "could do anything but restrict output, raise prices and retard innovation"; because such an approach ignores "the distinct interests of over 200 million American consumers in lower prices and higher product quality" most consumers should "start counting their silverware").

[34] See Samuelson, *supra* n. 30 (Congress and the FCC are "manipulating deregulation to advance pet agendas").

[35] Sort of like the process of forcing fruit through a juicing machine—you need to break up each individual juice cell to get the maximum amount of juice.

[36] Indeed, our "profound national commitment to the principle that debate on public issues should be uninhibited, robust and wide-open" is reflective of the fundamental understanding that "[c]ompetition in ideas and governmental policies is at the core of our electoral process." See, e.g., *Elrod* v. *Burns*, 427 U.S. 347, 357 (1996); *Saxbe* v. *Washington Post Co.*, 417 U.S. 843, 862–63 (1974) (Powell, J., dissenting) ("[S]urest course for developing sound national policy lies in a free exchange of views on public issues. And public debate must not only be unfettered; it must also be informed."); see also *United States* v. *NTEU*, 513 U.S. 454, 469–76 (1995).

exercise? Is it just to reallocate wealth and maintain "benevolent" regulation over one or more industries, or do we really want to maximise consumer welfare?

If the true goals of the WTO are to: (a) "open markets" and (b) move from monopoly to competition, then the appropriate regulatory focus should be on simple litmus test: do telecoms policies promote entry or deter entry? Clearly, however, the concept of "open markets" is subjective. In particular, "open markets" does not *a fortiori* mean "competitive" markets—i.e., markets may be technically/legally "open" to new entry but entry may nonetheless still be unattractive for new entrepreneurs (e.g., sufficient entry barriers and entry costs remain as to make entry unprofitable). As such, the question must also be asked if regulators are taking any affirmative steps to enact policies that encourage new entry by eliminating unnecessary endogenous entry costs (*e.g.*, removing geographic build-out requirements and geographic averaging; removing extra "entry" fees just to dig up the street to lay new networks; removing "franchise fees" for new entrants; not imposing additional hidden fees for spectrum auctions, implementing and enforcing meaningful interconnection and collocation rules; meaningfully review industry horizontal reconcentration and vertical integration, etc.).

Why is new entry important? Telecoms—unlike the legal or real estate brokerage business—is a business characterised by high margins. Moreover, with such technological advances, these margins are actually on the rise. For example, "Plain Old Telephone Service" ("POTS") used to be the only source of revenue for the local loop operator. Moreover, the price for POTS was fixed by the regulator. Let's assume for the sake of argument that the rate for POTS is US $30/month. Clearly, with such a *di minimis* revenue stream, additional entry would not be profitable. However, with technology and liberalisation, you can now also provide over that same line long-distance/international service (assume US $100) and a broadband, xDSL service for (US $80). Thus, a line that was worth only US $30 five years ago can now be worth well over US $200! [$30 + $70 + $100 = $200].

The ostensible purpose of restructuring, therefore, is to accelerate new entry and thereby have competitive pressures decrease these margins nearer to cost. Indeed, if the ostensible public policy goal is to move from a market characterised by monopoly to a market characterised by multiple firms, then entry of *more* firms is the *sine qua non* of this entire exercise.

With the growing regulatory cynicism discussed above, it is apparent that most regulatory initiatives post-WTO have *not* sought to promote tangible new entry, however, but rather to reallocate the above-mentioned rents among various segments of the industry to buy their silence to advance pet agendas. Thus, we do not have either competition or meaningful de-regulation, but rather a "static, incumbent-centric perpetual resale model" characterised by "fair, competition-like outcomes accompanied by the benevolent use of market-friendly regulation." Thus, why have "competition" when you can have "choices"? Moreover, if rent allocation is sufficient to buy silence from both the private and public sector, then why even think about meaningful structural solutions to the competitive problems of today?

As such, so long as the various public and private special interest groups get their share of the pie, there continues to be no real constituency for meaningful competition. Instead, we are left tragically with a "static, incumbent-centric perpetual resale model" under which everyone is simply reselling the same crappy service. Thus, consumers do not have a true choice of competitors—rather, their only choice is to whom they would like to write their monthly subscription checks out. If overall consumer welfare is ever to be improved, therefore, then such cynicism can no longer be condoned.

Accordingly, although legislation or EU directives may require it, neither competition law nor economic regulation should be used to achieve some sort of a "fair" outcome or establish "a level playing field."[37] Even though many European Directives and American state statutes use the term "fair competition," from an economic point of view, "fair," to any self-respecting competition lawyer or economist, should be yet another obscene, four-letter word that begins with the letter "F".[38] "Competition" requires *rivalry*—there is no notion of "equity" in this term.[39] (Indeed, there are no "white hats" in this business.) Similarly, we should discard the irrational notion that antitrust or economic regulation should "level the playing field," for the market never was, nor ever will be, supposed to be reduced to a zero-sum game with relatively equal

---

[37] See Reed Hundt & Charlene Barshefsky, "FCC Isn't Backpedaling on Telecommunications Deal", *New York Times*, 17 Aug. 1997, at F36 ("The FCC remains committed . . . to adopting *fair* rules that live up to American international commitments, while safeguarding the public interest and insuring *full and fair competition* in telecommunications markets in the United States. The executive branch fully supports this view" (emphasis supplied)).

[38] See Hazlett & Ford, *supra* n. 21.

[39] See *Town of Concord* v. *Boston Edison Co.*, 915 F.2d 17, 21–22 (1st Cir. 1990), *cert. denied*, 499 U.S. 931 (1991) ("[A] practice is not 'anticompetitive' simply 'because it harms competitors'— after all, the whole purpose of competition is to "advance a firm's fortunes at the expense of its competitors." Rather, "a practice is 'anticompetitive' only if it 'harms the competitive process' by obstructing the "achievement of competition's basic goals—lower prices, better products and more efficient production methods"); see also Ocean State Physicians Health Plan, Inc. v. Blue Cross & Blue Shield of R.I., 833 F.2d 1101, 113 (1st Cir. 1989), *cert. denied*, 494 U.S. 1027 (1990) ("[T]he desire to crush a competitor, standing alone, is insufficient to make out a violation of the antitrust laws . . . As long as [the defendants'] course of conduct was itself legitimate, the fact that some of its executives hoped to see [the plaintiff] disappear is irrelevant."); *Olympia Equipment Leasing Co.* v. *Western Union Tel. Co.*, 797 F.2d 370, 379 (7th Cir. 1986), *cert. denied*, 480 U.S. 934 (1987) ("[I]f conduct is not objectionably anticompetitive, the fact that it was motivated by hostility to competitors ('these turkeys') is irrelevant."); *Hawaiian Telephone* v. *FCC*, 498 F.2d 771 (D.C. Cir. 1974) ("equity" considerations cannot substitute for thorough legal and economic analysis when invoking "competition" principles under the public interest standard).

competitors.[40] If we do not, then the only thing accomplished is the reallocation of wealth among competitors, without producing a single benefit for consumers.[41]

So why should we be concerned? After all, isn't this just business as usual? The answer to this question should be a straightforward no, and let us tell you why.

While we all would like to realise the utopian goal of "private competition and public interest benefits," the word "public" in the term "public utility" cannot be stretched to such an absurd point that economic policies fail to realise that all of the various segments of the telecoms industry—terrestrial, wireless, satellite, etc.—are high stakes *businesses* as well. If reasonable business people perceive that the costs and risks of entry outweigh the potential financial benefits, then these firms will choose not to enter, or remain in, the market.

Yet, the preceding paragraph highlights the primary challenge and great oxymoron about telecoms industry restructurings: the simple fact that the deliberate inclusion of the word "public" in "public utilities" likewise cannot be ignored. Like it or not, we must accept the fact that consumers around the globe consider cheap and reliable (if not outright free) telephone, cable television, (and apparently now "broadband access" as well)—unlike any other lawful business—to be some kind of an inherent birthright. Thus, in addition to viewing these industries from a strict dollars and cents perspective, we need to view these industries (and the policies designed to restructure them) from a *societal* perspective as well.

That is to say, as explained above, in truly competitive markets, inefficient firms will be eliminated. However, while both politicians and consumers love to extol the benefits and necessity of competitive telecoms markets, if the power or phones go out, consumers tend to become quite upset. When they do, these angry consumers call their local politicians, who then call other politicians, who then call utility and telephone company CEOs and scream at them for letting some little old lady sit in a cold dark room with no way of calling: "Help, I've fallen and I can't get up!" Accordingly, because consumers consider cheap and reliable telephone, video, and broadband as an inherent birthright, if consumers

---

[40] See Easterbrook, *supra* n. 24 (those "who see economic transactions as zero-sum games are likely to favor 'fair' divisions of the gains and losses"); see also Joseph Farrell, "Creating Local Competition", 49 *Fed. Comm. L.J.* 201, 212 (1996); John Berresford, Future of the FCC: Promote Competition, Then Turn Out the Lights? (Economic Strategy Institute, 1997) 21–2. Berresford states that the "playing field is never 'even' to begin with, and bringing in a lot of regulatory landscape architects and earth-moving equipment will, in most cases, only postpone the emerging competition and the benefits it would bring to consumers." Thus, once regulators start to level the playing field to be "fair" to one competitor, "all the other competitors will find something unfair to them and will want their valleys to be filled and their mountains and hills to be brought low. The process can become an endless one and, if carried to its logical conclusion, makes the regulator into a cartel manager. This guarantees jobs for the regulators, lawyers and lobbyists, and oligopoly for the so-called competitors, but it will do little for consumers."

[41] See also Glassman, *supra* n. 22 ("We work in order to eat, not visa versa. In other words, an economy should, first and foremost, benefit consumers, not producers—individuals rather than the established interests of business and labor").

perceive a sufficient diminution in quality or increase in price, they will demand swift and demonstrable action. When the cacophony of consumer outrage becomes sufficiently loud (and it always does), then there is a distinct and strong possibility that legislators and regulators will take some kind of "punitive" action.[42]

As an initial, "less intrusive" measure, government and industry may work out a deal that creates the "appearance" of immediate competitive benefits, but which will, in fact, act as a net detriment to overall consumer welfare in the long-run.[43] If "voluntary" commitments prove inadequate to alleviate political pressure, government could also impose some sort of "punitive" regulation—specifically, new regulation that will (1) be far more intrusive and costly than the system we operate under now and contribute absolutely nothing to improving consumer welfare, but (2) nonetheless make great points with voters back home.[44]

---

[42] See Thomas G. Dolan, "Editorial Commentary: The Antitrust Delusion—The Federal Trade Commission Explains it All to You", *Barrons*, 7 July 1997, at 46 (noting that when public criticism reaches this boiling point, "such criticism helps undermine the antitrust delusion and establishes the deeper truth that all antitrust cases are political first, based on economics last"); see also Eleanor M. Fox, "Lessons From Boeing: A Modest Proposal to Keep Politics Out of Antitrust", *Antitrust Report*, Nov. 1997, at 19 ("the antitrust experts did their job, while the politicians trivialized antitrust, reinforcing the popular notion that any big case that matters is political"; moreover, "it doesn't have to be [this] way, but counteracting politicisation requires heavy leaning against the wind").

[43] See, e.g., Scott Cleland, "The 'Real Story' Behind the FCC's Subsidy Reform Decision?" *Telecom Bulletin* (Washington Research Group, 9 May 1997) ("[O]nly 'escape route' possible from the 'political trap' of appearing to be increasing the nation's telephone rate burden to pay for new school subsidies" was for FCC to enter into a "last minute 'deal'" with AT&T," which, in "return for public promises from AT&T to pass on any access charge reductions to basic consumers for the first time in years, the FCC would decrease the local telcos' price caps by an additional $750 million." This " 'deal,' combined with a slower phase-in of the new universal service fund, enabled the FCC to defensively claim 'offsetting savings' for both long distance and local customers to pay for the $3 billion in new subsidies.").

[44] For example, because the Cable Television Act of 1992 regulates cable companies' rates on a *franchise-by-franchise* basis, the economic compliance costs far out-weigh any conceivable public interest benefit (i.e., actual amount of refunds achieved are often *de minimis*—generally a couple of thousand dollars). Thus, if government is really so concerned about the ability of cable monopolies to gouge consumers over a few thousand bucks, then government should simply write consumers a check for this amount instead. More disturbing, however, is that this costly regime does absolutely *nothing* to improve the overall performance of the larger "Multichannel Video Programming Distribution (MVPD) market. See Annual Assessment of the Status of Competition in the Market for the Delivery of Video Programming, Third Annual Report, FCC 96–496 (rel. Jan. 2, 1997) at 4. ("Local markets for the delivery of video programming generally remain highly concentrated, and structural conditions remain in place that could permit the exercise of market power by incumbent cable systems." Thus, it remains "difficult to determine to what extent these markets will be characterized over the long term by vigorous rivalry"). Accordingly, consumers are also pressuring lawmakers to explain why this regime has not produced any benefits. See, e.g., Ron Podell, "Cable Company Hikes Rates", *Montgomery J.*, 21 May 1997, at A1; "Murdoch Plans Total Local Carriage From DBS Platform", *Satellite Week*, 14 Apr. 1997 (reporting that Commerce Committee Chairman Senator McCain (R-Ariz) held hearings on status of competition in MVPD market because he is "concerned that passage of the Telecom Act last year didn't result in lower prices and more competition in the video market, particularly since telcos dropped plans to enter video distribution market").

The problem with this approach is that given the large sunk costs required for new entry, additional new capacity (e.g., undersea cable capacity, alternative local distribution networks, cable "overbuilds," satellite constellations) cannot come on line to relieve constrained facilities whenever politicians want them. These projects are both very time and capital intensive. Thus, without forward-looking policies designed to promote and encourage tangible, facilities-based entry, as demand expands and supply stays constant (or, in some cases, shifts in as outdated facilities go off line and are not replaced), consumers may very well experience an increase in price and a diminution in choices or quality of services, rather than the opposite result, which they were originally promised and fully expect to realise.[45] When this happens, the lives of everyone involved with the process—politicians, industry, and especially consumers—become just a little bit more miserable. Accordingly, those who advocate the "neo-competition" and "neo-mercantile" view that consumer welfare is best "promoted" or "protected" by increased government intervention into the market—absent any articulation on their part that such intervention is both required and specifically tailored to eliminate a clear "public policy" barrier to entry—simply cannot have their cake and eat it too.

V. CASE STUDY: THE UNITED STATES' INTERNATIONAL TELECOMS POLICY

Perhaps a textbook case of the regulatory cynicism we write about in this book can be found in the US government's (and in particular, its Federal Communications Commission's) approach to international telecoms. Indeed, the FCC—despite its rhetoric—over the past several years has launched an aggressive (and indeed hypocritical) campaign to erode—if not outright abrogate—the United States' obligations under various international telecoms agreements, including both the WTO Agreement on Basic Telecommunications Services and the International Telecommunication Union (ITU) treaty.

In fact, the FCC—after admitting publicly that it did not trust the market-opening efforts and commitments of other countries—unilaterally issued stringent regulations (including naked price controls), to the dismay of the international telecoms community. The FCC's aggressive, unilateral actions have engendered much ill will among America's trading partners, who see those actions as mercantilist and find them hypocritical, given the slow advance of competition in US telecoms markets.

As we also show in this book, the FCC's actions were not limited to that, however. The FCC also opened up fronts in the international telecoms trade war in such diverse areas as international satellite spectrum policy; universal

---

[45] As explained above, "neo-comps" *a fortiori* reject any criticisms that their policies are, in fact, barriers to entry. Well, perhaps this criticism may be over-reaching just a bit. "Neo-comps," just like everyone else, love to proclaim that they want the doors open wide—the only problem with this statement is that they also want to say hello (and, if possible charge an entry fee) to everyone who walks by.

service; cable landing petitions; and review of international mergers, acquisitions ands joint ventures.

Sadly, you need not take just our word for it. According to United States Federal Reserve Chairman Alan Greenspan, he "regrets" personally that:

"[D]espite the remarkable success over a near half century of GATT, the General Agreement on Trade and Tariffs, and its successor, the World Trade Organisation, in reducing trade barriers, *our trade laws and negotiating practices are essentially adversarial.* They presume that a trade concession extracted from us by our trading partners is to their advantage at our expense, and must be countered. Few economists see the world that way. And I am rash enough to suggest we economists are correct, at least in this regard: *trade is not a zero-sum* game. If trade barriers are lowered by both parties, each clearly benefits. But if one lowers barriers and the other does not, the country that lowered barriers unilaterally would still be better off having done so. Raising barriers to achieve protectionist equality with reluctant trading partners would be neither to our benefit, nor to theirs. The best of all possible worlds for competition is for both parties to lower trade barriers. The worst is for both to keep them up. For these reasons, I am concerned about the recent evident weakening of support for free trade in this country. Should we endeavour to freeze competitive progress in place, we will almost certainly slow economic growth overall, and impart substantial harm to those workers who would otherwise seek more effective longer-term job opportunities. Protecting markets from new technologies has never succeeded. Adjustments to newer technologies have been delayed, but only at significant cost. *Even should our trading partners not retaliate in the face of increased American trade barriers, an unlikely event, we do ourselves great harm by lessening the vigour of American competitiveness.* The United States has been in the forefront of the post-war opening up of international markets, much to our, and the rest of the world's, benefit. It would be a great tragedy were that process reversed."[46]

Chairman Greenspan's words simply reinforce the old adage that *"two wrongs do not make one right."* Everyone in this business knows that there are some countries, to state it politely, which are adverse to competition. They make interconnection difficult, they insist upon high (and sometimes asymmetrical) settlement rates to benefit incumbent carriers, they prohibit foreign entry, etc. Does this mean that the international community should condone such actions? Of course not. As shown passim, this whole book is about various failures to promote true competition and deregulation.

At the same time, however, if such conduct occurs, then it does not also *a fortiori* mean that the United States can retaliate with equal (or worse conduct). Again, *"two wrongs still do not make one right."*

---

[46] Remarks by Chairman Alan Greenspan before the Dallas Ambassadors Forum, Dallas Texas (16 April 1999) (emphasis supplied). Sadly, recent press reports indicate that the FCC has no intentions of departing from business as usual. See, e.g., Theresa Foley, "Profile: Trade Warrior's Hands-on Approach to Regulation", *Comm. Wk. Intn'l* (4 Oct. 1999) ("A veteran trade warrior has taken the helm of the International Bureau at the FCC in Washington, D.C., Don Abelson, 49, doesn't have a telecoms or satellite background, but having notched up two decades at the US Trade Representatives' office . . . he is well versed in the ways of international trade.") (Emphasis supplied.)

Why is this? Because such naked cynicism towards the policy-making process sends the completely wrong message to those counties in Europe and elsewhere who are attempting to privatise and restructure their domestic markets from monopoly to competition. Indeed, why should the Federal Communications Commission be accorded great deference as the global industry "expert" when this agency refuses to articulate a cohesive analytical framework to solve the problems raised by US telecommunications industry restructuring? If the US— ostensibly the bright light and leader of the Free World—hypocritically refuses to engage in meaningful reform and instead bases its decisions on cynicism and political pressure, then why should the rest of the community of nations engage in meaningful structural solutions on their part as well?[47]

Such issues are rapidly coming to the forefront of the debate. Numerous sovereign countries and international organizations currently are of the firm belief that the US' unilateral international telecoms initiatives are hypocritical because, in their view, the US is far from complying with its own WTO and other international telecoms commitments.[48] As such, the US cannot preach

[47] See, e.g., Maev Sullivan, "Bottom Line: Why the USTR is too Quick to Cry Foul", *Comm. Wk. Int'l* (22 May 2000) ("[G]iven that the United States took about three years to turn the vision of unbundling into reality, the USTR out to know better than to beat up foreigners trying to do their best, albeit belatedly.")

[48] See, e.g., Focus Group to ITU-T Study Group 3 "Final Report" regarding "Accounting Rate Principles for International Telephone Service" (November 6, 1998) criticizing heavily and directly the FCC's unilateral approach to IMTS telecoms reform. This Final Report takes the formal form of a new draft Annex E to ITU-T Recommendation D.140 and is available at <http://www.itu.int/intset/focus/index.html>. See also Reply Comments of the European Community to the Commission's Third NPRM in the Amendment of Section 2.106 of the Commission's Rules to Allocate Spectrum at 2 GHz for Use by the Mobile-Satellite Service, (FCC 98–309) in Docket No. ET 95–18at 10 criticizing FCC's proposal to impose unilaterally spectrum clearing costs on new entrants:

> "The EC would like to reaffirm that it will remain attentive to the treatment given to European-based satellite systems in the U.S. The EC will be *particularly attentive to any behaviour which is contrary to the spirit or letter of the commitments undertaken by the U.S. within the WTO agreement on basic telecommunications services.*" (Emphasis supplied.)

Similarly, the Japanese government stated specifically that the "Enhanced Initiative on Deregulation and Competition Policy is to be conducted on the principle of reciprocity, *but the US has done virtually nothing towards the fulfilment of its end of the bargain.*" 2 April 1999, comments by the Japanese Ministry of Posts and Telecommunications on the Annual Review under Section 1377 of the US Trade Act (Telecommunications Clause) and the 1999 USTR National Trade Estimate Report on Foreign Trade Barriers (or NTE Report, Barrier Report), http://www.mpt. go.jp/pressrelease/english/general/news990402.html.

Sadly, as shown passim, these developments have been the hallmark of the FCC's international telecoms policies under the Clinton/Gore Administration. See, e.g., David Molony, "WTO Basic Agreement Put on Hold as Signatories Clash over Timetable", *Comm. Wk. Intn'l*, Jan. 9, 1998, at 1 (reporting that "signatories to the treaty claim the United States wants to take advantage of the current position by gaining early access to its trade partners' markets on more favorable terms, without having to open its own markets to foreign carriers"); "EU Presses US To Change Telecoms Rules", *Reuters*, 5 Aug. 1997, available in LEXIS, News Library, Wires File (reporting that the European Commission warned that the United States "risks violating its world trading obligations" if it continues with mercantile-type policies—i.e., the FCC's continued policy of maintaining "broad and unclear 'public interest' factors" regarding foreign participation in the US domestic telecommunications market and, in particular, the fact that the FCC allows factors such as law enforcement, foreign policy, or trade concerns to be taken into consideration, as well as accepting the concept of "*ideal-politick*" but practice "*real-politick*" without any consequences. Indeed, so long as the US continues to engage in a hypocritical approach towards both trade and economic policies, the strength of these arguments continues to diminish in the eyes of the international community. Thus, much like the "boy who cried wolf", even where a truly legitimate WTO violation occurs, the merits of the case generally fall on deaf ears.

"very high risk to competition" as a reason for a license refusal); Albert P. Halprin, "Two Steps Backward on Open Markets", *New York Times*, 20 July 1997, at F13 ("FCC, citing the supposed requirements of Federal communications law, is . . . backpedal[ing] on major American commitments in the deal. If our nation fails to live up to its end of the bargain, so will other signatories, and this historic opportunity will be lost."); Guy Daniels, "Huffing and Puffing", *Comm. Intn'l*, Oct. 1998, at 8 ("As a possible trade war looms and Uncle Sam blusters over compatibility issues, . . . the European Community is holding firm in the face of determined U.S. efforts to muscle-in on the third generation mobile standards agenda"); Robert Aamoth, "One Law for the Rich", *Comm. Intn'l*, Nov. 1998 ("The U.S. Federal Communications Commission's international settlement rate policies have caused such disquiet in the global telecoms community that . . . several of the world's largest carriers—and their governments—are prepared to go to law to get things changed"); David Molony, "EC and US To Clash over Universal Service Funds", *Comm. Wk. Intn'l*, 6 Apr. 1998, at 1, 30.

2

Why Restructure?

MERRIAM-WEBSTER'S DICTIONARY defines the act of "restructuring" as "to change the makeup, organisation or pattern" of the subject at hand.[1] If this telecoms restructuring process is to succeed, therefore, then policy-makers need to find constructive ways to change the underlying market structure from one characterised by monopoly (i.e., *one* firm) to a market structure capable of sustaining competition (i.e., *many* firms). As such, the core issue at hand is not a question of technological "development" or "convergence" *per se* (indeed, technical entrepreneurship has always been the least of the market's problems) but specifically about how regulators can promote affirmatively and effectively new advanced competitive infrastructure entry.

Indeed, the problems facing the telecoms industry in most markets continue to stem from dominant firms controlling access to monopoly local plant. That situation cannot be solved through "better pricing" of that plant, however— ultimately, *it can only be solved by entry of new, alternative rival suppliers.* Accordingly, for structural problems, final structural solutions are required.

II. IDENTIFY OPTIONAL LONG-TERM MARKET STRUCTURE

If policy-makers are truly serious about promoting "deregulation" and "competition" and abandoning their current efforts to promote improperly "neo-competition (*aka*, "fair, competition-type outcomes accompanied by the benevolent use of 'market-friendly' regulation"), then the first step in the process must be to formulate, articulate and implement policy paradigms designed to establish, to the extent practicable, a structural framework conducive to competitive entry and rivalry, under which firms will be unable to engage in strategic anticompetitive conduct—even if they try.[2]

In a market structure conducive to vigorous rivalry, efficient firms (*i.e.*, those firms that can lower their costs, innovate to make new products, and regularly offer consumers more choices) should, in theory, be able to make *more* money as the market becomes more competitive. Such an outcome is infinitely superior to the probable performance of a market that—even though it lacks a structural framework conducive to competitive rivalry—the regulator believes with sufficient intervention is nonetheless capable of achieving a level of "workable" market performance which "mimics" competition.

Stated another way, different market structures induce different types of rivalrous conduct. That is, because firms seek to always maximise profits, if the underlying structure is conducive to competitive rivalry, then firms will be forced to innovate and compete, thus maximising consumer welfare. Conversely, if a structure is *not* conducive to competitive rivalry, then firms will have the incentive to engage in strategic anticompetitive conduct. As such, if a firm lives in a "toxic" market, then it will make "toxic" decisions.

Clearly, because of such rapid technological advancement in the telecoms industry, undertaking a dynamic perspective can be quite challenging. As such, we must not focus on picking winners and losers and achieving one particular outcome—indeed, as we learned from the Soviet experiment, central planning just doesn't work—but we should instead try to create a market structure which exhibits the the characteristics are usually associated with a market producing good economic performance. Specifically, we would like to see:

(1) Vigorous price competition;
(2) Vigorous non-price competition;
(3) Elastic supply and demand;
(4) Low switching and search costs among providers; and
(5) Low barriers to entry and exit.

If policy-makers aim towards achieving this goal, then the market will tell us how many firms it can sustain efficiently, rather than government.[3]

---

[1] "Restructuring" is a very different concept from "liberalisation", however. "Liberalisation" simply refers to transforming a state-run monopoly to a privately-run monopoly. While the former is more interested in maximising employment for local citizens and the latter is more concerned with maximising monopoly rents—the end result is the same.

[2] See generally *Brooke Group Ltd.* v. *Brown & Williamson Tobacco Corp.*, 509 U.S. 209, rehearing denied, 509 U.S. 940 (1993); *A.A. Poultry Farms Inc.* v. *Rose Acre Farms Inc.*, 881 F.2d 1396, 1401 (7th Cir. 1989) ("Market structure offers a way to cut the inquiry [of potential, anticompetitive strategic vertical conduct] off at the pass. . . ."). See also F.M. Scherer & David Ross, *Industrial Market Structure And Economic Performance* (3d. ed., Boston, Houghton Mifflin, 1990) (despite antitrust's focus on structural measures such as the HHI, economic concentration is only one aspect of market structure; other relevant features of market structure include product differentiation, barriers to entry, cost structures, vertical integration, and diversification).

[3] For example, there are no federal regulatory commissions or comprehensive consent decrees in such industries as camera film (Kodak sells 70 per cent of the film sold in the U.S.), pasta (4 firms comprise 77 per cent of the market); commercial airplane manufacturing (3 firms control 97 per cent of the market), soft drinks (2 firms control 71 per cent of the market) or toothpaste (4 firms control 90 per cent of the market). See Michael L. Katz & Harvey S. Rosen, *Microeconomics* 508 (2d ed., Irwin, 1994); John E. Kwoka, Jr., "Regularity and Diversity of Firm Size Distribution in U.S. Industries", 34 *J. Econ. & Bus.* 391. Indeed, if there is sound economic evidence that indicates that a market is performing well in markets with low barriers to entry—e.g., static economic efficiencies in the form of declining prices and dynamic economic efficiencies in the form of increasing technological innovation and new services—it may be appropriate to let one firm earn high profits in the short term because, in the long term (a) new firms will have a greater incentive to enter and compete, and (b) the existing firm will have the incentive to innovate to retain its leadership position. However, if it is demonstrated that, over the long term, this same firm can erect barriers to entry by foreclosing key inputs of production, then some sort of intervention-antitrust or regulatory-may be appropriate.

A. Case Study: The US verses the European Mobile Industry

A classic example of how the policy-makers refused to undertake such a dynamic analysis can be found in the US mobile industry. There, because the FCC was more interested in revenue raising through its auction process than ensuring the most efficient use of spectrum, the FCC botched any possibility of quickly having a ubiquitous nation-wide mobile network that consumers would view as a close substitute to the copper public switched transport network (PSTN).[4]

For example, rather than getting any useful block of spectrum (both in terms of geographic scope and amount of bandwidth) into the market immediately, the FCC acted like a good "frequency monopolist" and dribbled out bits and pieces of spectrum. In so doing, the FCC spurred "buyers euphoria" in the bidding process and increased revenue potential. While such a strategy was designed to provide consumers with the ephemeral appearance of a "win-win-win",[5] in fact the FCC could have taken far more aggressive steps to promote consumer welfare. Specifically, by adopting the "bits and pieces" approach to spectrum management, the FCC delayed unnecessarily the creation of nation-wide and ubiquitous mobile networks. Instead, the limited number of nation-wide mobile networks had to be cobbled slowly together via mergers and acquisitions, thus again raising entry costs for new firms.[6]

Second, in addition to driving up the auction price, for many of the auctions, the FCC also often improperly forces new entrants to pay spectrum relocation fees to incumbent spectrum users (i.e., broadcasters) when spectrum cannot be

---

[4] Tragically, several European countries, such as the UK and France, appear to be reproducing this mistake in its auction of 3G wireless licences. (See, e.g., "France May Ask Entry Fee for 3G Bidders", *Reuters*, 18 April 2000 (reporting that France is considering asking bidding candidates to pay an "entry fee" as well as a yearly rental charge.); Andrew Gliniecki, "Editorial: A Taxing Process", *Comm. Wk. Int'l*, 17 April 2000. (While the UK UMTS auction bids have produced bids "way beyond the scale invisaged", such bids represent a "tax" on UK mobile consumers because the proceeds will be spent on "anything the British Government chooses—and political expediency is boundto play a big part.")) It will be interesting to follow the future differences between the results of the UK's and France's approach—expensive licences that will be ultimately be paid by consumers or market failure—versus the approach of Finland, which was a beauty contest without further licensing fees. A prediction: Finland will continue to be the success story of the wireless world while the UK and France will mysteriously lag behind take up of 3G services, perhaps prompting more regulatory intervention.

[5] Indeed, former FCC Chairman Reed Hundt was fond of saying that the FCC's PCS auctions policies were a "win-win-win" scenario:

> Consumers win because a competitive marketplace will mean lower prices and better service. Industry wins because licenses are going to be awarded more quickly to those who are most likely to invest in and provide these new services. And taxpayers win because auction revenues go directly to the U.S. Treasury.

See, e.g., Statement of Chairman Reed E. Hundt before PCIA Convention (September 23, 1994) (http://www.fcc.gov/Speeches/Hundt/spreh428.txt)

[6] See, e.g., FCC News Release, *FCC Bureaus Approve Bell Atlantic/Vodaphone and Voice-Stream/Aerial License Transfers and Assignments—Two New National Wireless Competitors to be Created* (March 30, 2000).

shared. As discussed in more detail in Chapter 16, such a policy simply deters entry (especially to those rural areas who need it the most) and may, in the international context, violate many of the market-opening commitments made by the United States.

Finally, as if the previous two examples were bad enough, the FCC further exacerbated the problem by setting aside two significant blocks of spectrum (the C and F blocks) exclusively for "small businesss" (aka minority and women-owned businesses)—including providing bidding credits to help these small entities afford the cost of entry. While this scheme makes nice hyperbole, given the huge endogenous and exogenous entry costs associated with the telecoms industry, the reality is that it simply does not make economic sense to operate a mobile company exclusively on a small, regional basis. Thus, if we peer beneath the veneer, it is clear that this set-aside scheme is simply designed to provide certain constitutencies with an opportunity to "flip" this valuable spectrum at a significant profit after a mandatory waiting period to another operator who can actually make the most efficient use of this capacity.

As expected, the FCC's C block auctions turned into a complete fiasco. In the FCC's own words, it just recently conceded that:

> three C block licensees, NextWave Personal Communications, Inc. ("NextWave"), GWI PCS Inc. ("GWI"), and DCR PCS, Inc. ("DCR"), filed for bankruptcy protection. Other C block licensees defaulted on payments owed for their licenses. Bankruptcy filings and payment defaults by other C block licensees followed the auction; and, to date, a total of 232 C and F block licenses, covering a population ("pops") of approximately 191 million, have been involved in bankruptcy proceedings and/or defaulted on license payments. *It appears that the vast majority of the defaulted licenses have never been placed into service.*[7]

The pathetic results of the FCC's spectrum policies speak for themselves.[8] Rather than have a mobile market (such as that found in Europe) characterised by low switching costs and numerous close substitutes (i.e., to switch wireless carriers in the US, one generally has to purchase a completely new phone), the US mobile market is characterised not only by multiple standards, but by multiple frequencies as well. (Dual-mode phone, unfortunately, does not mean both GSM and CDMA.)[9] Moreover, this lack of leadership essentially prevents the majority of US wireless users (non-GSM) from seamlessly using their wireless

---

[7] In re Amendment of the Commission's Rules Regarding Instalment Payment financing for Personal Communications Services (PCS) Licensees. Further Notice of Proposed Rulemaking, FCC 00–197 (rel. June 7, 2000) at ¶ 10.

[8] The "parade of horribles" does not end here, unfortunately. Other contributing factors as to why it is unlikely that mobile telephony will ever become a close substitute for fixed wired access in the United States include the lack of "calling party pays", and the fact that the FCC has permitted many incumbent LECs (e.g., Verizon (formerly GTE and Bell Atlantic) and SBC/Bell South to own large mobile operators,companies which have absolutely no incentive to convert a profitable *complementary service* (wireless) to become a true *competitive substitute* for their core fixed access service in which they dominate.

[9] See Steven Brull and Catherine Yang, "Cell Phones: Europe Made the Right Call", *Business Week* 7 Sept. 1998.

phones in over 133 countries abroad (especially, from personal experience, Europe). And, as if this was not bad enough, the US has used this issue to open up yet another from in the growing telecoms trade war in the on going battle to determine a world-wide 3G mobile standard.[10] Thus the fact that there may be five mobile providers in a market does not *a fortiori* mean that this market is.

Now contrast such performance with the European Mobile Market, where mobile penetration has increased exponentially in many European countries—so much so that mobile is actually becoming a close substitute for fixed-line service in many countries. For example, in the specific case of Sweden, the OECD posited that:

> mobile subscriptions are being used instead of second lines in primary residences, as first lines in holiday homes, and to create mobile offices for some users who would otherwise require a fixed line. In addition some new customers for telephone service in Scandinavia are opting for a cellular connection as their first line and later perhaps migrating to a fixed line . . . If current trends continue, finland is likely to be the first country where the number of mobile subscriptions exceeds the number of fixed access lines.[11]

B. The Structure—Conduct—Performance Paradigm

Perhaps the best way of formulating a long-term view of market structure is to use the "Structure-Conduct-Performance" ("SCP") Paradigm of Industrial Organisation Economics as a basic "checklist" of the state of the market. The SCP teaches us that a market structure conducive to competitive rivalry is the key to a competitive marketplace. As illustrated by Figure 1 below, market *performance* depends on the *conduct* of sellers and buyers in such matters as pricing policies, investment decisions, and the like. Conduct in turn depends upon the *structure* of the relevant market, characterised by the number and size of sellers and buyers, product differentiation, and the presence (or lack thereof) of barriers to entry. Moreover, market structure is affected by a variety of *basic conditions*, which include everything from the sophistication of the consumers and the business culture in the market to technology and product durability. The concept of "basic conditions" takes on even greater significance when attempting to measure the progress of WTO implementation, because, for example, the culture, state of technology, and political environment in the US are very different from the basic conditions found in New Zealand or Uzbekistan.

Under any scenario, however, government intervention—such as regulation, international trade rules, taxes and subsidies, price controls, competition law

---

[10] See Guy Daniels, "Huffing and Puffing", *Comm. Week Int'l*, Oct. 1998, at 8 ("As a possible trade war looms and Uncle Sam blusters over compatibility issues, . . . the European Community is holding firm in the face of determined US efforts to muscle-in on the third generation mobile standards agenda").

[11] *OECD Communications Outlook* 1999, at 66–67, 76.

enforcement, reporting requirements, etc.—affects each leg of the paradigm chain and its potential for both good and bad cannot be discounted in any analytical framework.[12]

Fig. 1. *The Structure-Conduct Performance Paradigm*

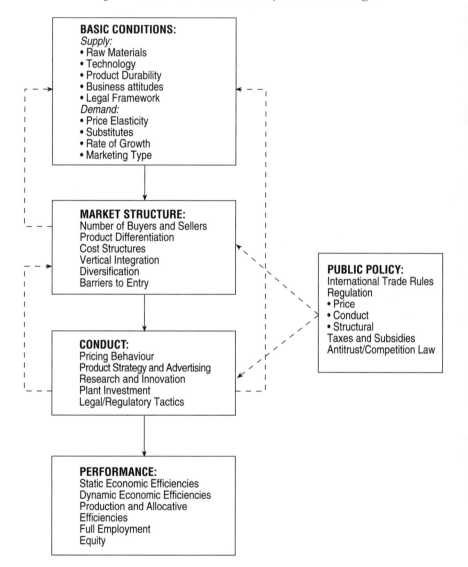

---

[12] Scherer & Ross, supra n. 2 at 4–6.

C. The Concept of Transaction Cost Economics

As an analytical complement to the SCP "check-list," policy-makers should also understand the concept of "transaction cost" economics set forth by Oliver Williamson in his seminal book, *The Economic Institutions of Capitalism.*[13] Transaction cost economics attempts to determine optimal (*i.e.*, most efficient) institutional organisational arrangements that minimise transaction costs under different sets of circumstances. Transaction cost economics is based on the cognitive assumption of "bounded rationality"—*i.e.*, economic actors are assumed to be "*intendedly* rational, but only *limitedly* so."

Thus, for example, a vertically integrated telephone company has the incentive to engage in strategic anti-competitive conduct by foreclosing rival's access to unbundled loops in order to protect its market share as well as other sunk investments. In contrast, a firm that is in the exclusive business of selling access to the home on a wholesale basis has the incentive to sell as many loops as possible because as more firms purchase its products and services, the more profitable its business becomes.

Transaction cost economic also submits that corporate internal governance (a "firm") and markets are *alternative* methods of resource allocation and, therefore—depending on given factual circumstances—the most efficient organisation of a business would be *either*: (a) to enter the market and contract with other businesses for goods and services on a transaction-specific basis; or, alternatively, (b) bring transactions "out of the market" and "into a firm" (*i.e.*, either produce these goods and services on an vertically integrated, in-house basis or, to a lesser extent, enter into long-term supply contracts that effectively achieve the same goal). To make this determination, every transaction can be viewed through three criteria:

(1) *How often is the transaction to be carried out?* If the transaction is to be carried out with great frequency, then perhaps it is better to bring the transaction into the firm (*e.g.*, the need for skilled labour). On the other hand, if the transaction is infrequent (*e.g.*, new plant construction), then the most efficient allocation of resources would be to go into the market and complete the transaction by contract.

(2) *Asset Specificity—i.e., how unique is the asset to facilitate a particular transaction?* Again, the more specific the asset (*i.e.*, sunk network facilities), the more sense it makes to bring the asset out of the market and into the firm. Conversely, the less asset specificity is required (*e.g.*, wholesale long-haul capacity), then it is more efficient for a firm to conduct the transaction in the open market.

(3) *Degree of Uncertainty—i.e., how big is the risk?* Intuitively, if the risk is large, then vertical integration into a firm is the more efficient organisation

---

[13] (Free Press 1985).

of the business. If the product is fungible and easily replicated, however, then the more efficient organisation of the business is to conduct the transaction in the open market.

Accordingly, properly thought-out pro-competitive regulatory policies have the potential to change market structure for the greater good.[14] As such, unless and until policy-makers articulate a clear vision of long-term industry organisation within these parameters *for the unique contours of their respective markets*, realisation of the information society will remain an ephemeral dream. For example, different countries and regions have markedly different economic basic conditions and, as such, a "cookie-cutter" approach to regulation is both arbitrary and capricious—e.g., country A is imposing unbundling, so therefore we in country B must also impose unbundling. Moreover, not only do basic conditions and structural frameworks differ widely, from country to country and region to region, but also not all elements of a telecoms network share homogeneous economic characteristics. Similarly, most telecoms companies are not *single output* firms. Instead they are *multi-product* firms.[15] Finally, as if the process is not confusing enough, as various distribution technologies converge, competition also correspondingly becomes multi-dimensional (e.g., do we allow the cable industry to reconcentrate in order to provide hopefully, competition against the local phone company?) Naturally, this convergence will require policy-makers to undertake a careful balancing of various policy choices. To reiterate this point therefore, *the starting point of the analysis requires policy-makers to articulate a clear vision of market structure—such choices may not be made in a vacuum.* Think about it. Without articulating a clear cohesive view of long-term industry structure, then how will policy-makers know what kind of regulation is necessary in the first instance? Similarly, without articulating such a long-term view, it will be extremely difficult for policy-makers to evaluate the success of their efforts to "promote competition." Only by spelling out specifically such a view, therefore, can policy-makers know when market performance is satisfactory enough to justify the eventual elimination of its regulatory intervention—i.e., truly responsible public policies will, first, correctly and precisely identify whatever structural elements actually frustrate competition, and then (after concluding that the economic costs of the intervention do not outweigh the competitive benefits), narrowly tailor the remedy to mitigate that specific harm.

---

[14] See, e.g., the FCC's successful efforts to bring competition to the U.S. long-distance market through its *Competitive Carrier* paradigm and its efforts to promote competition for information services by aggressively "carving out" the terminal equipment and customer premises equipment markets via stringent structural rules such as standard technical interfaces.

[15] See "Reorienting Economic Analysis of Telecommunications Markets After the 1996 Act", *Antitrust Magazine* (American Bar Association, Spring 1997).

D. Public Policy Should Seek to Promote Good Market Performance

The next step policy-makers must take is to ask (a) how the markets under their jurisdiction are actually *performing*; and, if necessary, (b) what steps can they affirmatively take to promote additional infrastructure entry and thereby improve this performance over the long-term. As explained in more detail above, "good" market performance is usually characterised by the presence of static economic efficiencies (declining prices), dynamic economic efficiencies (innovation in new services or technologies), or both. If a market is performing well, therefore, then consumers will enjoy other societal benefits such as the long-term growth of real income per person.[16] More important, however, is that if a market is performing well, *then the need for stringent government intervention should be unnecessary.*[17]

Notice that the operative word here is *"well"*—not *"perfectly."* Indeed, various economic factors make it *impossible* to achieve "perfect competition" in certain regulated network and public utility industries. For example, because the telecoms business is characterised by high fixed and sunk costs, marginal cost pricing (the *raison d'être* of perfect competition) makes "perfect competition" impossible to achieve.[18] Also, the presence of network externalities (i.e., the value of the network increases with the number of users) makes "perfect competition" difficult to obtain. Finally, as argued throughout, residual "public interest" regulation—unrelated to promoting economic efficiency—will continue to distort market performance by affecting both the structure of many markets and the conduct of firms within those markets.[19]

---

[16] See F.M. Scherer & David Ross, supra n. 2 at 4–5.

[17] *Cf.,* Walter Adams, Public Policy in a Free Enterprise Economy, in Walter Adams (ed.), *The Structure of American Industry* (7th ed., Macmillan, 1986) (primary purpose of economic public policy paradigms should be to "perpetuate and preserve, in spite of possible cost, a system of governance for a competitive, free enterprise economy" where "power is decentralised; . . . newcomers with new products and new techniques have a genuine opportunity to introduce themselves and their ideas; . . . [and] the 'unseen hand' of competition instead of the heavy hand of the state performs the basic regulatory function on behalf of society").

[18] See generally David Evans & Richard Schmalensee, "A Guide to the Antitrust Economics of Networks", *Antitrust*, Spring 1996, at 36, 38. The authors explain that because many network industries are characterised by high fixed costs and low marginal costs, firms that price at marginal cost "would not recover their fixed costs, which are often the costs of developing innovative new products and services. To survive, they have to price well in excess of marginal cost. And, since they are making a profit at the margin on almost every unit, they often engage in price discrimination such as volume discounts, special deals, and complex pricing systems."

[19] See Jerry Hausman, "Taxation by Telecommunications Regulation", in *Tax Policy and the Economy* (1998) ("Because of significant economies of scale and scope, the first best prescription for setting price equal to marginal cost would require government subsidies or would lead to bankruptcy of local phone companies. In the US, government subsidies have not been used, and regulators have set price in excess of marginal cost for some services to allow regulated telephone companies to cover their fixed and common costs *and to provide a subsidy to basic residential service.*" (citations omitted and emphasis supplied)); see also Stephen Martin, *Industrial Economics: Economic Analysis and Public Policy* 16 (Macmillan, 1988) ("[perfect] competition is a Shangri-La up to which no real-world market can measure").

E. Many Policy-Makers Have Neither Articulated a Long-Term View of Industry Structure nor Sought Aggressively to Improve Market Performance (and Eventual De-Regulation) of Telecoms Markets

Some critics may argue that having the regulator work towards a specific long-term goal of market structure is just a venue for government control of the market. Conversely, other people argue that with "convergence," articulating a clear, long-term view of market structure is a nearly impossible task. Both pedantic views simply are not correct, however. There is a significant difference between central planning and having policy-makers develop a long-term industry structure—based upon what we know today and what is likely to happen tomorrow—that produces good market performance. As explained above, a market that demonstrates good market performance is typically characterised by a structure where there is vigorous price and non-price competition, low barriers to entry and exit, low switching costs among providers, and elastic supply and demand. Thus, it is really immaterial exactly what the market ends up looking like so long as consumers receive the benefits of both static and dynamic economic efficiencies.

Sadly, many regulators appear to be doing their best to deter any meaningful improvement for those markets currently characterised by poor economic performance (e.g., local loop competition; the multi-channel delivered video programming industry) and, more egregiously, to impair those markets demonstrating good economic performance (e.g., the US long-distance industry).[20] Despite their rhetoric that they want more "competitors," the reality is that many regulators continue to attempt to control the industries under their jurisdiction from an "incumbent-centric" approach. Stated another way, many regulators appear to hold to the erroneous view that capacity can be viewed from a static perspective, and therefore existing loop capacity—via resale and unbundling—is sufficient to handle all comers. The problem with this approach is that it prevents sufficient competition to develop to warrant true de-regulation—ostensibly the whole purpose of this massive "restructuring" exercise. In doing so, these policies inadvertently give firms the bizarre incentive to throw themselves eagerly into the proverbial "briar-patch" of regulation, rather than the appropriate incentive to innovate, create new infrastructure, cut costs, and compete.[21] It is no wonder, therefore, that neither incumbents nor new entrants

---

[20] See, e.g., *In re Low-Volume Long-Distance Users, Notice of Inquiry*, CC Docket No. 99-249, Notice of inquiry, FCC 99-168, (rel. July 20, 1999).

[21] To wit, look at the recent trend of industry reconcentration with seemingly little regulatory oversight. Indeed, because the FCC is using involuntary "voluntary" commitments as a proxy for a thorough inquiry, we never get to ask the fundamental question of whether, after conducting a detailed legal and economic analysis, the increasing trend in industry reconcentration is really in the public interest. See Reconcentration of Telecommunications Markets after the 1996 Act: Implications for Long-Term Market Performance (Second Edition) Phoenix Center Policy Paper No. 2 (July, 1998) (http://www.phoenix-center.org/pcpp/pcpp2.doc).

(both of which would like to deploy additional infrastructure and new technologies to capture increasing margins) benefit from a perpetual incumbent-
centric, resale model (including both total product resale and UNE-platform
entry), because such a paradigm fails to alter the *status quo* by appropriately
promoting an overall shift in the supply curve itself (i.e., new infrastructure
development).[22]

In fact, many regulators' actions (especially those of the FCC) actually appear
to be designed exclusively to *maintain* the *status quo,* because many policy-
makers still believes erroneously that competition is a "zero-sum" game—i.e.,
the discredited notion that one firm cannot be made better off unless another
firm is made worse off. If public-policy officials would instead properly focus
their attention on entry and *expanding*—rather than improperly attempting to
split—the overall market, then this flawed notion need not be true.

III. POLICYMAKERS MUST SEEK TO PROMOTE ENTRY AGGRESSIVELY

As stated above, the ostensible public policy goal is to move from a market characterised by monopoly to a market characterised by multiple firms, then entry
of *more* firms is the *sine qua non* of this entire exercise. More firms, however, is
not the equivalent of more *"choices."* As leading one leading telecoms economist recently observed about the US experience:

> One explanation for the failure of the [1996 Telecoms] Act is that an important inter-
> mediate step between monopoly and competition has been overlooked. If consumers
> are to have a choice in local phone markets, the entry of new firms selling local
> telecommunications services to a broad base of residential and small business con-
> sumers is required. "Choice" in any context implies alternatives. *In fact, while the
> term "competition" has become somewhat synonymous with the Act, the Act is really
> much less about competition than it is about competitive entry.*[23]

Indeed, while there may be multiple firms "competing" against one another, *so
long as these firms are scrambling to use the same underlying network facilities*
(e.g., the incumbent local exchange carrier or "ILEC's" local loop), it does not
a fortiori mean that "more" firms will produce "more" competition—i.e., better market performance as measured by lower prices or more services.[24] As
such, an act of Congress or a Directive from the European Commission:

> cannot force firms to compete, but can alter industry structure in such a way as to
> make entry profitable and, therefore, viable competition more likely. For example,
> legislation that reduces entry barriers can increase the number of firms in an industry,

---

[22] Antitrust courts also recognise that for network industries characterised by high fixed costs,
consumer welfare is unlikely to benefit so long as constrained supply, in the long-run, remains static. *Cf. City of Anaheim* v. *Southern California Edison Co.,* 955 F.2d 1373, 1380–81 (9th Cir. 1994).

[23] George S. Ford, "Opportunities for Local Exchange Competition Are Greatly Exaggerated",
Electric Light & Power (April 1998) at 20–1 (emphasis supplied) (http://www.phoenix-center.org/
library/ford_1.doc)

[24] Indeed, the dictionary simply defines "competition" as the "act of competing."

and the presence of many firms selling similar products and services will inevitably lead to price and quality competition. *Without entry, however, competition in the local exchange market will remain nothing more than a fabrication of incumbent monopolists and their representatives.*[25]

If we have learned anything from history, therefore, is that it is a metaphysical impossibility to have "competition without change." Instead, new, tangible entry—wired *or* wireless—is required.

For example, one of the primary problems with the concept of unbundling today is the issue of incentives—i.e., under current market structure, the incumbent LEC has absolutely no incentive to sell the primary input of production (the loop) to its rivals.[26] Conversely, its rivals also have no desire to purchase loops from a competitor (ILEC or otherwise). However, the economics of the telecoms business may make construction of a new network on a stand-alone basis cost prohibitive. What may solve this problem is the entry of one or more alternative distribution companies or "ADCos" (essentially a "carriers'-carrier" on the line side of the switch) which sells loops and other network services to all comers (i.e., it aggregates the demand) on a non-discriminatory basis in direct competition with the ILEC.

What makes the ADCo story so attractive from a policy perspective is that the entry of an ADCO would provide a tremendous incentive for the ILEC to divest *voluntarily* its loop functions from its marketing functions, because the ILEC would simply find it more efficient to do so under such changed market structure.[27]

To wit, there is great talk currently about forcing incumbent telephone operators to "fundamentally unbundle" their network operations from their marketing arms, such that the ILEC's marketing division would have to buy their network elements from the "LoopCo." Political and legal issues make this an unlikely scenario, however. Yet, as technology continues to progress and advance, it may be possible for a new entrant to contemplate an entry strategy where they would act as a competitive and ubiquitous alternative *wholesale* distribution provider (i.e., "ADCos"), rather than an entry strategy where they would attempt to act simply as just another end-to-end *retail* service provider. If this strategy is successful, then the overall structure of the distribution market will shift as supply becomes elastic. As this structural change occurs and the incumbent faces an increasingly higher own-price elasticity of demand, the incumbent may no longer have the incentive to engage in entry-deterring strategies but rather have the incentive to disaggregate *voluntarily*—rather than by intrusive regulatory fiat—its loop plant from its marketing activities because it

---

[25] Ford, *supra* n. 19, (emphasis supplied).

[26] Indeed, this emotional dilemma presented by mandatory unbundling is just like telling a child to go become an Olympic swimmer, but not to get wet in the process. An efficiently organised market, where transaction costs are minimised, would relieve this dilemma.

[27] See, e.g., Oliver Williamson, *supra* n. 9.

will be a more *efficient* (i.e., *profitable*) way to organise its business. That is to say, the incumbent may find under this altered market structure that it will make *more* money because: (1) its network operation will be able to sell more loops to more providers; and (2) its marketing operation will be able to provide cheaper service because it will always be able to by loops from competitive infrastructure providers.

A. Case Study: Terminal Equipment

A classic example of how changing the underlying structure of the market can force firms to "voluntarily" disaggregate can be found in AT&T's spin-off of Lucent Technologies (né Bell Cabs). To wit, back when AT&T had a total monopoly over everything short of the spoken word, it was very efficient for AT&T to bring the terminal equipment sector of the industry "out of the market and into the firm"—i.e., manufacture its terminal equipment on a vertically-integrated basis. In the mid-Eighties, however, as long distance competition was in its infancy, a more forward-looking FCC realised that competitors should have more than one source of terminal switching equipment (i.e., AT&T/Bell Labs). As such, through stringent structural regulation such as standard interfaces and plugs, the FCC essentially carved-out the terminal equipment market to allow for competing suppliers.

By the mid-1990's, the market for terminal equipment was flourishing. Not only was there Bell Labs/AT&T, but also other vendors such as Cisco, Siemens and Nortel and a wide variety of other niche technology players as well. As the result of this competition for terminal equipment, the equipment vendor side of AT&T found it was losing customers because, as a corporate entity, it was prohibited from selling to would-be rivals, and the network/marketing side of AT&T was limited only to what Bell Labs came up with. Given this changed market structure, it was now more efficient (i.e., more profitable) for AT&T to disaggregate *voluntarily* Bell Labs (now Lucent) from AT&T's telephone business (i.e., bring the transaction out of the firm and into the market). In so doing, both firms are better off, as Lucent can now sell to a wide variety of customers, and AT&T now has a choice of competing terminal equipment vendors who distinguish themselves on both a price and/or service quality or technological basis.

B. Case Study: Customer Premises Equipment (CPE)

Prior to the break-up of AT&T, customer premises equipment (i.e., your home telephone) in the United States literally was hard-wired into, and therefore an integral part of, the entire AT&T nation-wide PSTN network. For reasons similar to those found in the terminal equipment market, the FCC believed it could also "carve-out" the CPE market with stringent structural regulations. This process was not as easy it seemed, however.

The FCC justified its intrusion into the CPE market by noting that because there was a "long history of untrained telephone users"—i.e., Dad with a pair of pliers and a Phillips-head screwdriver—of installing equipment (such as extension telephones, automatic answering machines, etc.) that "damaged the reliability of the network," it was in the public interest to promulgate standard plugs and jacks. When the FCC first embarked on this process, the FCC purposefully declined *sua sponte* to impose specific standard plug/jack designs in the belief that mutually acceptable designs would be voluntarily arrived at by cooperative action of the affected industry—i.e., telephone carriers and telephone equipment managers. In fact, the FCC (naively perhaps) fully expected that such entities would meet and arrive at suitable designs without FCC involvement.[28]

Wrong. Citing to industry "confusion" regarding this issue, the FCC established a Notice of Proposed Rulemaking (NPRM) to ease the process along, in which all of the interested parties filed comments. Low and behold, just three months after the FCC released its original NPRM, the FCC, after reviewing all of the competing designs, released an order adopting the AT&T-sponsored plug that we all use today.[29]

Now we are sure that many of you are wondering why we are making such a big deal over this tiny little plug. Well, let us tell you why: this plug was the tiny acorn from which the mighty telecommunications and information services oak sprang forth. Think about it. Without a standard, inexpensive phone plug, we would still be renting our phones from the phone company and, moreover, these phones would come in basic black. There would be no princess phones, cordless phones, or even those nice football phones you get when you order a new subscription of Sports Illustrated. The explosion of the customer premises equipment market was just the beginning however. Without a standard interconnection jack, the development and proliferation of the quintessential fax machine we all take for granted today might never have occurred.

Finally, this plug, as small and inexpensive as it may be, was crucial to the creation of the global information superhighway we now enjoy. In the first instance, the standard plug permits consumers to easily access the Internet through a phone modem from any location they may choose. However, the real beauty of the standard plug is that—just like the variety of telephone models and prices available to consumers that mentioned above—consumers are not limited to a single monopoly supplier of computer or Internet services. In fact, the standard plug helps contribute to exactly the type of market performance we

---

[28] See Revision of Part 68 of the Commission's Rules to Specify Standard Plugs and Jacks for the Connection of Telephone Equipment to the Nationwide Telephone Network, 62 FCC 2d 735, Docket No. 20774 (rel. 12 July 1976) at 2–3.

[29] Ibid. at 7.

should want—i.e., a rivalrous computer and modem industry characterized by sustained trends of declining prices and new products and innovations.

IV. THE ECONOMICS OF ENTRY: THE "ENTRY CONDITION"

As both the European Commission and the FCC often have recognised ostensibly in the past, regulation has both *costs* and *benefits*.[30] Accordingly, regardless of the merits of any rule or regulation imposed on the market, it does not *a fortiori* mean that consumers suddenly will be awash in "waves" of competition. Entry is an extremely time and capital intensive endeavour, and will only occur if the new entrant believes that entry will be profitable.[31] A firm's decision to enter any market can be described as the "entry condition"—i.e., entry will only occur when:

(1) Post-Entry Profit (d) minus
(2) Inherent (exogenous) Entry Costs (x) minus
(3) Incumbent or Regulation-Induced Entry Costs (endogenous) (e) plus any
(4) Spillover Effects (s) i.e., when some firms can enter more cheaply than others
(5) Are greater than Zero[32]

This maxim can be represented by the formula:

$$d - x - e + s > 0$$

Post entry profits might be (loosely) defined as revenues minus average cost (excluding amortised sunk costs). This margin must be sufficient to cover any sunk costs (x, e) the firm must incur upon entry (and, to possibly, exit). Sunk costs are akin to a non-refundable deposit, and as such substantially increase the risk of entry. Sunk costs can be either a results of the capital expenses for technology and marketing necessary to enter a market (exogenous sunk costs) or the result of incumbent behaviour and regulatory decisions (endogenous sunk costs). The effects on (e) of regulation deal specifically with sunk costs, but regulators are not limited to that.

---

[30] See, e.g., *In re Competition in the Interstate Interexchange Marketplace*, 6 FCC Rcd 5880 (1991) at 80 (finding that when there is no economic nexus between regulations imposed and current market conditions, regulation can have a variety of adverse effects on market performance, including, inter alia: (1) denying a firm flexibility to react to market conditions and customer demands; (2) regulatory delays and uncertainty which reduce the value of a firm's service offerings; (3) affording competitors advanced notice of another firm's price and service changes which fosters a "reactive market, rather than a proactive one," and thus reduces the incentives for firms to "stay on their competitive toes"; and (4) by negating, in whole or in part, a heavily-regulated firm's incentive and ability to become a "first-mover" in the market.)

[31] Indeed, entreprenuership—defined by the dictionary those people who are willing both to organize a business venture and to assume the risk for it—needs to be affirmatively encouraged and promoted by policy-makers, not ignored (or worse, effectively, albeit unintentionally, quashed).

[32] Ford, *supra* n. 19.

One real-world example of an endogenous sunk cost is the cost of physical collocation in an ILEC central office. That space can, because of regulation, only be used to provide telecommunications services—once procured, a new entrant cannot readily convert collocation space to a condo or a youth education centre. ILECs know this, and rationally price collocation in a manner akin to an "entry tax." Currently, these construction costs are lightly and ineffectually regulated (if at all) and, in the US, oftentimes are in excess of $100,000 for each central office. With that type of entry tax, it is not surprising that there has been little entry into smaller or rural central offices.

Accordingly, *virtually every decision*, past and present, the regulator makes alters one or more variables in the entry equation (with the exclusion, by assumption, of exogenous entry costs (x)).[32a] That is to say, if a firm is contemplating the construction of a new advanced network, on what factors does regulation have a direct (or at minimum indirect) effect? Obviously, nearly *everything*. Among other things, the quintessential elements required to construct a new advanced telecoms network—but whose costs and availability are affected by regulation—include:

(1) Cost-based interconnection rates on a forward-looking basis (domestic and international);
(2) Effective OSS and standard technical interfaces;
(3) Timely and adequate collocation;
(4) Cost-based backhaul, IRUs, and leased lines on a forward-looking basis;
(5) Access to rights of way, poles, ducts, etc.;
(6) The ability to dig up streets without a hassle[32b];
(7) Building access/inside wiring;
(8) Non-discriminatory call origination for internet access;
(9) Number portability or, more accurately, number termination flexibility[32c]; and *depending on a firm's particular entry strategy*,
(10) Non-discriminatory and cost-based access to unbundled copper loops at any technically feasible point.

[32a] For example, unchecked incumbent horizontal reconcentration and vertical re-integration can reduce spillover effects.

[32b] Unfortunately, politicians in the United States continue to raise entry costs for new firms to build advanced facilities-based networks. See, e.g., Lyndsey Layton, "D.C. to Charge Cable Firm for Street Damage" *Washington Post*, 22 March 2000 at B01 (reporting that in response to disruptions of the city's roadways, Washington D.C. would impose fees ranging from [U.S.] $739 to $2,059 *per mile*); Lyndsey Layton, "Hidden Cost of Road Tear-Ups" *Washington Post*, 16 March 2000 at A1 (reporting that Prince George's County Maryland imposed a franchise fee of 5% of a company's revenue for digging up the street to lay new cable.

[32c] That is to say, it makes little sense to think about "number portability" from a demand-side perspective (i.e., a consumer has a single number which follows him or her for the rest of their life) because nobody really cares how many telephone numbers they may have. (Plus, having one number permanently assigned to you for life raises a rather unsavoury Orwellian connotation as well.) Instead, truly efficient number portability is *not* the ability for residential consumers to take one number with them from provider to provider , but instead *for consumers to have one number that can route to them wherever they are in the world.*

And, as if the preceding list is not large enough, regulators can, and often do, control post entry profits (d) (revenue minus variable cost) through regulation. (Indeed both phone rates and collocation prices, loop prices, USF/USO taxes, etc. are direct controls over (d).) Thus if regulators fail to get their pricing policies right in the first instance, then any contemplated entry decision by a new firm might just become a "non-starter."

A. Case Study: Utility Entry into Telecoms

As stated above, spillover effects i.e., where some firms can enter more easily than others can, if sufficiently large, offset otherwise entry prohibiting costs. Take, for example, electric and gas utilities. These firms generally have significant existing *sunk* (and indeed *ubiquitous*) infrastructure to provide alternative, competitive distribution facilities and services. Moreover, utilities, given their corporate culture of understanding exactly what truly means to be a "public utility," are the perfect candidates for successful ADCos.

Unfortunately, however, regulation (either deliberately or by accident) often stymies utilities' ability to maximise the spillover effects. That is to say, not only do utilities have to overcome the already high barriers to entry into the telecoms sector that other new entrants must face, but utilities must also uniquely overcome bizarre "public-interest" arguments that have absolutely no bearing on consumer welfare.

Two of the most powerful tools in these opponents' arsenal is to perpetuate improperly what has been described as the "cultural myth"—i.e., utilities, because of their established brand name, existing assets, and market position in a wholly separate and distinct industry (electricity) somehow have a competitive advantage in telecoms and therefore their entry into telecoms would be "unfair"—or the "cross-subsidisation myth"—i.e., utilities are using assets that were paid for by captive ratepayers, and therefore any profits derived from ancillary business must *a fortiori* be passed back to consumers, not shareholders. While these sector-specific issues are clearly beyond a telecom regulator's ken, readers must nonetheless recognise that these barriers do exist, are deterring utility telecoms entry decisions, and are harming consumer welfare by denying them access to alternative competitive choices. Both of these arguments are specious at best.

For example, in the former category, you often see in the United States utilities having to justify the use of their own brand name to enter competitive ancillary businesses. For example, the Georgia Public Service Commission actually prohibited Atlanta Gas Light from using their historical brand-name (ostensibly paid for by captive ratepayers, of course) because the utility's use of its historical brand-name for its gas marketing affiliate would confer an "unfair advantage" and lead to "consumer confusion" in a competitive market.[33] As noted

---

[33] See, e.g., Georgia Public Service Commission Press Release (20 Aug. 1998).

passim, however, the notion that "competition" must be "fair" is just rubbish. There is no notion of equity in competition—competition requires rivalry, because only through aggressive rivalry will firms be forced to innovate and lower costs. Used in this context, therefore, because regulation has deterred the entry of a significant new competitor, "fair" has once again become another obscene four-letter word that begins with the letter "F."

Moreover, the notion that a utility's "obligation to serve" its captive ratepayers with reliable service at just and reasonable rates must have a higher priority over a utility's equally legally binding duty to uphold its fiduciary duty to its shareholders is just as ridiculous. Indeed, if this argument is taken to its (il)logical conclusion then, by definition, a utility would technically own no tangible assets and instead would exist only as a service company to manage the grid. Unfortunately, such a position just does not square with reality. For example:

If a utility's captive rate-payers are the ones who actually paid for, and therefore own, rate-base facilities, does this also mean *a fortiori* that anyone who bought a vehicle from General Motors—and not GM's shareholders—actually own GM's plants and facilities, because GM used the revenue stream it received from the sale of vehicles to pay for the costs of its plants and operating expenses and provide itself with a profit?

If the utility serves only as a "service company"—because the captive ratepayers technically own all of the corporation's assets—then why are the utility's shareholders (and not captive ratepayers) liable for all of the debt incurred to build and maintain the facilities in the first instance?

Similarly, if a utility really serves only as a "service company" to manage the grid, then should not this company also have the ability to exit the market quickly with *de minimis* costs if it so chooses?

Finally, utility-bashing is one of the most time-honoured campaign techniques used by aggressive politicians to win poplar support at election time. Why? Just think about it. Utility assets are very large, visible and (to some) extremely unaesthetic things to look at. Moreover, as the dictionary's definition of "sunk costs" is often nothing more than a large picture of a nuclear power plant, a utility's ability to exit the market (to put it politely) is limited at best. As such, because utilities are not going anywhere (and everybody knows it) it is very easy to rally the proletariat against the big bad utility to gain political popularity.

Believe it or not perhaps the greatest master of this game was none other than America's own beloved President, William Jefferson Clinton, when he was active in state politics. If you think that we are kidding, let's just go to the proverbial video tape. During Governor Clinton's first term as governor of Arkansas, his administration's most famous and most popular battles were fought against Arkansas Power & Light (AP&L). In fact, he was known then as a so-called "reform governor", complete with his own "whiz kids" to run a newly-created Arkansas Energy Department. However, as he and his whiz kids apparently also decided to reform not only the Arkansas electric utility industry, but several other major sectors of the Arkansas economy as well, Governor Clinton upset too many industries and lost a supposedly easy re-election. Despite this loss, the former Governor Clinton knew that utility-bashing was still a strong, populist hot-button issue. As such, former Governor Clinton campaigned strongly on utility issues when he sought, and eventually won, re-election to the Governor's office.

Back in office after his involuntary hiatus, newly elected Governor Clinton apparently picked up right where he left off. His *piece de la resistance* of utility bashing came in the Grand Gulf nuclear plant litigation (affectionately known to many of us in America as "Grand Goof"). Specifically, Governor Clinton challenged the US Federal Energy Regulatory Commission's (FERC's) decision that Arkansas ratepayers—as part of the overall Middle South (now Entergy) System—should have to pay for their *pro rata* share of the cost of Middle South's Grand Gulf nuclear plant (which just happened to be located in Louisiana). The press reports from this time indicate that Governor Clinton unleashed an unending stream of vitriolic attacks against AP&L and FERC. Moreover, Governor Clinton often publicly threatened that if this rate-case was not settled to his satisfaction, Arkansas would actually seek to take over (i.e., condemn) AP&L from Middle South. Unfortunately, this type of improper "strong-arm" regulatory approach is very similar to the one employed by many NRAs (especially FERC) today.

The only problem with this political rhetoric was it was just that: rhetoric, without any serious analytical backing. Thus, while Governor Clinton was arguing that FERC and AP&L were evil incarnate to seek political favour with constituents, the United States Supreme Court reached the exact opposite conclusion. Indeed, not only did the Supreme Court uphold FERC's allocation decision, but it also found that FERC's allocation proceedings pre-empted a prudence inquiry by affected state commissions. Despite this resounding loss, however, a few months after the Supreme Court's decision, Mr Clinton launched his first successful run for the US presidency.[34]

V. AGGRESSIVELY PROMOTING ENTRY IS THE *SINE QUA NON* OF THIS
ENTIRE EXERCISE

Despite the analytical challenge outlined above, the nearly four years since telecoms restructuring has started to move forward aggressively in Europe and in

---

[34] For a further exegesis of all of these issues (complete with citations and references), please see "Utility Entry Into Telecommunications: Exactly How Serious Are We?" *Phoenix Center Policy Paper Series No. 1* (July 1998) (http://www.phoenix-center.org/pcpp/pcpp1.doc); "Three Reasons Why Utilities Need Telecommunications Expertise—Whether They Like it or Not", *Infrastructure*, (American Bar Association, Section of Public Utility Law, Spring 1998) (http://www.phoenix-center.org/library/ 3_reasons.doc); "Is Entry Into Telecoms The Right Strategy For Your Utility?" *Power Economics* (Dec. 1998) (http://www.phoenix-center.org/library/ power_econ.doc).

the United States, it often appears that regulators have not adequately considered the effects of their decisions, from basic rules to merger approvals, on the entry decisions of firms.[35] Instead, their decisions have been too focused on details perceived as required to implement the 1996 Act or various EC Directives, *rather than focused on implementing the underlying physical construct* (i.e., *the promotion of infrastructure entry*). Indeed, rather than undertake any meaningful analysis and set forth any constructive or innovative solution, regulators often try to avoid the issue by attempting either to "draw a line straight down the middle"[36] or by determining whether a proposed merger is "eminently thinkable."[37] While any opportunity to take a *tabla rasa* approach to contemplate the most optimal way to restructure the telecommunications industry would certainly be nice at this point, however, the eggs are unfortunately already too far scrambled.[38]

---

[35] What is particularly sad is that the FCC had at one point set forth a rational litmus test for regulatory intervention: the "Public Policy Barrier to Entry." That is, the FCC acknowledged five years ago in its first Cable Competition Report, not every perceived barrier to entry is one that requires an immediate regulatory response—only those barriers that are "policy-relevant." To determine whether a particular structural condition is a policy-relevant barrier to entry, the Commission stated that it must engage in a cost-benefit analysis that identifies, inter alia:

> all possible economic efficiencies, if any, that might result from the presence of the barrier to entry; (2) all offsetting economic efficiencies that might be attributable to the barrier to entry, if any; (3) all relevant positive and negative network externalities; and (4) the estimated economic cost of eliminating the barrier to entry or minimizing its effects.

See In re Implementation of Section 19 of the Cable Television Consumer Protection and Competition Act of 1992, Annual Assessment of the Status of Competition in the Market for Delivery of Video Programming, 9 FCC Rcd 7442, App. H at 29–31 (1994); see also Jerry Duvall & Michael Pelcovits, "Reforming Regulatory Policy for Private Line Telecommunications Services: Implications for Market Performance", *Federal Communications Commission OPP Working Paper No. 4* (1980) (analysis should focus on market performance, rather than on market participants' residual market power). Sadly, the FCC has never mentioned this test again.

[36] See "Industry Told To Avoid "Spins" In Arguing Legislative Intent", *Communications Daily* (26 February 1996) (quoting then-FCC General Counsel (and now-Chairman), William Kennard told industry executives that his office will take the "bowling ball" or "straight down the middle" approach in interpreting the 1996 Act.)

[37] See Reed Hundt, "Thinking About Why Some Communications Mergers are Unthinkable", Delivered to the Brookings Institution, Washington D.C. (19 June 1997); 24 June 1998 Statement From FCC Chairman William E. Kennard On AT&T And TCI Proposed Merger ("If AT&T and TCI make a strong commitment to bring residential consumers more choice in local telephone and high speed Internet access services, then this proposed merger is eminently thinkable."); but c.f., *Hawaiian Telephone* v. *FCC*, 498 F.2d 771, 776–77 (D.C. Cir. 1974) (FCC "cannot merely assert the benefits of competition in an abstract, sterile way").

[38] In the now-famous words of Justice Scalia in *AT&T Corp. et al.* v. *Iowa Utilities Bd. et al.*, 525 U.S. 366, 119 S.Ct. 721, 738 (1999)

> It would be gross understatement to say that the Telecommunications Act of 1996 is not a model of clarity. It is in many important respects a model of ambiguity or indeed even self-contradiction. That is most unfortunate for a piece of legislation that profoundly affects a crucial segment of the economy worth tens of billions of dollars. The 1996 Act can be read to grant (borrowing a phrase from incumbent GTE) "most promiscuous rights" to the FCC *vis- & agrave; -vis* the state commissions and to competing carriers *vis- & agrave; -vis* the incumbents—and the Commission has chosen in some instances to read it that way. But Congress is well aware that the ambiguities it chooses to produce in a statute will be resolved by the implementing agency. We can only enforce the clear limits that the 1996 Act contains. . . .

Citations omitted.

Moreover, recent initiatives do not provide any indication that regulators are going to depart from "business-as-usual." Indeed, rather than undertake the type of rigorous economic analysis suggested above, regulators now simply hold public forums to gauge the political winds. If policy-makers want to encourage new entry, however, then they cannot use a static "5-Year Plan" for broadband deployment—i.e., a "regulatory deal" between a few big-time industry players and the government to deploy a modicum of interesting new services conveniently in time for the next election. The public interest requires more.[39]

A. Case Study: The New Zealand Residential Market

When the New Zealand government decided to restructure its telecoms industry, they decided to do something radical. Fully aware of the dangers of regulatory capture, they adopted essentially a two-prong approach. First, New Zealand would mitigate the incumbent's residual market power by vigorous enforcement of existing competition law. Second, and more importantly, New Zealand decided to promote aggressively new entry by reducing, to the extent practicable, all regulatory barriers to entry. Among the most significant pro-entry policies is New Zealand's efforts to remove barriers to new facilities-based build-out. Indeed, Rather than extort concessions from new entrants to build new advanced broadband networks (such as that found in the United States), in 1989 the Government introduced a special provision called "Network Operator Status" to provide new entrants the right to apply for a court order to install telecommunications plant on public and private property. Not only is Network Operator status not a pre-requisite for conducting business as an end-to-end carrier, but also designation is automatic on application for those that qualify. Moreover, not only are there no licensing requirements in New Zealand, but New Zealand—unlike the United States—has an open-door policy that encourages—rather than deters—foreign entry into the market as well.

As a result of this pro-investment climate, numerous foreign firms have entered significantly into the New Zealand market on a facilities basis. For example, British Telecom has invested NZ $160 million and Vodafone has invested NZ $200 million in advanced technologies. But, perhaps most encouraging of all, Saturn and Telstra (the dominant firm in Australia) have recently announced their investment of more than NZ $1 billion dollars in a broadband network which will pass *over two thirds of all homes* in New Zealand.

The significance of the Telstra/Saturn investment in particular cannot be overstated. First, the Telstra/Saturn investment again demonstrates that competition—rather than regulation—has a significant impact on the price for local telephone services. The Wellington region has experienced a significant decrease

---

[39] See, e.g., *Northeast Utilities Service Co. v. FERC*, 993 F.2d 937, 951 (1st Cir. 1993) (the "public interest" may not be used to benefit a particular individual or group; rather, an agency's actions must be consistent with the interest of "the public" as a whole).

in price as a result of competition, and the rollout of the remainder of the network will no doubt put downward pressure on overall prices. Indeed, as the New Zealand Ministry of Commerce noted late last year, OECD figures show that the "relative performance [of the New Zealand residential telecommunications market] *is considerably better than the OECD average.*"[40] Contrast this performance with that found in the United States, where, as mentioned above, local call prices are actually on the rise due to the imposition of fees on consumers' bills such as a "subscriber line charge" and a "universal connectivity charge" and there is no competitive pressure from rival infrastructure providers.

Second, this massive investment shows that new entrants believe entering the New Zealand market on such a large scale especially with increased revenues from selling advanced, broadband services, will be *profitable*. As such, given the unique economic conditions (both geographic and demographic) of the New Zealand market, other entry-promoting incentives such as local loop unbundling are probably not needed.

IV. SO WHY ARE SO MANY REGULATORS REALLY AGAINST NEW ENTRY?

There are many theories why government may not want true competition. For example, government may not like the outcome that a market may produce.[41] Alternatively, government belligerence towards competition can result from outright naked regulatory capture.[42] Over the last seven years, however, there has been new and troubing third approach on the horizon: naked regulatory cynisim designed to reallocate wealth and achieve political pork.[43]

Think about it. Entry eliminates economic rents. Without economic rents, however, government has no levereage to extract "voluntary" concessions to reallocate wealth and perpetuate individual political narcissism. Stated another way, current regulatory policies appear to be designed *not* to dissipate market power via entry and competition but instead to *transfer* existing market power to the regulators themselves. Why? Because if the market can efficiently allocate resources, then regulators will have no patronage to dole out whenever the

---

[40] New Zealand Minister of Telecommunications, Telecommunications Services Regulatory Regime (9 December 1999) at 22.

[41] See Scherer & Ross, *supra* n. 2 at 9.

[42] That is to say, once an industry has a recognized organization that it can lobby on its behalf for regulation to its liking—in particular, either regulation that provides protection from outside the group or public programs to support it, etc.—industry has a powerful tool to lock in the status quo. See, e.g., Richard R. Nelson, "Recent Evolutionary Theorizing About Economic Change", (1995) 33 *Journal of Economic Literature* 48, 77; see also Julie Pitta, "Format Wars", *Forbes* (7 July 1997) at 262, providing examples of where regulatory capture prevented the introduction of new products and services for consumers.

[43] See, e.g., Gordon Tullock, "The Welfare Cost of Tariffs, Monopolies and Theft", *Western Economic Journal* (1967).

mood suits them.[43a] As such, why have "competition" when you can have "choices"? If consumer welfare is ever to be improved, however, then such cynicism can no longer be condoned.[44]

[43a] See, e.g., Kevin J Delaney "France Government Withdraws an Amendment on Local Calls" *Wall Street Journal*, 27 April 2000 (reporting that the French government withdrew a legislative amendment that would have opened France Telecom to new competition via unbundling following a request by communist party leaders); see also *European Union's Fifth Report on the Telecommunications Regulatory Package* (1999) at pp. 10–11 (http://europa.eu.int/comm/information_society/policy/telecom/
5threport/index.en.htm) where the European Commission presents a virtual laundry list of regulatory failures across the Community including, but certainly not limited to, the lack of regulatory independence due to a Member State having an equity share in the indigenous dominant incumbent; NRA's who are prone to regulatory delay; and an overall lack of resources and qualified staff.

[44] See, e.g., Reed Hundt, Statement on Westinghouse's Children's Educational Television Announcement, WDC, Sept. 20, 1995 (visited Nov. 4, 1998) <http://www.fcc.gov/Speeches/Hundt/spreh527.txt> ("Westinghouse's assurance that it will deliver three hours of children's educational TV on CBS underscores the tremendous importance of teaching our kids, instead of harming them, with broadcast TV." In the words of President Clinton, American children must not "lose 'countless opportunities to learn' from quality educational TV delivered by commercial networks for free to every home in the country.") (Note: The FCC attempted to act deceptively when Disney sought to acquire ABC/Cap Cities. Considering Disney's well-documented record with creating children's programming, however, Mr. Hundt could only argue that "it remain[ed] to be seen" whether Disney could still do something more to help America's children.); Statement of Reed Hundt in Response to AT&T's Pledge of $150 Million to Help Put the Nation's Schools on the Information Superhighway, 1995 FCC LEXIS 7113, Oct. 31, 1995 ("We at the FCC hope that AT&T's gift," mysteriously made concurrent with the FCC's decision to declare AT&T as a non-dominant carrier for domestic service "of free internet access and voice-mail to all the children of America will catalyze a nationwide public/private partnership to network all classrooms as the President and Vice President have challenged.").

3

Analytical Framework

GIVEN THE RAPID change in technology, telecoms regulators and practitioners now realise that they must approach telecoms restructuring efforts from a different perspective. Indeed, the changes set in motion over the last several years will present far more complicated analytical problems of economic issues than before, when these issues seemed to be familiar and clearly delineated— i.e., "evil" monopolists or "dominant firms" with a "helpless" fringe. Now, with the potential convergence of technologies and bundling of products, the lines between customers and competitors will become increasingly blurred. In light of these sweeping changes, economic analysis of telecommunications markets will have to account for this evolving competitive landscape.

Further, as the world of telecommunications rapidly continues to change, it will become more and more difficult to determine exactly what is the market we are analysing. As telecommunications markets become increasingly "multidimensional" (both horizontally and vertically), attempting to apply economic "first principles" (i.e., defining the relevant markets, evaluating the elasticities of supply and demand, identifying barriers to entry, etc.) to analyse the power in, and performance of, telecommunications markets initially may be frustrating to both neophytes and old hands alike.

The purpose of this chapter is to try to highlight some of the ways technology may change the structural and behavioural characteristics of telecommunications markets. As explained *passim*, correctly identifying the structural characteristics of telecommunications markets in the post-WTO world is the key to determining accurately whether firms are—or can—engage in some kind of strategic, anticompetitive conduct (e.g., collusive behaviour, raising rivals' costs, price squeezes, erecting barriers to entry, etc.) that warrants intervention by the courts or regulators.

II. BASIC ECONOMIC CHARACTERISTICS OF DYNAMIC VERSES STATIC MARKETS

At bottom, the current debate about the future of the Information Society does not revolve primarily around the issue of about monopoly pricing, but on the future of new innovation itself—i.e., the notion that in high technology, a company that establishes itself as a dominant standard in one critical market can leverage this market power into other markets to the disadvantage of competing technologies and products that may be superior.[1] Yet, if the pundits' prolific claims that because we are really in a dynamic technological revolution (i.e., nothing really lasts forever) are true, then should we care from a public policy perspective that one or more firms may have a "dominant" position in the first instance?[2]

Indeed, the economic literature explains that because of the rapidly dynamic and evolutionary nature of technology, there may in fact be multiple economic equilibria, all of which may completely possible. This market structure is unlike those markets characterized by goods that are homogeneous and unchanging, where "stabilizing" forces (i.e., diminishing returns) may appear to operate to correct market distortions and bring the market back into equilibrium—i.e., supply will equal demand. In the case of a dynamic product, "positive feedback" (i.e., increasing returns) makes for *many* positive equilibria, and therefore there is no guarantee that the particular economic outcome selected from among the many alternatives will be the "best" one. Moreover, once random economic events select a particular path, the choice may become locked in regardless of the advantages of the alternatives. Thus, if one product in a competitive market place gets ahead by "chance," it tends to stay ahead and even increase its lead and, as such, shared markets are no longer guaranteed.[3] This phenomenon is now often referred to as the concept of "network externalities"—*i.e.*, a product or network becomes more valuable as the number of people using the product or network increases.

---

[1] See "Microsoft: What's Really at Stake", *Business Week* 19 Jan. 1998 at 96.

[2] See, e.g., Gary S. Becker, "Let the Marketplace Judge Microsoft", *Business Week* (6 April 1998) ("Rapid turnover of monopolies in dynamic industries such as computing suggests that antitrust policy should not focus on whether companies have large market shares but rather on how soon they are likely to be replaced by others with superior technologies.")

[3] See W. Brian Arthur, *Increasing Returns and Path Dependence in the Economy* (University of Michigan Press, 1994) at 1. To illustrate this point, Arthur provides the following examples to illustrate these two respective market scenarios. In the former, "negative feedback" analysis, consider the relationship between a utility executive's decision to use either coal or hydro—two technologies performing the same function—to generate electricity. As hydro plants take more of the market, engineers must exploit more costly dam sites, thereby increasing the chance that a coal-fired plant would be cheaper. As coal plants take more of the market, they bid up the price of coal (or trigger the imposition of costly pollution controls), and so tip the balance toward hydropower. Thus, you end up with a market in which two technologies share in a predictable proportion that best exploits the potentials of each. Ibid., at 2.

In the latter, "positive feedback" approach, consider the battle between VHS and Beta. Both standards were introduced at about the same time at about the same price. Each format could therefore realize increasing shares as their respective market shares increased—i.e., the more VHS recorders there were, the greater the incentive for video rental stores to stock more pre-recorded tapes in VHS format, and therefore increasing the value of owning a VHS recorder and leading more people to buy one. In this way, a small gain in market share would improve the competitive position of one system and help it improve its lead. Yet, as market shares fluctuated early on because of external circumstances, "luck," and corporate manoeuvring, increasing returns on early gains eventually tilted the competition towards VHS: it accumulated enough of an advantage to take over the entire VCR market. Ibid.

Understanding the concept of network externalities may not be as simple as it seems, however. Indeed, as the concept of network externalities becomes yet another of the current *en vogue* analytical buzzword *du jour*, it is very important for everyone to identify carefully those situations where true network externalities exist (which may or may not have pro- or anticompetitive implications) and to distinguish those cases from situations where the traditional *per se* prohibition against tying arrangements of related products is more appropriate. This analytical caution is especially crucial as technology products and networks continue to proliferate, because concerns over "network externalities" can be inferred in a wide range of industries. If this careful identification is not made, then any legitimate concerns about network externalities may in fact be nothing more than arguments to prohibit economies of scope.

As explained *passim*, network externalities play a significant role in the telecommunications industry, because consumers are generally better off if different individuals buy similar or compatible products.[4] Because each user of a communications network is strongly interested in having other users have compatible products, therefore, if network externalities are present, then these externalities may lend an advantage to a variant that just happens to attract a number of customers early.[5] Similarly, if a new firm seeks to enter the telecommunications or video market, without an established base of "committed" customers, then it is unlikely that a new entrant could sufficiently sustain a "critical mass" of core customers to make the project economically viable.[6] The issue of network externalities is also extremely important when discussing the creation and availability of standard telephone network "Operational System Support" (OSS) software.

III. IMPORTANCE OF A DYNAMIC PERSPECTIVE

Obviously, as technology continues to advance, people attempting to analyse (or even discuss) the economics of sophisticated technology may feel like they are trying to hit a moving target or nailing Jell-O to a wall. Because we are not talking about cars, wheat or pork bellies, however—where a particular market equilibrium marks the "best" possible outcome under the circumstances—public policy-makers are going to have to think about what they want the structure of the market to look like in the future before any new paradigms are adopted and the damage caused by its intervention cannot be rectified.

---

[4] For this reason, you often see telecommunications carriers offer packages where it is cheaper to call someone "on-network" than "off-network" in order to attract and maintain customers—e.g., MCI's old "Friends And Family" tariff, Vodaphone's current mobile tariffs.

[5] See, e.g., Richard R. Nelson, "Recent Evolutionary Theorizing About Economic Change", (1995) 33 *Journal of Economic Literature* 48, 77 at 74.

[6] See James Olson & Lawrence Spiwak, "Can Short-Term Limits on Strategic Vertical Restraints Improve Long-Term Cable Industry Market Performance?" (1995) 13 *Cardozo Arts & Ent. L. J.* 283, 285.

Accordingly, policy-makers must continually account for the real potential for change that characterises telecommunications markets.[7] Indeed, because both demand and supply appear to be rapidly expanding,[8] simply focusing the analysis on current market conditions may not reveal an accurate picture of what is (or may be) occurring. In the new telecommunications environment, we must now explicitly account for the potential for change in assessing the extent of competition in telecommunications markets.[9]

Why is a dynamic forward-looking approach so important? Failure to account for such change may not provide a paradigm that detects and promotes good market performance over the longer term.[10] In an industry that manifests the potential for rapid technological change and innovation, such as telecommunications, an economic analysis should not focus too narrowly or exclusively on promoting the best use of society's resources from the standpoint of today's technology and resources availability—i.e., static economic efficiency. Rather, telecommunications, with its significant potential for rapid technological advance, should be viewed from a dynamic perspective.[11] A static analysis, when used as a substitute for a comprehensive dynamic review, can actually impose significant economic costs on an industry characterised by rapid change, because any remedy imposed will not be able to adapt easily to future market conditions.[12]

That is to say, static economic efficiency conceptually refers to an "optimal" allocation of scarce resources, such that the processes of production and the consumption of goods and services by consumers cannot be reorganised in any

---

[7] The particular time period used for such a forward-looking analysis is irrelevant to the broader issue of considering a dynamic approach. Depending on the purpose of the analysis, the two-year time period specified in the 1992 Merger Guidelines may be sufficient (§ 3.2), or an even longer period may be necessary to adequately measure future market performance in an industry characterised by rapid change.

[8] For example, on the demand side, telecommunications and, in particular, interexchange services, is a growing industry. This is evident from the substantial increase in choices available to consumers. On the supply side, technological change is ongoing. Moreover, the cost of underlying technology is becoming less significant (e.g., the cost of fibre optic continues to fall), while the costs of billing, advertising, and access continue to fluctuate.

[9] See Burton H. Klein, *Dynamic Economics* (Harvard University Press, 1977) 35, ("The essential difference between static and dynamic economic efficiency is that whereas the former is the result of making choices along a production-possibilities frontier, the latter is the result of extending the frontier by exploiting as fully as possible a technological potential").

[10] See, e.g., *United States* v. *FCC*, 652 F.2d 72, 106 (D.C. Cir. 1980). There, the FCC, specifically rejecting arguments in opposition raised by the DOJ and FTC, approved a satellite joint venture between IBM and Comsat to offer integrated voice, data, and digital image transmission service. The FCC found that the potential competitive benefits would outweigh any alleged current anticompetitive affects created by the proposed joint venture. The FCC's forward-looking approach made a significant contribution to the performance of this market.

[11] See Walter G. Bolter et al., "Telecommunications Policy For The 1980's: The Transition To Competition" (Prentice Hall, 1984) 360.

[12] See Friedrich A. Hayek, *The Fatal Conceit: The Errors Of Socialism* (Routledge, 1988) 85 ("What cannot be known cannot be planned"); see also *In re Motion of AT&T Corp. to Be Reclassified as a Non-Dominant Carrier*, FCC 95–427, 11 FCC Rcd 3271 at 32 n.90 (rel. Oct. 23, 1995).

way to increase the economic welfare of one or more individuals without simultaneously decreasing the economic welfare of some other individual. Static efficiency assumes that the quantity of factor inputs is fixed and the state of technical knowledge is given and unchanging.[13] In contrast, "dynamic economic efficiency describes the optimality of the allocation of resources as both the quantity of factor inputs and the state of technological knowledge varies."[14] Put another way:

> "The essential difference between static and dynamic efficiency is that whereas the former is the result of making choices along a production- possibilities frontier, the latter is the result of extending the frontier by exploiting as fully as possible a technological potential."[15]

However, the realisation of static economic efficiency may conflict with the attainment of dynamic economic efficiency; thus, it is realistic to expect that the attainment of dynamic economic efficiency may require the sacrifice of some static economic efficiencies in the short-run.[16] Accordingly, Bolter, et al., warned nearly fifteen years ago that:

> "Where static and dynamic economic efficiency conflict as public policy goals, policy makers should assess the potential for technological change in the industry subject to their jurisdiction. An industry that manifests potential for rapid technological change and innovation should not be guided by policies focused too narrowly on promoting the best use of society's resources from the standpoint of today's technology and resources availability, i.e., static economic efficiency. Rather, an industry with significant potential for rapid technological advance should not be constrained by regulatory or legislative policies that place too little weight on the importance of dynamic economic efficiency. The telecommunications industry in nearly all market segments is presently and prospectively characterised by rapid technological change. Policy makers, therefore, should carefully assess policy choices such that dynamic economic efficiency is given substantial priority in the decision making process."[17]

Notwithstanding the above, the advent of admittedly truly remarkable new advanced broadband technologies does not *a fortiori* mean that regulators can continue to duck meaningful analysis of the competitive problems underlying current market structure by promising consumers the ephemeral benefits of "convergence" in an era of "technological marvel" and even the shifting of

---

[13] Such an economically efficient allocation of resources is also sometimes referred to as "Pareto-optimal" or "Pareto-efficient". See James M. Henderon & Richard E. Quandt, *Microeconomics Theory: A Mathematical Approach* (3rd ed. McGraw Hill, 1986) at 286 .

[14] Walter G. Bolter et al., *supra* n. 11, at 359.

[15] Burton H. Klein, *supra* n. 9, at 35.

[16] See Joseph A. Schumpeter, "Capitalism, Socialism and Democracy" (Unwin Paperbacks 1987) (Original, 1943) at 83. Schumpeter explains:

> A system—any system, economic or other—that at every given point of time fully utilizes its possibilities to the best advantage may yet in the long run be inferior to a system that does so at no given point of time, because the latter's failure to do so may be a condition for the level or speed of long-run performance. Ibid. (emphasis in original).

[17] Walter G. Bolter et al., *supra* n. 11, at 360 (emphasis in original).

tectonics plates. Indeed, "convergence" and "choices" are no substitutes for tangible, competition that can be sustained for the long term.[18] Such a cynical "snake oil" sales pitch of a technology utopia—and concurrent "light-handed regulation" or dominant players—disserves both the market (to wit, consider the incredible valuation of dot.com start-ups with outrageously high Price/Earnings ratios) and, by definition, to consumer welfare as a whole.

All of these advanced technologies need some form of distribution mechanism and, therefore, placing priority on "service" competition" rather than facilities-based competition simply makes no sense. Why? Because the mere promise of technology does not and cannot mitigate market power when there is only one distribution source. Instead, as explained more fully in Chapter 2, policy makers must focus more on removing residual barriers to entry for a wide variety of distribution mechanisms (e.g., alternative terrestrial networks, wireless options, etc.) rather than focusing exclusively on splitting up the existing PSTN among various firms.

More importantly, even though technology can certainly hasten the restructuring process (and as it is in fact so doing) effective restructuring of a market characterised by monopoly for over sixty years still takes *time*—it simply cannot happen overnight as politicians may desire or promise.[19] Thus, as discussed *passim*, by cynically promising the appearance of an "Information Economy" in the short-term at the expense of true structural change in the long-run (and thus maximise consumer welfare via true sustainable competition and de-regulation), current policy-makers pervert the caveat spelled out above.

IV. CASE STUDY: DYNAMIC CHANGE AND THE NEED FOR THE 1996
US TELECOMS ACT

The rapidly changing market conditions of telecommunication industries are one of the driving forces behind the 1996 US Telecoms Act's modification of the Modified Final Judgement (MFJ) regime. While the break up of the old AT&T monopoly was probably one of the most pro-competitive achievements of the 20th century, the MFJ also created a scheme in which one segment of the telecommunications industry (i.e., the activities of the regional Bell Operating Companies or "BOCs") was effectively regulated by a static consent decree for the last fifteen years, which provided neither the court nor the DOJ with the ability or incentive to review the competitive effects of the MFJ beyond its narrow scope.[20] With the increasing development of new telecommunications

[18] To wit, if we really are living in an era of "infinite bandwidth," then why are we still paying high access and interconnection charges in so many markets? Similarly, if bandwidth is so ubiquitous (and free), why build any new facilities at all?

[19] For example, it took nearly 15 years for the US long-distance market to become competitive.

[20] See generally A. Douglas Melamed, "Antitrust: The New Regulation", *Antitrust*, Fall 1995, at 13, 14 ("The MFJ has become, in effect, a device for Antitrust Division regulation of both the wired and wireless industry"). In *SBC Communications Inc.* v. *FCC*, 56 F.3d 1484, 1491 (D.C. Cir. 1995),

technologies, this static regulation was not able to effectively adapt to, and account for, long-term market performance in adjacent markets, such as wireless telecommunications.[21]

The 1996 Act is, at bottom, expressly designed to change this regime. Specifically, the DOJ is stripped of its "pseudo-regulator" status, while the FCC is required to establish the structural framework to accelerate competition.[21a] The FCC's framework will attempt to achieve this goal by eliminating structural and regulatory barriers to entry by requiring, among other things, incumbent local exchange carriers to offer competitors interconnection, unbundled network elements, resale of exchange carrier services, and number portability.[21b] Once there is a sufficient level of rivalry, a substantial portion of current FCC regulation should presumably no longer be necessary.[22] At that point, the FCC is supposed to use its new forbearance authority contained in the 1996 Act and eliminate the unnecessary regulation.[22a]

V. UNDERSTANDING THE ROLE OF GOVERNMENT

A. Defining the Roles: Who Does What?

As with any other strategic plan, given the plethora of interests at stake with this endeavour, politicians need to figure out "who-should-do-what" during the restructuring process. Thus, before legislators even commit pen to paper (or, perhaps more accurately, get ideas from industry lobbyists during a free lunch

---

the D.C. Circuit, in affirming the FCC's disposition of the AT&T/McCaw merger, rejected both BellSouth's argument that the FCC failed to consider the MFJ as a "special circumstance affecting competition" and BellSouth's notion that the Commission should impose MFJ restrictions on McCaw. Using the FCC's own words, the court reasoned that "assuming [with BellSouth] . . . that the MFJ restricts competition in undesirable ways, expanding its application to the BOC's competitors would only compound the harm."

[21] As explained more fully below, when the MFJ was implemented, the various parties agreed to create "local access and transport areas" or "LATAs." LATAs are not uniform in shape or size and can be both interstate and intrastate. At the time, the LATAs were a convenient way to divide the assets of the old Bell system and to delineate the respective service areas of the BOCs. However, the MFJ, and the LATA boundaries in particular, were imposed on the BOC's cellular companies, even though the MFJ and LATA boundaries had been created without any thought of cellular service and the former bore no relation to the latter's. See generally *United States* v. *Western Elec. Co.*, 578 F. Supp. 643 (D.D.C. 1983). To fit the cellular square peg into the MFJ round hole, a waiver procedure involving both the court and the DOJ was created which, in one case, required nearly five years for the innocuous addition of one small county to an existing cellular system's coverage area. The net result of this procedure was the unnecessary denial of competition in cellular service for the residents of this county and the unnecessary delay of seamless cellular service between New York and Washington. See 141 Cong. Rec. S7881–02, 7884 7 June 1995 (statement of Sen. Pressler).

[21a] See 47 U.S.C. §152 note.

[21b] See 47 U.S.C. §251.

[22] However, enforcement by the FCC to ensure that carriers continue to provide interconnection, unbundled network elements, resale, and number portability will probably continue for years to come.

[22a] See 47 U.S.C. §§160, 161.

at the Palm), it is crucial to understand the proper and respective roles of the antitrust enforcement agencies and those agencies responsible for economic regulation of a particular industrial sector.

Probably the most misunderstood issue regarding the proper roles of antitrust and economic regulation is the exact scope and definition of the "public interest" standard included in many US laws and EC Directives and the relationship of this standard to the enforcement of the US antitrust and European competition laws. Clearly, regulatory agencies such as the FCC or the Information Society Directorate are not (nor should they be) responsible for enforcing the antitrust or competition laws. Rather, these tasks are explicitly and appropriately left this task to the Department of Justice or the Federal Trade Commission in the United States and to the Competition Directorate in the EC. These regulatory agencies have a separate and distinct duty from these enforcement agencies, and, as such, they have "significantly different" standards.[23]

1. The Role of the Antitrust and Competition Law Enforcement Agencies

Authorities responsible for enforcing the antitrust or competition laws serve in a *prosecutorial* role and bring actions on a case-by-case basis. To facilitate their objective, they often have certain powers bestowed on them, such as confidentiality and subpoena provisions. However, because the enforcement agency, and not the defendant, has the burden to demonstrate to a court that either that a specific transaction would substantially lessen competition under current market conditions or that one or more parties have engaged or attempted to engage in anticompetitive conduct, these enforcement agencies typically view economic analysis through a "static" model. That is to say, their determinations generally utilize narrow market definitions and short time periods because they assume that the quantity of inputs is fixed and the state of technology is given and unchanging.[24]

2. The Role of Administrative Agencies Responsible for Economic Regulation

In contrast to the antitrust and competition law enforcement agencies, the FCC and the Information Society Directorate and individual National Regulatory

---

[23] See, e.g., *ABC Cos. Inc.*, 7 FCC 2d 245, 249 (1966) ("Antitrust Division is charged with the enforcement of the antitrust laws . . . while the Commission is charged with effectuating the policies of the Communications Act."); see also Dissenting Statement of FTC Commissioner Mary L. Azcuenaga in *Time Warner Inc.*, FTC File No. 961–0004 (14 Aug. 1996) (because FCC already had rules in place prohibiting discriminatory prices and practices, there was "little justification" for the FTC to require Time Warner to "comply with communications law" and, therefore, to the extent that the proposed consent order offered "a standard different from that promulgated by Congress and the FCC, it arguably is inconsistent with the will of Congress"; as such, "*[t]here is much to be said for having the FTC confine itself to FTC matters, leaving FCC matters to the FCC*" (emphasis supplied)).

[24] Notwithstanding the above, however, antitrust enforcement agencies often cannot overcome the temptation to become pseudo-regulators. This trend appears to have increased exponentially over the last several years, as the various antitrust enforcement agencies on several occasions simply have ordered the defendants to obey applicable FCC regulation(s).

Authorities serve as independent *regulatory* bodies. In other words, interested parties must first seek their approval before they may engage in a jurisdictional activity. In contrast to the procedure for competition law enforcement, therefore, the burden rests with the moving parties—and not with the regulatory agencies— to show that a particular transaction meets the relevant statutory criteria.

Notwithstanding this procedural difference, because regulators serve as both investigators and adjudicators, regulatory agencies must examine, *inter alia*, all of the relevant facts, and must make clear the "basic data and the 'whys and wherefores' of [their] conclusions."[25] Moreover, these regulatory agencies must take great care to ensure procedural due process for all parties in a proceeding.[26]

At bottom, these regulatory agencies—be it the FCC, the Information Society Directorate, or any other NRA for that matter—should be concerned about solving two basic economic problems: (1) assuring that the regulated firms under their jurisdiction do not engage in anticompetitive behavior or charge captive ratepayers monopoly prices; and (2), where practical, formulating regulatory paradigms designed to improve overall market performance in both the short-run and especially, given the huge sunk costs inherent to the telecommunications and related industries, the long-run.[27] Given this daunting and difficult task, the powers of many regulatory agencies responsible for economic regulation can be significantly *broader* than those of the antitrust enforcement agencies, because they are "entrusted with the responsibility to determine when and to what extent the public interest would be served by competition in the industry."[28]

[25] See, e.g., *City of Holyoke Gas & Electric Dept.* v. *FERC*, 954 F.2d 740, 743 (D.C. Cir. 1992) ("Since it is already doing the relevant calculation, it is a small matter to abide by the injunction of the arithmetic teacher: Show your work! For the Commission to do less deprives the [consumer] of a rational explanation of its decision.").

[26] In the US, if the FCC fails in any or all of these responsibilities, a reviewing court may reverse and remand the agency's decision as arbitrary and capricious. *Ibid.*

[27] It should be noted, however, that the FCC's challenge is made more complex because telecommunications is clearly an industry characterized by rapid change and innovation. This challenge is now exacerbated with the passage of the Telecommunications Act of 1996. See, e.g., *Turner Broadcasting System Inc.*, v. *FCC*, 117 S. Ct. 1174, 1189 (1997) (regulatory schemes concerning telecommunications have "special significance" because of the "inherent complexity and assessments about the likely interaction of industries undergoing rapid economic and technological change"); *Denver Area Educational Telecommunications Consortium Inc.*, v. *FCC*, 116 S. Ct. 2374, 2385 (1996) (Court is "aware . . . of the changes taking place in the law, the technology, and the industrial structure, related to telecommunications, see, e.g., Telecommunications Act of 1996 . . . ."); *Columbia Broadcasting Inc* v. *Democratic National Committee*, 412 U.S. 94, 102, 93 S. Ct. 2080, 2086 (1973) ("The problems of regulation are rendered more difficult because the . . . industry is dynamic in terms of technological change"); *FCC* v. *Pottsville Broadcasting Co.*, 309 U.S. 134, 138 (1940) ("Communications Act is not designed primarily as a new code for the adjustment of conflicting private rights through adjudication. Rather it expresses a desire on the part of Congress to maintain, through appropriate administrative control, a grip on the dynamic aspects" of the telecommunications industry).

[28] *FCC* v. *RCA Communications Inc.*, 346 U.S. 86, 93–95 (1953); *Northeast Utils. Serv. Co.* v. *FERC*, 993 F.2d 937, 947–48 (1st Cir. 1993) (public interest standard does not require agencies "to analyze proposed mergers under the same standards that the [DOJ] . . . must apply" because administrative agency is not required to "serve as an enforcer of antitrust policy in conjunction" with the DOJ or FTC; thus, while agency "must include antitrust considerations in its public interest

B. Harmonising Economic Regulation and Competition Law

Despite the fact that economic regulation and antitrust approach and analyse market performance from different perspectives—i.e., economic regulation seeks to promote competitive rivalry directly "through rules and regulations" while antitrust or competition law enforcement seeks to foster competitive rivalry "indirectly by promoting and preserving a process that tends to bring them about"[29]—both regimes should fulfill identical public-policy goals. According to (now) US Supreme Court Justice Stephen Breyer, these goals are "low and economically efficient prices, innovation, and efficient production methods."[30]

As such, those who argue that there is no relationship between antitrust/competition law and economic regulation completely miss the point.[31] Congress and the European Commission clearly intended this "direct/indirect" dual regime approach, because there are often situations where certain market conditions or an individual firm's conduct may not satisfy the requisite legal criteria to violate the antitrust or competition laws but nonetheless may have a direct negative impact on market performance. These conditions are sometimes referred to as "policy-relevant" barriers to entry—i.e., those situations where government intervention may be warranted, because the economic costs of imposing remedial regulation will not exceed the existing economic costs created by the barrier if no government intervention occurs.[32] If a "policy-relevant" barrier to entry is

calculations . . . it is not bound to use antitrust principles when they may be inconsistent with the [agency's] regulatory goals"). See also *National Broadcasting Co.* v. *United States*, 319 U.S. 190, 219 (1943) (Congress, through the Communications Act, "gave the Commission not niggardly but expansive powers."); Craig O. McCaw, Memorandum Opinion & Order, 9 FCC Rcd. 5836 (1994) at 7, *affirmed*, *SBC Communications* v. *FCC*, 56 F.3d 1484 (D.C. Cir. 1995) (FCC's "jurisdiction under the Communications Act gives us much more flexibility and more precise enforcement tools that the typical court has").

[29] *Town of Concord* v. *Boston Edison Co.*, 915 F.2d 17, 22 (1st Cir. 1990) (Breyer, J.), *cert. denied*, 499 U.S. 931 (1991).

[30] *Ibid.* Accord *United States* v. *FCC*, 652 F.2d 72, 88 (D.C. Cir. 1980) ("basic goal of direct governmental regulation through administrative bodies and the goal of indirect governmental regulation in the form of antitrust law is the same—to achieve the most efficient allocation of resources possible"); see also Hausman "Taxation by Telecommunications Regulation" in *Tax Policy and the Economy* (1998) ("The public interest standard should recognize economic efficiency as one of its primary goals. Economic efficiency implies not assessing unnecessary costs on U.S. consumers and firms").

[31] See *United States* v. *AT&T*, 498 F. Supp. 353, 364 (D.D.C. 1980) (Green, J.) (it is "not appropriate to distinguish between Communications Act standards and antitrust standards" because "both the FCC, in its enforcement of the Communications Act, and the courts, in their application of the antitrust laws, guard against unfair competition and attempt to protect the public interest").

[32] That is to say, from a public policy perspective, not all impediments to entry are necessarily barriers to entry that require some type of government intervention or remediation. Thus, when analyzing whether a particular structural characteristic is a "policy-relevant" barrier to entry, policy makers will have to engage in a cost-benefit analysis that identifies, *inter alia*: (1) all possible economic efficiencies, if any, that might result from the presence of the barrier to entry; (2) all offsetting economic efficiencies that might be attributable to the barrier to entry, if any; (3) all relevant positive and negative network externalities; and (4) the estimated economic cost of eliminating the barrier to entry or minimizing its effects. *Ibid.*

present, then regulatory intervention may be appropriate.[33] What legislators in both Europe and the United States did not intend by this dual review process is wasteful redundancy of government and taxpayer resources.[34]

This concept is the *raison d'être* of regulation—i.e., (again, just to emphasize the point) that economic regulation is supposed to be a *substitute for*, and *not a complement of*, competitive rivalry. It is not, contrary to popular belief, "*because we can.*"[35] In other words, economic regulation is appropriate only when one or more firms are capable of successfully exercising market power (charging monopoly prices or restricting output) for a sustained period of time and additional entry is unlikely.[36] If this caveat is ignored, then it may very be that the government intervention will probably do more to create distortions in market performance than the public interest benefits policy-makers are attempting to produce.[37]

If regulation is, in fact, warranted, however, it does not mean that government suddenly has a "green light" to prescribe specific prices for goods or

[33] For example, while ESPN, CNN, HBO or Showtime appropriately should not be considered to be an "essential facility" under the antitrust laws, without these popular channels, new entrants will find it extremely difficult to establish a viable, rival distribution system for delivered multi-channel video programming. As such, Congress in the 1992 Cable Act required, inter alia, parties to an exclusive programming distribution contract to demonstrate that such contract is in the public interest, see 47 U.S.C. § 548. When undertaking this review—just like under antitrust precedent—the Commission must weigh the procompetitive benefits of an exclusive distribution contract against its likely anticompetitive harms. Evidence has borne out that this short-term regime has contributed significantly to the deconcentration of the MVPD market. See James Olson & Lawrence Spiwak, *supra* n. 6.

[34] Again, as now-U.S. Supreme Court Justice Breyer once wrote, an "antitrust rule that seeks to promote competition but nonetheless interferes with regulatory controls could undercut the very objectives the antitrust laws are designed to serve." As such, where regulatory and antitrust regimes coexist, "antitrust analyses must sensitively 'recognize and reflect the distinctive economic and legal setting' of the regulated industry to which it applies." *Town of Concord*, 915 F.2d at 22. See also *Gulf States Utils. Co.* v. *FPC*, 411 U.S. 747, 760 (1973) ("Consideration of antitrust and anticompetitive issues by [regulatory agencies,] moreover, serves the important function of establishing a first line of defense against those competitive practices that might later be the subject of antitrust proceedings.").

[35] But *cf.* Hoecker Cites "Misconceptions," *Electric Utility Week*, 31 Mar. 1997 (reporting that U.S. Federal Energy Regulatory Commission Chair James Hoecker issued a "strong defense" for a continuing role for regulators in deregulated markets. According to Hoecker, some view the concept of "regulated competition [as] an oxymoron like 'postal service' or 'airline food'. . . . [However,] I prefer to think of regulation as evolving into a guardian and guarantor of competition, *instead of its substitute.*" emphasis supplied.)

[36] For example, there are certain types of "procompetitive" regulation which, when properly constructed, can produce more public interest benefits than the economic costs the regulation imposes on the market. See, e.g., Part 68 of the FCC's rules, 47 C.F.R. § 68.1 et seq., which, by requiring standard technical interfaces, permits competition in the terminal equipment market.

[37] See, e.g., *In re Motion of AT&T Corp. to Be Reclassified as a Non-Dominant Carrier*, FCC 95–427, 11 FCC Rcd. 3271 (1995) at 32 ("When the economic costs of regulation exceed the public interest benefits, the Commission should reconsider the validity of continuing to impose such regulation on the market."); see also Joseph Kattan, "Beyond Facilitating Practices: Price Signalling and Price Protection in the New Antitrust Environment", (1994) 63 *Antitrust L.J.* 133, 136; Nina Cornell, Peter Greenhalgh & Daniel Kelley, "Social Objectives and Competition in Common Carrier Communications: Incompatible or Inseparable?", *Federal Communications Commission OPP Working Paper No. 1* (1980); John Haring & Kathleen Levitz, "What Makes the Dominant Firm Dominant?", *Federal Communications Commission OPP Working Paper No. 25* (1989).

services. Indeed, if economic regulation is truly supposed to be a substitute for competition, then, just as in competitive, non-regulated markets, regulation should permit a range of prices for a particular product or service, each of which accounts for different consumer preferences and purchasing capabilities (e.g., volume discounts, superior service quality, etc).

As explained below, basic ratemaking principles instruct that there cannot be one, single, generic industry-wide price under the common "just and reasonable" standard. Rather, the "just and reasonable" standard requires only that rates fall within a "zone of reasonableness"—i.e., rates must only be neither "excessive" (rates that permit the regulated firm to recover monopoly rents) nor "confiscatory" (rates that do not permit the regulated firm to recover its costs).[38] From an economic point of view, they need not—just like caviar or Rolls Royce limousines—be "fair" or "affordable" for everyone.

Thus, if we are truly serious about "deregulation," then we need to formulate policy paradigms designed to establish, to the extent practicable, a structural framework conducive to competitive rivalry, under which firms will be unable to engage in strategic anticompetitive conduct—even if they try.[39] Think about it. In a market structure conducive to vigorous rivalry, efficient firms (i.e., those firms that can lower their costs, innovate to make new products, and regularly offer consumers more choices) should, in theory, be able to make *more* money as demand and supply continue to shift down and to the right. Such an outcome is infinitely superior to the probable performance of a market that—even though it lacks a structural framework conducive to competitive rivalry—government believes with sufficient intervention is nonetheless capable of achieving a level of "workable" market performance that "mimics" competition.

Yet, despite the fact that government has a wide variety of tools to help it accomplish this goal, it is also crucial to recognize that government intervention, no matter how innocuous, *de minimis,* or well-meaning, will impose significant economic costs on society. These economic costs include administrative and compliance costs, the possible deterrence or delay of innovation, the creation of market structures that can promote collusive behaviour and, as discussed in more detail below, the often denied, yet highly ubiquitous (and insidious) issue of "regulatory capture."[40]

---

[38] See *Farmers Union Central Exchange Inc.* v. *FERC*, 734 F.2d 1486, 1504 (D.C. Cir.), *cert. denied*, 469 U.S. 1034 (1984) (the concept of "just and reasonable" must clearly be more than a "mere vessel into which meaning must be poured").

[39] See generally *Brooke Group Ltd.* v. *Brown & Williamson Tobacco Corp.*, 509 U.S. 209, *rehearing denied*, 509 U.S. 940 (1993); A.A. Poultry Farms, Inc. v. Rose Acre Farms, Inc., 881 F.2d 1396, 1401 (7th Cir. 1989) ("Market structure offers a way to cut the inquiry [of potential, anticompetitive strategic vertical conduct] off at the pass . . . ."). See also F.M. Scherer & David Ross, *Industrial Market Structure and Economic Performances* (3d ed., Houghton Mifflin, 1990) (despite antitrust's focus on structural measures such as the Herfindahl-Hirschman Index (HHI), economic concentration is only one aspect of market structure; other relevant features of market structure include product differentiation, barriers to entry, cost structures, vertical integration, and diversification).

[40] See, e.g., *In re Competition in the Interstate Interexchange Marketplace*, 6 FCC Rcd. 5880 (1991) at 80 (finding that when there is no economic nexus between regulations imposed and current

As such, government intervention must be wielded like a scalpel rather than a blunt-edged sword—i.e., truly responsible public policies will, first, correctly and precisely identify whatever structural elements actually frustrate competition, and then (after concluding that the economic costs of the intervention do not outweigh the competitive benefits) narrowly tailor the remedy to mitigate that specific harm. However, if either antitrust enforcement officials or regulators fail to conduct such an analysis—because of the economic costs mentioned above—then poorly conceived or outdated regulation or antitrust conditions can actually create more distortions in market performance than the public interest benefits the regulation or conditions are designed to achieve.[41]

VI. DEFINING THE RHETORIC: WHAT DO WE MEAN?

So if antitrust and economic regulation are supposed to achieve the same goals, why all the fuss? The debate about the appropriate roles of antitrust and economic regulation stems from a long line of cases which stand for the proposition that an administrative agency charged with the economic regulation of one or more industrial sectors must, in the exercise of its responsibilities, "*make findings related to the pertinent antitrust policies, draw conclusions from the findings, and weigh these conclusions along with other important public interest considerations.*"[42] The big question, therefore, is how to define "antitrust policies" and "other public interest factors"?

A. "Competition"

Before we start, however, perhaps it is a good idea—again, starting *tabula rasa*—to try to assign some analytical concept to the term "competition" itself.

market conditions, regulation can have a variety of adverse effects on market performance, including, *inter alia*: (1) denying a firm flexibility to react to market conditions and customer demands; (2) regulatory delays and uncertainty which reduce the value of a firm's service offerings; (3) affording competitors advanced notice of another firm's price and service changes which fosters a "reactive market, rather than a proactive one," and thus reduces the incentives for firms to "stay on their competitive toes"; and (4) negating, in whole or in part, a heavily-regulated firm's incentive and ability to become a "first-mover" in the market.

[41] See, e.g., *Clamp-All Corp* v. *Cast Iron Soil Pipe Institute*, 851 F.2d 478, 484 (1st Cir. 1988), *cert. denied*, 488 U.S. 1007 (1989) (Breyer, J.) (rejecting argument that antitrust policies warrant the imposition of stringent conditions to remedy interdependent pricing, "not because [interdependent] pricing is desirable (it is not), but because it is close to impossible to devise a judicially enforceable remedy for 'interdependent' pricing. How does one order a firm to set its prices without regard to the likely reactions of its competitors?"); *In re Motion of AT&T Corp. to Be Reclassified as a Non-Dominant Carrier*, FCC 95–427, 11 FCC Rcd. 3271 (1995) at 32 ("When the economic costs of regulation exceed the public interest benefits, the Commission should reconsider the validity of continuing to impose such regulation on the market."); see also Joseph Kattan, Beyond Facilitating Practices: Price Signaling and Price Protection in the New Antitrust Environment, *supra* n. 30 at 136; Nina Cornell, Peter Greenhalgh & Daniel Kelley *supra* n. 30; John Haring & Kathleen Levitz, *supra* n. 37.

Unfortunately, while numerous people in both the private and public sectors seem to enjoy bandying this phrase about, it is increasingly evident that many of these people have no real idea about its exact meaning. "Competition" is neither some utopian destination like Xanadu or Nirvana nor a tangible object that we can reach out and touch and comfort ourselves with. Indeed, because economic terms actually have technical meaning, the mere ability to conjugate the verb "to compete" in the same sentence with the word "market" does not necessarily mean that one understands economic theory—e.g., how the presence of high sunk costs affects both entry decisions and strategic behavior to protect sunk assets; the economic costs of residual "public interest" obligations such as "universal service" or an "obligation to serve"; and the economic costs of advanced tariffing and reporting requirements.

In fact, the dictionary simply defines "competition" as the "act of competing." However, the fact that there may be multiple firms "competing" against one another does not necessarily mean that this rivalry will produce lower prices or more services. For example, there may be types of market structures in which a very efficient fringe is vigorously competing with a dominant firm, yet the underlying structural characteristics of the market prevent the realization of static and dynamic economic efficiencies. Conversely, there may be market structures that may look to the inexperienced as being *prima facie* incapable of producing competitive rivalry, yet nonetheless demonstrate sustained trends of dynamic and static economic efficiencies.

As such, the more appropriate question to ask is how a market is actually *performing*. "Good" market performance is usually characterized by the presence of static economic efficiencies (declining prices), dynamic economic efficiencies (innovation in new services or technologies), or both. If a market is performing well, then consumers will enjoy other societal benefits such as the long-term growth of real income per person.[43] More important, however, is that under the rationale of regulation explained above, if a market is performing well, *then the need for stringent government intervention should be unnecessary*.[44]

---

[42] *United States* v. *FCC*, 652 F.2d 72, 81–82 (D.C. Cir. 1980) (*en banc*) (quoting *Northern Natural Gas Co.* v. *FPC*, 399 F.2d 953, 961 (D.C. Cir. 1968)). See also *FCC* v. *National Citizens Comm. for Broad.*, 436 U.S. 775, 795 (1978); *Gulf States Utils. Co.* v. *FPC*, 411 U.S. 747, 755–62 (1973) (regulatory agencies must consider "matters relating to both the broad purposes" of their enabling statutes "and the fundamental national economic policy expressed in the antitrust laws"); *FCC* v. *RCA Communications Inc.*, 346 U.S. 86 (1953) ("There can be no doubt that competition is a relevant factor in weighing the public interest.").

[43] See Scherer & Ross, *supra* n. 39 at 4–5.

[44] See also Walter Adams, Public Policy in a Free Enterprise Economy, in Walter Adams (ed.), The Structure of American Industry (7th ed., Macmillan, 1986) (primary purpose of economic public policy paradigms should be to "perpetuate and preserve, in spite of possible cost, a system of governance for a competitive, free enterprise economy" where "power is decentralized; . . . newcomers with new products and new techniques have a genuine opportunity to introduce themselves and their ideas; . . . [and] the 'unseen hand' of competition instead of the heavy hand of the state performs the basic regulatory function on behalf of society").

B. "Antitrust Policies"

What exactly are "antitrust policies"? The answer should be rather simple: It has long been established that administrative agencies responsible for economic regulation must support their decisions with sound legal and economic reasoning, rather than with cursory conclusions.[45] Merely stating, without more, that "competition" is a "national policy," however, does not satisfy this burden.[46] Thus, as outlined above, because: (1) both economic regulation and antitrust are supposed to be the marriage between law and economics; and, as such, (2) the legal and economic analyses and the public policy end-goals of each discipline are the same (low prices/more services); then (3) it would therefore seem highly logical that economic regulators should look to relevant antitrust precedent (where a judge may have already grappled with a similar issue) to help guide their independent analysis, rather than reinvent what smarter people have already traveled to Stockholm and received prizes for.[47] (For example, the laws of supply and demand are pretty much established and cannot be ignored, regardless of any worthy motivations behind current public policy initiatives.)

C. "Other Public Interest Factors"

The big issue rests with the definition of "other public interest factors." If the regulatory analysis is (properly) focused on maximizing consumer economic welfare, "other public interest factors" should be limited only to those "policy-relevant" barriers to entry explained above. Providing an appropriate definition for the phrase "other public interest factors" becomes more complicated, however, whenever our society, through our elected representatives, believes that it is important to impose other "public interest" obligations—unrelated to promoting competitive rivalry—that will directly affect market structure, conduct and performance.[48]

---

[45] See, e.g., *Cincinnati Bell Tel. Co.* v. *FCC*, 69 F.3d 752, 760 (6th Cir. 1995) (reversing Commission decision because the order contained no "expert economic data, or [analogies] to related industries in which the claimed anticompetitive behavior has taken place" but instead justified its conclusions as "simply 'common sense'").

[46] See *RCA Communications*, 346 U.S. at 93–95 (Frankfurter, J.) (FCC's economic analysis may not primarily rely on a "reading of national policy" because agency's actions were simply "too loose and too much calculated to mislead in the exercise of the discretion entrusted to it").

[47] See, e.g., *Northern Natural Gas* v. *FPC*, 399 F.2d 953, 961 (D.C. Cir. 1968) ("In short, the antitrust laws are merely another tool which a regulatory agency employs to a greater or lesser degree to give 'understandable content' to the broad statutory concept of the 'public interest.'"). *But cf.* "FERC Chair Hoecker Delivers Scary Halloween Message for Industrials", *Foster Electric Report, No. 125* (5 Nov. 1997) (reporting that FERC Chair Hoecker argued that "regulated competition" is wholly appropriate because FERC will not "race headlong towards 'de-regulation' that is based largely on untested theories about the behavior of competitive markets" (emphasis supplied)).

[48] See also Harold Demsetz, "Barriers to Entry", (1982) 72 *Am. Econ. Rev.* 37–47; William J. Baumol et al., *Contestable Markets and the Theory of Industry Structure* (Harcourt Brace Janovich, 1988) 362.

Now, let us be very clear here: there is absolutely nothing wrong with this concept. But what we should not do is to continue dressing up these otherwise legitimate public policies in the guise of "economic-style" rhetoric. Many of the current "public interest" policies have nothing to do with the promotion of good market performance. To the contrary, these policies—once implemented— often impose substantial detrimental effects on a properly working market by deliberately reallocating wealth to whatever the intended beneficiaries of these policies are intended to be.[49] Thus, just as US Supreme Court Justice Stephen Breyer noted in his concurrence in the case of *Turner Broadcasting Systems, Inc. v. FCC*, government should be honest about its actions, rather than trying to turn economically irrational policies into something they are not.[50]

Notwithstanding the above, it would be very naïve for us to ignore the reality that government intervention into the market has been going on since the concept of government first began. In fact, the economic literature indicates that government often decides to intervene in the market—either by antitrust or economic regulation—simply because it is dissatisfied with a particular outcome or, even though markets may be working well, those who have political power are often displeased by the results or they may consider some good or service to be too important to be priced and allocated by unfettered market processes.[51] Given this history, many people argue that we should be reluctant to criticize the current policy paradigms (a.k.a. "the system's bigger than me, so why rock the boat" approach). The problem with this argument, however, is that—if taken to its logical conclusion—it nearly always does not lead us down the road to good, long-term market performance, but instead only down the proverbial "primrose path."[52]

---

[49] See Frank Easterbrook, "The Court and the Economic System", (1984) 98 *Harv. L. Rev.* 4, 15–16 ("[P]eople demand laws just as they demand automobiles, and some people demand more effectively than others. Laws that benefit the people in common are hard to enact because no one can obtain very much of the benefit of lobbying for or preserving such laws." As such, because "cohesive groups can get more for themselves by restricting competition and appropriating rents than by seeking rules that enhance the welfare of all . . . we should expect regulatory programs and other statutes to benefit the regulated group. . . ." Accordingly, these groups "need not 'capture' the programs, because they owned them all along. The burgeoning evidence showing that regulatory programs increase prices for consumers and profits for producers supports this understanding." (emphasis supplied and citations omitted)); see also George Stigler, "The Theory of Economic Regulation", (1971) 2 *Bell J. Econ. & Mgmt. Sci.* 2–21.

[50] See, e.g., *Turner Broad. Sys. Inc. v. FCC*, 117 S. Ct. 1174, 1204 (1997) (Breyer, J., concurring) (the "anticompetitive rationale" of majority's opinion upholding federal statute that cable companies "must carry" local broadcast stations has no economic basis; rather, Congress's clearly articulated "public interest" objectives contained in the Cable Act of 1992 are sufficient grounds to uphold the rules); Richard Posner, "Taxation by Regulation", 2 *Bell J. Econ. & Mgmt. Sci.* 22, 47 (1971) ("[I]f we are stuck with taxation by regulation," then agencies and reviewing courts should insist that the "amount and cost of the subsidy, together with the identity of the recipients and payors, be calculated and placed in the public record." While this approach might "eliminate some of the more captious instances of the phenomenon; at least it would bring an important issue of public policy out in the open.").

[51] See Scherer & Ross, *supra* n. 39 at 9.

[52] See Posner, *supra* n. 50 (while debate over the purpose and effect of regulation usually revolves around arguments that regulation either: (a) is needed to protect captive consumers; or (b) is

That is to say, once this "economic-style" analysis becomes accepted, it is very difficult to "re-introduce" the legal and economic "heavy-lifting" necessary to get policies back on track. Public policy officials do not live in a vacuum and are continually lobbied by various constituencies to reach a resolution favorable to their interests. As such, while such an analysis may permit officials to brag to the public that government is there to help them, a weak analysis will actually harm consumers more when major players manipulate the regulatory process to have some of that re-allocated wealth sent their way. Indeed, the presence of "regulatory capture" or other political pressures on policy makers just exacerbates the tendency to make decisions without regard to the effect of government intervention on economic performance.[53]

After reviewing recent major antitrust enforcement and restructuring initiatives in both the United States and European Union, it is clear that political pressure and regulatory capture are increasingly successful in influencing policy decisions. Indeed, when examining many of the current policies, it is often difficult to discern whether the intended rationale and purpose behind government's actions are supposed to be the appropriate promotion of "competition" or instead the inappropriate promotion of "competitors." True competition means the ability to succeed *and* the ability to fail. However, because many current policies often permit inefficient firms to remain in (and are, in fact, specifically designed to prevent any possible exit of these inefficient firms from) the market, such policies add nothing more than additional impediments to the successful creation of a properly working market. If we have learned anything from history, it is that it is impossible to have "competition without change."[54] Accordingly, any notion that we can "protect competition by protecting competitors" is entirely flawed.[55]

Indeed, we all know (or should) the "golden rule" of competition law: Antitrust is supposed to protect *competition—not competitors.*[56] However,

procured only by "politically effective groups which are assumed to be members of the regulated industry itself for their own protection," neither view "explains an important phenomenon of regulated industries: the deliberate and continued provision of many services at lower rates and in larger quantities than would be offered in an unregulated market or, a fortiori, in an unregulated monopolistic one").

[53] See also Easterbrook, *supra* n. 49; Stigler, *supra* n. 49.

[54] Moreover, the desire to achieve "competition without change" is not limited to the protection of inefficient rivals. In the effort to ease consumers' "transition to competition," very often regulated firms must accept "voluntary" conditions if they want to become "deregulated" so as to mitigate any potential consumer "rate shock" when prices are actually set using unfettered market forces. See also *In re Motion of AT&T Corp. to Be Reclassified as a Non-Dominant Carrier*, FCC 95–427, 11 FCC Rcd 3271 at (rel. Oct. 23, 1995) at 84.

[55] One of the counter-arguments to this position is the often-misguided notion that the naked "protection of competitors" is analytically the equivalent to attempting to promote tangible new entry into a market currently dominated by a monopoly incumbent. It is not. As the FCC's former chief economist recently argued, it is very "important that the playing field should be leveled upwards, not downwards" because "rules that forbid a firm from exploiting efficiencies just because its rivals cannot do likewise" do nothing but harm, rather than improve, consumer welfare. Joseph Farrell, "Creating Local Competition", (1996) 49 *Fed. Comm. L.J.* 201, 212.

[56] See, e.g., *Brunswick Corp. v. Pueblo Bowl-O-Mat Inc.*, 429 U.S. 477, 488, 97 S. Ct. 690, 697, 50 L. Ed. 2d 701 (1977) (quoting *Brown Shoe Co. v. United States*, 370 U.S. 294, 320, 82 S. Ct. 1502, 1521, 8 L. Ed. 2d 510 (1962)).

because many people fail to realize that this golden rule should apply equally to economic regulation, regulatory proceedings should also not be used to advance the interests of competitors—through "voluntary" commitments or "involuntary" conditions—at the expense of consumer welfare.[57]

[57] Hard to believe, but the U.S. Ninth Circuit Court of Appeals recognised this basic principle nearly *sixty* years ago in *Pacific Power & Light Co.* v. *FPC*, 111 F.2d 1014, 1016 (9th Cir. 1940). There, the Ninth Circuit specifically rejected the argument of the Federal Power Commission (FERC's predecessor) that an applicant's burden to show that a particular proposal is consistent with the public interest "requires something more than a showing of convenience to the applicant, and can reasonably be interpreted as indicating that the Congress intended that there be a showing that benefit to the public will result from the proposed merger of facilities before it should receive Commission approval." In particular, the court rejected the FPC's argument that it may reject a merger application if the parties cannot show that "the consuming public will be benefited thereby." According to the court, the "phrase 'consistent with the public interest' does not connote a public benefit to be derived or suggest the idea of a promotion of the public interest. The thought conveyed is merely one of compatibility." As such, the court concluded that it is "enough if the applicants show that the proposed merger is compatible with the public interest. The Commission, as a condition of its approval, may not impose a more burdensome requirement in the way of proof than that prescribed by law."

Courts have applied this rule equally to FCC decisions. For example, in *Hawaiian Telephone* v. *FCC*, 498 F.2d 771 (D.C. Cir. 1974), the U.S. Court of Appeals for the D.C. Circuit found the FCC's grant of a Section 214 certificate to RCA for service between the U.S. mainland and Hawaii to be arbitrary and capricious. According to the court, a legal and economic analysis of competitive issues under the public interest standard must be more than an inquiry into "whether the balance of equities and opportunities among competing carriers suggests a change." The court reversed and remanded the FCC's decision, finding that it was "all too embarrassingly apparent that the Commission has been thinking about competition, not in terms primarily as to its benefit to the public, but specifically equalising competition among competitors." *Ibid.*, at 775–6.

Similarly, in the FCC's positive disposition of the AT&T/McCaw merger, various RBOC opponents argued on appeal that the Commission erred because it did not impose on the merged entity the same MFJ restrictions that the RBOCs were subject to. The court, citing Hawaiian Telephone, rejected the RBOCs' argument, finding that the application of the MFJ restrictions to the merged entity would "serve the interests only of the RBOCs rather than those of the public." As such, the court made it explicitly clear that when the Commission deliberates whether a proposed merger serves the public interest, the "Commission is not at liberty . . . to subordinate the public interest to the interest of 'equalising competition among competitors.' " SBC Communications, 56 F.3d at 1491 (citing *Hawaiian Telephone, supra*; *W.U. Telephone Co.* v. *FCC*, 665 F.2d 1112, 1122 (D.C. Cir.1981) ("equalisation of competition is not itself a sufficient basis for Commission action")).

However, with the increasing politicisation of regulatory proceedings and the corresponding increase of analytical laziness, the FCC increased its policies of extracting large "voluntary commitments" as a surrogate for meaningful analysis. To wit, look at the recent trend of industry reconcentration with seemingly little regulatory oversight. Indeed, because the Commission is using involuntary "voluntary" commitments as a proxy for a thorough inquiry, we never get to ask the fundamental question of whether, after conducting a detailed legal and economic analysis, the increasing trend in industry reconcentration is really in the public interest. See Reconcentration of Telecommunications Markets after the 1996 Act: Implications for Long-Term Market Performance (2nd ed., Phoenix Center Policy Paper No. 2, 1998) (http://www.phoenix-center.org/pcpp/pcpp2.doc).

For example, in the FCC's adjudication of the merger between Bell Atlantic and Nynex Corporation, the FCC—rather than require applicants to demonstrate that a proposed merger was in the public interest because the transaction would, for example, generate efficiency savings that could be passed on to consumers, or at least make the merged entity a more effective competitor— the FCC stated that "[i]n order to find that a merger is in the public interest, we must . . . be convinced that it will *enhance competition*. A merger will be pro-competitive if the harms to competition . . . are outweighed by the benefits that *enhance competition*. If applicants cannot carry this burden, the applications must be denied" emphasis supplied). See *Applications of NYNEX*

1. Case Study: A Tale of Two Footnotes

As stated *passim*, there is a growing cynicism towards the regulatory process that is now impossible to ignore. An excellent European example of such cynicism can be found in the Access Notice experience.[58] To wit, the EC's Draft Access Notice noted that ECJ judgments and European Commission decisions in the transport field have followed the principle "that a firm controlling an essential facility must give access in certain circumstances."[59] In order to determine if a telecommunications operator is abusing a dominant position by denying access to an essential facility, the European Commission would begin the analysis by identifying the existing or potential relevant market,[60] then determine whether access to the requested facility is essential in order to compete.[61]

The Draft Access Notice inserted at footnote at this point that should be examined in its entirety:

> Community law protects competition and not competitors, and therefore, it would be insufficient to demonstrate that one competitor needed access to a facility in order to compete in the downstream market. It would be necessary to demonstrate that access is necessary for all except exceptional competitors in order for access to be made compulsory.[62]

While the statement that competition law "protects competition and not competitors" is a fundamental principle of economic theory, due to political considerations, this concept is not very well-established in European law. As European restructuring efforts move forward, recognition of this principle in EC jurisprudence would be a welcome addition as an emphasis on competition should lead to consistent and coherent economic results.

Upon closer reading, however, the footnote actually mischaracterises the distinction between "competition" and "competitors." The Draft Access Notice footnote quoted above implies that "competition" means a number of competitors, not one single competitor. A better definition of "competition" would be the maximisation of consumer welfare, which are "such things as low prices, innovation, choice among differing products—all things we think of as being good for consumers."[63] As argued *passim*, the maximisation of consumer welfare occurs through the most efficient marketing structure, companies, or company, not by dictating that a certain number of competitors must be present in a market.

Corporation and Bell Atlantic Corporation for Consent to Transfer Control, Memorandum Opinion & Order, FCC 97–286 (rel. Aug. 14, 1997) at 2. Sadly, such extortions did not end there. See also chapter 2.

[58] Access Notice.

[59] Access Notice, *supra* n. 58, para. 88.

[60] *Ibid.*, para. 91.

[61] *Ibid.*, para. 91a.

[62] Draft Access Notice on the Application of the Competition Rules to Access Agreements in the Telecommunications Sector, Framework, Relevant Markets and Principles, COM(96)649 final para. 79, n. 58.

[63] Robert H. Bork, *The Antitrust Paradox: A Policy At War With Itself* (Free Press, 1993) at 61.

To make matters worse, when the EC issued its Final Access Notice, the EC even further perverted the "competition not competitors" language cited in the footnote above. Instead, the EC altered this language to mean that:

> "It would be insufficient to demonstrate that one competitor needed access to a facility in order to compete in the downstream market. It would be necessary to demonstrate that access is necessary for all except exceptional competitors in order for access to be made compulsory."[64]

Did the authors of the Access Notice realise the dangers inherent in a statement supporting competition over the interests of competitors? Certainly, if competition does not take a backseat to the interests of competitors, micromanagement of the market is not possible. With real competition, competitors would have to actually produce a superior product or find real efficiencies to offer lower prices, rather than relying on the artificial subsidies provided by enforcement officials and regulators—subsidies that must be ultimately paid by consumers.

VII.   HOW SHOULD WE MOVE FORWARD?

As both the FCC and European Commission have recognised, poorly conceived or economically expensive regulations (regardless of any worthy intentions behind them) may actually harm—rather than promote—consumer welfare. As such, regulators must explicitly account for how its policies—*e.g.*, the economic costs of residual "public interest" obligations such as "universal service" or an "obligation to serve"; mandatory geographic rate averaging and build-out requirements; the economic costs of advanced tariffing and reporting requirements, *etc.*—will affect firms' decisions to commit the substantial sunk costs necessary to enter and compete.

Because market structures are not homogeneous, any regulation imposed by regulators must not be homogeneous as well. As such, a "one-size fits all" approach ultimately will prove in practice to be both naïve and arbitrary. *Instead, the appropriate approach is for the regulator to contour its regulation to account for (and, if possible, pro-competitively change) the structure of the market, not the other way around.* Accordingly, because different remedies are needed for different types of harms, regulators must understand that appropriate scope and type of regulation will depend exclusively on the specific set of market conditions. Depending on the facts of the specific case, therefore, the appropriate regulatory response may be a combination, and different degrees, of price, conduct and structural regulation, a combination of only two types of the aforementioned regulation, *or simply none at all.*[65]

---

[64] Access Notice, *supra* n. 58, para. 91a n. 68.

[65] For example, stock markets are not subject to price regulation, but they function efficiently because of stringent conduct and structural regulation.

Moreover, despite their own dicta, most regulators often fail to recognise in practice that government intervention, no matter how innocuous, *de minimis*, or well-meaning, may impose significant economic costs on society. As noted above, these economic costs include administrative and compliance costs, the possible deterrence or delay of innovation, the creation of market structures which can promote collusive behaviour and the often denied, yet highly ubiquitous (and insidious), issue of "regulatory capture." Accordingly, because economic regulation has both costs and benefits, any regulation imposed must have a *direct nexus* to a specific anticompetitive harm and, moreover, must be narrowly tailored to mitigate only that specific anticompetitive harm. As stated colloquially *passim*,

> "Economic regulation is supposed to be a substitute for, and not a complement of, competitive rivalry. It is not, contrary to popular belief, *'because we can.'* "

In other words, economic regulation is only appropriate where one or more firms are capable of successfully exercising market power (charging monopoly prices or restricting output) for a sustained period of time, and additional entry is unlikely.

As such, in order to help regulators formulate a cohesive regulatory framework, perhaps it would therefore be useful to go over (again) each type of regulation at their disposal, and the appropriate circumstances for each, briefly below:[66]

A. Price Regulation

Price regulation is only appropriate where one or more firms can exercise market power by raising prices above competitive levels. If price regulation is, in fact, warranted, however, then it does not mean that the regulator suddenly has a "green light" to prescribe specific prices for goods or services. Indeed, if economic regulation is truly supposed to be a substitute for competition, then, just as in competitive, non-regulated markets, then the regulator should permit a range of prices for a particular product or service, each of which accounts for different consumer preferences and purchasing capabilities (*i.e.*, volume discounts, superior service quality, *etc.*). Thus, for example, so long as a regulator requires geographic averaging of interexchange telecommunications or cable rates, then a new entrant has absolutely no incentive to enter—even on a limited "foothold" basis to compete for high-volume (*i.e.*, high revenue) customers. Geographic averaging requirements serve only to buy incumbents time from competitive entry and ultimately disserve the residential, rural and poor consumers these restrictions were ostensibly designed to protect.

---

[66] Indeed, time and space constraints prevent a detailed critique of every single FCC and EC *faux pas* in this book. Besides, as noted above, the onus to formulate a cohesive pro-competitive public policy falls on the regulator—and not the industry—in the first instance.

Moreover, regulators must abandon the flawed notion that rates must be "affordable." "Affordability" is completely subjective in nature.[67] What regulators must understand is that the "just and reasonable" standard only requires that prices fall within a "zone of reasonableness"—*i.e.,* that these rates are neither "excessive" (rates that permit the firm to recover monopoly rents) nor "confiscatory" (rates that do not permit the regulated firm to recover its costs). They need not—as stated supra—be *"fair"* or *"affordable"* for everyone.[68]

Accordingly, because regulation is supposed to be the substitute for, and not the complement of, competitive rivalry, regulators should attempt to set a rate that approximates the equilibrium price (*i.e.,* where supply equals demand) that a rivalrous market would produce, including a rational allocation of fixed and shared costs (a task often impossible to do with great accuracy in practice[69]). But if regulators truly want to make prices for a "public" good or service more "affordable"—regardless of whether the end-price for this product or service is set by regulation or not—then regulators need to focus their priorities on promoting entry and rivalry, such that firms will be forced to innovate and lower costs and, with such innovation and increased efficiency, force supply and demand to move down and to the right. If this shift occurs, then the entire "zone" should therefore also be forced down and to the right over time. So long as regulators maintain a static, "incumbent-centric" approach, however (*i.e.,* the incumbent is the only source of distribution), it will provide firms with no real incentive to innovate and lower costs and, as such, true de-regulation and competition will never occur.

Similarly, regulators are going to have to determine whether the firm(s) under their jurisdiction are single-output or, more likely in today's era of "convergence," multi-product firms. As such, whenever a regulator attempts to define a firm's rate (*i.e.,* define the zone of "zone of reasonableness"), a primary focus on a multi-product firm's *aggregate* profits is irrelevant. Rather, the appropriate scope of the regulator's inquiry must be whether the specific profits derived from providing *regulated* products and services (and *not* from ancillary businesses or investments) are the result of the regulated company's ability to charge an excessive (*i.e.,* monopoly) rate for the regulated product or service—*i.e.,* the product

---

[67] Perhaps one of the primary reasons for the proliferation of the concept of "affordability" stems from current policy-makers' erroneous belief that competition is "one dimensional"—i.e., price competition. There are, in fact, other types of competition such as quality and innovation.

[68] See *Farmers Union Central Exchange Inc.* v. *FERC*, 734 F.2d 1486, 1504 (D.C. Cir.), *cert. denied, sub nom.,* 469 U.S. 1034 (1984) (the concept of "just and reasonable" must clearly be more than a "mere vessel into which meaning must be poured."); but c.f., *Southwestern Bell Telephone*, ("Access charges imposed on IXCs that include the LECs' universal service cost are not 'above cost' since universal service contributions are a real cost of doing business.") (Emphasis supplied.) It would be very interesting to find out, however, exactly which hornbook or what theorist the court is referring to that recognises or perhaps even defines the concept of "real" as a legitimate type of economic cost.

[69] See Thomas W. Hazlett and George S. Ford, "The Fallacy of Regulatory Symmetry: an Economic Analysis of the 'Level Playing Field' " in *Cable TV Franchising Statutes* (unpublished, 1997) (notion of "fair, competition-like outcomes" is ridiculous because regulators will never "choose 'efficient' prices, outputs, and quality costlessly and with perfect information.").

or service over which it can raise price or strict output absent regulation. If the rate reflects the regulated company's true costs of providing the regulated product or service, but the regulator nonetheless believes that this "just and reasonable" rate is "too expensive," "unfair," or not sufficiently "affordable," then it is therefore wholly improper for the regulator to require the regulated firm to "subsidise" the price it charges consumers for its regulated service with ancillary profits just to make the rate more politically "affordable" or "fair." When this occurs, "affordable" simply becomes an excuse for the regulator to set unlawfully confiscatory rates instead.[70]

Another consequence of multi-product offerings is that cost-allocations decisions will be increasingly important if a regulator decides to engage in price regulation. In the United States for instance, recent attempts by ILECs to allocate *all* local loop costs to its monopoly voice service customers and away from its competitive xDSL services—despite the fact that the same loop facility support both services—must be examined carefully and resolved if the FCC believes that rate regulation has a place in this environment.[71] Otherwise, the exercise of reviewing these ILEC tariffs will be a worthless and counter-productive exercise, because approval of these bogus tariffs would confer a modicum of regulatory approval of this practice.

B. Conduct Regulation

Conduct regulation is usually used to mitigate various types of strategic, anti-competitive behaviour, such as undue discrimination to bottleneck facilities, input foreclosure, raising rivals' costs, *etc*. Again, because market structures are not homogeneous, conduct regulation also can take many forms. For example, there may be "passive" types of conduct regulation, where the regulator may impose special reporting requirements on one specific class of firms (*e.g.*, "dominant" firms). Similarly, the regulator may permit the rates of "non-dominant" firms to go into effect immediately, but require any new tariffs from "dominant firms" to endure prolonged notice and comment periods before the rates may go into effect. Conduct regulation may take more "active" forms as well. For example, a firm may have to demonstrate that the economic costs resulting from an exclusive distribution contract do not outweigh the efficiency benefits created by

---

[70] See, e.g., Christopher Stern, "FCC Chief Eyes Cable Rate Cap", *Reuters* 14 Jan. 1998 (Reporting that Kennard is "pondering" limits on amount of programming costs cable companies may pass on to consumers. Kennard questioned whether it was "right" to permit cable companies to pass on all programming costs to consumers, adding: "Should the consumer shoulder all the increased costs of programming?" As a possible mitigation measure, Kennard suggested that increased programming expenses should be offset for consumers through other revenues including advertising, commissions, and payments by programmers for carriage.)

[71] See, e.g., GTE Telephone, GTOC Tariff No. 1, GTOC Transmittal No. 1148, CC Docket No. 98–79.

this exclusion.[72] Similarly, a firm might be obligated to provide rivals non-discriminatory access to its network based on a particular cost methodology.

Under any scenario, however, the concept of conduct regulation always implies that the regulator will take enforcement action against one or more firms only when it comes to the regulator's attention—either by complaint or *sua sponte*—that the regulated firm has acted contrary to the regulator's rules. In other words, enforcement of alleged acts of anticompetitive conduct will essentially occur on a case-by-case basis and, moreover, the responsibility for effective enforcement lies squarely on the regulator's shoulders. The big problem, however, is that most regulators have a very poor track record for effective and judicious enforcement against one or more firms' ability to exercise market power.[73] Thus, as US Circuit Court Judge Frank Easterbrook wrote over ten years ago, the "principle that regulation must extend to catch all substitutions at the margin has a corollary: *if you're not prepared to regulate thoroughly, don't start.*"[74]

C. Structural Regulation

Structural regulation attempts to affect positively market performance by establishing "bright line" tests that firms may not cross. In so doing, structural regulation can remove much of the subjectiveness of the regulator so prevalent in price and conduct regulation. Typical examples of structural regulation include ownership limits, standard technological interfaces and standards,[75] and various forms and degrees of structural separation. Like all other forms of regulation, however, structural separation is also not a homogenous regulatory tool. Rather, like all forms of economic regulation, structural separation is question of degree: the stricter the regulatory requirement of "separateness," the higher the cost to the regulated firm. As such, depending on the specific harm the regulator wants to mitigate or the particular long-term market structure the regulator wants (but has yet to articulate) to achieve, the regulator can avail itself of four primary forms of "structural separation" (each of which is listed in order of most significant economic costs to least imposed economic costs): (1) "line-of-business" restrictions; (2) mandatory separate subsidiaries with outside equity participation; (3) wholly-owned separate subsidiaries; and (4) mandatory

---

[72] For a detailed exegesis of the FCC's program access rules, see James W. Olson & Lawrence J. Spiwak, *supra* n. 6.

[73] See Thomas W. Hazlett and George S. Ford, *supra* n. 69 (notion of "fair, competition-like outcomes" is ridiculous because regulators will never "choose 'efficient' prices, outputs, and quality costlessly and with perfect information."); Harold Demsetz, "Information and Efficiency: Another Viewpoint", *J.L. & Econ.* (Apr. 1969) at 1–22; Paul McNulty, "Economic Theory and the Meaning of Competition", (1968) 82 *Q.J. Econ.* 639–656) and *cf. European Union's Fifth Report on the Telecommunications Regulatory Package* (1999) at pp. 10–11.

[74] See Frank Easterbrook, *supra* n. 49, 40 (emphasis supplied).

[75] See, e.g., Part 68 of the FCC's rules, 47 C.F.R. §§ 68.1 *et seq.*, which, by requiring standard technical interfaces, permits competition in the terminal equipment market.

separate corporate divisions. As a regulatory alternative to strict structural separation, however, it is also possible to impose strict accounting requirements accompanied by various conduct restrictions or mandates.

Yet, if the regulator routinely fails to undertake the prerequisite cost/benefit analysis necessary to determine—in light of where the regulator wants to see the future market structure to be—what the costs and benefit are of the structural rules the regulator wants to impose, then any regulatory initiative will deter rather than accelerate, new infrastructure entry. Unfortunately, promulgating "rules for the sake of rules" is no substitute for reasoned public policy decision-making.

For example, one of the most significant barriers to entry for new infrastructure development are regulatory and legislative "buildout" requirements"—*i.e.*, requirements that a new entrant must serve *all* of the franchise territory before it can begin providing service, rather than using an entry strategy that initially targets select areas.[76] This barrier is simply exacerbated when the buildout requirements also require new entrants to build capacity in excess of their own needs for the benefit of potential competitors (*see, e.g.*, the FCC's "Open Video System" build-out requirements). Indeed, considering the considerable sums new entrants must sink (and accordingly risk) to enter an already concentrated market, any requirement that a new entrant must also build additional capacity *for its competitors* well in excess of its own needs simply makes entry unattractive. Moreover, these requirements seem to contradict regulations imposed on the telephone side, where, for example, the FCC has attempted ostensibly to spur immediate competition through resale and UNEs, thus permitting new firms to enter in limited areas without having to complete a full overbuild of the incumbent's network.[77]

---

[76] See, e.g., U.S. Cable Act s. 621(a)(3), and by implication, Cable Act s. 621(a), which provide in pertinent part that:

(3)In awarding a franchise or franchises, a franchising authority shall assure that access to cable service is not denied to any group of potential residential cable subscribers because of the income of the residents of the local area in which the group resides.

(4)In awarding a franchise, the franchising authority—shall allow the applicant's cable system a reasonable period of time to become capable of providing cable service to all households in the franchise area.

Thus, for example, under current rules, if a SMATV strings a line over a public right of way, it becomes a cable operator and therefore subject to cable rules and obligations—including buildout requirements. Yet, one of the quickest services of cable competition in many areas would be from SMATVs serving adjacent buildings and neighbourhoods, because there are few alternative firms that already possess the sufficient economies of scale and scope (e.g., perhaps a LEC or maybe a public utility) necessary to pass existing buildout requirements (i.e., the new entrant must serve an entire franchise area before having a single customer) to make immediate entry likely.

[77] For example, if the FCC really wanted to encourage additional cable MSO overbuilds, it could take such steps as, inter alia: (1) Streamlining and overhauling its OVS Rules to make entry more attractive (indeed, if Internet video is to become a reality, FCC must be *semper vigilans* regarding rivals' attempts to impose access charges on Internet providers); (2) Encouraging new entrants to bundle telephone and video services using Ramsey-pricing methodology (because video is very profitable, such bundling may actually promote additional facilities-based entry for new telephone service); (3) Eliminating DBS exogenous costs (e.g., elimination of restrictions on retransmission of

broadcast and network signals by DBS providers); (4) Continuing not to impose "public interest" broadcast requirements on MVPD providers; (5) Waging a battle against local governments using the franchising process and other regulatory forums as a way to extract revenue, obtain "free" coverage of zoning board meetings, and delay entry overall; (6) Ensuring that local fees for digging up the streets should be non-discriminatory; (7) Eliminating must-carry for "qualified low power" stations (i.e., MSOs should be permitted to "chase the eyeballs"—as such, there is no need to continue to subsidise HSN *et al.*); and (8) Eliminating Leased Access and PEG Channel requirements (i.e., the economic rationale for eliminating these programs is the same for the elimination of PTAR in broadcasting and for the elimination of must-carry for low-powered stations).

4

Evaluating Competition in
A Post-WTO World

I. STRUCTURAL MARKET CONDITIONS IN THE POST-WTO WORLD—GENERIC
ANALYTICAL FRAMEWORK

As DETAILED IN the preceding chapters, technological advancement and convergence can make an accurate analysis of telecoms markets an increasingly difficult endeavour. Accordingly, given the significant changes that may result from the WTO Basic Agreement on Telecoms Services, how should we think about applying economic "first principles" to assess market power in, or the market performance of, telecommunications industries? A good starting point is to try to identify some of the prominent structural characteristics of various telecommunications markets.

A. Domestic Markets

1. *Products and Producers*

In most telecoms markets, many telecommunications firms—like most other firms—are not single-out-put providers. This observation is more significant than merely recognising that many telecommunications firms sell multiple outputs using different technologies—e.g., wired and wireless telephone service, and cable and satellite video programming. Rather, a more sophisticated analysis of telecommunications providers often reveals that while many telephone companies appear to provide a homogeneous telephony service—either local or long-distance—the reality is that these carriers provide a number of discrete telephone services (at different prices) in the form of residential, business, toll, and wholesale services, such as local exchange access for use by interexchange carriers. Moreover, products are further differentiated by the number and availability of various calling plans.

From the supply side, many of the facilities used to provide various services are identical; yet from a demand-side perspective, residential customers generally do not view business services as an acceptable substitute or vice-versa. In addition, the demand characteristics are often very different for each service, as business customers are often more sophisticated and, therefore, may have a higher own price elasticity of demand than residential customers. Finally, although the service may appear to be homogeneous, the presence of switching costs (i.e., searching out new providers, abandoning a traditional brand, and administering the switch) also demonstrates that there is substantial product differentiation among telecommunications services.[1]

2. Market Definitions

Given the above, it is extremely important to avoid the use of overly narrow or broad market definitions when analyzing the structure of telecommunications markets, because the convergence of technologies makes "traditional" telecommunications market definitions increasingly irrelevant. For example, it makes no sense to discuss a single "cable" or similar technology market, when cable actually competes with broadcast television, direct broadcast satellite systems, LMDS systems, and the like.[2]

Similarly, it is becoming increasingly questionable in the US domestic markets to define distinct homogeneous "long-distance" or "local" telephone markets with the eventual re-integration of the long-distance and local business as permitted by the US 1996 Telecoms Act.[3] This distinction becomes even more blurred now that companies are beginning to bundle additional telecommunications or information products and services into a single package, such as wireless service, paging, Internet access, video, or even alarm monitoring.[4]

Finally, because various distribution technologies are capable of serving widely-different service territories (e.g., a single satellite can cover an entire continent, but xDSL needs close proximity to a central office/local exchange and access to house-specific loops to work effectively), it also makes little sense to draw overly broad, or—more importantly—overly narrow geographic market definitions.

For example, in the United States, with the increasing convergence of telecommunications services and products into a variety of bundled offerings, the boundaries created by the Modified Final Judgement (MFJ) increasingly reflect a dated economic picture of the market. When the MFJ was implemented, the various parties agreed to create "local access and transport areas" or "LATAs." Although these lines were completely arbitrary, the LATAs were a convenient way to delineate the respective service areas of the Regional Bell Operating Companies ("RBOCs"). The creation of these boundaries under the MFJ therefore argued for three distinct economic markets: (1) local; (2) intra-LATA toll; and (3) inter-LATA or "long-distance" service. While these boundaries may have made sense at the actual time of divestiture, the LATA

---

[1] See W. Kip Viscusi *et al.*, *Economics Of Regulation And Antitrust* (2d ed., MIT Press, 1995), 17–78.

[2] See Chapter 14 discussing the EC's use over overly-narrow market definitions in their Access Notice; see also "Time Warner, Turner Seek Peace with FTC While Girding for War", *Wall St. J.*, 27 June 1996, at A1 (reporting that parties object to narrow "cable" market definitions).

[3] See 47 U.S.C. § 271.

[4] See "MCI Launches All-in-One Communications Package", 29 Apr. 1996, CNNFN.

boundaries were never intended to be definitive (or permanent) economic boundaries for purposes of measuring market power. Accordingly, given the radical changes set in motion by the 1996 Act, the MFJ approach does not accurately reflect a market where firms offer "one-stop shopping" for a variety of telecommunications services.

To wit, most US consumers appear to take a more simplistic approach towards telephone service: there is the local (fixed-charge) call (near) and the more expensive (per minutes of usage) long-distance toll call (far). To consumers, there is no significant difference between an intra-LATA toll call and an inter-LATA toll call-they are both toll calls. Thus, the fact that consumers tend to view both toll calls as one product, rather than distinct services, argues against the automatic use of LATAs as appropriate market definitions for antitrust or regulatory purposes.

The increasing use of wireless and satellite service also argues against the use of LATAs as appropriate market definitions. Wireless service, by definition, can extend beyond artificial LATA boundaries. Accordingly, if wireless service eventually replaces, or at minimum is viewed as a close substitute for, wired local service, then LATAs again will not accurately reflect the economic boundaries of the market.[5]

3. Relevance of Market Share

In analyzing the structural characteristics of telecommunications markets, it is also important not to exaggerate the relevance of the Herfindahl-Hirschman Index (HHI).[6] Given the technology of the telecommunications industry, many

---

[5] See *United States* v. *Western Elec. Co.*, 578 F. Supp. 643 (D.D.C. 1983).

[6] Under the Herfindahl-Hirschman Index (HHI) of market concentration, the squares of the individual market shares of all the participants are summed, thus giving proportionately greater weight to the market shares of the larger firms, in accord with their relative importance in competitive interactions.

For example, a market consisting of four firms with market shares of 30 per cent, 30 per cent, 20 per cent and 20 per cent has an HHI of 2600 ($30^2 + 30^2 + 20^2 + 20^2 = 2600$). The HHI ranges from 10,000 (in the case of a pure monopoly) to a number approaching zero (in the case of an atomistic market). Although it is desirable to include all firms in the calculation, lack of information about small firms is not critical because such firms do not affect the HHI significantly.

The increase in concentration as measured by the HHI can be calculated independently of the overall market concentration by doubling the product of the market shares of the merging firms. For example, the merger of firms with shares of 5 per cent and 10 per cent of the market would increase the HHI by 100 ($5 \times 10 \times 2 = 100$). The explanation for this technique is as follows: In calculating the HHI before the merger, the market shares of the merging firms are squared individually: $(a)^2 + (b)^2$. After the merger, the sum of those shares would be squared: $(a + b)^2$, which equals $a^2 + 2ab + b^2$. The increase in the HHI therefore is represented by $2ab$.

Typically, antitrust enforcement agencies (such as the US Department of Justice) divide the spectrum of market concentration as measured by the HHI into three regions that can be broadly characterized as unconcentrated (HHI below 1000), moderately concentrated (HHI between 1000 and 1800), and highly concentrated (HHI above 1800). The high the concentration ratio, the more likely that it would take an enforcement action. For a full copy of the US Department of Justice 1992 (as revised in 1997) Horizontal Merger Guidelines, see http://www.usdoj.gov/atr/public/guidelines/horiz_book/hmg1.html

markets will probably be characterized by the presence of one or more firms with a predominant market share. Under well accepted precedent, this basic condition alone does not indicate that a market is performing poorly.[7] Similarly, the fact that there may be multiple firms in a market also does not *a fortiori* mean that a market is performing well (e.g., the US website industry.) This is why, in the context of telecommunications, the analysis must always move beyond HHIs and towards the evaluation of the elasticities of supply and demand and, in particular, the presence (or lack) of barriers to entry.[8]

For example, consider the FCC's deregulation of AT&T for domestic long-distance services.[9] In that proceeding, many parties argued that AT&T had market power simply by virtue of having a 60 percent market share. Upon review, however, the FCC found that while AT&T did have a very large market share, AT&T nonetheless faced a very elastic demand curve, in which consumers were very likely to switch carriers in the event of a price increase or unsatisfactory service. The FCC further found that AT&T no longer controlled any bottleneck facilities, and supply was highly elastic both in terms of excess capacity and the number of competing firms. The FCC also found strong evidence of nonprice competition in the form of frequent-flyer points or tie-ins with other products. Given such a market structure, the Commission found that it would be difficult for AT&T to successfully engage in strategic anticompetitive conduct.[10]

---

[7] See, e.g., *United States* v. *Baker Hughes Inc.*, 908 F.2d 981, 986 (D.C. Cir. 1990) (Thomas, J.) (market share statistics "misleading" in a "volatile and shifting" market); *Southern Pac. Communications Co.* v. *AT&T*, 740 F.2d 980, 1000 (D.C. Cir. 1984), *cert. denied*, 470 U.S. 1005 (1985) (When a "predominant market share may merely be the result of regulation, and regulatory control may preclude the exercise of market power . . . in such cases market share should be at most a point of departure in determining whether market power exists."); *Metro Mobile CTS, Inc.* v. *New Vector Communications Inc.*, 892 F.2d 62, 63 (9th Cir. 1989) ("Reliance on statistical market share in cases involving regulated industries is at best a tricky enterprise and is downright folly where . . . the predominant market share is the result of regulation").

[8] See generally Duncan Cameron & Mark Glick, "Market Share and Market Power in Merger and Monopolization Cases", (1996) 17 *Managerial & Decision Econ.* 193 (legal precedent requiring courts to draw inferences about market power based primarily or exclusively on market shares and/or market concentration can often be misleading; the only alternative to such bright-line rules is to utilize modern economic tools to undertake more extensive competitive analyses).

[9] *In re Motion of AT&T Corp. to Be Reclassified as a Non-Dominant Carrier*, FCC 95–427, 11 FCC Rcd 3271 (rel. 23 Oct. 1995).

[10] Similarly, take the situation where two contiguous cable systems want to merge (or "cluster") in order to achieve the sufficient size and scope necessary to provide competitive telephone service to the incumbent local exchange carrier. Prior to the merger, each cable firm will probably have a respective HHI of around 10,000 for its respective service areas, as each enjoyed a lawful monopoly in the form of a franchise for many years. When the two companies merge, the merged entity will continue to be the dominant provider of cable service and, as such, the HHIs for cable service will probably remain at 10,000. However, if the merged firm now attempts to provide competition for local telephone service, its market share in the "local loop" market will be zero as a new entrant. Therefore, should a competitive inquiry be based upon a static analysis of a "cable" merger within arbitrary franchise territories, or rather upon the more dynamic possibilities that a new cable "cluster" may facilitate local phone competition in a regional area? Clearly, the answer should lie with the latter approach. See, e.g., *In re Cox Cable Communications Inc. and Times Mirror Co.*, Transfer of Control and Petition for Special Relief, DA No. 94–1570, 10 FCC Rcd 1559 at 16–19 (rel. 22 Dec. 1994).

4. Residual Regulation

There is one additional structural characteristic of telecommunications markets that simply cannot be ignored in any thorough economic analysis—i.e., the continuing presence of some sort of "public interest" regulation by the government. While regulation of telecommunications markets is supposed to decrease as more competition develops, residual regulation of telecommunications industries will nevertheless probably continue well into the future. It will, therefore, be crucial to account for such regulation and to examine the effects of such regulation on the various market participants.[11]

For example, the 1996 Act requires the FCC to impose residual regulations—unrelated to competition—designed to advance certain public policy objectives that will have a direct effect on market performance.[12] Perhaps one of the most significant of these residual regulatory mandates is the Act's requirement that telecommunications firms provide "universal service" to, among other entities, rural health care providers, educational providers and libraries.[13] The 1996 Act defines "universal service" as those telecommunications products or services which: (a) are essential to education, public health, or public safety; (b) are subscribed to by a substantial majority of residential consumers; (c) are being deployed in telecommunications networks; and (d) are consistent with the public interest, convenience and necessity.[14] Unlike most other rate prescription statutes in the United States—where rates must only be "just and reasonable"—the rates for universal service must be "just, reasonable *and affordable*."[15] According to the statute, "affordable" appears to mean rates that are

> "*less than* the amounts charged for similar services to other parties . . . that the [FCC] . . . and the States . . . determine is appropriate and necessary to ensure *affordable access* to and use of such services by such entities."[16]

---

[11] See *Town of Concord* v. *Boston Edison Co.*, 915 F.2d 17, 22 (1st Cir. 1990) (Breyer, J.), cert. denied, 111 S. Ct 1337 (1991). The court held that the differing "administrative considerations" between courts and regulatory agencies must be taken into account when adjudicating competitive issues in regulated industries. According to the court, although regulators and the antitrust laws "typically aim at similar goals . . . , [e]conomic regulators seek to achieve them directly by controlling prices through rules and regulations; antitrust seeks to achieve them indirectly by promoting and preserving a process that tends to bring them about"

> An antitrust rule that seeks to promote competition but nonetheless interferes with regulatory controls could undercut the very objectives the antitrust laws are designed to serve. Thus, where regulatory and antitrust regimes coexist, antitrust analysis must sensitively "recognize and reflect the distinctive economic and legal setting" of the regulated industry to which it applies.

[12] For a full discussion of this issue, see Chapter 15 *infra*.
[13] See 47 U.S.C. § 254.
[14] See 47 U.S.C. § 254(c)(1).
[15] See 47 U.S.C. § 254(b)(1) (emphasis supplied).
[16] Emphasis added, see 47 U.S.C. § 254(h)(1)(B).

Thus, under this mandate, regulation will continue to be an important factor that can affect firms' conduct, because even if there is a "competitive" price, that competitive price has no meaning if it is not "affordable."[17]

B. International Markets

While the WTO focuses exclusively on opening domestic markets, the degree of "openness" of domestic origination and termination markets has a direct and material effect on the market for international telecoms. As such, in order to put the concept of "international telecommunications" into context, it is also necessary to identify some of the major structural characteristics and basic economic conditions of the market for International Message Telecommunications Service (IMTS).[18]

1. Relevant Markets

First, try not to visualize the market for international telecommunications products and services as some sort of generic, global information superhighway. Rather, this market is made up of a series of individual country-route markets between "originating" countries and "destination" or "terminating" countries.[19] Both supply-side and demand-side factors lead to this view.

From a supply-side perspective, because carriers need to obtain operating agreements and/or regulatory approval from each terminating-country market, a carrier cannot freely provide service to a given country merely if it wishes to do so. In addition, it is very difficult for a carrier to shift its facilities from serving one country to serving another based upon market conditions because the use of relatively few cable and satellite facilities often provides less flexibility than the broader-based domestic facilities. Before reducing or adding facilities, carriers often have to obtain the acquiescence of the foreign correspondent in

---

[17] As one leading telecommunications antitrust lawyer wrote, "[u]niversal service, as defined in the new Act, and competitive markets cannot coexist, where the goods produced have many substitutes or where the technology is dynamic." Thomas G. Krattenmaker, "The Telecommunications Act of 1996", (1996) 49 *Fed. Comm. L.J.* 1, 41–43 (emphasis added). In Krattenmaker's judgment, "it is both bad competition policy and bad regulatory policy to think that one can achieve properly functioning telecommunications markets while a regulator sees to it that these same markets generate subsidized pro-societal benefits." Ibid.

[18] The "MTS" in IMTS was AT&T's old name for standard switched telephone service.

[19] For example, while some US residential customers may have a significant number of friends or relatives in several different destination markets (and therefore have a need for an inexpensive, generic worldwide IMTS calling plan), most residential US-outbound calls are generally made to relatives and friends left back in the old country. *Ibid.* Indeed, there is quite a bit of data that indicates that the majority of US-outbound calls from northern California are often to the Pacific Rim; the majority of US-outbound calls from southern California and the Gulf Coast are commonly to Latin America; the majority of US-outbound calls from Florida are generally to Latin America and the Caribbean; and the majority of US-outbound calls from the Northeast are generally to Europe, the Caribbean, and Asia. See Krattenmaker, *supra* n. 17.

both the countries in which facilities were reduced and in which they were increased.

A demand-side perspective also supports a country-pair approach. Because the demand for residential international telecommunications services tends to be very "country-specific," consumers do not generally view international service as a homogeneous, worldwide service. Rather, demand tends to be targeted to those countries where friends and relatives may be. This demand characteristic is quite different from the demand for domestic long-distance service, where consumers tend to view the market as a single, nationwide market. For example, a US consumer in Chicago (the rough mid-point of the United States) will want to be able to call New York City just as easily as California.

Given the above, the conventional way to view IMTS markets is from a *vertical* perspective, either unilaterally-originated service on country-pair specific routes, or on specific country-pair routes including both domestic and foreign originating traffic. As such, most US regulatory initiatives are ostensibly concerned with preventing, or mitigating, the effects from the economic harms traditionally associated with vertical integration. These harms often include (1) raising rivals' costs (e.g., forcing rivals to enter at two levels or input foreclosure); (2) cross-subsidy/predation; or (3) a "price squeeze." This is not to say, however, that vertical integration cannot produce pro-competitive benefits. The most frequently acknowledged benefits of vertical efficiency include: (1) economies of scale and scope; (2) eliminating free-rider problems; (3) spreading the risk of investing/losing sunk costs; (4) coordination in design and production; (5) the elimination of double mark-up of costs; and (6) the minimisation of efficiency losses suffered by foreclosed competitors.[20] Accordingly, under conventional economic and legal thought, when reviewing vertical issues, decision-makers must balance pro-competitive effects against likely anticompetitive harms.[21]

2. Supply and Demand Elasticities

As explained more fully below, there is a sufficient amount of public data to support the conclusion that US carriers face a high own-price elasticity of demand, such that customers will readily switch carriers if there is an increase in price or diminution in service. However, this demand is characterized by country-specific preferences, rather than by a preference for a homogeneous worldwide market.[22] Regarding the elasticity of supply of international facilities, there has been a demonstrable upward trend in both the numbers of suppliers as well as in underlying facilities. This is not to say, however, that there have not been

---

[20] See James W. Olson & Lawrence J. Spiwak, "Can Short-Term Limits on Strategic Vertical Restraints Improve Long-Term Cable Industry Market Performance?", (1995) 13 *Cardozo Arts & Ent. L.J.* 283.

[21] See *supra* n. 11 and accompanying text.

[22] See *supra* n. 19 and accompanying text.

short-term supply shortages from time to time. Given the incredible increase in international traffic minutes, there have been several periods where undersea cable capacity has in fact been constrained. In each case, however, the FCC has determined that these shortages would only be temporary as both additional capacity and new technologies would relieve these constraints.

3. Major Endogenous Regulatory Factors

It is impossible to discuss international telecommunications without understanding the international settlement-of-accounts regime. The international settlement-of-accounts regime was developed in 1865 by twenty European countries to provide for a standard, common method to divide the revenues for international telecommunications service between originating and destination countries.[23]

Specifically, the accounting rates system was established under the authority of the International Telecommunication Union (ITU) and has been in place for many years. Member States of the ITU are bound by a treaty, periodically renewed. Under the terms of the treaty, ITU Regulations are promulgated. Under the ITU regulations:

> "For each applicable service in a given relation, administrations [or recognized private operating agenc(ies)] shall by mutual agreement establish and revise accounting rates to be applied between them, in accordance with the provisions of Appendix 1 and taking into account relevant CCITT Recommendations and relevant cost trends."[24]

By implication, therefore, accounting rates are established by international treaty, to which all ITU members (including the United States and the Member States of the EU) are signatories, as the means of inter-operator transporting and paying for termination of international traffic. As such, refiling (i.e., routing traffic through a third party to arbitrage competing rates) is forbidden unless paid for as if it had been routed via the normal method. This is not to say that refilling does not occur, however. As markets across the globe continue to liberalse, competition is forcing firms to find the cheapest way to terminate a call as possible. Moreover, although illegal, because refilling places downward pressure on accounting and termination rates, most governments tend to acquiesce to refilling with a "wink and a nod."

However, neither the "accounting" nor the "settlement" rate is a rate charged to end consumers. Instead, the rate charged to end consumers is called the *collection* rate, which is often regulated directly by NRA's. In contrast, the "accounting rate" is the privately negotiated internal price between originating and terminating carriers. The accounting rate is related, sometimes very loosely,

---

[23] See Chapter 3, Box 3.1 of *Direction of Traffic 1996*, (ITU/Telegeography inc., (1996) visited 1998) <http://www.itu.int/intset/whatare/howwork/pdf> [hereinafter Direction of Traffic].

[24] Final Acts of the World Administrative Telegraph and Telephone Conference Melbourne, 1988 (WATTC–88) International Telecommunications Regulations, art. 6.2.1.

to the carriers' end-to-end facilities cost. The carriers then agree to a "settlement" rate—usually one-half of the accounting rate—to hand-off and terminate traffic to each other in the middle of the ocean (hence the phrase "half circuit"). If there is an exact equal amount of traffic exchanged between the originating market and the destination market, then the originating and terminating carriers' "settlement of accounts" will be zero.

Unfortunately, for those countries which generally have more outbound traffic than incoming traffic for nearly every international route (e.g., the United States), these settlement rates—which, because of the foreign carrier's monopoly or dominant position, are often set far above the actual costs of terminating a call—can create a substantial subsidy from the originating market's consumers to the destination market. When this occurs, the carrier who has to "settle-up" its account with its foreign correspondent effectively has to pay more to terminate a call—which therefore means it must offer a higher price for service to potential customers. Thus, if a carrier can bypass having to pay a settlement rate to its foreign correspondent, then that carrier will have a significant cost advantage over its rivals.

The significance of this "dual price" system for international telephony (i.e., regulated collection rates and privately negotiated accounting rates) on market conduct and performance cannot be underestimated, because carriers' net revenue for international service is a function of *both* their accounting rates as well as their collection charges. Thus, if traffic is balanced on a particular route, then the value of the accounting rate is essentially irrelevant since no settlement is necessary and each carrier's revenue will depend directly on its collection charge. On the other hand, however, where traffic is imbalanced, the accounting rate may have a significant effect on the commercial options of the two carriers.

For example, if a carrier has a significant incoming traffic deficit, then the settlement payments which it must make to its foreign correspondent limit its ability to reduce its collection charges. Conversely, a carrier with a net traffic surplus has little incentive to operate more efficiently or to reduce the accounting rate because of the net settlement benefits it receives under the *status quo*. For this reason, carriers that have relatively lower collection charges, often due to the competition from other carriers, and a net traffic deficit, are dissatisfied with the current accounting rate regime because the *status quo* tends to subsidize high cost monopoly carriers at the expense of lower cost carriers and end-users from competitive regimes.[25]

Prior to global liberalisation, one of the major problems confronting the industry was the ability of a monopolist in a foreign destination market to play the various carriers of another country against each other to gain higher rates. This practice is known as "whipsawing." To mitigate this distortion, regulators such as the FCC developed, mechanisms to mitigate this strategic conduct by requiring such measures as (1) the equal division of accounting rates; (2)

---

[25] See Direction of Traffic, *supra* n. 23.

nondiscriminatory treatment of US carriers; and (3) proportionate return of inbound traffic.[26] As explained in more detail in Chapter 6, however, these types of mechanisms can impose significant costs on the market as well.

With the growth of liberalisation, however, there are now two ways a carrier can currently bypass the settlement-of-accounts regime. First, carriers can elect to build and own the entire "full" circuit between the originating and the destination/terminating market. Second, an originating carrier could merge with a foreign correspondent, and therefore also obtain a full circuit (the originating half plus the foreign termination half). Under either scenario, however, because one carrier can bypass the international settlement-of-accounts regime while other rivals (for a variety of reasons) cannot, the bottleneck now shifts away from the half circuit to the point(s) of interconnection with the network in the destination market. Thus, without standard, cost-based interconnection rates for *all* carriers (both indigenous and foreign) in the destination/terminating market, a monopoly or "dominant" carrier in a terminating market with an affiliate in a high-volume originating market could potentially engage in some kind of strategic, anticompetitive behavior on that particular route.[27] As mentioned above, such strategic conduct could include, *inter alia*, raising their rivals' costs by forcing them to enter the terminating market at two different levels, a potential "price squeeze" or, depending on the structural characteristics of the originating and terminating markets, some kind of predatory conduct by a local affiliate of a dominant foreign firm.

C. Getting a Grip on "Convergence"

According to FCC Chairman William E. Kennard's home-page: "The telecommunications marketplace is dramatically changing our world. Cable lines will

---

[26] See "Implementation and Scope of the International Settlements Policy for Parallel International Communication Routes, Report and Order", (1986) 51 *Fed. Reg.* 4736, modified in part on recons., 2 F.C.C.R. 1118, 62 Rad. Reg. 2d (P & F) 408 (1987) [hereinafter ISP Report and Order], further recons., 3 F.C.C.R. 1614, 64 Rad. Reg. 2d (P & F) 956 (1988). See also "Regulation of International Accounting Rates, Phase I, Report and Order", (1991) 6 *F.C.C.R.* 3552, 69 *Rad. Reg.* 2d (P & F) 241, on recons., 7 F.C.C.R. 8049, 71 Rad. Reg. 2d (P & F) (1992). The FCC's ISP also requires US carriers to file copies of all contracts, agreements and arrangements that relate to the routing of traffic and the settlement of accounts.

[27] That is to say, while the ability to bypass the settlement-of-accounts regime certainly will enable a vertically integrated firm to realise certain economies of scale and scope that competitors may not be able to achieve immediately (and, like any other lawful business, this is not necessarily a bad thing), if a foreign correspondent also has, for example, the ability to control return traffic or charge different interconnection rates to rivals, then any alleged efficiencies resulting from vertical integration are not necessarily the result of improved operational efficiencies, but rather of strategic, anticompetitive conduct. Thus, without standard, cost-based interconnection rates for all carriers at the foreign end, given the structural characteristics discussed above, vertical integration by any carrier that is either a monopolist or a dominant carrier in both the originating and terminating markets could significantly distort the market performance of those IMTS routes, which are in high demand by consumers in its core territory (e.g., U.S./U.K., U.S./Japan, U.S./Germany, U.S./Mexico, U.S./Jamaica). *Ibid.*, (citation omitted).

carry phone calls, phone wires will deliver movies and the airwaves will carry both. This convergence of technology will transform how we live, work, play and shop. It will blur traditional industry lines." If this argument is taken to its logical conclusion, therefore, then the issue moves away from industry-specific regulation of individual distribution mechanisms towards a focus on some sort of homogeneous, all-powerful broadband "bit stream."

Stated another way, at present, while the various types of distribution technologies provide some sort of Internet access, Internet access is not the primary product provided—i.e., the PSTN network primarily provides switched-voice; wireless provides mobile communications; cable provides multi-channel delivered programming, etc. (See diagram on p. 81). As such, because of the respective endogenous and exogenous cost characteristics, technical limitations and regulatory restrictions imposed on each type of distribution mechanism, consumers currently do not generally view these various technologies as *close substitutes* for each other—e.g., if a cable operator in the US raised its price for video service, because satellite operators were previously prohibited by law from carrying local broadcast stations, consumers still would not necessarily switch to a satellite provider.

With technological convergence and regulatory reform, however, consumers are starting to view various distribution mechanisms as close substitutes. For example, mobile penetration is equal to (and probably about to surpass) landline usage in many countries.[28] Similarly, with the recent passage of the Satellite Home Viewer Improvement Act—which permits satellite carriers to offer their subscribers local TV broadcast signals through the option of providing "local-into-local" service—Digital Satellite Service service in the US can now be a substitute for, rather than a complement of, existing cable operators. Accordingly, if the market really boils down to just broadband "bit-stream" as policy-makers predict, then bit-stream should be a homogenous and fungible product.

Given this convergence, what will this new market look like? As just discussed, given such technological advancement, it makes little sense to view the problem from a supply-side perspective. Again, perhaps we should view the problem from a demand-side perspective instead. Indeed, *consumers do not buy facilities*, they buy *service*. That is to say, if the promise of convergence holds true, then we should be evaluating competition from a "delivered" product

---

[28] As highlighted in chapter 2 above, the OECD reports that the "number of [fixed] access lines in Austria, Japan and Sweden have decreased for 1996–97" (1999) *OECD Communications Outlook* at 76. This, coupled with the extraordinary increase in mobile penetration in those countries, leads to the inescapable conclusion that mobile service is can be a substitute for fixed line service if the policy-makers get it right. For example, in the specific case of Sweden, the OECD posited that "mobile subscriptions are being used instead of second lines in primary residences, as first lines in holiday homes, and to create mobile offices for some users who would otherwise require a fixed line. In addition some new customers for telephone service in Scandinavia are opting for a cellular connection as their first line and later perhaps migrating to a fixed line . . . If current trends continue, Finland is likely to be the first country where the number of mobile subscriptions exceeds the number of fixed access lines" at 66–67; In the case of Japan, the *Financial Times* reported 8 Apr. 2000 that Japanese mobile phone subscribers outnumbered fixed-line users for the first time.

perspective—i.e., what choices do consumers have of broadband "bit-stream"? If we get the process correct, then the market should produce a wide variety of competitive price and service choices for broadband bit-stream that best fits each consumer's individual demand.[29]

So how do we get there from here? Let's refer back to the "entry condition" explained in Chapter 2. Once again, entry will only occur when:

(1) Post-Entry Profit (**d**) minus
(2) Inherent (exogenous) Entry Costs (**x**) minus
(3) Incumbent or Regulation-Induced Entry Costs (endogenous) (**e**) plus any
(4) Spillover Effects (**s**)
(5) Are greater than Zero.

However, the entry condition affects each different access technology differently. Putting aside both the various technical limitations of each respective technology and the usual exogenous costs which all of these technologies generally share (e.g., marketing, construction, billing systems, etc.), all of these technologies have different—although all significant—endogenous costs imposed upon them as a precondition of entry. For example, to provide wireless service, a firm needs (among other things) spectrum and government permission to locate tower sites. For satellite service, these costs are increased exponentially as these firms must also obtain approval from each nation in which they want to provide service. On the other hand, if a firm wants to build an alternative network and provide service on an end-to-end basis, it must often obtain approval from local authorities to dig up the streets,[30] permission from local authorities to provide video service, and subject itself to other regulatory "shakedowns" such as geographic build-out-requirements, geographic averaging, and "voluntary contributions" to wire local schools. Moreover, if this firm wants to provide international service, it must obtain, among other things, multiple licenses and permission to land cable facilities.

Accordingly, if we really want to realise this world of bit-stream "convergence," the key still boils down to removing, to the extent possible, all regulatory barriers to entry. Like it or not, "convergence" is no substitute for "competition." Until policy-makers understand this fact, the Information Society will remain an ephemeral dream.

---

[29] A similar example can be found in the computer market. On one side, it is currently possible to purchase a desktop computer with a 1 Gb hard drive and a 1 Ghz chip for a reasonable amount of money. Such a device is only good for those users who do not need mobility. On the other hand, for those of us who need mobility, we will probably trade off capability and price for a portable laptop. For the third sector of society who does not need anything fancy but instead needs something only for e-mail retrieval and rudimentary web-surfing, there is a whole class of computers designed for them. Under such a structure, therefore, consumers benefit from both price and service competition.

[30] See, e.g., Lyndsey Layton, "Hidden Cost of Road Tear-ups", *Washington Post*, 16 March 2000 at A1 (reporting that Prince George's County Maryland imposed a franchise fee of 5 per cent of a company's revenue for digging up the street to lay new cable); Lyndsey Layton, "D.C. to Charge Cable Firms for Street Damage", *Washington Post*, 22 March 2000 at B1 see p. 36 above.

Local Access Technology	Incumbent Telecoms Operator	CLEC	Data LEC or "PCLEC"	Cable MSO	Mobile	Satellite
Examples of Major Endogenous Entry Costs	"Carrier of last resort" obligations; Stringent price, conduct and structural regulation	Interconnection; Build-out requirements Building Access; Local government "user" fees; USO Obligations; Lack of regulatory harmonization among various jurisdictions	Loops; Collocation; Provisioning; Loop conditioning	Programming; Franchise certification authority	Spectrum; Interconnection; Tower siting; Tech. standards • GSM • TDMA • CDMA • 3G	Spectrum; Interconnection; Tower siting; Tech. standards; Int'l approval for each country in which to seek to do business
Technical advantages and limitations	Excellent for voice; Good for "broadband" (xDSL); Poor for multi-channel video programming	Ability to build state-of-the-art network; thus, has potential to be excellent for voice, video and/or "broadband" depending on business conditions	Good for "broadband"; Poor for voice; Poor for multi-channel video programming	Excellent for multi-channel programming; Excellent for "broadband"; Poor for voice	Excellent for voice; OK for data; Poor for video; But very advantageous because it is *MOBILE*	Excellent for video; Excellent for data OK for voice; OK for "broadband"; Can be either mobile or fixed

RESIDENTIAL CONSUMER

Substitutes or Complements?

II. POTENTIAL CONDUCT IN THE POST-WTO WORLD

Once the relevant structural characteristics of the relevant market are defined, the question becomes whether this structure will permit firms to exercise market power to the detriment of consumers.[31] In the context of telecommunications, there are specific factors that can indicate whether competitors can engage successfully in anticompetitive conduct. On one hand, telecommunications industries are currently enjoying unparalleled investment in both capital infrastructure and research and development. Advertising revenues are currently up in many sectors,[32] and many telecommunications firms are also heavily competing in areas other than price, such as frequent-flyer miles, bar association discounts, credit cards, etc. These factors are consistent with the conclusions that there are high elasticities of supply and demand in these markets.

On the other hand, with the increasing trend of attempted and actual vertical and horizontal reintegration among telecommunications providers and/or services (e.g., MFS/WorldCom, AT&T/McCaw, Sprint/DT-FT, NYNEX/Bell-Atlantic, Bell Atlantic/NYNEX, Bell Atlantic/GTE, SBC/Ameritech, SBC/PacTel, MCI/Worldcom, Sprint/Worldcom, Telia/Telinor), firms may attempt to raise rivals' costs by, *inter alia*, foreclosing key inputs of production.[33] In addition, so long as the current regulatory cynicism continues unchecked, many firms will nonetheless continue to attempt to manipulate the regulatory system for their individual benefit and to the detriment of good market performance.[34]

For example, economies of scope can certainly have pro-competitive benefits; however, economies of scope can also create the ability to engage in strategic anticompetitive conduct. Therefore, because of the significant costs of entry, entry rarely occurs in "waves of competition" on a large-scale basis. Rather, entry usually occurs in pinpoint attacks wherever the incumbent may be the most vulnerable. Yet, if the incumbent enjoys significant economies of scope, it may attempt to allocate the defence costs of these attacks over a much wider customer base where competitive pressures may not be present. The more captive customers an incumbent may have, the more the per-unit share of defence costs will decrease. If there are enough customers to make the per-unit/customer share sufficiently *de minimis*—such that neither captive consumers nor regulators notice (or care about) this *de minimis* increase in price—then the incumbent

---

[31] See, e.g., *Town of Concord* v. *Boston Edison Co.*, 915 F.2d 17, 21–22 (1st Cir. 1990) (Breyer, J.), *cert. denied*, 111 S. Ct 1337 (1991); see also *Southern Pac. Communications Co.* v. *AT&T*, 740 F.2d 980, 1000 (D.C. Cir. 1984), *cert. denied*, 470 U.S. 1005 (1985) ("Ultimately, a court should focus directly upon the ability of the regulated firm to control prices or exclude competition."); *In re Review of Commission's Regulations Governing Television Broadcasting, Further Notice of Proposed Rulemaking*, 10 FCC Rcd 3524, 3534 (rel. Jan. 17, 1995).

[32] See generally, Douglass A. Galbi, "The Price of Telecom Competition: Counting the Cost of Advertising and Promotion", (1999) 1 *Info* 133.

[33] See generally James W. Olson & Lawrence J. Spiwak, *supra* n. 20 at 294.

[34] See generally Bruce M. Owen & Ronald Braeutigam, *The Regulation Game: Strategic Use of the Administrative Process* (Ballinger Pub. Co., 1978).

has used its economies of scope both to deter entry and evade regulation successfully.[35]

Similarly, with the massive reconcentration of the industry now underway, a significant challenge in evaluating firms' conduct will be determining whether the structure of telecommunications markets now permits firms to engage successfully in some sort of oligopolistic pricing harmful to consumers. Clearly, if discovery reveals a "smoking gun" demonstrating overt collusion, then the inquiry is at its end. But what happens if no smoking gun is found, and there is a clear pattern of parallel pricing? Is it evidence of overt collusive attempts of joint-profit maximization (that should therefore properly be a violation of the antitrust laws) or is it simply Cournot pricing (and therefore probably not a violation)?[36]

As a general matter, an industry, such as telecommunications, that is subject to rapid technological change and innovation is usually less susceptible to oligopolistic co-ordination because technological change and innovation can introduce differences in product lines, production costs, and demand conditions—i.e., the pace and direction of innovation is difficult to predict. Indeed, the more rapidly producers' cost functions are altered through technological change and the more unevenly those changes are diffused throughout the industry, the more likely it is that there will be conflict among competitors regarding pricing choices.[37] However, despite this generalization, there may be some telecommunications market structures that could facilitate successful joint profit maximization.

Accordingly, the ability to make an accurate determination of firms' conduct will depend directly on the accurate identification of the market's basic conditions and structure referenced above. Specifically, are there homogeneous

---

[35] See *Reconcentration of Telecommunications Markets After the 1996 Act: Implications for Long-Term Market Performance* (2nd Edition) Phoenix Center Policy Paper Series, Policy Paper No. 2, (July, 1998) at 32, <http://www.phoenix-center.org/pcpp/pcpp2.doc> [hereinafter Phoenix Center Policy Paper]; but compare NYNEX Corp. and Bell Atlantic Corp., Memorandum Opinion and Order, 12 F.C.C.R. 19,985, para. 16, 9 Comm. Reg. (P & F) 187 (1997) [hereinafter NYNEX/Bell Atlantic Memorandum Opinion and Order], where an increase in market concentration can apparently enhance "regulatory efficiency" as well. (The FCC found it necessary to impose stringent reporting requirements as a condition of merger. "As diversity among carriers declines, both this Commission and state commissions may lose the ability to compare performance between similar carriers that have made different management or strategic choices" because, in the FCC's view, the "Bell Companies, being of similar size, history, and regional concentration have, to date, been useful benchmarks for assessing each other's performance.").

[36] See, e.g., *Market Force Inc.* v. *Wauwatosa Realty Co.*, 906 F.2d 1167, 1172 & n.8 (7th Cir. 1990); *Clamp-All Corp* v. *Cast Iron Soil Pipe Inst.*, 851 F.2d 478, 484 (1st Cir. 1988), *cert. denied*, 488 U.S. 1007 (1989); *E.I. du Pont de Nemours Co.* v. *FTC*, 729 F.2d 128, 139 (2d Cir. 1984); *City of Tuscaloosa* v. *Harcros Chems. Inc.*, 877 F. Supp. 1504, 1524 (N.D. Ala. 1995); see also Louis Phlips, *The Economics Of Imperfect Information* (Cambridge University Press, 1988) ch. 6 ; Joseph Kattan, "Beyond Facilitating Practices: Price Signaling and Price Protection Clauses in the New Antitrust Enforcement Environment", (1994) 63 *Antitrust L.J.* 133, 136.

[37] See F.M. Scherer & David Ross, *Industrial Market Structure And Economic Performance* 285 (3rd. ed., Houghton Mifflin, 1990); Alexis Jacquemin & Margaret Slade, "Cartels, Collusion and Horizontal Merger", in (1989) 1 *Handbook Of Industrial Organization* 420 (eds) (Richard Schmalensee & Robert Willig).

products? Are supply and demand elastic? How sophisticated are consumers? And is there an adequate signalling mechanism? If the structure of the market indicates procompetitive conditions—i.e., high elasticities of supply and demand, sophisticated consumers, no asymmetrical or advanced tariffing requirements to act as price signals, etc.—then firms will probably not be able to succeed in strategic conduct, even if they try.[38]

Again, examine the case of the US domestic long-distance marketplace. Most customers avail themselves of a variety of discount plans, rather than "basic" service, which indicates that actual market prices are not homogeneous. Considering the complexities of a modern tariff, exact prices are extremely difficult to replicate. This pattern is further exacerbated by the fact that discount plans are often bundled with non-price incentives, such as reward programs, which are often hard to quantify in making a price comparison. Moreover, because supply continues to expand in terms of both the number of competitors and the amount of fiber transmission capacity that is available, firms are motivated to protect their sunk investments by competing for new customers. Similarly, there is a tremendous amount of consumer "churn" among carriers' various discount plans, which is consistent with a conclusion that firms face a high elasticity of demand. Finally, with the FCC's increasing trend towards the elimination of asymmetrical regulations and attempts at de-tariffing of telecommunications services, effective signalling mechanisms are rapidly disappearing.[39]

Some observers, however, continue to maintain that the interexchange market will become "truly competitive" only when the BOCs can enter this market. As support for this position, proponents often cite the fact that "basic" rates for long-distance service appear to have increased in "lock-step" over the past several years.[40] Focusing exclusively on basic rates, however, ignores the fact that most customers who spend more than the average amount for long- distance service (e.g., greater than $20 a month) are on some kind of discount plan.

In contrast to the rise in basic rates, real prices for discount plans have fallen dramatically over the last several years. Thus, given the structural attributes of the interexchange market discussed above, this evidence supports the conclusion that strategic coordinated behavior is difficult to achieve, because firms must aggressively compete to retain (or possibly increase) market share and protect sunk investments.[41]

---

[38] See generally *Brooke Group Ltd.* v. *Brown & Williamson Tobacco Corp.*, 509 U.S. 209 (1993).

[39] See Jerry Duvall et al., "Market Performance in the Long Distance Telecommunications Industry: The AT&T Non-Dominance Petition", Paper Presented at 2nd Annual Conference of Consortium for Research on Telecommunications Policy, Evanston, Ill. (11 May 1996) http://www.phoenix-center.org/library/longdist.doc

[40] See generally Paul M. Macavoy, *The Failure Of Antitrust And Regulation To Establish Competition In Long-Distance Telephone Services* (MIT Press, 1996).

[41] Ibid.

III. MARKET PERFORMANCE IN THE POST-WTO WORLD

In addition to looking at the structure of the relevant markets and the conduct of firms within these markets, we should also look at the current and potential performance of these markets to determine whether some sort of intervention—antitrust or regulatory—is warranted to ensure that consumers receive lower prices or new products and services.[42] As explained in the preceding chapters, the inherent technological characteristics (e.g., economies of scale and density) of many telecommunications markets make it unlikely that imposing remedial conditions in either a consent decree or a regulatory order will achieve "perfect" competition. As many economists have recognized, telecommunications markets typically are characterized by high fixed and sunk costs, making marginal cost pricing (the *raison d'être* of perfect competition) impossible to achieve.[43] Also, the presence of network externalities—i.e., the value of the network increases with the number of users-makes "perfect" competition difficult to obtain. Finally, residual "public interest" regulation will continue to distort market performance by affecting both the structure of many markets and the conduct of firms within those markets.[44]

Rather than pursuing the ethereal goal of "perfect" competition by regulation or antitrust, however, the critical question should instead be whether competitive rivalry in telecommunications markets is generating either static economic efficiencies (are prices for telecommunications services going up or down) or dynamic economic efficiencies (is there innovation in new telecommunications technologies) or both. If technology is improving and costs are going down, will competition create sufficient incentives for firms to provide societal benefits to consumers, such as educational Internet service, in order to attract and maintain market share, or must government continue to mandate that these firms do so?

[42] See, e.g., Jerry Duvall & Michael Pelcovits, *Reforming Regulatory Policy for Private Line Telecommunications Services: Implications for Market Performance* (OPP Working Paper No. 4, 1980) (analysis should focus on market performance, rather than on market participants' residual market power); Thomas DiLorenzo & Jack High, "Antitrust and Competition, Historically Considered", (1988) 25 *Econ. Inquiry* 423, 433 (rivalry focuses on behavior associated with the verb "to compete," whereas perfect competition focuses on properties of equilibrium; "[b]ut if [perfect competition model] conclusions are substantially different from conclusions based on rivalry, then the competitive model has very likely misdirected the profession, at least as far as . . . policy is concerned"); see also *In re Implementation of Section 19 of the Cable Television Consumer Protection and Competition Act of 1992*, Annual Assessment of the Status of Competition in the Market for Delivery of Video Programming, 9 FCC Rcd 7442, App. H at 31 (1994) (focus should be on "policy-relevant" barriers to entry); Department of Justice & Federal Trade Commission Antitrust Guidelines for the Licensing of Intellectual Property (1995).

[43] See generally William J. Baumol & David F. Bradford, "Optimal Departures From Marginal Cost Pricing", (1970) 60 *Am. Econ. Rev.* 265

[44] See generally John Haring & Kathleen Levitz, *What Makes the Dominant Firm Dominant?* (OPP Working Paper No. 25, 1989).

5

The WTO and the Reference Paper: An Ostensible Blueprint for Entry

THERE ARE FEW international bodies more full of promise or more misunderstood than the World Trade Organisation (WTO), the successor to the procedures established under the General Agreement on Tariffs and Trade (GATT). The GATT, first established by a 1947 treaty, unified and streamlined tariff classifications, provided a mechanism for international trade disputes, and generally promoted freer international trade. With the establishment of the WTO as well as the adoption of the Agreement on Trade-Related Aspects of Intellectual Property Rights (TRIPS), fruit of the Uruguay Round of trade talks, and the earlier extension of the GATT through the General Agreement on Trade in Services (GATS), the stage was set for extension of free trade principles to telecommunications.

The adoption of the WTO Telecoms Treaty (as an Annex to the GATS) in 1997 (becoming effective in February 1998) has, however, failed to live up to the promise of a border-less telecommunications market. Prospects for free trade in general under the auspices of the WTO have dimmed with nationalistic and protectionist bickering, often disguised as concerns for consumers, the environment, or labour rights, becoming the rule. Disputes between the developed and developing nations are also holding the effectiveness of the WTO back, as highlighted by the failure of the Member nations to reach consensus on a full-term leader of the organisation. Although it is too early to write off the WTO, it is apparent that Member nations need to recommit to principles of free trade and good faith dispute resolution if the organisation is to be saved from degenerating into a pulpit for political grandstanding. This is especially true in an area like telecommunications, so vitally important to the modern economy, so recently emerging from monopoly situations, and so newly open to principles of free trade and competition.

The rules of economics do not change just because telecommunications markets or international trade is involved. Mercantilism does not lead to the creation of wealth, even for the nations misguided enough to practice it. A policy of "beggar thy neighbour" will likely impoverish both the neighbour and the practitioner. It is important to remember primary economic principles when examining international telecommunications. This is particularly the case in that the WTO Telecoms Treaty is designed to accelerate a movement away from the old International Telecommunication Union (ITU) system, based on exchanges among sovereign national monopolies and heavily weighted with subsidy policies, towards a market-based international order allowing foreign entry into home markets and promoting competition. There is a danger that the old system designed to protect national interests and subsidise favoured industries or groups might endure or mutate into more subtle forms of mercantilism; the danger intensifies if the WTO Telecoms Treaty and the liberalisation it promises is undermined before it has a chance to establish itself. Recent regulatory developments such the FCC's Benchmarks Order do not auger well for the future.

While a good faith application of the WTO Telecoms Treaty can do much to lessen trade tension, promote market entry and increase consumer welfare, the Treaty in and of itself cannot solve all of the problems confronting the telecommunications industry and regulators. The WTO is not a super regulator and, scare tactics notwithstanding, it is not the purpose or the role of the WTO to substitute itself for national regulation and remedies. Nor is the WTO Telecoms Treaty the sole answer for potential entrants. The reality of the Treaty can only be understood by first examining WTO structures and procedures, and how the system has functioned in recent disputes. It will then be appropriate to turn to the provision of the Telecoms Annex and the Regulatory Reference Paper.

II. A BRIEF HISTORY OF THE WTO TELECOMS TREATY AND THE GATS

The WTO Basic Telecommunications Agreement was concluded under the framework established by the General Agreement on Trade in Services (GATS), which is one of the agreements negotiated in conjunction with the creation of the WTO.[1] For the first time, the GATS brought trade in services within the international trading regime established for trade in goods by the General Agreement on Tariffs and Trade (GATT) after the Second World War. The GATS consists of general obligations and specific sectoral commitments contained in individual Member Schedules.

---

[1] The WTO came into being on 1 January 1995, pursuant to the Marrakesh Agreement Establishing the World Trade Organisation. Final Act Embodying the Results of the Uruguay Round of Multilateral Trade Negotiations, 15 Apr. 1994, *The Results of the Uruguay Round of Multilateral Trade Negotiations: The Legal Texts 2* (GAT Secretariat, 1994), (1994) 33 *I.L.M.* 1125 [hereinafter Final Act]. The Marrakesh Agreement consists of multilateral agreements on trade in goods, services, intellectual property and dispute settlement. See General Agreement on Trade in Services, 15 Apr. 1994, Marrakesh Agreement Establishing the World Trade Organisation [hereinafter WTO Agreement], Annex 1B, *The Results of the Uruguay Round of Multilateral Trade Negotiations: The Legal Texts 325* (GAT Secretariat, 1994), (1994) 33 *I.L.M.* 1167 [hereinafter GATS]. There are currently about 130 Members of the WTO.

A. The GATS

1. Analytical Construct

The GATS is composed of three major components. The first component consists of general obligations and disciplines that apply to all WTO Members. The second component is comprised of specific commitments relating to market access, national treatment, and other commitments, which are embodied in individual WTO Member Schedules of Specific Commitments.[2] The final component sets out exemptions from the general obligations embodied in Lists of Article II (Most-Favoured-Nation (MFN)) Exemptions.[3]

2. Most Favoured Nation

The most important of the general obligations and disciplines that apply to all WTO Members is the requirement in Article II of the GATS to accord MFN treatment to like services and service suppliers of all other WTO Members, no matter what specific commitments a WTO Member has made. MFN is essentially a non-discrimination rule that requires each WTO Member to treat like services and service suppliers from all other WTO Members similarly.[4] In addition to the MFN obligation, all WTO Members undertake transparency obligations in accordance with Article III (Transparency) of the GATS, which requires prompt publication of all laws and regulations applicable to the provision of services.[5]

3. Market Access

GATS Article XVI (Market Access) requires each WTO Member to "accord services and service suppliers of any other [WTO] Member treatment no less favourable than that provided for under the terms, limitations and conditions agreed and specified in its Schedule" and to refrain from imposing certain types of quantitative restrictions, economic needs tests or local incorporation requirements, in those sectors where the WTO Member has undertaken specific

---

[2] The Schedules of Specific Commitments form an integral part of the GATS. The Schedules containing commitments on basic telecommunications services are available on the WTO Web page at <http://www.wto.org>. GATS, *Ibid.*

[3] The Annex on Article II Exemptions specifies the conditions under which a WTO Member is exempted from its MFN obligations under paragraph 1 of Article II. The United States excluded from its market access commitments and national treatment obligations and took an MFN exemption for the provision of direct-broadcast satellite services, direct-to-home satellite services and digital audio radio satellite services. GATS, Annex on Article II Exemptions, WTO Agreement, Annex 1B, *The Results of the Uruguay Round of Multilateral Trade Negotiations: The Legal Texts* 352 (GAT Secretariat 1994), (1994) 33 I.L.M. 1196.

[4] Article II of the GATS requires WTO Members to accord "to services and service suppliers of any other [WTO] Member treatment no less favourable than that it accords to like services and service suppliers of any other country." GATS, *supra* at n. 1 art. II.

[5] *See Ibid.*, art. III.

market access commitments.[6] This means that a Member may not maintain limits such as the number of service suppliers or the corporate form in which a service can be provided unless the Member has specifically listed such limitations in its Schedule. Article XVII (National Treatment) is a non-discrimination rule that requires a WTO Member to treat like services and service suppliers from other WTO Members no less favorably than it treats its own services and service suppliers.[6a] Under GATS Articles II (MFN) and XVII (National Treatment), treatment of domestic and foreign service suppliers need not be identical to accord MFN or national treatment. The critical aspect of an MFN or national treatment analysis is whether the treatment accorded modifies the conditions of competition in favour of certain foreign or domestic suppliers. Thus, dissimilar treatment can be consistent with MFN or national treatment obligations if it does not put the foreign supplier at a competitive disadvantage to another foreign supplier or a domestic supplier.

4. The Big Rub: Monopolies and Exclusive Service Suppliers

Perhaps one of the biggest issues of contention currently among the various WTO Members is the thorny issue of how to deal with state-controlled monopolies. Does the WTO, and the subsequent Agreement on Basic Telecoms Services, permit or prohibit them?

As explained *infra*, the Regulatory Reference Paper attached to the Agreement on Basic Telecoms Services requires that regulatory agencies be "separate from, and not accountable to, any supplier of basic telecommunications services." Moreover, the regulator's decisions and procedures "shall be impartial with respect to all market participants".[6b] Clearly, in Europe alone, residual state equity positions in incumbent monopolists—although permitted by treaty[6c]—have done much to impede regulatory independence and *a fortiori*, rapid new entry on a pan-continental basis.[6d]

---

[6] *Ibid.*, art. XVI. A quantitative restriction is a cap on the number of permitted suppliers; an economic needs test is a limitation on the number of service suppliers based on an assessment of whether the market will be able to absorb new service suppliers without harm to existing service suppliers.

[6a] Article XVII states that "[i]n the sectors inscribed in its Schedule, and subject to any conditions and qualifications set out therein, each Member shall accord to services and service suppliers of any other Member, in respect of all measures affecting the supply of services, treatment no less favourable than that it accords to its own like services and service suppliers." *Ibid.*, art. XVII (citation omitted).

[6b] World Trade Organisation, Reference Paper on Regulatory Principles [hereinafter Reference Paper] <http://www.wto.org/english/tratop_e/tel23.htm>.

[6c] See discussion in Chapter 10 *infra*.

[6d] In fact, the European Court of Justice recently found that Italy violated numerous provisions of the EC Treaty for attempting to give itself "special powers" to control the actions of Telecom Italia in order to block potential acquisitions by foreign entities. Case C-58/99 *Commission of the European Communities* v. *Italian Republic* 23 May 2000; see also Communication from the Commission to the European Parliament, the Council, the Economic and Social Committee and the Committee of the Regions, Fifth Report on the Implementation of the Telecommunications Regulatory Package, 11 November 1999 [hereinafter Fifth Report] at pp10–11. <http://europa.eu.int/comm/information_society/policy/telecom/5threport/pdf/5threp99_en.pdf>.

Several influential US lawmakers contend that this provision of the Regulatory Reference Paper "somehow impliedly" requires all WTO members to privatise any state-owned monopolies.[6e] Although privatisation is certainly the best way to eliminate conflicts of interests and ensure true regulatory independence, did the members of the WTO really agree that privatisation is "somehow impliedly" required? Apparently not.

Under Article VIII of the GATs, each WTO member only "shall ensure that any monopoly supplier of a service in its territory does not, in the supply of the monopoly service in the relevant market, act in a manner inconsistent with that member's obligations under Article II and specific commitments".[6f] Moreover, where "a member's monopoly supplier competes, either directly or through an affiliated company, in the supply of a service outside the scope of its monopoly rights and which is subject to that Member's specific commitments, the Member shall ensure that such a supplier does not abuse its monopoly position to act in its territory in a manner inconsistent with such commitments".[7] Accordingly, it appears that it is *not a per se* WTO violation if a WTO Member government merely holds an equity stake in a dominant incumbent provider, but it is a WTO violation if the WTO Member government permits that monopoly provider to "abuse its monopoly position to act in its territory" in a manner inconsistent with the Member's individual commitments.

III. WTO DISPUTES AND RESOLUTION PROCEDURE

The WTO is an organisation of nations, called Members in WTO documents. It is important to remember that only Members—i.e. nations—have rights under the WTO treaties. An individual or company that considers that a nation is not living up to its WTO obligations cannot successfully sue that nation in a WTO court. Recourse is only available through the WTO process if the aggrieved party can interest a Member nation in bringing a complaint. Therefore, the reality is that political connections do count. A well-connected firm may easily convince its government that another nation has violated a treaty. On the other hand, matters of diplomacy or unrelated international politics undoubtedly influence a government's decision whether to initiate proceedings and how aggressive it will be in pursuing a case.

The WTO encourages Members to settle disputes on an informal basis before complaints are filed. Once proceedings are instituted, the parties are still encouraged to seek the "good offices" of the WTO to resolve the matter. Mediation

---

[6e] See 7 September 2000 Oversight Hearing of the US House of Representatives Subcommittee on Telecommunications, Trade and Consumer Protection—Foreign Government Ownership of American Telecommunications Companies (transcript available at time of press).

[6f] Article VIII, ¶ 1.

[7] Article VIII, ¶ 2.

and conciliation are also available. Formal resolution procedures are set out in an Understanding on Rules and Procedures Governing the Settlement of Disputes, sometimes referred to as the Disputes Settlement Understanding (DSU). Overall administrative responsibility for procedures rests with the Dispute Settlement Body (DSB).[8] Once a Member comes forward with a complaint clearly demonstrating that another Member nation has not carried out duties required under a WTO agreement, a *prima facie* case has been made and the target of the complaint then has the burden of disproving the charge.[9]

The first step in filing and resolving a complaint is known as a request for a consultation.[10] The filing of a request for a consultation is to be in writing and state the grounds for the complaint against the other Member nation. The recipient has ten days to respond, or settlement negotiations may start during a 30-day period after the request is filed. Assuming the recipient enters into settlement negotiations, or consultations as they are called, the complainant can take no further action for 60 days. Highlighting a common complaint about WTO proceedings, their lack of openness, it is stated that the consultations are to be confidential.[11] While confidentiality may be helpful in encouraging Members to be more forthcoming and reduce chances of impolite or embarrassing statements causing political difficulties, it does little to enlighten the public about the WTO's obscure proceedings. At the end of the 60-day consultation time period, or sooner if the parties agree, a panel—in effect a judicial board—may be requested by the complaining party. The process may be accelerated in case of urgency, such as cases involving perishable goods.

The DSB then selects a panel, composed of three or five individuals and refers the case to this panel for examination.[12] The WTO Secretariat nominates panelists from a list composed of qualified governmental and non-governmental individuals who are expert in trade-related matters.[13] The parties can veto a panelist for compelling reasons, presumably such as demonstrated prejudice. In line with a general policy of sensitivity to the concerns of developing nations, if a developing nation is a party to the dispute, at least one panelist must be from a developing nation if so requested. Third parties—i.e. other Member nations— interested in the case may make submissions to the panel. Panels are charged with making findings of fact and conclusions consisting of interpretation of the agreements and practices in question.[14]

During the six months (less if a matter is designated as urgent, or up to nine months if the panel cannot issue its report in six months) after the panel is selected, the panel is to meet with the parties, encourage settlement, accept writ-

---

[8]   The WTO, like all bureaucratic bodies, relies heavily on acronyms.

[9]   WTO Understanding on Rules and Procedures Governing the Settlement of Disputes, art. 3.8 [hereinafter DSU] <http://www.wto.org/english/docs_e/legal_e/28-dsu.pdf>.

[10]   *Ibid.*, art. 4.

[11]   *Ibid.*, art. 4.6.

[12]   *Ibid.*, arts. 6–8.

[13]   *Ibid.*, art. 8.

[14]   *Ibid.*, art. 11.

ten submissions, possibly seek information from experts as well as individuals, companies, Member nations or other "bodies" (but the panels are not given any right of subpoena),[15] and issue interim and final reports.[16] Panels are instructed to be sensitive to the concerns of developing nations.[17]

As is the case with the consultation procedure, it is specified that the panel deliberations shall be confidential.[18] Panel reports, however, are published and available on the WTO's Internet site.[19] Final panel reports are circulated to the Member nations; parties are given a right to circulate written objections, and the panel report is to be adopted by the DSB within 60 days of its circulation unless notice of an appeal is filed by one of the parties or if by consensus the DSB decides to reject the panel report.[20]

The Appellate Body, composed of seven members, three members of whom are selected to hear an individual appeal, is charged with hearing on ruling on appeals within 60 days of the filing of the notification of appeal.[21] The review is limited to issues of law. Like the panel procedure, proceedings, submissions and deliberations are confidential. The Appellate Body can uphold, reverse or modify the findings of the panel, and recommend ways for the offending Member to bring itself into compliance with the WTO agreements. While the parties have no recourse from the decision of the Appellate Body, the DSB can decide by consensus to reject the Appellate Body's findings. The entire process from the time a panel is selected to hear a dispute until the final report of the Appellate Body should take no more than one year,[22] a very fast resolution particularly considering that complex issues of international trade, interpretation of treaties, and likely highly technical industrial matters will be under consideration. By comparison, complex or even routine litigation in national courts may ordinarily take several years to be tried and appeals exhausted.

After a final ruling, the Member nation has an obligation to implement the ruling, beginning with notifying the DSB as to how and when the implementation will occur.[23] Of course there can be further disputes about what is meant by the decision of a panel or Appellate Body and whether measures the losing party proposes are adequate to address the problem, in which case there are further procedures to send the matter back to the original panel for consideration.[24]

Assuming the guilty Member nation does not alter the offending practice, the aggrieved Member nation that brought the action may retaliate, referred to as

---

[15] *Ibid.*, art 13.
[16] *Ibid.*, art 12.
[17] *Ibid.*, art. 12.11.
[18] *Ibid.*, art 14.1.
[19] <http://www.wto.org/english/tratop_e/dispu_e/distab_e.htm>.
[20] DSU, *supra* n. 9, art. 16.
[21] *Ibid.*, art. 17.
[22] *Ibid.*, art. 20.
[23] *Ibid.*, art. 21.
[24] *Ibid.*, art. 21.5.

suspending concessions,[25] or seek compensation from the other party. The DSU is to be kept informed of and authorise the proposed retaliation. The target of the retaliation may invoke an arbitration procedure lasting no more than 60 days, before the original panel, if possible.

Although the dispute resolution procedure sounds complicated and cumbersome, it is difficult to imagine how the process might be substantially improved given the realities of international politics and commerce. It is designed to be fast and fair to all of the involved nations. Ample opportunity is given to be heard, make written submissions, or settle the matter. The lack of openness may hurt the perception of the WTO's resolution procedures, but being away from the view of the media and special interests may encourage truthfulness and the ability to find workable solutions behind closed doors. Not posturing for the folks back home might lead to better results.

IV. WTO RESOLUTION: ILLUSTRATIVE CASES

The best way to judge the effect of the WTO and its dispute resolution procedure is to examine some actual cases. Perhaps because of the end of the Cold War, trade disputes seem to have become more common in recent years. These disputes could be more visible because international commerce is more important. The existence of the WTO and the accompanying new dispute resolution procedure could also be a factor.

A. Kodak versus Fuji equals United States versus Japan

Kodak, the US photographic company, had publicly and repeatedly complained that it was impossible for it to break into the Japanese film market. Fuji, a Japanese company, held a dominant position in its home film market. Kodak claimed that Fuji's dominance was maintained by various actions of the Japanese government designed to hurt film imports and protect domestic Japanese companies. The US government, apparently persuaded of the justice of Kodak's position, brought an action against Japan in September 1996 alleging violation of GATT provisions. The WTO panel report,[26] issued in March 1998, concluded that Japan had not violated the GATT. In effect, the panel held that Kodak's failure to succeed in the Japanese market was not due to unfair trade practices. The case is interesting in that it shows how a single firm, with no direct rights before the WTO, can nevertheless bring a WTO action, if its government is sympathetic to its cause. It also shows that failure to crack a

---

[25] *Ibid.*, art. 22.

[26] World Trade Organisation, *Japan—Measures Affecting Consumer Photographic Film and Paper*, (Report of the Panel, WT/DS44/R, 31 March 1998 <http://www.wto.org/english/tratop_e/dispu_e/ 44r00.pdf>).

foreign market, standing alone, is not enough to establish a WTO violation. Finally, it shows that despite the fast procedures called for under the DSU, resolution can still take some time: the US requested a panel (in effect filed a complaint) in September 1996, and the panel did not file its report until March 1998.

B. Is it a Computer, a Telephone or a TV?

Different products are subject to different import tariffs. Classification of products within a product grouping is therefore of vital interest to importers. Often it is difficult to determine precisely where a product belongs in existing classification lists, particularly for new products in high-technology fields. The problem is made worse by the process of convergence among telecommunications, media and computers. This was the problem confronted by the WTO in the US's complaint against product classification practices of the EU.[27] Earlier negotiations had led to favourable tariff treatment for computers. Subsequently, products such as routers used to link computers together and form local area networks (LANs), began to be imported into the EU in substantial numbers prompting the question of whether such devices were computers or telephone transmission equipment, and thereby subject to a higher tariff. The EU also classified another new product, multimedia computers, as televisions rather than as computers. The US, a major manufacturer and exporter of both LAN devices and multimedia computers, opened proceedings against the EU, requesting that the WTO rule that the products in questions should be classified as computers. The panel found that while LAN equipment should properly be classified as computers, multimedia computers could legitimately fall under the television classification. The EU referred the matter to the Appellate Body, who delivered an opinion that the EU was justified in classifying LAN equipment as telecommunications equipment.[28] There was evidence that EU Member States had classified LAN equipment as both computer and telecommunications equipment, so the US assertion that LAN equipment had been consistently treated in the past as computer equipment was incorrect.

It is precisely this sort of dispute that the WTO is well-positioned to resolve. Problems of tariff classification are best solved by an independent international body. The alternative would have been for the exporters to attempt to challenge the classifications either with the Member States or with the EU, jurisdictions having a financial interest in the outcome. The case also illustrates the problem of dealing with new products that will not conveniently fit in existing categories.

[27] World Trade Organisation, *European Communities—Customs Classification of Certain Computer Equipment* (Report of the Panel, WT/DS62/R, WT/DS67/R, and WT/DS68/R, 5 February 1998, <http://www.wto.org/english/tratop_e/dispu_e/comp.pdf>).

[28] World Trade Organisation, European Communities—Customs Classification of Certain Computer Equipment, Report of the Appellate Body, WT/DS62/R, WT/DS67/R, and WT/DS68/R, 5 June 1998 <http://www.wto.org/wto/english/tratop_e/dispu_e/62abre.pdf>.

C. Meat on the Table

The most contentious recent trade disputes have concerned food. This is perhaps understandable given that food touches everyone's lives and raises not only commercial issues, but also health safety, national pride, and policy issues such as promotion of an agricultural lifestyle. The powerful imagery of the family farm runs deep in many cultures. There are also European specific concerns over food as witnessed by the problems involving mad cow disease and British beef, food contamination in Belgium as well as the growing concerns over genetically modified foods. It is against that backdrop that the dispute between the US and the EU over the EU's ban on importation of hormone treated beef should be viewed. The EU eventually lost this protracted dispute, and the US was authorised by the WTO to impose sanctions totally US$ 116.8 million per year.[29] Nevertheless, the EU has indicated that it will continue its ban against hormone-treated beef, and that scientific evidence (rejected by the WTO) of the health dangers of hormone-treated beef justifies its actions. For now, however, European exporters will suffer through payment of increased tariffs to support the EU, and ultimately to support the European beef producers who benefit from the ban. Domestic politics, here the power of European agricultural interests, often prevail over promotion of free international trade. Farm subsidies remain a difficult problem, and not only internationally. Both the US and the EU have powerful farm lobbies. Subsidies to farmers constitute a large part of the EU's budget, and the problem will have to be addressed before the EU expands its membership to include former-Soviet bloc states. Including these nations within the EU's Common Agricultural Programme would break the EU budget. The US likes to publicly call for freer international trade in the agricultural sector, but US farmers receive subsidies as well.

D. Yes, We Have a Banana War

Probably the best-known and most intractable trade dispute the WTO has dealt with is over importation of bananas into the EU. As a part of its colonial legacy, the EU has preserved a quota and preference system to favour importation of bananas from certain former colonies of EU Member States and therefore protect and subsidise the banana industry in those countries. Bananas from non-favoured nations could only be imported in limited numbers and subject to higher tariffs. The result has been fewer opportunities for other banana producing countries as well as for fruit companies owned by US interests to sell

---

[29] World Trade Organisation, *European Communities—Measures Concerning Meat and Meat Products (Hormones)* (original Complaint by the United States, Recourse to Arbitration by the European Communities Under Article 22.6 of the DSU, Decision by the Arbitrators, WT/DS26/ARB, 12 July 1999 <http://www.wto.org/english/tratop_e/dispu_e/48arb.pdf).

bananas in the EU. The result has also been lower quality bananas made available at higher prices for European consumers. The US, joined by Ecuador, Guatemala, Honduras, and Mexico, complained that the banana quota and preference system contravened the GATT agreement. An initial panel report was favourable to the position of the US and the other complaining parties, as was the subsequent decision of the Appellate Body and various arbitrations.[30] Suffice it to say that the EU exhausted every possible avenue of appeal and delay.

The EU claimed that its quota and preference system was authorised under the pre-existing Lomé convention, a development treaty between the EU and many African, Caribbean, and Pacific nations. The EU also claimed that the quota and preference system as practised was essential for the economies of the benefiting developing nations. In the accompanying publicity war, the EU portrayed the struggle as between the poor nations and the exploitative rich US fruit corporations. This characterisation ignored the presence of the other complaining Member nations, all developing nations themselves. This characterisation also ignored the profits reaped by European fruit distributors from the quota system. The result was that the EU will be able to maintain at least a portion of its quota and preference system for the present, but it will be diminished over time. At the time of this writing, it is unsure whether a settlement will be worked out or if the US will enforce sanctions against the EU.

The stubbornness of both sides of the banana war over what at first glance seems a ridiculous issue is emblematic of both how important international trade is and how selfish interests can work against finding common sense solutions. Although it sounds noble for the EU to fight for developing nations, the banana quota system hurts other developing nations, a classic case of attempting to benefit by beggaring a neighbour. Furthermore, the quota and preference system is supposed to help certain developing nations, but should subsidies be given to encourage inefficient behaviour? That is, if the beneficiaries of the preferences could not sell their fruit without subsidies, then they should not be producing this fruit. This may seem like a cold attitude, but it is only facing reality. Propping up an industry that cannot succeed in the market, be it automobile manufacturing or banana growing, only delays inevitable failure and creates a cost that must be paid by someone. In the case of bananas, it is European consumers who pay more for inferior fruit. If the EU wishes to subsidise favoured developing nations, it should do so out of general tax revenue. That would be more honest and more efficient. It is more politically expedient, however, to pay the subsidy in an inefficient, but hidden way by increasing everyone's food bill. It is still a cost to the economy; it is a lie to the people of Europe, and it is also unfair to the supposed beneficiaries of the EU's good intentions. What does it profit anyone to artificially maintain banana production? Conditions will not

[30] World Trade Organisation, *European Communities—Regime for the Importation, Sale and Distribution of Bananas* (Panel Reports, WT/DS27/R/ECU, WT/DS27/R/GTM, WT/DS27/R/HND, WT/DDS27/R/MEX, WT/SDDS27/R/USA, 27 May 1997; Appellate Body Report, WT/DS27/AB/R, 25 September 1997 <http://www.wto.org/english/tratop_e/banana_e.htm> *et seq*).

magically change in the future so as to suddenly make banana production profitable in these countries. Rather, if the EU really wants to help these nations, rather than maintaining them in a state of colonial-like dependence, it would be better to spend its money investing in opportunities likely to bear real fruit of technical progress and economic efficiency. Assistance in creating a pro-business climate would help more than the cleverest quota scheme ever devised.

V. THE WTO TELECOMS TREATY

A. The Inclusion of Telecommunications Under the GATS

At the conclusion of the negotiations creating the WTO in April 1994, the United States and other WTO Members made commitments to allow market access for a broad range of services—including such diverse industries as construction services, professional services (such as legal and medical services), distribution services, and value-added (or enhanced) telecommunications services.[31] Basic telecommunications, however, was one of a limited number of service sectors for which negotiations were extended beyond April 1994.[32] WTO Members recognised the economic importance of basic telecommunications services and established a separate, sector-specific negotiation for these services that were scheduled to conclude by April 30, 1996. Because the negotiations had made insufficient progress by that date, the WTO agreed to extend the deadline for concluding the negotiations to February 15, 1997. This extension resulted in the final WTO Telecoms Treaty that became effective in February 1998. [33]

[31] The United States adopted the FCC's definition of enhanced services for purposes of its GATS obligations, that is, "services, offered over common carrier transmission facilities . . . which employ computer processing applications that act on the format, content code, protocol or similar aspects of the subscriber's transmitted information; provide the subscriber additional, different, or restructured information; or involve subscriber interaction with stored information." 47 C.F.R. § 64.702 (1997).

[32] The other sectors were financial services and maritime services.

[33] For a truly excellent summary of the negotiations, political backstabbing and other events leading up to the Telecommunications Annex, see Cynthia A. Beltz, *The Borderless Economy* (AEI, 1999). For example, if the second round of WTO negotiations fell apart, the United States was fully prepared to blame its "friendly neighbours to the north"—the Canadians—for seeking to impose stringent indigenous content restrictions on broadcast and satellite services. See David Molony, "U.S. Guns for Canada at WTO", *Comm. Wk. Int'l*, 3 Feb. 1997, at 1. Not only is this act alone outrageous (after all, how is one more choice—even if it is Canadian rules football or repeats of SCTV's "Great White North"—actually bad for American consumers), but it is especially hypocritical given Canada's long track record of broadcasting "acceptable" children's educational programming—one of the Clinton/Gore/Hundt Administration's primary regulatory agendas. See, e.g., Statement by FCC Commissioner Susan Ness on the Death of Shari Lewis, 1998 WL 439268, Aug. 4, 1998 ("lament[ing]" that Shari Lewis "had to go to Canada to find funding for educational children's programming"); see also Reed Hundt, "Statement on Westinghouse's Children's Educational Television Announcement", *WDC*, 20 Sept. 1995 (visited Nov. 4, 1998) <http://www.fcc.gov/ Speeches/Hundt/ spreh527.txt> ("Westinghouse's assurance that it will deliver three hours of children's educational TV on CBS underscores the tremendous importance of teaching our kids, instead

B. General Framework

As just mentioned, the WTO Telecoms Treaty was signed in 1997 and became effective in February 1998.[34] As stated above, the Treaty is formally an Annex to the General Agreement on Trade in Services. It is divided into two parts, the actual Annex on Telecommunications and an accompanying Reference Paper on Regulatory Principles,[35] a commitment entered into by fewer Member nations than the Annex on Telecommunications. Not all Member nations agreed to all of the provisions of either the Annex or the Reference Paper, for example some Member nations wish to maintain a telecom operator's monopoly position or limit foreign investment in telecommunications companies for a limited time.[36] For purposes of this discussion, the documents will be considered in their entirety. Information about the extent of a particular nation's conformity to the Annex and the Reference Paper can only be obtained by examining that nation's individual commitment.

The Telecommunications Annex begins with a recognition of the importance of the telecommunications industry, both as a specific sector as well as a means of transport for communications, a vital part of modern economies. Beyond this high level objective, the Annex is given a broad scope as well, applying "to all

of harming them, with broadcast TV." In the words of President Clinton, American children must not "lose 'countless opportunities to learn' from quality educational TV delivered by commercial networks for free to every home in the country.") (Note: The FCC attempted to act deceptively when Disney sought to acquire ABC/Cap Cities. Considering Disney's well-documented record with creating children's programming, however, Mr. Hundt could only argue that "it remain[ed] to be seen" whether Disney could still do something more to help America's children.); Statement of Reed Hundt in Response to AT&T's Pledge of $150 Million to Help Put the Nation's Schools on the Information Superhighway, 1995 FCC LEXIS 7113, 31 Oct. 1995 ("We at the FCC hope that AT&T's gift," mysteriously made concurrent with the FCC's decision to declare AT&T as a nondominant carrier for domestic service "of free internet access and voice-mail to all the children of America will catalyze a nationwide public/private partnership to network all classrooms as the President and Vice President have challenged.").

[34] World Trade Organisation, General Agreement on Trade in Services, Annex on Telecommunications [hereinafter Telecommunications Annex] <http://www.wto.org/english/docs_e/legal_e/26-gats.pdf>.

[35] Reference Paper <http://www.itu.int/newsarchive/press/WTPF98/WTORefpaper.html>.

[36] Indeed, it is particularly interesting to note that, contrary to the plethora of press reports and politicians' statements, that the Telecommunications Annex accounts for approximately 90 per cent of world telecommunications revenue, the actual scope and depth of the Telecommunications Annex may be far less than suggested. See William J. Drake & Eli M. Noam, "The WTO Deal on Basic Telecommunications: Big Bang or Little Whimper?", (1997) 21 *Telecomm. Pol'y* 799, 811 (While the Telecommunications Annex is a "step in the right direction," it is "quite another matter to declare it, as credit-grabbing victory bulletins did, a revolution, a breakthrough, a telecommunications D-Day" because "the people directly involved in the drafting, lobbying, analyzing, and implementing of the agreement have worked hard to seal the deal, and it is therefore natural for them to believe that the result of their attention has been a monumental change rather than a monumental effort."). To wit, the United States, Japan, and the European Union alone account for 74 per cent of total volume. Moreover, those signing the agreement account for less than 55 per cent of the WTO membership and the world's population. In fact, as of the time of this writing, China and Russia are not signatories to the Telecommunications Annex, *primarily because they are not even Members of the WTO.*

measures of a Member that affect access to and use of public telecommunications networks and services."[37] There is a limitation on the applicability of the Annex in that it is not to be concerned with radio or television distribution, however, presumably the use of cable television networks for telecommunications purposes as is technically feasible and becoming increasingly common, would be covered by the Annex.

Neither the signatory states nor telecommunications providers under the jurisdiction of the signatories may be required under the Annex to provide any services or give access to telecommunications infrastructure other than what is offered to the general public.[38] This provision may be important when considering whether the Annex requires Member nations or incumbent telecoms operators to give entrants access to unbundled local loops. It is doubtful that an ordinary subscriber, the general public, would be able to purchase or lease a local loop. A subscriber can obtain service over a local loop, but that is a different matter from provision of and rights to use the raw copper or transmission rights that go with unbundled loops. Lease or use of high capacity lines, referred to in the industry as leased lines or private lines, is dealt with separately in another section of the Annex.

Among the defined terms in the Annex, of particular interest is "public telecommunications transport service." The definition covers voice and data, but may exclude communications that do not occur in real-time, or where the form or content of the end-user's information is altered, or that are not between two or more points. A similar definition for basic voice service in the EU's regulatory framework led the EU Commission to conclude that Internet telephony was not subject to the licensing and universal service requirements of voice service since Internet telephony did not occur in real-time, was altered in form, and might not occur between two points in a network.[39] It is at least arguable whether Internet communications fall under the WTO's definition of a public telecommunications transport service.

Member nations are under obligations to ensure publication of criteria for supplier access to public networks, tariffs and conditions of service, standards and technical interface requirements, as well as rules of licensing, registration or notification by service providers.[40] Access to public telecommunications networks must be on a reasonable and non-discriminatory basis are further specified as most-favoured nation and national treatment.[41]

Left open by the WTO is whether the duty of non-discrimination extends on an *intra*-country basis. That is, does the WTO require its members to ensure that domestic network providers give access to domestic competitors on the same terms it itself enjoys? Such internal non-discrimination requirements are

---

[37] Telecommunications Annex, *supra* n. 34, art. 2(a).

[38] *Ibid.*, art. 2(c).

[39] Commission Notice concerning the Status of voice communications on Internet under community law and, in particular, pursuant to the Services Directive [1998] OJ C6/4.

[40] Telecommunications Annex, *supra* n. 34, art. 4.

[41] *Ibid.*, art. 5.

very difficult to implement and oversee, particularly regarding entities, such as state-owned monopolies that might not have a tradition of strict accounting or regulatory oversight. Given, however, the limited nature of the definition of facilities that service suppliers must be given access to ("public transport networks and services"), it appears that the WTO signatories intended that there be non-discrimination for interconnection on an *intra*-Member State basis.

The remainder of Article Five spells out interconnection rights of foreign service suppliers in greater detail. (Let's face it, this business is still, at bottom, all about handing off traffic from one network to another.) This includes a right to access and use network facilities within or across the border of the Member nation.[42] In practice this means a right to use leased lines or private lines on either a domestic or international basis, answering the question of whether access to this type of infrastructure was contemplated within the definition of public networks.

This provision does, however, raise a further question as to whether use of international facilities means that international interconnection should also be available. International traffic has traditionally been routed via the accounting rates system under the auspices of the International Telecommunication Union rather than by interconnection contracts. This section of the Annex implies that international interconnection should be an option to accounting rates. An interconnection right, not specified as restricted to domestic or international traffic, is granted in this Annex Article.[43]

As might be expected, there are restrictions as to access and use of public networks by foreign entrants. As a starting point, Member nations may not be forced to allow services other than as set forth in that Member's commitment, a statement of the obvious under WTO rules. Member nations can take actions to protect the security and confidentiality of messages, ensure the "public service responsibilities" of providers as well as protect the technical integrity of the network.[44] While these sorts of provisions are standard in telecommunications laws, care needs to be taken to ensure that these exceptions do not become lightly disguised anti-competitive devices. For example, telecommunications incumbents commonly fight the typical first wave of competition, that of supply of end-user equipment, by claiming that allowing allegedly low quality telephones to be used would damage the telecommunications network.

In support of the general principles such as technical integrity set out above, Members are more specifically allowed to place restrictions on telecommunications services.[45] These may include "restrictions of resale or shared use" of telecommunications services.

A restriction on sharing would kill any attempt to use this Annex as support for more liberal unbundling schemes such as the FCC's line sharing rules for

[42] Telecommunications Annex, *supra* n. 34, art. 5(b).
[43] *Ibid.*, art. 5(b)(ii).
[44] *Ibid.*, art. 5(d) and (e).
[45] *Ibid.*, art. 5(f).

local loop unbundling. While sharing telephone lines among customers or different types of services may arguably cause technical problems, it is difficult to envisage what sort of problems the drafters may have had in mind in connection with the allowed ban on resale. Member nations might attempt to rely on this provision to justify prohibitions on competitors using leased lines to serve end-users, as that would be a type of resale. In addition to restricting resale or sharing, Member nations may require competitors to observe certain technical interfaces and standards in their service offerings. It is curious, however, that Member nations are allowed to maintain "restrictions on inter-connection of private leased or owned circuits with such networks or services or with circuits leased or owned by another service supplier."[46] It is to be hoped that this allowance is to be interpreted as only justified when the Member nation can meet the general policy of technical interference or safeguarding public responsibilities, etc. Otherwise, such an interpretation would defeat any interconnection obligation. This section of the Annex ends with an endorsement of the right of Member nations to maintain requirements of notification, registration and licensing.

Developing nations are given special rights to "place reasonable conditions on access" that are "necessary to strengthen its domestic telecommunications infrastructure" as well as to "increase its participation in international trade in telecommunications services."[47] This is another provision with obscure meaning. The reference to international trade could be a recognition of the emphasis that developing nations place on maintaining high accounting rates for termination of international telephone traffic within their borders. These high rates are a traditional source of revenue for developing nations.

It is argued by developing nations and their advocates that this subsidy is necessary for developing nations to modernise their networks. As the subsidy system has been in place as long as there have been international telephone calls, it is questionable whether it has been effective in modernising telecommunications networks. Developing nations' accounting rates remain high; it costs a lot to call these nations, and therefore international business involving those nations suffers as well. The telecommunications networks in these nations as a rule remain poor. God knows where the subsidy money ends up, but it is obviously not being spent on better telecommunications infrastructure. Although it may not be politically palatable to say so, privatisation and competition work better than subsidies in promoting technical progress and consumer welfare. This is true in the developing world as well as everywhere else.

C. The Reference Paper

More attention has focused on the Reference Paper, sort of an annex to the Telecommunications Annex, than on the Annex itself. This is understandable as the Reference Paper is revolutionary. Although the WTO is not a regulatory

---

[46] *Ibid.*, art. 5(f)(v).
[47] *Ibid.*, art. 5(g).

agency, the signatory nations commit themselves to a common telecommunications regulatory framework, and the WTO is the ultimate enforcer of this commitment. In addition, the Reference Paper commits the signatories to prohibit certain anti-competitive practices. A possible area for WTO expansion has been in the area of antitrust law. Some nations have proposed that a WTO Treaty for signatory states to meet minimum standards of antitrust protection be agreed, much like what was done in the TRIPS Treaty for intellectual property law. The Reference Paper has already taken this step, at least in the telecommunications sector, and therefore the Reference Paper may be considered the first international antitrust code.

A question in general about the Reference Paper is whether the law or regulation of any one nation may be used to fill in the gaps in the Reference Paper's framework. The Reference Paper is relatively short, much shorter than national telecommunications law and regulations as might be found in, for example, the 1996 US Telecommunications Act alone, not counting all of the regulations and interpretations that Act spawned. Soon after the Reference Paper was adopted, US trade officials stated that the 1996 US Telecommunications Act should be used to fill in the gaps in the Reference Paper, as the 1996 Act was the "gold standard" for telecommunications regulation in the world.[48] Under this position, US telecommunications suppliers would carry the 1996 Act with them wherever they went, sort of like a flag.

The reaction of the rest of this world to this assertion of "1996 Act imperialism" may be guessed. Officials of the EU had a similar assertion for application of the EU telecommunications regulatory framework; the reasoning was perhaps marginally better than that of the US. The EU position was that since the Reference Paper was under negotiation at the same time the EU regulatory framework was being finalised, the drafters of the Reference Paper had the EU framework in mind. Contemporary negotiations and practices are noted by the WTO in its dispute settlements procedures.

To be fair to both the US and the EU, a detailed examination of the Reference Paper reveals elements of both the 1996 Act and the EU framework. Neither regime should be able to impose its regulatory law on the rest of the world, however. The Reference Paper should be interpreted in light of each Member nation's law. There must of course be minimum standards that the Members must maintain. These are to be found in the "definitions and principles" that are the entire substance of the Reference Paper.

The definitions section of the Reference Paper contains three terms, "users", "essential facilities", and "major supplier".

---

[48] See Reed Hundt, Statement of FCC Chairman Reed Hundt Concerning WTO Agreement on Telecom Services, 1997 WL 63345 (Feb. 18, 1997). Unfortunately, given the current success record of the 1996 Act, it can be seen why the world eliminated the gold standard.

1. Definitions

Users—The most non-controversial term is that of "users". Under the Reference Paper, "users" are defined so as to include both end users (consumers) as well as suppliers.

Essential Facilities—The most interesting term is essential facilities and it is defined in the Reference Paper as follows:

> "Essential facilities mean facilities of a public telecommunications transport network or service that are exclusively or predominantly provided by a single or limited number of suppliers; and cannot feasibly be economically or technically substituted in order to provide a service."

"Essential facilities" is a term originally used in US antitrust law, coming from cases involving such things as competitor access to railroad bridges operated by other railroad companies. As US Courts originated the doctrine and its application, the US certainly has an argument that "essential facilities" should be interpreted in accordance with US antitrust law. The EU has also adopted a form of the essential facilities doctrine, but most other countries in the world, being relatively new to even concepts of antitrust law, have not. It must be considered as quite an accomplishment that this term figures so prominently in the Reference Paper. The actual use of the term essential facilities within the Reference Paper is limited, however, as will be discussed below. Further the question remains unresolved as to whose law will fill in the gaps for application of the essential facilities doctrine, even as to its (current) limited use. There are also important differences, particularly regarding pricing of access to essential facilities, even in the US and EU doctrines. Greater differences may be expected in those nations that until now have no experience of the doctrine. While application issues may be rare now due to the limited application of the essential facilities doctrine in the Reference Paper, if the doctrine is extended, perhaps to include such areas as competitor access to unbundled loops, then resolution of the question, "whose essential facilities doctrine?" will be of critical importance.

Major Supplier—The final definition, that of a "major supplier", seems to derive more from EU concepts, specifically that of a provider with significant market power. The EU regulatory framework presumes that a telecoms operator having at least a 25 per cent market share has significant market power and is therefore subject to certain obligations. The Reference Paper definition is more flexible and in line with principles of monopolist determination, that is the ability to act independently of competitors or customers in setting price and supply conditions. The Reference Paper defines a "major supplier" as one who can "materially affect" price or supply in the market because of that supplier's control over essential facilities or use of its market position. Major suppliers, like the EU's significant market power providers, have special duties.

2. *"Comparative Safeguards"*

Article 1 of the Reference Paper consists of competitive safeguards, directed at practices of major suppliers. A question is raised in that this section is targeted at "suppliers who, alone or together, are a major supplier. . ." It should have been safe to assume that by "major suppliers" the Reference Paper had incumbent operators, the former monopolies, in mind. This language of "alone or together" calls this assumption into question. Does this mean when operators act together in a conspiracy to deny opportunities to other competitors, a type of group boycott? Is this an expression of the EU's concept of joint dominance? If the language is meant to be taken literally, then all telecommunications suppliers would be considered as major suppliers, for if they are considered together then they have a 100 per cent market share, can obviously control the market, and possess essential facilities. It would, however, be a misuse of competition law principles to apply rules designed for monopolists to all participants in a market for the sole reason that the market is a heavily regulated one.

The Reference Paper specifies that Member nations must have safeguards against anti-competitive practices, including cross-subsidisation, anti-competitive use of competitor information, and withholding of necessary technical information.[49] This is rather a short list, but it should be emphasised that this is a minimum list. Member nations are certainly free to add more stringent safeguards. Indeed, in could be argued that these three areas are only given as examples; signatory states may be under a duty to do more in the absence of specific reservations in their commitments. While it may be argued that Member nations should require more, perhaps to the level of safeguards as set forth in the US 1996 Telecommunications Act or the EU's regulatory framework, it is doubtful that such a position would prevail in a WTO dispute. As discussed in Chapter 14, *infra*, however, universal service disputes have become a growing front in the "telecoms trade war."

The second safeguard heading, that of forbidding incumbents from improperly using competitor information, should be a necessity in any regulatory regime, though it will be very difficult to enforce. By their very position as operators on the public telecommunications network and server of most customers, incumbent operators are in a position to gather a great deal of information about the activities, customers and intentions of competitors. Not only would it offend competition law principles for incumbents to make whatever use they chose of this information, it could also impact the privacy rights of end-users.

On the other hand, there are valid reasons for incumbent operators to have access to and use competitor information. The network must be provisioned and maintained. Current and forecasted use of the network from all operators and end-users must be considered. In effect, incumbent operators might have to erect walls between those having a legitimate need to access competitor information and those who might use this information to gain an improper advantage in the market.

---

[49] Reference Paper, *supra* n. 35, art. 1.2.

Moreover, policing these walls will be very difficult. Regulators will be forced to practically rely on creation of protective measures inside an incumbent's operations, such as appropriate structural separation, and then the good faith of the incumbent. In-house compliance programmes will obviously have a role to play. It must also be borne in mind that every interconnection is two-way; competitors gain information about customers of the incumbent operator with every call and interconnection between the customers of the competitor and the incumbent operator. To use the concept of the level playing field, it is not equal to subject incumbent operators to regulation and let entrants off with no obligation. As calling information inevitably involves end-users and hence individual calls, perhaps the neutral requirements of data protection and privacy regulation are best suited to act in this area.

The last of the specified competitive safeguards is a prohibition of major suppliers withholding technical information about essential facilities as well as "commercially relevant information" from competitors.[50] This is the sole reference to "essential facilities" in the body of the Reference Paper, so perhaps there will not be much argument over the contentious issue of defining essential facilities, since not much is really at stake in this Reference Paper. Technical information should be read as interface requirements and so forth so that interconnection can take place. "Commercially relevant information" is a vaguer concept, and it is difficult to imagine what the drafters had in mind. Competitors would consider all marketing plans, internal accounts and strategic plans of the incumbent to be commercially relevant, however, the drafters could not have intended that this degree of information be provided. Rather, the included modifier "necessary for [competitors] to provide services" should place a burden on competitors to demonstrate that the requested information is in fact necessary.

3. Interconnection

The next section of the Reference Paper deals with interconnection, an area of vital importance as competition develops. If end-users are not able to effectively communicate with each other, such communication being the essence of interconnection, then it is impossible for competition in telecommunications to exist. It is not enough, however, to mandate that interconnection must be allowed. Details of interconnection, particularly regarding interconnection prices must be considered, implemented and written into contracts. Another important factor is where physical interconnection will take place. Incumbent operators might make things difficult for competitors by requiring that all interconnection take place at one location, requiring competitors to route all of their traffic to that one, perhaps distant location. Conversely, an incumbent might attempt to require competitors to interconnect at many locations throughout a nation and thereby incur significant construction and maintenance costs.

[50] *Ibid.*, art. 1.2(c).

The Reference Paper would leave the choice of interconnection points with competitors and require major suppliers to allow interconnection "at any technically feasible point in the network."[51] This requirement of interconnection at any technically feasible point is identical to language found in the US 1996 Telecommunications Act setting forth the interconnection duties of incumbent local exchange carriers.[52] Interestingly, this language differs from the EU interconnection regime which requires significant market power providers (those with a greater than 25 per cent market share) to "meet all reasonable requests for" interconnection "including access at points other than the network termination points offered to the majority of end-users."[53]

The US requirement of technically feasible and therefore the language of the WTO is more favourable to competitors than the EU requirement of meeting reasonable requests at non-majority points. It remains to be seen if this difference will be of any real effect. Certainly it supports a US claim that the 1996 Telecommunications Act must be considered under the Reference Paper. Language very similar to the EU regime, requiring interconnection at points other than those offered to the majority of end-users is included in the Reference Paper, along with a provision allowing charges for additional construction that might be needed to honour such a request.[54]

The Reference Paper further specifies that interconnection is to be granted on non-discriminatory terms, not only among competitors but also non-discriminatory when compared with the incumbent's own internal interconnection rates and conditions.[55] The 1996 Act requires that incumbent local exchange carriers provide interconnection of a quality that is at least equal to that it provides itself,[56] and "rates, terms and conditions" are to be "just, reasonable, and nondiscriminatory,"[57] but nothing is mentioned about the incumbent charging competitors the same rates that it charges itself. Such internal pricing, referred to as transfer pricing, is in line with the EU principles of non-discrimination, nevertheless, even the EU regulatory framework recognises that interconnection charges may include a reasonable rate of return for the incumbent operator.[58] As both the EU and the US, surely the most competitor friendly regimes in the world, do not require a strict type of internal non-discrimination regarding interconnection prices, perhaps a claim against a Member nation based on failure to require internal non-discrimination would not succeed. Nevertheless, the language of the Reference Paper is there.

---

[51] *Ibid.*, art. 2.2.

[52] 47 U.S.C. 251(c)(2)(B).

[53] Directive 97/33/EC of the European Parliament and of the Council of 30 June 1997 on Interconnection in Telecommunications With Regard to Ensuring Universal Service and Interoperability Through Application of the Principles of Open Network Provision (ONP) [1997] OJ L199/32 art. 4.1 [hereinafter Interconnection Directive].

[54] Reference Paper, *supra* n. 35, art. 2.2(c).

[55] *Ibid.*, art.2.2(a).

[56] 47 U.S.C. 251(c)(2)(C).

[57] 47 U.S.C. 251 (c)(2)(D).

[58] Interconnection Directive, *supra* n. 52, art. 7.2.

Further provisions of the Reference Paper require that interconnection be provided on a timely basis and at cost-oriented prices. Once again, we enter an area where the US and the EU are in general agreement: interconnection should be priced at a cost-oriented basis. This, however, does not answer the question of what will be the methodology used or even the more fundamental question of why this requirement of cost-orientation exists. Does cost-orientation, or as it is sometimes expressed cost-based prices, mean that the cost for interconnection must mirror the incumbent's actual costs? Is a reasonable profit allowed, as in the EU regime? Does cost-orientation mean the actual cost for the incumbent? What sort of mark-up is allowed within the range of cost-orientation? How are costs to be determined?

4. Cost Determination

This last point, that of cost determination, is key, and has been difficult for regulators throughout the world. There are many different methods of cost determination, from fully allocated costs to various methods of forward looking and marginal costs. While the method used might very well influence the final prices paid for interconnection, so will the inputs into whatever costing model is adopted. The choice of accountant might be just as important as the costing model in determining the final interconnection price.

One other provision is of particular interest here. The Reference Paper requires that the interconnection be "sufficiently unbundled so that the supplier [competitor] need not pay for network components or facilities that it does not require for the service to be provided."[59] Does this require local loop unbundling?[60] A competitor might allege that it needs interconnection at the point of the end-user and at a central office (local exchange); it does not require network elements such as switching generally included in leased lines. The competitor's interconnection needs are in effect for unbundled local loops. The reference to "sufficiently unbundled" is not explained further. Unbundling is a word that is usually used in the telecommunications industry to refer to competitor use of incumbent local loops. If the US 1996 Act is viewed as controlling legal authority, then indeed this might mean local loop unbundling, as this is required under the 1996 Act. On the other hand, the EU's regulatory framework, very similar to the interconnection language contained in the Reference Paper, but not including this reference to "sufficiently unbundled," did not require full local loop unbundling.[61]

---

[59] *Ibid.*, art. 2.2(b).

[60] The United States has taken the public view with the EC that unbundling, as contemplated in the US Telecoms Act, is required by the WTO. See US 11 February 2000 Comments in the 1999 Review, http://www.ispo.cec.be/infosoc/telecompolicy/review99/comments/usgov16b.htm. Moreover, at the time of this writing, the US is also contemplating whether to bring a claim against the over access to British Telecom's local network for third-party digital subscriber line charges. See Jane Dudman, "US Slams BT over DSL Access", *Comm. Wk. Int'l*, 17 April 2000.

[61] Communication from the Commission to the European Parliament, the Council, the Economic and Social Committee and the Committee of the Regions, "Towards a New Framework for

The remainder of the Reference Paper's measures concerning interconnection mandate that major suppliers make its procedures for interconnection application as well as its terms and conditions publicly available,[62] and that there be available an independent body to resolve interconnection disputes.[63]

5. Universal Service

Universal service policies are explicitly recognised by the Reference Paper, and implicitly included is the right of Member nations to establish a universal service support fund.[64] Such funding, however, is not to be more than is necessary to meet the Member nation's universal service policy requirements. The Reference Paper is silent as to whether such a universal service policy and fund may include such elements as funding Internet access for schools and libraries as required under the US universal service policy and accompanying tax (the so-called e-rate).[65]

6. Transparency

Transparency is stressed in the section of the Reference Paper dealing with licensing criteria. Member nations are to make publicly available criteria for licensing and how long an applicant might expect to wait to receive a license.[66] Nothing is said about the cost of license, which can be high and constitute a barrier to entry. Terms and conditions of individual licenses are also to be made publicly available.

Member nations are to maintain an independent regulatory body.[67] As many nations still have state ownership of the incumbent provider, it is questionable how independent in fact a regulator can be when both the regulatory body and the regulated entity report to the same government. The government, and hence the regulator, has an interest in seeing that the state owned operator succeeds and continues to provide jobs.[67a] The situation may even be made worse, at least temporarily, as former government owned telcos privatise. In the period before a sale, the government would be under economic pressure to favour the incumbent in order to maximise the value of a sale. Strengthening the incumbent though lenient regulation will bring more money into the treasury when the incumbent is sold. Moreover, as explored in this chapter, whether or not the issue of regulatory transparency and independence "impliedly" requires complete privatisation is an issue of merger contention among Member Nations.

Electronic Communications Infrastructure and Associated Services", *The 1999 Communications Review*, COM (1999) 539, §4.2.3.

[62] Reference Paper, *supra* n. 35, arts. 2.3 and 2.4.
[63] *Ibid.*, art. 2.5.
[64] *Ibid.*, art. 3.
[65] For a full discussion of universal service issues, see Chapter 15 *infra*.
[66] *Ibid.*, art. 4.
[67] *Ibid.*, art. 5.
[67a] See p. 42, n. 43a in this volume.

7. Allocations of Scarce Resources

The final provision of the Reference Paper requires that allocation of scarce resources such as telephone numbers, frequencies, and access to rights of way be accomplished in an "objective, timely, transparent and non-discriminatory manner."[68] In nations that have liberalised their telecommunications markets, there do not seem to be major problems in this area. Number portability is being carried out according to regulation, and competitors have access to numbers, indeed more than they can use which is causing a problem as available numbers exhaust.

Frequency allocation is usually accomplished today via auctions that have the advantage of using market forces to decide winners. The alternative is the beauty contest; this may not bring as much money into the treasury, but it should lead to lower prices in the market, at least in theory. Prices for frequency rights, and hence ultimately end-user prices, decided via auction may be rather high, as shown by the fact that winners in FCC frequency auctions have subsequently gone bankrupt.[68a] The UK's auction of third generation mobile licenses is another example of high spectrum prices. There is also a problem of leveling the playing field for providers who paid for their frequency rights when earlier licensees received their rights for free. The EU Commission, in a series of decisions, held that the proper remedy was for the earlier licensees to match the latter auction award price, a type of rough justice that the beneficiary governments surely did not object to. Concerning equal access to rights of way, this also does not seem to be a major problem except for the public who suffer through repeated torn up streets.

In conclusion, although the Reference Paper is not as detailed as the 1996 Act or the EU's regulatory framework, it does set an ambitious standard to promote the rights of telecommunications competitors. It remains to be seen how the Telecommunications Annex and the Reference Paper will fare in the WTO's dispute resolution process.

D. Apparent International Policy Objectives

Notwithstanding the above, the real questions to ask are: what type of telecoms industry market structure is supposed to emerge post-WTO, and what kind of performance can we expect from this particular market structure? After reviewing the Telecommunications Annex, the general policy objectives of the WTO seem to be the following: (1) the creation of market structure for switched "international message telecoms service" (IMTS) traffic characterised by multiple vertically integrated providers of bundled IMTS telecommunications prod-

---

[68] *Ibid.*, art. 6.
[68a] See discussion in chapter 2.

ucts and services; (2) full "point-to-point" service between country-pairs; (3) the abolition of the international settlement-of-accounts regime; (4) the abolition of economically expensive "anti-whipsawing" provisions (i.e., the FCC's international settlements policy); (5) elimination of domestic monopolies; and, especially, (6) good market performance.[69] The obvious residual question, therefore, is whether the signatories to the Telecommunications Annex will implement both the letter and spirit of their respective commitments, such that the end goals of the WTO can be achieved.

On one hand, the WTO promises to open up local markets to competition. While it is indeed true that several countries in fact agreed to permit some kind of foreign ownership or control of *local* telecommunications services and facilities by 1998, a close examination of the WTO commitments reveals that investment into local markets may not be as easy as it may seem. That is to say, for those countries that committed to permit foreign ownership by 1998, most of those countries prohibit foreign investment in the dominant incumbent provider. Therefore, in these aforementioned countries, it appears that new entrants are certainly welcome to invest in local facilities, but they must do so from the ground up. Moreover, several countries did not promise to permit foreign ownership by January 1, 1998, but instead only agreed to permit foreign ownership beginning in 1999 or well beyond. Similarly, ten countries agreed to permit only limited foreign ownership or control in certain telecommunications services, and ten countries did not agree to permit foreign control under any circumstances.

As discussed more fully in chapters 2–4, however, under the best of conditions entry into local markets is a very expensive endeavour—for example, high sunk costs, incumbent's first-mover advantage, subsidised "local" service, marketing costs, etc.[70] Indeed, as evidenced by the US experience of cable overbuilding or the current struggle to establish facilities-based competition for local telephone service, sometimes the economics just do not justify the investment and the risks. The difficulty of creating a successful business case for local entry is often exacerbated in those poor countries where there really is not much money to be made providing service to, and keeping on the network thereafter, people who probably cannot even afford to buy food—much less basic telephone service.

On the other hand, however, so long as the *huge* revenue stream generated by above-cost accounting rates continues, the real profit source in international telecoms is the market for IMTS service. As such, it should also come as no surprise that while thirty-one countries in fact agreed to "guarantee" market access to *international* telecommunications services and facilities in 1998, a substantial number of countries on high-volume routes only agreed to permit competition

---

[69] See generally Rules and Policies on Foreign Participation in the U.S. Telecomm. Market, Report and Order on Reconsideration, 12 F.C.C.R. 23,891, 10 Comm. Reg. (P & F) 750 (1997) [hereinafter Foreign Participation Order].

[70] George S. Ford, "Opportunities for Local Exchange Competition Are Greatly Exaggerated", *Electric Light & Power*, Apr. 1998, at 20–21.

for IMTS service originating from their markets until well into the future. These range from Peru (1999) to the most egregious offer of Jamaica (2013).[71] Moreover, six countries are open only for "selected" international service, and eight countries have limited or no market access commitments for international service.

But what about the promise of the Regulatory Reference Paper? Nearly seventy countries agreed to guarantee some or all of the "pro-competitive" regulatory principles stated in the Regulatory Reference Paper. As mentioned above, these principles include the adoption of competitive safeguards, interconnection, publicly available licensing criteria, independent regulators, the "objective, timely, transparent and non-discriminatory" allocation and use of "scarce resources" (e.g., frequencies, numbers and rights-of-way) and, of course, universal service.[72]

It is important to note, however, that of the total number of these countries, only fifty-four countries agreed to guarantee all of these regulatory principles. Moreover, three countries only agreed to adopt an ill-defined amount of the "pro-competitive" regulatory principles in the future, eight countries agreed to adopt "some" amount of "pro-competitive" regulatory principles, and three countries stated that they would make no additional regulatory commitments. Moreover, it is also very important to note that among those countries that agreed to guarantee these regulatory principles *are many of the very countries that refused to agree to open their markets.*

As such, it would seem that any international multilateral agreement in which, on one hand, the signatory countries agree to uphold certain "pro-competitive regulatory principles" yet, at the same time, these signatory countries also condone other signatory countries which refuse to allow any new

---

[71] See "C&W Sees Threat", *The Jamaica Gleaner*, 13 Aug. 1998 (visited 1998) <http:// 204.177.56.98/gleaner/19980813/f1.html> (reporting that the President and Chief Executive Officer of Cable & Wireless Jamaica (aka "Telecommunications of Jamaica" or "ToJ") said that the monopoly on telecommunications enjoyed by the company through its exclusive license was the only model which could deliver the infrastructure required by the country: " 'We feel that the model has worked for Jamaica and is the only model that will deliver the type of infrastructure that Jamaica will require to enter the 21st century.' "); "Bunny [Wailer] Bewails ToJ Monopoly", *The Jamaica Gleaner*, 27 Jan. 1998 (visited Nov. 4, 1998) <http://www.204.177.56.98/gleaner/19980127/ news/n3.html> ("'Jamaica cannot afford to be observed as being alienated from international competitiveness in the telecommunications market by practices that corrupt goodwill and fair trade.'").

[72] Reference Paper, *supra* n. 35. Several scholars are sceptical about the true efficacy of the principles set forth in the Regulatory Reference Paper. For example, Drake and Noam argue that:

> Much is made over the acceptance of a regulatory reference model, making it seem like the adoption of some universal charter of telecommunications freedom. The reality is more modest. The "model" principles are mostly procedural, not substantive. They speak of "independence" of the regulator, but this merely refers to the independence from the monopolist, not from politics. As if formal independence prevents capture. The principles speak of openness, public licensing criteria, transparency, and objective allocation procedures. All this sounds good, but is worth little because of its vagueness, if a government drags its feet. For example, an openness of process can mean very little outside the public "sunshine" on the senior staff level before ceremoniously reaching the official decision event.

See William J. Drake & Eli M. Noam, "The WTO Deal on Basic Telecommunications: Big Bang or Little Whimper?", (1997) 21 *Telecomm. Pol'y* 799, 811.

competitors to enter their market, at first blush, the WTO agreement may not appear to be really such a great bargain after all.

Actually, such a conclusion may not necessarily be entirely correct. At the end of the day, presumably no one would disagree that open markets are the best way to maximise consumer welfare. Yet as noted above there are numerous countries that are, to state it politely, a bit recalcitrant to open their markets. So long as these incumbents' monopoly power remains unchecked, therefore, they can engage in whipsawing and other numerous price and non-price discrimination strategies against or among carriers in competitive markets.

Unfortunately, because the goal of promoting good market performance is not always complementary to the goal of promoting trade issues, numerous constituencies are more concerned about promoting mercantile agendas than focusing on the economic issues at hand. The problem of such an arrogant approach is that it will not gain any ground. In these situations, basic international law is pretty clear about enforcement options: barring evidence that one country is using its territory to stage a military attack against another, one country may not interfere in the internal domestic affairs of another.[73] Thus, the best way to mitigate unilateral, strategic anti-competitive conduct for IMTS service is to convince the recalcitrant country to establish, *inter alia*, standard, cost-based accounting rates and transparent regulation to mitigate against non-price discrimination. This is precisely what the hard-fought WTO Agreement achieves. As such, from an economic point of view, whether or not a foreign carrier has the ability to set up a rival network in a WTO Member destination country should be irrelevant to the question of whether a foreign firm can successfully engage in strategic conduct for IMTS traffic on that country-route. Instead, substantial priority should appropriately be dedicated to effective implementation of the WTO regulatory principles; issues of entry can be addressed at a subsequent time.

VI. THE FUTURE OF THE WTO TELECOMS TREATY?

This is indeed a pressing question. As of this writing, no dispute has been brought before the WTO under the Telecoms Treaty. There has, however, been a good deal of sabre rattling, particularly by the US, alleging that several Member nations throughout the world are violating its provisions. The US has focused its allegations on interconnection terms. Perhaps it would be good for a few cases to actually go through the dispute resolution process in order that some precedent exist and Member nations as well as industry participants can obtain a surer understanding of what the language of the Annex and the Reference Paper actually mean. Until then, we are left with guesses and threats.

---

[73] The 1999 NATO intervention in Yugoslavia however, calls this principle into question.

A. The Future of the WTO: The Debacle in Seattle

Recent developments have not been good for the WTO. There was controversy between industrial and developing nations over the selection of a new Director-General for the WTO. Mike Moore of New Zealand was eventually selected, but only after an agreement was reached that his term be split with someone from a developing nation. Part of the problem is the consensus procedure that the WTO labours under. Another part of the problem is a backlash against the feared process of globalisation, and this was starkly clear at the WTO meetings in Seattle.

Leading up to the Seattle meetings, many were optimistic about what could be accomplished. E-commerce, labour, environmental standards, agricultural, foreign investment and competition codes were all mentioned as possible areas for new agreements. The reality was somewhat different. Nothing of any value was accomplished with the possible exception of vague commitments to greater transparency in WTO proceedings. It would have been difficult under the best of circumstances to reach agreement in such contentious areas as agricultural subsidies, but the best conditions were not present. Instead self-styled anarchists were allowed to terrorise delegates while large-scale protests were mounted by labour and environmental groups.

Many people lay the blame for this debacle squarely at the feet of the Clinton/Gore Administration's hypocritical neo-mercantile approach to free trade and open markets. For example, a scathing piece by *The Economist*[74] found essentially three culprits behind the Seattle fiasco: The first culprit according to *The Economist* was US Trade Representative Charlene Barshefsky who insisted on both chairing the talks and concurrently leading America's negotiating team. Moreover, according to *The Economist*, she was "clumsy" and her "abrasive style proved ill-suited to achieving consensus." Among her more egregious gaffes was her hard-line instance that the Seattle talks be renamed the "Clinton Round."[75]

The second culprit according to *The Economist* was President Clinton, as he infuriated almost all of the government delegates by expressing sympathy with many of the anti-WTO demonstrators besieging Seattle—so much so that Sir Leon Brittan, until recently the EU's trade commissioner, remarked that Mr. Clinton's intervention dealt a "body blow" to the negotiations.[76]

The third culprit according to *The Economist* was Vice President Al Gore. As *The Economist* reported:

> "The administration's overriding aim in Seattle was to boost, or at least to avoid harming, Mr. Gore's presidential campaign rather than to advance America's wider

[74] FT McCarthy, "A Global Disaster", *The Economist*, 11 December 1999.
[75] See Bob Davis and Helene Cooper, "Round and Round they Go, to Name New Trade Talks", *Wall Street Journal*, 29 November 2000 at A1.
[76] *The Economist, supra* n. 74.

interest in launching a new round. This 'no body bags' trade policy explains America's refusal to give any ground. . . . In the end, America chose to walk away from a potential deal rather than make any compromises that might be politically risky."[77]

Such cynical conduct on the part of the Clinton/Gore Administration is once again unconscionable. Pandering to the US labour movement—a key voting block essential for realising Al Gore's desire to succeed Bill Clinton—Al Gore has caused a rift with the developing world that rightly views labour standards as a disguised attempt to restrict imports from developing nations. It may sound righteous to insist that all workers have decent working conditions and wages, but the best way to help workers in developing nations is first to help them have jobs, and that can be ensured by freer trade. Labour movements as a rule do not want freer trade as shown by the rhetoric about jobs moving offshore and the reflexive support by labour of protectionism. Cynicism and promoting antiquated protectionist systems will not help workers or industry, either at home or abroad.

Post-Seattle signs have been somewhat encouraging. Governments and WTO officials appear determined to press on with more talks, on a less-ambitious scale, and perhaps a more secure location should be selected for any subsequent rounds. As a sign of cooling rhetoric, a dispute between the EU and the US over imposition of trade sanctions under the US Section 301 law (yet another fallout of the interminable banana war) ended with the WTO panel condemning the law in principle as it allows the US to retaliate outside the WTO process, yet accepting the US assurances that the law in fact would not be used to impose sanctions outside the WTO process. Both the EU and the US announced that they were pleased with the result,[78] surely a red-letter day. It is to be hoped that all concerned realise just how much they have to lose if world trade is seriously damaged by childish antics.

---

[77] *Ibid.*
[78] "Both EU, US For Once, Accept Ruling by WTO," *The Wall Street Journal Europe*, 28–29 January 2000, at 12.

PART II

US EFFORTS TO PROMOTE TELECOMS COMPETITION

6

From International Competitive Carrier *Paradigm to* Effective Competitive Opportunities: *The FCC's International Policies Pre-WTO*

THE FIRST MAJOR attempt by the FCC to promote competition for international telecoms can be found in the self-titled *"International Competitive Carrier"*[1] proceeding, which was nothing more that the FCC's introduction of its domestic *"Competitive Carrier"* paradigm[2] to the international market.

---

[1] International Competitive Carrier Policies, Notice of Proposed Rulemaking, 100 F.C.C.2d 1270 (1985) [hereinafter *Int'l Competitive Carrier NPRM*], *Report and Order*, 102 F.C.C.2d 812, 59 Rad. Reg. 2d (P & F) 283 (1985) [hereinafter Int'l Competitive Carrier Report and Order], *recons. denied*, 60 Rad. Reg. 2d (P & F) 1435 (1986).

[2] *See* Policy & Rules Concerning Rates for Competitive Common Carrier Servs. & Facilities Authorisations Therefor, *First Report and Order*, 85 F.C.C.2d 1, 52 Rad. Reg. 2d (P & F) 215 (1980) [hereinafter *Competitive Common Carrier First Report and Order*], *Second Report and Order*, 91 F.C.C.2d 59, 52 Rad. Reg. 2d (P & F) 187 (1982), *Order on Reconsideration*, 93 F.C.C.2d 54, 53 Rad. Reg. 2d (P & F) 735 (1983), *Third Report and Order*, 48 Fed. Reg. 46,791 (1983), *Fourth Report and Order*, 95 F.C.C.2d 554, 56 Rad. Reg. 2d (P & F) 1198 (1983), *vacated*, AT&T v. FCC, 978 F.2d 727 (D.C. Cir. 1992), *cert. denied*, MCI Telecomm. Corp. v. AT&T, 509 U.S. 913 (1993), *Fifth Report and Order*, 98 F.C.C.2d 1191, 56 Rad. Reg. 2d (P & F) 1204 (1984), *Sixth Report and Order*, 99 F.C.C.2d 1020, 57 Rad. Reg. 2d (P & F) 1391 (1985), *rev'd*, MCI Telecomm. Corp. v. FCC, 765 F.2d 1186 (D.C. Cir. 1985).

As explained in more detail in Annex I, The idea behind the FCC's *Competitive Carrier* paradigm was relatively simple: AT&T, as the "dominant" carrier, would be subject to all existing regulations—i.e., rate of return and then later price cap regulation, all new tariffs would continue to be suspended for 45 days before any new rate could go into effect, numerous reporting requirements, and the like. However, in order to accelerate entry into the long-distance market (and therefore improve market performance to a level of sufficient rivalry such that regulation could eventually be removed altogether), the FCC basically removed all regulatory barriers to entry for new entrants.

In addition, the FCC—via its 1980 MTS/WATS resale decision, see, e.g., Resale and Shared Use of Common Carrier Domestic Public Switched Network Servs., *Report and Order*, 83 F.C.C.2d 167, 48 Rad. Reg. 2d (P & F) 1067 (1980)—helped new entrants, *inter alia*, to appear to consumers that they had a nation-wide, facilities-based presence until their networks could be completed. As a result of this paradigm, the long-distance market was transformed from a market characterised by a single dominant firm with a small competitive fringe, to a market characterised by a highly elastic supply (both in capacity and in the number of competing firms), an extremely high churn rate, and a demonstrated trend of declining prices and increasing services. Given these market conditions, the FCC eventually decided to remove the asymmetrical regulation previously imposed on AT&T, realising that the economic harms created by asymmetrical dominant carrier regulation outweighed the

Significantly, this decision marks the first clear statement by the FCC that, with proper regulatory incentives and constraints, it was possible to promote competition for international service—in addition to domestic long-distance service. In other words, in the FCC's opinion, there was finally sufficient competitive rivalry in the international market to impose "streamlined" Title II common carrier regulation on non-dominant international carriers of international service.

A. Relevant Product Markets

The FCC basically divided the international market into two groups: International Message Telecommunications Service (IMTS) and non-IMTS service.[3] The FCC found the latter market competitive; the former it did not. For purposes of analysis, therefore, this chapter will focus exclusively on IMTS services from this point forward.

B. Relevant Geographic Market

Because of the significant regulatory approvals and individual operating agreements required to provide IMTS service to more than one country, the FCC concluded that each country-pair IMTS route should be considered to be a separate, distinct geographic market.[4]

C. Definition of Market Power

The FCC decided to adopt the same standard to define market power in the IMTS context as it used in the domestic context—that is, the "power to control prices or exclude competition."[5] Moreover, the FCC recognised that while any determination of an international carrier's dominance or non-dominance is not "scientifically precise," there are several nonexclusive factors, such as market share, control of bottleneck facilities, rate of return, as well as the existence of actual or potential competition that could indicate the possession of market power.[6]

public interest benefits the dominant carrier regulation was originally intended to achieve. See Motion of AT&T Corp. to be Reclassified as a Non-Dominant Carrier, *Order*, 11 F.C.C.R. 3271, 32 Rad. Reg. 2d (P & F) 605 (1995).

[3] The FCC found that IMTS and non-IMTS were discrete product markets because, inter alia, from a demand substitutability perspective, the FCC found that customers simply did not view the two types of services as acceptable substitutes for one another. See Int'l Competitive Carrier NPRM, *supra* n. 1, paras. 13–20.

[4] See *ibid.*, para. 29.

[5] *Int'l Competitive Carrier Report and Order, supra* n. 1, para. 40 (quoting *United States* v. *E.I. DuPont de Nemours & Co.*, 351 U.S. 377, 391 (1956)).

[6] See *ibid.*, para. 42; *Int'l Competitive Carrier NPRM, supra* n. 1, para. 32.

D. Merits

After review, the FCC concluded that: (a) American Telephone and Telegraph (AT&T) was dominant in the provision of IMTS; and (b) all other IMTS providers (i.e., Sprint, MCI) were not dominant. While the FCC recognised that market share is not determinative of market power, given current market conditions the FCC nonetheless held that it was "a clear indication of dominance for AT&T's provision of IMTS."[7] For example the FCC found that at the time of the *Report and Order*, AT&T was still the only provider of IMTS between the US mainland and a majority of foreign countries. Moreover, in those countries where there were other IMTS providers, the FCC found that AT&T still had an overwhelming market share. Indeed, the FCC specifically rejected AT&T's argument that it faced actual or potential competition, stating that "[m]erely because more than one carrier provides service to a given geographic area does not automatically mean that all carriers providing service to that area are non-dominant."[8] Additionally, the FCC noted that while it was adopting a country-by-country approach, the question of how many different countries the new entrants served was a factor in determining if AT&T (or any other carrier) faced effective competition. According to the FCC:

> "[t]here is clearly some competitive marketing advantage to be gained if a carrier has the ability to serve all or most foreign points because a subscriber is more likely to take service from a carrier with the more comprehensive coverage."[9]

In light of the foregoing, the FCC concluded that the IMTS market was not yet sufficiently competitive to ensure that AT&T was unable to manipulate rates in a way to discourage competition. Thus, held the FCC:

> "until such time as competition in the provision of IMTS more fully develops so as to negate AT&T's ability to control prices or exclude competition, it is necessary to continue the full scale regulation of AT&T for its IMTS offerings to all countries."[10]

To determine whether there was such competition, the FCC stated that it would look, on a country-by-country approach

> "at a variety of factors including the number of entrants, market penetration for both inbound and outbound traffic, regional and global market positions, refiling and transiting arrangements, control of facilities and the potential for non-competitive pricing."[11]

---

[7] As an important point, the FCC noted "that not all operating agreements obtained by AT&T's IMTS competitors provide (or initially provided) for the handling of U.S. inbound traffic. Because the handling of U.S. inbound traffic and the receipt of one half of the agreed upon accounting rate directly influences a route's profitability as well as the U.S. carrier's collection rate for outbound traffic," the FCC stated that "any analysis of market power which looks at market share must consider both outbound and inbound traffic shares." *Int'l Competitive Carrier Report and Order, supra* n. 1, para. 44 & n. 44.

[8] *Ibid.*, para. 44.

[9] *Ibid.*, para. 45.

[10] *Ibid.*, para. 46.

[11] *Ibid.*

II. THE FCC'S FIRST ATTEMPTS TO CONTROL FOREIGN CARRIERS

A. Statutory Authority

Under Section 214 of the US Communications Act of 1934,

> No carrier shall undertake the construction of a new line or an extension of any line, or shall acquire or operate any line or extension thereof, or shall engage in transmission over or by means of such additional or extended line, unless and until there shall first have been obtained from the Commission a certificate that the present or future public convenience and necessity.[12]

This statute was originally intended to prevent AT&T—as the exclusive phone company—from improperly padding its rate-base by improperly constructing unnecessary (a.k.a. "imprudent") plant. With the break-up of the old AT&T monopoly, the introduction of price cap regulation for ILECs and no price regulation for non-dominant carriers, the continued use of having to get a Section 214 certificate as a pre-condition of entry is increasingly making little sense in the domestic US context. In the international context, however, the FCC's Section 214 authority is the only regulatory "hook" over foreign carriers at its disposal. As we shall see subsequently, the FCC has used its best intellectual gymnastics to construe its Section 214 to heights heretofore thought unimaginable.

B. The FCC's Foreign Affiliate Rules[14]

This proceeding was designed to modify the original international dominant/ non-dominant framework for IMTS services as set forth in *International Competitive Carrier*. Specifically, the FCC stated that it wanted to move away from a policy under which it always presumed that:

> "foreign-owned US common carriers [were] dominant in their provision of all international services to all foreign markets in favour of a policy that regulates US international carriers, whether US-owned or foreign-owned, as dominant only on those routes where their foreign affiliates have the ability to discriminate"[15]

in "favor of [their] US affiliate in the provision of services or facilities used to terminate US international traffic."[16] Indeed, the FCC reaffirmed its tentative

---

[12] See 47 U.S.C. § 214.

[14] Regulation of International Common Carrier Services, Notice of Proposed Rulemaking, 7 F.C.C.R. 577 (1992) [hereinafter *Regulation NPRM*], *Report and Order*, 7 F.C.C.R. 7331, 71 Rad. Reg. 2d (P & F) 717 (1992) [hereinafter *Regulation Report and Order*].

[15] *Regulation NPRM, supra* n. 14, para. 2.

[16] *Regulation Report and Order, supra* n. 14, para. 4.

conclusion in the *NPRM* that its then-current international dominant policy was "*overbroad, unnecessarily burdensome and may be detrimental to competition.*"[17] As such, the FCC believed it appropriate to redirect its

> "regulation to those instances where a relationship between a US international carrier and a foreign carrier may present some substantial risk of anticompetitive conduct, [in an effort to] promote competition in the US international service market by reducing the costs of entry and operation, while continuing to protect unaffiliated US carriers from discrimination by foreign carriers."[18]

First, the FCC addressed what it would consider as "control" of a US carrier. The FCC stated that it would treat a US carrier "as an affiliate of a foreign carrier when the US carrier controls, is controlled by, or is under common control with a foreign carrier."[19] In adopting this standard, the FCC recognised "the concern that a less-than-controlling interest by a foreign carrier in a US carrier could give the foreign carrier the financial incentive to favour its US affiliate."[20] However, the FCC also recognised that "the foreign carrier would not be in a position to direct the actions of the US carrier," and that "the US carrier would be unlikely to risk sanctions by this Commission for participating in discriminatory conduct that violated Commission rules or policy, or any conditions of its Section 214 certificate."[21]

Moreover, the FCC noted:

> "US carriers will be subject to ongoing reporting requirements that are designed to detect discrimination by foreign carriers or administrations in favour of specific US carriers,"

and that the FCC retained "the option to impose or reimpose dominant carrier regulation on a particular carrier that is found to have engaged in anticompetitive conduct."[22]

Finally, the FCC recognised that the US Department of Justice continues to have the authority to take enforcement action under the antitrust laws in appropriate cases.[23] Accordingly, the FCC concluded that, on balance, it did not believe the:

> "possibility of anticompetitive collusion poses enough of a threat to competition to impose dominant carrier regulation absent control by a foreign carrier of a US carrier, particularly in light of the substantial competitive benefits that can result from lifting the burden of current regulation."[24]

In so holding, the FCC specifically declined to craft:

---

[17] *Ibid.*, para. 6 (emphasis added).
[18] *Ibid.*
[19] *Ibid.*, para. 10.
[20] *Ibid.*
[21] *Ibid.*
[22] *Ibid.*
[23] *Ibid.*
[24] *Ibid.*

> "an affiliation standard that would capture certain non-ownership arrangements between a US and foreign carrier, such as co-marketing agreements for the provision of telecommunications services or joint ventures for the provision of non-telecommunications services."[25]

According to the FCC, although these arrangements could provide a financial incentive for carriers to act jointly in pursuit of marketing objectives, neither carrier has the ability to direct the actions of the other or to derive a direct financial benefit with respect to the other's telecommunications operations. Moreover, the US carrier would "in all cases be subject to the ongoing regulatory requirements" imposed by the FCC on all US international carriers."[26] Therefore, concluded the FCC, "submission and evaluation of such arrangements would appear to require an unnecessary expenditure of Commission and carrier resources."[27] As such, the FCC held that these arrangements do not present a substantial possibility of anticompetitive effects such that "these relationships need be addressed in the context of deciding whether to regulate a carrier as dominant or non-dominant."[28] Rather, the FCC stated that it would instead "rely on [its] Section 208 complaint procedures and sanctioning authority to remedy any anticompetitive consequences that might arise once a carrier gains access to the US market."[29]

Having thus defined "affiliate," the FCC next turned to its definition of a dominant carrier. As noted above, the FCC held that it intended:

> "to regulate US international carriers as dominant only on those routes where a foreign affiliate has the ability to discriminate in favor of its US affiliate through control of bottleneck services or facilities in the destination market."[30]

To achieve this end, the FCC adopted a three-part threshold to determine the level of regulatory scrutiny it would apply to a given carrier. First, the FCC stated that it would presume that "carriers that have no affiliation with a foreign carrier in the destination market . . . [are] non-dominant for that route."[31] Second, the FCC stated that it would presume that all "carriers affiliated with a foreign carrier that is a monopoly in the destination market . . . [are] dominant for that route."[32] And third, the FCC stated that "carriers affiliated with a foreign carrier that is not a monopoly on that route receive closer scrutiny by the Commission."[33] Finally, the FCC stated that it "will place the burden of proof on any party, applicant or petitioner, that seeks to defeat the presumptions in the first two categories."[34]

However, for those carriers covered by the third category that seek to be regulated as non-dominant, the FCC stated that those carriers:

> "bear the burden of submitting information to the FCC sufficient to demonstrate that their foreign affiliates lack the ability to discriminate against unaffiliated US carriers."[35]

---

[25] *Regulation Report and Order, supra* n. 14, para. 11.　　[26] *Ibid.*
[27] *Ibid.*　　　　　　　　　　　　[28] *Ibid.*　　　[29] *Ibid.*
[30] *Ibid.*, para. 19.　　　　　　　[31] *Ibid.*　　　[32] *Ibid.*
[33] *Ibid.*　　　　　　　　　　　　[34] *Ibid.*　　　[35] *Ibid.*, para. 20.

Indeed, the FCC specifically stated that it fully expects:

> "carriers to address the factors that relate to the scope or degree of their foreign affiliate's bottleneck control, such as: the duopoly or oligopoly status in the foreign affiliate's country; and whether the affiliate has the potential to discriminate through such means as preferential operating agreements, preferential routing of traffic, exclusive or more favorable transiting agreements, or preferential domestic access and interconnection arrangements."[36]

Moreover, the FCC stated that it also expects carriers to address whether public regulation in the destination market can be relied upon effectively to constrain the affiliate's ability to discriminate. According to the FCC,

> "[t]here would appear to be no substantial risk of discrimination, for example, where a US carrier is affiliated with a foreign carrier that operates solely through the resale of an unaffiliated foreign carrier's services in a destination market that provides equivalent resale opportunities."[37]

Finally, the FCC addressed the issue of potential anticompetitive harm resulting from "third-country leveraging."[38] Given the structure of the international market, the FCC stated that it could not "rule out the possibility that an affiliated US carrier [would] attempt to gain an unfair competitive advantage on affiliated or unaffiliated routes through the negotiation of exclusive arrangements with foreign carriers or administrations."[39] As such, the FCC amended Part 63 of the Rules to require that Section 214 applicants with a foreign carrier affiliate in any market certify in each application filed with the FCC that they

> "have not agreed to accept special concessions directly or indirectly from any foreign carrier or administration with respect to traffic or revenue flows between the US and any destination market served under the authority of their Section 214 certificates and have not agreed to enter into such agreements in the future."[40]

The FCC held that it would "define 'special concession' as any arrangement that affects traffic or revenue flows to or from the US that is offered exclusively by a foreign carrier or administration to a particular US carrier and not also to similarly situated US international carriers authorised to serve a given route."[41]

III. THE FCC'S FOREIGN CARRIER OR "ECO" ORDER[42]

On November 30, 1995, the FCC released an *Order* clarifying its "public interest" analysis for international service applications.[43] According to the FCC, this

---

[36] *Ibid.*
[37] *Ibid.*
[38] *Ibid.*, paras. 25–26.
[39] *Ibid.*, para. 27.
[40] *Ibid.*, (citations omitted).
[41] *Ibid.*
[42] Market Entry and Regulation of Foreign-affiliated Entities, *Report and Order*, 11 F.C.C.R. 3873, 1 Comm. Reg. (P & F) 459 (1995) [hereinafter *ECO Order*].
[43] *Ibid.*

public interest analysis was comprised of two distinct parts: (1) an "effective competitive opportunities" or "*ECO*" analysis; and (2) an analysis of additional public interest factors that could counter-balance (i.e., override) an adverse *ECO* finding.[44] The FCC stated that it undertook this initiative with the hope that this policy would both promote entry by US carriers on the foreign end and also promote foreign entry into the US market.[45] In reality, the *Foreign Carrier Order* marked the debut of naked (of course, relative to the commonly accepted, historically implicit) trade concerns—rather than consumer welfare concerns— as the top priority for FCC international telecoms policies.

A. The Rise of Naked Trade Concerns

The FCC reasoned that its desire to promote potential new entry of US firms abroad was legitimate public policy because, in the FCC's opinion, the option of entry into the US telecommunications market was such

> "a significant advantage, especially for those [foreign carriers] who are trying to establish their US market position largely through their own marketing organization,"

the FCC assumed *a fortiori* that

> "a foreign carrier would[, therefore] have a significant incentive to encourage its government to liberalize sufficiently to meet the effective competitive opportunities test for facilities-based or resale entry if that were necessary for the carrier to control an end-to-end network service."[46]

Indeed, the FCC found that there was "significant value in being able to establish a substantial investment relationship with a US carrier" because

> "[p]artnerships with US carriers, cemented by large equity holdings, [would] provide foreign carriers with lower cost options for pursuing the US customer base. The partnerships also [would] provide immediate access to the established customer base of the US affiliate."[47]

Moreover, reasoned the FCC, such partnerships would

> "greatly strengthen the capacity to offer the benefits of one-stop shopping for all global needs, including a single customized billing and cost control system for all global services, and specialized service and software designed to meet the special needs of the client."[48]

In short, argued the FCC, these partnerships offered "important strategic capabilities in a critical global market" and, therefore,

---

[44] *ECO Order.*
[45] *Ibid.*
[46] *Ibid.*, para. 32.
[47] *Ibid.*, para. 33.
[48] *Ibid.*

"the ability to invest substantially in the US affiliate/partner [would permit] the foreign carrier to strengthen its partner's capabilities in the US market while creating a management structure that better safeguards its competitive interests in the joint venture."[49]

Thus, concluded the FCC,

"the ability of a foreign carrier to acquire a substantial equity position in a US carrier can be an important advantage in a major world market. This advantage can provide a significant incentive for a foreign government to support liberalization."[50]

B. The Improper Redefinition of Market Power

Given the sales pitch above, the FCC explained that it would apply its new "effective competitive opportunities" standard to foreign carriers or their US affiliates of IMTS service *only whenever a foreign carrier has market power on the foreign end.*[51] This inquiry, stated the FCC, would be applied on a route-by-route basis.[52] If a foreign carrier or its US affiliate failed this test, then the FCC would deny permission to provide service on the particular route.[53] According to the FCC, possession of market power "may include the home market of the foreign carrier, but it also includes all other destination markets where it has the ability to leverage market power."[54]

In contrast to the definition of market power it used in *International Competitive Carrier* and in the domestic context, however, the FCC changed the definition of "market power" for purposes of the *ECO* test.[55] No longer would the FCC use a variation of the traditional test of whether a carrier has the power to control prices or exclude competition. Now, as naked trade concerns became the obvious top priority of FCC IMTS policies, the FCC stated that it would define market power as

"*the ability of the carrier to act anticompetitively against unaffiliated US carriers through the control of bottleneck services or facilities on the foreign end.*"[56]

The FCC then defined "bottleneck services or facilities" as those facilities "that are necessary for the provision of international services, including inter-city or local access facilities on the foreign end."[57]

---

[49] *Ibid.*
[50] *Ibid.*
[51] See *ibid.*, para. 21.
[52] *Ibid.*
[53] See *ibid.*, para. 36.
[54] *Ibid.*, para. 116.
[55] *Ibid.*
[56] *Ibid.*, (emphasis added).
[57] *Ibid.*

C. The New ECO Standard

Under the new *ECO* standard, the FCC stated that it would examine the following six factors:

> "(1) whether US carriers can offer in the foreign country international facilities-based services substantially similar to those that the foreign carrier seeks to offer in the United States; (2) whether competitive safeguards exist in the foreign country to protect against anticompetitive and discriminatory practices, including cost-allocation rules to prevent cross-subsidization; (3) the availability of published, nondiscriminatory charges, terms and conditions for interconnection to foreign domestic carriers' facilities for termination and origination of international services; (4) timely and nondiscriminatory disclosure of technical information needed to use or interconnect with carriers' facilities; (5) the protection of carrier and customer proprietary information; and (6) whether an independent regulatory body with fair and transparent procedures is established to enforce competitive safeguards."[58]

D. Other "Public Interest" Factors

The FCC also held, however, that it would consider several other "public interest" factors, in addition to its *ECO* test, that might "weigh in favor of, or against, authorizing a foreign carrier to serve destination countries where [such carrier] has market power."[59] According to the FCC, there may be occasions when the public interest requires that these additional factors actually override an *ECO* determination to either allow or deny entry.[60] These factors included, *inter alia*, (1) "the general significance of the proposed entry to the promotion of competition in the US communications market"; (2) as discussed more fully *infra*, and perhaps most inflammatory to the international community, any "national security, law enforcement, *foreign policy, and trade concerns raised by the Executive Branch*"; and (3) the "presence"—*but not an absolute requirement of*—cost-based accounting rates.[61]

E. Accounting Rate Issues

As just mentioned one of the most significant aspects of the FCC's *ECO Order* was that it would *not* require the presence of cost-based accounting rates as a precondition of entry. Quite to the contrary, the FCC was of the opinion that requiring the presence of cost-based accounting rates:

---

[57] *ECO Order.*
[58] *Ibid.*, para. 40.
[59] *Ibid.*, para. 61.
[60] *Ibid.*, para. 62.
[61] *Ibid.*, (emphasis added).

"could preclude otherwise qualified candidates from competing in the US international services market. It would become, in effect, a barrier to market entry. Such a result would be contrary to [its] objective of encouraging competitive entry and, thereby, reducing industry concentration on both ends of US international routes."[62]

In fact, the FCC argued that:

"[a]dditional competition should produce service alternatives and price competition in the US market which should in turn stimulate US outbound demand. This, in turn, will make foreign carriers more amenable to further reducing their accounting rates, in that they will experience less of a loss in settlement revenues. This reduces the per minute settlements burden on US consumers."[63]

Moreover, the FCC specifically rejected the argument that, absent a requirement of cost-based accounting rates, a US affiliate of a foreign carrier would be able to price its services without the full cost of settlements with its foreign parent and, thereby, would have some kind of anticompetitive advantage (in this docket, an alleged price squeeze) over other unaffiliated US carriers.[64] The FCC gave several reasons to support this conclusion. First, the FCC stated outright that it was:

"not convinced that dominant foreign carriers can set the 'input' accounting rate level unilaterally. These rates are established by negotiation between a US and foreign carrier. Competitive pressures from end users and carriers, as well as [its] International Settlements Policy, have strengthened the position of US carriers during accounting rate negotiations, and [it] expect[s] this trend will continue.[65]

Second, the FCC explained that:

"[e]ven assuming *arguendo* that a dominant foreign carrier can unilaterally set an accounting rate, a squeeze will not succeed if the high price of a particular input can be offset by lower prices for other inputs, or economies of scale and scope, or other efficiencies."[66]

Where such offsets are possible, "the integrated firm will have little or no ability to inflict substantial harm on competitors via a squeeze."[67] Moreover, "the affiliated US carrier must maintain low prices and high accounting rates over a sufficiently long time period so as to inflict substantial economic harm to competitors."[68]

Third, because the FCC found that no party had demonstrated conclusively under the record of this proceeding that:

---

[62] *Ibid.*, para. 67 (emphasis added).
[63] *Ibid.*, (citation omitted).
[64] *Ibid.*, para. 68.
[65] *Ibid.*, para. 69 (emphasis added).
[66] *Ibid.*, para. 70.
[67] *Ibid.*
[68] *Ibid.*

"above-cost accounting rates on particular routes where a carrier has an affiliate on the foreign end realistically jeopardize the ability of unaffiliated carriers to compete on those routes or in the US international services market as a whole,"

the FCC found that "the possibility of such harm is [actually] outweighed by the benefits of additional price and service competition that will result from further US market entry."[69]

F. Joint Marketing Agreements

The FCC was also concerned about the competitive effects of "global alliances." On one hand, the FCC specifically refused to apply its *ECO* test to both exclusive and non-exclusive non-equity arrangements between a US international carrier and a foreign Post, Telegraph, and Telephone Administration (PTT) because the FCC found that "foreign carrier participation in such alliances did not constitute entry into the US international services market as a common carrier."[70] Moreover, the FCC held that application of the *ECO* test in such circumstances could actually have negative consequences, as "[s]uch an application could deny US consumers the competitive benefits of the services of such alliances and would do little to open foreign markets."[71] Indeed, the FCC specifically recognised that such non-equity arrangements can actually attenuate the potential for collusive conduct because while:

"[n]on-equity arrangements can provide a financial incentive for carriers to act jointly in the pursuit of marketing objectives . . . neither carrier [will derive] a direct financial benefit with respect to the other's telecommunications operations."[72]

On the other hand, however, the FCC found no evidence:

"to contradict the conclusion that *exclusive* co-marketing or other agreements affecting the provision of US basic international services pose an unacceptable risk of anticompetitive harm where the agreement is between a US carrier and a dominant foreign carrier."[73]

The FCC held that it would

---

[69] *ECO Order.* As explained more fully *infra*, the significance of the FCC's specific refusal to require cost-based accounting rates as a precondition of entry cannot be understated. Much to the dismay of the international community, while the FCC has steadfastly insisted on retaining the "national security, law enforcement, foreign policy and trade concerns raised by the Executive Branch" component of its public interest inquiry, political pressure subsequently fueled these fires by convincing the FCC to reverse completely its decision not to require cost-based accounting rates as a precondition to entry. The FCC announced in its Foreign Participation proceeding that the United States will now charge an entry fee—i.e., the FCC's "benchmarks" condition.

[70] *Ibid.*, para. 95 (citation omitted).

[71] *Ibid.*, (citation omitted).

[72] *Ibid.*

[73] *Ibid.*, para. 255.

"view such exclusive agreements as within the scope of the 'no exclusive arrangements' condition [it has] placed on numerous Section 214 authorizations and cable landing licenses."[74]

This condition requires that

"[the] carrier shall not acquire or enjoy any right for the purpose of handling or interchanging traffic . . . that is denied to any other US carrier."[75]

The FCC also held that it would "view such exclusive agreements as prohibited by the special concessions prohibition applied to foreign-affiliated US carriers under Section 63.14 of [its] rules."[76] According to the FCC, it would:

"continue to enforce these provisions to prohibit any exclusive co-marketing agreement or joint venture between a US and a dominant foreign carrier that, either on its face or in practice, grants exclusive rights to the US carrier for the provision of basic telecommunications services originating or terminating in the United States."[77]

However, the FCC also stated that it would look

"favorably on requests to waive these provisions where the US carrier can demonstrate that its allied foreign carrier lacks market power, i.e., the ability to discriminate among US international carriers in the provision of bottleneck services or facilities used to terminate US international traffic."[78]

G. Trade and the "Public Interest"

Finally, the FCC made clear that it had jurisdiction to adopt an *ECO* analysis under both Section 214 and Section 310(b)(4) of the US Communications Act of 1934.[79] Moreover, the FCC reasoned that its *ECO* paradigm is "consistent with [its] responsibilities under the Clayton Act to consider anticompetitive issues under the public interest standard."[80] First, the FCC rejected commenters' arguments that it was adopting nothing more than a naked trade reciprocity requirement under Section 214.[81] In the FCC's words, it was "not adopting a reciprocity requirement" but was, instead, simply:

"adopting a public interest analysis that is comprised, in part, by an effective competitive opportunities analysis for those Section 214 applications filed by US carriers

[74] *Ibid.*
[75] *Ibid.*, (citation omitted).
[76] *Ibid.*, (citation omitted).
[77] *Ibid.*
[78] *Ibid.*
[79] *Ibid.*, para. 222.
[80] *Ibid.*, (citation omitted) (Readers' note: The Clayton Act is the U.S. statute under which the Department of Justice, the Federal Trade Commission reviews mergers and acquisitions and, in very limited and rarely used circumstances, the FCC for mergers and joint ventures involving common carriers.)
[81] *Ibid.*, para. 227.

affiliated with foreign carriers that have the ability and incentive to discriminate against unaffiliated US carriers, thereby harming US consumers and businesses."[82]

The FCC reasoned that it did not formulate this policy paradigm:

> "to secure open markets as an end in itself, but rather to ensure that US consumers and businesses realize the benefits of effective competition in the provision of their international telecommunications services."[83]

In support of this position, the FCC reasoned that:

> "effective competitive opportunities on the foreign end of US international routes are necessary to limit the potential for anticompetitive conduct by foreign carriers and to ensure that their entry promotes rather than hinders competition in the US international services market."[84]

Thus, concluded the FCC,

> "[t]he fact that Congress did not require us to consider specifically the openness of foreign markets under Section 214 in no way implies that this factor is not relevant under the broader concept of the public interest, convenience and necessity."[85]

Second, the FCC also concluded that the *ECO* test is a "permissible component" of the public interest analysis required by Section 310(b)(4) of the Communications Act.[86] According to the FCC, under Section 1 of the Communications Act, it has:

> "a general mandate to promote the availability to US consumers of a 'rapid, efficient, Nation-wide and world-wide wire and radio communication service with adequate facilities at reasonable charges,' and a specific mandate under Section 310(b)(4) to allow foreign investment above the benchmark level unless the Commission determines that the investment is inconsistent with the public interest.[87]

Thus, reasoned the FCC, the *ECO* test will:

> "promote increased competition in the US telecommunications market, thus furthering the public interest by reducing rates charged to consumers, increasing the quality of services, and encouraging the development of new and innovative services for US consumers."[88]

Moreover, the FCC rejected arguments that in adopting the *ECO* test, the FCC was, in fact, engaging in trade issues which are outside the FCC's mandate. According to the FCC, the *ECO* paradigm:

---

[82] *ECO Order.*
[83] *Ibid.*
[84] *Ibid.*
[85] *Ibid.*, (citation omitted).
[86] *Ibid.*, para. 238.
[87] *Ibid.*, (citation omitted).
[88] *Ibid.*

"is fully consistent, not only with [its] responsibility to promote the US public interest, *but also with the responsibility of the Executive Branch to formulate and execute US international trade policy.*"[89]

The fact that under US law the FCC is supposed to be an independent regulatory agency and not part of the Executive Branch was apparently lost on (or more accurately, deliberately ignored by) the Commission however. Of course, keeping with the trade-centric theme of this *Order*, the FCC specifically declined to apply its *ECO* test to US carriers' investments overseas because, in the FCC's words, "such scrutiny would not further the goals underlying this proceeding."[90] In the FCC's view however:

"a substantial investment by a US carrier in a dominant foreign carrier may raise competition concerns with respect to traffic between the foreign country and the United States, there are established Commission rules and policies, as well as antitrust laws, that address such concerns."[91]

As such, the FCC stated that while it has "confidence" in its own ability to address any such competitive concerns with its own safeguards, including its dominant carrier safeguards, it lacked such confidence in other regulators' ability to regulate to the same standard of excellence over issues outside the FCC's jurisdiction.[92] Moreover, the FCC professed that it did "not want unnecessarily to impede the flow of US telecommunications carriers' investment and entry into foreign markets."[93] In the FCC's opinion, the "presence of US carriers not only benefits those carriers' US customers, but also may foster liberalization efforts."[94] Why? Because, in the FCC's view:

"such a restriction on US investment in foreign carriers would be tantamount to an export control and would be directly contrary to long-standing US policy in favor of US investment abroad."[95]

The FCC further argued that it was wholly appropriate for it to apply a different regulatory approach to US carrier investment in foreign carriers because its *ECO* analysis distinguishes between US carriers and foreign carriers for three separate reasons. First, "the same anticompetitive concerns [did not] exist where a US carrier invests in a foreign carrier as where a foreign carrier invests in a US carrier."[96] In circumstances where "a US carrier has a substantial investment in a dominant foreign carrier and uses its influence over the foreign carrier to obtain an anticompetitive advantage on the affiliated route," the FCC has "jurisdiction over the US carrier, through its licenses and authorizations in the United States, to redress its behavior," but, in contrast,

"where a dominant foreign carrier has a substantial investment in, and influence over, a US carrier, [it did] not have similar jurisdiction over the foreign carrier, through its

---

[89] *Ibid.*, para. 239 (emphasis added).   [90] *Ibid.*, para. 103 (citation omitted).
[91] *Ibid.*, para. 105 (citation omitted).   [92] *Ibid.*, (citation omitted).
[93] *Ibid.*   [94] *Ibid.*   [95] *Ibid.*   [96] *Ibid.*, para. 106.

foreign licenses and authorizations, to redress any anticompetitive use of its bottleneck facilities."[97]

Second, the FCC argued that applying its ECO analysis to "a US carrier seeking to invest abroad would be contrary to US policy."[98] Finally, the FCC maintained that any application of the *ECO* analysis "to a US carrier investor simply would not serve the market opening goals of this proceeding."[99]

IV. QUESTIONS OF DOMINANCE AND EFFECTIVE COMPETITIVE OPPORTUNITIES

A. Generic Worldwide Dominance: The AT&T International Non-Dominant Petition[100]

In this *Order*, the FCC finally granted AT&T's petition to be declared a non-dominant carrier for all US-based IMTS routes.[101] At the time of this *Order*, "dominance" for AT&T meant that AT&T, for every single international route, was subject to stringent FCC reporting requirements, price cap regulation, and any new tariff AT&T filed was subject to a forty-five-day notice and comment period before it could go into effect.[102]

First, the FCC found that AT&T's market share for IMTS service has declined consistently over the past several years (indeed, AT&T actually lost market share faster for IMTS service than for domestic service). This pattern of sustained reductions of AT&T's market share suggested intense rivalry for IMTS service.[103] Second, the FCC found that, as of the time of this *Order*, demand was highly elastic for IMTS service; in fact, the FCC held that consumers are even more price sensitive for international services than they are for domestic services.[104] Third, the FCC analysed the elasticity of supply of the IMTS market, in terms of both the number of operators and the amount of capacity available. In both cases, the FCC found that there were sufficient competitive alternatives available to mitigate against any successful exercise of market power by AT&T.[105] In fact, the FCC found that to the extent that barriers to entry continued to exist, they were not so great as to bar effective com-

---

[97] *ECO Order*.   [98] *Ibid.*   [99] *Ibid.*

[100] *Motion of AT&T Corp. to be Declared Non-Dominant for International Service*, Order, 12 F.C.C.R. 17,963, 3 Comm. Reg. (P & F) 111 (1996) [hereinafter *AT&T Order*].

[101] *Ibid.*, para. 98. However, because there were four markets with *de minimis* revenues, the FCC decided to forbear from imposing dominant carrier regulation on those routes. *Ibid.*, paras. 94–97.

[102] As explained *infra* in Chapter 18, the FCC's concept of dominance was widely inconsistent depending on its political mood *du jour*. That is, even though AT&T controlled no bottleneck facilities at the time the FCC was debating over whether to de-regulate AT&T for IMTS service, the FCC had already approved BT's (i.e. at that time, a government monopolist) investment in MCI on the condition that MCI's rates for the US-UK route with only one-day's notice and comment; and Deutsche Telecom's and France Telecom's investment (again two state owned monopolists) on the condition that Sprint's rates for France and Germany be put out for fourteen days notice and comment.

[103] AT&T Order, *supra* n. 100, paras. 37–39.

[104] *Ibid.*, paras. 42–47.   [105] *Ibid.*, paras. 48–51.

petition, nor were they particular to AT&T.[106] As such, the FCC found that the

> "increasing availability of both multiple operating agreements and of alternative means for US facilities-based carriers to route their traffic support[ed] a finding to reclassify AT&T as non-dominant on all but the four US international routes"

on which it exercised its new authority to forbear from imposing dominant carrier regulation.[107]

B. Does the FCC View Competition/Antitrust Laws as Effective as Regulation? The Telecom New Zealand ECO Case[108]

In this *Order*, the FCC granted, subject to certain conditions, Telecom New Zealand Limited's (TNZL) application to obtain section 214 authority to acquire US half-circuits in transoceanic cables and satellite capacity in order to provide services between the United States and New Zealand on a full-circuit basis.[109] TNZL proposed to "terminate its facilities at a point of interconnection on the West Coast of the United States, outside the geographic areas served by the local exchange telephone companies of Bell Atlantic Corporation and

---

[106] *Ibid.*, paras. 56–57. While the FCC readily agreed "that U.S. international calling prices are at the very high end of the 'zone of reasonableness'" (indeed, the FCC noted that residential IMTS pricing was (and continued to be) significantly higher and more profitable than U.S. domestic long-distance calling prices, and some IMTS prices had risen over the past several years), the FCC concluded that because: (a) the record in the *ECO Order* suggested that "high international calling prices result[ed] more from problems with the structure, conduct and performance of the international market than from market power unique to AT&T; [and (b) there was] evidence in the record to support [a] conclusion that residential IMTS customers [were] very price sensitive," and could be expected to switch international carriers in response to price promotions, the FCC therefore found that "AT&T alone could not raise and sustain prices above a competitive level for residential services without risking loss of its customers to its competitors." *Ibid.*, para. 83. In particular, the FCC stated that it was "especially concerned about the apparently large profits that U.S. international carriers make as a result of imperfections in the U.S. international market." *Ibid.* Indeed, the FCC found that "AT&T's competitors, including WorldCom, could choose to sacrifice some of their profitability to increase their market share, but have not done so." *Ibid.*, (citing report that "WorldCom and its predecessor companies, for example, provided a total return to investors of 57.3 per cent per year during the past decade." *Wall Street Journal*, 19 Feb. 1996, at D2.) To remedy this situation, the FCC stated that it would continue to take steps to "expedite the entry of additional U.S. competitors to the U.S. international services market as provided for under the 1996 Act," because, in the FCC's own words, "[a]dditional competition is the best way to reduce high U.S. international calling prices." *Ibid.*, para. 86.

[107] *Ibid.*, para. 51. See also Streamlining Report and Order, *supra* n. ???, para. 49. There, the FCC streamlined its procedures for discontinuing international service because it found that the "increase in the number of international carriers and competition in international services means that customers can switch to another international carrier if service is discontinued by their current carrier."

[108] Telecom New Zealand Limited, Application for Authority under Section 214 of the Communications Act of 1934, *Order, Authorisation and Certificate*, 12 F.C.C.R. 19,379, 6 Comm. Reg. (P & F) 1 (1996).

[109] *Ibid.*

Ameritech Corporation," which held indirect minority ownership interests in TNZL at the time of this *Order*.[110]

The FCC reasoned that because TNZL was a "foreign carrier" within the meaning its rules, it had to examine TNZL's application under the framework established in *ECO*—that is, whether it should apply *ECO* if TNZL had sufficient market power in its home market that could potentially be leveraged to the detriment of unaffiliated US carriers providing service to those countries.[111] After reviewing: "(1) TNZL's market share; (2) the supply elasticity of the market; (3) the demand elasticity of TNZL's customers; and (4) TNZL's cost structure, size and resources,"[112] the FCC concluded that because TNZL "controlled the only ubiquitous local exchange network in New Zealand," TNZL therefore had market power in the local access market and, as such, it was appropriate (and necessary) to conduct an *ECO* analysis.[113]

The first public interest factor the FCC examined was whether New Zealand had any legal barriers to entry for US carriers to provide international telecommunications services. After review, the FCC concluded that there were none.[114] The FCC found that all applicants (indigenous and foreign alike) seeking to provide international service in New Zealand simply had to register with, and pay a registration fee to, the Communications Division of the Ministry of Commerce, "in circumstances where the applicant (other than a 'call-back' operator) proposes to interconnect international facilities to the public switched network."[115] The FCC further found that as of the time of this *Order*, ten companies had registered as international service operators in New Zealand (five of which were facilities-based) and, moreover, that no applicant had been denied registration as an international service operator as of the date of the *Order*.[116]

Next, the FCC examined New Zealand's terms and conditions for interconnection. The FCC stated that while the New Zealand interconnection regime may not have been designed as the FCC preferred, it appeared that—based on existing laws and regulations, the existence of multiple international facilities-based carriers (including one with 23 per cent market share), and most importantly on favourable toll interconnection rates—US carriers had the opportunity to obtain interconnection on reasonable and non-discriminatory terms for the provision of international facilities-based service.[117] Indeed, the FCC stated that while it was "concerned" that

---

[110] Communications Act of 1934, *Order, Authorisation and Certificate*, 12 F.C.C.R. 19,379, 6 Comm. Reg. (P & F) 1 (1996), para. 3 (citation omitted).

[111] *Ibid.*, para. 5.

[112] *Ibid.*, para. 8 (citations omitted).

[113] *Ibid.*, para. 9.

[114] *Ibid.*, para. 11.

[115] *Ibid.*, (citation omitted).

[116] *Ibid.*, para. 12.

[117] *Ibid.*, para. 17.

"New Zealand [did] not have standard rates for toll interconnection, accompanied by a pricing methodology that enables carriers seeking such interconnection to determine whether prices are cost-based,"

the FCC nonetheless believed that

"[o]ther aspects of New Zealand's regulatory regime and market performance . . . weigh[ed] in favor of finding that New Zealand satisfi[ed] this aspect of [the] ECO test."[118]

Specifically, the FCC found that

"New Zealand relies primarily on its Commerce Act 1986—its general competition law—to regulate telecommunications."[119]

"In particular, section 36 of the statute prohibits entities with a dominant position in a market from using their position to restrict or eliminate competition."[120]

In addition, the FCC noted that New Zealand had issued some sector-specific legislation, including the Telecommunications Act of 1987:

"which, along with subsequent amendments, liberalized the provision of telecommunications services, authorized the government to regulate international services and required [incumbent carriers] to disclose financial and interconnection information."[121]

Moreover, the FCC found that the New Zealand government has published several sets of regulations regarding telecommunications, including: (1) the Telecommunications (Disclosure) Regulations of 1990; and (2) the Telecommunications (International Services) Regulations of 1994.[122] In addition, the FCC noted that while "[i]nterconnection arrangements in New Zealand are negotiated on a private contractual basis, . . . several factors [nonetheless] help protect against discriminatory conduct."[123] In the FCC's view, such factors included:

"(1) the legal requirement that [the incumbent carrier] provide interconnection on terms that are not unreasonably discriminatory; (2) public and private remedies for anticompetitive conduct, and the apparent willingness of the New Zealand government to utilise such public remedies;[124] (3) the requirement that the incumbent carrier publish its prescribed services and all interconnection agreements on a quarterly basis; and (4) emerging competition in the New Zealand local exchange market."[125]

Notwithstanding the above, the FCC could not resist taking several cheap pot-shots at a country that decided to take a different regulatory approach than

---

[118] *Ibid.*
[119] *Ibid.*, para. 18.
[120] *Ibid.*, (citation omitted).
[121] *Ibid.*
[122] *Ibid.*
[123] *Ibid.*, para. 19.
[124] *Ibid.*
[125] *Ibid.*, (citations omitted).

that adopted by the United States. To wit, even though the FCC found that there was, in fact, adequate regulatory oversight in New Zealand (particularly when considered in combination with the expanding list of competitors in the New Zealand international telecommunications market), the FCC stated that it believed that "*competition in the New Zealand telecommunications market would be better served if the government played a more direct role in oversee-ing interconnection arrangements*"[126] as the US government had "*concerns about the effectiveness of the New Zealand regulatory regime.*"[127] Indeed, the FCC felt compelled to comment that, in its humble, expert opinion, "*competi-tion would be better assured if the Ministry took a more active regulatory approach.*"[128] The fact that the FCC made these statements while priding itself as the leader in "de-regulatory" and "pro-competitive" initiatives is comical at best.

V. WHO NEEDS MARKET POWER TO APPLY ECO? THE *MAP* AND *APC PCS*
ECO ORDERS[129]

On 16 May 1997, the FCC's International Bureau issued two *Orders* which approved a foreign investment into a US personal communications services (PCS) company that would exceed the 25 per cent benchmark contained in section 310(b)(4) of the US Communications Act of 1934. In the first *Order*, the FCC approved the investment by an Australian company into MAP Mobile Com-munications, Inc., a US PCS company; in the second, the FCC approved the invest-ment of a German company in APC PCS, another US PCS company. What is significant about these *Orders* is not the fact that the FCC made no mention of the possibility of having either the dominant firm from Australia or Germany leverage its foreign market power into the US PCS market, *but the fact that in the absence of such a concern*, the FCC performed an *ECO* analysis of the German and Australian wireless markets nonetheless.[130] What is also significant to note is that the FCC decided to apply the reciprocal *ECO* test in these two situations despite the fact that both Germany and Australia had signed on to the WTO Telecom-munications Treaty and, in particular, the Regulatory Reference Paper.[131]

[126] Communications Act of 1934, *Order, Authorisation and Certificate*, 12 F.C.C.R. 19,379, 6 Comm. Reg. (P & F) 1 (1996), para. 20 (emphasis added).

[127] *Ibid.*, para. 35 (emphasis added).

[128] *Ibid.*, para. 34 (emphasis added).

[129] MAP Mobile Comm., Inc. Petition for Declaratory Ruling Concerning Section 310(b)(4), *Order*, 12 F.C.C.R. 6109 (1997) [hereinafter *MAP Order*]; APC PCS d/b/a Am. Personal Comm. Petition for Declaratory Ruling Concerning Section 310(b)(4) of the Comm. Act of 1934, as amended, *Declaratory Ruling and Order*, 12 F.C.C.R. 6535 (1997) [hereinafter *APC Declaratory Ruling and Order*].

[130] See *MAP Order, supra* n. 129, para. 7; *APC Declaratory Ruling and Order, supra* n. 129, paras. 8–9.

[131] See *MAP Order, supra* n. 129, para. 19; *APC Declaratory Ruling and Order, supra* n. 129, paras. 17–18, 21; cf. *ECO Order, supra* n. 42, para. 187 ("We do not believe it is unfair to hold for-eign carriers accountable for the policies of their home governments.").

VI. SETTLEMENT RATE DISPUTES: THE TELINTAR TRADE WAR

The seeds of the Telintar "trade war" were first planted when AT&T's settlement rate agreement with Telintar—the monopoly provider of IMTS service in Argentina at the time of this *Order*[132]—expired, and the parties could not come to a new agreement (under the previous contract, the parties had agreed to an accounting rate of $1.47 per minute).[133] Although the parties agreed to an interim extension of the contract, the parties nonetheless immediately started to engage in surreptitious conduct against each other.[134]

On Telintar's part, it allegedly: (a) blocked 180 of AT&T's circuits over this period, thus preventing the use of those circuits by AT&T for outbound US international calls to Argentina; (b) "disabled AT&T's USADirect® Service from Argentina"; and (c) "re-routed a portion of AT&T's return traffic to other carriers."[135] Not without its own arsenal, however, AT&T petitioned for, and in the end received, help from the US government in this matter. This help included communications from both the State Department and the FCC to the Argentine regulator, the National Telecommunications Commission (CNT).[136] Unfortunately, the US diplomatic efforts failed, as Telintar continued to refuse to restore service.[137]

With the failure of regulatory diplomacy, the United States—through the FCC—decided to take stronger measures to protect its flagship telephone company. As its opening salvo, the FCC announced to the IMTS community that:

"This Commission will not allow foreign monopolists to undermine US law, injure US carriers or disadvantage US consumers. Telintar, of Argentina, is attempting to do just that. We must use our regulatory authority to prevent this effort from being successful."[138]

To back this fiery rhetoric up, the FCC ordered *all* US carriers to suspend settlement payments to Telintar effective immediately and, moreover, directed all

---

[132] AT&T Corp., Proposed Extension of Accounting Rate Agreement for Switched Voice Service with Arg., *Order*, 11 F.C.C.R. 18,014, para. 1 n. 1 (1996). In addition, "Telefonica of Argentina and Telecom Argentina, Argentina's two regional monopoly providers of local telephone service, each own[ed] 50 percent of Telintar" at the time of this Order. *Ibid.*

[133] *Ibid.*, para. 4.

[134] See *Ibid.*, paras. 4–5.

[135] *Ibid.*, para. 5.

[136] *Ibid.*, para. 6.

[137] *Ibid.* The casualties of this trade war unfortunately spilled beyond the AT&T/Telintar theatre. As this fight was going on, Telintar allegedly refused to grant WorldCom adequate facilities to terminate all of WorldCom's traffic destined for Argentina which forced WorldCom to overflow as much as 25% of its traffic to other carriers for termination in Argentina. However, WorldCom did advise the FCC "that the additional capacity it requires could be accomplished by means of circuit multiplication, and that no additional investment in cable or satellite facilities [wa]s required." *Ibid.*, para. 7.

[138] *Ibid.*, para. 1 (emphasis added) (citation omitted).

US carriers to continue this suspension until AT&T's circuits were no longer blocked and its USADirect® Service was restored.[139]

Yet, it appeared that the FCC only used rubber (rather than real) bullets in this skirmish. Specifically, Telintar would suffer no direct financial damage because the FCC instructed US carriers to pay Telintar any settlements that had been withheld.[140] Moreover, the FCC set a maximum interim accounting rate that US carriers could pay of $1.43 per minute. While this rate was still higher than the FCC's prior maximum benchmark rate of $1.20, this rate reflected the lowest level agreed to by Telintar with a US carrier (i.e., MCI and Sprint). In the FCC's view, $1.20 "appear[ed] generous as an interim accounting rate."[141]

When the dust cleared, however, the "power of the purse" won this trade war in the end. Apparently finding that its immediate need for a consistent and substantial stream of above-cost accounting rate revenue outweighed its willingness to stand on principle and suspend service indefinitely as a matter of national pride, Telintar restored the blocked circuits. As soon as it did, the FCC permitted US carriers to resume payments.[142]

VII. SUMMARY AND ANALYSIS

The *Orders* analysed in this chapter demonstrate a clear and wholly improper shift in US government priorities toward protecting domestic US *competitors* rather than *competition* (i.e., consumers).[143] Indeed, even though *International Competitive Carrier* focused on the ability of AT&T's rivals to obtain an operating agreement with a foreign correspondent, the FCC did not attempt to force foreign markets open for the benefit of these carriers. By adopting a naked reciprocity approach as a precondition of foreign entry in *ECO*, however, the FCC improperly changed its policy objectives of IMTS regulation from ensuring that US carriers charge US consumers just and reasonable rates, to acting as a wholly-owned subdivision of the US Trade Representative and the Executive Branch to promote international trade for the benefit of these very same carriers.[144]

As explained *passim*, the FCC often makes use of its broad "public interest" standard as support for its various IMTS policy initiatives. With the rise of naked trade concerns as a primary emphasis of these policy initiatives, the ques-

---

[139] *MAP Order, supra* n. 129, para. 19; *APC Declaratory Ruling and Order,*, para. 15.

[140] *Ibid.*, para. 11.

[141] *Ibid.*, para. 12.

[142] See FCC News Release, International Action AT&T Circuits to Argentina Reactivated; Settlement Payments to Resume, Rep. No. IN 96–9, 1996 FCC LEXIS 1498 (Mar. 27, 1996).

[143] See discussion *supra* pp 129–38.

[144] See Reed Hundt & Charlene Barshefsky, "FCC Isn't Backpedaling on Telecommunications Deal", *New York Times*, 17 Aug. 1997, at F36 ("FCC will continue to show deference to the executive branch on matters concerning foreign policy and trade . . ." and the "executive branch fully supports this view.")). As we observed in passim, such a statement is really quite interesting, given the fact that the FCC is supposed to be an *independent* regulatory agency.

tion of whether or not trade may be a legitimate public interest factor must therefore be resolved. While the FCC has stated that trade may be a permissible component of the public interest standard, established legal precedent and economic theory indicate a contrary conclusion.

As explained earlier in Part I of this book, it is very important to remember that, as a general proposition, economic regulation and trade policy seek to promote *very* different goals. Antitrust and regulatory policy appropriately focuses on *consumers*—not competitors.[145] Trade policy, on the other hand, by its very definition seeks to promote *competitors* (i.e., competitors of the "domestic" sort). Thus, while antitrust is certainly one of a number of policies affecting international trade, the various national trade policies (which very often are not even in harmony with each other) may at times be in tension with antitrust policies.[146] Accordingly, because economic regulators have the responsibility to maximise consumer welfare, and therefore these regulators—just like under antitrust jurisprudence—are similarly not at liberty to subordinate the public interest to the interest of equalising competition among competitors, trade considerations correspondingly should not be a legitimate public interest factor in regulatory decision-making.

By becoming "captured" by the Executive Branch—rather than fighting to maintain its independence—the FCC took its first giant step in dislodging the dominant carrier paradigm from its analytical anchors established in the domestic *Competitive Carrier* and *International Competitive Carrier* proceedings; the FCC made final divorce from any analytical foundation in the adjudications and rulemakings discussed *infra*. Indeed, by removing the analytical underpinnings of the dominant carrier paradigm, the FCC has now apparently turned the concept of dominance into a regulatory term of convenience.

While such an approach may make great press release headlines, the reality is that any argument that reciprocity can actually improve consumer welfare is specious at best. As discussed in more detail in Part I of this book, by adopting an aggressive "America First" approach, both foreign governments and carriers will probably have a (if not exacerbating an existing) substantial *disincentive* to engage in good faith negotiations with US carriers to enter their home markets (which, paradoxically, is supposed to be the whole goal of such an approach in the first place). Accordingly, cultivating foreign recalcitrance is precisely the one thing that the FCC's IMTS policies have managed to accomplish successfully.[147]

---

[145] See, e.g., *Brunswick Corp.* v. *Pueblo Bowl-O-Mat Inc.*, 429 U.S. 477, 488 (1977) (quoting *Brown Shoe Co.* v. *United States*, 370 U.S. 294, 320 (1962)); *Hawaiian Tel. Co.* v. *FCC*, 498 F.2d 771, 775–76 (D.C. Cir. 1974); *SBC Comm. Inc.* v. *FCC*, 56 F.3d 1484, 1491 (D.C. Cir. 1995) (citing *W.U. Tel. Co.* v. *FCC*, 665 F.2d 1112, 1122 (D.C. Cir. 1981) ("equalization of competition is not itself a sufficient basis for Commission action")).

[146] See American Bar Association *Antitrust Law Developments* 991 (4th ed., American Bar Assocation, 1997).

[147] See Scott Blake Harris, "Why the EC Has Got Its Priorities All Wrong", *Comm. Wk. Int'l*, 19 Jan. 1998, at 9, where the former (and inaugural) Chief of the FCC's International Bureau lambasted the European Commission for suggesting the need for a European-wide approach to licensing and

other basic regulatory issues. In Mr. Harris' purported expert opinion, the "EC has a very long way to go before it could possibly be qualified to act as a regulator. Indeed, it would need radically to reorient its thinking so that it focuses more on fairness and openness, and less on industrial policy." *Ibid.* In fact, Mr. Harris appears shocked at the notion that a regulator, in particular the European Commission and Directorate General XIII (now the Information Society Directorate)—would apparently "consider the promotion of European industry to be the motivating rationale for competition and open markets." *Ibid.* This view, admonished Mr. Harris, "squarely conflicts with the role of a regulator, which is to bring consistency, fairness, and openness to the decision-making process." *Ibid.* (emphasis added). To help guide our European friends, therefore, Mr. Harris suggested that the European Commission look to the FCC as the very model of a pareto optimal regulatory body. For example, Mr. Harris noted that as "a regulatory agency, the FCC is not allowed to play favorites. It must treat [foreign firms] no better, and no worse, than it treats other [domestic] applicants." *Ibid.* Most importantly, argued Mr. Harris, is that "the FCC cannot strike deals with other governmental agencies favoring" either domestic or foreign firms. Ibid. Thus, concluded Mr. Harris, [t]o put it mildly, such trade-offs have no place at any regulatory agency. Let's hope this is just a misunderstanding. But do not be shocked if it is not. The EC still thinks its role is to protect European industry, and its respect for independent regulatory processes seems to be mere talk. . . . If it ever hopes to be a regulator—or have respect from regulators—the EC must understand that the fair and open application of rules to facts is what regulators do. Looking out for "client" industrial interests is not. We believe the correct legal and economic term to describe accurately this argument can be summarized in one word—"chutzpa."

7

US Policies Post-WTO Part I—
Benchmarks and Entry Fees

I. EXACTLY HOW OPEN ARE US MARKETS POST-WTO?

IN THE NEXT two chapters, we discuss probably the most contentious battle in the growing telecoms trade war—the FCC's unilateral decision to impose settlement rate benchmarks on the rest of the international community. Claiming that such "competitive safeguards" were necessary because it did not trust the rest of the WTO community to meaningfully enforce their respective Member Commitments, the next two chapters show that both the FCC's economic rational behind these actions and the legal justification upholding the FCC's orders were flimsy at best.

A. The FCC's Benchmarks Final Order[1]

Despite the conclusion of the landmark WTO Agreement on Basic Telecoms Services, the FCC—after admitting publicly that it did not trust the market-opening efforts and commitments of other Member Countries—decided to unilaterally establish settlement rate benchmarks to the dismay of the international telecoms community. In the FCC's view, however, it was doing no such thing. Instead, it was only seeking to "govern the international settlement rates US carriers may pay foreign carriers to terminate international traffic originating in the United States."[2] In doing so, the FCC stated that the actions it took in this *Benchmarks Order*, along with its *Flexibility Order*[3] and its proceedings implementing the February Accord, "substantially complete[d its] plan to restructure the economics of the market for US international telecommunications services."[4]

The FCC reasoned that this restructuring would "promote the low cost, technologically innovative interconnectivity serving all the world's consumers that

---

[1] International Settlement Rates, *Report and Order*, 12 F.C.C.R. 19,806, 9 Comm. Reg. (P & F) 1 (1997) [hereinafter *Benchmarks Order*], *recons. pending, appeal filed, Order*, 13 F.C.C.R. 9188 (1998). <http://www.fcc.gov/Bureaus/International/Orders/1999/ fcc99073.txt>.

[2] *Ibid.*, para. 1.

[3] *Flexibility Order, Regulation of International Accounting Rates*, CC Docket No. 90-337, Phase II, *Fourth Report and Order*, 11 FCC Rcd 20, 063 (1996).

[4] *Benchmarks Order, supra* n. 1, para. 1.

should be the hallmark of a Global Information Infrastructure."[5] While the FCC emphasised that it would prefer to achieve its goals through a multilateral agreement on accounting rate reform, it argued that it must take unilateral action to reform the current international settlement-of-accounts regime in order to (a) fulfill its "duty to ensure reasonable rates for US consumers";[6] (b) "allow consumers in all countries to receive higher quality service [and] more service options";[7] and (c) "benefit every carrier [regardless of nationality] that provides international services by stimulating growth of those [IMTS] services."[8]

1. Pricing Methodology and Application

The FCC reaffirmed its belief that it should use the "Tariffed Components Price" (TCP) methodology—that is, the tariffed prices carriers charge to their own domestic customers—set forth in its *International Settlement Rates NPRM* to establish settlement rate benchmarks in the absence of carrier-specific cost data.[9] The FCC reasoned that by "[r]elying on publicly available tariff data and information published by the ITU," it would both be able "to make some progress in achieving the goal of cost-oriented settlement rates" and to "treat foreign carriers fairly."[10] To wit, the FCC reasoned that the TCP methodology is appropriate not only because it relies on carriers' publicly available "tariffed rates and information published by the ITU," but because the TCP methodology is "based on a framework that [already] received consensus approval from

---

[5] *Benchmarks Order*, *supra* n. 1, para. 1.

[6] *Ibid.*, para. 5.

[7] *Ibid.*, para. 7 (citation omitted).

[8] *Ibid.* It is also interesting to note the FCC's opinion about the efficacy of participating in international organisations, especially the ITU, to achieve accounting rate reform. The FCC stated that while it had "contributed actively to the work of multilateral organizations and agreed that [it] should continue to work vigorously with these organizations to pursue accounting rate reform, . . . [it] did not . . . agree that [its] contribution to multilateral efforts should be [its] exclusive means of addressing accounting rate reform." *Ibid.* Indeed, the FCC recognised that even though it must take action as the implementation process of the commitments made by the United States in the WTO Basic Telecommunications Agreement moves forward, it nonetheless believed that it "must also take action domestically in the interim to reduce settlement rates to a more cost-based level." *Ibid.* Yet, according to the FCC, the unilateral action taken in this proceeding was "concurrent with [its] continued efforts to achieve reform of the accounting rate system in the ITU and other multilateral organizations." *Ibid.*, para. 18 (citation omitted).

[9] According to the FCC, it used the following three network components to calculate the "tariffed component price" for each country basket: (1) the "international facility component," consisting of "international transmission facilities, both cable and satellite, including the link to international switching facilities" (the FCC included "only the half-circuit on the terminating end," however, because it reasoned that "originating carriers have traditionally been responsible for the half circuit on the originating end of a call"); (2) the "international gateway component," consisting of "international switching centres and associated transmission and signalling equipment"; and (3) a "national extension component," consisting of "national exchanges, national transmission, and the local loop facilities used to distribute international service within a country." *Ibid.*, para. 49.

[10] *Ibid.*, para. 66.

the members of the ITU."[11] Moreover, reasoned the FCC, "[r]eliance on tariffed prices also means that US carriers are treated fairly" because "nondiscriminatory treatment of US carriers would require that foreign carriers assess US carriers a comparable charge for the network elements necessary for international termination services as they charge their own domestic customers."[12]

Rather than establish country-specific benchmarks, however, the FCC decided to establish benchmarks categories based on a particular country's level of economic development, as defined by gross national product (GNP) per capita: (1) "high income" countries (GNP per capita of $8,956 or more); (2) "upper-middle income" countries (GNP per capita of $2,896–$8,955); (3) "lower-middle income" countries (GNP per capita of $726–$2,895); and (4) "lower income" countries (GNP per capita of less than $726).[13] The FCC opted for this "basket" approach because it believed that there were "certain shortcomings of using tariff data that make reliance on each country's TCP to establish individual country benchmarks inappropriate."[14] Using the simple average of the TCPs for all countries for which it had data in each category, the FCC adopted the following benchmark for each respective category:[15]

upper income countries	$0.15
upper-middle income countries	$0.19
lower-middle income countries	$0.19
lower income countries	$0.23

However, notwithstanding the fact that the FCC stated that it would "revise and update [its] benchmarks periodically as necessary," (according to the FCC, "periodic revisions are necessary to avoid the problem in the future of [its] benchmarks not keeping pace with cost reductions, and to encourage further movement toward cost-based settlement rates"),[16] the FCC also stated— over substantial international opposition—that it would not forbear from

[11] *Ibid.*, para. 67 (citations omitted).
[12] *Ibid.*
[13] *Ibid.*, para. 120.
[14] *Ibid.*, para. 101. According to the FCC, "[t]he primary shortcoming of using tariff data to calculate settlement rate benchmarks is that any inefficiencies in foreign carriers' tariffed prices are captured in its TCP." *Ibid.*, para. 102. For example, the FCC maintained that "carriers' tariffed prices in many cases do not reflect the underlying cost of providing the tariffed service" because "the tariffs reflect social policies such as universal service goals." *Ibid.* Similarly, argued the FCC, "many countries have rate structures that use high international and domestic long distance charges to offset below-cost local service fees." *Ibid.* Another reason the FCC believed that "tariffed rates reflect inefficiencies is that, in many countries, telephone service is provided by monopoly carriers whose tariff rates may reflect protected market positions and an ability to charge prices not related to underlying costs. Because tariffed rates vary widely as a result of these inefficiencies, similarly situated countries could have substantially different individual TCPs." *Ibid.*, (citation omitted). Moreover, reasoned the FCC, "using tariff data to calculate settlement rate benchmarks" could be inaccurate because a foreign "country could attempt to influence the level of its future benchmark rate by changing its carriers' tariff rates." *Ibid.*
[15] *Ibid.*, para. 111.
[16] *Ibid.*, para. 112 (citation omitted).

applying its settlement rate benchmarks "*on any route, including routes where competition has been introduced.*"[17] As support for this position, the FCC noted that because, as a general matter, "it will take time for vigorous competition to create efficient pricing," it therefore could not "rely entirely on the development of competitive markets to reduce settlement rates to more cost-based levels in a timely manner."[18]

As to why it would not forbear its benchmarks policy where there is fully developed competition, the FCC dismissed opposing arguments by presuming that in such circumstances, settlement rates would likely be below its benchmarks. Thus, reasoned the FCC, "whether the settlement rate benchmarks should be implemented on those routes would be a moot question."[19] Moreover, the FCC maintained that

> "with the increasing market liberalization that will result from implementation of countries' commitments made in the WTO Basic Telecom Agreement, [its] benchmarks policy [would] have minimal impact on most WTO Member countries."[20]

Because the FCC lacked "the incremental cost data or a costing methodology necessary to calculate a precise estimate of carriers' incremental cost of terminating international traffic," however, the FCC stated that it would "use the TCP methodology to calculate the top end of its benchmark ranges."[21] As a proxy for the low end of its benchmark ranges, therefore, the FCC announced that it would instead adopt a "best practice" rate that it would enforce "to the extent carriers seek authorization to provide facilities-based service from the United States to affiliated markets and to provide private line resale service" as a safeguard when it detects a distortion in the US market for IMTS.[22] Yet, "[b]ecause [it] did not have [any] data to establish an accurate cost-based rate," the FCC stated that it would "use a market-based rate as a substitute."[23] In the FCC's words, this would be a "'best practice rate' that is based on the lowest, commercially viable, settlement rate paid today by US carriers to an overseas carrier from a competitive market."[24] This "best practice" rate would "be a presumptive rate that [would] apply in cases of market distortion until evidence is

---

[17] *Benchmarks Order, supra* n. 1, para. 114 (emphasis added).

[18] *Ibid.*

[19] *Ibid.*, para. 115.

[20] *Ibid.* As an interesting side note, the FCC rejected arguments that its benchmarks policy is inconsistent with its flexibility policy. According to the FCC, its flexibility policy is supposed to create a more "flexible regulatory framework that permits carriers to take their international traffic off the traditional settlement system where effective competitive conditions permit and to negotiate alternatives for terminating international calls that do not comply with the FCC's ISP." *Ibid.*, para. 116. By contrast, argued the FCC, "the goal of [its] benchmarks policy is to reduce settlement rates where market forces have not led to more cost-based settlement rates." *Ibid.* The FCC stated, however, that to the extent it "may in the future need to consider the application of the two policies in individual circumstances, [it would] examine those situations at the time they arise, on a case-by-case basis." *Ibid.* (citation omitted).

[21] *Ibid.*, para. 130.

[22] *Ibid.*, para. 132.

[23] *Ibid.*, para. 133.

[24] *Ibid.*

presented that other factors should be taken into consideration."[25] After review, the FCC eventually settled on the rate of $0.08 offered by Sweden as a best practice settlement rate.[26]

2. Timing and Implementation

To implement these benchmarks, the FCC allotted a certain period of time for US carriers to negotiate settlement rates with their foreign correspondents for each income category discussed above. Significantly, the FCC added one additional category for those:

> " 'least telecommunications developed' " countries, where it would use teledensity (as measured by lines per one hundred inhabitants) rather than GNP data.[27] The FCC reasoned that if a country has "a level of teledensity [that is] less than one, [such data] is generally a strong indication that a country's telecommunications infrastructure is severely underdeveloped."[28]

Depending on the specific country category, therefore, the FCC required US carriers to negotiate settlement rates with their foreign correspondents in accordance with the following schedule:[29]

carriers in upper income countries	1 year from implementation of this *Order*[30]
carriers in upper-middle income countries	2 years from implementation of this *Order*
carriers in lower-middle income countries	3 years from implementation of this *Order*
carriers in lower income countries	4 years from implementation of this *Order*
carriers in countries with teledensity less than 1	5 years from implementation of this *Order*

In order to avoid the situation where US carriers are unable to negotiate settlement rate reductions until the end of the applicable transition period,

---

[25] *Ibid.*

[26] *Ibid.*, para. 134. The FCC chose Sweden for a variety of factors. First, it found that "the lowest settlement rate that U.S. carriers currently pay on average is with Sweden, at 0.06 SDR ($0.08)." *Ibid.*, (citation omitted). Second, the FCC concluded that this rate is "commercially viable," in that "[t]his rate [was] in effect since March 1996 and during that time, Sweden had experienced sustainable, vibrant, pro-competitive development of its telecommunications industry." *Ibid.* Third, the FCC found that Sweden offered "effective competitive opportunities ('ECO') for U.S. carriers to offer facilities-based switched and private line services." *Ibid.* As such, concluded the FCC, the "vibrant pro-competitive development of the Swedish telecommunications sectors indicates that its settlement rate with the United States is economically feasible and sustainable." *Ibid.*

[27] *Ibid.*, paras. 163–64.

[28] *Ibid.*, para. 164 (citation omitted).

[29] *Ibid.*, para. 165.

[30] The FCC set the effective date of this *Order* as January 1, 1998, which is the accepted implementation date of the WTO Accord on telecommunications. *Ibid.*, para. 165 n.294.

however, the FCC stated that it would "expect"—but not mandate—US carriers to negotiate proportional annual reductions in settlement rates.[31] In particular, the FCC stated that it would expect "US carriers [to] negotiate twenty per cent reductions annually of the spread between a carrier's current settlement rates and the relevant benchmark for carriers with a five year transition period. For carriers with a four year transition period," an annual 25 per cent reduction in the spread; "for carriers with a three year transition period," an annual reduction of 33 per cent in the spread; and "for carriers with a two year transition period," an annual reduction in the spread of 50 per cent.[32] Moreover, the FCC stated that it would:

> "consider providing additional transition time for negotiations with foreign carriers in countries for which annual reductions in settlement rates, according to [its] transition schedule, would entail a loss of greater than 20 per cent of the country's annual telecommunications revenue."[33]

It also appeared that the FCC was just as unwavering about the sanctity of its implementation schedule as it was about the sanctity of the benchmark calculations themselves. For example, the FCC rejected arguments that its transition periods were unrealistic given historical experience (including that of the United States). While the FCC once again "recognize[d] that the transition to competition takes time and requires difficult adjustments," it simply responded that the transition periods required by this *Order* were:

> "not intended to be schedules for implementation of competition in other countries. Rather, they [were] intended to provide some time for carriers in all countries, even those that have not introduced competition, to make the adjustments necessary to transition to a more cost-based system of accounting rates."[34]

Similarly, the FCC explicitly refused to adopt its original proposal in its *Notice* "to provide additional flexibility in implementation of the benchmarks beyond [its] transition periods for US carriers and their correspondents in developing countries"—even if those countries had "demonstrated an actual commitment to fostering entry and promoting competitive market environments."[35] The FCC gave two reasons for its reversal. First, it believed that its:

> "transition periods adequately take into account the challenges faced by developing countries in moving to more cost-based rates, especially given the longer transition periods [it] adopt[ed] here for lower-middle income countries and countries with teledensity lower than one."[36]

---

[31] *Benchmarks Order, supra* n. 1, para. 172.

[32] *Ibid.*

[33] *Ibid.*, para. 174 (citation omitted). However, the FCC did "emphasize . . . that [it might] take enforcement action if a U.S. carrier is unable to make any progress in negotiating settlement rate reductions during the transition periods and settlement rates remain well in excess of [its] benchmarks." *Ibid.*, para. 173.

[34] *Ibid.*, para. 168.

[35] *Ibid.*, para. 175 (citation omitted).

[36] *Ibid.*, para. 176.

Second, it was:

"concerned that a policy which would create an exemption based on market conditions in the destination market . . . [might] not be consistent with [its] MFN obligations under the GATS."[37]

3. Enforcement

Notwithstanding the above, however, the FCC was a bit more oblique as to actual enforcement mechanisms for its benchmark paradigm. While the FCC stated that it would both: (a) identify recalcitrant carriers and work with the responsible government authorities;[38] and (b) "allow the US international carrier to ask [it] to consider stronger steps,"[39] it declined in this particular *Report and Order* to "adopt any set enforcement mechanism."[40] Instead, the FCC stated that it would "consider the individual circumstances surrounding each carrier-initiated petition to determine the appropriate enforcement action to take."[41] However, the FCC made clear that

"whatever enforcement action [it] take[s] with regard to a complaint about a foreign correspondent's unwillingness to negotiate a settlement rate at or below the relevant benchmark, [this action would] apply to all US international carriers' dealings with that foreign correspondent."[42]

Yet, while the FCC was unwilling to impose a specific enforcement mechanism directly in this proceeding, it was willing to impose two enforcement mechanisms ("competitive safeguards") indirectly. First, the FCC stated that it would condition any and all facilities-based switched and private line Section 214 authorisations (existing and prospective) of carriers seeking to serve affiliated foreign markets from the United States on the requirement that the affiliated foreign carrier offer all "US carriers a settlement rate [for] terminat[ing] US-originated traffic on the affiliated route that is at or below the

---

[37] *Ibid.*, (citation omitted). The FCC did state, however, that if, in the future, there is an alternative "multilateral consensus on a substantially equivalent international measure" that would achieve the United States' "goals of a cost-based system of settlements in a timely manner, [then it would] waive enforcement of the benchmark settlement rates." *Ibid.*, para. 190; see also *ibid.*, para. 5.

[38] In particular, the FCC stated that it would convey its "concern about continued high settlement rates and the lack of meaningful progress," as well as "emphasize the need for co-operation in achieving the goal of cost-based rates, enlist their active support in achieving that goal, cite relevant ITU recommendations such as Recommendation D.140, and suggest further discussions that may be necessary." *Ibid.*, para. 185.

[39] *Ibid.*, para. 186. According to the FCC, "a U.S. international carrier may file a petition that: (1) demonstrates that it has been unable to negotiate a settlement rate with its foreign correspondent that complies with the rules and policies we adopt in this Order; and (2) requests enforcement measures be taken to ensure that no U.S. carrier pays that foreign correspondent an amount exceeding the lawful settlement rate benchmark." *Ibid.*

[40] *Ibid.*, para. 187.

[41] *Ibid.*

[42] *Ibid.*, (citation omitted).

relevant benchmark."[43] The FCC stated that such a generic condition was necessary in order to mitigate potential anti-competitive distortions in the US market—in particular, predatory price squeeze behavior.[44]

To determine whether a market distortion has occurred, the FCC:

> "establish[ed] a rebuttable presumption that a carrier has engaged in price squeeze behavior that creates distortions in the US market for IMTS if . . . any of a carrier's tariffed collection rates on an affiliated route are less than the carrier's average variable costs on that route."[45]

Further

> "If any tariffed collection rate is less than average variable costs, [the FCC would] presume that the carrier is engaging in anticompetitive price squeeze behavior and [as such would] take enforcement action."[46]

The FCC stated that its presumption of market distortion could be rebutted, however, if a carrier demonstrates that it had "an economically justifiable reason for pricing below average variable costs" (e.g., "a carrier could show that its pricing strategy is a time limited promotion in order to gain market share").[47] If

---

[43] *Benchmarks Order, supra* n. 1, para. 207. In fact, for those U.S. carriers that served affiliated markets with existing Section 214 certificates, the FCC required these affiliated carriers to negotiate with all U.S. carriers and have *"in effect within ninety days of the effective date of this Order"* a settlement rate for the affiliated route that is at or below the appropriate benchmark. *Ibid.,* para. 228 (emphasis added).

[44] *Ibid.,* paras. 208–16. What is particularly interesting to note is that the FCC performed almost a perfect 180-degree reversal of its price squeeze analysis in the *ECO Order.* As discussed above, the FCC concluded in *ECO* that it was unnecessary to impose such a condition to mitigate against a successful price squeeze. According to the FCC, its "balance of considerations has changed significantly" since *ECO* because its action in this proceeding "comes after the time period for implementation of ITU Recommendation D.140 has concluded, yet settlement rates remain far above cost-based levels." *Ibid.,* para. 218. Against this backdrop, the FCC maintained that "the prospect of freer entry into the US market after January 1, 1998 pursuant to [its] rulemaking proposals implementing the WTO Basic Telecom Agreement increases [its] concern that foreign carrier entry could create competitive distortions in the US market." *Ibid.* Moreover, the FCC argued that such a reversal was appropriate because "[it could] not find on that record persuasive evidence that foreign carriers that entered [the US] market pursuant to [its] *ECO* framework could successfully engage in a price squeeze." *Ibid.,* para. 217. The FCC nonetheless found that the concerns raised in the record in this proceeding were "serious enough for [it] to take the preventive measure of adopting a Section 214 authorisation condition at this time." *Ibid.,* para. 218.

[45] *Ibid.,* para. 224.

[46] *Ibid.*

[47] *Ibid.,* para. 225. For purposes of this bright line test, [the FCC] define[d] a carrier's average variable costs on the affiliated route as the carrier's net settlement rate plus any originating access charges [because t]hese are the two primary expenses that a carrier would not incur in the short term if it stopped providing IMTS from the United States to its affiliated market . . . [and m]ost other expenses are fixed in the short term, and would be incurred regardless of whether the carrier provided service. *Ibid.,* para. 224 (citations omitted). The FCC reasoned that: "recovery of average variable costs [was] an appropriate threshold standard for determining the existence of price squeeze behavior because in the short run carriers can increase their profits (or minimize their losses) by offering service at a price at or above average variable costs. Thus, any price below that floor would indicate that the carrier is losing money by providing service. Alternatively, in the case of a U.S. affiliate of a foreign carrier, any price below the floor could indicate that the U.S. affiliate is attempting a price squeeze. Because the U.S. affiliate's net settlement payments are an intracorporate

this presumption was triggered and not rebutted, however, the FCC stated that it may, *inter alia*, require that "the settlement rate of an affiliated carrier for the route be at a level equal to or below its best practices rate" (again, $0.08), or revoke "the authorization of the carrier to serve the affiliated market."[48]

The second section 214 authorization condition the FCC imposed was a requirement that any carrier that provides switched basic services over international facilities-based or resold private lines between the United States and foreign destination countries must ensure that the "settlement rates for at least 50 per cent of the settled US billed traffic on the route or routes are at or below the appropriate benchmark."[49] Again, the FCC warned that if it determines that competition "has been distorted," it may, *inter alia*:

> "prohibit carriers from using their authorizations to provide switched services over private lines on that route until settlement rates for at least 50 per cent of the settled US billed traffic on the route are at or below the . . . best practice rate of $0.08, or revocation of the carrier's authorization."[50]

As a triggering mechanism, the FCC established a presumption that a

> "market distortion exists, [that is,] inbound switched traffic is being diverted from the accounting rate system to facilities-based or resold private lines, if the ratio of outbound (US-billed) to inbound (foreign-billed) settled traffic increases 10 or more per cent in two successive quarterly measurement periods."[51]

The FCC reasoned that such a condition was required in order to mitigate the threat of "one-way bypass" of the international settlement-of-accounts regime.[52] Yet, as the FCC itself noted, "[t]he provision of switched services over private lines has strong pro-competitive effects in the marketplace."[53] Indeed, according to the FCC,

> "a more liberal policy with respect to resale of international private lines will allow new entities to enter the market and offer services such as IMTS. This new entry will compel carriers at both ends of the circuit to bring their prices closer to cost to avoid losing their current customers to resale providers."[54]

---

transfer and not a true cost, the U.S. affiliate could price its service in the U.S. market below average variable costs." *Ibid.*, para. 225.

[48] *Ibid.*, para. 231.

[49] *Ibid.*, para. 243.

[50] *Ibid.* What is particularly interesting to note here is the fact that while Sweden may have one of the lowest rates for interconnection, the EC nonetheless found that Sweden had among the highest rates for least lines for all of Europe.

[51] *Ibid.*, para. 249. As an example, the FCC stated that its "presumption of market distortion would be met if the traffic ratio at the beginning of a quarterly measurement period was 60 per cent outbound traffic and 40 per cent inbound traffic and the traffic ratio at the end of the subsequent quarterly measurement period (i.e., six months later) had changed to 65 per cent outbound traffic and 35 per cent inbound traffic." *Ibid.*

[52] *Ibid.*, para. 242.

[53] *Ibid.*

[54] *Ibid.*, (citation omitted).

The FCC resolved its self-described "dilemma" by weighing the "pro-competitive effects of private line resale . . . against the market distorting effects of one-way bypass."[55] After review, the FCC held that the latter condition posed a greater public interest burden. According to the FCC, the:

> "threat of one-way bypass of the accounting rate system cannot be ignored [because] it has significant implications for competition in the US market for IMTS, and consequently, for US consumers. One-way bypass exacerbates the US net settlements deficit and ultimately increases the burden on US ratepayers through higher rates for IMTS."[56]

The FCC also rejected the notion that the threat of one-way bypass was ephemeral just because it had yet to take action against carriers for such conduct. Quite to the contrary, the FCC argued proudly:

> "[t]he reason [it had] been able to avoid one-way bypass in the past [was its] equivalency policy. [The] policy permits private line resale only to countries that afford resale opportunities equivalent to those available under US law."[57]

II.   THE FCC'S *FOREIGN PARTICIPATION ORDER* (WTO IMPLEMENTATION PROCEEDING)[58]

In this *Order*, the FCC stated that it was abolishing its *ECO* test and replacing it with an "open entry standard" for applicants from WTO Member countries.[59] In particular, the FCC adopted, as a factor in its public interest analysis, a rebuttable presumption that applications for Section 214 authority from carriers of WTO Members do not pose concerns that would justify denial of an application on competition grounds.[60] The FCC also adopted a:

> "rebuttable presumption that such competitive concerns are not raised by applications to land and operate submarine cables from WTO Members or by indirect ownership

---

[55] *Benchmarks Order*, *supra* n. 1, para. (citation omitted).

[56] *Ibid.*

[57] *Ibid.*

[58] *Foreign Participation Order*, reference required.

[59] *Ibid.*, para. 9.

[60] *Ibid.*, para. 69. Significantly, the FCC also concluded that it would apply its post-WTO entry policy "equally to U.S. carrier investments in foreign carriers as well as foreign carrier investments in U.S. carriers." *Ibid.*, para. 70. The FCC recognised that while it previously found in ECO that "it was unnecessary and contrary to the goals of that proceeding to apply the ECO test to U.S carrier investments in foreign carriers" (indeed, the FCC feared that the application of its ECO test on U.S. carriers would actually *"frustrate* U.S. policy of encouraging foreign investment by U.S. companies"), its subsequent experience indicated that, "there is a likelihood of competitive harm from an international carrier operating in the U.S. market that possesses sufficient foreign market power in a market for services necessary for the provision of U.S. international services to adversely affect competition on the U.S. end of the route, regardless of whether the entity is U.S. or foreign owned." *Ibid.*, (emphasis added) (citation omitted). Of course, the fact that the FCC also feared "that continuing to treat foreign carrier investments in U.S. carriers differently from U.S. carrier investments in foreign carriers could be viewed as inconsistent with U.S. GATS obligations." *Ibid.*, (citation omitted).

by entities from WTO Members of common carrier and aeronautical radio licensees under Section 310(b)(4) of the Act."[61]

Yet, despite substantial international objection, the FCC stated that it would, in appropriate situations, deny entry to a WTO Member country if "other public interest factors" (i.e., the general significance of the proposed entry to the promotion of competition in the US communications market, the presence of cost-based accounting rates, and any national security, law enforcement, foreign policy and trade policy concerns brought to its attention by the Executive Branch) warrant.[62] The FCC was quick to disclaim, however, that "other public interest issues" would be present only in "very rare circumstances."[63]

Notwithstanding the above, the FCC stated that because, in its view, the circumstances that existed when it adopted its *ECO* and *Flexibility Orders* did not change sufficiently with respect to non-WTO Member countries, it continued "to serve the goals of [its] international telecommunications policy to apply [its] ECO and equivalency tests in the context of non-WTO Member countries."[64] Significantly, the FCC specifically rejected the argument that its sole focus in this proceeding should have been on the "potential harm to competition in the US markets."[65] In the FCC's view, "[i]t continues to serve the public interest to maintain policies directed at encouraging non-WTO Member countries to open their telecommunications markets to competition."[66]

Along a similar vein, the FCC also stated that it would henceforth apply the *ECO* test to a route whenever a carrier or its foreign affiliate,

"without regard to whether the applicant, or its affiliate, is a US carrier, . . . controls, is controlled by, or is under common control with a carrier that has market

---

[61] *Ibid.*, para. 50.

[62] *Ibid.*, para. 65. For example, the FCC recognised that while foreign indirect investment in U.S. common carrier wireless markets is unlikely to raise anti-competitive dangers (as those markets are, for the most part, wholly domestic and therefore, there is no possibility of levering foreign bottlenecks in order to create advantages for some competitors in U.S. markets) and, in fact, could *promote* competition in the U.S. market, foreign ownership of U.S. spectrum may raise national security concerns. As such, the FCC accepted the FBI's concerns that even small investments in publicly traded securities could, if aggregated, nevertheless create a degree of control or influence over a licensee that would be contrary to U.S. national security or law enforcement interests that Executive Branch agencies may need an opportunity to evaluate before a grant of section 310(b)(4) authority. The FCC also found similar concerns for foreign ownership of aeronautical en route and fixed services licenses. *Ibid.*, paras. 111–18.

[63] *Ibid.*, para. 50. Moreover, given the substantial criticism received by the FCC that it was inappropriately stepping beyond its mandate, the FCC was also quick to emphasise that it would only "make an independent decision on applications to be considered and [would] evaluate concerns raised by the Executive Branch agencies in light of all the issues raised (and comments in response) in the context of a particular application." *Ibid.*, para. 66. The FCC was equally quick to point out, however, that it expected "that the Executive Branch [would] advise [it] of concerns relating to national security, law enforcement, foreign policy, and trade concerns only in very rare circumstances, [and that those concerns] . . . must be communicated in writing and [would] be part of the public file in the relevant proceeding." *Ibid.*, (citation omitted).

[64] *Ibid.*, para. 124 (citation omitted).

[65] *Ibid.*, para. 125.

[66] *Ibid.*

power in a destination market, where that destination market is a non-WTO country."[67]

In the FCC's opinion, as a

"more liberalized environment [emerges] from the WTO Basic Telecommunications Agreement, it will become increasingly difficult to define a 'US carrier' for the purpose of distinguishing between US-carrier and foreign-carrier ownership of carriers,"

and, "[i]n light of those difficulties, [it could] no longer rely on [its] greater ability to redress anticompetitive conduct by US carriers as compared to foreign carriers."[68]

Again, the FCC specifically rejected the argument that the application of the *ECO* test to third countries exceeds its statutory mandate because when:

"a foreign carrier that controls bottleneck facilities controls, is controlled by, or is under common control with a carrier that is affiliated with a US carrier, there is a danger that the bottleneck facilities will be used to discriminate against unaffiliated US carriers"

and, absent the application of its *ECO* test in these circumstances, the "US affiliate of a foreign carrier that enters various markets through wholly owned subsidiaries would be able to serve all of those subsidiaries' routes."[69] In such a case, reasoned the FCC, the:

"other subsidiaries would have the ability and incentive to use their market power to discriminate against unaffiliated US carriers by routing traffic in ways that take advantage of their market power."[70]

Moreover, reasoned the FCC, "applying the ECO test to non-WTO countries [would] encourage non-WTO countries to open their markets to competition in addition to privatising their telecommunications carriers."[71] In the FCC's opinion:

"[b]ecause privatization without liberalization neither promotes competition nor reduces the risk of anticompetitive conduct, [its] goal is to encourage simultaneous privatization and liberalization. . . . If the ECO test lowers the value of an exclusive arrangement in a privatization, it would thereby encourage simultaneous liberalization and privatization."[72]

In light of this new "open entry" approach, the FCC stated that it was appropriate to revisit, review, and modify its:

---

[67] *Benchmarks Order, supra* n. 1, para. 139.
[68] *Ibid.*, para. 140.
[69] *Ibid.*, para. 141.
[70] *Ibid.*
[71] *Ibid.*, para. 142.
[72] *Ibid.*

"competitive safeguards governing foreign-affiliated carrier provision of basic telecommunications services in the US market and, more broadly, US carrier dealings with foreign carriers."[73]

The FCC stated that it would, in particular, focus its examination of its "rules preventing the exercise of foreign market power in the US market" in order "to monitor and detect anticompetitive behaviour in the US market without imposing regulations that are more burdensome than necessary."[74] According to the FCC:

"[c]oncerns about potential anticompetitive conduct generally [would be] triggered where one party has sufficient market power to cause harm to competition and consumers in the US market."[75]

Significantly, however, the FCC moved away from its definition of market power it used in previous international *Orders* (i.e., "'the ability to act anti-competitively against unaffiliated US carriers through the control of bottleneck services or facilities on the route in question'")[76] to the more conventional definition of market power as "a carrier's ability to raise price by restricting its output of services."[77] The FCC maintained that such a clarification was necessary because the regulatory framework it adopted in this proceeding focused

"on dealings with foreign carriers that possess sufficient market power on the foreign end of a US international route to affect competition adversely in the US international services market."[78]

In particular:

"telecommunications services that originate or terminate in, or transit the United States . . . includ[ing] the US market for global, seamless network services that increasingly are being used by US businesses." [*The FCC's*] *primary concern in this proceeding, however, involves the ability of US carriers to terminate traffic on the foreign end of an international route.*[79]

Yet, despite the regulatory commitments agreed to in the WTO Telecommunications Treaty, the FCC rejected the view that it should eliminate competitive safeguards altogether. In the FCC's opinion, absent effective regulation in the US market:

"a foreign carrier with market power in an input market on the foreign end of a US international route [could] exercise, or leverage, that market power into the US market to the detriment of competition and consumers."[80]

---

[73] *Ibid.*, para. 143 (citation omitted).
[74] *Ibid.*
[75] *Ibid.*, para. 144.
[76] *Ibid.*, (quoting *ECO Order*, para. 116).
[77] *Ibid.*, (citation omitted).
[78] *Ibid.*
[79] *Ibid.*, (alteration in original, citations omitted, emphasis added).
[80] *Ibid.*, para. 145.

Such anti-competitive conduct could, in the FCC's view, include, *inter alia*, price discrimination, non-price discrimination, and price squeeze behaviour.[81]

The first competitive safeguard the FCC imposed was to modify its "No Special Concessions" rule, under which US carriers were prohibited from entering into exclusive arrangements with any foreign carrier affecting traffic or revenue flows to or from the United States.[82] Yet, because the FCC again recognised "that special concessions granted by a foreign carrier [could] serve the public interest in appropriate circumstances" (e.g., "[s]uch arrangements . . . [could] involve innovative services or operational efficiencies that reduce the rates for US international services or increase the quality of such services"), the FCC modified its rule to prohibit only "US carriers from agreeing to accept special concessions granted by foreign carriers that possess market power in a relevant market on the foreign end of a US international route."[83] In the FCC's view, such an approach "strike[s] an appropriate balance" between "encourag[ing] such arrangements," yet deterring arrangements that result in an "unacceptable risk of harm to competition and consumers in the US international services market."[84]

However, because the FCC believed that "determinations of market power on the foreign end of an international route can involve extensive analysis," the FCC decided to establish a "bright-line test." [85] This test would be:

> "a rebuttable presumption that foreign carriers with less than 50 per cent market share in each relevant market on the foreign end lack sufficient market power to affect competition adversely in the US market."[86]

> "If a US carrier seeks to use the under–50 per cent market share presumption as the basis to accept a special concession from a foreign carrier, it must file data with the FCC to substantiate that claim for the relevant input markets on the foreign end of the international route."[87]

In addition, the FCC found that it would be beneficial to delineate the types of exclusive arrangements that the modified No Special Concessions rule would prohibit. After consideration, the FCC decided to limit its No Special Concessions rule to:

---

[81] *Benchmarks Order, supra* n. 1, paras. 145–49.

[82] See 47 C.F.R. § 63.14 (1997).

[83] *Foreign Participation Order*, all references needed here, para. 156 (citations omitted).

[84] *Ibid.*, (citation omitted).

[85] *Ibid.*, para. 159 (citation omitted).

[86] *Ibid.*, para. 161 (citation omitted).

[87] *Ibid.*, para. 163 (citation omitted). See *ibid.*, paras. 156–62. Although the FCC did not specify exactly what "share" it was concerned about (e.g., minutes? revenues? facilities?), it recognised correctly nonetheless that "market share is but one factor in a traditional market power analysis." *Ibid.*, para. 161. Yet, because the FCC believed that "market share data is more readily available" than other information, market share would "serve as a sufficient approximation of foreign market power for purposes of satisfying [its] rebuttable presumption." *Ibid.*

"exclusive dealings involving services, facilities, or functions on the foreign end of a US international route that are necessary for the provision of basic telecommunications service."[88]

In the FCC's view, the rule would therefore:

"prohibit any US carrier from agreeing to accept from a foreign carrier with market power any special concession not offered to similarly situated US-licensed carriers involving: (1) operating agreements for the provision of basic services; (2) distribution arrangements or interconnection arrangements, including pricing, technical specifications, functional capabilities, or other quality and operational characteristics, such as provisioning and maintenance times; and (3) any information, prior to public disclosure, about a foreign carrier's basic network services that affects either the provision of basic or enhanced services or interconnection to the foreign country's domestic network by US carriers or their US customers."[89]

Next, the FCC again believed it necessary to impose competitive safeguards for those US carriers affiliated with a foreign carrier with market power in the destination market. As such, the FCC stated that it would condition any authorisation to serve an affiliated market on the requirement that the foreign carrier offer US-licensed international carriers a settlement rate for the affiliated route at or below the relevant benchmark adopted in the *Benchmarks Order*.[90] Significantly, however, the FCC "decline[d] to apply [its] settlement rate benchmark condition to switched resale providers."[91] The FCC rationalised this conclusion by noting that because its:

"goal in this proceeding [was] to adopt a regulatory framework that is narrowly tailored to address identifiable harms to competition and consumers in the US market,"

it approached

---

[88] *Ibid.*, para. 165. Unfortunately, this case was one of several "pavlovian" attempts by the FCC to rely on market share as a bright-line test, even though using market share as a bright-line test in these circumstances is a "tricky enterprise" at best. See, e.g., *Phoenix Center Policy Paper*, full reference at 32; Spiwak, *Economic Analysis*, full reference at 34 & n.14. Tragically, the European Union is not much better in this regard, where the EU's blind reliance on market shares alone also has produced some truly absurd regulatory decisions. See Mark Naftel, "How Does One Say "Dominance" in European?", *Antitrust Rep.*, Oct. 1997, at 2. http://www.phoenix-center.org/library/naftel_dom.doc.

[89] *Foreign Participation Order*, *supra* n. 83, para. 165. Significantly, the FCC took great pains to clarify that its modified "no special concessions rule" would prohibit "one-stop shopping." *Ibid.*, para. 167. According to the FCC, "the rule does not prevent a U.S. carrier and a foreign carrier from offering end-to-end services. It does, however, prohibit U.S. carriers from entering into exclusive arrangements with certain carriers for certain services." *Ibid.* To illustrate this point, the FCC stated that, for example, "a U.S. carrier cannot agree to enter an exclusive 'one-stop shopping' arrangement in which the U.S. carrier acts as an agent on behalf of its U.S. customers in obtaining private line service from a foreign carrier with market power, where the foreign carrier refuses to recognize other U.S. carriers as agents." *Ibid.* In the FCC's view, "[t]his type of exclusive arrangement would preclude competing U.S. carriers from serving an important segment of the U.S. international services market." *Ibid.*

[90] See discussion *supra* pp. 147–56 and n. 1.

[91] *Foreign Participation Order*, *supra* n. 83, para. 194.

"critically any request for conditions that would impose additional burdens on the manner in which companies could provide service to the US market and thereby provide consumers with additional choices."[92]

Specifically, the FCC stated it would not impose its benchmarks condition on resellers because it did not find the same degree of danger of anti-competitive effects resulting from a switched reseller's provision of service to an affiliated market as it did regarding the "ability of a facilities-based US affiliate of a foreign carrier to 'price squeeze' its competitors because of its relationship with the foreign affiliate."[93] The FCC gave two basic reasons in support of this conclusion. First, the FCC believed that "a switched reseller has substantially less incentive to engage in a predatory price squeeze strategy than a facilities-based carrier."[94] Second, the FCC believed that "it is easier to detect a predatory price squeeze in the switched resale context than in the facilities-based context."[95] Thus, reasoned the FCC:

"[e]asier detection should deter switched resellers from attempting a predatory price squeeze and will allow [it] or other authorities to take action in the event a carrier does attempt a predatory price squeeze."[96]

Finally, the FCC believed that the:

"benefits to consumers of additional new entrants and existing switched resale providers in the US market outweigh the minimal risk to competition from a possible predatory price squeeze or other anticompetitive behavior by a switched resale provider providing service to an affiliated market."[97]

Third, given the WTO Telecoms Treaty, the FCC found it appropriate to modify the safeguards it applied to US carriers classified as dominant due to an affiliation with a foreign carrier that has market power in a relevant market in the following ways: (1) the FCC replaced the fourteen-day advance notice tariff filing requirement with a one-day advance notice requirement and accorded these tariff filings a presumption of lawfulness;[98] (2) the FCC removed the prior

---

[92] *Foreign Participation Order, supra* n. 83, para. 194.
[93] *Ibid.*
[94] *Ibid.*, para. 195.
[95] *Ibid.*
[96] *Ibid.*
[97] *Ibid.*; see also *ibid.*, paras. 193–94, 198–206.
[98] *See ibid.*, paras. 240–45. As discussed above, the FCC had recently modified the tariff filing requirements it imposed on dominant and non-dominant foreign-affiliated IMTS carriers. In the former case, the FCC shortened the advance notice period for dominant carriers to 14 days; in the latter case, the FCC shortened the advance notice period for non-dominant carriers of IMTS service to one day. *Ibid.*, para. 242. Yet, while the FCC recognised that "retaining the existing tariff filing requirements possibly could constrain the ability of a dominant foreign-affiliated carrier to engage in anticompetitive conduct," the FCC reasoned that "the fact that these requirements might help to deter anticompetitive behavior [was] not, by itself, sufficient to retain these measures." *Ibid.*, para. 243. In the FCC's view, "[it] should also consider whether and to what extent these regulations would dampen competition and whether other regulatory provisions accomplish the same objectives." *Ibid.*
After review, the FCC concluded that, on balance, "retaining the fourteen-day notice period

approval requirement for circuit additions or discontinuances on the dominant route;[99] (3) the FCC required a limited form of structural separation between a US carrier and its foreign affiliate;[100] (4) the FCC retained its quarterly traffic and revenue reporting requirement;[101] (5) the FCC replaced its provisioning and maintenance record-keeping requirement with a quarterly reporting requirement that summarises the provisioning and maintenance services provided by the foreign affiliate;[102] and (6) the FCC required dominant carriers to file a quarterly circuit status report.[103] The FCC declined, however, to ban exclusive arrangements involving joint marketing, customer steering, and the use of foreign market telephone customer information.[104]

Again, however, the FCC reaffirmed the appropriateness of its unilateral policy perspective. For example, the FCC stated that it would "not consider the effectiveness of foreign regulation as a separate matter when making a determination of a foreign-affiliated carrier's regulatory classification" because "the benefits derived from such evaluations [did not] outweigh the costs incurred."[105] In the FCC's opinion, "such attempts at evaluating the effectiveness of regulation in a foreign market impose significant burdens on the Commission," and its "experience has shown that obtaining sufficiently reliable and timely information about a foreign regulatory regime is a difficult, resource-intensive, and time-consuming process."[106]

Similarly, the FCC stated that it would maintain its dominant carrier safeguards for US affiliates of foreign carriers from WTO Member countries that agreed to adopt the regulatory principles contained in the Reference Paper— *even where the settlement rate may be within the FCC's benchmark range*— because, in the FCC's opinion:

[would] significantly inhibit[] a dominant foreign-affiliated carrier's incentive to reduce prices, because competitors can respond to pro-consumer price and service changes before the tariff would become effective." *Ibid.*, para. 244 (citation omitted). The FCC believed that a "one-day notice period, coupled with a presumption of lawfulness, [would] provide carriers with additional flexibility to respond to customer demands. To the extent that a foreign-affiliated carrier has the ability to engage in a predatory price squeeze," however, the FCC maintained that "the existence of a tariff filing requirement, regardless of the length of the advance notice, [would] serve to deter such behavior." *Ibid.*, (citations omitted). Moreover, the FCC argued that "in the unlikely event that a foreign-affiliated dominant carrier files an unlawful tariff, remedial action"—either by complaint or on its own motion—"[could] be taken after the tariff becomes effective." *Ibid.*, para. 245.

   [99] See *ibid.*, paras. 246–51.
   [100] See *ibid.*, paras. 252–69.
   [101] See *ibid.*, paras. 270–73.
   [102] See *ibid.*, paras. 274–80.
   [103] See *ibid.*, paras. 281–86.
   [104] See *ibid.*, paras. 287–92.
   [105] *Ibid.*, para. 230 (citations omitted).
   [106] *Ibid.*, (citation omitted). The FCC did state, however, that "[i]n making a foreign market power determination, . . . [it would] consider the presence and degree of barriers to entry or expansion, which may relate to the foreign regulatory regime." *Ibid.*, (citation omitted).

"removal of foreign entry barriers alone will be insufficient to prevent foreign carriers with market power from seeking to leverage their market power into the US market, especially in the short term."[107]

According to the FCC, because the WTO Reference Paper:

"expressly provides that governments have the right to adopt rules to prevent anti-competitive behavior by carriers that, alone or together, control 'essential facilities or otherwise have the ability to affect the market adversely,' "

it was wholly appropriate for the FCC to adopt an

"open entry policy for carriers from WTO Member countries with an understanding that the public interest mandates that [it] ensure against the leveraging of foreign market power into the US market."[108]

Moreover, argued the FCC, even where a settlement rate may be within the FCC's benchmark range, the:

"achievement of settlement rates does not address all forms of anticompetitive conduct, such as non-price discrimination, that [its] dominant carrier safeguards are intended to address."[109]

Finally, the FCC believed that it was also appropriate to modify the framework it adopted in its *Flexibility Order*[110] for approving alternative settlement arrangements in light of the WTO Telecoms Treaty. As such, the FCC stated that it would no longer apply its *ECO* test as the threshold standard "for determining when to permit accounting rate flexibility with carriers from WTO Member countries."[111] Instead, the FCC established "a rebuttable presumption that flexibility is permitted for carriers from WTO Member countries."[112] In order to rebut its presumption in favour of permitting flexibility, the FCC stated that:

"a party must demonstrate that the foreign carrier is not subject to competition in its home market from multiple (more than one) facilities-based carriers that possess the ability to terminate international traffic and serve existing customers in the foreign market."[113]

However, in order to mitigate its residual concerns that a foreign carrier with market power may discriminate among US carriers in settlement rate negotiations—even if the foreign carrier is subject to competition in its home market—the FCC retained the safeguards it imposed in its *Flexibility Order*.[114]

---

[107] *Foreign Participation Order, supra* n. 83, para. 237.
[108] *Ibid.*, (citation omitted).
[109] *Ibid.*, para. 236 (citation omitted).
[110] See discussion *supra* p. 147 and n. 20.
[111] *Ibid.*, para. 132.
[112] *Ibid.*
[113] *Ibid.*, para. 307.
[114] *Ibid.*, para. 308; *see ibid.*, paras. 302–12. For a detailed analysis of these safeguards, see discussion *supra* pp. 153–6.

III. SUMMARY AND ANALYSIS

The cases examined in the preceding section represent perhaps the nadir of FCC international telecoms policy decision-making. The passage of the Telecommunications Act of 1996 (1996 Act) and the conclusion of the WTO Telecoms Accord presented the FCC with a truly unique and once-in-a-lifetime opportunity to lay, virtually *tabula rasa*, the foundations for an underlying market structure conducive to tangible, competitive facilities-based rivalry and only *de minimis* prophylactic regulation. Yet, because the FCC tragically succumbed to both industry pressure and political narcissism, the FCC squandered this unique opportunity because it attempted improperly to play Metternich-style "power politics" rather than attempting properly to seize this singular opportunity to maximise consumer welfare *a la* Grotius [**better explain this**]. Critiques of the most glaring examples are outlined below.

A. Problem No. 1: "Mercantilism Rising"—that is, It Is Arguably More Difficult To Enter US Markets Post-WTO than It Was Under *ECO*

As highlighted in Chapter 6, the FCC stated specifically in its *ECO Order* that it would not make the presence of cost-based accounting rates a *per se* precondition of entry. Rather, the FCC would permit foreign entry to occur if it found either: (a) that US carriers could avail themselves of "effective competitive opportunities" in the foreign destination market; and (b) *even in the absence of such effective competitive opportunities*, if it found that certain countervailing "public interest factors" were present.[115] In the FCC's *Foreign Participation Order*, however, the FCC decided to apply a *completely opposite standard for foreign entry into US markets*.[116] That is to say, in its *Foreign Participation Order*, the FCC stated specifically that it would not undertake any analysis of the basic economic conditions and structure of foreign markets of WTO Member countries (and, in particular, the effectiveness of regulation or other protections on the foreign end), but that it would simply charge a substantial entry fee—that is, the FCC's infamous "benchmark condition"—to any WTO Member country that wants to participate in US markets.[117]

[115] See, e.g., *Sprint Declaratory Ruling and Order*, full reference required here.
[116] *Foreign Participation Order, supra* n. 83.
[117] *Ibid.*, para. 230. As noted in Chapter 5 *supra*, those non-WTO Member countries that want to enter U.S. telecommunications markets (e.g., China and Russia) will be subject to the worst of both regulatory worlds—an *ECO* analysis and the mandatory acceptance of the Benchmarks condition. But *cf. ibid.*, paras. 125–26 ("Since 1995, our application of the ECO test has provided incentives for foreign governments to allow U.S. participation in their markets, and it played a part in the WTO negotiations that resulted in the Basic Telecom Agreement. We believe that continuing to apply the ECO test to non-WTO Member countries may encourage some of those countries to take unilateral or bilateral steps toward opening their markets to competition and may provide incentives for them to join the WTO.").

Yet, because the FCC stated specifically that it would not undertake any analysis of the basic economic conditions and the structure of foreign markets of WTO Member countries (and, in particular, the effectiveness of regulation or other projections on the other end), then any time the FCC classifies a firm as a "dominant" carrier (and with such classification, the additional regulatory constraints associated with this status) *a fortiori* simply has no analytical foundation.[118] That is, without performing an economic analysis to determine whether a firm has the ability to raise prices anti-competitively or restrict output, the FCC has essentially reduced the concept of "dominance" to nothing more than "I don't like you."[119] Accordingly, although it may *prima facie* appear that entry into US markets is easier post-WTO, the cases above indicate that due to the myriad of complex (and not too subtly hidden) new regulatory hurdles that foreign firms must nonetheless overcome, there is a strong argument that these additional regulatory compliance costs actually make the process far more difficult than before. Given the above, therefore, perhaps the more appropriate and accurate nomenclature to describe the FCC's attempt to make its rules consistent with the United States' WTO obligations should be the ("We don't want any") *Foreign Participation Order*.

B. Problem No. 2: Despite Rhetoric, FCC *Orders* Reveal that the United States Apparently Has Little Desire To Move to a Full-Circuit World and Eliminate the International Settlement-of-Accounts Regime

The cases discussed in the preceding section are replete with prolific pronouncements from the FCC about how the world is moving away from monopolies to "competitive" markets—in particular, IMTS country-route markets characterised by: (a) numerous suppliers (with each carrier using their own full-circuits), (b) standard cost-based interconnection rates, and (c) a transparent and independent regulator on both the originating and terminating end of the routes and, with this purported competition, the elimination of (if not only a *de minimis* requirement for) both the international settlement-of-accounts regime and the FCC's International Settlements Policy (ISP) (replete with proportionate return requirements). While this vision is certainly a worthy social goal, once practitioners read past the introductory sections of these extremely lengthy *Orders* where these rhetorical "sound-bites" are contained, it unfortunately appears that the substance of the FCC's policies are never intended to reach this purported outcome.

In particular, the cases discussed above appear to indicate that despite its "pro-competition" rhetoric, the FCC nonetheless intends to continue to unilat-

---

[118] But *cf.* Motion of AT&T Corp. to be Reclassified as a Non-Dominant Carrier, *Order*, 11 F.C.C.R. 3271, 1 Comm. Reg. (P & F) 63 (1995).

[119] See *supra* n. 62 Spiwak, "Antitrust, the 'Public Interest' and Competition Policy: The Search for Meaningful Definitions in a Sea of Analytical Rhetoric" *Antitrust Report* (Matthew Bender, December 1997), at 25 n.15.

erally impose settlement rate "benchmarks" and maintain its ISP in a full-circuit world. The problem with this policy approach, however, is that it is wholly inapposite to the very reasons the international community agreed to the WTO Telecoms Treaty in the first place—that is, once Member countries fully implement all of the regulatory principles contained in the Reference Paper, the international settlement-of-accounts regime is ostensibly supposed to be eliminated. Likewise, any unilateral regulation by the FCC to impose benchmarks to constrain the settlement-of-accounts regime and to perpetuate its ISP should, *a fortiori*, essentially be unwarranted under such a market structure as well.

To get around this metaphysical inconvenience, the *Orders* discussed above reveal that the FCC's policy response is simply to make the requisite conditions precedent for "flexibility" as difficult as possible to satisfy. For example, under the FCC's "No Special Concessions" rule, while joint ownership of end-to-end facilities is prohibited, it is apparently perfectly acceptable under current FCC rules to have a single firm own the entire full circuit using two affiliates—one US, the other foreign—each affiliate owning 100 per cent of its respective "half" of the circuit. Under this arrangement, however, the two affiliates are nonetheless forced to correspond with each other using the traditional international settlement-of-accounts regime and, *a fortiori*, the FCC's benchmarks. Of course, while the parent carrier is certainly welcome to petition the FCC for "flexibility" on that route, the FCC nonetheless imposes benchmarks on a portion of "flexible" traffic; it therefore appears that the FCC *never intends to let firms out of the very regime it is allegedly trying so hard to eliminate.*

To readers unfamiliar with the inner politics of the IMTS business, it does indeed seem a bit incredulous that the FCC would actually seek to circumvent the very policy outcome it has publicly promised to achieve. There are, however, several explanations for this paradoxical behaviour. First, contrary to their public admonitions, the large, "traditional" US carriers actually tend to like the ISP and would therefore like to see it retained. Why? Because under oligopolistic market conditions, carriers' profits rise with a co-ordinated increase in price/cost margins across all competitors that is, a publicly known, date-certain reduction in termination prices provides a co-ordinated increase in price/cost margins across the industry.[120] Moreover, because it is highly unlikely in the short-term that there will be either a radical redistribution of market share among the big firms or a mysterious, radical jump in minutes, the ISP provides a very convenient mechanism for corporate finance officers to forecast somewhat accurately their firm's expected revenue stream.

It must also be noted, however, that it is not appropriate to lay the entire blame for industry pressure to perpetuate the ISP upon the collective feet of the big US IMTS carriers, because proportionate return favours carriers with small market share, and therefore new entrants are also likely to seek to perpetuate

---

[120] See Douglas A. Galbi, "Cross-Border Rent Shifting in International Telecommunications" (1998) 10 *Information Economics & Pol'y* 515, 527–531 at para. 20–22.

such a regime.[121] Finally, because it is a well-known (but nonetheless unfortunate) fact that regulators are only truly happy when they have something to regulate, if those firms subject to the regulator's jurisdiction are actually begging to be thrown voluntarily into the proverbial "briar patch," then what self-respecting regulator could really refuse such a generous offer?[122]

C. Problem No. 3: Bringing Settlement Rates in Line with "Costs" Does Not *a fortiori* Mean that Either: (a) Prices Will Decline; or (b)Telecom Providers' Revenues Will Increase.

Under the cases outlined *supra*, it appears that the following logic underlies the FCC's actions.

(1) Settlement rates are "above costs";
(2) Regulation can bring settlement rates in line with "costs";
(3) Once settlement rates are in line with costs, collection rates to end-users will fall;
(4) A reduction in end-user rates will spur an increase in demand;
(5) An increase in demand will cause providers' net revenue to rise;
(6) The FCC's policies are a good idea because both carriers and consumers will be better off in the long run.

Wrong. First, even if the overall logic of this paradigm were true, because the FCC has deliberately failed to articulate exactly what "costs" it is talking about, it is metaphysically impossible to bring anything into line that is ephemeral at best.[123] Instead, the concept of economic costs appears to be tragically reduced to yet another regulatory term of convenience to facilitate predetermined social outcomes.[124]

---

[121] Douglas A. Galbi, "Cross-Border Rent Shifting in International Telecommunications" (1998) 10 *Information Economics & Pol'y* 515, 527–531 at para. 20–22.

[122] See Spiwak, "The Search for Meaningful Definitions", *supra* n. 119, at 1–12; Frank H. Easterbrook, "The Supreme Court, 1983 Term: Foreword: The Court and the Economic System", (1984) 98 *Harv. L. Rev.* 4, 15–16 ("People demand laws just as they demand automobiles, and some people demand more effectively than others. Laws that benefit the people in common are hard to enact because no one can obtain very much of the benefit of lobbying for or preserving such laws." As such, because "cohesive groups can get more for themselves by restricting competition and appropriating rents than by seeking rules that enhance the welfare of all, . . . we should expect regulatory programs and other statutes to benefit the regulated group . . . ." *Ibid.*, at 16. Accordingly, these groups "need not 'capture' the programs, because they owned them all along. The burgeoning evidence showing that regulatory programs increase prices for consumers and profits for producers supports this understanding." (emphasis added and citations omitted)); see also George J. Stigler, "The Theory of Economic Regulation", (1971), 2 *Bell J. Econ. & Mgmt. Sci.* 3. It would seem, therefore, that U.S. carriers are now protected by "market-friendly" regulation.

[123] See, e.g., *City of Holyoke Gas & Electric Dept.* v. *FERC*, 954 F.2d 740, 743 (D.C. Cir. 1992) ("Since it is already doing the relevant calculation, it is a small matter to abide by the injunction of the arithmetic teacher: Show your work! For the Commission to do less deprives the [consumer] of a rational explanation of its decision.").

[124] See, e.g., Adri den Broeder, "KPN Must Eliminate Corporate Discounts Says Regulator",

Moreover, the FCC should take care concerning what it wishes. As discussed below, the FCC has taken great pains to hide both the scope and scale of the economic costs relating to its current flawed and controversial universal service program. Much to everyone's surprise, however, the FCC recently won one battle relating to universal service in court, where it convinced the US Eighth Circuit Court of Appeals that access charges (the domestic version of settlement rates) imposed on long-distance providers that include LECs' universal service costs are not "above-cost" "*since universal service contributions are a real cost of doing business.*"[125] Yet, if the logic of the Eighth Circuit is followed, then current settlement rates are similarly not "above-cost," since international settlement rates are also simply "a real cost of doing business."

More significant, however, is the FCC's misunderstanding about the relationship between per-minute prices for international calls and the international settlement-of-accounts regime. Foreign carriers and regulators (i.e., parties reaping the benefits from the above-cost settlement rates) are unsurprisingly reluctant to reduce settlement rates. Yet, even though economic theory indicates that prices are related to cost, for US carriers the settlement rate does *not* measure the settlement cost of providing a minute of IMTS service. With multiple carriers and proportionate returns, the cost relevant to the setting of prices is not only a function of the settlement rate but of the input-output ratio (the ratio of inbound to outbound IMTS traffic) and the carrier's market share.[126] Only for a monopolist is the settlement rate equal to the marginal settlement cost of the carrier. Given the absence of monopoly in the United States, therefore, there is no reason to expect that the IMTS prices of US carriers should be directly related to the settlement rate. In other countries, however, where monopoly is prevalent, the marginal settlement cost *is* the settlement rate, and, as such, any reduction in the settlement rate will unambiguously reduce the marginal settlement cost of the carrier, other things constant.[127] Thus, rather than develop constructive solutions for the problem, the debate over the relationship between

TotalTele.Com (Oct. 2, 1998) <http://www.totaltele.com/news/view.asp?articleID=19554&Pub=TT> ("Dutch telecommunications regulator OPTA said telecommunications company Royal KPN NV must eliminate discounts for corporate telephone-service clients by January 1, and base its charges on costs.").

[125] *Southwestern Bell Telephone* v. *FCC*, 153 F.3d 523, 554 (8th Cir. 1998) (emphasis added).

[126] Specifically, the marginal settlement cost is $S([1 - IO((1 - w)]$ where S is the settlement rate, IO is the input-output ratio, and w is the market share of the carrier. Note that for a monopolist, (where w = 1), the marginal settlement cost is equal to the settlement rate. Given proportionate returns, the cost function of the U.S. carrier to a particular country is $S(q - S(F(q/Q))$ where q is the carrier's outbound minutes, F is the industry inbound minutes, and Q is the industry outbound minutes so that q/Q is the market share of the carrier. We are grateful to George Ford PhD, Adjunct Fellow of the Phoenix Center, for this economic analysis.

[127] The common argument proffered by foreign carriers and regulators against the reduction of settlement rates that U.S. carrier's IMTS prices bear no relationship to the settlement rate (since prices are not related to the settlement rates) and therefore, reductions in the settlement rates offer no benefit is equally specious. Under basic economic theory, the reduction of a price or rate substantially above marginal cost is unambiguously welfare *improving*.

prices and cost tragically continues to be fuelled by the FCC's lack of understanding of what the true settlement costs are.

D. Problem No. 4: In the FCC's View, What Is Good for the Goose Apparently Does Not Necessarily Have To Be Good for the Gander—Even When the Goose Refuses To Lay Any Eggs

To get around the jurisdictional issues associated with its *Benchmark* conditions, the FCC stated that its settlement rate benchmarks applied only to the charges paid by US carriers to their foreign correspondents, and not to the foreign correspondents themselves. At the end of the day, however, the big question of what will the United States do if a foreign carrier simply refuses to co-operate with the FCC's unilateral actions remains unresolved. Indeed, if a foreign carrier refuses to negotiate a settlement rate at or below the FCC's benchmarks within the exact time specified by the FCC, is a US carrier really going to ask the FCC to declare their own rates unlawful? Hardly.

History has taught that if countries are going to engage successfully in *realpolitic* diplomatic manoeuvres, words must be backed with demonstrable and swift action. In the US case, however, while there certainly is no shortage of fiery neo-mercantile rhetoric to create (if not exacerbate an existing) substantial *disincentive* for both foreign governments and carriers to engage in good faith negotiations with US carriers to enter their home markets (which, paradoxically, is supposed to be the whole goal of such an approach in the first place),[128] the FCC's rhetoric is backed up with nothing more than threats to punish rogue international carriers either by: (1) public identification; (2) working with (i.e., complaining to) the offending carrier's government; or (3) allowing US international carriers to petition the FCC to consider stronger steps. As such, both US consumers and business should really not be surprised when the economic costs of neo-mercantilism outweigh the very economic benefits the FCC promised that they would receive.

As mentioned above in Chapter 1, the economic costs of mercantilism can be substantial. These include as a general matter the *creation*—rather than the *elimination*—of significant barriers to entry for both new firms into US domestic telecommunications markets and US firms into foreign markets; and, with such barriers, increased investment "uncertainty" for international telecommunications development projects. When this occurs, consumers are forced to pay higher prices to reflect both this increased cost of capital and the firm's incentive to *raise* its prices to ensure that it can recover its costs in the shortest time possible.

Accordingly, from a policy and economic point of view, any proposal that advocates that the FCC should set prices *sua sponte* in the first instance—espe-

---

[128] *Ibid.*, at 19.

cially a unilateral attempt to set international settlement rates that were negotiated privately between parties, one of which the FCC clearly does not have jurisdiction over—has odious implications. Permitting government to unilaterally set prices over products and services—especially without first determining the actual underlying costs of these products and services—is a proven way to eliminate innovation and harm competition.[129] As mentioned above, this issue is especially acute in the international context because US public policy should not remove any incentive for competitive reform in other countries. Similarly, because US consumer demand for IMTS service continues to grow exponentially, mandating specific prices does not improve market performance either; rather, it simply guarantees US carriers a substantial revenue stream (they make up the lost revenues by increased volume) and thus removes any incentive for them to compete.[130] And, of course, as mentioned repeatedly above, so long as the FCC wants to play the "trade" game as well as the "regulation game," any unilateral attempt to prescribe prices over people not subject to the United States' jurisdiction will only create, and more likely exacerbate an existing, recalcitrance by foreign carriers to do business with US carriers, which was the whole goal of this exercise in the first place.[131]

---

[129] See, e.g., *Competitive Telecomm. Ass'n v. FCC*, 87 F.3d 522, 529–30 (D.C. Cir. 1996) ("The test of a competitive market is whether consumers are offered the lowest possible prices or more or better services. . . . As [such], the goal of the agency 'is to promote competition in the interchange marketplace, not to protect competitors.'" *Ibid.*, at 530 (citations omitted)); see also *Central Iowa Power Corp.* v. *FERC*, 606 F.2d 1156, 1163 (D.C. Cir. 1979) (holding simply because a tariff may be unduly discriminatory or preferential does not automatically mean that a tariff may be, in fact, anticompetitive).

[130] Considering the fact that the FCC's former Chairman stated publicly that the FCC would not be in the business of setting rates on the domestic side, it does seem a bit hypocritical for the FCC to rationally believe that it could otherwise lawfully set prices in the international context. See "Competition: Walking the Walk and Talking the Talk", Statement of FCC Chairman Reed Hundt before Alex. Brown & Co.'s "Media & Communications '96 Conference" Waldorf-Astoria Hotel, NY, 1996 WL 529213 (Sept. 17, 1996) (What "our interconnection order does not do is set any specific prices new entrants will pay for leasing elements of the existing network, like unbundled loops and switching capacity. These will be set in state arbitrations or through negotiations between the parties.").

[131] See *supra* n. 60; see also Dataquest, "Gunship Diplomacy: The FCC's International Settlement Rate Policies", *Public Telephony Services North America Market Analysis* 9 Feb. 1998 available at <http://www.gartner11.gartnerweb.com/dq/static/dq.html> ("[W]hile the traditional accounting rate system must be reformed, . . . the adversarial structure designed by the FCC is bound to fail in the long term. The FCC does not appear to want to work co-operatively in international forums but, instead, mandates onerous rates, terms, and conditions concerning international settlement rates. The FCC's rigid policies and benchmark rates to improve the international accounting rate system have set off an international firestorm, and this could come back to haunt the FCC as it strives to effect a competitive international marketplace.").

8

US Policies Post-WTO Part 2—The Naked Politicisation of the American Legal System

I N THE PRECEDING chapter, we examined in detail the FCC's *Benchmarks Order* in which the FCC unilaterally imposed maximum benchmarks on the amount US carriers may pay their foreign correspondents to hand off US-originated International Message Telecommunications Service (IMTS) traffic. As that chapter demonstrated, the FCC's actions raised serious questions from both a legal and overall policy perspective.

In this chapter, we examine the United States Court of Appeals for the District of Columbia's decision in *Cable & Wireless* v. *FCC* (*C&W*) which—to the unbridled giddiness of the FCC and to the dismay of various parties representing over 100 foreign governments, regulators, and telecommunications companies[1] —upheld the FCC's *Benchmarks Order* in its "entirety."[2] In doing so, the D.C. Circuit has not only placed major areas of previously settled US case law in flux, but—even assuming *arguendo* the court ruled correctly—also has approved nakedly the FCC's role of "cartel manager" and destroyed what little chance there was to avoid an all-out international telecommunications trade war.

A. The Court's Decision

In upholding the FCC's *Benchmarks Order*, the *C&W* court's arguments essentially fell into two broad categories: In the first category, the court concluded that the FCC reasonably exercised its rate-making authority under the Communications Act.[3] In support of this decision, the court held that: (a) the FCC had sufficient jurisdiction under the US Communications Act of 1934 to impose settlement rate benchmarks; (b) the FCC had adequately demonstrated

---

[1] *Statement of FCC Chairman William E. Kennard on Today's Court Decision Upholding the FCC's Benchmarks Order*, 12 Jan. 1999 <http://www.fcc.gov/Speeches/Kennard/Statements/stwek902.html>; *cf.* Heather Fleming, "C&W Loses Battle for Higher U.S. Interconnect Rates", *Bloomberg News*, 13 Jan. 1999, available at <http://www.totaltele.com>.

[2] *Cable & Wireless P.L.C. v. FCC*, 166 F.3d 1224, 1226 (D.C. Cir. 1999).

[3] *Ibid.*

its use of the Tariff Components Rate methodology; and (c) the FCC's actions were a legitimate exercise of its authority under the *Mobile-Sierra* doctrine. As demonstrated below, however, the court was only able to reach this conclusion by ignoring well-settled ratemaking jurisprudence.

In the second category, the court apparently concluded that if the political stakes are high enough, mercantile trade concerns can trump legal precedent, economic theory, and the factual record itself. To wit, the court both upheld the FCC's argument that benchmarks were necessary to protect US firms against ephemeral price squeeze behaviour by foreign firms and found that—international comity aside—the FCC's actions *in toto* did not violate international law. Indeed, in finding that the FCC's actions "to strengthen the bargaining position of domestic telecommunications companies in negotiations with their foreign counterparts" were a legitimate exercise of the FCC's "public interest" authority, the court violated the heretofore golden rule that the "Commission is not at liberty . . . to subordinate the public interest to the interest of 'equalising competition among competitors.' "[4] Each category is discussed more fully below.

B. The Demise of US Ratemaking Law

1. *Jurisdictional Issues*

The court held that there were essentially three reasons why the FCC could assert jurisdiction to impose settlement rate benchmarks. First, the court held that the FCC was not asserting jurisdiction over foreign carriers or foreign telecommunications in violation of the US Communications Act of 1934.[5] Rather, the FCC was asserting jurisdiction only over the settlement rates that US carriers must pay their foreign corespondents for termination of US-originated traffic. While the court was quick to point out that both it and the FCC were engaging in legal hair-splitting—that is, "that regulating what domestic carriers may pay and regulating what foreign carriers may charge appear to be opposite sides of the same coin"[6]—the court reasoned that:

> "by focusing only on the *Order*'s effects on foreign carriers, petitioners overlook the crucial economic reality that makes the Commission's position that it is only regulating domestic carriers reasonable: Because domestic carriers operate in a competitive market, they face a serious dilemma when they bargain with monopolist foreign carriers. As a group, US carriers would be best off if each decided not to accept settlement rates higher than FCC benchmarks. But if one US carrier maintained this position to

---

[4] *SBC Comm. Inc.* v. *FCC*, 56 F.3d 1484, 1491 (D.C. Cir. 1995) (citing *Hawaiian Tel. Co.* v. *FCC*, 498 F.2d 771, 776 (D.C. Cir. 1974) (finding that it was "all too embarrassingly apparent that the Commission has been thinking about competition, not in terms primarily as to its benefit to the public, but specifically with the objective of equalising competition among competitors")); *see also Western Union Tel. Co.* v. *FCC*, 665 F.2d 1112, 1122 (D.C. Cir. 1981).

[5] *Cable & Wireless*, 166 F.3d 1229

[6] *Ibid.*

the point of impasse in negotiations with a foreign carrier, a competing US carrier would make the foreign carrier a higher offer".[7]

The preceding analysis raises two significant concerns. First, the language cited above indicates that the court either did not understand accurately (or petitioners' counsel did not explain sufficiently), the basic facts of the case. For example, the court assumes that the United States is the only country in the world with a significant outpayment deficit. Contrary to popular belief, however, this assumption simply is *not* true. Indeed, this "victim" mentality is a bit disingenuous considering the facts that, for example, Japan-based carriers have large deficits with Taiwan, the Philippines, South Korea, Singapore, and other major Asian countries. Similarly, France Télécom has large outflows to Africa, the Middle East, and even Latin America. Moreover, the same holds true for British Telecom, Deutsche Telekom, Telecom Italia, and other large overseas telephone companies.[8] Similarly, the court again appears to assume that the United States is the only "competitive" market. Again, this is not so. Numerous other countries such as the United Kingdom, New Zealand, Sweden, and Denmark would probably both beg to differ and take great umbrage with the court's blanket conclusion. Moreover, if the court wants to make blanket conclusions, then it should look at the local termination markets in the United States, which, unfortunately, are still characterised by dominant providers and are likely to remain so for the foreseeable future.[9]

The second concern is perhaps more egregious: The court's language cited above blatantly condones and indeed encourages the FCC's efforts to help US firms engage in a group boycott against foreign firms. Clearly, this stretches any reasonable interpretation of either the *Noerr-Pennington*[10] or "State Action" doctrines.[11]

[7] *Ibid.*

[8] See "International Communications Survey Memorandum Re: Addressing the 'Accounting Rates Challenge' ", *Telecomm. Pol'y Rev.*, 5 Jan. 1997.

[9] See, e.g., George S. Ford, "Opportunities for Local Exchange Competition Are Greatly Exaggerated", *Electric Light & Power*, Apr. 1998, at 20–21; see also Reconcentration of Telecommunications Markets After the 1996 Act: Implications for Long-Term Market Performance (2nd Edition), Phoenix Center Policy Paper Series, Policy Paper No. 2 (July, 1998) at 36. <http://www.phoenix- center.org/pcpp/pcpp2.doc> (noting that Ray Smith, Chairman of Bell Atlantic, proclaimed proudly on CNN the very night the FCC approved the merger between Bell Atlantic and NYNEX that the merged company "accounts for 50 per cent of all the European international traffic" originating and terminating in the United States); "The Busiest Bell", *Bus. Wk.*, 11 Jan. 1999, at 80 (naming Ed Whitacre of SBC among its top-10 executives of the year, citing Whitacre's SBC-Ameritech deal, which, once the deal closes, "Whitacre will head a telecom giant with some 57 million local phone lines—*almost a third of all phone lines in the country*." (emphasis added). According to the article, "It's all part of Whitacre's plan to take on AT&T and MCI Worldcom. 'We can sit here and get picked on,' he says, 'or get bigger and have more clout.'").

[10] The Noerr-Pennington Doctrine is a defence under U.S. antitrust law which takes its name from two court cases: *Eastern R.R. Conference* v. *Noerr Motor Freight*, 365 U.S. 127 (1961) and *United Mine Workers* v. *Pennington*, 381 U.S. 657 (1965). Basically, this doctrine attempts to reconcile U.S. antitrust law and the First Amendment to the U.S. Constitution. In its simplest form, it precludes grounding antitrust liability for private parties' efforts to petition the government or regulatory agencies for relief.

[11] The "state action" is the converse of *Noerr-Pennington* doctrine, at it provibides for a defence

Moreover, if the court applies its factual assumptions to its reasoning, then the court actually concedes its point that US firms are always at the mercy of foreign monopolists. Quite to the contrary, given the huge amount of revenue US traffic represents, when US firms act as a cartel, they actually have significant monopsony power—or more accurately, economic *bargaining* power—with foreign firms and should be (and are) able to exercise this power to their advantage.[12] If readers recall from Chapter 6, this is precisely what happened in the "Telintar Trade War."[13]

The court next reasoned that even if the FCC was taking jurisdiction over foreign entities, this action was essentially benign because the FCC lacked an effective enforcement mechanism. Indeed, reasoned the court,

> "Far from threatening foreign carriers with enforcement actions, the *Order* at most states that the FCC will contact 'responsible [foreign] government authorities' to 'seek their support in lowering settlement rates.' Given the structure of the global telecommunications industry and its resulting incentives, we find reasonable the Commission's view that the *Order* regulates domestic carriers, not foreign carriers."[14]

As explained in more detail in the preceding chapter, however, the lack of an effective enforcement mechanism is one of the major problems with the FCC's policies, primarily because a US carrier is hardly going to ask the FCC to declare its own rates unlawful if a foreign carrier refuses to negotiate a settlement rate at or below the FCC's benchmarks within the exact time specified by the FCC. Indeed, the whole reason why the international telecommunications community entered into treaties such as the International Telecommunication Union (ITU) in the first instance was to mitigate the risk that traffic would be interrupted if the "negotiations" referenced by the court prove unsuccessful. As such, by flagrantly violating its international commitments, the only thing the FCC's mercantile rhetoric has achieved is the creation (if not the exacerbation) of a substantial *disincentive* for both foreign governments and carriers to engage in good faith negotiations with US carriers to enter their home markets (which, paradoxically, is supposed to be the whole goal of such an approach in the first place). As such, both US consumers and business should really not be surprised when the economic costs of neo-mercantilism outweigh the very economic benefits the FCC promised that they would receive.

---

under U.S. antitrust laws for private actions supposedly ordered directly by a state law or regulation. See *Parker* v. *Brown*, 317 U.S. 341 (1943).

[12] See, e.g, David Kaut, *US-Australian War of Words Highlights Global Dispute Over Internet Compensation* (Bureau of National Affairs, 30 May 2000) (reporting that when Australia complained in international fora about "the bullying tactics of major US carriers" regarding international internet peering traffic payments and charges into and out of the US, FCC International Bureau Chief Don Abelson responded with a vicious and ad hominem attack, claiming (erroneously) that Australia was attempting to subject Internet traffic to the telephone accounting rate regime and this was nothing but an attempt by "monopolies" to thwart competition and "regulate" the internet.

[13] *See* Chapter 6 *supra*.

[14] *Cable & Wireless*, 166 F.3d at 1230 (citation omitted, alteration in original).

Finally, the court gave the "so what" defence to the FCC's actions. In the court's own words, while the "practical effect" of the FCC's *Order* will be to reduce settlement rates charged by foreign carriers, "the Commission does not exceed its authority simply because a regulatory action has extraterritorial consequences."[15] Thus, reasoned the court, the FCC's actions in the *Benchmarks Order* are identical to the situations where

> "the Environmental Protection Agency regulates the automobile industry when it requires states and localities to comply with national ambient air quality standards, or [when] the Department of Commerce regulates foreign manufacturers when it collects tariffs on foreign-made goods."[16]

This analogy simply is not accurate—rather, it is inapposite. First, a trade tariff is nothing more than a naked barrier to entry, usually imposed by xenophobic and protectionist policymakers to insulate domestic firms from (and thus deny domestic consumers the benefits of) the lower prices and additional choices resulting from cheaper goods produced off-shore (hence the derogatory term for this conduct—*dumping*).[17] Because lower prices and more choices are supposed to be *good* for consumers, however, such mercantile actions are anticompetitive and harm consumer welfare.[18] Similarly, the FCC's actions in the *Benchmarks Order* are not akin to imposing national environmental standards because while the US Constitution clearly provides the US government with preemption authority over states and localities for such environmental issues,[19] as explained in more detail *infra*, the US government does *not* have the right under

---

[15] *Ibid.*, (citations omitted).

[16] *Ibid.*

[17] See Paul Magnusson, "Getting a Grip on Trade Sanctions", *Bus. Wk.*, 17 Nov. 1997, at 115. Magnusson reports that "[i]n the past four years, President Clinton has signed 62 laws and executive actions targeting 35 countries." These numbers account "for more than half the sanctions imposed [by the United States] in the past 80 years." *Ibid.*, (emphasis added). Moreover, Magnusson reported that "the direct cost to U.S. exporters in lost sales in 1995 alone was as high as $20 billion [, a]n estimated 250,000 [U.S.] jobs also disappeared, and *no one can measure the damage to relations with angry allies.*" *Ibid.*, (emphasis added).

[18] See, e.g., James C. Miller, III, "Reindustrialization Through the Free Market", (1984) 53 *Antitrust L.J.* 121. Miller argues that when government takes "an activist," collaborative approach to work with industry in order to promote "competition," it is virtually impossible to avoid the inevitable conclusion that the outcome of such policies "could do anything but restrict output, raise prices and retard innovation." *Ibid.*, at 125. Because such an approach ignores "the distinct interests of over 200 million American consumers in lower prices and higher product quality," most consumers should "start counting their silverware." *Ibid.*, at 124–25. As such, argues Miller, "*Why kick Santa Claus in the fact?* If other countries foolishly subsidise U.S. consumers . . . why should we object? It could only be a distortion of our economy if they had any chance to achieve monopoly power to recoup the subsidies we would now be enjoying." *Ibid.*, at 126 (footnote omitted, emphasis added).

[19] See, e.g., *California* v. *FERC*, 495 U.S. 490 (1990); see also *AT&T Corp.* v. *Iowa Utils.*, 525 U.S. 721, 119 S.Ct. 721, 732 (1999), where the US Supreme Court upheld the FCC's jurisdiction to prescribe rate methodology for states, finding that: "[t]he FCC's prescription, through rulemaking, of a requisite pricing methodology no more prevents the States from establishing rates than do the statutory "Pricing standards" set forth in § 252(d). It is the States that will apply those standards and implement that methodology, determining the concrete result in particular circumstances. That is enough to constitute the establishment of rates", *ibid.*

either express international treaty or the legal concept of comity to contemptuously trump *another co-sovereign entity* by unilaterally prescribing international settlement rates.

In contrast, the FCC's Benchmarks policy is a situation where the US international telecommunications cartel essentially petitioned the US government to reduce a common input, even when the FCC's own International Settlements Policy (with its proportionate return requirements eliminating the possibility of whipsaw effects) is expressly designed to keep the cartel "fat and happy" and deter foreign entry—a point that the *C&W* court seems to ignore deliberately. Accordingly, contrary to the court's analogy, the instant situation is more akin to the hypothetical situation where the US shippers pressure the US Maritime Commission to formulate a single universal fee (based on their internal proprietary data provided by the largest US carrier), and then have the US government "force" them to only pay that universal fee whenever US-flagged ships seek to enter foreign ports—regardless of the underlying cost structure of the individual harbours.

2. Tariff Components Price Methodology

The court also upheld the FCC's use of the tariff components price methodology (TCP). In doing so, the *C&W* court specifically rejected petitioners' arguments that:

> "the TCP methodology fails to produce cost-based settlement rates because it does not use data on the actual cost of foreign termination services, petitioners claim that the calculated rates under-compensate foreign carriers."[20]

According to the court, the record overwhelmingly indicated that "the Commission meticulously documented and carefully considered a wide range of public comments concerning the TCP methodology" and, moreover, that the "final *Order* contains several passages explaining why the method more than fully compensates foreign carriers."[21]

What particularly troubled the court, however, is the fact that, in the court's view:

> "Throughout the rulemaking process . . . petitioners [that is, foreign carriers] withheld the very cost data that would have enabled the FCC to establish precise, cost-based rates"

despite "repeated[]" invitations from the FCC "to suggest alternative methods for calculating settlement rates."[22] Thus, reasoned the court:

> "Since petitioners refused to let the Commission see their cost data, and since the Commission thoroughly explained why 'the TCP methodology provides a reasonable

---

[20] *Cable & Wireless*, 166 F.3d at 1232.
[21] *Ibid.*, (citations omitted).
[22] *Ibid.*, at 1233.

basis for establishing settlement rate benchmarks in the absence of carrier-specific cost data,' we have no firm basis for accepting petitioners' claim that the benchmark rates are not fully compensatory."[23]

Similarly, the court rejected the notion that the FCC used non-record data—in particular, US outgoing call distribution data provided by AT&T on a confidential basis to calculate country-by-country prices for national extension services (one of the three TCP components)—even though: (1) this data was made available for inspection for only a two-week period; (2) the FCC refused to lengthen the comment period on the grounds that the data was concise and easy to understand; and (3) that at least one party submitted comments criticising the FCC's reliance on the data.[24] According to the court:

> "foreign carriers had in their hands all the incoming call distribution data they needed to contest the accuracy of the Commission's calculated price for national extension services. In other words, even if the Commission's handling of the AT&T data was less than ideal, it did not impair the ability of foreign carriers to challenge the national extension component of the benchmark rates."[25]

So what really happened here? Not to anyone's surprise, the FCC cleverly and expectedly took jurisdiction over just US carriers (despite its "extraterritorial" effects), and the court upheld the FCC's actions. As discussed in greater detail *infra* (and as history is replete with examples of), however, just because the FCC can regulate something still does not necessarily mean that it is actually a good idea. Yet, looking beyond this question for the moment, the *C&W* decision raises two significant questions that have yet to be answered.

First, accepting the court's logic for the moment *arguendo*, it is unclear how foreign firms were ever to escape the FCC's jurisdictional "Catch–22"—that is, the *Benchmarks Order* states (and *C&W* upholds) that if foreign carriers fail to come forward with proprietary evidence about their costs, then the FCC can assume those costs for them (even though it admittedly does not know what those costs are). Yet, if the foreign carriers decide to come forward to produce their costs (which, under the clear language of the FCC's invitation they did not have to do because this proceeding only applied to US carriers), then by doing so they would effectively waive their jurisdiction in the first instance.

Second, even though the court correctly stated that the FCC may prescribe a ratemaking methodology[26] and chastised foreign carriers for failing to produce country-specific data, the court fails to answer why it is also acceptable to use average costs based on teledensity. It is black-letter law that administrative agencies must account for different market conditions when analysing rates,[27] and teledensity—which measures only the amount of telephone *penetration*—

---

[23] *Ibid.*, (citations omitted).
[24] *Ibid.*, at 1232–24
[25] *Ibid.*
[26] See *AT&T Corp.* v. *Iowa Utils. Bd.*, *supra* n. 19.
[27] See, e.g., *City of Batavia* v. *FERC*, 672 F.2d 64, 90 (D.C. Cir. 1982).

cannot by definition reveal what the underlying costs are for serving individual countries.

More important, however, is the fact that the court failed to recognise that the use of teledensity actually harms—rather than promotes—consumer welfare (albeit the consumers of developing countries). That is to say, under the FCC's *Benchmarks Order*, the FCC requires countries to negotiate lower settlement rates over a five-year period of time, depending on teledensity—that is, the lower the teledensity, the longer a foreign firm may charge higher settlement rates. Accordingly, rather than appropriately *encouraging* infrastructure development in those very countries that need it the most, the FCC's *Benchmarks Order* instead provides monopoly incumbents (which are State owned or controlled) from developing countries with the perverse incentive to *delay*—rather than accelerate—new infrastructure development in order to maximise revenues.

3. The Evisceration of the Mobile-Sierra Doctrine

There are, moreover, many significant legal issues associated with these policies of which practitioners may not be aware. For example, settlement rates are set by privately negotiated agreements among US carriers and their foreign correspondents. After the parties reach an agreement, the FCC accepts that rate and permits the US carrier to pass that cost component (if any) through to end consumers in the collection rate.[28] However, by unilaterally imposing mandatory settlement benchmarks calculated by the FCC on a *sua sponte* basis, the FCC has essentially modified the parties' private agreement. In doing so, the FCC may have violated the parameters of the *Mobile-Sierra* doctrine.[29]

Under the *Mobile-Sierra* doctrine, the FCC has the power to prescribe a change in contract rates when it finds them to be unlawful and "to modify other provisions of private contracts when necessary to serve the public interest."[30] As US Judge Robert Bork once explained:

> "Although the legal standard for changing contract rates (they must be 'unlawful') differs from the standard for changing other contract provisions (they must disserve 'the public interest'), in fact the two standards are not very different. Before changing rates, the Commission must make a finding that they are 'unlawful' according to the terms of the governing statute, which typically requires a finding that existing rates are unjust, unreasonable, unduly discriminatory, or preferential. . . . But as the Supreme Court recognised in *Sierra*, complaints about existing rates do not concern the Commission unless the problems raised are sufficiently serious to 'adversely affect the public interest'."[31]

[28] See generally 47 C.F.R. § 43.51 (1997).
[29] See *United Gas Pipe Line Co.* v. *Mobile Gas Serv. Corp.*, 350 U.S. 332, 339–43 (1956); *FPC v. Sierra Pac. Power Co.*, 350 U.S. 348, 353–55 (1956).
[30] *See Western Union Tel. Co.* v. *FCC*, 815 F.2d 1495, 1501 (D.C. Cir. 1987).
[31] *Ibid.*, at 1501 n.2 (citations omitted).

Despite this authority, however, courts have held that *Mobile-Sierra's* "public interest" standard is "practically insurmountable."[32] Indeed, courts require an exceptionally high burden of proof to show why a contractual term is not in the public interest[33]—that is, the anticompetitive basis resulting from the contract outweigh the perpetual public interest benefits. Moreover, satisfying this burden is simply made more difficult by the fact that the FCC lacks jurisdiction over one of the signatories (i.e., the foreign correspondent) and that most of these agreements deliberately do not contain either a "choice of law" or a "choice of venue" provision.

Notwithstanding this precedent, the court held nonetheless that the FCC's actions were appropriate and did not violate the *Mobile-Sierra* doctrine. Indeed, even though the D.C. Circuit relied specifically on Judge Bork's decision in *Western Union*, nowhere in the *C&W* court's opinion is either *Papago* mentioned specifically or *Western Union* cited accurately. Instead, stretching *Chevron's* mandate that courts must give administrative agencies great deference (in this case, upholding expressly the FCC's role of cartel manager), the court upheld the FCC's actions with limited discussion.[34]

Accordingly, by eviscerating the law, the D.C. Circuit now essentially has given every regulatory agency *carte blanche* to abrogate a contract that it believes subjectively to be against the "public interest." As demonstrated throughout this book, the "public interest" should not be an arbitrary standard that regulators may use to promote political pet projects, however. So long as the US government erects barriers to entry in the name of promoting competition, however, such policies will provide US firms with no real incentive to innovate and lower costs and, as such, true deregulation and competition will never occur.

Moreover, (and perhaps without realising it), the court's decision on this issue will have lasting and far-reaching implications beyond the boundaries of this case because the *Mobile-Sierra* doctrine also applies to a wide variety of circumstances in addition to just international settlement rates. For example, this case will impact significantly how the FCC resolves issues of reciprocal compensation.[35] More importantly, however, this case will have significant implications for the US electric utility and natural gas industries (the industries from

[32] See, e.g., *Papago Tribal Authority v. FERC*, 723 F.2d 950, 954 (D.C. Cir. 1983); but *cf. Northeast Utils. Serv. Co. v. FERC*, 55 F.3d 686, 691 (1st Cir. 1995) ("We do not think that Papago, read in context, means that the 'public interest' standard is practically insurmountable in all circumstances. It all depends on whose ox is gored and how the public interest is affected.").

[33] See, e.g., *Western Union Tel.*, 815 F.2d at 1501–02 (holding the FCC was not justified in abrogating settlement agreement which established compromise rates for leasing special access facilities and set specific procedures for changing those rates in the future).

[34] Indeed, the court curiously focused primarily on counsel's argument that *Mobile-Sierra* somehow was contingent on the underlying transaction of the contract rate in question, rather than attempting to determine whether the FCC had presented sufficient justification to escape *Papago's* "practically insurmountable" test.

[35] See, e.g., Remarks of William E. Kennard, Chairman of the FCC, to the National Association of Regulatory Commissioners, Orlando, Florida, 11 Nov. 1998 <http://www.fcc.gov/Speeches/Kennard/spwek 833.html>. "I know that a large number of states have already weighed in on the issue of reciprocal compensation between local carriers handling Internet traffic. I believe that those

which the *Mobile-Sierra* doctrine arose), for this case will now give the US Federal Energy Regulatory Commission (FERC) even greater license to abrogate contracts to implement its flawed restructuring paradigms.[36]

Perhaps more troubling, however, is that the US judicial branch has affirmed the FCC's hubris that it may proscribe, *sua sponte*, specific, long-term prices under both the US Communications Act and international law on a unilateral basis in the first instance.[37] While the FCC certainly has the legal authority to proscribe a particular ratemaking *methodology*,[38] the FCC's authority to proscribe rates is much more limited. Under existing precedent, courts have held that it is only permissible for the FCC to proscribe specific *interim* settlement rates because "any harm caused by the interim rates [can] be remedied."[39] Moreover, the FCC may not exercise its proscription authority in a vacuum. Under the plain language of the US Communications Act, *the FCC may exercise its authority to proscribe interim rates under section 205 only after it has first rejected rates initially proposed by carriers as unjust and unreasonable.*[40] Thus,

states have been right to decide that issue when it has been presented to them and I do not believe it is the role of the FCC to interfere with those state decisions in any way.

Parties should be held to the terms of their agreements, and if a state has decided that a reciprocal compensation agreement provides for the payment of compensation for Internet-bound traffic, then that agreement and that decision by the state must be honoured.

Now the debate over reciprocal compensation of course raises the issue of jurisdiction. I fully respect the interests of state and local government and its regulators to protect the state's vital interests and consumers. At the same time, in this global economy, vital national interests are also at stake. We must not allow our mutual legitimate interests be used to divide us as we pursue our mutual and consistent goals." *Ibid.*

[36] See, e.g., Lawrence J. Spiwak, *FERC Merger Analysis Post-Order No. 888: Where Do We Go from Here?*, (Phoenix Center Policy Paper Series, Policy Paper No. 3 1998), at 13–14 http://www.phoenix-center.org/wps.html; Lawrence J. Spiwak, You Say ISO, I Say Transco, Let's Call the Whole Thing Off: Why Current Electric Utility "Unbundling" Initiatives Work Without Fundamental Change (Phoenix Center Policy Paper Series No. 4, 1999) (http://www.phoenix-center.org/pcpp/pcpp4.doc) (also excerpted in March 15, 1999 issue of *Public Utilities Fortnightly*); Lawrence J. Spiwak, "FERC, Put Economics First: Additional Thoughts on Functional Unbundling", *Public Utilities Fortnightly* (Aug. 1999).

[37] Specifically, the FCC's actions may, in fact, violate the International Telecommunication Union (ITU) regulations, a treaty to which the United States is party and for which the FCC is the U.S. enforcement authority under U.S. domestic law. 47 U.S.C. § 303(r) (1998). See, e.g., International Telecommunication Regulations, 9 Dec. 1988, S. Treaty Doc. No. 102–13, art. I, para. 1.5 (1991) [hereinafter ITU]. ("Within the framework of the present Regulations, the provision and operation of international telecommunications services in each relation is pursuant to *mutual agreement* between administrations [or RPOAs]."); ITU, *supra*, art. 6.2.1 ("For each applicable service in a given relation, administrations [or RPOAs] shall by *mutual agreement* establish and revise accounting rates to be applied between them, in accordance with the provisions of Appendix 1 and *taking into account relevant CCITT Recommendations and relevant cost trends*.") (emphasis added).

[38] See *Farmers Union Cent. Exch., Inc. v. FERC*, 734 F.2d 1486 (D.C. Cir. 1984).

[39] *FTC Comm. v. FCC*, 750 F.2d 226, 232 (2d Cir. 1984); *Western Union Int'l v. FCC*, 652 F.2d 136, 144 (D.C. Cir. 1980); *cf.* discussion *supra* Part IV.C.3 (indicating FCC conceded that it only had authority to proscribe interim rates). Of course, "interim" rates in the telecommunications context can often last for quite a long time.

[40] See *Ralph Nader v. FCC*, 520 F.2d 182, 198 (D.C. Cir. 1975); *AT&T v. FCC*, 449 F.2d 439, 450–53 (2d Cir. 1971); *Western Union Tel.*, 815 F.2d 1495. See also Communications Act of 1934, ch. 652, § 205, 47 U.S.C. § 205, which provides in relevant part that: "Whenever, after full

because it is still the carrier who has the burden to justify that its specific rates are just and reasonable, basic ratemaking principles instruct that there cannot be a single, generic industry-wide rate under the common "just and reasonable" standard.[41] Accordingly, the FCC's "one-size"—or, more accurately "five-sizes" —"fits all" approach to settlement rate determination is specious at best. The costs of wiring Uzbekistan are simply not the same as the costs of wiring Uruguay, and, moreover, if either Uzbekistan or Uruguay fail to meet the FCC's benchmarks, *the costs of wiring either country are still not the same as the (US) $0.08 the FCC thinks is the cost of wiring Sweden.*

This process is not as difficult to satisfy as it may seem. In order for a rate to be "just and reasonable," prices only need to fall within a "zone of reasonableness"—that is, that these rates are neither "excessive" (rates that permit the firm to recover monopoly rents) nor "confiscatory" (rates that do not permit the regulated firm to recover its costs).[42] Yet, while this standard is not very precise, the phrase "just and reasonable" is clearly more than a "mere vessel into which meaning must be poured."[43] Rather, the delineation of the "zone of reasonableness" in a particular case will involve a "complex inquiry into a myriad of factors."[44] These myriad of factors, however, may include both *cost and non-cost* factors to determine whether particular rates fall within the zone.[45] Thus, had the FCC recognised the legitimacy of the basic notion that different countries have different economies and, *a fortiori*, different cost structures—much as the ITU did in its recent proposal discussed in Chapter 15—the FCC's unilateral approach would have stood on much firmer footing.

---

opportunity for hearing, upon a complaint or . . . on its own initiative, the Commission shall be of opinion that any charge, classification, regulation, or practice of any carrier or carriers is or will be in violation of any of the provisions of this chapter, the Commission is authorised and empowered to determine and prescribe what will be the just and reasonable charge or . . . charges to be thereafter observed".

   [41] See 47 U.S.C. § 203 (1998). See also *New England Tel. & Tel. Co.* v. *FCC*, 826 F.2d 1101, 1104 (D.C. Cir. 1987).

   [42] *Farmers Union*, 734 F.2d at 1502. Courts generally give administrative agencies substantial discretion to define this zone. Indeed, as the D.C. Circuit Court once explained, when examining an agency's determination that a particular rate falls within the zone of reasonableness, it is not a court's "function . . . to impose [its] own standards of reasonableness upon the Commission, but rather to ensure that the Commission's order is supported by substantial record evidence and is neither arbitrary, capricious, nor an abuse of discretion." *Nader*, 520 F.2d at 192 (citations omitted). However, the court was also quick to point out that, "[i]n terms of ratemaking, the agency's expertise allows us to accept its judgement after it defines the zone of reasonableness; *but we cannot rely on claims of judgement to explain how the agency arrived at the zone.*" *Ibid.*, at 193 (emphasis added).

   [43] See *Farmers Union*, 734 F.2d at 1504.

   [44] *Ibid.*, at 1502.

   [45] *Ibid.* When considering the latter, courts have upheld the legitimate role non-cost factors may play in order to achieve a particular public policy objective (e.g., a desire to establish additional supply), so long as the agency specifies the nature of the relevant non-cost factor and offers a reasoned explanation of how the factor justifies the resulting rates. *Ibid.*, at 1502–03 (citations omitted); see also *National Ass'n of Regulatory Utility Comm'rs* v. *FCC*, 737 F.2d 1095, 1137 (D.C. Cir. 1984); *National Rural Telecom Ass'n* v. *FCC*, 988 F.2d 174, 182–83 (D.C. Cir. 1993) (affirming price cap regulation although not tied directly to cost).

III. HOW POLITICS NOW TRUMPS LAW, ECONOMICS, AND FACTS

As highlighted above, much of the *C&W* court's reasoning was justified by inferring an "America-first" rationale (e.g., only the United States has outpayment deficit; only the US market is competitive; the FCC needs to protect US competitors, not competition; US firms need to engage in joint boycotts against foreign firms, etc.) In this section, however, one can see how the court justified its actions with "explicit" mercantile arguments.

A. The FCC Apparently Believes that the Mere Potential for Foreign Carriers to Think "Evil Thoughts" is Sufficient Justification to Impose Stringent Regulation as a Precondition of Entry

1. Price Squeeze-Type Conduct

As noted above in the preceding chapter, the FCC concluded (contrary to conclusions made in its earlier international proceedings and other domestic proceedings)[46] that because a foreign carrier supposedly has the *per se* ability to engage in "price squeeze" behaviour, the mere fact that a foreign carrier might also have the "*incentive*" to engage in price squeeze behaviour is sufficient grounds to justify the imposition of its "*Benchmarks* condition" as a prophylactic device. The problem with this analysis, however, is that it runs completely inapposite to established antitrust and regulatory price squeeze precedent.

That is to say, a predatory price squeeze plaintiff generally has two options available. First, a plaintiff may apply for an administrative remedy from the regulatory administrative agency with jurisdiction over the alleged anticompetitive rate.[47] Alternatively, the plaintiff may elect to sue under section 2 of the Sherman Act in federal district court. However, because of the different roles of antitrust and regulation, each avenue has different criteria for success and different remedies.[48]

On one hand, as explained *supra*, it is well established that the role of an administrative remedy is to ensure that rates are just and reasonable.[49] As such, if a plaintiff seeks an administrative remedy from the regulator, then the regulator typically is not required to focus its examination on the firm's intent, but rather on the anticompetitive effects of the alleged price squeeze on the wholesale customer/retail competitor and whether they are outweighed by the effect

---

[46] See chapter 7 *supra*.

[47] Lawrence J. Spiwak, "Is the Price Squeeze Doctrine Still Viable in Fully-Regulated Energy Markets?", (1993) 14 *Energy L.J.* 75, 77.

[48] See *ibid*.

[49] *Ibid*. Notwithstanding this precedent, as mentioned elsewhere, the FCC now believes erroneously that its "public interest" authority may be far broader and, as such, has created its own trade division to address its regulatory constituents' concerns.

on the supplying firm's financial viability and its ability to serve its customers.[50] If a plaintiff successfully proves a price squeeze claim, however, then the regulator may remedy the price squeeze only by reducing the offending jurisdictional rate within a "zone of reasonableness."[51]

In contrast, a section 2 claim seeks to remedy some kind of intentionally imposed anticompetitive harm.[52] A section 2 plaintiff must show more than a general intent, however; rather, under section 2, this plaintiff must show that the defendant had some degree of monopolistic intent, as well as some demonstrable harm to competition.[53] If both prongs of the test are met, then treble damages are available to punish the offender (and, moreover, the plaintiff will not have to share this award with any other potential similarly-situated plaintiffs not party to the suit because rate reductions benefit *all* customers receiving service under the regulated firm's tariff).[54]

The FCC's approach to price squeeze conduct, unfortunately, requires neither a showing of specific intent nor—even more importantly—any showing of anticompetitive harm. Rather, the FCC seems to believe that it may set prices over firms clearly not under its jurisdiction simply because they have the more *potential* to think "anticompetitive thoughts" in their hearts. Indeed, the FCC's anticompetitive concerns appear unfortunately to be far more ephemeral than probable. By deliberately choosing not to undertake a detailed economic analysis of the structural conditions in a WTO Member country's home market, therefore, it is difficult to discern exactly any clear nexus between the regulation imposed by the FCC and the specific anticompetitive harms this regulation is supposed to mitigate.

2. Posing a "Very High Risk" to Competition

Not content with the market opening commitments of the WTO, along with its own ISP and "No Special Concessions" Rule, the FCC stated nonetheless that it could not "rule out the possibility" that its various "regulatory safeguards" would be "ineffective at preventing anti-competitive conduct in a particular context, *and* that, as a result, a carrier would be able to raise the costs of its rivals to the degree that end-user customers would be injured."[55] As such, the FCC also decided to adopt yet one more regulatory mechanism by introducing a brand new term into the legal and economic lexicon—that is, a presumption that "an application does not pose a risk of competitive harm that would justify

---

[50] *Ibid.*, (citation omitted).
[51] *Ibid.*
[52] *Ibid.*, (citations omitted).
[53] *Ibid.*
[54] *Ibid.*, (citation omitted).
[55] See generally Rules and Policies on Foreign Participation in the U.S. Telecomm. Market, *Report and Order on Reconsideration*, 12 F.C.C.R. 23,891, 10 Comm. Reg. (P & F) 750 (1997) [hereinafter *Foreign Participation Order*] at para. 51.

denial unless it is shown that granting the application would pose . . . a *very high risk to competition*."[56] The big problem, however, is the FCC's failure to provide a precise definition of the heretofore-unknown standard of "very high risk to competition."[57]

According to the FCC, a "very high risk to competition" in the US market occurs whenever there is a situation which "cannot be addressed by [its] safeguards or conditions, and would therefore warrant denial of a license."[58] In order to have the ability to pose such a risk, however, "an applicant must possess the ability to harm competition in the US market in addition to the ability to exercise its foreign market power."[59] While the FCC was quick to point out various situations that it would not consider a "very high risk to competition,"[60] this standard is just too vague (and gives the regulator far too much subjective discretion) to have any analytical anchoring.

The D.C. Circuit ignored this precedent, however, and instead affirmed the FCC's actions by setting forth what amounts to an *ad homonym* attack on the international telecoms community. In a naked statement of neo-mercantilism, the court reasons that the FCC's Benchmark Condition is necessary to mitigate the ephemeral "price squeeze-type" behaviour of all foreign firms because:

> "foreign carriers with US affiliates can use their monopoly power to distort competition in the United States. This occurs when a foreign carrier and its US affiliate act together as an integrated firm, competing in the US market as a provider of international long-distance services while serving as a monopoly supplier of a necessary input, i.e., termination services in the foreign country. By extracting above-cost settlement rates from US carriers, the foreign carrier enables its US affiliate to undercut its competitors, since the above-cost portion of the settlement rate is essentially an internal transfer for the foreign-affiliated US carrier; *for other competitors, it represents a real cost*. Economically, this 'price squeeze' behavior has the same effect as if the foreign carrier engaged in price discrimination by charging its US affiliate a lower settlement rate than it charged all other US carriers."[61]

---

[56] *Foreign Participation Order*, (emphasis added).

[57] Indeed, is this standard the same as "very very high risk to competition?" Or, conversely, somehow less dangerous than a plain old "high risk" to competition?

[58] *Foreign Participation Order*, *supra* n. 55 at para. 52.

[59] *Ibid.*

[60] For example, the FCC stated that it would find it "highly unlikely" that a "very high risk to competition" was present: (a) when an acquisition of less than a controlling interest in a U.S. carrier by a foreign carrier occurs; (b) when a carrier from a WTO Member country has "open, competitive markets and a procompetitive regulatory regime in place"; or (c) that the FCC would deny entry " 'based solely on [the applicant's] market share.' " *Ibid.*, (citations omitted).

[61] *Cable & Wireless P.L.C. v. FCC*, 166 F.3d at 1227 (emphasis added). For example, the court found that in the case of Hong Kong: "The Commission's Order assigns Hong Kong's international carrier, HKTI, a settlement rate of $0.15 per minute—a rate which, according to petitioners, cannot possibly compensate HKTI for the $0.29 per minute government-mandated charge that it must pay Hong Kong's local carrier for terminating each incoming international call. But, according to the intervenors on behalf of the FCC, HKTI is a wholly owned subsidiary of Hong Kong Telecom, and Hong Kong Telecom owns Hong Kong Telephone Company, the monopoly provider of local service in Hong Kong. The $0.29 per minute charge is therefore simply a "left pocket-right pocket" transaction between two subsidiaries of the same company. Asked about this at oral argument, petitioners had no response." *Ibid.*, at 1233 (citation omitted).

Moreover, the court went on to reason that even though the FCC originally believed that its "Effective Competitive Opportunities" test would be sufficient to "reduce the monopolist leverage essential for price squeeze behaviour," by 1997:

> "at least two things had changed. First, because the United States had committed to allowing foreign competitors freer entry into the US market pursuant to the World Trade Organization Basic Telecom Agreement of February 1997, the Commission had proposed eliminating the effective competitive opportunities test. Second, despite the Commission's expectation that increased global competition would drive rates toward cost-based levels, 'settlement rates remain[ed] far above cost-based levels.' *In light of these changed conditions*, we think the Commission reasonably adopted its current section 214 authorisation *policy to deal with the heightened risk of price squeeze behavior*."[62]

There are several major problems with the D.C. Circuit's analysis from both an antitrust and factual perspective, however.

As explained *supra*, the primary problem with the FCC's price squeeze analysis is that it ignores the very bedrock of price squeeze law (both regulatory cases and cases brought under section 2 of the Sherman Act)—that is, *that the alleged squeeze must be capable of producing a tangible antitrust injury*[63]—i.e. a firm must be able to *both* anticompetitively drive its rivals from the market and after doing so raise prices above competitive levels. As further shown *supra*, under the current and emerging structure of international telecommunications markets, any attempt at a price squeeze is unlikely to succeed for US-originated traffic.

To begin, even if a foreign firm could succeed in driving its *rivals* from the market, residual price regulation should be able to prevent this firm from charging supra competition prices. In other words, if a firm can successfully charge supra competitive prices after a price squeeze, then it is more accurately an issue of *regulatory failure* on the part of the FCC in prohibiting the firm from unlawfully charging rates that are unjust, unreasonable, and unduly discriminatory. Moreover, if the court thought about it for a moment, then not only is it highly unlikely that any foreign firm is actually going to harm competition by being able to drive out a US firm and then recouping super-competitive prices via a "price squeeze," but if US consumers start to switch over to the supposedly "cheaper" foreign supplier—subsidised ostensibly by those above-cost settlement rate outpayments—then US firms would *a fortiori* lose traffic, and the subsidies to foreign firms would therefore concurrently decline, thus preventing foreign firms from offering service at cheaper rates. As such, the whole notion is

---

[62] *Ibid.*, at 1234 (citations omitted, emphasis added, alteration in original).

[63] See, e.g., *Cities of Anaheim* v. *FERC*, 941 F.2d 1234 (D.C. Cir. 1991); *Town of Concord* v. *Boston Edison Co.*, 915 F.2d 17 (1st Cir. 1990); *Boroughs of Ellwood City* v. *FERC*, 731 F.2d 959, 979 (D.C. Cir. 1984) ("It is primarily the effects of the price squeeze and its prospective remedy that should guide the Commission's exercise of discretion . . . ."); *City of Batavia* v. *FERC*, 672 F.2d 64 (D.C. Cir. 1982).

a *self-defeating exercise.* As explained *passim,* if the FCC wants to mitigate strategic vertical conduct by a foreign firm, then the key is to get standard interconnection rates at the terminating end—the key objective of the World Trade Organisation (WTO) but inapposite to the FCC's mercantile policy of mandating entry by US firms.

The court, however, had no real understanding (nor apparently did counsel for the petitioners again succeed in educating the court) of these facts or economic theory. By affirming the FCC's flawed analysis, therefore, the D.C. Circuit has changed price squeeze law to mean that plaintiffs need not show antitrust injury to prevail; rather, they need only show that the defendant had "evil" in his heart and that there was some ephemeral "very high risk to competition."

There are other significant factual errors in the D.C. Circuit's price squeeze analysis as well. For example, the court essentially affirms the FCC's erroneous assumption that settlement rates suddenly will become more "affordable" if they are priced in line with "true costs." As explained in chapter 7, however:

> "Foreign carriers and regulators (i.e., parties reaping the benefits from the above-cost settlement rates) are unsurprisingly reluctant to reduce settlement rates. Yet, even though economic theory indicates that prices are related to cost, for US carriers the settlement rate does *not* measure the settlement cost of providing a minute of IMTS service. With multiple carriers and proportionate returns, the cost relevant to the setting of prices is not only a function of the settlement rate but of the input-output ratio (the ratio of inbound to outbound IMTS traffic) and the carrier's market share. Only for a monopolist is the settlement rate equal to the marginal settlement cost of the carrier. Given the absence of monopoly in the United States, therefore, there is no reason to expect that the IMTS prices of US carriers should be directly related to the settlement rate."[64]

As such, both the court's and the FCC's notion of "perfect competition" is just "a Shangri-La up to which no real-world market can measure."[65]

The factual and theoretical errors do not end there, however. For example, the court also assumes that—even in the post-WTO world—(1) every country aside from the United States is characterised by a monopoly provider (which is simply not true); and (2) even assuming *arguendo* point (1), it is impossible for regulators to formulate adequate safeguards to mitigate transfer-pricing abuses with a dominant incumbent. Yet, as the court itself admits, if things are actually getting *better* as a direct result of the WTO and other international liberalisation efforts, and as the FCC's own admission that "increased global competition

---

[64] See chapter 7.

[65] Stephen Martin, *Industrial Economics: Economic Analysis and Public Policy* 16 (Prentice Hall, 1988); see also *AT&T Corp.* v. *Iowa Utils. Bd., AT&T Corp. et al.* v. *Iowa Utilities Bd. et al.*, 525 U.S. 366, 119 S.Ct. 721, 735 (1999) ("In a world of perfect competition, in which all carriers are providing their service at marginal cost, the Commission's total equating of increased cost (or decreased quality) with 'necessity' and 'impairment' might be reasonable; but it has not established the existence of such an ideal world.").

would drive rates towards cost-based levels,"[66] then why is *more* regulation needed to deal with a "heightened risk of price squeeze behaviour"?[67]

On the other hand, however, assuming *arguendo* that the court's factual and theoretical assertions are correct, then *a fortiori* the FCC should also be incapable of formulating an adequate methodology to protect firms from transfer-pricing abuses from America's very own dominant suppliers of local access—the regional Bell operating companies—from successfully engaging in price squeeze behaviour. This is not so. In the FCC's domestic *Access Charge Reform Order*, the FCC found specifically that "although an incumbent LEC's control of exchange and exchange access facilities may give it the incentive and ability to engage in a price squeeze,"[68] the FCC's regulatory safeguards, coupled with the structural conditions of the market, make a successful price squeeze unlikely to occur.[69] Moreover, when this *Order* was challenged in court, the US Circuit Court of Appeals for the Eighth Circuit held specifically that the FCC's access charges (the domestic version of settlement rates) imposed on long-distance providers that include LECs' universal service costs are not "above-cost" "since universal service contributions are a real cost of doing business."[70] Accordingly, if international settlement rates are—as the D.C. Circuit posits— "real costs,"[71] and if the logic of the Eighth Circuit is followed, then current settlement rates are similarly not "above-cost," since international settlement rates are also simply "a real cost of doing business."[72] Once again, therefore, the FCC erroneously believes that the letter "D" in "domestic" also stands for "different."

B. Evisceration of International Law

According to the *C&W* court, the FCC's *Benchmarks Order* does not violate the International Telecommunication Union's 1998 Melbourne Treaty (ITU

---

[66] *Cable & Wireless P.L.C.* v. *FCC*, 166 F.3d 1234.

[67] *Ibid.* Sadly, this illogical "things-are-better-so-we-need-more-regulation" attitude was also the centrepiece of the FCC's adjudication of the since-aborted BT/MCI merger. See chapter 18, *infra*.

[68] See Access Charge Reform; Price Cap Performance Review for Local Exchange Carriers; Transport Rate Structure and Pricing End User Common Line Charges, *First Report and Order*, 12 F.C.C.R. 15,982, para. 278, 7 Comm. Reg. (P & F) 1209 (1997).

[69] *Ibid.*, paras. 275–82. As the FCC explained, a price squeeze is possible in the domestic context if the incumbent LEC could: "rais[e] the price of interstate access services to all interexchange carriers, which would cause competing in-region carriers to either raise their retail rates to maintain their profit margins or to attempt to maintain their market share by not raising their prices to reflect the increase in access charges, thereby reducing their profit margins. If the competing in-region, interexchange providers raised their prices to recover the increased access charges, the incumbent LEC's interexchange affiliate could seek to expand its market share by not matching the price increase. The incumbent LEC affiliate could also set its in-region, interexchange prices at or below its access prices. Its competitors would then be faced with the choice of lowering their retail rates for interexchange services, thereby reducing their profit margins, or maintaining their retail rates at the higher price and risk losing market share." *Ibid.*, para. 277.

[70] *Southwestern Bell Tel. Co.* v. *FCC*, 153 F.3d 523, 554 (8th Cir. 1998).

[71] *Cable & Wireless*, 166 F.3d at 1227. Of course, the great unanswered question is from which economics hornbook did these courts derive the definition of "real costs."

[72] See *supra* p. 166.

Treaty), which sets the ITU's International Telecommunication Regulations (ITR).[73] In the court's opinion:

> "Although the treaty provides that carriers 'shall by mutual agreement establish and revise accounting rates to be applied between them,' . . . a separate provision 'recognize[s] the right of any member, subject to national law . . . to require that administrations and private operating agencies, which operate in its territory and provide an international telecommunication service to the public, be authorized by that member'."[74]

Moreover, the court agreed with the FCC that

> "the right to authorize a carrier to provide service in a given country necessarily includes the right to attach reasonable conditions to such authorization to safeguard the public interest"

finding that the ITU Treaty's preamble "makes clear that 'it is the sovereign right of each country to regulate its telecommunications.' "[75]

Once again, the court in *C&W* is just plain wrong. First, the court (like most American regulators) has blatantly misread and misconstrued the ITU Treaty.[76] As mentioned *supra*, the court upheld the FCC's actions on the ground that the ITU Treaty's preamble states that "'*it is* the sovereign right of each country to regulate its telecommunications.'"[77] This reading is not true. Had the court taken the time to read the actual language of the preamble, it would have found that there is no such absolute right because the words "it is" do not even appear.[78] Rather, the preamble provides the exact opposite:

> "While the sovereign right of each country to regulate its telecommunications is fully recognised, the provisions of the present Regulations supplement the International Telecommunication Convention, with a view to attaining the purposes of the International Telecommunication Union in promoting the development of telecommunication services and their most efficient operation while harmonising the development of facilities for world-wide telecommunications."[79]

---

[73] The International Telecommunication Regulations (Melbourne, 1988) were ratified by the United States on 23 December 1992, and became effective on 6 April 1993, the date of deposit with the ITU. International Telecommunication Regulations, 9 Dec. 1988, S. Treaty Doc. No. 102–13 (1991). Together with the Radio Regulations, they compose the "administrative regulations" of the ITU, some version of which is binding on all ITU Members (see, e.g., Constitution and Convention of the International Telecommunication Union, Dec. 22, 1992, S. Treaty Doc. No. 104–34, art. 4 (1996)). Compared with the Radio Regulations (now a four-volume set), the ITR are brief—12 pages of text supplemented by eight pages of integrated annexes. They are to the wireline world roughly what the Radio Regulations are to the radio world.

[74] *Cable & Wireless*, 166 F.3d at 1230 (citations omitted, alteration in original).

[75] *Ibid.*, (citation omitted).

[76] To add insult to injury, the court also did not even have the professional courtesy of spelling out the ITU's formal name correctly, erroneously describing the ITU as the "International *Telecommunications* [sic] Union."

[77] *Ibid.*, (emphasis added) (citation omitted).

[78] Consistent with the Clinton/Gore Administration's penchant for legal hair-splitting, we find ourselves once again arguing over what the definition of the word "is" is.

[79] International Telecommunication Regulations, 9 Dec. 1988, S. Treaty Doc. No. 102–13, preamble (1991) (emphasis added).

In other words, by signing the ITU Treaty (*aka* a "contract" among sovereign nations), member states agreed to *waive*—and *not* to reserve—some of their sovereign rights in the telecommunications arena in order to fulfil the broader goals of the ITU. Thus, taking the court's gross misinterpretation of the preamble that parties agreed to reserve, rather than waive, their sovereign rights, there would be no need for a treaty and no need for a dispute settlement agreement since no party to the treaty could ever be wrong or in violation of the treaty—it would simply be exercising its sovereign rights.

Second, even assuming *arguendo* the court read and interpreted the Melbourne Treaty correctly, the court once again ignores the facts. As demonstrated *passim*, the United States is *not* the only country with a net settlement outpayment deficit. If the court's logic is followed to its (il)logical conclusion, therefore, and if those countries that also have substantial settlement outpayments deficits enact similar measures, then these countries' actions would also be perfectly acceptable and legal, despite the FCC's inevitable argument that such action would be nothing more than an anticompetitive effort to codify above-cost subsidies to foreign monopolists. Thus, to avoid this inevitable conflict, the ITU's International Telecommunication Regulation (ITR) regime deliberately envisions and requires (yet the FCC and *C&W* court consistently ignore) that there be "mutual agreement" on a route-by-route and service basis (rather than unilateral action based on country groupings).[80] This regulation is especially important given the fact that while there is often general agreement that settlement rates should be "cost based," there often remains the question as to what costs should be included or how those costs should be calculated.

That is to say, section 6.2.1 of the ITR provides that:

"For each applicable service in a given relation, administrations [or recognised private operating agency(ies)] shall by *mutual agreement* establish and revise accounting rates to be applied between them, in accordance with the provisions of Appendix 1 . . . ."[81]

As discussed above and in the original article, the FCC's actions have clearly ignored this requirement. Similarly, these same "administrations or recognised private operating agency(ies)" must also "tak[e] into account relevant CCITT [now TSB] Recommendations and relevant cost trends."[82] As explained in the main article, however, the ITU specifically recommended in a new draft Annex to ITU Recommendation D.140 *against* adopting the FCC's benchmark regime, finding, *inter alia*, that:

"The FCC methodology makes no allowance for dependence on net settlement payments. In almost all cases the average rate of reduction necessary under the FCC's methodology is steeper than even the worst case under the Focus Group methodology"

[80] *Ibid.*, art. 6.2.1.
[81] *Ibid.*, (emphasis added).
[82] *Ibid.*

and, therefore, in marked contrast to the FCC's "exacting" draconian unilateral actions in which rates are prescribed arbitrarily, the ITU recommended that "[t]he exact form that a smoother transition path could take is better left to bilateral negotiations."[83]

Moreover, this issue can be particularly acute in the case of universal service payments. As explained more fully in Chapter 15 *infra*, the international community is already dismayed (including specific statements by the ITU) over the fact that every time a call is terminated in the United States, a caller must pay into the FCC's universal service fund. As further explained *supra*, the Eighth Circuit has held that these universal service charges, when rolled into access charges, are not "above cost" because they are a "real cost of doing business." Yet, given its actions and policies to date, it is highly doubtful that the United States would react positively if, for example, a country hypothetically defined its internal version of universal service as "a wireline phone to every family unit with installation and usage charges not to exceed those in the United States, 90% funded by international carriers in the settlement-of-account process based on their volume of calls terminating in US territory," even though such a universal service program would seem to meet all the criteria of the WTO Reference Paper.

Fourth, the court ignores the fact that the ITU offers several (albeit admittedly under-utilised and perhaps even completely ineffective) dispute settlement mechanisms.[84] If the US government had laid an appropriate predicate, then it would have been an option open to immediate action.

Finally, the *C&W* court completely ignores the concept of international "comity" and the importance of this concept in American jurisprudence. *Black's Law Dictionary* defines "comity of nations" as:

"The recognition which one nation allows within its territory to the legislative, executive, or judicial acts of another nation, having due regard to international duty and

---

[83] See "Methodological Note on Transition Paths to Cost-Orientation: Revision 1 of Contribution from the ITU Secretariat", 9 Nov. 1998 <http://www.itu.int/intset/focus/transition_path%20rev1.pdf>. Indeed, the significance of the fact that the ITU—the official telecommunications agency of the United Nations—went so far as to actually use exclamation points in its critique (i.e., a diplomatic communiqué) of the FCC's actions cannot be discounted. (As a measure of comparison, even U.N. Security Council resolutions condemning Saddam Hussein have yet to include any exclamation points in the text).

[84] The first two paragraphs of Article 56 of the ITU Constitution are quoted below. The third paragraph deals with a compulsory settlement arrangement (in the form of a protocol attached to the Constitution) to which the United States is not party.

(1) Members may settle their disputes on questions relating to the interpretation or application of this Constitution, the Convention or of the Administrative Regulations by negotiation, through diplomatic channels, or according to procedures established by bilateral or multilateral treaties concluded between them for the settlement of international disputes, or by any other method mutually agreed upon.
(2) If none of these methods of settlement is adopted, any Member party to a dispute may have recourse to arbitration in accordance with the procedure defined in the Convention.

Constitution and Convention of the International Telecommunication Union, Dec. 22, 1992, S. Treaty Doc. No. 104–34, art. 56 (1996); see also *ibid.*, art. 41.

convenience and to the rights of its own citizens or of other persons who are under the protection of its laws."[85]

The primary reason to provide comity is to avoid the pitfalls of mercantilism that Adam Smith warned about nearly 200 years ago, and, as such, both courts[86] and enforcement agencies must consider international comity when enforcing the US antitrust laws and policing other disputes.[87] Like it or not, because there exists for international telecommunications services an international legal regime that describes the rights and obligations of countries in terms of reaching "mutual agreement," there is a significant comity problem in this case that simply cannot be ignored.[88]

C. Implications for the Future

The above discussion shows that the D.C. Circuit's decision in *C&W* has dire implications for the future of telecommunications law. Just for the sake of argument, however, assume that the D.C. Circuit was correct and the FCC's actions are wholly lawful. In this hypothetical case, was it still the right thing to do? We submit that, from a policy perspective, it was not.

[85] *Black's Law Dictionary* 267 (6th ed. 1990).

[86] See, e.g., *Timberlane Lumber Co. v. Bank of America*, 549 F.2d 597 (9th Cir. 1976).

[87] See U.S. Dep't of Justice & FTC, *Antitrust Enforcement Guidelines for International Operations* (US DOJ and FTC 1995) where both the DOJ and the FTC must, "in determining whether to assert jurisdiction to investigate or bring an action, or to seek particular remedies in a given case, . . . take into account whether significant interests of any foreign sovereign would be affected." *Ibid.*, § 3.2; see also *ibid.*, § 3.2 n. 73 (noting that both the DOJ and the FTC have agreed to consider the legitimate interests of other nations in accordance with the recommendations of the OECD and various other bilateral agreements).

Specifically, section 3.2 requires that:

In performing a comity analysis, the [DOJ and the FTC must] take into account all relevant factors, [including inter alia:] (1) the relative significance to the alleged violation of conduct within the United States, as compared to conduct abroad; (2) the nationality of the persons involved in or affected by the conduct; (3) the presence or absence of a purpose to affect U.S. consumers, markets, or exporters; (4) the relative significance and foreseeability of the effects of the conduct on the United States as compared to the effects abroad; (5) the existence of reasonable expectations that would be furthered or defeated by the action; (6) the degree of conflict with foreign law or articulated foreign economic policies; (7) the extent to which the enforcement activities of another country with respect to the same persons, including remedies resulting from those activities, may be affected; and (8) the effectiveness of foreign enforcement as compared to U.S. enforcement action.

Ibid., § 3.2. For a full discussion of comity in relation to agency enforcement of antitrust laws, see *Ibid.*, § 3.2, at 20–22.

[88] Indeed, assuming *arguendo* there were no international legal regime applicable to the commodity or service in question, would the United States be affronted if a foreign government were to act unilaterally so as to limit the ability of U.S.-domiciled entities to contract freely with their foreign counterparts in the supply and delivery of a necessary good or service? Would the United States be likely to consult with its allies regarding an appropriate response if a foreign entity took comparable unilateral action affecting all OECD countries? All ITU Members? All WTO Members? Obviously, because the answer to each one of these rhetorical questions is "Yes," there is a comity problem.

First, and perhaps most egregiously, the D.C. Circuit essentially lawfully codifies the notion that "FCC" should, in fact, stand for "Facilitating Cartels and Collusion." Indeed, by openly approving the fact that the whole purpose of the FCC's actions was to "strengthen the bargaining position of domestic telecommunications companies in negotiations with their foreign counterparts" and by encouraging and condoning US carriers' efforts to engage in what amounts to a group boycott, the D.C. Circuit has bastardised the "public interest" standard into a concept that inappropriately promotes individual (domestic) competitor interests over competition and American consumer welfare. To argue that by "protecting competitors we *a fortiori* protect competition" just does not pass the economic giggle test.

Second, this case (along with other recent US Trade Representative and FCC actions) sent a clear signal to the international telecommunications community that the United States now considers the 1997 WTO Telecom Treaty essentially to be worthless.[89] Indeed, the rest of the WTO's signatories certainly did not agree to commit to an arrangement where the United States would be "first among equals" and, more insulting, that their own respective efforts would be discounted by both US regulators and courts. As such, US firms should not be surprised if they find their international counterparts suddenly less co-operative and foreign regulators and courts suddenly more hostile to their interests.[89a]

III. SO WHAT'S REALLY GOING ON HERE?

Clearly, when all of actors in a market get together to reduce a common input of production, policy-makers should take note. Indeed, the preceding two Chapters raise an unusual question: If the FCC's International Settlements Policy is expressly designed to keep the US IMTS "cartel" fat and happy, then why were all of the US carriers nonetheless jointly lobbying for a *reduction* in cost of a common input?

Indeed, these "above cost" settlement rates had little adverse effect on the performance of the US IMTS market. For example, when George Ford evaluated

---

[89] See, for example, the FCC's attempts to back-pedal against Mexico's admittedly poor WTO offer. See also the plethora of material on the FCC Web page dedicated to the FCC's International Bureau Actions Concerning Accounting Rates on the U.S./Mexico Route and Potential Violations Telmex/Sprint Communications' Authorisation to Serve Mexico <http://www.fcc.gov/Bureaus/International/News_Releases/1998/telmex-sprint.html>. Moreover, the FCC recently fined Telmex, the Mexican dominant carrier, $100,000 for "*apparently* wilfully and repeatedly" violating the terms of its Section 214 to provide international switched resale services, even though Mexico had specifically excluded ISR from its WTO offer (emphasis supplied.) See In *re Telmex International Ventures, USA, Inc., Notice of Apparent Liability for Forfeiture*, DA 0057 (Enforcement Bureau, rel. 13 Jan. 2000). If the FCC suddenly realises this fact and wants to get out of a bad deal, however, then maybe it should not have accepted such a poor offer in the first instance.
[89a] See e.g., "US–Australian War of Words Highlights Global Dispute over Internet Competition" (Bureau of National Affairs, 30 May 2000).

the flow through of settlement costs to US IMTS prices, he found that there was "strong evidence that IMTS prices are closely related to settlement costs, and that these prices fully reflect differences in settlement costs." So much so, that Ford found that the US IMTS industry to be "far more competitive than the standard Cournot model would imply, and very close to perfect competition."[90]

Alternatively then, perhaps the unilateral push for Benchmarks was just an industry attempt to cultivate some regulatory good will? Indeed, it is an easy (yet pedantic) story to convey to regulators that US carriers (which are certainly not struggling or nascent firms and, as demonstrated above, have tremendous economic bargaining power) are some how the victims of the foreign monopolist correspondents. Such a "victim" mentality seems a bit disingenuous, however, given the fact that US-based carriers are not the only ones faced with large settlement imbalances. As shown previously, Japan-based carriers have large deficits with Taiwan, the Philippines, South Korea, Singapore, and other major Asian countries. Similarly, France Telecom has large outflows to Africa, the Middle East, and even Latin America. Moreover, the same holds true for British Telecom, Deutsche Telekom, Telecom Italia, and other large overseas telephone companies.[91]

Perhaps the more likely reason was—just like the motivations behind *ECO* and its progeny—US carriers' and government officials' xenophobia of foreign competition. In their view: (a) under the existing international settlement-of-accounts regime, the US traffic imbalance effectively forces US firms to subsidise—via above-cost settlement rates—foreign firms' activities; which subsidy (b) allegedly permits foreign firms to build a "full circuit" and therefore bypass the international settlement-of-accounts regime (i.e., provide IMTS service at *lower cost*); and because (c) the ability for any firm to achieve lower costs must be *a fortiori* "anticompetitive," the US government should make it as difficult as possible for foreign firms to enter the US market.

As such, the *Orders* discussed in the preceding Chapters appear to demonstrate a desire by the United States to not put all of its "promoting US investment abroad" eggs into the reciprocity basket. To wit, the FCC in *ECO* at least made the pretence of stating that entry into the United States would be conditioned on reciprocal effective competitive opportunities for US carriers abroad. With the release of the *Benchmarks Order,* the FCC stated that would set a fee for entry as well.

As such, let's just call the FCC's Benchmarks policy as it really is. As former FCC Chief Economist William T. Melody summarised correctly:

"The international revenue settlement subsidy, as asserted by the US operators and the FCC is not only a myth, it is a harmful and pernicious myth. The so-called subsidy

---

[90] George Ford, Phoenix Centre Public Policy Paper No. 7: *Flow-Through and Competition in the International Message Telephone Service Market* (2000).

[91] See, e.g., Maev Sullivan, "Why Is the United States Whining About Its Own Creation?", *Comm. Wk. Int'l,* 20 Jan. 1997.

payments are monopoly profits realised by operators in foreign countries from termination traffic at high prices, a common practice in all countries, including the US. Unsatisfied with realizing the highest rate of profit of any country from terminating international traffic, the US operators have gone after the profits of the operators terminating US traffic in foreign countries, and particularly the developing countries. The FCC Benchmarking Order facilitates that objective extremely well, even to the point of requiring many high cost poor countries to subsidise the termination of US traffic in their countries."[92]

The industry should therefore thank the Clinton/Gore Administration for giving them exactly what they wished for—ensuring that US firms will be perceived immediately as the "ugly American" every time they enter a foreign counterpart's or regulator's office. As such, everyone should get out his Nehru jacket and get used to the catcalls of "Yanqui Go Home" because free trade, competition, and deregulation are the last things the FCC's international telecommunications policies are ever going to produce.

---

[92] William H. Melody, "Telecom Myths: The International Revenue Settlements Subsidy", (2000) 24 *Telecommunications Policy Online* (http://www.tpeditor.com/melody.htm).

9

"Do As I Say, Not As I Do"—US Efforts at Promoting Local Telecoms Competition

As noted in Chapter 5, former FCC Chairman Reed Hundt was fond of saying that with the passage WTO Agreement on Basic Telecoms Services, the world had adopted the US model as its "gold standard."[1] (After all, we Americans have elevated regulation to an art form.) In order to ensure that this vision was carried out correctly, the FCC under Mr. Hundt's hand-picked successor—Mr. William E. Kennard—issued *"Connecting the Globe: A Regulator's Guide to Building a Global Information Community."*[2]

In this manifesto, the FCC argues that in "order to achieve the benefits of competition described above, governments and regulators must establish an appropriate policy framework to govern the telecommunications sector."[3] According to the FCC, creating this policy framework requires a three-step process: (1) governments should remove legal barriers that protect existing monopoly providers from competition by new entrants; (2) policymakers should take affirmative steps to promote competition in sectors of the market that were previously closed to competition; and (3) policymakers should consider introducing competitive safeguards to protect against the exercise of market power by incumbent carriers during the transition to competition.[4] The FCC went on to state that regardless of the individual method of entry—*i.e.*, facilities-based entry, unbundled network elements or resale—interconnection (and presumably subsumed therein, issues of collocation)—is the "key to competitive success."

While all of these statements are certainly true from a theoretical perspective, actions speak louder than words. Accordingly, if the FCC is intent on pontificating to the rest of the world how they should restructure and liberalise their indigenous markets, then it is also entirely legitimate to evaluate briefly the success and failure of the FCC's efforts to implement these criteria in its own

---

[1] See Reed Hundt, "Statement of FCC Chairman Reed Hundt Concerning WTO Agreement on Telecom Services", 1997 *WL* 63345 (18 Feb. 1997).
[2] See http://www.fcc.gov/connectglobe
[3] *Ibid*. Part V.
[4] *Ibid*.

domestic markets to date. Indeed, as one leading telecoms economist recently quipped, "while the US Telecoms Act made competition legal, the big question is whether the FCC made it possible." As explained below, however, the FCC's admonitions to the rest of the world hypocritically amount to nothing more than "do as I say, not as I do."

Just as in the international context, the FCC has been recalcitrant to promote additional entry in the domestic context. As noted *passim*, telecoms is a business characterized by high margins.[5] The ostensible purpose of restructuring, therefore, is to accelerate new facilities-based entry and thus have competitive pressures decrease these margins nearer to cost. Indeed, if the ostensible public policy goal is to move from a market characterized by monopoly to a market characterized by multiple firms, then (as repeated *passim*) the entry of *more* firms is the *sine qua non* of this entire exercise.

Mr. Kennard's policies (like Mr. Hundt's policies before him) have not sought to promote tangible new entry, however, but rather to reallocate rents among various segments of the industry to buy their silence to advance pet agendas such as politicising universal service to require an annual multi-billion dollar subsidy to provide Internet service to schools, libraries and Indian reservations or to ensure that broadcasters (i.e., incumbent users of spectrum) "voluntarily" transmit three hours of "acceptable" children's television each week. (Of course, as explained in Chapters 6–8, for international telecoms, the FCC makes sure that all of these rents vest to US firms.)[6] Thus, we do not have either competition or meaningful de-regulation in the US, but, once again, "fair, competition-like outcomes accompanied by the benevolent use of market-friendly regulation."

To provide some insight into recent FCC decisionmaking, one can look to several statements by current FCC Chairman William E. Kennard. The first statement was made several years ago when Mr Kennard was FCC General Counsel (under then FCC-Chairman Reed Hundt) when he remarked that when it came to formulating US telecoms policy, he would take will take a "bowling ball" or "straight down the middle" approach.[7] Recently, now-Chairman Kennard defended this approach by claiming that this "is the correct policy for a world of new technologies and convergence, where the primary objective is to protect consumer choice."[8] Such milquetoast statements are truly telling, as it confirms that that the FCC never had any intention of developing a long-term vision of a pro-competitive market structure.[9] Instead, the FCC simply prefers

---

[5] Price per unit minus variable costs per unit.

[6] See also William H. Melody, "Telecom Myths: The International Revenue Settlements Subsidy", 24 *Telecommunications Policy Online*, Feb. 2000 (http://www.tpeditor.com/melody.htm).

[7] "Industry Told to Avoid "Spins" in Arguing Legislative Intent", *Communications Daily*, 26 Feb 1996.

[8] "Readers' Report", *Business Week* 8 Nov. 1999.

[9] See discussion in Chapter 6 *supra*.

to attempt to appease everyone in the industry with consumer welfare left out of the question entirely.[10]

Indeed, a look at the FCC's actions *in toto* over the last several years reveal a disturbing trend of *quid pro quo* among incumbents and new entrants which reveals little analytical cohesion: First, one for the new entrants—the FCC issues interconnection and unbundling rules under the 1996 Telecoms Act; next, one for the incumbents—the FCC approves the almost total horizontal reconcentration of the ILEC, cable and broadcast industries in the US; next, one for the new entrants—the FCC orders incumbents to provide "line sharing" virtually at no cost to new entrants; next, one for the incumbents—the FCC approves the re-vertical integration of the market by granting Bell Atlantic's petition to provide in-region long-distance service in New York.

Accordingly, when viewing the FCC's domestic restructuring initiatives as a whole, there is no demonstration of any cohesive long-term view of industry structure. Instead, it appears that whatever efforts the FCC makes to promote competition with one hand, it takes away with the other. It is no surprise, therefore, that *both* incumbents and new entrants are dissatisfied with current policies, because neither side can figure out how to formulate a long-term business plan.

Let's review each of the FCC's policy decisions *in seriatim*.

II. UNBUNDLING

Call it what you will—"unbundled network elements" or ("UNEs"), "access to raw copper", "bit-stream unbundling" or "shared access"—but forcing

---

[10] A classic example of the FCC under the Clinton/Gore Administration's cynical efforts to just "settle everything away" can be found in the FCC's recent approach to access charge reform. On 31 May, the FCC proudly announced that it was going to reduce access charge fees paid by long-distance companies to local exchange carriers. See *In re Access Charge Reform*, FCC Rcd FCC 00–193 (rel, 31 May 2000). To make a complicated story short, the FCC accepted a backroom deal (a fact disdainfully noted by FCC Commissioner Hard Furchtgott-Roth) offered up by certain industry participants—i.e., the "Coalition for Affordable Local and Long Distance Service" or "CALLS"— whereby in exchange for eliminating multiple access charges paid by consumers to long-distance companies, US consumers would instead pay an increased flat monthly "subscriber line charge" (SLC) directly to the ILECs of $4.35 per line ending up at $6.50 per line in two years. While there may be *de minimus* relief for consumers, the reality is that long-distance companies are happy because it appears that their rates are declining (and therefore competitive against eventual RBOC entry into long-distance), and ILECs are happy because —considering the slow pace of residential competition in the United States—they have guaranteed themselves a steady revenue stream that is likely to continue for the forseeable future. In this way, the FCC cynically has rid itself of a thorny issue in a way that appears to lower user charges but without materially hurting the Bells' revenues.

Such a cynical and political approach to such an important issue stands in stark contrast to the FCC of fifteen years ago, where these difficult issues were approached with solemnity and academic rigour. Indeed, if readers want to see what a constructive, well-reasoned and analytically honest access charge reform proprosal should look like, then they should read the proposal set forth by former FCC Commissioner Anne P. Jones nearly twenty years ago. In the Matter of MTS and WATS Market Structure, CC Docket No. 78–72, Phase I, *Third Report And Order*, FCC 82–579, 93 F.C.C.2d 241 (1983), Separate Statement of Commissioner Anne P. Jones.

incumbents to provide rivals with access to elements of the local loop (either "à la carte" or by full resale) is one of the cornerstones of current telecoms restructuring efforts. While unbundling and interconnection may seem simple in concept, in reality unbundling is an extremely complex story and, more importantly, must be viewed in the context of broader telecoms restructuring efforts.

A. The "Micro-Level"

Before we turn to the public policy merits of unbundling, let's first view unbundling from the "micro-level." Specifically, how exactly does one go about splitting-up the existing public switched telephone network ("PSTN")?

Moreover, once you decide what network elements to split up and parse out, what about the all-important issue of pricing? On one hand, how do you determine the correct price for each unbundled element such that it will not be so high as to make entry unprofitable, yet at the same time be high enough to encourage facilities-based entry? On the other hand, how do you determine the correct price for each unbundled element such that the rate encourages resale entry (thus, as explained infra, creating new, non-incumbent demand to make new "wholesale" facilities-based entry profitable), yet at the same time not so low as to be confiscatory for the incumbent?

Indeed, policy makers must understand that when it comes to pricing decisions, they have to make a very important choice between two visions of the market. Do they want competition *"in the market"*—i.e., price competition; or would they prefer competition *"for the market"*—i.e., "innovation competition." One cannot have both in the short-run.[11]

That is to say, if policy-makers want *price competition*, because both fixed and sunk costs are important in telecommunications, they must understand that entry is really a *two-stage game*—i.e., (1) an entrant decides to enter the market and commit to making a substantial sunk cost in plant capacity; and then (2) the entrant makes a pricing strategy consistent with the first decision. As such, the decision to enter depends on the interplay between the fixed and sunk setup costs incurred in Stage 1 and the anticipated intensity of price competition that firms face in Stage 2.[12]

On the other hand, if policymakers want competition "for the market" (i.e., *innovation competition*), then they will have to implement a different set of policy paradigms. Specifically, policymakers must understand that telecommunications products and services tend to reflect the attributes of high-technology, namely: (1) *network effects*, such that the growing acceptance of a product by

[11] See Jerry B. Duvall, "Adapting Concepts of Competition Changes in Public Policy: Lessons from Federal Telecommunications Regulatory Experience in the United States", presented at the Phoenix Center For Advanced Legal & Economic Public Policy Studies 1999 Symposium on Managing the Strategic Impact of Competition Law in Telecoms, Brussels Belgium (8 February 1999).

[12] *Ibid.*

consumers increases its value to other consumers; (2) *economies of scale* in production such that marginal cost is less than average costs; (3) *large uncertainty* regarding the success or failure of new products; and (4) *large sunk costs* in the research and development of new products. Accordingly, competition "for the market" may be viewed as a dynamic process resulting in "winner take all" outcomes and strong critical mass effects.

The two policy decisions conflict because the attributes of high-technology markets tend to limit the intensity of price competition while encouraging firms to leapfrog, pre-empt, or otherwise introduce product innovations in order to attain market dominance. (For example, Microsoft's practice of "giving away" free copies of its Internet browser, thus making its overall Microsoft Office Suite of products more valuable to consumers.) Thus, although both price competition and innovation competition provide benefits to consumers, there tends to be a trade-off between the two types of competition. When public policy makers attempt to "have their cake and eat it too,"—i.e., formulate policies that only contemplate an open entry price competition framework—may inadvertently affect the mix of competition for the market and in the market.[13]

Finally, and perhaps most important of all, no matter what threat of regulation and punishment may lurk in the details, how do you get a firm (i.e., the incumbent) to provision its rivals with their key input (i.e. loops) of production on a timely basis when it is completely against their self-interest to do so in the first instance? Indeed, no amount of regulatory performance standards can really mitigate the incentive for strategic, anticompetitive conduct under current market conditions. As shown below, therefore, the physical act of obtaining "unbundled" elements of the incumbent's network is a rather difficult and technically complex process.[14]

1. What Should We Unbundle?

The first public policy decision to be made about unbundling is to decide exactly what "elements" of the local loop we want to "unbundle." In the case of the United States, Section 251(c)(3) of the 1996 Telecoms Act imposes a duty on all incumbent local exchange carriers (ILECs)—with a few exceptions—to provide to competitors with "non-discriminatory access to network elements on an unbundled basis at any technically feasible point on rates, terms and conditions that are just, reasonable and non-discriminatory. . . ." Under the Act, these elements are those components that give a new entrant the "ability . . . to provide the services it seeks to offer."[15] The FCC, after much deliberation, interpreted Section 251 to mean that incumbent LECs must make available, on an unbundled basis, the following network elements:

---

[13] *Ibid.*

[14] Moreover, as unbundling continues to become an increasingly technically complex exercise with the introduction splitters, restoration and testing issues, etc., resolving unbundling disputes is perhaps best left in the engineers' hands rather than those of lawyers and economists.

[15] See Communications Act Section 251(d)(2)(B); 47 U.S.C. § 251(d)(2)(B).

(1) local loops;
(2) network interface devices;
(3) local switching;
(4) interoffice transmission facilities;
(5) signalling networks and call-related databases;
(6) operations support systems; and
(7) operator services and directory assistance.

Although the 1996 Act imposes a duty on the incumbent to make certain network elements available on an unbundled basis, this duty is not unfettered, however. Instead, the FCC must determine, at minimum, whether:

(A) access to such network elements as are proprietary in nature is *necessary*; and
(B) the failure to provide access to such network element would *impair* the ability of the telecommunications carrier seeking access to provide the services that it seeks to offer."[16]

This test has now colloquially become known as the "'necessary" and "impair'" test. Suffice it to say, there has been zesty debate between incumbents and new entrants over the scope of this test.

In its *Interconnection Order* implementing Section 251,[17] the FCC attempted to deal with this problem by defining the term "necessary" to mean "an element is a prerequisite for competition,"[18] and by defining the term "impair" to mean "to make or cause to become worse; diminish in value."[19] The FCC also determined that a requesting carrier's ability to offer service is "impaired" ("diminished in value") if "the quality of the service the entrant can offer, absent access to the requested element, declines" or if "the cost of providing the service rises."[20]

Making a very long story short, the US Supreme Court—although upholding the FCC's generic authority to promulgate interconnection rules—concluded that the FCC had not adequately considered the "necessary" and "impair" standard of section 251(d)(2). The Court found, among other things, that the FCC in deciding which elements must be unbundled, did not adequately take into consideration the "availability of elements outside the incumbent's network." The Court also faulted the FCC's

> "assumption that any increase in cost (or decrease in quality) imposed by a denial of a network element renders access to that element 'necessary,' and causes the failure to provide that element to 'impair' the entrant's ability to furnish its desired services."

---

[16] 47 U.S.C. § 251(d)(2).

[17] Full reference required.

[18] *Ibid.*, 11 FCC Rcd at 15641–42, ¶ 282.

[19] *Ibid.*, 11 FCC Rcd at 15643, ¶ 285 (quoting Random House College Dictionary 665 (rev. ed. 1984)).

[20] *Ibid.*, 11 FCC Rcd at 15643, ¶ 285.

In addition, the Court criticised the FCC's interpretation of section 251(d)(2) because it "allows entrants, rather than the FCC, to determine" whether the requirements of that section are satisfied.[21]

The FCC responded to the Supreme Court's remand in the following ways.[22] First, the FCC determined that it is generally no longer necessary for ILECs to provide CLECs with access to their operator and directory assistance services. According to the FCC, because the market had developed since 1996 to where competitors can and do self-provision these services, or acquire them from alternative sources, there was no longer any reason to mandate access.

Second, the FCC also concluded, in light of competitive deployment of switches in the major urban areas, that—subject to certain conditions—incumbent LECs need not provide access to unbundled local circuit switching for customers with four or more lines that are located in the densest parts of the top 50 Metropolitan Statistical Areas (MSAs).

Third, the FCC addressed the unbundling obligations for network elements that were not on the original list in 1996. To the FCC's credit, the FCC required incumbents to provide unbundled access to subloops, or portions of loops, and dark fiber optic loops and transport. The FCC declined, however, except in limited circumstances, to require incumbent LECs to unbundle the facilities used to provide high-speed Internet access and other data services, specifically, packet switches and digital subscriber line access multiplexers (DSLAMs).

2. How Much Should it Cost?

Next, the parties (i.e., the incumbent and its "competitors" who seek to cannibalise its network) have to agree on how much these unbundled network elements are worth in the market. The popular methodology with regulators today is to require incumbents to sell these elements at prices based upon some form of forward-looking cost models (TELRIC, LRIC, *etc.*) and, moreover, that incumbents offer some sort of discount for full resale rather than on an "à la carte" basis.

The FCC held that the incumbent must make these unbundled elements available on a non-discriminatory basis using the local telephone companies' respective Total Service Long Run Incremental Cost of a particular network element, which the FCC calls "Total Element Long-Run Incremental Cost" (TELRIC), plus a reasonable share of forward-looking joint and common costs.[23]

---

[21] *AT&T Corp. et al.* v. *Iowa Utils. Bd. et al.*, 119 S.Ct. 721 (1999).

[22] *In re Implementation of the Local Competition Provisions of the Telecommunications Act of 1996, Third Report and Order and Fourth Further Notice of Proposed Rulemaking*, FCC No. 99–238 (rel. Nov. 5, 1999).

[23] Implementation of the Local Competition Provisions of the Telecommunications Act of 1996, CC Docket No. 96–98, *First Report and Order*, 11 FCC Rcd 15499 (1996) (Local Competition First Report and Order) at ¶ 29. Just as this book was going to press, the US Eighth Circuit Court of Appeals ruled on the FCC's choice of a forward-looking cost methodology. *Iowa Utilities Board et*

However, a new entrant may also elect to purchase all of these elements on a total "resale" bundled basis.[24] Under this scenario, full resale service is not priced by aggregating the cost of each individual element, but via a mandatory 17 per cent to 25 per cent discount below retail rate levels.[25]

How have the FCC's policy initiatives played out to date? First, as shown below, just getting the incumbent to provision a line has proven frustrating. Second, even assuming arguendo that a rival can get an incumbent to provision a full loop on a timely basis, given the FCC's pricing policies, if a firm wants to enter as an alternative voice provider in the US, stating it bluntly, full resale is a "dog"—*i.e.*, it is highly *unprofitable*. In the US, the average revenue of local telephone service is approximately $25. Even with a discount of 20 per cent (US $5), however, the other costs associated with capturing a customer are around $10. In other words, although it costs you $30 [$20 + $10] to provide service, you can only get $25 in revenue—*a net loss*.[26] Accordingly, *absent greater discounts or higher revenue potential, entry via resale is unprofitable.* As a consequence (along with continued incumbent recalcitrance to provision timely loops), entry via total resale into US domestic markets to date has been *de minimis*.[27] Thus,

al. v. *FCC*, No. 96–3321 (and consolidated cases) (8th Cir. Filed July 18, 2000). Although the court approved in principle the FCC's use of TELRIC, it did so with an important caveat.

In particular, the court rejected the FCC's use of a "hypothetical network standard"—i.e., that the "[t]he total element long-run incremental cost of an element should be measured based on the use of the most efficient telecommunications technology currently available and the lowest cost network configuration, given the existing location of the incumbent LEC's wire centers." (Slip op. at 6) According to the court, such a hypothetical standard violates the plain meaning of the 1996 Telecoms Act, because "Congress was dealing in reality, not fantisizing about what might be." Instead, reasoned the court,

> It is the cost to the ILEC of providing its existing facilities and equipment either through interconnection or by providing the specifically requested existing network elements that the competitor will in fact be ob taining for use that must be the basis for the charges. The new entrant competitor, in effect, piggybacks on the ILEC's existing facilities and equipment. It is the cost to the ILEC of providing that ride on those facilities that the statute permits the ILEC to recoup. This does not defeat the purpose of using a forward-looking methodology as the intervenors assert. Costs can be forward-looking in that they can be calculated to reflect what it will cost the ILEC in the future to furnish to the competitor those portions or capacities of the ILEC's facilities and equipment that the competitor will use including any system or component upgrading that the ILEC chooses to put in place for its own more efficient use. In our view it is the cost to the ILEC of carrying the extra burden of the competitor's traffic that Congress entitled the ILEC to recover, and to that extent, the FCC's use of an incremental cost approach does no violence tothe statute. At bottom, however, Congress has made it clear that it is the cost of providing the actual facilities and equipment that will be used by the competitor (and not some state of the art presently available technology ideally configured but neither deployed by the ILEC nor to be used by the competitor) which must be ascertained and determined. (Slip op. at 7–8)

However, the court refused to reach the question of whether rates set under TELERIC were confiscatory in this decision as unripe, because the "consequences of the FCC's choice to use TELRIC methodology cannot be known until the resulting rates have been determined and applied. . . ."

Given the important of the issues involved in this decision, appeal for a writ of *certiorari* to the US Supreme Court is virtually ensured.

[24] See 47 U.S.C. § 251(c)(4).

[25] Local Competition *First Report and Order* at ¶ 910. Not to mention that the epistemological foundation for these calculations lack cohesive, empirical strength.

[26] Stating this notion graphically, $D - X - E > 0$. Because D is revenue minus costs; revenue = $25, then Cost = 20 [$25(1–0.20)]+$10 (CLEC costs) = $30. In other words, $D < 0$ so entry does not occur.

[27] "AT&T's Armstrong Says Small Resale Discounts Delay Residential Competition",

while some firms are certainly entering via resale service—absent a proprietary technology that can enhance overall revenue potential by "souping up" basic resale service via web-based applications such as voice mail, "communications centres," and the like—a full resale strategy can only be short-term under current market conditions.

On the other hand, the economics of entry via using select unbundled elements—such as xDSL—are much different. That is to say, a xDSL provider needs only a conditioned copper loop to provide service, and not all of the other bells and whistles inherent to providing voice service. As such, even though loop rates and customer acquisition costs are still high, revenue is sufficiently higher ($40 to $80) so as to make entry profitable. Thus, given all of the hassles it takes to be a true "Competitive Local Exchange Carrier" ("CLEC") in the US (including, but not limited to, high exogenous and endogenous entry costs, USO obligations, build-out requirements, E–911, etc.), we do not see a lot of new entrants for voice service. Instead, we see the rise of a new kind of animal—the self-described "PCLEC" or "Data LEC." In other words, a firm that, under the current conditions of the market, has no rational incentive whatsoever of providing anything other than DSL services and who would not consider going near a Class 5 voice switch with a 10-foot pole.

3. Co-location

Finally, once you have a product to buy and sell (loop elements) and a price at which you can buy or sell these products for, then you then need to resolve the thorny issue of co-location. If you think this is easy, readers should note that it took the FCC *over three years* to promulgate finally a clear set of co-location rules, and the matter continued to be litigated before the courts and the FCC even as this book goes to press.[28]

While discussing the academic merits of unbundling is always interesting, the real challenge comes when a new entrant actually shows up at the incumbent's central office/local exchange and asks the incumbent's uncooperative employees to please pass the interconnection cable through the chicken-wire. Indeed, obtaining hassle-free physical collocation in the incumbent's central office/local exchange/local exchange is among one of the most significant entry costs for new firms.[29]

TeleCompetition Report 26 Feb. 1998 (Reporting that AT&T Chairman Michael Armstrong statement that because the current average discount rate of 22 per cent offered for wholesale local service, coupled with the "lack of [an unbundled network element platform]" means that no one can afford to go into the local exchange business. . . ." As such, Armstrong stated that because AT&T was losing $3 a month on each customer, AT&T was "not going to spend money on this fool's errand, and that's what [total service resale] is today."); "MCI Halts Drive into Residential Market Using Resale, Joins AT&T in Shift", *Communications Daily* 23 Jan. 1998.

[28] See, e.g., *GTE Services Corp.* v. *FCC*, 205 F3d 416 (D.C. Cir. 2000)(remanding portions of FCC's collocation order as arbitrary and capricious).

[29] Indeed, U.S. incumbents know this, and rationally price collocation in a manner akin to an "entry tax." These construction costs are lightly and ineffectually regulated (if at all) and oftentimes

In April 1999, the FCC responded finally to some (but clearly not all) of these issues by revising its collocation rules.[30] Under the FCC's new collocation rules:

(1) Incumbent LECs must make available to requesting competitive LECs shared cage *and cageless* collocation arrangements. Moreover, when collocation is exhausted at a particular LEC location, incumbent LECs must permit collocation in adjacent controlled environmental vaults or similar structures to the extent technically feasible.

(2) The FCC held that it would presume that a collocation method used by one incumbent LEC or mandated by a state commission is also technically feasible for any other incumbent LEC.

(3) Incumbent LECs may adopt reasonable security measures to protect their central office/local exchange/local exchange equipment.

(4) Incumbent LECs may not require competitive LEC equipment to meet more stringent safety requirements than those the incumbent LEC imposes on its own equipment.

(5) Incumbent LECs must permit competitors to collocate all equipment used for interconnection and/or access to unbundled network elements (UNEs), even if it includes a "switching" or enhanced services function, and incumbent LECs cannot require that the switching or enhanced services functionality of equipment be disengaged.

(6) Incumbent LECs must permit a competitive LEC to tour the entire central office/local exchange in which that competitive LEC has been denied collocation space. Incumbent LECs must provide a list of all offices in which there is no more space. Incumbent LECs must remove obsolete, unused equipment, in order to facilitate the creation of additional collocation space within a central office/local exchange.

However, provisioning delays and other operational shenanigans by incumbents' employees (*e.g.*, requiring new entrants to build a parking lot to accommodate ostensibly the increased traffic to the central office/local exchange; forcing new entrants to build an *external* four-story staircase to the central office/local exchange because permitting new entrants to use the internal elevator would raise too many "security" concerns, *etc.*) continue to delay entry.

4. How Have the FCC's Unbundling and Collocation Policies Worked to Date?

So exactly how successful have the FCC's unbundling and collocation efforts been four years after the passage of the 1996 Act? Sadly, they have been a dismal

are in excess of (U.S.) $100,000 for each central office/local exchange. With that type of entry tax, it is not surprising that there has been little entry into smaller or rural central office/local exchanges in the U.S.

[30] See *In re Deployment of Wireline Services Offering Advanced Telecommunications Capability*, First Report & Order and Further Notice of Proposed Rulemaking, FCC 99–48 (rel. 31 March 1999).

failure. Because the FCC and state commissions have failed to aggressively enforce these rules, even after nearly four years, the US unbundling experience has been a total disaster. In fact, the FCC conceded in its August 1999 Local Competition Report (even with tables updated as of 10 September 1999) that the aggregate amount of loops made available on an unbundled basis since the passage of the US Telecoms Act nearly four years ago is *"a still-small 0.2 per cent of total [Incumbent] lines."*[31] Moreover, according to the same report, there are even some states in which no lines have been provided on an unbundled basis.

This pitiful progress has improved only marginally over time. When the FCC released its most updated numbers in March 2000 just as this book was going to press, ILECs reported leasing lines to CLECs under UNE arrangements increased by 90 per cent in the first half of 1999, but nonetheless "remained a small 0.4 per cent of total ILEC lines—about 0.7 million lines as of June 30, 1999." Moreover, this report again indicated that in states such as Idaho, South Dakota and Wyoming, *no lines* (i.e., zero) were provided under UNE arrangements.[32]

Resale does not fare much better. According to this same report, the rate of increase of resold ILEC services has slowed, no doubt as the result of the FCC's pricing policies.[33] Moreover, although the FCC does not receive from CLECs data on the number of customer lines they provide solely over their own facilities or data about the types of customers they serve over their own facilities or by means of leased UNE loops, the FCC found that most CLECs had more success reselling selling specialized services, such as special access and local private line services, than they have had selling basic switched local service to end users.[34] In other words, *they bleed red ink.*

B. The "Macro-Level"

Now, however, let's view "unbundling" from the macro-level. In other words, while all of the details discussed above are nice, exactly what do we hope to achieve from such a draconian policy initiative? Indeed, imposing unbundling must have a purpose aside from the vague notion that it would be a "good idea" or, worse yet, simply because some other country may be imposing unbundling as well.

[31] Local Competition: August 1999, Federal Communications Commission, Common Carrier Bureau, Industry Analysis Division at Table 3.3 (http://www.fcc.gov/Bureaus/Common_Carrier/Reports/FCC-State_Link/IAD/lcomp99–1.pdf).

[32] Trends in Telephone Service (March 2000), Industry Analysis Division, Common Carrier Bureau, Federal Communications Commission at 9–3, http://www.fcc.gov/Bureaus/Common_Carrier/Reports/FCC-State_Link/trends.html

[33] According to the Report: the 17 per cent increase during the first six months of 1999 compares to a 25 per cent increase during the last six months of 1998 and a 40 per cent increase during the first six months of 1998. *Ibid.*, at 9–2.

[34] *Ibid.*, at 9–1.

The answer is easy: unbundling should be one of several tools in the policy-makers arsenal of pro-entry policies that hopefully will lead eventually to facilities-based infrastructure competition (on either a wholesale or vertically-integrated basis). Once this demand is realised and facilities-based competition exists, however, mandatory asymmetrical unbundling should, in theory, no longer be necessary.[35] In other words, because regulation has both costs and benefits, there should be an end-purpose to any government intervention into the market. Unbundling should not be used to create a "static, incumbent-centric perpetual resale model" where everyone purchases their primary input from a single monopoly provider.

So how does unbundling come into play to accelerate new entry? The idea behind unbundling is that because there are high entry barriers into the local access market are so high, unbundling—i.e., a weak form of divestiture—seeks to "leapfrog" those barriers to accelerate the pace of competition.[35a] In its most simplest form, unbundling is supposed to lead to new facilities-based competition by providing new entrants initially with the appearance of "ubiquity" and economies of scope necessary to enter a very costly business—i.e., the entrant would first develop its customer base, and (because it has no desire to purchase its primary inputs of production from its rivals) would then build-out as conditions warrant. Such a strategy is often referred to as a "smart-build" approach.[36] This is precisely what the FCC did in its *1980 MTS/WATS Resale Decision* to great success for the US long-distance market.

Unfortunately, however, given the huge sunk costs and risks associated with constructing a new, alternative residential access network, many firms will not (or cannot) afford the "smart-build" approach. What do we do now? Again, the answer is easy: Use unbundling to create sufficient new alternative "non-incumbent" demand such that an alternative distribution company ("ADCo") discussed in previous chapters economically attractive and viable to serve this consolidated demand.

---

[35] This is not to say that some form of mandatory resale should continue in perpetuity. Resale serves many important functions in a market. For example, it provides an entry strategy for a firm who may seek to introduce new technologies into the market. In addition, a vibrant resale market also can keep the market it check by differentiating themselves with better customer service, etc. Given the pathetically slow progress of unbundling both in the US and in Europe, however, any suggestion that market conditions have changed so significantly that it is appropriate to sunset unbundling initiatives at this time is both premature and specious at best.

[35a] From a transaction cost economic perspective, probably the most efficient (and actually value-enhancing) policy would be to impose mandatory divestiture of the incumbent's loop plant from its marketing arm, rather than go the current agonizing process of heaping massive amounts of price, structural and conduct regulation attempting to force the incumbent into conduct against its (perceived) self-intent. As demonstrated *passim*, this option is a political non-starter.

[36] Take for example the U.S. experience, where the most likely entrants into the local market (i.e., those with the greatest spillover effects)—the big three long-distance companies of AT&T, MCIWorldcom and Sprint—have, at the time of this writing, refused to construct alternative advanced networks from the ground-up. AT&T instead has bought numerous cable monopolies; MCIWorldcom is adopting a short-term approach of full resale for only its largest long-distance customers (i.e., the only way to offset the net loss of full resale pricing on a stand-alone bass) and sought to merge with Sprint.

To wit, assume arguendo that after a new firm performs its initial cost modelling, the numbers reveal that a new facilities-based entrant will need a 40 per cent market share to survive. (In other words, the market is only capable of sustaining 2.5 firms.)[37] As noted above, given the huge costs of entering this business, few firms would be willing to risk their capital for such an endeavour (e.g., AT&T, MCIWorldcom and Sprint). However, who says that only one firm has to provide all of this entire market share? If unbundling is successful, then it is entirely possible for four firms to provide 10 per cent of the market; 10 firms provide 4 per cent of the market; 40 firms serve 1 per cent of the market, etc. and then have an ADCO enter and consolidate and serve this new demand.

Accordingly, unbundling is supposed to be a two-stage process: (1) unbundle and stimulate new alternative, non-incumbent demand; and (2) have new facilities-based entry to serve this consolidated demand. Where the FCC's current efforts fail, among other things, is their apparent belief that unbundling is sufficient, *in-and-of-itself*, to solve telecoms' current ills and therefore they need also not do anything else affirmatively to promote additional facilities-based-entry. Wrong. So long as regulators do absolutely nothing to provide alternative mechanisms of delivery (especially as technology grows and develops), then consumers will suffer in the long-run with the current "static, incumbent-centric perpetual resale model" now in place because neither incumbents nor new entrants will have any incentive whatsoever to invest in new plant.

To wit, as explained in Chapter 3, as a general matter, telecoms is a very expensive, capital-intensive business to be in (i.e., very high exogenous entry costs). For example, not only does a new firm have to incur such costs as the construction of facilities, but also must develop a billing system as well. Perhaps, however, the largest expense to any new entrant is marketing and customer retention, costs that can actually be expected to *increase* as competition takes hold.[38] So long as a new entrant continues to perceive that it will make more money than it costs to provide the service, however, then entry will nonetheless continue to occur.

---

[37] *CF.* John Sutton, *Sunk Cost and Market Structure* (MIT Press, 1991). Basically, there exist an equilibrium number of firms in an industry (N*). This equilibrium number of firms depends on: (1) The size of the market in expenditures (+); (2) The size and nature of production cost (−); and (3) The intensity of price competition (−). This can be represented as:

$$N^* = \frac{1}{\text{Minimum Market Share}}$$

Thus, the larger are economies of scale and sunk costs, the larger is the market share required to justify entry. In the case of telecoms, the minimum market share for a facilities-based local provider of mass market local service is large, suggesting high concentration in that market—i.e., facilities based entrant for mass market will require large market share (20–50 per cent). The telecoms market therefore stands (for example) in contrast to the market for fast food or "take away" restaurants (e.g., McDonalds) where in any given city, you see numerous burger-joints all within one square mile of each other because they need a *de minimis* market share to survive.

[38] *Cf.* Douglas A. Galbi, "The Price of Telecoms Competition: Counting the Cost of Advertising and Promotion", (1999) 1 *Info* 133.

But this is not the end to the entry story in the telecoms business. As also discussed in Chapter 3, there are also significant endogenous entry costs (i.e., incumbent or regulation induced entry costs) that also can and do act as significant barriers to entry. As such, whatever good may come from an aggressive unbundling regime, these benefits have no meaning so long as these other policy-relevant barriers to entry are not concurrently removed.

The common regulatory excuse for this lack of policy priority on concurrently promoting aggressively new infrastructure entry essentially boils-down to a "ripeness" argument. That is to say, many regulators argue that giving priority (either equal or superior) to infrastructure investment over unbundling—*i.e.*, promoting a "Build it and They Will Come" entry strategy—is just, as the cinema title goes, a "Field of Dreams." Instead, regulators argue that entry will occur *only* if new entrants are permitted first to enter by resale in order to stimulate and consolidate alternative demand.

Sadly, this is not a policy of "Field of Dreams" but of "Waiting for Godot." That is to say, many regulators contend that because no new entrant will build any facilities unless it is assured of a customer base and revenue stream, entry will occur only if new entrants are permitted first to enter by resale in order to stimulate and consolidate alternative demand. As such, these regulators argue that giving priority (either equal or superior) to infrastructure investment over unbundling improperly promotes wasteful and duplicative facilities.[39] This position is just plain wrong and, as noted above, the discounts that are available are not sufficient for a viable resale business in local exchange distribution.

Let's be quite clear: we are not talking about Malaysian real estate here. We are talking about an industry with an almost insatiable demand for new capacity. Indeed, the demand in many markets is there and is screaming to be satisfied! Unfortunately, however, this demand will never be satisfied so long as regulators continue to impose barriers to entry such as (but definitely not limited to) geographic build-out and rate averaging requirements, failing to resolve building access/inside wiring issues, and permitting all of the industries under its jurisdiction to reconcentrate.

The pro-competitive reasons why policy-makers must also concurrently promote new infrastructure entry are undeniable. As discussed in chapter 4 *supra*,

---

[39] The FCC's approach is in direct contrast to the approach adopted in New Zealand. As explained in more detail in Chapter 2, for better or for worse, the New Zealand government established a series of bright-line structural rules with residual anticompetitive conduct addressed by competition law. What really distinguishes the New Zealand approach from that adopted by the U.S., however, is that New Zealand also took aggressive steps to reduce endogenous entry barriers by, *inter alia*, creating the notion of "Network Operator Status," which provides a company with the right to apply for a court order to install telecommunications plant on both public and private company. Moreover, designation is automatic on those that qualify, and no fee is payable. See New Zealand Telecommunications Information Publication No. 6, Minister of Commerce, Resources and Networks Branch (December 1998) at ¶ 28 and Annex I. As the result of such pro-entry policies, Telstra (the Australian incumbent) plans to construct an advanced broadband network that will pass over two-thirds of all New Zealand residences. Thus, if the end goal of facilities-based competition has been achieved, there is no need for asymmetrical unbundling in this case.

perhaps the most compelling reason is that to the extent the market can sustain additional providers of alternative local-loop distribution companies ("ADCos") who can actually supply reliable loops on a non-discriminatory wholesale basis, then the overall structure of the distribution market will shift. As this shift occurs and the underlying market structure becomes more competitive, the incumbent will no longer have the incentive to engage in entry-deterring strategies, but rather have an incentive to disaggregate voluntarily—rather than by intrusive regulatory fiat—its loop plant from its marketing activities because it will be a more efficient and profitable way to organise its business. That is to say, the incumbent will find under this market structure that it will make more money by disaggregation because its network operation will be able to sell more loops to more providers, and because its marketing operation will be able to provide cheaper service since it will be able to buy loops from competitive infrastructure providers.

But what is happening in the United States? Because "convergence" is taking priority over competition, we see the bizarre outcome of American consumers having the appearance of a "choice" among data providers selling a US $80 broadband service over resold unbundled loops from the same carrier, but residential telephone rates continue to rise due to the imposition of fees on consumers' bills such as a "subscriber line charge" and a "universal connectivity charge" and there is no competitive pressure from rival infrastructure providers. Had the FCC focused more appropriately on reducing (and not imposing more) regulatory barriers to facilities-based entry instead of inappropriately promoting the interests of specific competitors over those of consumers as a whole, competition for local access in the US would be a lot further along.

In sum, if telecoms regulators truly want restructuring to work, then they must view unbundling in the correct context. Remember, what we don't need are more "competitors" or "choices" *per se*—what we need are *more loops*.

III.   INCUMBENT RECONCENTRATION

A. Analytical Framework

When discussing issues of horizontal concentration, it is crucial to avoid resorting to the populist arguments that government intervention is appropriate merely because a particular company is too "big" or makes "too much money." Under long-standing US antitrust law precedent, it is perfectly acceptable for a firm to gain market power by superior business acumen or even historical accident.[40] Market power, like all human endeavours, is really a question of *degree*.

Accordingly, the appropriate inquiry should not focus on whether a particular firm *has* market power, but rather on whether the firm has the ability to *exercise* this market power successfully (*i.e.*, raise prices or restrict output) and

---

[40] *Eastman Kodak Co.* v. *Image Tech. Serv. Inc.*, 112 S.Ct. 2072, 2089 (1992); *United States* v. *Grinnell Corp.*, 384 U.S. 563, 570–71 (1966).

affect adversely market performance (*i.e.*, consumer welfare). Stated another way, policy-makers should look to see if increased horizontal concentration will permit the merged firm to raise prices or restrict output and, in particular, erect or maintain barriers to new entry. Indeed, high levels of market concentration *may* reflect (1) the effects of price competition; and (2) the attributes of high-technology products on innovation competition. As such, market concentration is not necessarily inimical to consumer welfare in markets where innovation competition is important. Quite to the contrary, given the quantitative significance of both exogenous sunk set-up costs and endogenous sunk costs in modern telecommunications networks, it is likely that local telecommunications, even in the longer term, will be highly concentrated, not withstanding public policies intended to foster competitive entry.[41]

However, although economies of scope can certainly have pro-competitive benefits, economies of scope can also enhance the ability of a dominant firm to engage in strategic anti-competitive conduct. That is to say, because of the significant costs of entry (especially for residential, local telephone competition), entry rarely occurs in "waves of competition" on a large-scale basis. Rather, entry usually occurs in "pin point" attacks wherever the incumbent may be the most vulnerable. Yet, if the incumbent enjoys significant economies of scope, then it may attempt to allocate the defence costs of these attacks over a much wider customer base where competitive pressures may not be present—*i.e.*, the more captive customers an incumbent may have, the more the per unit share of defence costs will decrease. If there are enough customers to make the per unit/customer share sufficiently *de minimis*—such that neither captive consumers nor regulators notice (or care about) this *de minimis* increase in price—then the incumbent has used successfully its economies of scope to both successfully deter entry and evade regulation.[42]

The ability to engage in such strategic conduct is also exacerbated by the number of jurisdictions a firm provides service in. That is to say, as the number of independent regulatory bodies increases, then the easier it may be for the regulated firm to play one public utility commission (or, in the case of Europe, a National Regulatory Authority) off of another—in other words, *regulatory evasion*. When this occurs, those captive ratepayers who live in rural or high cost areas where competitive entry may not be (to put it politely) immediate, may inadvertently end up paying higher rates against their own interests.[43]

---

[41] See Jerry B. Duvall, *supra* n. 11.

[42] Indeed, it is the potential to use strategically economies of scope successfully to deter new entry is significant reason why the 1996 Act (and the MFJ before that) prohibited the BOCs from interLata entry but permitted other LECs such as SNET and Cincinnati Bell (with their relatively small footprint) or GTE (with its very diverse yet non-contiguous footprint) to enter the long-distance market immediately.

[43] It is also equally important to recognise the converse of this rule: Legitimate concerns about regulatory evasion are similarly not an excuse for increased government intervention to maximise "regulatory"—as opposed to "economic"—efficiency. See *infra* n. 63.

B. Statutory Authority

The FCC is vested with broad jurisdiction to review telecommunications industry transactions through a number of statutory provisions. These provisions are:

(1) Communications Act Section 310(d), § 47 USC. 310(d). Under this statute,
no construction permit or station license may be transferred, assigned or
disposed of in any manner, "voluntarily or involuntarily, directly or
directly, *or by transfer or control of any corporation holding such license
or permit*" to any person "except upon application to the Commission
and upon finding by the Commission that the public interest, convenience
and necessity will be served thereby."

(2) Communications Act Section 310(b)(4), 47 USC. § 310(b)(4). Under this
statute, no broadcast or common carrier license may be controlled,
directly or indirectly, by a foreign entity if the FCC finds that "the public
interest will be served by the refusal or revocation of such license."

(3) Communications Act Section 214, 47 USC. § 214. Under section 214, no
common carrier shall acquire any line "unless and until there shall first
have been obtained from the Commission a certificate that the present or
future public convenience and necessity require or will require" the operation of the line.

(4) Communications Act Section 221(a), 47 USC. § 221(a). Under section
221(a), if the FCC finds that a "proposed consolidation, acquisition, or
[acquisition of] control" of "telephone companies" "will be of advantage
to the persons to whom service is to be rendered and in the public interest, it shall certify to that effect; and thereupon any Act or Acts of
Congress making the proposed transaction unlawful shall not apply."[44]
The statute expressly preserves any state jurisdiction over mergers.[45]

(5) Communications Act Section 314, 47 USC. § 314. Section 314 of the
Communications Act forbids anticompetitive acquisitions of certain

---

[44] The section has various other requirements: the telephone companies must apply for the
antitrust exemption; and the FCC must give notice to the Governor and state Commission of each
affected state, must accept comments, and must hold a public hearing in certain circumstances.
    The FCC has held the "public hearing" requirement to be satisfied by its notice and comment pro-
cedures. *Pacific Northwest Bell Tel. Co.*, Memorandum Opinion and Order (ENF 85–52), 1986 WL
292012 (¶¶ 5–9) (Com. Car. Bur. 1986) (hereinafter "PNB"), reconsideration granted in part and
denied in part, 2 F.C.C. Rcd. 2019 (Com. Car. Bur. 1987). This is consistent with numerous holdings that "hearing" means an opportunity for interested persons to make their views known. Except
in the rare case where witnesses' factual perceptions are in dispute (such as "who had the green
light?"), a "hearing" need not be a "trial-type" evidentiary hearing. *United States v. Florida East
Coast Railway Co.*, 410 U.S. 224, 243–46 (1973); *The Bell Telephone Co. of Pennsylvania v. FCC*,
503 F.2d 1250, 1266 (3d Cir. 1974), *cert. denied*, 422 U.S. 1026 (1976). Only statutes that require a
"hearing on the record" confer the right to the latter kind of hearing. See *United States v. Florida
East Coast Railway Co.*, 410 U.S. 224 (1973).

[45] It states: "Nothing in this subsection shall be construed as in any way limiting or restricting the
powers of the several States to control and regulate telephone companies."

international carriers. No reported court or FCC decision has interpreted this statute in more than a cursory way, or has found a violation of it.

(6) Clayton Act Section 11, 15 USC. § 21. Under this provision, the FCC is vested with the authority to enforce section 7 of the Clayton Act over common carriers.[46] If the FCC elects to use its section 7 authority, it must issue an administrative complaint alleging a violation of Section 7 of the Clayton Act, and set the matter for hearing.[47] However, unlike the mandatory requirements of sections 214 and 310 above, the FCC's section 7 authority is discretionary. Moreover, The FCC has only "limited" experience under Section 11.[48]

C. The FCC's Approach to Mergers Under the Clinton/Gore Administration

Despite the FCC's various attempts to write "pro-competitive rules" (the FCC refuses to acknowledge that because it is a regulatory body, it writes *regulations* that have both costs and benefits) to further the interests of "competition, community and common sense,"[49] the empirical evidence unfortunately supports the conclusion that the FCC's efforts (as well as the efforts of the United States' Department of Justice) to date on reviewing incumbent reconcentration have been a dismal failure.[50] Indeed, since the passage of the 1996 Act, the telecoms

---

[46] Section 7 of the Clayton Act prohibits a firm from acquiring stock and assets "in any line of commerce in any section of the country the effect of [which] may be substantially to lessen competition, or to tend to create a monopoly." 15 U.S.C.A. § 18.

[47] The language of section 11 and cases involving the enforcement activities of other agencies suggest that the FCC must await an agreement between the parties (though not the consummation of the agreement) before bringing an administrative complaint. See *FTC* v. *Dean Foods Co.*, 384 U.S. 597, 605 (1965); *United States* v. *Manufacturers Hanover Trust Co.*, 240 F. Supp. 867 (S.D.N.Y. 1965). However, the FCC may seek a preliminary injunction from the Court of Appeals under the All Writs Act to prevent consummation of the agreement pending prosecution of the administrative proceeding. *FTC* v. *Dean Foods Co.*, 384 U.S. at 605. (Court of Appeals has jurisdiction to issue a preliminary injunction preventing consummation of an agreement upon a showing that effective remedial action post-consummation would be virtually impossible, rendering enforcement of final divestiture decree futile).

[48] See H.R. Rep. No. 580, 86th Cong., 1st Sess. 20 (1959), cited in *United States* v. *FCC*, 652 F.2d 72, 85 n.65 (D.C. Cir. 1980)(en banc). Thus, as discussed below, while the FCC's Clayton Act authority is often alluded to in FCC orders involving industry transactions, the FCC typically acts either under Section 310 or 214 of the Communications Act. Accordingly, we are unaware of any recent case where the FCC actually brought a Clayton Act administrative complaint. See, e.g., *In re Applications of NYNEX and Bell Atlantic for Consent to Transfer Control*, Memorandum Opinion and Order, FCC 97–286 (rel. Aug. 14, 1997) at ¶ 29; *In re Applications of Ameritech and SBC Communications for Consent to Transfer Control*, Memorandum Opinion and Order, FCC 99–279 (rel. Oct. 8, 1999) at ¶ 53.

[49] See "Kennard Takes Helm of FCC, Sounds Pro-Consumer Themes", *TR Wireless News* 13 November 1997 ("In his first public statements last week as chairman of the FCC, William E. Kennard set a pro-consumer tone, vowing to make 'competition, community, and common sense' his watchwords.") While this is certainly very nice, readers should note how the word "consumers" is conspicuously absent.

[50] If you really think about it, we really should not be so surprised by this considering the fact that the FCC was headed by a self-described antitrust lawyer who stated publicly that three incumbents could actually produce more competition. See Jared Sandberg & Steven Lipin, "Bell Atlantic and GTE Boards Approve Plans for a Merger", *Wall Street Journal*, 28 July 1998, at A3 (according

industry in all segments has undergone—in the FCC's own words—"unprecedented consolidation."[51] In the telecoms/cable markets alone, not only have the FCC and the DOJ approved the near total reconcentration of the ILEC industry (e.g., Bell Atlantic/NYNEX, SBC/PacTel, SBC/Ameritech,[52] Bell Atlantic/GTE), but also have given their acquiescence to new entrants' attempts to acquire dominant local access players as well (e.g., AT&T/TCI, AT&T/Media One,[53] Quest/US West, Global Crossing/Frontier).[54]

So what kind of market structure is emerging in the US post- the 1996 Act? Not a very good one. With the merger of Bell Atlantic/GTE (now Verizon), the US government has permitted the creation of a telecoms behemoth that controls more than one third of all local access lines in the United States nationwide and, like in cable, a near monopoly of local lines in their core territories. As if this reconcentration is not bad enough, we must also remember that when the FCC

to Mr. Hundt, the spate of recent consolidations (in particular, AT&T/TCI, Ameritech/SBC, and Bell Atlantic/GTE) "would mean a triumvirate of telecom giants is likely to emerge, resulting in more competition.") (emphasis added).

[51] See FCC Press Release 12 January 2000, "FCC Implements Predictable, Transparent and Streamlined Review Process". For example, consider the case of the US radio industry. Because Congress eliminated the FCC's radio ownership rules in the 1996 Act, the FCC (with the full acquiescence of the US Department of Justice) apparently believes that it has a green light to permit many radio markets to reconcentrate down to a clear duopoly (i.e., two firm) market. The running joke about this broadcast reconcentration among US communications lawyers is that under the FCC's old (and inaccurate) radio nomenclature, "duopoly" meant that one simply owned two stations in the same market. As the FCC apparently refuses to engage in any reasoned decision-making by applying economic theory correctly to the market, at least it is nice to see that the FCC is attempting to have the market fit the correct economic definition of duopoly.

[52] Indeed, despite the "pro-competitive voluntary" commitments the FCC extracted from the merging parties, this merger nonetheless leaves the combined company with control of almost one third of all access lines in the U.S. According to SBS CEO Ed Whitacre, however, such a reconcentration was necessary because only a merger would enable SBC to take on the likes of AT&T and MCI. In Mr. Whitacre's words, "We can sit here and get picked on, or get bigger and have more clout." "The Top Executive", *Business Week* 11 Jan. 1999.

[53] This merger now gives AT&T 30 per cent of the US multichannel delivered programming market. While this may not seem like a lot, readers must realise that cable service is offered on a local franchise basis, of which AT&T will be the dominant, if not exclusive, provider in its core territories. What makes this decision so cynical however, is that it represents the exact opposite result from what was so vigorously promised to us seven years ago by the Hundt/Kennard adminstration—that is, meaningful competition for multichannel delivered programming. So what happened? Basically the FCC—through inept policies and actions—never developed a coherent policy paradigm and, as such, used up its political capital with both the industry and the Congress. Afraid to take a stand therefore, the FCC essentially gave up on promoting competition and tried to obfuscate the issue with rhetoric that cable "clustering" will provide both immediate and effective competition to local phone monopolies.

Hardly. US cable systems were never designed to carry two-way voice traffic over a "star" architecture network using coaxial cable. Thus, overcoming the challenge of upgrading these systems to send voice is proving both costly and technologically frustrating. Such a situation stands in stark contrast to Europe, where many cable operators constructed their systems originally with both a twisted pair and a coaxial cable to the home. As such, US consumers should not be holding their breath in expectation of their cable operators —and industry that is notorious for poor quality and customer service —offering reliable and competitive voice service at any time soon.

[54] Specific mergers in which trade concerns trumped any form of competitive analysis are discussed in greater detail in Chapter 18 *infra*.

and DOJ approved SBC/Ameritech in December 1999, it gave that merged company control over another third of all local access lines in the United States.

What is more incredulous, however, is that the FCC officials attempt to rationalise this unprecedented reconcentration on the ground that the FCC can use the merger review process to extract sufficient "voluntary commitments" from the merging parties to make the proposed transaction ostensibly *accelerate* the pace of competition.[55] If these "voluntary commitments" were really so draconian, however, then why would any incumbent have an incentive to merge in the first instance? As such, forcing the incumbents to do what they already required by law to do (and what the FCC is required to enforce in the first instance) does not make almost total industry reconcentration any more acceptable.[56]

In a similar vein, the FCC rationalises this total industry reconcentration by arguing that these mergers are in the public interest because the increase in scale and scope will help these merged entities to compete outside of their core territory. However, given the fact that these companies enjoy a near monopoly control in their profitable and growing home markets, to think that one monopolist would have any real incentive to enter into another monopolist's territory (other than by acquisition) for example, take Verizon's (formerly Bell Atlantic) recent deal with Northpoint Communications. Under the terms of this deal, in exchange for fifty-five per cent ownership in Northpoint, Verizon will contribute its DSL assets to Northpoint as well as [US] $800 million. Although the deal will purportedly benefit the DSL business of both Verizon and Northpoint, this is not the whole of the story—this deal also resolves some pressing regulatory issues for Verizon as well. Specifically, as part of its various merger conditions, Verizon had agreed to spend [US] $500 million on out of region expansion, and this deal certainly falls within this ambit. More significantly, however, by placing its DSL into a publicly-held, separate affiliate with forty-five per cent outside equity ownership, Verizon has very cleverly attempted to

[55] See, e.g., Press Statement of FCC Chairman William E. Kennard Regarding SBC-Ameritrech Merger 6 Oct. 1999:

"The option we choose today not only balances the contending issues at stake but it moves forward, in a concrete wave, virtually the entire telecommunications industry. The conditions to which SBC and Ameritech agreed, after arduous but entirely professional and good faith discussions with Commission staff, will change the status quo to the benefit of telecommunications consumers. These conditions will create an irreversible momentum to open local markets, both inside and outside of the SBC-Ameritech territories, while freeing all industry participants to compete fully and fairly to offer advanced telecommunications services to all Americans. The conditions will also expedite the deployment of high speed Internet access and other broadband services to consumers in low income and rural areas."

[56] See Frank Easterbrook, "The Court and the Economic System", (1984) 98 *Harv. L. Rev.* 4, 39:

"Often an agency with the power to deny an application (say, a request to commence service) or to delay the grant of the application will grant approval only if the regulated firm agrees to conditions. The agency may use this power to obtain adherence to rules that it could not require by invoking statutory authority. The conditioning power is limited, of course, by private responses to the ultimatums—firms will not agree to conditions more onerous than the losses they would suffer from the agency's pursuit of the options expressly granted by the statute. The firm will accept the options expressly granted by the statute. The firm will accept the conditions only when they make both it and the agency (representing the public or some other constituency) better off. Still, though, the agency's options often are potent, and the grant of an application on condition may greatly increase the span of the agency's control."

assuage regulators' concerns about affiliate-self dealing and the like,[57] in order to meaningfully compete for local service — as the FCC promises — is just wishful thinking.[57a]

Accordingly, it does not take a rocket scientist to realize that there is something dreadfully wrong with this picture. Rather than promote new entry, the FCC simply condones state-sanctioned, horizontal market division (previously regarded as a *per se* violation of competition laws around the world) and engages in backroom deals to preserve economic rents all in the guise of promoting consumer welfare.

This is not to say, however, that the FCC has not attempted to develop some kind of pseudo-analytical cover to convince both naïve consumers and naïve politicians on Capitol Hill that they are firmly out to protect and promote the public interest from increased industry reconcentration. In a speech narcissistically entitled *Thinking About Why Some Communications Mergers are Unthinkable* delivered at the Brookings Institution, former FCC Chairman Reed Hundt proudly announced his vision (or, more accurately, the revision) of how the FCC should analyse telecommunications industry mergers post-1996 Act— *i.e.*, the "effectively precluded competitor" framework.[58]

Yet, because, as Mr Hundt's title clearly implies, the *EPC* framework was designed, at bottom, to provide nothing more than political cover for the FCC's then-anticipated (and pre-determined) dispositions of *BT-MCI* ("thinkable" if "neo-mercantile" trade objectives are achieved),[59] Bell Atlantic/NYNEX and SBC/Ameritech ("thinkable" if enough voluntary commitments are obtained), this "framework"—by its very purpose—was forced to abandon any firm legal or economic analytical foundation when precedent or first principles conflicted with the pre-determined outcome.[60] In doing so, the FCC unnecessarily subjected itself

---

[57] See Anna-Maria Kovacs et al, *Janny Montgomery Scott Investment Report* (9 August 2000).

[57a] The FCC believes that it can impose "voluntary" commitments to alleviate this problem however. For example, in the Bell Atlantic/GTE merger order, the merged entity agreed to a "voluntary commitment" that would require them, within 36 months of closing, to spend at least (US) $500 million to provide competitive local service and associated services outside of the Bell Atlantic and GTE legacy service areas. If the merged entity fails to comply with this "voluntary commitment" however, then the merged entity "will be subject to voluntary payments to the US Treasury in the amount of 150 per cent of any shortfall in its out-of-region expenditure." See *In re Application of GTE Corporation, and Bell Atlantic for Consent to Transfer Control of Domestic and International Sections 214 and 310 Authorizations and Application to Transfer Control of a Submarine Cable Landing License, Memorandum Opinion and Order*, FCC 00–221 (rel. 16 June 2000) at ¶¶319–323.

[58] See, Reed Hundt, "Thinking About Why Some Communications Mergers are Unthinkable", (Delivered to the Brookings Institution, Washington D.C. 19 June 1997); but see *TV Communications Network, Inc.* v. *Turner Network Television, Inc.*, 964 F.2d 1022, 1026 (10th Cir.), *cert. denied*, 113 S. Ct. 601 (1992); *Hawaiian Telephone* v. *FCC*, 498 F.2d 771, 776–77 (D.C. Cir. 1974) (FCC "cannot merely assert the benefits of competition in an abstract, sterile way").

[59] See chapter 1 *supra*.

[60] Unfortunately, the FCC's subjective, arbitrary approach to merger review continues to this day. See June 24, 1998 Statement From FCC Chairman William E. Kennard on AT&T And TCI Proposed Merger ("If AT&T and TCI make a strong commitment to bring residential consumers more choice in local telephone and high speed Internet access services, then this proposed merger is eminently thinkable.") Indeed, now that the cow is essentially out of the barn regarding ILEC, cable

to claims of arbitrary and capricious decision-making—especially when the FCC's policy objectives could have been achieved equally using a more "analytically honest" approach.[61]

What is even more disturbing, however, is the fact that the FCC has used successfully its *EPC* framework as political/analytical cover to extract sufficient "voluntary" concessions or "involuntary" conditions to "buy off" opposing parties from contesting the case. "Regulatory shakedowns" should not be the centrepiece of the FCC's litigation-avoidance strategy. At the end of the day, the FCC simply cannot use "voluntary" commitments to make either economically (*i.e.*, when the FCC's own competitive analysis concludes that the merger should not be permitted to move forward) or politically (*i.e.*, where trade concerns outweigh the economic evidence) "unthinkable" mergers "thinkable" at the expense of consumer welfare.

Accordingly, so long as the political hyperbole remains the centrepiece of the FCC's merger analyses, therefore, then whenever the FCC does conduct an accurate economic analysis regarding the potential pro- and anticompetitive effects on industry re-concentration post-1996 Act, these important conclusions will simply be lost in the morass. This loss is quite sad, given the fact that the FCC truly had an opportunity to advance the analytical debate about the form of industry structure post-1996 Act. Moreover, as stated above, the FCC could have achieved its policy objectives just as easily and effectively—and garnered the respect and admiration of the professional and academic communities in the process as well—had the FCC adopted a more straight-forward analytical approach. This vacuum in analysis and leadership is even more acute today, given the plethora of recent impediments that have deterred the implementation of the goals of the 1996 Act. Accordingly, if the FCC is going to continue to apply its *EPC* framework on a generic industry-wide basis, then several key "elements" of the *EPC* framework need to be refined and re-considered substantially to make the framework more legally and economically supportable in the future.

D. So Should the FCC Review Mergers at All?

Much has been argued lately about how the FCC has no business reviewing the competitive effects of telecommunications industry mergers, acquisitions and joint ventures. As explained in specific detail both in Chapter 3 and 18, such an

MSO and broadcast industry reconcentration, it is nice to see that Chairman Kennard is attempting to close the door by talking tough on IXC reconcentration (even though that market has been competitive for over 10 years and the FCC is about to permit ILECs to re-integrate via Section 271 of the 1996 Telecommunications Act even though local markets are far from competitive.) See, e.g., 5 October 1999 Statement of FCC Chairman William E. Kennard Statement on Proposed Merger of MCI Worldcom, Inc. and Sprint Corp. ("American consumers are enjoying the lowest long distance rates in history and the lowest Internet rates in the world for one reason: competition. Competition has produced a price war in the long distance market. This merger appears to be a surrender. How can this be good for consumers? The parties will bear a heavy burden to show how consumers would be better off.")

argument is just plain wrong. Just to recap the point, under existing case law, the FCC must take competitive considerations into account as part of it public interest considerations—i.e., in exercising its public interest mandate under the Communications Act, the FCC is required to "make findings related to the pertinent antitrust policies, draw conclusions from the findings and weigh these conclusions along with other important public interest considerations."[62] This does not mean that the FCC is responsible for enforcing the antitrust laws under its Title II and Title III responsibilities. Rather, as the FCC recognized nearly thirty years ago, "the standards governing [the Department of Justice] and the action of the FCC are significantly different. The Antitrust Division is charged with the enforcement of the antitrust laws . . . , while the Commission is charged with effectuating the policies of the Communications Act."[63]

Thus, if we remember the discussion in Chapter 3, the FCC's responsibilities under the Communications Act are significantly broader than those of the antitrust enforcement agencies, because the FCC is "entrusted with the responsibility to determine when and to what extent the public interest would be served by competition in the industry."[64] That is to say, the FCC's:

"determination about the proper role of competitive forces in an industry must therefore be based, not exclusively on the letter of the antitrust laws, but also on the 'special considerations' of the particular industry. As the Supreme Court has said, resolution of the sometimes-conflicting public interest considerations 'is a complex

---

[61] For a detailed exegesis of this flawed paradigm, see *Reconcentration of Telecommunications Markets After the 1996 Act: Implications for Long-Term Market Performance* (2nd ed., Phoenix Center Policy Paper Series No. 2, 1998) (http://www.phoenix-center.org/pcpp/pcpp2.doc).

[62] *United States* v. *FCC*, 652 F.2d 72, 81–82 (D.C. Cir. 1980) (en banc) (quoting *Northern Natural Gas Co.* v. *FPC*, 399 F.2d 953, 961 (D.C. Cir. 1968)); see also *Gulf States Utilities Company* v. *FPC*, 411 U.S. 747, 755–62 (1973).

[63] *ABC Cos. Inc.*, 7 FCC 2d 245, 249 (1966); *U.S.* v. *FCC*, 652 F.2d at 88 (citations omitted)(while "the basic goal of direct governmental regulation through administrative bodies and the goal of indirect governmental regulation in the form of antitrust law is the same—to achieve the most efficient allocation of resources possible," the FCC is not responsible for enforcing the antitrust laws); *U.S.* v. *AT&T*, 498 F.Supp. 353, 364 (D.D.C. 1980)("[I]t is not appropriate to distinguish between Communications Act standards and antitrust standards on the basis that the former are in the 'broad public interest area' and while the latter serve the interests of 'competition.' Although technically the Communications Act focuses on public necessity and convenience and the Sherman Act on competition, in a very real sense both the FCC, in its enforcement of the Communications Act, and the courts, in their application of the antitrust laws, guard against unfair competition and attempt to protect the public interest."); *Town of Concord* v. *Boston Edison Co.*, 915 F.2d 17, 22 (1st Cir. 1990), cert. denied, 499 U.S. 391 (1991)(while public regulation and the federal antitrust laws "typically aim at similar goals"—i.e., low and economically efficient prices, innovation and production methods," economic regulation seeks to achieve these goals directly "through rules and regulations; [while] antitrust seeks to achieve them indirectly by promoting and preserving a process that tends to bring them about."); see also *Northeast Utilities Service Co.* v. *FERC*, 933 F.2d 937, 947–48 (1st Cir. 1993) (agency is not required to "serve as an enforcer of antitrust policy in conjunction with the Department of Justice or the Federal Trade Commission"; while agency "must include antitrust considerations in its public interest calculations . . . it is not bound to use antitrust principles when they may be inconsistent with the [agency's] regulatory goals").

[64] *U.S.* v. *FCC*, 652 F.2d at 88 (citations omitted, emphasis added).

task which requires extensive facilities, expert judgment and considerable knowledge of the . . . industry. Congress left that task to the Commission'."[65]

Accordingly, because the FCC serves a different function from that of the DOJ or the FTC, the FCC need not either defer to those agencies, or undertake exactly the same analysis or utilize exactly the same procedures as these agencies.[66] Rather, both the requirements of Title III of the Communications Act and the FCC's discretionary application of the Clayton Act "are satisfied when the Commission seriously considers the antitrust consequences of a proposal and weighs those consequences with other public interest factors."[67]

While FCC decisionmakers may not always be consciously undertaking such an approach, using a dynamic economic model, rather than the static economic model used by competition law enforcement agencies, is nothing revolutionary. As explained above in chapter 8, US courts have long recognized that the FCC is endowed with broad and flexible powers in order to determine the optimal manner in which to regulate a dynamic industry.[68]

For example, in *FCC v. RCA Communications, Inc.*,[69] the Supreme Court stated that while "[t]here can be no doubt that competition is a relevant factor in weighing the public interest," the FCC must make an "independent conclusion" on matters before it that takes into account "the trends and needs of this industry."[70] The Court distinguished the general antitrust laws from the FCC's expert role in regulating the communications industry:

> "What may substantially lessen competition in those areas where competition is the main reliance for regulation of the market cannot be automatically transplanted to areas in which active regulation is entrusted to an administrative agency; for reasons we have indicated above, what competition is and should be in such areas must be read in light of the special considerations that have influenced Congress to make specific provision for the particular industry."[71]

For this reason, the FCC has engaged in numerous analyses of the competitive effects (and has imposed conditions to mitigate these anticompetitive effects) resulting from mergers, acquisitions and joint ventures s over telephone and

---

[65] *Ibid.*, (citing *McLean Trucking Co.* v. *United States*, 321 U.S. 67, 87 (1984)); accord *FCC v. RCA Communications Inc.*, 346 U.S. 86, 98 (1953); *Equipment Distributor's Coalition Inc.* v. *FCC*, 824 F.2d 1197, 1201 (D.C. Cir. 1982).

[66] See *Bilingual Cultural Coalition* v. *FCC*, 595 F.2d 621, 630–31 (D.C. Cir. 1978) (FCC's discretion in gathering information in radio licensing proceedings is broad and FCC need only obtain "sufficient information to make an informed decision").[67] *U.S.* v. *FCC*, 652 F.2d at 88; *Equipment Distributors*, 824 F.2d at 1201; see also *Northeast Utilities*, 993 F.2d at 947 (public interest standard does not require agencies "to analyze proposed mergers under the same standards that the Department of Justice . . . must apply").

[68] See, e.g., *P&R Temmer* v. *FCC*, 743 F.2d 918, 932 n.12 (D.C. Cir. 1984) (Bork., J.); *United States* v. *Storer Broadcasting Co.*, 351 U.S. 192, 203 (1956); *National Broadcasting Co.* v. *United States*, 319 U.S. 190, 219 (1943); *FCC* v. *Pottsville Broadcasting Co.*, 309 U.S. 143, 138 (1940).

[69] 346 U.S. 86 (1953).

[70] *Ibid.*, 346 U.S. at 93–95.

[71] *Ibid.*, 346 U.S. at 98.

cable industry mergers for the past 30 years,[72] To argue now that the FCC actually lacks such jurisdiction under the Communications Act simply misreads the law. (Whether the FCC should be stripped of this authority due to its analytical and procedural ineptitude is an other matter altogether, however.)

And, as these were not enough, courts have also upheld the FCC's actions even *over* the Department of Justice's specific objections. For example, in *United States v. FCC, supra*, the FCC, over the strenuous objections of the DOJ, permitted a joint venture between the largest manufacturer of computers (IBM) and the largest supplier of satellite facilities (Comsat) in order to spur immediate entry into a market previously occupied by a single firm. In conducting a dynamic economic analysis, the FCC balanced the possible anticompetitive effects of the joint venture in the domestic land-line market against the potential pro-competitive effects of spurring rapid entry in a highly concentrated, monopolistic market with poor performance. The net result of this decision is now a vibrant, competitive market for satellite services.

So is competition law a true substitute for regulatory action in the United States? After reviewing the Department of Justices actions over the last eight years, the answer is definitely no. Indeed, the blame for the near total reconcentration of the telephone, cable and broadcast industry cannot not lie exclusively with the FCC, because the Antitrust Division at the Department of Justice also botched any opportunity to stem the recent merger tide. In the case of the Department of Justice, they hid behind a narrow reading of Section 7 of the Clayton Act (the US competition law which evaluates mergers), which basically states that a merger is unlawful if it "substantially lessens competition." In the

---

[72] See, e.g., *TelePrompTer Transmission of Kansas-H&B*, 25 FCC2d 469 (1970); *ATC-Time/Life Cable TV Merger*, 43 F.C.C.2d 983 (1973); *In re Athena Communications*, 47 F.C.C. 2d 535 (1974); *Teleprompter-Group W*, 87 FCC 2d 531 (1981), *aff'd on recon.*, 89 FCC2d 417 (1982).

[73] What is truly amazing is that former FCC Commissioner Johnson warned close to thirty years ago that the FCC should be vary careful not to permit industry reconcentration in the fact of political pressure. See *ATC-Time/Life Cable TV Merger*, 43 F.C.C.2d 983 (1973). In ATC, the FCC, without discussion, authorized the staff to grant applications for the transfer of CARS and business radio station licenses from Time-Life Cable to ATC, in what at the time was one of the largest mergers in the cable industry—the acquisition by ATC, than the country's 4th largest MSO with 315,000 subscribers, of Time-Life's 11 systems having 45,000 subscribers for $11 million. The matter was presented to the FCC as a routine item for "information and/or discussion." In a scathing dissent, objecting to the FCC's routine approval of the transfers, Commissioner Johnson stated: "The infant cable industry is very rapidly coming into the mold of the conventional American oligopolistic pattern—where imitation rather than innovation comes from "competitor," and inflation rather than price competition greets the consumer. The FCC has already created monopolies and oligopolies in two of its other major regulated industries—telephone and television. . . . But those industries have taken 50 years or more to reach their current status. It is shocking that an infant industry like cable television, which has scarcely begun to toddle under the FCC's broadcaster-protective cable regulations, has already made such strides toward oligopolistic status. At our Commission meeting discussion of this item I made a formal motion that the Commission at least ask the Department of Justice, if it might possibly have any antitrust objections to this further reduction in cable competition. The disinterest of the Commission in antitrust issues is reflected in the startling fact that such a motion could not even garner a second." *Ibid.*, at 985–986. We wonder what the good Commissioner would say to the developments of the last several years.

DOJ's view, because two contiguous incumbent monopolists never really competed against one another, there was no competition to "substantially lessen."

Accordingly, the issue is not whether the FCC has or lacks authority to review and remedy the competitive effects of industry mergers, because—as shown *passim*—the case law is quite clear that it does. Instead, the primary issue is that the FCC over the last eight years simply has handled industry reconcentration extremely *poorly*. Indeed, we would not see such massive reconcentration if the merging parties had any inkling that the FCC (or Antitrust Division of the DOJ) would actually say no instead of a belated—but nonetheless assured and possibly politically qualified with "voluntary" commitments—yes. [73] Given this regulatory behaviour, we are left with two policy choices: (a) have the FCC do a better job; or (b) remove the FCC's authority to review mergers in their entirely. Under any case, however, we need remove the political garbage from the overall dialectic and return to first principles before the omelette becomes too firm to unscramble.

IV. LINE SHARING

A. The FCC's Decision

In November 1999, frustrated with the incumbents' recalcitrance to unbundle an entire loop,[74] the FCC took the additional draconian step of ordering "line sharing"—that is, forcing incumbents to "unbundle" the high frequency portion of the loop to permit alternative suppliers to sell ADSL services on top of the voice incumbent's service as the incumbent LEC continues to provide POTS services on the lower frequencies.[75] In this way, consumers will now ostensibly have a "choice" in ADSL providers.[76]

According to the FCC, line sharing was necessary because competitive LECs seeking to deploy xDSL-based service to customers subscribing to the incumbent LEC's voice telephone service could not deploy their xDSL with the same efficiency or at the same cost—especially because incumbent LECs did not permit competitive LECs to access the high frequency portion of the loop to provide xDSL-based services, even though the incumbent LECs utilised the high frequency portion of the loop to deploy their own services. In the FCC's view, "this situation materially diminishes the competitive LEC's ability to provide

---

[74] Indeed, U.S. incumbents really had no one to blame but themselves for mandatory line sharing at no cost. In a nut shell, the incumbents—through their recalcitrance to provision loops in a timely fashion and demands that CLEC's pay exorbitant and—in the case of requiring new entrants to build everything from new parking lots to external four-story fire escapes—ridiculous non-recurring charges, they simply pushed the FCC too far. In other words, punishment by rent reallocation.

[75] Reference required here.

[76] *In re Deployment of Wireline Services Offering Advanced Telecommunications Capability and Implementation of the Local Competition Provisions of the Telecommunications Act of 1996*, Third Report & Order in CC Docket No. 98–147; Fourth Report and Order in CC Docket No. 96–98, FCC No. 99–355 (rel. Dec. 9, 1999) (hereinafter "Line Sharing Order").

the particular type of xDSL-based service that it seeks to offer." In contrast, however, the FCC also concluded that competitors were not impaired when they sought to deploy those versions of xDSL-based services that require a dedicated local loop, such as SDSL or HDSL, because they can procure unbundled loops to deploy such service.[77]

The FCC provided several reasons why purchasing or self-provisioning a second loop is not possible as a practical, operational or economic matter. First, the FCC reasoned that second loops are not ubiquitously available and an ILEC's refusal to unbundle the high frequency portion of the loop in this situation forecloses competitive access to the segment of consumers that lack additional copper pairs to their homes or small businesses. In the FCC's opinion, lack of access to the high frequency portion of the loop reduces the efficient use of existing loop plant and diminishes the scope of potential customers to whom competitive LECs can market xDSL-based service, thereby limiting the competitive choices available to consumers for whom additional copper loops are not available. In addition, reasoned the FCC, such lack of access can accelerate the depletion of copper loops in entire communities, necessitating inefficient capital expenditures that will increase costs imposed on consumers and competitors alike. Even if there are spare pairs in the "drop" to a home or business, there are not corresponding pairs in the feeder plant connecting the neighborhood to the central office/local exchange.[78]

Second, the FCC reasoned that if competitive LECs were to purchase or self-provision a second unbundled loop to provide voice-compatible xDSL-based services, their provisioning of service would be materially more costly, and coincidentally less efficient, than purchasing the unbundled high-frequency portion of the loop. According to the FCC, the inability of competing carriers to provide xDSL-based services over the same loop facilities that the incumbents use to provide local exchange service makes the provision of competitive xDSL-based services to customers that want a single line for both voice and data applications—typically small businesses and mass market residential consumers—not just marginally more expensive, but so prohibitively expensive that competitive LECs will not be able to provide such services on a sustained economic basis.[79]

Third, the FCC reasoned that a competitive carrier faces a competitive disadvantage in providing xDSL over a second line when competing against the incumbent's single line offering. The incumbent is able to market its own service to customers as a quick and convenient add-on service, while the competitive carrier must persuade the customer to purchase a second line. In comparison, consumers that desire to obtain xDSL service from competitive LECs must encounter complications and expenses, including the need to arrange for a technician to install service, that do not arise if they procure the exact same service from the incumbent LEC. Providing competitive LECs with access to the high

---

[77] *Ibid.*, at ¶ 33.
[78] *Ibid.*, at ¶ 38.
[79] *Ibid.*, at ¶ 39.

frequency portion of the loop would remove that additional burden from consumers that prefer to obtain xDSL service from competitors.[80]

Finally, the FCC addressed the all-important issue of pricing. With regards to line sharing, the big question is how much of the cost of the local loop should be assigned to the provision of DSL service when the line is "shared" with local service? That is to say, DSL and voice are "joint products," because DSL and voice "share" the loop, using non-overlapping frequencies and the frequencies for DSL and voice are jointly supplied (i.e., fixed proportions). Because every loop is capable of both, one more voice loop implies one more DSL loop. (For example, if you order a chicken in a restaurant, you also get both two wings and two breasts.) Given his basic condition, the FCC wants nonetheless to imitate "competitive" pricing (i.e., TELRIC).[81] Accordingly, what is the "competitive" price for jointly supplied goods (voice and xDSL)?

On one hand, the demand for a loop is the (vertical) summation of the demand for both Voice and DSL. Prices are determined by the intersection of supply and demand. According to the FCC, however, the "cost of [the loop] is already being recovered through charges for jurisdictional services."[82] If the FCC's statement is followed to its logical conclusion, therefore, then the price of the DSL portion must be $0.[83]

Notwithstanding the above, the FCC also goes on to state that the DSL-specific costs should be recovered separately from the joint facility (i.e. the local loop)[84] yet also ensure that what ever prices are set in the long-run, also ensure policy goals are met (i.e., promote competition in the provisioning of xDSL-based services.[85] But what about the huge amount of subsidies that affect materially the true price of local phone service? If subsidies are included in the average cost of the loop, then DSL *may* have to bear some costs, this decreasing the total amount of the subsidy. The only solution is to have the FCC treat DSL-specific costs independently of loop costs. Thus, if the demand for DSL grows, then DSL may eventually bear a positive portion of loop costs.

B. Broader Policy Implications Raised by Line Sharing

According to the FCC, unbundling the high frequency portion of the loop will not deter investment by facilities-based competitive LECs that plan to offer a

---

[80] *Ibid.*, at ¶ 42.

[81] *In re Deployment of Wireline Services Offering Advanced Telecommunications Capability and Implementation of the Local Competition Provisions of the Telecommunications Act of 1996,* at ¶132.

[82] *Ibid.*, at ¶138.

[83] See Kim Sunderland, "Rhythms Cuts Deal with US West on Line Sharing Costs", *X-Change Magazine* 11 April 2000 (Reporting that Rhythms NetConnections, Inc. (a PCLEC) gets to pay absolutely nothing to US West for line sharing in exchange for "vowing not to oppose US West's merger with Qwest Communications International.")

[84] Line Sharing Order at ¶ 136.

[85] *Ibid.*, at ¶135.

full range of services to consumers, including both voice and data services. Instead, the FCC expects that that such carriers would be able to differentiate themselves from competitive LECs offering only data services by offering consumers the benefits of one-stop shopping, or by providing access to superior facilities or technology. In addition, the FCC disagreed with those parties who argued that providing competitors with the option to deliver data services would permit incumbent LECs to become entrenched in the provision of voice service. In the FCC's view, "product integration and technological innovation will, over time, enable competitive LECs to continue to compete with incumbents for the provision of a full range of services."[86] But will such policies really create sufficient alternative, non-incumbent demand to warrant the entry of another facilities-based provider?[87]

The FCC's decision to impose line-sharing adds a significant twist to the economics of the unbundling paradigm. That is, as explained supra, a new entrant can enter either by full resale or on an à la carte basis by purchasing individual UNEs. Either way, the new entrant still has to deal with provisioning and collocation hassles with the incumbent. Thus, because you can add a voice switch subsequently to a loop conditioned for xDSL,[88] if a PCLEC purchases a loop on a UNE basis and does all of the initial grunt work and incurred all of the start-up entry costs to create a national footprint, then there is nothing stopping that PCLEC from selling or leasing that underlying voice switch of the loop to a company who has expertise in marketing the *entire* product (e.g., a long-distance company).[89] In other words, the PCLEC benefits because it has just reduced its exogenous costs (marketing) by maximising another firm's spillover effects (e.g., an retail operator's established brand name and marketing expertise) and, conversely, the other firm benefits because the arrangement has lowered its endogenous entry costs.

With the FCC's new notion on line sharing, however, the promise is that although the incumbent would still control the underlying voice switch, new technology ostensibly makes it possible for the PCLEC to provide not only high-speed data on the high-frequency portion of the loop, but also multiple voice

---

[86] *Ibid.*, at ¶ 57.

[87] Perhaps the FCC's application of the consolidated, alternative non-incumbent demand story in regards to line-sharing is this: (1) consumers will be attracted to the broadband market initially by a "competitive" entry-level (and, by definition, least expensive) ADSL service; (2) consumers like their ADSL service so much (and, because of their prior poor experience with the incumbent) they then decide to upgrade to a higher version of xDSL or other broadband technology from non-incumbent suppliers; (3) now that the new non-incumbent demand has been created, new facilities-based entry will occur to serve this consolidated demand.

[88] In the old days, because voice was the primary product provided over the copper loop, the mere possibility of using the same line for data as well was referred to as "DUV"—i.e., "Data Under Voice."

[89] Indeed, because a PCLEC will be targeting and serving a customer who has no problem paying $60 to $80 for xDSL service, it would be reasonable to assume that this same customer would be a high-volume telephone customer as well.

switches as well.[90] However, for the same reasons why a PCLEC may not want to go near the voice side of the business under the "traditional" model, a PCLEC may want to "sub-contract" out those "virtual voice switches" on the high frequency portion of the loop to a firm that has expertise in such areas. Thus, under the FCC's new line-sharing model, it is now conceivably possible to have *three* firms sharing the same line (all at virtually no cost to the PCLEC/CLEC joint venture).

While the promise of multiple lines and high-speed data at *de minimis* cost sounds great in concept, several potential problems remain. First, as the incumbent continues to have little incentive to provision an entire loop, the incumbent certainly has little incentive to share a line at essentially no cost with a rival. (Remember that the incumbent wants to receive the $40–$80 subscription fee for the service for itself.) Second, the FCC's pricing decision for shared lines just adds further fat to the fire on the proverbial "buy verses build" debate. (Indeed, if one can get line-sharing for free from the incumbent, no matter how much alternative, non-incumbent demand is created, an ADCO may still not find entry profitable because it certainly cannot sell on a stand-alone basis the high-frequency portion of its loops for free.) Finally, if the PCLEC decides to add voice as well, significant issues of reliability remain—i.e., because consumers will tolerate net outages or congestion but will not tolerate a quality diminution for POTS, determining who is responsible for a faulty line might become an administrative and technical nightmare.

V. VERTICAL RE-INTEGRATION

Just as with horizontal mergers, as a general economic matter, there is absolutely nothing wrong will vertical integration in and of itself. Vertical integration can allow a firm to realise many economies of scale and scope.[91] (Indeed, to the best of anyone's knowledge, the United States appears to be the only country that currently has an artificial distinction between "local" and "long-distance" markets.) The competitive problems arise whenever the economic costs of vertical integration outweigh the efficiencies gained from such integration. Accordingly, if the "re-integrated" structure of post-1996 Act telecommunications markets permit one or more firms to engage successfully in strategic, anticompetitive conduct against its rivals, then the consumers are unlikely to enjoy the purported benefits that politicians promised them prolifically they would receive.

---

[90] See, e.g., John Shinal, "Voice is the Killer DSL App", *Forbes.com* 2 Feb. 2000; Om Malik, "DSL Finds its Voice", *Forbes.com* 14 March 2000.

[91] See, e.g., *In Re Applications of Capital Cities/ABC, Inc., (Transferor) and The Walt Disney Company, (Transferee)*, Memorandum Opinion & Order, 11 F.C.C.R. 5841 (rel. Feb. 8, 1996); See also James Olson & Lawrence Spiwak, "Can Short-Term Limits on Strategic Vertical Restraints Improve Long-Term Cable Industry Market Performance?" (1994) 13 *Cardozo Arts & Ent. L.J.* 283.

In the United States, when the US government broke up AT&T in the mid-1980s, they essentially "carved out" the long distance market (i.e., everything on the trunk-side of the switch) because they knew that this market—absent the constraints of one or more firms' dominant control of constrained local loop facilities—could be (and in fact has turned out to be) capable of vigorous competition. With the passage of the 1996 Telecoms Act, however, the US Congress decided affirmatively that dominant control of local loop facilities was not a per se barrier to re-vertical integration, so long as an incumbent LEC could satisfy the "competitive checklist" contained in Section 271 of the Telecoms Act. According to this "competitive checklist", an RBOC must first demonstrate that it:

(1) provides interconnection in accordance with the requirements of sections 251(c)(2) and 252(d)(1) of the Act;

(2) provides nondiscriminatory access to network elements in accordance with the requirements of sections 251(c)(3) and 252(d)(1) of the Act;

(3) provides nondiscriminatory access to the poles, ducts, conduits, and rights-of-way owned or controlled by the Bell operating company at just and reasonable rates in accordance with the requirements of section 224 of the Act;

(4) provides local loop transmission from the central office/local exchange to the customer's premises, unbundled from local switching or other services;

(5) provides local transport from the trunk side of a wireline local exchange carrier switch unbundled from switching or other services;

(6) provides local switching unbundled from transport, local loop transmission, or other services;

(7) provides nondiscriminatory access to (a) 911 and E911 services; (b) directory assistance services to allow the other carrier's customers to obtain telephone numbers; and (c) operator call completion services;

(8) provides White pages directory listings for customers of the other carrier's telephone exchange service;

(9) until the date by which telecommunications numbering administration guidelines, plan, or rules are established, provides non-discriminatory access to telephone numbers for assignment to the other carrier's telephone exchange service customers. After that date, compliance with such guidelines, plan, or rules;

(10) provides non-discriminatory access to databases and associated signalling necessary for call routing and completion;

(11) until the date by which the FCC issues regulations pursuant to section 251 to require number portability, interim telecommunications number portability through remote call forwarding, direct inward dialling trunks, or other comparable arrangements, with as little impairment of functioning, quality, reliability, and convenience as possible. After that date, full compliance with such regulations;

(12) provides non-discriminatory access to such services or information as are necessary to allow the requesting carrier to implement local dialling parity in accordance with the requirements of section 251(b)(3);

(13) provides reciprocal compensation arrangements in accordance with the requirements of section 252(d)(2); and

(14) telecommunications services are available for resale in accordance with the requirements of sections 251(c)(4) and 252(d)(3).

The process does not end here, however. After the RBOC makes its filing demonstrating that it satisfies the "competitive checklist," then—after consultation with the US Attorney General and the relevant state public utility commissions—the FCC must then find not only that the RBOC has proved its submission, but also that the application is nonetheless "consistent with the public interest, convenience and necessity."

In Chapter 3 *supra*, we went through a lengthy exegesis over what the appropriate scope of the "public interest standard" should mean. In the particular case of the re-vertical integration of the US markets, however, this inquiry takes on even greater significance. First, it is very important to recognise that because entry is far easier into the long-distance market than it is into the local market, incumbents have a significant cost advantage over their rivals for vertically integrated service offerings. In contrast to the local market, entry into the "long-distance" is far less expensive. That is to say, the long distance network by design is a non-ubiquitous, facilities-concentrated, usage-based, mass-market network where high capital costs are spread among huge number of customers who in turn indirectly heavily subsidise the local loop. In contrast, the local loop by design is ubiquitous, more facilities-dispersed, generally fixed-cost, retail market where high cost rural areas are subsidised by urban and suburban areas and from long-distance access charges indirectly via access charges and universal service fees.[92] Moreover, given the demand characteristics of the market, as spelled out in Chapter 3, a pre-mature re-vertical integration of the market could reduce a new entrant's spillover effects and thus deter new entry for local service.

Moreover, there is a huge differential in the capital cost involved in replicating the local loop verses the long-distance network. At the time the 1996 Telecommunications act was passed, in the United States, the local loop had roughly 6,200,000 km of all types of cable plant, while the long-distance industry had roughly 150,000 km of cable plant. This approximately amounted to a 41:1 kilometre differential. This differential was magnified if one considered the physical and regulatory costs of digging up America's cities. Indeed, the total value of the local plant aat the time of the 1996 Act was roughly \$270 billion while the total value of the long-distance plant was roughly \$40 billion. These widely disparate costs resulted in a valuation differential of approximately 7:1.[93]

---

[92] See Scott Cleland, "Telecomplexity: navigating the New Telecom Law for Investment Advantage" *The Washington Research Group* 25 March 1996 at 13.

[93] *Ibid.*

Given the above, Congress appeared to recognise that it will be quite expensive for new entrants to enter the market at "two" (*i.e.*, "local" and "long-distance") levels. If an incumbent could use this structure to its strategic advantage, therefore, then an incumbent could further deter new entry.[94] For example, without competitive alternatives for "local service," ILECs would still dominate local access facilities that they may use to deter entry into the "bundled, vertically-integrated" market. Moreover, not only did the incumbent LEC have significant cost and access advantages (the economic "yin and yang" of bottleneck facilities), but it also had significant other "first mover" advantages over new entrants—*i.e.*, ILECs had virtually 100 per cent of the residential traffic "pre-reintegration"—and, as such, they had brand loyalty and an established local presence that other new entrants probably did not possess. If other potential entrants concluded that the risks associated with attempting to provide both long distance and create nascent "local" competition was simply too great (*i.e.*, uneconomical), then entry might not occur.[95] If entry did not occur or was delayed, then it was (and continues to be) highly probable that an ILEC would be able to grab immediately a substantial—if not an outright majority—share of the "bundled service" market before any of its rivals.[96]

Given the FCC's actions over the last five years, it appears unfortunately that this scenario has come to pass, in that the US telecoms market is rapidly developing into the undesirable outcome of several regional markets (*i.e.*, the ILECs' original service territory) characterised by a "dominant firm/fringe" model for "bundled" products ("been there/done that" on a national basis with AT&T fifteen years ago), rather than the preferred outcome of a national market characterised by multiple vertically-integrated, facilities-based carriers and a healthy competitive niche fringe which sustains a level of rivalry sufficient to make stringent regulation unnecessary.

Finally, what is truly remarkable to note about the 1996 Act's so-called "competitive checklist" is that the US Congress effectively ignored the fundamental reason why the FCC's *Competitive Carrier* paradigm (both domestic and international) were so successful fifteen years ago—the realisation that who ever dominates local access facilities and also engages in a retail operation has both

---

[94] Indeed, a long-distance company seeking to transform itself into a provider of "bundled" services faces a difficult strategic decision: It can either pass on pursuing the local loop while its core business is invaded, or it can counterattack with a time-consuming costly build-out of alternative facilities all over the country or it can resell the local loop wholesale break-even or at a loss. See Scott Cleland, *supra* n. 92 at 10.

[95] See, e.g., John Greenwald et al., "Hung Up on Competition Cable Television, Utilities, Railroads—Everyone Was Going to Provide Local Phone Service. But Until AT&T and the Baby Bells are Cleared to Compete Head-On, Customers will Still Pay Monopoly Prices", *Time Magazine* 21 July 1997 at 50 ("[S]peed is key" to get a head-start in the race to sell customers a bundle of branded services).

[96] See, e.g., *ibid.*, reporting that because GTE—which has some 20 million local customers scattered across 29 states and sales that exceeded $21.3 billion in 1996—was not required to open its local markets before it may provide in-region, inter-LATA service under Section 271, GTE aggressively signed-up more than 1.25 million long-distance subscribers (most from AT&T) within only one year of the enactment of the 1996 Act.

the incentive and ability to engage in strategic anticompetitive conduct against its rivals.[97]

That is to say, in 1980 (pre-MFJ), the FCC completely re-thought the way it regulates the domestic, long-distance service industry. In order to promote competition for long-distance service, the FCC devised a regulatory scheme designed, in part, to spur new entry into the marketplace. The mechanism derived was the dominant/non-dominant regulatory scheme.[98] Under this process, if the FCC determined that a common carrier could exercise market power (i.e. AT&T), then the FCC would classify this carrier as a "dominant". If the FCC found that a carrier lacked market power (i.e. everybody else), however, then the FCC would classify the carrier as "non dominant". The advantage of a non-dominant carrier classification was that the regulatory requirements imposed on non-dominant carriers were substantially reduced—if not outright eliminated. Such "streamlined" regulation included, but was not limited to: (a) a presumption that the rates charged by a non-dominant carrier would be *per se* just and reasonable; and (b) reduced notice periods for non-dominant carrier tariff filings.

The centre-piece of the FCC's dominant/non-dominant inquiry was whether or not a carrier controlled "bottleneck facilities"[99] and, as such, had the ability to exercise market power.[100]

The FCC defined control of bottleneck facilities as whenever:

"a firm or group of firms has sufficient command over some essential commodity or facility in its industry or trade to be able to impede new entrants. Thus, bottleneck

---

[97] For a brief analysis of the major cases from the FCC's remarkable *Competitive Carrier* Paradigm, please see Appendix.

[98] See Policy & Rules Concerning Rates for Competitive Common Carrier Services and Facilities Authorisations Therefore, CC Docket No. 79–252 ("Competitive Carrier Proceeding"), Notice of Inquiry and Proposed Rulemaking, 77 FCC 2d 308 (1979); *First Report & Order*, 85 FCC 2d 1 (1980); Further Notice of Proposed Rulemaking, 84 FCC 2d 445 (1981), *Second Report & Order*, 91 FCC 2d 59 (1982); recon. 93 FCC 2d 54 (1983); Second Further Notice of Proposed Rulemaking, FCC 82–187, released April 21, 1982; Third Further Notice of Proposed Rulemaking, Mimeo No. 3347, released June 14, 1983, 48 Fed. Reg. 28,292 (June 21, 1983); *Third Report & Order*, Mimeo No. 46,791, released October 6, 1983; 48 Fed. Reg. 46,791 (Oct. 6, 1983); *Fourth Report & Order*, 95 FCC 2d 554 (1983); Fourth Further Notice of Proposed Rulemaking, 96 FCC 2d 1191 (1984); *Fifth Report & Order*, 98 FCC 2d 1191 (1984); *Sixth Report & Order*, 99 FCC 2d 1020 (1985), rev'd, MCI v. FCC, 765 F.2d 1186 (D.C. Cir. 1985).

[99] In re Policy and Rules Concerning Rates for Competitive Common Carrier Services and Facilities Authorisations Therefor, Docket No. 79–252, 85 FCC 2d 1 (1980).

[100] According to the FCC, "Market power refers to the control a firm can exercise in setting the price of its output. A firm with market power is able to engage in conduct that may be anticompetitive or otherwise inconsistent with the public interest. This may entail setting price above competitive costs in order to earn supranormal profits, or setting price below competitive costs to forestall entry by new competitors or to eliminate existing competitors. In contrast, a competitive firm, lacking market power, must take the market price as given, because if it raises price it will face an unacceptable loss of business, and if it lowers price it will face unrecoverable monetary losses in an attempt to supply the market demand at that price." *First Report & Order* at ¶ 56. See also 47 C.F.R. § 61.3(o)("dominant carrier" is defined as any "carrier found by the Commission to have market power (i.e., power to control prices)").

control describes the structural characteristics of a market that new entrants must either be allowed to share the bottleneck facility or fail."[101]

According to the FCC, control of bottleneck facilities was "prima facia evidence of market power requiring detailed regulatory scrutiny."[102] The FCC's "control of bottleneck facilities" test was also they key factor in determining whether AT&T was non-dominant for international services as well.

When it comes to evaluating whether an incumbent can exercise market power by their control of "bottleneck facilities" before it should be permitted to re-vertically integrate and enter the long-distance market, both Congress and the FCC conveniently ignore this inquiry, however does the FCC evaluate the performance of the market as part of its "public interest" inquiry? Sadly, no. Instead, the FCC engages simply in a "head count" of how many agreements the local ILEC has entered into with CLECs and PCLECs to see if competition is sufficient.[103]

This deliberate omission is an abrogation of the FCC's basic mandate to maximise consumer welfare. Indeed, if the FCC is not going to evaluate the current and likely performance of the market post-integration, then why did Congress provide a "public interest" finding as a competitive backstop? Recent developments show the foolishness of the FCC's premature re-integration of the market. To wit, when the FCC's enforcement Bureau provided evidence that Bell Atlantic had almost immediately after it had received its Section 271 authorisation engaged in strategic, anticompetitive conduct against its rivals (and thus also supporting the notion that perhaps the FCC's decision in this case was in fact premature), Bell Atlantic agreed to make to make a "voluntary contribution to the US Treasury" of (US) $3 million with an additional liability of up to $24 million.[104]

VI. CONCLUSION

As noted above in Chapter 2, this naked desire to preserve and allocate rents reveals the depth of the FCC's cynicism under the last two FCC Commissions. Once again, viewing the FCC's policies in toto over the last several years, the Clinton/Gore Administration appears to prefer "choices" over "competition." Moreover, if rent allocation is sufficient to buy silence from both the private and public sector, then why even think about meaningful structural solutions to the competitive problems of today?

---

[101] *Ibid.*, at ¶ 59.

[102] *Ibid.*, at ¶ 58.

[103] See, e.g., *In re Bell Atlantic New York for Authorization Under Section 271 of the Communications Act to Provide In-Region, InterLATA Services in the State of New York*, FCC No. 99–404 (rel. 22 Dec. 1999).

[104] In *re Bell Atlantic New York for Authorization Under Section 271 of the Communications Act to Provide In-Region, InterLATA Services in the State of New York*, FCC No. 00–92 (9 March 2000).

Like it or not, the ephemeral promise of "convergence" is no substitute for tangible "competition." So long as the various public and private special interest groups get their share of the pie, therefore, there continues to be no real constituency for meaningful competition. Instead, we are left with a "static, incumbent-centric perpetual resale model" under which everyone is simply reselling the same crappy service. Thus, US consumers do not have a true choice of competitive substitutes—rather, their only "choice" is to whom they would like to write their monthly subscription checks out. In other words, the US experience, *substantively*, in turn is not one that should be exported for international consumption on an "as is" basis.

Perhaps Judge Frank Easterbrook summed it up best over fifteen years ago.

"The principle that regulation must extend to catch all substitutions at the margin has a corollary: *if you're not prepared to regulate thoroughly, don't start.*"[105]

Certainly words to live by.

---

[105] See Frank Easterbrook, "The Court and the Economic System", (1984) 98 *Harv. L. Rev.* 4, 40 (emphasis supplied).

PART III

EUROPEAN EFFORTS TO PROMOTE TELECOMS COMPETITION

10

EU Foundations, Institutions and Policies

I. INTRODUCTION

As the european Union (EU) governance system and institutions are rather complicated, some background about EU procedures may be helpful in understanding both the powers and the limitations of the EU in its efforts to promote competition in telecommunications markets. Basic information about EU governance policies should clarify the EU's role in telecommunications regulation as well as give some clues as to why the EU has adopted certain policies and to what its direction may be in the future.

II. THE BIRTH OF A NEW KIND OF NATION

The EU is a recent creation as far as governments go, and it is unique in its hybrid state formation. Born as the European Economic Communities (EEC), and originally popularly known as the "Common Market", the EU has its constitutional underpinnings in the Treaty of Rome of 1957.[1] The most recent amendments to the Treaty of Rome contained in the Treaty of Amsterdam changed the numbering of Treaty Articles. Treaty Articles as enumerated in the Treaty of Amsterdam will be used in this book.

Since the date of the Treaty of Rome, the European Community[2] (EC), as it was called until the Maastricht amendments of 1992 introduced the term "European Union,"[3] has grown steadily both in terms of the number of participating nations (Member States) and its concurrent influence over legal and economic affairs of the Member States. The Treaty of Rome established principles of free movement of goods among the Member States (Articles 28–30), freedom to provide services (Article 49), and undistorted competition (Article 3(g)).

---

[1] Consolidated Version Of The Treaty Establishing The European Community [1997] OJ C340/173–308 [hereinafter EU Treaty] <http://europa.eu.int/eur-lex/en/treaties/dat/ec_cons_treaty_en.pdf>.

[2] The original treaties established the European Coal and Steel Community, the European Economic Community and Euratom—hence the plural "Communities." Legally, "Community" is still part of the entity's title and "Community law" is still referred to.

[3] EU Treaty, *supra* n. 1, at 145–172.

III. EU INSTITUTIONS, LAW AND POLICY

A. The Council and the European Commission

The EU governing process is complex. At the top is the Council of Ministers, composed of one appropriate minister from each Member State, depending on the subject matter before the Council.[4] Legislative proposals are passed either unanimously or under a weighted voting system known as a qualified majority.[5] The European Commission is the administrative institution of the EU, proposing legislation, administering existing EU funds and programs, and investigating violations of Community Law.[6] The European Commission considers itself the guardian of the Treaty. The President of the European Commission, currently Romano Prodi, holds the closest position the EU has to a chief executive.[7] There are two divisions, or Directorates-General (DGs), of the European Commission that are of particular importance in telecommunications matters. First, the Competition Directorate-General[8] is charged with implementation of EU competition law through investigations and enforcement actions (including fines), and has a limited power to issue directives on its own.[9] It also maintains the Merger Task Force, which is responsible for receiving and reviewing merger notifications. The Competition Directorate-General might be considered equivalent to the Antitrust Division of the US Department of Justice. Second, the Information Society Directorate-General[10] is in charge of EU telecommunications regulation, postal services, and research and information services, and might be considered equivalent to the US Federal Communications Commission (FCC). The Information Society Directorate-General drafted much of the telecommunications regulatory framework.

B. EU Legislation

The basic EU legislation is a directive. Member States are required to implement directives, not necessarily by enacting them word for word, but by accomplishing the object of the directive.[11] In general, the European Commission proposes directives, the Council adopts them, and Member States implement them. The European Commission can take action against Member States for failure to

---

[4] EU Treaty, *supra* n. 1, arts. 202–210.
[5] *Ibid.*, art. 95.
[6] *Ibid.*, art. 211.
[7] *Ibid.*, arts. 211–219.
[8] Formerly known as DG IV.
[9] EU Treaty, *supra* n. 1, art. 86.
[10] Formerly known as DG XIII.
[11] EU Treaty, *supra* n. 1, art. 10.

implement directives,[12] and certain directives are considered to have direct effect, even if Member States fail to implement them.[13]

Another more recent and informal source of law should be mentioned as it is of increasing importance in telecommunications regulation. That is soft law. Soft law can consist of guidelines or recommendations from the European Commission. Troubling from the standpoint of legal certainly, soft law can provide regulators with expeditious tools to react to perceived market difficulties, or to implement pet projects that might not survive the usual legislative process. Soft law is also of doubtful enforceability, basically being the opinion of the European Commission. Recommendations are just that, recommendations, and some Member States may choose not to accept a recommendation of the European Commission, leaving the European Commission with a dilemma of whether to attempt enforcement of a recommendation, perhaps doubtful of whether the European Courts will uphold its opinion, or to accept different rules in different Member States, leading to a fragmentation of the market.

C. Parliament

The European Parliament, chosen by popular election every five years in the Member States, has limited powers to propose amendments to contemplated legislation, to approve certain budgets, and to submit written questions to the European Commission.[14] The constitutional powers and influence of the European Parliament have grown steadily, partially due to attempts to address the "democratic deficit" in the EU. The European Parliament is the only European institution whose members are directly elected. Among the powers of the European Parliament are to approve the composition of the top members of the European Commission and upon a two thirds majority vote to censure, that is to dismiss, these members.[15] It was the Parliament's power of censure that led to the European Commissioners' mass resignation in the spring of 1999 in the face of corruption allegations.

D. The Court

The European Court of Justice (ECJ), composed of fifteen judges, rules on Community law.[16] Its cases are composed mainly of actions brought by the Commission against Member States or questions of Community Law referred by national courts.[17] No evidentiary hearings are conducted. There is also a

---

[12] *Ibid.*, art. 226.
[13] Case 152/84 *Marshall* v. *Southampton Area Health Auth.* [1986] ECR 723, 728.
[14] EU Treaty, *supra* n. 1, arts. 189–201.
[15] *Ibid.*, art. 201.
[16] *Ibid.*, art. 221.
[17] *Ibid.*, art. 230.

lower court, known as the Court of First Instance[18] that often initially hears competition law cases.

The ECJ's procedure is interesting. The Treaty calls for the ECJ to be assisted by Advocates General who are required to submit opinions or "reasoned submissions" to assist the court.[19] Although the court is not obligated to follow the Advocate General's opinion, often the opinions are influential. This is particularly the case in that the ECJ's rules require that its opinions be signed by all the presiding judges, in effect a requirement of unanimity.[20] This results in compromise opinions, and the opinion of the Advocate General, when followed, can often give a clearer picture of the opinion of the majority of the court's judges than the actual final opinion. In cases where the opinion of the Advocate General is not followed, it might be considered as a type of dissenting opinion.

The ECJ holds that Community law is supreme over national law,[21] and this position has been accepted by Member States' courts. The European Commission also has the power to issue quasi-judicial decisions, including levying fines of up to ten per cent of the involved firm(s) worldwide annual turnover for violations of competition law.[22] There is a right of appeal to the ECJ for review of fines.[23] Community law, including competition law, should not be considered criminal in nature.

E. Remaining Policies

Some important EU policies should also be mentioned, as these policies are reflected throughout EU legislation, European Commission actions, and court judgments. The "four freedoms": freedom of movement of goods, services, persons, and capital throughout the EU are fundamental. Closely connected is the idea of the single market: that the EU consists of a single market, and EU policy should break down national or regional barriers. For example, attempts to limit distribution of goods to specific Member States are viewed harshly. Economic and technical progress is to be promoted.[24]

---

[18] EU Treaty, *supra* n. 1, art. 225.

[19] *Ibid.*, art 222.

[20] Rules of Procedure of the Court of Justice of the European Communities of 19 June 1991, art. 64, [1991] OJ L176/7, and L 383 (corrigenda) of 29.12.1992, with amendments published in [1995] OJ L44/61, and in [1997] OJ L103/1 and 3, and [1997] OJ L351 (corrigenda).

[21] Case 6/64 *Costa* v. *ENEL* [1964] ECR 585, 588.

[22] Council Regulation No. 17/62 implementing Articles 85 and 86 [81 and 82] of the EC Treaty [1962] OJ L13/204.

[23] *Ibid.*, art 17.

[24] EU Treaty, *supra* n.1, art. 81(3) includes the statement that an agreement, otherwise objectionable under competition law shall be allowed "which contributes to improving the production or distribution of goods or to promoting technical or economic progress, while allowing consumers a fair share of the resulting benefit". This policy statement may be considered as the rough EU equivalent of the US antitrust rule of reason under which there is a weighing of pro and anti-competitive effects.

IV. EU COMPETITION POLICY AND THE CONCEPT OF DOMINANCE

As the European Commission used its competition law enforcement power to put European telecommunications markets on the road to competition, a close examination of this law and policy is warranted. Not only is competition law important from an historical perspective, but also on an on going basis as many battles are fought between incumbent and entrant telecoms companies on the basis of competition law principles. As these battles are usually fought on the basis of an incumbent's alleged abuse of a dominant position, this discussion will focus on the concept of dominance. The principle of dominance and its determination should become even more important in the future as competition law begins to replace regulatory law in telecommunications markets.

A. Competition Law Provisions of the Treaty of Rome

Antitrust or competition rules are more specifically set out in Treaty Articles 81 and 82. Article 81 prohibits agreements affecting trade between Member States having "as their object or effect the prevention, restriction or distortion of competition." A list of *per se* violations including price fixing and market sharing follows. Article 81(2) declares agreements contrary to Article 81 automatically void. Article 81 may be considered roughly equivalent to section one of the US Sherman Antitrust Act.[25] Article 82 condemns any "[a]buse by one or more undertakings of a dominant position," followed by a non-exhaustive list of examples. Article 82 may be considered equivalent to section two of the US Sherman Antitrust Act.[26] Article 86 of the Treaty allows government monopolies, but states that they are subject to Treaty competition rules to the extent that "the application of such rules does not obstruct the performance, in law or in fact, of the particular tasks assigned to them." The European Commission is given authority to oversee this provision concerning government monopolies and "address appropriate directives or decisions to Member States." This authority became vitally important in introducing telecommunications competition.

B. Dominance

European law does not forbid a business from having a dominant position as such in a market. Rather, it prohibits the abuse of a dominant position. Still, an essential first step for enforcement officials to prove a violation of Article 82 or to take action to forbid or modify a proposed merger is to determine whether a

---

[25]   15 U.S.C. §1 (1995).
[26]   15 U.S.C. §2 (1995).

firm is dominant. The Treaty gives no guidance as to what constitutes a dominant position. The European Commission and the European courts have filled this vacuum through case law. Legislation and guidelines have been adopted, largely based on judicially enunciated principles, helping define what is meant by dominance.

1. High Level Definition of Dominance

To those who find themselves on the receiving end of a Commission investigation, it may seem that "the concepts of dominant position and abuse of such a position in Article 86 [82] are among the most indeterminate and vague concepts both in Community law and in the national law of the Member States."[27] Nevertheless, a degree of certainty can be obtained through examining enabling legislation and case law.

A dominant firm is not necessarily a complete monopoly, but it should have a position enabling it "if not to determine, at least to have an appreciable influence on the conditions under which that competition will develop, and in any case to act largely in disregard of it."[28] In principle then, dominance consists of the ability to act independently of the market. The ECJ defined dominant position, for purposes of Article 82, as "a position of economic strength enjoyed by an undertaking which enables it to prevent effective competition being maintained on the relevant market by giving it the power to behave to an appreciable extent independently of its competitors, customers and ultimately of consumers."[29]

What is meant by the ability to behave independently? It is the "power to determine prices or to control production or distribution for a significant part of the products" in the market.[30] Imposing unfair prices or selling conditions and limiting production or markets are listed as abuses of a dominant position in Treaty Article 82. Therefore, the ability to act in an abusive manner is evidence of dominance. Part of the process to determine dominance consists of examining "facts put forward as acts amounting to abuses without necessarily having to acknowledge that they are abuses."[31] In other words, it is possible determine if an undertaking is dominant by seeing if it acts like a dominant firm—that is in an abusive manner.[32] There is a logical and economic appeal to this argument, circular though it may be. Presumably, a firm would not engage in abusive behavior, such as charging excessive high prices, unless it enjoyed a position of competitive independence.

---

[27] Case 85/76 *Hoffmann-La Roche and Co.* v. *Commission* [1979] ECR 461, para. 4.
[28] *Ibid.*, para. 39
[29] Case 22/76 *United Brands Company* v. *Commission* [1978] ECR 207, para. 65, and *Hoffmann-La Roche and Co.* v. *Commission, ibid.*, para. 38.
[30] *United Brands Company* v. *Commission, ibid.*, para. 65.
[31] *Ibid.*, para. 68.
[32] Case T–30/89 *Hilti* v. *Commission* [1991] ECR II–1439, para. 87.

2. *Market Share Definition*

While there is a high level definition of economic independence that influences conclusions regarding dominance, in reality European enforcement officials and courts employ a test based on market shares to determine the existence of dominance.[33] A straightforward approach is employed whereby first the relevant product market or markets is determined, then the relevant geographic market.[34] Once market shares are determined, the position of the alleged dominant firm on the market can be ascertained and analysed.[35]

a. The Relevant Product Market

A first step in an Article 82 case is the determination of the relevant product market. The ECJ has held that competitive conditions should be judged by examining products that are "particularly apt to satisfy an inelastic need and are only to a limited extent interchangeable with other products."[36]

On occasion, a test of the sustainability of a theoretical small price increase is used to help determine the relevant product market. If it is found that price increases of perhaps five to ten per cent could be sustained for one or more products, then those products will be included within the range constituting the relevant product market. This is sometimes expressed as a "cross-price-elasticity test."

The theory behind this test is that if the price increase could not be sustained, there exists substitutability with other products that would need to be included within the relevant product market. Purchasers would have substituted other products rather than pay the price increase. It also might have been possible that producers attracted by the price increase have entered the market. The European Commission has indicated that it will use this test to help determine the relevant product markets in the area of telecommunications.[37]

The European Commission considers that the cross-price-elasticity test is "a synthesis of all the factors that properly determine whether two different products can properly be said to be in the same relevant market."[38] In fact, the cross-price-elasticity test is more of a subjective judgment of separate demand and supply side substitutability, with a heavy emphasis on demand side substitutability. Commission Form A/B, currently used to notify agreements that might fall under European competition law, states that the relevant product

---

[33] *United Brands Company v. Commission, supra* n. 27, and *Hoffmann-La Roche and Co.* v. *Commission, supra* n. 29.

[34] *United Brands Company v. Commission, supra* n. 27, para. 11.

[35] *Hilti* v. *Commission, supra* n. 32, para. 46.

[36] *Ibid.*, para. 64.

[37] Notice on the Application of the Competition Rules to Access Agreements in the Telecommunications Sector, Framework, Relevant Markets and Principles, 31 March 1998 [1998] OJ C265/2 para. 40 [hereinafter Access Notice] <http://europa.eu.int/Smartapi/cgi/Sga_doc?Smartapi!celexplus!prod!CELEXnumdoc+lg=en+numdoc=31998Y0822(01)>.

[38] *Hilti* v. *Commission, supra* n. 32, para. 53.

market is determined on the basis of interchangeability from the standpoint of the consumer.[39]

Leading European judgments stress the importance of determining markets from the consumers' standpoint.[40] The ECJ tends to accept narrowly drawn, even product-specific, markets.[41]

The European Commission issued guidelines recognising the difficulties inherent in defining markets in an area of rapid technological change such as telecommunications,[42] and stating that relevant product markets could only be determined on a case-by-case basis after examining factors of substitutability and "the competitive conditions and the structure of supply and demand on the market."[43] The European Commission indicated that it would tend to draw narrow product markets with distinct product markets "for terrestrial network provision, voice communication, data communication and satellites."[44] Nevertheless, there was a recognition that, at least regarding services such as mobile, paging and cordless telephones, technology was causing a blurring and consequent heightened interchangeability from a consumer standpoint.[45]

The European Commission also issued guidelines for competitors' access to telecommunications facilities containing a definition of distinct markets of provision of telecommunications services and access to facilities necessary to provide such services.[46] In effect, the European Commission asserted that telecommunications competition itself, manifested in the form of access to facilities necessary to compete, constitutes a separate market. To its credit, the Access Notice concedes that as telecommunications competition develops, market definitions, and therefore much of the Access Notice's analysis and conclusions, may change as well.[47] Given the above, the presence (or lack thereof) of alternative access networks should become increasingly important.

b. The Relevant Geographic Market

Once the relevant product market has been determined, the next step is to conduct an economic assessment of the relevant geographic market. The result will be conclusive as to market shares in that area, thereby enabling a decision as to

---

[39] Commission Regulation (EC) No. 3385/94 of 31 December 1994 on the form, content and other details of applications and notifications provided for in Council Regulation 17, § 6, [1994] OJ L 377/28. The notification system may be altered or eliminated in the future by reforms under consideration. White Paper On Modernisation of the Rules Implementing Articles 85 And 86 [81 and 82] of the EC Treaty Commission Programme No 99/027, 28.04.99.

[40] *United Brands Company* v. *Commission, supra* n. 29, para. 11.

[41] *Hilti* v. *Commission, supra* n. 32.

[42] Guidelines on the Application of EEC Competition Rules in the Telecommunications Sector, para. 25, [1991] OJ C 233/2 [hereinafter Telecommunications Competition Guidelines] <http://europa.eu.int/comm/competition/lawliber/en/91c2331.htm>.

[43] *Ibid.*, para. 26.

[44] *Ibid.*, para. 27.

[45] *Ibid.*, para. 30.

[46] Access Notice, *supra* n. 37, para. 44.

[47] *Ibid.*, para. 53.

dominance.[48] A short definition of the relevant geographic market is that in which trading conditions are similar.[49] This has been expressed as an "area where the objective conditions of competition applying to the product in question must be the same for all traders."[50] This is not to say that conditions of competition must be perfectly homogenous. "It is sufficient if they are 'the same' or 'sufficiently homogenous'."[51]

A designation of relevant markets is coloured by the European policy of promoting a single European market through breaking down national barriers to trade. Attempts to divide the market and discourage inter-Member State trade (prohibition of parallel imports) are viewed harshly. When faced with an unusual plea of national geographic markets, the ECJ held that national markets were not established in spite of the existence of national subsidiaries, customers' practice of buying at the local level, and price differences between nations. The Court reasoned that these differences were artificial and resulted from an attempt to divide the European market along national lines rather than from genuine different national markets.[52]

According to the Court, there were three factors determinative of the existence of a Community-wide relevant geographic market: (1) significant demand was stable throughout the Community; (2) customers could obtain machinery or cartons from other Member States; and (3) there was low cost of transport.[53] National markets have been found for telecommunications, but the European Commission expressed the belief that national markets will begin to break down and a European-wide geographic market emerge.[54]

c. The Relationship of Market Shares to Dominance

There is not a bright line test for how large a market share is necessary for a conclusion of dominance, but EU authorities have been forthcoming about the establishment of presumptions concerning the relationship of market shares to dominance. As might be expected, the existence of very large market shares is more likely to result in a determination of dominance.[55] The ECJ held that although large market shares, standing alone, are not always conclusive proof of dominance, they are, except in exceptional circumstances, evidence of the existence of a dominant position. A large market share held for a considerable period of time places a firm "in a position of strength which makes it an unavoidable trading partner," giving it "that freedom of action which is the especial feature of a dominant position."[56]

---

[48] *Hilti* v. *Commission, supra* n. 32, para. 79.
[49] *Ibid.*
[50] *United Brands Company* v. *Commission, supra* n. 29, para. 44.
[51] Case T–83/91 *Tetra Pak International S.A.* v. *Commission* [1994] ECR II–764 para. 92.
[52] *Ibid.*
[53] *Ibid.,* para. 94.
[54] Telecommunications Competition Guidelines, *supra* n. 42, para. 32.
[55] *Hilti* v. *Commission, supra* n. 32, para. 90.
[56] *Hoffmann-La Roche and Co.* v. *Commission, supra* n. 27, para. 109.

How large of a market share is necessary to be considered dominant in and of itself? The European Commission has considered a market share of 90 per cent to constitute "irrefutable evidence of dominance."[57] In this neighborhood, the ECJ has held that an 87 per cent market share results in an automatic determination of dominance.[58] Below this point, the language used to describe market shares changes. Shares of between seventy to eighty per cent may be seen as "a clear indication of the existence of a dominant position."[59] However, other factors might be considered in this range, including the relationship of the firm's market share with the shares of its competitors.[60] Shares of between fifty-four and fifty-eight per cent were found to be dominant when these shares were much larger than other competitors.[61] There is not a strict mathematical test for comparing the size of market shares of the subject and its competitors. Yet the ECJ has held that the market share of a company "equal to the aggregate of the shares of its two next largest competitors, proves that it is entirely free to decide what attitude to adopt when confronted by competition."[62]

As market shares decline further, other factors assume greater importance in dominance determinations. Market shares of between forty to fifty per cent have been held not to constitute dominance when there was evidence that the subject's market shares were declining, the impact of imports was being felt in the market, and there was no other evidence or even arguments presented as to why dominance should be found.[63] The presumption of dominance vanishes with a market share somewhere in the forties.[64]

There is at least one case where a European court has upheld a finding of dominance with a market share in the specific relevant product market of around forty per cent.[65] However, the subject held high market shares in neighbouring markets, and the Court reasoned that a finding of dominance in the neighbouring market had a type of spill-over effect, reinforcing the firm's economic power and justifying a finding of dominance.[66] In the Court's view, the high market share meant that the firm could concentrate its efforts where it had a lower market share. Therefore, it acted like a dominant firm and could be considered as dominant even though it did not have the market share of a dominant firm in that particular market. This result seems contrary to other cases in which courts have examined narrow markets and submarkets within the same industrial sector and found firms to be dominant in some, but not all, of the relevant product markets.[67] To be fair to the Court, it did also find a disparity between

[57] *Tetra Pak International S.A.* v. *Commission, supra* n. 51, para. 105.
[58] *Hoffmann-La Roche and Co.* v. *Commission, supra* n. 27, para. 55.
[59] *Hilti* v. *Commission, supra* n. 32, paras. 91–92.
[60] *Hoffmann-La Roche and Co.* v. *Commission, supra* n. 27, para. 60.
[61] *Ibid.*, para. 66.
[62] *Ibid.*, para. 51.
[63] *Ibid.*, paras. 57–58.
[64] *United Brands Company* v. *Commission, supra* n. 29, para. 109.
[65] *Tetra Pak International S.A.* v. *Commission, supra* n. 52, para. 120.
[66] *Ibid.*, para. 114.
[67] *Hoffmann-La Roche and Co.* v. *Commission, supra* n.27.

the firm's market shares and that of its nearest rival and that its position of strength was reinforced by its technological advantages.[68]

3. *Joint Dominance*

A concept of EU competition law that does not have a counterpart in US antitrust law is joint dominance. Treaty Article 82 speaks of "abuse by one or more undertakings of a dominant position"[69], leading to the conclusion that Article 82 can be applied against firms that are jointly dominant, that is oligopolies. Conceptually, this is hard to reconcile with the high level definition of dominance, that of market independence. How can more than one firm be independent of its competitors? Either a firm is dominant and can control the market or it is not. If there is agreement or a concerted practice among firms to behave anti-competitively, then this should be punished under Article 81. Pushed to its conclusion, the concept of joint dominance would mean that any firm, no matter how small its market share, was dominant, for all of the firms in a market, when considered together, obviously are dominant.

Unfortunately, the trend of EU policy and case law in this area is away from recognition of the illogic of joint dominance. Early case law indicated that there should be substantial links between the firms involved. For example, a parent may be held responsible for a subsidiary's abuse of a dominant position.[70] Indeed, perhaps the parent-subsidiary relationship was what was meant by "one or more firms." The European Commission and the ECJ, however, have taken a broader view of joint dominance. In the *Italian Flat Glass*[71] case, The ECJ held that independent firms may be jointly dominant.

> "There is nothing, in principle, to prevent two or more independent economic entities from being, on a specific market, united by such economic links that, by virtue of that fact, together they hold a dominant position vis-à-vis the other operators on the same market. This could be the case, for example, where two or more independent undertakings jointly have, through agreements or licences, a technological lead affording them the power to behave to an appreciable extent independently of their competitors, their customers and ultimately of their consumers."[72]

This comes very close to saying that an anti-competitive agreement is enough to confer dominance. The reference to licensing is also troublesome. EU authorities view the exercise of intellectual property rights with suspicion and have on occasion required mandatory licensing. Under the *Italian Flat Glass* rationale, if the holder of an intellectual property right licenses its competitor, perhaps to avoid an allegation of abuse of a dominant position, it runs a risk that it will be

---

[68] *Tetra Pak International S.A.* v. *Commission, supra* n. 51, para. 121.

[69] EU Treaty, *supra* n. 1, art 82.

[70] *Hilti* v. *Commission, supra* n.32.

[71] Case T–68, 77, and 78/89 *Società Italiana Vetro SpA* v. *Commission* [1992] ECR II–1403 [hereinafter *Italian Flat Glass*].

[72] *Ibid.*, para. 358.

held to be jointly dominant with its competitor by so acting. This is not a mere academic exercise. Holders of dominant positions are forbidden from doing such things as price discrimination that might be engaged in by non-dominant providers.

More recently, the European Court of First Instance has broadened the scope of joint dominance even further. *Gencor*[73] was an appeal from an adverse ruling of the European Commission regarding a proposed concentration of platinum producing companies. Among other issues, the Court considered whether the EU Merger Regulation applies in cases of alleged joint dominance. The European Commission banned the merger holding that it "would lead to the creation of a situation of oligopolistic dominance in the market concerned."[74]

The parties to the proposed merger argued that the prohibitions contained in the EU Merger Regulation, forbidding the creation or strengthening of dominant position, did not apply to cases of joint dominance. The Court disagreed, finding that proposed mergers can be forbidden even when the new creation alone would not have a dominant position. The Regulation could apply

> "to cases where concentrations lead to the creation of strengthening of a collective dominant position, that is to say a dominant position held by the parties to the concentration together with one or more undertakings not party thereto."[75]

Thus the European Commission is empowered to prohibit mergers that would lead to the creation or strengthening of an oligopoly.

With this reading of the Merger Regulation, it is not surprising that the Court found that it was not necessary that the proposed merger alone have a large market share in order for dominance to be found. While market share was important, in the eyes of the Court, it was not the only factor to be considered. Also important are market structure, means of production, relative size of market shares, as well as other factors that would give the parties "a position of strength which makes it an unavoidable trading partner and . . . that freedom of action which is the special feature of a dominant position."[76] Perhaps in response to the argument that more than one firm cannot be independent, the Court then immediately discounted the importance of market shares when considering a potential oligopoly.

> "It is true that, in the context of an oligopoly, the fact that the parties to the oligopoly hold large market shares does not necessarily have the same significance, compared to the analysis of an of an individual dominant position, with regard to the opportunities for those parties, as a group, to act to a considerable extent independently of their competitors, their customers and, ultimately, of consumers. Nevertheless, particularly in the case of a duopoly, a large market share is, in the absence of evidence to the contrary, likewise a strong indication of the existence of a collective dominant position."[77]

[73] Case T–102/96 *Gencor* v. *Commission* [1999] ECR II–753.
[74] *Ibid.*, para. 18.
[75] *Ibid.*, para. 125.
[76] *Ibid.*, para. 205.
[77] *Ibid.*, para. 206.

It is difficult to make sense of the foregoing paragraph, but the Court seems to say that oligopolies may have smaller market shares than individual firms and still be dominant. From a mere adding of market shares, that is facially correct. One firm with a hundred per cent market share would equal four firms with a twenty-five per cent market share each. The analysis fails, however, in market power terms. In the absence of collusion, the four firms would lack market power. The necessary collusion is a violation of Treaty Article 81. It should be sanctioned as such instead of perverting the concept of dominance. It might as well be argued that every violation of Article 81 is also a violation of Article 82, for every agreement having its "object or effect the prevention, restriction or distortion of competition",[78] if successful, allows the involved firms to act outside of normal market forces and hence independent of competitors and customers.

The proposed merging parties argued that the *Italian Flat Glass* judgment should be interpreted as requiring structural links between firms alleged to be collectively dominant. The Court again disagreed, holding that the reference to structural links in *Italian Flat Glass* was no more than an example of the type of "economic links" necessary to find joint dominance,[79] economic links presumably being looser than structural links. The Court held that the existence of an oligopoly itself is enough to show economic links. That is, few firms in a market is *per se* joint dominance.[79a]

> "Furthermore, there is no reason whatsoever in legal or economic terms to exclude from the notion of economic links the relationship of interdependence existing between the parties to a tight oligopoly within which, in a market with the appropriate characteristics, in particular in terms of market concentration, transparency and product homogeneity, those parties are in a position to anticipate one another's behaviour and are therefore strongly encouraged to align their conduct in the market, in particular in such a way as to maximise their joint profits by restricting production with a view to increasing prices. In such a context, each trader is aware that highly competitive action on its part designed to increase its market share (for example a price cut) would provoke identical action by the others, so that it would derive no benefit from its initiative."

The Court's holding reasons that a desire to form a price-fixing cartel or even an incentive to do so is enough to find joint dominance. This is simply a fantasy. While participants in every industry would doubtless like to keep prices high, more than "evil thoughts" should be necessary to warrant government intervention. The Court submits no proof that oligopolies are inherently subject to illegal actions. Indeed there is no such proof. When cartels exist, they should be punished as such, and Treaty Article 81 gives the European Commission the tools to do so. If firms are engaging in price signalling, improperly furnishing information to competitors,[80] or engaging in conscious parallel behaviour, an

---

[78] EU Treaty, *supra* n. 1, art. 85(1).
[79] *Gencor, supra* n. 73, paras. 274–275.
[79a] See discussion in chapter 4 of the importance of moving beyond analysis of mere market shares.
[80] Case T–34/92 *Fiatgri U.K. Ltd and New Holland Ford Ltd* v. *Commission* [1994] ECR II–905.

anti-competitive agreement or a concerted practice can be found and sanctioned.

The theory of joint dominance was unfortunately also accepted in the European Commission's Telecommunications Access Notice. Perhaps anticipating *Gencor*, the Access Notice took a broad view of what is necessary to find joint dominance. In the opinion of the European Commission it would be enough for the involved companies to "have links such as agreements for cooperation, or interconnection agreements."[81] As all telecoms operators in a geographic service area must have interconnection agreements for traffic to reach its destination, and since interconnection agreements are required by EU directives, this means all telecoms operators are at least potentially collectively dominant. The European Commission cannot seriously think that interconnection agreements demonstrate desire to collectively control prices or production in telecommunications markets, however, the Access Notice states that there "does not seem to be any reason in law or in economic theory to require any other economic link between jointly dominant companies."[82] This potential mass dominance finding was probably necessary for the Access Notice's position regarding access to essential facilities, discussed below.

4. Telecommunications

In the telecommunications sector, there may be an exception to the general presumptions of dominance determination with certain market shares. The Interconnection Directive—discussed in great detail in Chapter 11—states that telecommunications organisations "which have significant market power" are subject to duties such as meeting interconnection requests.[83] The phrase "significant market power" is another way of saying "dominance." The Directive goes on to state that "[a]n organization shall be presumed to have significant market power when it has a share of more than twenty-five per cent of a particular telecommunications market in the geographic area in a Member State within which it is authorized to operate."[84] No guidance is given as to the determination of the relevant product market for gauging this twenty-five per cent share. Not only does this create of presumption of market power with a market share of only twenty-five per cent, it also arbitrarily decides that the relevant geographic markets are national. This is contrary to the policy of creating European-wide markets, and goes against the promotion of technologies designed to erase national telecommunications boundaries such as mobile GSM service with its Europe-wide roaming capabilities. The Directive allows

[81] Access Notice, *supra* n. 37, para. 79.
[82] *Ibid.*
[83] Directive 97/33/EC of the European Parliament and of the Council of 30 June 1997 on interconnection in telecommunications ensuring universal service and interoperability through application of the principles on open network provision (ONP), art. 4(3), [1997] OJ L199/32 [hereinafter Interconnection Directive].
[84] *Ibid.*

national regulatory authorities to deviate from this presumption for telecommunications organisations with greater or less than a twenty-five per cent market share. If the regulatory authorities choose to conduct their own dominance test independent of the twenty-five per cent presumption, the Directive specifies that they are to consider "the organization's ability to influence market conditions, its turnover relative to the size of the market, its control of the means of access to end-users, its access to financial resources and its experience in providing products and services in the market."[85]

It is certainly questionable whether a market share of twenty-five per cent can be said to grant significant market power. There is no European judicial authority finding dominance with a market share of only twenty-five per cent. Commentators have stated that a finding of dominance with a market share of less than twenty-five per cent is almost inconceivable, while a finding of dominance with a market share of twenty-five to thirty-nine per cent rare but possible.[86] The European Commission's 1999 Telecommunications Review appeared to recognise this problem by calling for a distinction between significant market power duties with at least a twenty-five per cent market share and duties (such as cost-based pricing) to be imposed on dominant operators, designated as those having at least a fifty per cent market share. Determination of dominance and significant market power would be left to the national regulatory authorities.[87]

5. State Monopolies

Since Europe has a long tradition of state enterprises and monopolies, it is to be expected that legal monopolies might receive special treatment under European law. Indeed, there is a special Article of the Treaty of Rome—Article 86—which specifically allows state monopolies.[88] This Article, however, also declares that the competition rules apply to state monopolies, unless such application would interfere with the basic mission of the state enterprise. This provision was the vehicle by which the Commission ultimately required that state telecommunications companies be exposed to full competition. Under European law, the grant of a legal monopoly results in an automatic finding of dominance over the relevant geographic area of the entire nation where the monopoly exists.[89] This does not mean that an abuse will be found or that the monopoly will be broken up.[90] Nevertheless, legal monopolies have been challenged in

---

[85] *Ibid.*

[86] Christopher Jones and Enrique Gonzáles-Díaz, The EEC Merger Regulation 133 (1992).

[87] Communication for the Commission to the European Parliament, the Council, the Economic and Social Committee and the Committee of the Regions, Towards a new Framework for Electronic Communications infrastructure and associate services: The 1999 Communications Review, COM (1999) 539 §4.7.2 [hereinafter 1999 Telecommunications Review].

[88] EU Treaty, *supra* n. 1, art. 86.

[89] Case 41/90 *Höfner* v. *Macrotron* [1991] ECR I–1979 para. 28.

[90] Case 179/90 *Porto di Genova* [1991] ECR I–5889 para. 16.

such areas as telecommunications,[91] postal services,[92] employment services,[93] and provision of port facilities.[94] Telecommunications competition will result in abolition of exclusive rights to provide equipment or service, but special rights ("privileged access") granted for such things as favoured access to place facilities in the right of way might still confer dominance, in the opinion of the Commission.[95]

Public enterprises are not the only legal monopolies considered to confer a dominant position. Intellectual property rights, or at least their exercise, may also give rise to dominance, although the existence of an intellectual property right, standing alone, is not enough to lead to a conclusion of dominance. However, the existence of an intellectual property right, standing alone, is not enough to give rise to a conclusion of dominance.[96] The ECJ has drawn a distinction between the existence of an intellectual property right and its exercise, which might cause competition law problems. The case law in this area is confused, with the ECJ in one case ruling that to prohibit exclusive intellectual property rights might interfere with the very basis of the right granted.[97] More recently, the European courts, in a series of cases dealing with television listings, have concluded that not only may intellectual property rights confer dominance, but licensing of those rights to competitors may be obliged under certain circumstances. Third parties wishing to compete with the holder of the intellectual property right holder may be in a position of economic dependence characteristic of the existence of a dominant position.[98] The holder could prevent "the emergence of any effective competition on the market."[99] Patents have been construed as technical barriers, and in combination with other factors have justified a finding of dominance.[100]

6. *Other Evidence of Dominance*

A firm's size is meaningful, and not only in the relevant geographic market. The ECJ has indicated that it may consider worldwide production and market shares.[101] If in the court's opinion too much of a product is being produced and overcapacity exists, this can be evidence of dominance,[102] as can the expense to enter the market because of the necessity of large capital investments, distribu-

---

[91] Case 41/83 *Italian Republic* v. *Commission* [1985] ECR 873.

[92] Case 320/91 *Paul Corbeau* v. *PTT* [1993] I ECR I–2533 para. 9.

[93] *Höfner* v. *Macrotron, supra* n. 89, para. 28

[94] *Porto di Genova, supra* n. 90, para. 16.

[95] Access Notice, *supra* n. 37, para. 74.

[96] Joined Cases C–241/91 and C–242/91 *Radio Telefis Eireann* v. *Commission* [1995] ECR I–743 para. 46 [hereinafter *Magill*].

[97] Case 238/87 *Volvo* v. *Veng* [1988] ECR 6211.

[98] Case T–70/89 *British Broadcasting Corporation* v. *Commission* [1991] ECR II–535 para. 10.

[99] *Ibid.*, para. 51.

[100] *Tetra Pak International S.A.* v. *Commission, supra* n. 51, para. 110.

[101] *Hoffmann-La Roche and Co.* v. *Commission, supra* n. 27, para. 42.

[102] *Ibid.*, para. 51.

tion systems, long term planning, and high marketing costs.[103] And if large market shares have been retained for a considerable period of time, it may be evidence that a dominant position is being maintained.[104] This is consistent with a general prejudice under European law in favor of smaller firms. Policy considerations other than consumer welfare often enter competition law cases.

Although a large share in the relevant market is probably the most important fact in determining dominance, there are other factors that may be considered under European law. The general structure of a market and such things as production, supply, and demand may be considered in relation to market shares,[105] leaving authorities free to consider almost anything they choose to consider important.

Technological advantages are repeatedly mentioned by courts as conferring dominance. Patents[106] and research and development[107] have been viewed "as helping to maintain and reinforce a dominant position in the market.[108] The very success in the market as shown by technological advantages is enough to demonstrate "the consequence of the existence of obstacles preventing new competitors from having access to the market."[109] A "technical lead" through patents is unacceptable.[110] Advanced telecommunications technologies have been noted as a specific factor in a finding of dominance.[111] A firm under an accusation of dominance may not even try to improve its productivity.[112] This reasoning is paradoxical, as limitations on production or technical development are specifically mentioned as abuses under Article 82.[113] This is not a desirable policy. Punishing successful innovators does little to promote either technical development or consumer welfare. Technology itself can be a spur to competition as demonstrated in the telecommunications and information technology industries. As technology continues to develop, the growth of commercially feasible alternatives should also continue.

Other production and marketing successes may also be viewed suspiciously. Developing a distinctive trademark that is identified with a product consumers desire can be proof of dominance.[114] EU cases have also considered as dominant behavior an extensive and highly specialised sales network,[115] a strong and well-organised distribution system,[116] a diversity of sources of supply, the homogenous nature of products offered by a firm, and "the organization of its

---

[103] *United Brands Company v. Commission, supra* n. 29, para. 122.
[104] *Ibid.,* para. 44.
[105] *Hoffmann-La Roche and Co. v. Commission, supra* n. 29, para. 40.
[106] *Ibid.,* para. 42.
[107] *Hilti v. Commission, supra* n. 32, para. 86.
[108] *Ibid.,* para. 93.
[109] *Hoffmann-La Roche and Co. v. Commission, supra* n. 29, para. 48.
[110] *Ibid.,* para. 51.
[111] Telecommunications Competition Guidelines, *supra* n. 42, para. 81.
[112] *United Brands Company v. Commission, supra* n. 29, para. 82.
[113] EU Treaty, *supra* n. 1, art. 82(b).
[114] *United Brands Company v. Commission, supra* n. 29, para. 93.
[115] *Hoffmann-La Roche and Co. v. Commission, supral* n. 27, para. 42.
[116] *Hilti v. Commission, supra* n. 32, para. 19.

production and transport, its marketing system and publicity campaigns, the diversified nature of its operations and finally its vertical integration."[117]

On the other hand, EU authorities do not appear overly impressed by evidence of market failures as evidence that a dominant position does not exist. Arguments that falling prices in the market should be accepted as conclusive proof of the lack of dominance have not succeeded.[118] Even though the ECJ agreed that falling prices might indicate "lively competition" was present in the market, that did not necessarily preclude the existence of a dominant firm.[119] While falling prices were concededly incompatible with independent economic behavior, when the Court looked again at the high market shares held in a particular submarket, it convinced itself that the falling prices must have been part of the dominant firm's strategy rather than proof it was not dominant. The ECJ concluded that price variations bore "no relation to the existence of competition."[120] To this writer, the falling prices demonstrate that the relevant product market was drawn too narrowly by the Court, and the firm was probably not dominant. Even losses sustained over a period of time may not negate high market shares. There is no requirement that a dominant firm be profitable.[121] High market shares are more important.[122]

C. Essential Facilities

The European Commission has stated that possession of a facility essential for competition is prima facie evidence of dominance,[123] which raises the question of the contents and scope of any EU doctrine of essential facilities.

The concept of essential facilities was imported into EU competition law from US antitrust law[124] and remains a controversial position. It is debatable whether the essential facilities doctrine, named as such, is even a part of EU law.

---

[117] *United Brands Company* v. *Commission, supra* n. 29, para. 58.
[118] *Hoffmann-La Roche and Co.* v. *Commission, supra* n. 27, para. 37.
[119] *Ibid.*, para. 70.
[120] *Ibid.*, para. 78.
[121] *United Brands Company* v. *Commission, supra* n. 29, para. 127.
[122] *Ibid.*, para. 128.
[123] Access Notice, *supra* n. 37, paras. 63 and 69. This position is only logical since under the European doctrine of essential facilities, as advocated by the EU Commission there must be no commercially available alternative. It should be kept in mind, however, that alternatives, perhaps offered by developing technologies, negate an automatic finding of dominance for the possessor of the facility. For example, due to the current existence of commercially feasible alternatives to traditional telecommunications networks for potential competitors, such as cable TV networks or wireless technologies, it might not be proper to assume that dominance in the provision of telecommunications facilities exists.
[124] The US essential facilities test was summarised in *MCI* v. *AT&T*, a case instrumental in opening the AT&T monopoly to competition, as follows:

> The case law sets forth four elements necessary to establish liability under the essential facilities doctrine: (1) control of the essential facility by a monopolist; (2) a competitor's inability practically or reasonably to duplicate the essential facility; (3) the denial of the use of the facility to a competitor; and (4) the feasibility of providing the facility. *MCI Communications* v. *AT&T*, 708 F.2d 1081, 1132–33 (7th Cir. 1983).

The European Commission's Access Notice accepts the basics of the US law of essential facilities as expressed in the *MCI* case, but goes further: if a monopolist possesses an essential facility, it must provide these facilities to competitors at its own "price," not necessarily the usual retail price it charges on the open market.[125] It should be stressed that under the US essential facilities doctrine, even a successful claimant wins no more that the right to access the facilities at commercial (retail) prices. US antitrust law does not impose a burden of transfer prices on the alleged dominant supplier as the Commission's Access Notice would do. Certainly there is nothing in the essential facilities doctrine (as interpreted under US law) requiring a supply at cost represented by what a firm might in essence "charge" itself.

1. EU Law of Essential Facilities

It should first be considered whether, properly speaking, there is a European doctrine of essential facilities. The ECJ has never used the term. However, a Commission official involved in oversight of telecommunications markets has asserted that such a doctrine does in fact exist, and under whatever name, the judgments of the ECJ indicate that supply by a dominant party can be mandated by EU competition law,[126] perhaps under the general headings of refusals to supply or interruptions in usual supply arrangements.

The leading European case on refusal of supply is *Commercial Solvents*,[127] involving a monopolist's decision to withdraw supply of an ingredient necessary

[125] Access Notice, *supra* n. 37, paras. 86 and 104. This burden is not imposed under US law. *In Laurel Sand & Gravel Inc.* v. *CSX Transp. Inc.*, 924 F.2d 539 (4th Cir. 1991), the Court accepted, for purposes of its analysis, plaintiff's allegations that the defendant railroad was a monopolist in control of an essential facility, thereby fulfilling the first requirement of the four-part essential facilities test. *Ibid.*, at 544 (citing *MCI Communications* v. *AT&T*, 708 F.2d 1081 at 1132–33). However, the Court held that plaintiff could not meet the remaining three requirements. *Ibid.* Plaintiff "failed to show that it could not reasonably duplicate or pursue a reasonable alternative to the essential facility. *Ibid.* The Court found that alternatives might exist, including building other facilities (the Court admitted that this would be economically impractical), or purchasing service at the rates the railroad requested (a standard rate that included profit). *Ibid.* Plaintiff contended that it could not make a profit at the rate the railroad requested. *Ibid.* Plaintiff's desire for a more favorable rate did not mean that the railroad's price was unreasonable. *Ibid.*, at 545. This was true even though plaintiff could not profitably pay the railroad's rate. The Court held that "[t]he reasonable standard of the access factor can not be read to mean the assurance of a profit for" plaintiff. *Ibid.* Lastly, the Court interpreted the final requirement (the feasibility of providing the facilities) in terms of the normal business dealings of the railroad. *Ibid.* That is, the Court refused to intervene in the normal commercial activities of the alleged monopolist. The legitimate business reasons of the railroad, including existing sales relationships, should be considered and take precedence over a competitor's request, especially when the monopolist does not refuse the request, but only insists that its normal prices be paid. *Ibid.*

[126] John Temple Lang, "Defining Legitimate Competition: Companies' Duties to Supply Competitors and Access to Essential Facilities", (1994) 18 *Fordham Int'l L.J.* 437. However, as John Temple Lang states, the essential facilities doctrine "must be treated with caution, because the law normally allows a company to retain, for its own exclusive use, all advantages that it has legitimately acquired." *Ibid.*, at 439.

[127] Joined Cases 6 and 7/73, *ICI & CSC* v. *Commission* [1974] ECR 223 [hereinafter *Commercial Solvents*].

to make a downstream product after the monopolist decided to enter this market itself. The argument of the European Commission in that case was that:

> "there is a duty to supply at least when: the dominant company is a monopoly; the refusal affects one of the principal users, a former customer; no objective justification is apparent; and the refusal gravely affects the conditions of competition in the EC. If there is a duty to supply, there is, under Article [82] itself, a duty not to discriminate if the buyers are in competition with one another."[128]

Leaving aside the redundancy in the first part of the test ("the dominant company is a monopoly"), this is much the same as the US essential facilities test, except for the gloss as to nondiscrimination. The actual judgment stated that:

> "it follows that an undertaking which has a dominant position in the market in raw materials and which, with the object of reserving such raw material for manufacturing its own derivatives, refuses to supply a customer, which is itself a manufacturer of these derivatives, and therefore risks eliminating all competition on the part of this customer, is abusing its dominant position within the meaning of Article [82]."[129]

Likewise, in *United Brands* v. *Commission*,[130] a discontinuance of supply to a distributor in retaliation for promoting a competitor's products was condemned as an abuse of a dominant position. In other cases, notably *Magill*,[131] the ECJ has found a duty to license access to intellectual property rights. Commission decisions regarding ports and ferry service are also relevant, particularly given the Commission's reasoning in *B&I Line* v. *Sealink* that an operator of a port cannot give more favorable terms to its own ferry service than to its competitors.[132] *Sealink* is also an important case as it is the first decision employing the specific term "essential facilities."[133]

2. The Bronner Case

a. The Advocate General's Opinion

Bronner v. *Mediaprint*,[134] dealing with a competition law complaint from an Austrian newspaper company, is a timely and important case in the field of essential facilities. The following is an analysis of the Opinion of the Advocate General in the case. Although the opinions of the Advocate General have only persuasive weight in the judgments of the ECJ, this Opinion is worth a close

---

[128] Lang, *supra* n. 126, at 445 (citing *Commercial Solvents, ibid.*, at 250–51).

[129] *Commercial Solvents, supra* n. 127, at 251.

[130] *United Brands Co.* v. *Commission, supra* n. 29, at 217.

[131] *Magill, supra* n. 96.

[132] *See B&I Line* v. *Sealink* 5 CMLR 255, 265, 266 (1992). "A company in a dominant position may not discriminate in favour of its own activities in a related market." (quoting Case C–260/89 *Elliniki Radiophonia* v. *Commission* (unreported)).

[133] *Ibid.*, at 266.

[134] Case D–7/97 *Oscar Bronner GmbH & Co. KG* v. *Mediaprint Zeitungs—und Zeitschriftenverlag GmbH & Co. KG and Others* Opinion of Advocate General Jacobs delivered on 28 May 1998 [1998] ECR I–8333 [hereinafter *Bronner*].

review. It contains a thorough analysis of the essential facilities doctrine as applied under US antitrust law and European Commission decisions. There is also a well-reasoned argument as to proper formulation and application of EU competition law policy.

Bronner published the Austrian daily newspaper *Der Standard*, with a 3.6 per cent of the Austrian newspaper market.[135] Bronner filed a complaint against Mediaprint, accusing it of abusing its dominant position[136] by refusing to give Bronner access to Mediaprint's daily delivery system.[137] Bronner argued that access to Mediaprint's delivery system was essential for it to compete, and that Mediaprint discriminated against it by giving another competitor access.[138] Mediaprint responded that the delivery system was used for its own benefit, and that even assuming that it "is in a dominant position, it is not obliged to afford assistance to competitors."[139] Mediaprint responded to the allegations of discrimination by noting that it required the competitor to accept other services before delivering its newspapers: conditions that Bronner refused to accept.[140] In essence, Mediaprint admitted tying.

Bronner's position was that under the essential facilities doctrine Mediaprint could be forced to give competitors access to delivery system as "it is a prerequisite for effective competition on the market in daily newspapers."[141] The Advocate General summarised the essential facilities doctrine as follows:

> "According to that doctrine a company which has a dominant position in the provision of facilities which are essential for the supply of goods or services on another market abuses its dominant position where, without objective justification, it refuses access to those facilities. Thus in certain cases a dominant undertaking must not merely refrain from anti-competitive action but must actively promote competition by allowing potential competitors access to the facilities which it has developed."[142]

The Opinion correctly notes that the ECJ itself has never used the words "essential facilities" in its judgments,[143] but a number of cases have dealt with refusals to deal or a withdrawal of supply from competitors including *Commercial Solvents*,[144] *United Brands*,[145] *Télémarketing*,[146] and *GB-Inno-BM*.[147] The last two cases have particularly applicability to telecoms markets and were important in the Commission's liberalisation of telecoms markets.

---

[135] *Ibid.*, para. 2.
[136] *Ibid.*, para. 3. Mediaprint had 46.8 per cent of total Austrian circulation through its two newspapers.
[137] *Ibid.*, para. 4.   [138] *Ibid.*
[139] *Ibid.*, para. 5.   [140] *Ibid.*
[141] *Ibid.*, para. 33.
[142] *Ibid.*, para.34.
[143] *Ibid.*, para. 35.
[144] *Commercial Solvents*, *supra* n. 127.
[145] *United Brands* v. *Commission*, *supra* n. 29.
[146] Case 311/84 *Centre Belge d'etudes de marche—Télémarketing (CBEM) SA* v. *Compagnie Luxembourtgeoise de Télé diffusion SA and Information Publicité Benelux SA* [1985] ECR 3261.
[147] Case C–18/88 *Regie des Telegraphes et des Telephones* v. *GB-INNO-BM SA* [1991] ECR I–5941.

In *Télémarketing*,[148] the state television company insisted that all commercials employing a call in number must use the telephone number supplied by the television company. The television company argued that there was no abuse of a dominant position because competition had been removed in the area by law.[149] The ECJ, consistent with the provisions of Treaty Article 86, that even if a Member State removes areas from competition, Article 82 may still be applied so as to sanction anticompetitive conduct. The *Télémarketing* judgment was important in Competition Directorate-General's drive to liberalise the telecoms markets.

The *GB-Inno-BM*[150] case involved an attempt by the Belgian PTT to continue to link the provision of telephone service to sales of telephone sets by withholding approval of sets other than those offered by the Belgian PTT. The ECJ held that the PTT acting as judge and jury of what equipment could be attached to its network amounted to an abuse of a dominant position.[151] Both *Télémarketing* and *GB-Inno-BM* can be considered as tying rather than refusal to deal cases.

The *Bronner* Opinion also considered two intellectual property cases, *Volvo* v. *Veng*[152] and *Magill*.[153] European Community law recognises a difference between the existence of an intellectual property right that may confer exclusivity—indeed a type of monopoly—and the exercise of that right, which may violate competition law. While the *Volvo* judgment expressed a qualified right of intellectual property right holders to refuse to deal with competitors, *Magill* held that under certain circumstances, copyright holders could be forced to license to competitors.

Magill proves the truth of the old legal adage that bad facts make bad law. The intellectual property rights in question were no more than the copyright to television listings. When faced with a similar claim of copyright in telephone directory listings, the US Supreme Court decided that such listings were not worthy of copyright protection.[154] Unfortunately, that option was not available to the ECJ in *Magill* because, as a matter of national law, a national court had already determined that the listings were protected by copyright. The ECJ held that the exercise of the copyright had the effect of prohibiting the emergence of a new product on the market—in this case a comprehensive weekly TV guide—as opposed to the available daily listings.[155]

Magill was widely hailed as a landmark judgment, and imaginative lawyers rushed to assert sweeping claims to use competitors' property based on its rea-

---

[148] *CBEM* v. *CLT and IPB*, *supra* n. 146.
[149] *Ibid.*, 3271–72.
[150] *Regie des Telegraphes et des Telephones* v. *GB-INNO-BM SA*, *supra* n. 147.
[151] *Ibid.*, at para. 12.
[152] *Volvo* v. *Veng*, *supra* n. 97.
[153] *Magill*, *supra* n. 96.
[154] *Feist Publications, Inc.* v. *Rural Tel. Serv. Co.*, 499 U.S. 340, 363 (1991).
[155] *Magill*, *supra* n. 96, para. 54.

soning. There are indications, however, that European courts may not be as open to these arguments as the claimants might wish.

The *Bronner* Opinion analyzes the recent Court of First Instance holding of *Tiercé Ladbroke*,[156] in which it was held not to be an abuse of a dominant position for the holders of exclusive rights in certain televised horse races to refuse to license the rights in Belgium. The Court noted that televised horse races were already present in Belgium and were used in the market (betting) on which claimants were active. Therefore, the television rights were not essential for competition in the relevant market, nor was the emergence of a new product prevented.[157]

The *Bronner* Opinion therefore comprehensively traced the essential facilities doctrine from its origins in US antitrust law to the Commission decisions. The Advocate General found support for an EU essential facilities doctrine, a position increasingly found in the national law of the Member States as well.[158] Against that line is contrasted the right of private property and contract, recognised throughout the EU and often conferred with constitutional status.[159] Given these competing considerations, the Advocate General was reluctant to interfere with the commercial decision of a firm, even a firm that is dominant in a particular market. It should be stressed that the question before the Advocate General was only a refusal to supply. There were not other factors "such as cut-off of supplies, tying of sales or discrimination between independent customers."[160] *Magill* was distinguished "by the special circumstances of that case," specifically the prevention of the emergence of a new product.[161]

Most striking is the *Bronner* Opinion's statements regarding competition law policy. While not specifically recommending a judgment to the effect that the essential facilities doctrine does not exist in Community Law, the Opinion expresses grave reservations about its wholesale application.

First, the Opinion recommended that courts should be extremely careful about interfering with commercial decisions regarding the identity of one's trading partners.[162] Generally, a firm can sell to whomever it wishes. Furthermore, the facilities in question may be the result of substantial investment. Habitually compelling competitor access to facilities created only with considerable effort and expense will not create incentives for such efforts in the future.[163] Likewise, the Access Notice notes the importance of maintaining proper incentives for all, including incumbent telcos, to enjoy the fruit of investments as new products or services are introduced.[164]

---

[156] Case T–504/93 *Tiercé Ladbroke* v. *Commission* [1997] ECR II–923.
[157] *Ibid.*, para. 131.
[158] *Bronner, supra* n. 134, para. 53.
[159] *Ibid.*, para. 56.
[160] *Ibid.*, para. 54.
[161] *Ibid.*, para. 63.
[162] *Ibid.*, para. 56.
[163] *Ibid.*, para. 62.
[164] Access Notice, *supra* n. 37, para. 91.

Second, it might not be economically desirable to force a firm to supply its competitors because:

"In the long term it is generally pro-competitive and in the interests of consumers to allow a company to retain for its own use facilities which it has developed for the purpose of its business. For example, if access to a production, purchasing or distribution facility were allowed too easily there would be no incentive for a competitor to develop competing facilities. Thus while competition was increased in the short term it would be reduce in the long term. Moreover, the incentive for a dominant undertaking to invest in efficient facilities would be reduced if its competitors were, upon request, able to share the benefits."[165]

The Opinion would carve out an exception to these principles, and the Advocate General may have had telecommunications networks in mind.

"I do not rule out the possibility that the cost of duplicating a facility might alone constitute an insuperable barrier to entry. That might be so particularly in cases in which the creation of the facility took place under non-competitive conditions, for example, partly through public funding."[166]

Pubic ownership or state aids can certainly give a competitive advantage, and not only in creation of a facility such as networks. Publicly owned, but regulated entities can benefit immensely from the conflict of interest their regulators labour under. Regarding the historic state ownership of entities that have been since been privatised, as many European telcos have, it is debatable whether they should be placed in a worse position than other industries whose facilities might not have been "created" with public funds. When these telcos were privatised, did not their owners, the state, receive full market value from the purchasers? This price included the network assets. Therefore, any residual debt to the state, perhaps encompassing granting competitors access at favourable terms would be erased on privatisation. Otherwise, the buyers of these telcos, the current shareholders, did not receive what they bargained for.

The problem of whether telecommunications competition law and regulatory policy should favor creation of alternative infrastructure or force the allowance of competitor access to facilities such as local telephone loops is a pressing issue in the EU. The EU's approach to local loop unbundling is discussed in greater detail below in Chapter 11.

The third prong of the assessment portion of the *Bronner* Opinion constitutes a ringing declaration that consumer welfare should be the touchstone of proper competition law policy. "[T]he primary purpose of Article 86 [82] is to prevent distortion of competition—and in particular to safeguard the interests of consumers—rather than to protect the position of particular competitors."[167] Furthermore, the Opinion reasons that the proper focus should be on the state of competition in the downstream market rather than in the upstream market,

---

[165] *Bronner, supra* n. 134, para. 57.
[166] *Ibid.*, para. 66.
[167] *Ibid.*, para. 58.

where the dominant firm might control access to raw materials. If there is sufficient competition, perhaps through available substitutes, in the downstream market, then it is not an abuse for the dominant firm to refuse to supply the potential downstream competitors. The refusal would not harm competition.

If consumers are not suffering because there is adequate competition, why should the law care whether the request a particular competitor for access to raw materials is met? The key here may be the assessment of adequate competition. Presumably, if the benefits of competition in the downstream market exist, and an essential facility upstream is alleged, then the facility is not really essential, substitutes are readily available in the downstream market, or the market is relatively easy to enter. Interestingly, the Access Notice itself, while still regrettably failing to distinguish competition and the interests of competitors, at least agrees that the alleged necessity of an individual competitor for access to upstream facilites should not be sufficient to force access.[168] The Opinion also stresses that the essential needs of all competitors, rather than one that might not be able to duplicate the facilites in question should be deteminative.[169]

Also of interest is a comparison between the position of the Access Notice and the *Bronner* Opinion regarding division of upstream and downstream markets. The Access Notice considers there is a division of upstream (telecom facilities) and downstream (telecom services) markets.[170] On the other hand, the *Bronner* Opinion (quoting the Opinion of the Advocate General in *Commercial Solvents*), questioned whether consideration of positions on an upstream market is relevant when considering competition in a downstream market. The consumer is only interested in the end product.[171] Likewise, in telecommunications markets, consumers only care about the delivery of dial tone, not whether that dial tone is supplied by a fixed line local loop, co-axial cable, fibre rings, wireless local loops, GSM, satellite, Internet telephony, or whatever curent or future means of delivery can be conceived and put in place by competitors.

This is not to say that the *Bronner* Opinion gives a free pass to monopoly activity (as the efficiency doctrine is often mis-characterised as doing). The Advocate General stated that refusal of access may constitue an abuse "where access to a facility is a precondition for competition on a related market for goods or service for which there is a limited degree of interchangeability."[172] That is, the essential facilities doctrine should be reserved for exceptional cases, as most commentators recognise. The *Bronner* Opinion would put an end to the tendency to promote the essential facilities doctrine from a remedy of last resort to the prevailing policy of competition law.

---

[168] Access Notice, *supra* n. 37, para. 91a n. 68.
[169] *Bronner, supra* n. 134, para. 65.
[170] Access Notice, *supra* n. 37, para. 45.
[171] *Bronner, supra* n. 134, para. 59.
[172] *Ibid.*, para. 59.

Policy makers must carefully consider whether that point has been reached in telecommunications markets. Perhaps competition in some telecommunications markets, particularly local telephone service and end user access necessary for Internet access and broadband services, has not developed rapidly and extensively enough to call for imposition of this extreme remedy. Certainly telecommunications is important enough as a cornerstone of the information economy for the market to develop properly. Access policy, however, should be well thought out and consistently applied.

The Opinion draws a distinction between the exercise of intellectual property rights, which presumably are of a limited duration in time, and monopolies that might be expected to be of such duration as to be considered as permanent.[173] If the cost of duplicating the facilities in question is prohibitive for all potential competitors, then the Opinion asserts that access might be mandated as then there might exist an insurmountable barrier to entry. Whatever the alleged barriers, however, they must grant the dominant firm "a genuine stranglehold on the related market."[174] In markets of rapid technological progress like telecommunications, such strangleholds should be rare.

With these considerations in mind, there is no surprise in the Advocate General's recommendation that the alleged dominant firm, Mediaprint, did not have an obligation to allow Bronner access to its home delivery network.[175] Alternative, "albeit less convenient"[176] means of distribution were available. Nor was the substantial investment needed for nation-wide home delivery seen as dispositive. If Bronner wished to compete on equal terms with Mediaprint, then it might be necessary to make the investments required of a paper with a large circulation. The fact that Bronner was enjoying substantial growth in circulation was also seen as proof that access to Mediaprint's network was not so essential after all.[177] Most importantly, the Advocate General was not willing to put the EU on a path that would lead to detailed regulation of markets throughout Europe, including regulation of prices and conditions of supply.[178] Given the Commission's regulatory creep towards total regulation of telecoms markets, such fears are not misplaced.[179]

b. The ECJ's Bronner Judgment

The *Bronner* Judgment[180] was not as long or comprehensive as the Advocate General's Opinion. It can be viewed as an endorsement of the Advocate

---

[173] *Bronner, supra* n. 134, para. 64.

[174] *Ibid.*, para. 65.

[175] *Ibid.*, para. 66.

[176] *Ibid.*, para. 67.

[177] *Ibid.*

[178] *Ibid.*, para. 69.

[179] The European Commission's closer involvement with the telecoms market can be demonstrated by the intervention in such matters as prices for mobile licenses charged by Member States, interconnection pricing, and settlement rates for termination of international traffic.

[180] Case C–7/97 *Oscar Bronner GmbH & Co. KG* v. *Meida Zeitungs—und Zeitschrifenverlag GmbH & Co. KG* [1998] ECR I–8333 [hereinafter *Bronner* Judgment].

General's Opinion, but given the consensus nature of the ECJ's judgments (the language of the judgments must be unanimously agreed upon), it is not surprising that the Judgment is rather terse and cryptic at times.

The Court first considered a jurisdictional question: whether the Austrian Court properly referred the case to the ECJ for resolution of EU legal questions. Mediaprint and the EU Commission both argued that Austrian law alone should have disposed of the legal issues involved in the case and that the dispute did not affect trade among the Member States of the EU as required for Treaty Article 82 to apply. The ECJ replied that it was for the Member State referring court itself to gauge whether a question of European law was involved so as to refer the matter to the ECJ under Treaty Article 234.[181] The question of the potential effect on trade between Member States was considered a factual matter, presumably to be disposed of by the Austrian Court in any subsequent trial.[182]

The Court than moves to consideration of the main question, whether the holder of a large market share for daily newspapers and possessing the only home delivery network violates Article 82 by refusing to grant a rival access to this network.[183] The next step of the analysis was to define relevant markets. Bronner argued that separate markets existed for Austrian newspapers themselves and the service of home delivery.[184]

According to Bronner, separate markets existed and were proven by the fact that delivery was requested and offered separately from the newspaper itself.[185] Certainly Bronner requested delivery separately from Mediaprint, desiring only delivery services of its own newspaper, but can an end customer request delivery without a newspaper to be delivered?

The Court, however, does not deal fully with the issue of market definition at this point. Instead, in the same paragraph the Judgment considered the allegation that the delivery network constitutes an essential facility.[186] The Court placed the phrase "essential facilities" within quotation marks, so it is still uncertain whether the ECJ accepts the doctrine as such. Bronner asserted that the doctrine as established under *Magill* first dictated that "the service performed by placing a facility at the disposal of others and that supplied by using that facility in principle constitute separate markets."[187] It then followed that the holder of an essential facility was "obliged to allow access to the scheme by competing products on market conditions and at market prices."[188] Bronner also pled the more classic refusal to supply case, *Commercial Solvents*.[189]

[181] *Ibid.*, para.16.
[182] *Ibid.*, para. 21.
[183] *Ibid.*, para. 23.
[184] *Ibid.*, para. 24.
[185] *Ibid.*
[186] *Ibid.*
[187] *Ibid.*
[188] *Ibid.* Note that Bronner did not claim the right to access at a price representing Mediaprint's own cost. In contrast, the Access Notice, *supra* n. 37, paras. 86 and 104, would require incumbent telcos to supply access to essential facilities at their own cost (transfer prices).
[189] *Ibid.*, para. 25.

Mediaprint responded that an obligation to supply should only be imposed in exceptional circumstances, being an interference with a firm's freedom and ability to make business decisions, including decisions as to the identity of a firm's customers.[190] *Commercial Solvents* can be distinguished in that refusals to supply are only to be condemned when such refusal has the effect of leading to an elimination of all competition in a downstream market. Mediaprint asserted that was not the case for Austrian newspapers; there are alternatives for distribution other than Mediaprint's home delivery network.[191] Even if the Court found the required "exceptional circumstances," Mediaprint argued that a dominant firm might still deny access to a competitor if such refusal could be objectively justified, for example due to lack of capacity.[192]

From the Judgment, it appears that the position of the European Commission was that the Court needed to engage in a three part test. First, the ECJ would determine whether a separate relevant product market existed for home delivery of newspapers. The second question was whether Mediaprint was dominant in that separate market. Third was the question of whether Mediaprint's refusal constituted an abuse of a dominant position.[193] Assuming the first two conditions were met, the European Commission then would have the Court consider whether Mediaprint discriminated against Bronner, discrimination being a listed abuse according to the terms of Article 82(c).[194] As Mediaprint provided delivery services to another newspaper competitor, albeit in conjunction with printing services, the European Commission did not consider that a discrimination case was made out.[195]

At this point, rather confusingly, the ECJ returned to the question of defining the relevant market, stating that it is up to the referring national court to determine the relevant markets, and therefore whether a home delivery network constitutes a separate product market, or whether other distribution outlets are sufficiently interchangeable to be included within the relevant product market.[196] With this detour in the analysis, it might be expected that the ECJ would end the case by returning it to the Austrian court. The Judgment went on, however, first to state that if a separate market was found for home delivery, the national court could conclude that Mediaprint was dominant in that relevant product market. With a geographical product market designation of Austria as a whole, EU jurisdiction would be present so Treaty Article 82 would apply.[197]

---

[190] Case C–7/97 *Oscar Bronner GmbH & Co. KG v. Meida Zeitungs—und Zeitschrifenverlag GmbH & Co. KG* [1998] ECR I–8333, para. 26.

[191] *Ibid.*, para. 27.

[192] *Ibid.*, para. 28.

[193] *Ibid.*, para. 29.

[194] *Ibid.*, para. 30.

[195] Although briefly discussed in the Advocate General's *Bronner* Opinion, *supra* n. 134, para. 73, the issue of whether Mediaprint was unlawfully tying printing and distribution (Mediaprint delivered newspapers for a competitor it also provided printing service to) was never ruled upon by the ECJ, an interesting omission.

[196] *Bronner* Judgment, *supra* n. 180, para. 34.

[197] *Ibid.*, paras. 35–36.

This then set the stage for a discussion of essential facilities and refusal to deal—that is, whether Mediaprint's refusal to give access to its distribution network was an abuse under Treaty Article 82.[198]

The Court read *Commercial Solvents* and *CBEM*[199] as condemning refusals to deal only when the supply "is indispensable for the activity of another undertaking in a different market."[200] *Magill* was likewise narrowly presented as a case where:

> "Refusal by the owner of an intellectual property right to grant a licence, even if it is the act of an undertaking holding a dominant position, cannot in itself constitute abuse of a dominant position, but that he exercise of an exclusive right by the proprietor may, in exceptional circumstances, involve an abuse."[201]

The ECJ recalled that in *Magill* exceptional circumstances were found; the refusal of the holder of the intellectual property right in question (copyrighted TV listings) to license the rights prevented the emergence of a new product—weekly TV guides.[202] The Court also hinted that it might restrict *Magill* to its facts—or only to cases involving exercise of intellectual property rights.[203]

Nevertheless, the Court gave guidance as to when refusal to supply could constitute an abuse of a dominant position, proposing a four part test. First, the refusal must "be likely to eliminate all competition"[204] in the upstream market. Second, The refusal must not be objectively justified. Third, The service or product in question must be indispensable. That is, fourth, there must be "no actual or potential substitute in existence" for the requested service or product.[205]

The Court concluded that Bronner could not succeed under this test, even assuming there was only one home delivery network in Austria.[206] There were other methods of selling newspapers, such as sales in stores, even if these other methods are not as advantageous as home delivery.[207] Furthermore, it is not "impossible, or even unreasonably difficult," for potential competitors to set up their own competing home delivery network.[208] Technical, legal or economic barriers do not exist to the establishment of any such rival delivery system.

Very importantly, the Court emphasised that economies of scale alone are not enough for a plea by a smaller rival for access to the dominant providers distribution system.[209] The claimant cannot succeed by merely pointing out that its small size does not justify a nationwide delivery system. The Court would not

---

[198] *Ibid.*, para. 37.
[199] *CBEM v. CLT, supra* n. 146.
[200] *Bronner* Judgment, *supra* n. 180, para. 38.
[201] *Ibid.*, para. 39.
[202] *Ibid.*, para. 40.
[203] *Ibid.*, para. 41.
[204] *Ibid.*
[205] *Ibid.*
[206] *Ibid.*, para. 42.
[207] *Ibid.*, para. 43.
[208] *Ibid.*, para. 44.
[209] *Ibid.*, para. 45.

require the dominant provider to in effect subsidise the operations of the smaller competitor by granting the ability to deliver newspapers through the system established by the larger firm. That is merely a benefit of size that the Court was unwilling to characterise as an abuse. The Court quoted with approval the test suggested by the Advocate General in Paragraph 68 of his opinion, that the claimant would have to demonstrate impossibility of the establishment of a competing network by showing the economic impossibility of such distribution "with a circulation comparable to that of the daily newspapers distributed by the existing scheme."[210] If a competing network is impossible with a small share of the market, but not with a large share, the competitor must then labour to raise its circulation or find other means to efficiently distribute its products. This Court refused to give it a hand up in the marketplace.

The *Bronner* Judgment did not expressly reject or accept the essential facilities doctrine, but it clarified the test for determining when a dominant firm's refusal to supply a rival can amount to an abuse of that dominant position. By narrowing the scope of *Magill*, the Judgment did a great service in helping to curtail the more imaginative uses some claimants tried to bend that case to. The dose of economic reality represented by the recognition that economies of scale do not automatically mean an abuse of a dominant position is also most welcome.

D. Merger Regulation

As a system of formal merger approval is a relatively recent addition to the EU legal system, when the Merger Regulation[211] was adopted it contained many of the principles developed through European case law concerning dominance. Although the specifics of the Merger Regulation's procedure and application through important EU merger decisions are examined below in Chapter 18, the Merger Regulation is itself is therefore a good source for a concise list of important factors in determining dominance under European law. The Merger Regulation provides that if certain thresholds are met, mergers—that is "concentrations" under Community terminology—shall be appraised by the European Commission, and mergers that would tend to create or strengthen a dominant position are forbidden.[212] The European Commission is to consider the structure of all markets concerned and actual or potential competition from other firms.[213] As part of this appraisal, the European Commission is to examine:

> "the market position of the undertakings concerned and their economic and financial power, the alternatives available to suppliers and users, their access to supplies or mar-

---

[210] *Bronner* Judgment, para. 46.
[211] Council Regulation (EEC) 4064/89 of 21 December 1989 on the control of concentrations between undertakings [1990] OJ L257/14.
[212] *Ibid.*, art. 2(3).
[213] *Ibid.*, art. 2(1)(a).

kets, any legal or other barriers to entry, supply and demand trends for the relevant goods and services, the interests of the intermediate and ultimate consumers, and the development of technical and economic progress provided that it is to consumers' advantage and does not form an obstacle to competition."[214]

In applying this test, the European Commission's Merger Task Force has acquired a reputation for leniency, but several mergers have failed to win approval, notably in such high technology media areas as development of pay TV systems[215] and development and transmission of satellite TV programming.[216] Not only is the European Commission becoming more critical, but the reach of the Merger Regulation is extensive, as demonstrated by controversy over approval of the Boeing/McDonnell Douglas merger. Though Europeans have complained in the past about the US application of the effects doctrine, there is an equivalent under European competition law. A wise practitioner should keep the rules regarding dominance in mind when advising clients that may be subject to European law.

IV. CONCLUSION

This chapter began with a recognition that EU institutions, policies and law are complex. While a detailed examination of these subjects would require a book in and of itself, hopefully, some basic lessons can be drawn from EU policies, particularly in the area of competition law. There is a tension in EU competition law between sound economic policy, expressed in terms of consumer welfare, and policies designed to promote the interests of competitors, or "fair" competition rules. While the EU is making strides to ensure that its policies are implemented so as to economically benefit consumers, the policy tension still exists. The next chapter takes a closer look at how the EU began to apply competition law to the telecommunications sector and how EU telecommunications regulatory policy evolved.

---

[214] *Ibid.*, art. 2(1)(b).
[215] Case IV/M.469 *MSG Media Service* [1994] OJ L364/1.
[216] Case IV/M.490 *Nordic Satellite Distribution* [1996] OJ L53/20.

11

Europe's First Steps Towards Telecoms Competition

I. INTRODUCTION

E UROPE DOES NOT have a history of telecommunications regulation similar to the United States. Until recently, the telephone companies (often combined with postal services and collectively known as PTTs) were government-owned monopolies. Prices were charged to end-users based on political decisions rather than rate of return regulation or any rational market concerns. However, changes in the US telephone industry beginning in the mid–1960s were influential in Europe. With the AT&T divestiture, interested European competition law enforcement officials began to seek a way to bring the benefits of competition to European telecommunications. The weapon employed was the European Commission's Article 86 authority to unilaterally issue directives or decisions to Member States in cases involving anti-competitive conduct by state monopolies or entities granted special or exclusive rights.[1]

Before the European Commission began to issue its Article 86 directives, the stage was set by an investigation and subsequent decision against a European telecommunications operator. This first important telecommunications case involved forwarding telecommunications traffic to a third country before termination in the destination country.[2] This refiling of traffic is done in order to reduce amounts paid for international settlement rates. Refiling is a practice that continues today, but reductions in international settlement rates have reduced somewhat the incentive to engage in refiling as the available arbitrage margins have themselves reduced.

II. INTERNATIONAL TRAFFIC EXCHANGES AND THE *BRITISH TELECOM* JUDGMENT

Due to the structure of international telex charges, it was often cheaper to send messages through third countries, such as the UK, than to transmit them directly

---

[1] Consolidated Version Of The Treaty Establishing The European Community [1997] OJ C340/173–308 art. 86(3) [hereinafter EU Treaty]. "The Commission shall ensure the application of the provisions of this article and shall, where necessary, address appropriate directives or decisions to Member States."

[2] Case 41/83 *Italian Republic* v. *Commission* [1985] ECR 873 [hereinafter *British Telecom*].

between the country where the message originated and the country where the message was to terminate.[3] Recognising this anomaly, telex forwarding agencies were established in the UK and took advantage of developing technology to store a number of messages and transmit them in short bursts.[4] The International Telecommunication Union (ITU), composed of representatives of nations and private telephone companies, reacted by passing ITU recommendations and regulations calling on telecommunications administrations to deny service to telex forwarding agencies.[5] The ITU is world's oldest international intergovernmental organisation, currently under the authority of the United Nations, and established and maintained the system of settlement and accounting rates, which is still the primary method used to pay for termination of international telephone calls. Although the ITU is a treaty organisation, its authority is ill-defined. One of the forwarding agencies, when threatened with disconnection by British Telecommunications (BT), complained to the Competition Directorate-General of the European Commission. The European Commission investigated, using its Article 86 power to oversee the compliance of state monopolies with the Community's competition law. The European Commission charged BT with a violation of Article 82 (abuse of a dominant position). The European Commission's decision condemned the threatened disconnection,[6] but by that time BT was in the process of privatisation, and neither BT nor the UK government chose to enforce the ITU regulations in question.[7]

As allowed under the procedures of the European Court of Justice (ECJ), the Italian government and other Member States appealed the Commission's decision to the ECJ.[8] The opinion of the Advocate-General submitted in the case noted that the message forwarding agencies relied on an "an advanced technology" as well as price differentials to conduct their business. Therefore, the forwarding agencies were able to offer the public a higher quality service at lower prices. Enforcing the ITU regulations and putting the forwarding agencies out of business would have had the effect to curbing technological progress and increasing prices, contrary to EU competition law policy.[9]

The Court held that Community competition law did apply,[10] and took a narrow view of the ITU regulations, holding that BT could have complied with the regulation without threatening to disconnect the forwarding agencies in viola-

---

[3] Case 41/83 *Italian Republic* v. *Commission* [1985] ECR 873, at 875, Advocate General Opinion.

[4] *Ibid.*, para. 7.

[5] *Ibid.*, at 873–82, Advocate General Opinion.

[6] Case 82/861 *Telespeed Servs. Ltd* v. *United Kingdom Post Office* [1983] 1 CMLR 457, 458.

[7] *British Telecom*, *supra* n. 2, at 874–875, Advocate General Opinion. This also should have raised a question of whether Article 86 would apply to privatised former state monopolies. Article 86(1) states that it applies not only to public undertakings, but also to "undertakings to which Member States grant special or exclusive rights," a phrase that would be the subject of later litigation involving BT.

[8] *Ibid.*, at 874, Advocate General Opinion.

[9] *Ibid.*, at 875–79, Advocate General's Opinion.

[10] *Ibid.*, para. 38.

tion of Article 82.[11] Furthermore, the Court held the "modicum of competition" represented by the message forwarding agencies was a benefit to consumers and did not constitute interference with a state monopoly's position that might be legitimately preserved from competition under EC Treaty Article 86(2).[12]

Italy argued that a Member State has complete discretion over the reservation of areas for exclusive or special rights and that the application of Article 86(2) should be left to the discretion of the Member State. The ECJ disagreed, however, holding that the enforcement provisions of Article 86(3) allowing the European Commission to address directives or decisions to Member States when public undertakings transgressed competition law entrusted oversight of state monopolies to the European Commission, not to the Member States themselves.[13] The ECJ maintained that allowing message forwarding agencies to exist could decrease the absolute nature of the state telecommunications monopoly, but the small decrease in revenue potentially suffered by the state monopoly would not sufficiently jeopardise the performance of the tasks assigned to the state monopoly so as to justify exclusivity.[14]

The *British Telecom* judgment laid down several key principles that were to be instrumental in the forthcoming promotion of competition in the telecommunications sector: (1) the European Commission can enforce competition law against state monopolies, including telephone companies; (2) regulation, here in the form of ITU regulations, cannot be used as an excuse to justify anti-competitive behaviour; (3) the court recognised the importance of technical and economic progress, as well as consumer choice.

III. THE EUROPEAN COMMISSION'S TELECOMMUNICATIONS GREEN PAPER

Soon after the *British Telecom* judgment, the European Commission conducted a comprehensive study of the European telecommunications market, released as a Green Paper in 1987.[15] Dissatisfied with the then monopoly structure and performance of European telecommunications markets, the Green Paper called for

---

[11] *Ibid.*, para. 40.

[12] *Ibid.*, para. 25.

[13] *Ibid.*, para 30. Member State application of EU competition law is an area of continuing controversy. Commission Regulation 17 gives the European Commission the exclusive right to issue exemptions to the provisions of Article 81 as called for under Article 81(3). It was thought that Member State court and enforcement officials lacked experience in competition law matters, and that allowing Member State application might lead to inconsistent results throughout the Community. In 1999, the European Commission issued a White Paper proposing that Member States be granted limited powers of applying EU competition law. White Paper on Modernisation of the Rules Implementing Articles 85 and 86 [81 and 82] of the EC Treaty, Commission Programme No 99/027, Brussels, 28.04.1999.

[14] *British Telecom, supra* n. 2, para. 33.

[15] Towards a Dynamic European Economy: Green Paper on the Development of the Common Market for Telecommunications Services and Equipment, COM(87)290 final [hereinafter Green Paper].

immediate competition in all aspects of telecommunications with the important exception of basic voice telephony.

The starting point of the Green Paper was a recognition of the importance of telecommunications for economic progress and that in general the state of European telecommunications in terms of quality of service and prices was poor in comparison with the US and Japan.[16] Europe could improve the situation by joining the global trend toward promotion of competition and privatisation of telecommunications,[17] the cornerstone of which was asserted to be a separation between the regulation and operation of telecommunications administrations.[18] In Europe, not only did the PTTs have a monopoly over telecommunications services and equipment, but the same governmental agency that provided the services typically set prices and granted approval for provision of services and equipment.

The Green Paper did not call for full competition, or liberalisation, immediately. Remembering that Treaty Article 86 allowed Member States to maintain public undertakings or "revenue-producing" monopolies,[19] the authors might have been concerned that immediate full competition might be going too far, too fast. A requirement of full competition might have enabled Member States to argue that stripping their telephone companies of all their monopoly rights interfered with their ability to perform "the particular tasks assigned to them," in the language of Treaty Article 86(2). The argument that monopoly rights were necessary to maintain universal service was later used by Member States attempting to stave off competition, but as the European Commission did not insist on full competition in the short term, this argument was not effective.

While the Green Paper concluded that basic voice traffic might be reserved as a monopoly service, this reservation was to be temporary, allowing the PTTs to maintain universal service support while adjusting to meet the challenges of forthcoming competition.[20] New and advanced services and international voice traffic would have to open to competition.[21] Therefore, technological progress would not be constrained in new service areas. Competition would be a spur to the old monopolies themselves to deploy competing services rather than risk loss of market share. While the PTTs were not to be forbidden to enter new service areas—there was no recommendation of line of business restrictions as were imposed on the regional Bell companies (RBOCs) in the US after the break up of the monopoly Bell System. Instead, the European Commission decided the best way to combat PTT cross subsidisation of new services was through requirements of accounting separation.[22]

---

[16] Towards a Dynamic European Economy: Green Paper on the Development of the Common Market for Telecommunications Services and Equipment, COM(87)290 final.

[17] *Ibid.*, at 10.

[18] *Ibid.*, at 185.

[19] EU Treaty, *supra* n. 1, art. 6(2).

[20] Green Paper, *supra* n. 15, at 177–79.

[21] *Ibid.*, at 68.

[22] *Ibid.*, at 77–78, 184.

The incremental approach of the European Commission was based on political reality. Realism is a hallmark of EU institutions. The European Commission would have liked to immediately liberalise all telecommunications markets, however the objections of PTTs and their State owners made that impossible. Had the European Commission attempted to insist, the entire liberalisation process would have been in jeopardy. As it was, the European Commission realised its plan, albeit over time. The need for compromise is inherent in the EU system, as is the need for patience. These factors help explain the slow pace of change in European telecommunications regulation.

IV. THE EQUIPMENT DIRECTIVE AND MEMBER STATE CHALLENGE

In the Green Paper, the European Commission expressed a desire to eliminate the monopoly PTTs had on provision of telephone equipment, including basic telephone sets.[23] The PTTs generally required subscribers to obtain telephone sets from them as well: a classic case of tying similar to what AT&T required in the US. And like in the US, the European Commission did not accept the monopolists' plea that non-monopoly telephones would injure the telecommunications network. That is not to say that the PTTs gave up easily. As recently as 1995, the ECJ ruled that France's attempt to criminally prosecute a merchant for advertising "non-approved" telephone sets was prohibited under European law.[24] In that case, it was a division of France Télécom itself that was responsible for approvals, and had understandably not had time to approve the competitor's telephone equipment.

In 1988, the European Commission issued a directive under its Article 86 authority calling for competition in telecommunications terminal equipment,[25] that is consumer telephone sets, sometimes called POTS (plain old telephone service) sets. In its preamble, the Equipment Directive delineates its goals as technical progress, consumer choice, the elimination of restrictions on imports from other Member States, fair competition, and mutual acceptance of goods legally manufactured and marketed in other Member States,[26] many of the basic principles of the European Community and the Single Market. Member States were to withdraw special or exclusive rights to supply telecommunications equipment.[27] Telecommunications regulatory authorities could, however, ban

---

[23] *Ibid.*, at 14.

[24] Case 91/94 *France* v. *Tranchant* [1995] ECR I–3911. Incredibly, some European incumbent operators even today claim that end-user equipment, such as telephones, can harm telecommunications networks. Apparently the engineers working for these operators are not familiar with basic network interface and protection devices.

[25] Commission Directive 88/301 of 16 May 1988 on competition in the markets in telecommunications terminal equipment [1988] OJ L131/73 [hereinafter Equipment Directive] <http://europa.eu.int/comm/competition/liberalization/legislation/88301.htm>. Under the Directive, terminals are defined to include all end-user equipment.

[26] *Ibid.*, recitals 1–5.

[27] *Ibid.*, art. 2.

equipment not meeting the requirements of any forthcoming European harmonising directive for telecommunications equipment, or, alternatively, could have their own technical requirements, subject to the obligation that such requirements be non-discriminatory.[28] This exception was designed to meet the PTTs' ostensible concern that non-conforming telephones might harm their networks.

To counter the temptation of telecommunications organisations to ban all equipment they did not supply, Member States were required to separate the regulatory and operating functions of their telecommunications administrations,[29] a requirement that some Member States did not meet for some time as demonstrated by the *Tranchant* judgment cited above. End-users locked into long term service contracts with PTTs were given the right to terminate on one year's notice.[30] The practice of dominant firms of entering into long term contracts with customers is often viewed by enforcement officials as abusive.

Several Member States filed a challenge to the Equipment Directive, focusing on the power of the European Commission to issue such a directive under EU Treaty Article 86(3).[31] The ECJ opinion declared that state monopolies, although recognised under Article 86, must be considered a departure from the general rules of the EU Treaty and the specific rules of competition.[32] That is to say, the ECJ ruled that the interests of Member States in using state monopolies as instruments of economic or fiscal policy must be weighed against the policy of the Community, as expressed in the EU Treaty, of preserving fair competition and the unity of the Common Market.[33] The ECJ accepted the stated premise of the Equipment Directive that competition could be allowed in telecommunications terminals without jeopardising fulfillment of the PTTs' basic mission: the furnishing of a telecommunications network and services.[34] As none of the challenging Member States contested this assertion, the ECJ did not need to consider whether competition in telecommunications equipment might interfere with this mission.[35]

The challenging Member States argued that the European Commission exceeded its Article 86(3) power by issuing a directive of general application instead of proceeding against individual Member States as allowed by Article 226.[36] This Treaty article allows the European Commission to initiate proceedings against a Member States for failure to fulfil its obligations under the Treaty. The ECJ rejected this argument as well, holding that the European Commission

---

[28] Commission Directive 88/301 of 16 May 1988 on competition in the markets in telecommunications terminal equipment [1988] OJ L131/73, art 3.

[29] *Ibid.*, art 6.

[30] *Ibid.*, art 6.

[31] Case 202/88 *France* v. *Commission* [1991] ECR I–1223 [hereinafter *Telecommunications Terminals*].

[32] *Ibid.*, at 1263.

[33] *Ibid.*

[34] *Ibid.*

[35] *Ibid.*

[36] *Ibid.*, at 1264.

had power to act in response to general market conditions in Member States by establishing concrete obligations through directives applicable to all Member States.[37]

The challenging Member States further alleged that a directive of this scope should have been issued as a harmonising directive, that is, with the full participation of the Council of Ministers and the European Parliament.[38] Although the ECJ upheld the European Commission's authority to issue such a directive on its own, the political difficulties generated by the European Commission's solo action did not disappear. Eventually, the Council officially endorsed the European Commission's telecommunications liberalisation policy and urged that future appropriate regulatory directives be issued with full participation from the Council, Parliament, and Commission.[39]

The total effect of the *Telecommunications Terminals* judgment was an endorsement of the European Commission's philosophy as expressed in the Green Paper and its exercise of power in the Equipment Directive. The European Commission was now emboldened to take further steps to chip away at the power of state telecommunications monopolies. One year later, the ECJ again decided in favour of the European Commission's power to issue directives on its own initiative to liberalise telecommunications markets, this time in response to a Member State challenge to the Telecommunications Services Directive.[40]

V. THE SERVICES DIRECTIVE

In 1990, the European Commission issued the Services Directive[41] on the same day that the Council adopted a Directive on Open Network Provision (ONP).[42] ONP was equivalent to the US Federal Communications Commission's (FCC) Open Network Architecture requirements and was designed to require incumbent operators to unbundle network elements and make them available as building blocks to potential competitors.[43] The goal of both the Services Directive

---

[37] *Ibid.*

[38] *Ibid.*, at 1265–66.

[39] Council Resolution 93/1 of 22 July 1993 on the Review of the Situation in the Telecommunications Sector and the Need for Further Development in that Market [1993] OJ C213/1; and Council Resolution 94/3 of 22 December 1994 on the principle and timetable for the liberalisation of telecommunications infrastructures [1994] OJ C379/4.

[40] Joined Cases 271, 281 and 289/90 *Spain, Belgium, Italian Republic* v. *Commission* [1992] ECR I–5833.

[41] Commission Directive 90/388 of 28 June 1990 on competition in the markets for telecommunications services [1990] OJ L192/10 [hereinafter Telecommunications Services Directive] <http://europa.eu.int/comm/competition/liberalization/legislation/90388.htm>.

[42] Council Directive 90/387 of 28 June 1990 on the establishment of the internal market for telecommunications services through the implementation of open network provision [1990] OJ L192/1 [hereinafter ONP services Directive] <http://www.ispo.cec.be/infosoc/legreg/docs/90387eec.html>.

[43] *Ibid.*, at 2. Unbundling requirements did not extend to local loop elements.

and the ONP Services Directive was to allow the competitive provision of some telecommunications services to become a reality.

The Services Directive required Member States to open telecommunications services to competition, with the temporary exception of basic voice telephone service.[44] The definition of voice telephony[45] was therefore closely studied, and potential entrants attempted to tailor services so as not to fall under its definition and therefore within the monopoly reservation. For example, providing telephone service to closed user groups (CUGs), that is among parties who could claim a common commercial or other relationship, beyond that of an interest in receiving service from a non-incumbent provider, was not considered as basic voice telephony, and therefore had to be allowed by Member States. The European Commission also relied on the voice telephony definition when considering Internet telephony, as discussed in Chapter 13 below.[46]

The Services Directive did not originally apply to telex, mobile radiotelephony, paging, and satellite services,[47] and these services were not subject to immediate liberalisation, but through amendments, again issued under its Article 86 authority, the European Commission used the Services Directive as a vehicle to require full telecommunications competition by 1 January 1998.[48] The Services Directive was amended to cover satellite services,[49] the use of cable television networks for already competitive telecommunications services,[50] mobile services,[51]and basic conditions for the competitive telecommunications market.[52]

A. Liberalised Services

The Satellite Directive, Cable Directive, and Mobile Directive allowed greater competition by progressively narrowing the definition of services (known as

[44] Telecommunications Services Directive, *supra* n. 41, at 10.

[45] "voice telephony" means the commercial provision for the public of the direct transport and switching of speech in real-time between public switched network termination points, enabling any user to use equipment connected to such a network termination point in order to communicate with another termination point." *Ibid.*, at 15.

[46] Status of Voice Communications on Internet Under Community Law and, in Particular, Under Directive 90/388/EEC [1998] OJ C6/ 4.

[47] The Telecommunications Services Directive, *supra* n. 41, at 10.   [48] *Ibid.*

[49] Commission Directive 94/46/EC of 13 October 1994 amending Directive 88/301/EEC and Directive 90/388/EEC in particular with regard to satellite communications [1994] OJ L268/15 [hereinafter Satellite Directive] <http://europa.eu.int/comm/competition/liberalization/legislation/9446.htm>.

[50] Commission Directive 95/51/EC of 18 October 1995 amending Directive 90/388/EEC with regard to the abolition of the restrictions on the use of cable television networks for the provision of already liberalized telecommunications services [1995] OJ L256/49 [hereinafter Cable Directive] <http://europa.eu.int/comm/competition/liberalization/legislation/9551.htm>.

[51] Commission Directive 96/2 of 16 January 1996 amending Directive 90/388/EEC with regard to mobile and personal communications [1996] OJ L20/59 [hereinafter Mobile Directive] <http://europa.eu.int/comm/competition/liberalization/legislation/922.htm>.

[52] Commission Directive 96/19 of 13 March 1996 amending Directive 90/388/EEC with regard to the implementation of full competition in telecommunications markets [1996] OJ L74/13 [hereinafter Full Competition Directive] < http://europa.eu.int/comm/competition/liberalization/legislation/9619.htm>.

"reserved services") that Member States could keep free from competition. With the adoption of the Full Competition Directive in 1996, only two reserved services would temporarily remain free from competition: basic voice telephony and public telecommunications networks.

The European Commission urged that new services, such as innovative calling card services, voice mail, or certain call forwarding services should immediately be opened to competition by virtue of being considered non-reserved.[53] The Member States would have the burden of proof to justify reservation of new services to a dominant telecommunications organisation.[54] All of the defined elements of voice telephony had to be present to justify continued reservation.

The European Commission considered that the "public" requirement found in the Services Directive meant that telephone service, including voice, provided to corporate networks or CUGs should be considered competitive immediately as they were not offered to the public. The European Commission, in an early soft law document, defined "corporate networks" as "those networks generally established by a single organisation encompassing distinct legal entities such as a company and its subsidiaries or its branches."[55] The European Commission's difficulty in defining CUGs prompted it to decide that some sort of group activity or link was to exist, but an economic identity, such as a corporation, was not necessary. For example, a professional relationship among entities might qualify a group as a CUG. The internal communications needs of the group were to result from a professional relationship, not a shared desire to obtain telephone service from a discount provider. To clarify the qualifications for CUG status, the European Commission gave examples, including "fund transfers for the banking industry, reservation systems for airlines, information transfers between universities involved in a common research project, re-insurance for the insurance industry, inter-library activities, common design projects, and different institutions or services of intergovernmental organisations."[56]

The requirement that both ends of a phone conversation be at public switched network termination points meant to the European Commission that if a customer was connected via leased lines or perhaps through a CUG, then calls could be completed to points on the public network without being considered basic voice service.

---

[53] Commission Communication to the European Parliament and the Council on the Status and Implementation of Directive 90/388 on Competition in the Markets for Telecommunications Services, COM(95) 113 final at 3–4 [hereinafter Commission Competition Communication]. This document, issued independently by the European Commission, is a splendid early example of how the European Commission determined to extend the scope and effect of the regulatory framework.

[54] *Ibid.*, at 8.

[55] *Ibid.*

[56] *Ibid.*

B. The Full Competition Directive

One of the more controversial provisions of the Full Competition Directive authorised the use of alternative or self-provided infrastructure for telecommunications services already declared competitive.[57] Several larger Member States actively opposed this proposal, and France and Germany changed their opposition only when the European Commission conditioned approval for France Télécom and Deutsche Telekom participating in the Global One joint venture on France and Germany supporting the European Commission in its efforts regarding alternative infrastructure provision.[58] France and Germany were further required to licence alternative infrastructure providers. The European Commission has utilised approval of mergers and joint ventures on several occasions to obtain what are in essence political concessions. Another example of this is the pressure the European Commission placed on Spain to allow full competition before its derogation date of 2003 in exchange for the European Commission's approval of Telefónica's participation in AT&T's Unisource/Uniworld joint venture.[59] A more recent example is the European Commission conditioning approval of the Telia and Telenor merger on the merging parties as well as their owners, the Swedish and Norwegian States, agreeing to local loop unbundling in their territory.[60] This undertaking was rendered ineffective by the parties' subsequent decision not to implement the merger.

The basic approach of the Full Competition Directive is similar to the US Telecommunications Act of 1996, though not nearly as specific. The Member States were to require existing telecommunications organisations to publish the terms and conditions for interconnection by 1 July 1997.[61] Service providers would be free to accept those terms or to negotiate their own interconnection agreements. It was envisioned that the parties should first attempt to commercially negotiate terms of interconnection agreements, but if they are unable to reach agreement, the Member States were to adopt a decision setting the individual terms of interconnection. The Directive stated that the European Commission might revisit interconnection issues if a harmonising directive was adopted, and in fact such a harmonising directive, the Interconnection Directive was adopted.[62] Nevertheless, the Services Directive, as amended, might itself have been adequate to set conditions for telecommunications competition in 1998.

---

[57] Full Competition Directive, *supra* n. 50, art. 2.

[58] Commission Decision Relating to a Proceeding Under Article 85 [81] of the EC Treaty and Article 53 of the EEA Agreement [1996] OJ C195/1 [hereinafter *Atlas/Phoenix*].

[59] Commission Notification of a Joint Venture [1995] OJ C276/9 *Unisource*.

[60] COMP/M.1439 *Telia/Telenor* [2000] [hereinafter Telia/Telenor Decision].

[61] Full Competition Directive, *supra* n. 50, art. 2.

[62] Directive 97/33/EC of the European Parliament and of the Council of 30 June 1997 on Interconnection in Telecommunications With Regard to Ensuring Universal Service and Interoperability Through Application of the Principles of Open Network Provision (ONP) [1997] OJ L199/32 [hereinafter Interconnection Directive] <http://www.ispo.cec.be/infosoc/telecompolicy/en/dir97-33en.htm/>.

VI. ONP DIRECTIVES

The telecommunications harmonising directives that have been adopted are mainly under the rubric of ONP directives—legislation designed to force dominant telecommunications operators to unbundle network elements and make them available to potential competitive telecommunications providers. The ONP Services Directive[63] established the general principle that network elements necessary to provide non-reserved telecommunications services should be made available on non-discriminatory and publicly known terms.

A. The Leased Lines Directive

Prices for network elements, primarily leased lines, remained high throughout Europe, at least in the opinion of the European Commission, and in 1992 the Leased Lines ONP Directive[64] was adopted establishing a common technical standard for leased lines and requiring that leased lines be offered on a cost-oriented basis. There has been a great deal of debate over what constitutes cost-orientation. The traditional PTTs have experienced some difficulty in accounting for costs as they have typically been run like government agencies instead of rate of return utilities. Determining cost of service is very important not only in conforming to ONP requirements, but also in negotiating interconnection. In general, "cost-oriented" and "cost-based" are interpreted to mean cost plus a reasonable profit.[65] Still to be resolved is whether costs should be calculated to include historic costs or if an incremental basis is proper. Many cost decisions are left to national regulators, but through recommendations, the European Commission has let its views be known.

B. The ONP Voice Telephony Directive

ONP requirements were further specified by the ONP Voice Telephony Directive.[66] The Directive has caused some confusion as it draws a distinction between requirements of interconnection and special network access without

---

[63] ONP Services Directive, *supra*, n. 42.

[64] Council Directive 92/44 of 5 June 1992 on the establishment of the international market for telecommunications services through the implementation of open network provision [1992] OJ L165/27 [hereinafter ONP Leased Lines Directive] <http://www.ispo.cec.be/infosoc/legreg/docs/9244eec.html>.

[65] Interconnection Directive, *supra* n. 62, art. 7(2).

[66] Directive 98/10/EC of the European Parliament and of the Council of 26 February 1998 on the application of open network provision (ONP) to voice telephony and on universal service for telecommunications in a competitive environment [1998] OJ L101/24 [hereinafter ONP Voice Telephony Directive] <http://www.ispo.cec.be/infosoc/telecompolicy/en/dir98-10en.html>.

defining what is meant by "special network access."[67] This term has been and will doubtless continue to be a subject of controversy. It has been claimed that special network access includes a requirement to provide unbundled local loops, but the matter is far from settled. Soon after the ONP Voice Telephony Directive appeared, the conventional interpretation of the special network access term was that it referred to access needed by potential service providers. If a potential service provider, lacking its own network facilities, requests access to elements of the public telecommunications network, then the dominant operator will be under an obligation to provide the facilities in accordance with cost-orientation.

On the other hand, telecommunications providers having network facilities could be considered as requesting interconnection instead of special network access. Interconnection was to be a matter of commercial negotiation between the parties, subject to possible intervention by national regulatory authorities, and operators were to respect the principle of non-discrimination.

The ONP Voice Telephony Directive also focused on universal service, defined as a minimum set of specified quality services accessible to all at an affordable price.[68] The operative part of the Directive also placed duties on incumbent operators regarding their relations with competitors. Member States were to strictly observe the independence of the regulator and the provider.[69] Parties affected by a decision of a national regulatory authority were given a right of appeal to an independent body.[70] Regulatory authorities were to ensure that at least one source of unbundled leased lines is available on a cost-oriented tariffed basis at every geographic point in their Member State. [71]

C. The Interconnection Directive

The Interconnection Directive further fleshed out the rules for European interconnection. Member States were required to remove all restrictions on the ability of service providers to negotiate interconnection agreements, and telecommunications organisations were required to negotiate such agreements, subject to certain limited exceptions.[72] Telecommunications organisations with significant market power, presumed for any telecommunications operator with a greater than twenty-five percent market share in a given geographic area, must meet all reasonable requests for interconnection.[73] It is questionable, in compe-

---

[67] Directive 98/10/EC of the European Parliament and of the Council of 26 February 1998 on the application of open network provision (ONP) to voice telephony and on universal service for telecommunications in a competitive environment [1998] OJ L101/24, art. 16.

[68] *Ibid.*, art. 1.

[69] Interconnection Directive, *supra* n. 62, art.1(5).

[70] *Ibid.*, art. 1.

[71] *Ibid.*, art. 2.

[72] *Ibid.*, art. 3(1).

[73] *Ibid.*, art. 4(3).

tition law terms, whether market power should be assumed with a twenty-five percent market share. Incumbents might welcome this provision because it promises that significant competitors might become subject to the same interconnection requirements as they gain market share. In a similar manner to the procedure required by the US Telecommunications Act of 1996, an appeal could be made to the national regulatory authority and an arbitrated agreement imposed if the parties are unable to reach an interconnection agreement.[74]

Interconnection agreements might include charges in support of universal service (when imposed by a Member State) and must be issued on a non-discriminatory basis with equal conditions applied for similar service elements.[75] Proposed changes in interconnection arrangements must be announced six months in advance, and all interconnection agreements should be open for public inspection.[76] Charges for interconnection were to be cost-based, with two allowable elements: one-time costs for network configuration and regular usage charges.[77]

Network security, network integrity, guaranteed interoperability, and essential requirements such as scarcity of available frequencies could justify Member States limiting certain interconnection requirements.[78] Sharing rights-of-way and collocation were not required but encouraged, and Member States could impose collocation or presumably local loop unbundling under their dispute resolution authority.[79] Additionally, telephone numbers were to be allocated in a fair manner, but number portability would not be required in major European cities until January 1, 2003.[80] If service providers licensed by different Member States could not agree on the terms of interconnection agreements, either party could refer the matter to the Member States involved and their regulatory authorities were to coordinate efforts to resolve the dispute within six months of referral.[81]

D. The Licensing Directive

A common framework was also established for the grant of telecommunications service authorisations and individual licenses. The Licensing Directive stated a

---

[74] *Ibid.*, art 9(5).
[75] *Ibid.*, art. 5.
[76] *Ibid.*, art. 14.
[77] *Ibid.*, art. 7(2).
[78] *Ibid.*, art.10.
[79] *Ibid.*, art. 9(3).
[80] *Ibid.*, art. 12(5). This date was subsequently moved forward to 1 January 2000 under the provisions of the Number Portability Directive; Directive 98/61/EC of the European Parliament and of the Council amending Directive 97/33/EC with regard to operator number portability and carrier pre-selection [1998] OJ L 268/37 [hereinafter Number Portability Directive] <http://www.ispo. cec.be/infosoc/telecompolicy/en/98–61en.pdf>.
[81] Directive 97/13 of the European Parliament and of the Council on a common framework for general authorizations and individual licences in the field of telecommunications services [1997] OJ L117/15 art. 12(3) [hereinafter Licensing Directive] <http://www.ispo.cec.be/infosoc/telecompolicy/en/licences.htm>.

preference for a maximisation of the number of service providers in order to bring the benefits of competition to the largest number of consumers.[82] Therefore, the Member States were to allow potential service providers to follow a declaration procedure granting general authorisation to offer services whenever possible.[83] There were, however, areas involving allocation of scarce resources such as radio frequencies that the Directive admitted might call for limiting the number of participants in the market.[84] Only essential requirements such as access to scarce resources, network security, integrity, data protection, or environmental concerns would justify restricting the number of licensees for a particular service.[85] As technology developed, perhaps enabling radio spectrum to be shared by more providers, technical justification for restrictions on the number of licensees might diminish.

Consistent with the European Single Market principle, the Licensing Directive set forth limited steps to promote a one-stop shop for telecommunications authorisations and licenses.[86] A potential operator who wished to provide service or infrastructure in more than one Member State could request the national authorities to coordinate authorisations. If the operator was not satisfied with the coordination, a notification could be made to a European Union Telecommunications Committee, which would then reach a solution that could be implemented by the involved Member States. If not implemented, the European Commission was to be informed, but no real enforcement powers existed.

Likewise, the proposal for a one-stop shop for licenses was vague. The European Commission was to establish a clearinghouse at one physical location that would forward requests for licenses to the appropriate Member States, which would then decide on the request within six months. This would not be a true one-stop shop because an applicant might still be subject to different substantive and procedural rules within the general framework of the Licensing Directive. Perhaps the European Commission only intended to set up the principle of a one-stop-shop at this time and make it a reality later.

E. The Number Portability Directive

EU authorities demonstrated impatience with earlier established schedules for liberalisation measures. Notably, this has occurred in the area of number portability. A harmonisation directive was issued in 1998 requiring carrier preselection and moving forward the implementation of number portability

---

[82] Directive 97/13 of the European Parliament and of the Council on a common framework for general authorizations and individual licences in the field of telecommunications services [1997] OJ L117/15, recital 25.

[83] *Ibid.*, art. 3(3).

[84] *Ibid.*, art. 10.

[85] *Ibid.*, art. 12.

[86] *Ibid.*

requirements.[87] The Directive took the form of an amendment to the Interconnection Directive and accelerated the date of full number portability from 2003 to January 2000.[88] The type of portability required was operator portability, that is the ability of end-users to keep their fixed-line telephone numbers when changing from one operator to another. All operators, not just incumbents were required to meet the portability requirement, though presumably most changes requiring ported numbers would be for end-users moving from incumbent operators to entrants, at least at first. Churn for fixed line customers, and therefore end-user interest in number portability may be difficult to predict.

January 2000 was not the most opportune date to require full portability, as telecoms operators were struggling to make their computers Y2K compliant by that date, with all of the changes in computer systems and data base management that represented. The Directive allowed for Member States to apply to the European Commission for extension of the compliance date.[89]

Significant omissions from the Directive include such issues as costing of portability (who will pay for porting numbers and how much), establishment of numbering data bases, and administration of numbering plans. These unresolved issues will have to be addressed some day. For example, if two end-users, perhaps customers of two different operators, each claim the same telephone number, who will receive the number? More fundamentally, who will resolve such disputes?

There are similar unresolved issues regarding the Directive's other requirements of carrier selection.[90] While the Directive required cost-oriented pricing for carrier selection, what type of calls were covered is unclear. It is not specified whether international, national (long distance) and or local calls are included. By implication, all calls were included, and this is true for pre-subscription (the end-user selects a favourite operator). There was also a requirement that end-users be able to override the pre-subscribed choice on a call-by-call basis. Only significant market power operators were required by the Directive to provide carrier selection, however, perhaps not the most consumer friendly requirement, and not exactly a level regulatory playing field. There was nothing stopping Member State national regulatory authorities from going further and requiring all telecoms operators to honour pre-selection and call-by-call requests. This was true for mobile operations as well. Carrier selection requirements on all operators, whatever their market share and whatever their mode of service, would have a beneficial result on market usage (per minute) charges, and it is puzzling why the Directive did not thus fully extend the carrier

---

[87] Number Portability Directive, *supra* n. 80.

[88] *Ibid.*, art. 1.2.

[89] *Ibid.*, art. 1.4.

[90] *Ibid.*, art. 1.3. As of March 2000, the UK had not implemented carrier selection rules and "Oftel, the UK regulator, has said it will not be able to implement all the measures until the end of [2001]." Deborah Hargreaves, "Brussels acts over slow liberalisation of telecoms market," *Financial Times*, 30 March 2000, at 2.

selection requirement. In its desire to protect entrants and mobile operators, the EU may retard growth of a competitive market and hurt end-users who change their subscription to entrant services, surely a strange policy.

VII.   ONE LAST DIRECTIVE

A final directive worthy of mention, the Amended CATV Directive,[91] was issued by Directorate General—Competition under its Article 86 authority in 1999. The Amended CATV Directive can be viewed as completing this stage of the European Commission's work, before the proposals for revised and new legislation emerging from the 1999 Telecommunications Review.[92]

The first Cable Directive required Member States to allow CATV networks to be used for already liberalised services as well as to require certain telecoms companies also having CATV interests to maintain separate accounts, the idea being to discourage cross-subsidisation.[93] In subsequent studies, the European Commission voiced its displeasure with the amount of telecoms services actually provided over CATV networks.[94] The European Commission apparently considered requiring incumbent telcos to divest their CATV operations as was subsequently imposed as a remedy in the proposed Telia/Telenor merger.[95]

The Directive as finally adopted, however, only required dominant telcos also operating CATV networks to legally separate those operations,[96] again presumably to minimise the risk of cross-subsidisation. It is questionable how effective the requirement of separate legal entities alone will be in achieving the European Commission's competition goals. Will mere legal separation make the parent organisations more likely to use the CATV networks to roll out new and possibly competing services to those provided over the public telecommunications network? Also questionable is the Directive's legal basis, that incumbent telcos, even in liberalised markets, continued to enjoy "special or exclusive rights."[97] This issue will be discussed in greater detail in the following chapter.

---

[91] Commission Directive of 23 June 1999 amending Directive 90/388/EEC in order to ensure that telecommunications networks and cable TV networks owned by a single operator are separate legal entities [1999] OJ L175/39 [hereinafter Amended CATV Directive].

[92] Communication from the Commission to the European Parliament, the Council, the Economic and Social Committee and the Committee of the Regions, Towards a new Framework for Electronic Communications infrastructure and associate services: The 1999 Communications Review, COM (1999) 539 [hereinafter 1999 Telecommunications Review].

[93] Cable Directive, *supra* n. 50.

[94] Communication concerning the review under competition rules of the joint provision of telecommunications and cable TV networks by a single operator and the abolition of restrictions on the provision of cable TV capacity over telecommunications networks [1998] OJ C 71/4 <http://europa.eu.int/comm/competition/liberalization/legislation/98c71_en.html>.

[95] Telia/Telenor Decision, *supra* n. 60, paras. 390–391.

[96] Amended CATV Directive, *supra* n. 90, art. 1.

[97] *Ibid.*

VIII.   CONCLUSION

How did Europe do in its first steps towards telecommunications? Not bad, especially considering the entrenched, state-owned monopolies the European Commission faced. The European Commission was inventive and persistent in taking steps towards its goal. In measures of market success, however, Europe still lags behind the US. In general, basic telephone service costs less in the US than in the EU as does competitive building blocks such as leased lines.[98] Perhaps most importantly, there are indications that continued lack of effective telecoms competition is slowing Europe's uptake of the Internet, and this could have ill effects throughout the information based economy.

[98] *OECD Communications Outlook 1999*, at 163–164, and 188.

12

Does the EU Regulatory Framework Work in the Market?

ANY TEST OF regulatory efficacy must be in the real world. Given that standard, it is difficult to gauge the results of the EU's efforts to promote competition in telecoms markets. For one thing fifteen different national markets are involved, and the fifteen Member States vary in basic legislation as well as the vigour of their regulatory authorities. The EU has done no more than demand a minimum framework, although the European Commission has attempted to go further, notably through recommendations, guidelines, decisions, investigations and other forms of soft law. Unified telecoms regulation, however, does not exist in Europe. Market fragmentation or at least a slowing of the movement towards a single European telecoms market is therefore a danger.

Balanced against this mixed record must be the undeniable progress that has been made in lowering telecoms prices and increasing consumer choice in equipment, services and providers. Again, it is difficult to judge how much of this progress may be laid at the feet of the European Commission and how much might have occurred anyway (or even more) due to technological and commercial developments. It is useful to observe the European Commission's policies in action, in four soft law areas: international interconnection; definition and application of the term special and exclusive rights; the European Commission's Telecommunications Access Notice; and finally local loop unbundling.

I. INTERNATIONAL INTERCONNECTION

As an example of how the EU regulatory framework is functioning in its goal of promoting competition, an examination of the European Commission's experience in the field of international interconnection is useful. Furthermore, the European Commission's experience in this area demonstrates the influence of the telecoms trade war, here particularly expressed as rising tensions between the US and the EU over international telecommunications traffic exchanges.

A. The European Commission Recommendation

Following the passage of the EU's Interconnection Directive,[1] officials of the European Commission made public statements that this Directive allowed interconnection as a substitute for the accounting rates system for international traffic exchanges among the EU Member States, sometimes also known as cross-border interconnection. International interconnection was not clearly authorised under the Interconnection Directive, however, Article 3 of the Directive refers to "Interconnection at national and Community level." This provision states that Member States are to allow interconnection between telecommunications organisations "in the same Member State or in different Member States." Article 3.1. Annex II of the Directive also refers to Community-wide services. Nevertheless, the European Commission's assertion of the right of international interconnection came as a surprise, and a case could be made that the Directive did not call for international interconnection; that international interconnection was inconsistent with other provisions of EU law; that international interconnection was forbidden by pre-existing treaty obligations; and that international interconnection would have placed the EU in an unfavourable trading position.

The European Commission's views on international interconnection were further developed in the Interconnection Pricing Recommendation of October 1997.[2] The European Commission asserted that interconnection was to be allowed as an alternative for exchanges of international traffic under the settlement rates system and that the basis for international interconnection prices (or cross-border interconnection) should be the price for national termination.[3] Like other regulatory agencies worldwide, the European Commission was concerned with the high prices of international telephone calls. The European Commission also had a special interest in this area, particularly for intra-EU international calls, as it could be argued that continued high end-user prices for intra-EU calling was working against the achievement of the European Single Market.

In public presentations, officials of the European Commission made a comparison between the end-user price for a call of a certain distance within a nation with a call of the same distance between two EU Member States. That is, the officials implied that the price of an international telephone call between perhaps Brussels and Milan should cost the same as a call from Milan to Naples,

---

[1] Directive 97/33/EC of the European Parliament and of the Council of 30 June 1997 on Interconnection in Telecommunications With Regard to Ensuring Universal Service and Interoperability Through Application of the Principles of Open Network Provision (ONP) [1997] OJ L199/32 [hereinafter Interconnection Directive].

[2] European Commission Recommendation on Interconnection in a liberalised telecommunications market. Part 1—Interconnection Pricing, C(97) 3148, 15.10.97 [hereinafter Interconnection Pricing Recommendation] < http://www.ispo.cec.be/infosoc/telecompolicy/en/r3148-en.htm>.

[3] *Ibid.*, §5.1.2.

roughly the same distance. The international call in reality would cost significantly more, and European Commission officials concluded that the difference was the result of high accounting rates (which the officials began to call international interconnection or cross-border interconnection prices). The accounting rates regime is, however, not the same as international interconnection. There are many rules and procedures such as proportionate return that go with settlement rates. But the European Commission asserted that intra-EU calls should cost the same as national calls.

The Interconnection Pricing Recommendation stated that a party requesting international interconnection should be able to deliver traffic by any means to the border of a Member State. At that point of physical interconnection the delivering party can either use alternative means of transport or an operator with significant market power could be obliged to offer transit prices, presumably priced lower than leased lines prices, to deliver the traffic to a point of interconnection desired by the delivering party. Usual national interconnection prices would have to be given from the point of interconnection to the ultimate termination point. There would be two pricing elements: (1) transit (if requested) from the border, and (2) interconnection (identical to existing rates offered for intra-national traffic).

This proposed method of international traffic delivery differed significantly from then-existing methods of international traffic exchange. Typically there was one settlement rate for an entire nation (in some cases different zones were declared for discrete regions, such as in France). That is, traffic delivered to a terminating nation is no longer distance sensitive, as would presumably be the case under international interconnection. Traffic may be delivered via half circuits or to a border point where the terminating (national) operator takes the traffic and delivers it to its destination.

The Interconnection Pricing Recommendation stated that Member States could not assert licensing or authorisation requirements on parties requesting international interconnection. A party authorised to provide telecommunications services anywhere in the EU could originate traffic there and terminate it anywhere else in the EU without further authorisation required.[4]

B. The Accounting Rates Regime

As explained above in Chapter 4, because the accounting rates system is established by the ITU Treaty, to which all Member States of the EU are signatories, refiling, or indeed any delivery of traffic outside the accounting rates system is legally forbidden unless paid for as if it had been routed via the normal method. This is not to say that refiling does not occur, however. As markets across the globe continue to liberalise, competition is forcing firms to find the cheapest way

---

[4] *Ibid.*

to terminate all calls, including international calls. Moreover, although strictly speaking illegal, because refiling places downward pressure on accounting and termination rates, and therefore presumably on retail prices as well, most governments, at least in developed nations, tend to acquiesce with a "wink and a nod." It is undeniable that a certain amount of telecommunications traffic (doubtless growing) is also being delivered through alternative means and terminated at normal "national" interconnection prices.

The *British Telecom* judgment,[5] discussed in the previous chapter, not only paved the way for European telecommunications competition, it also contained an interesting analysis of international telecommunications traffic exchanges, the settlement rates system, and alternatives (refiling) that were already developing. One of the issues in the case was some Member States' claim that the ITU Treaty required that the telex forwarding agencies be denied service, and the forwarding service itself, as a type of refiling, was a violation of the ITU Treaty and regulations.

The European Court of Justice (ECJ) was faced with a difficult case. On the one hand, the Member States had obligations under the ITU Treaty. On the other hand, the threat to deny service to the forwarding agencies could be viewed as an abuse of a dominant position. The ECJ's judgment held as follows:

> "The Italian Republic maintains that the Commission disregarded the terms of Article 234 [now Article 307 of the Treaty of Amsterdam] of the Treaty [of Rome]. Article 234 resolves any conflict between Community law and the pre-existing rules of international law, by giving the latter precedence over the former. The applicant claims that the provisions of the ITC [the International Telecommunications Convention of 1947 establishing the current structure of the ITU] and its administrative regulations have always forbidden national administrations to allow the re-routing of the international traffic in telegraph or telephone messages when such re-routing is caused by the attempt of private forwarding agencies to evade the full charges due for the complete route."[6]

The Court found that British Telecom (BT) could have met its obligations under both the ITU and EC treaties. It also recognised that refiling might be unlawful under the ITU Treaty and presumably could be stopped.[7] The ECJ, however, failed to give any guidance as to how these facially conflicting obligations could be carried out. Presumably, the Member State governments themselves could have prosecuted the forwarding agencies rather than relying on dominant providers like BT to put the agencies out of business by denying them service.

From the foregoing, it may be concluded that the ECJ recognised that Member States have valid obligations arising from the ITU Treaty. The ECJ strove to reconcile the ITU Treaty and the Treaty of Rome. The ECJ most assuredly did not hold that the Treaty of Rome is supreme over the ITU Treaty.

---

[5] Case 41/83 *Italian Republic* v. *Commission* [1985] ECR 873 [hereinafter *British Telecom*].
[6] *Ibid.*, para. 36.
[7] *Ibid.*, paras. 40–42.

Therefore, Member States may legitimately honour obligations under the ITU Treaty.

It is questionable whether the ITU Treaty, or at least certain ITU regulations such as the prohibition of refiling, are in fact effective today. Although the settlement rates system remains in place and the bulk of international telephone traffic is exchanged under the accounting rates system, it would be foolish to pretend that increasing amounts of telephone traffic are not refiled through third countries or transmitted and terminated by methods other than the settlement rates system. Much of the traffic in this later group is probably terminated via interconnection rates, however, it is likely being declared and paid for as national traffic, not under (still non-existent) international interconnection.

Another major path for transmission of international traffic through means other than the settlement rates system is the Internet. Internet traffic is not declared under the settlement rates system, nor are termination charges paid for delivery of international Internet content. In fact, it is usually the recipient operator (the network hosting the "requesting" Internet service provider) who pays for the privilege of receiving Internet content.[8]

C. International Interconnection?

Fundamentally, it is necessary to consider what is meant by the term international interconnection. The European Commission envisioned international interconnection as a substitute for the existing accounting rates—for telephone calls originating and terminating within the confines of the European Union. That is, *intra*-EU traffic.[9]

The availability of international interconnection for intra-EU traffic is not clearly required by any of the telecoms regulatory or competition directives. The Interconnection Directive states that telecoms organisations negotiating interconnection agreements may be in the same or different Member States,[10] but this language may well refer only to the ability of telecoms providers to move throughout the EU's single market: no more than a recognition of the EU Treaty concept of the freedom to provide services. This is not to say that interconnection may be sought without satisfying the legitimate Member State licensing requirements.

Under the Licensing Directive, Member States are allowed to issue individual licenses and authorisations, and Member States are allowed to impose conditions for grant of individual licenses or authorisations.[11] Therefore, national

---

[8] This raises the issue of interconnection of Internet backbones, known as "peering" or "transit" of Internet traffic. Implications of interconnection of Internet backbones are discussed in the context of the MCI WorldCom merger in Chapter 18, *infra*.

[9] Interconnection Pricing Recommendation, *supra* n. 2, §5.1.2.

[10] Interconnection Directive, *supra* n. 1, art. 3.1.

[11] Directive 97/13 of the European Parliament and of the Council on a common framework for general authorizations and individual licences in the field of telecommunications services [1997] OJ L117/15 Annex I [hereinafter Licensing Directive].

regulatory authorities (NRAs) may legitimately decide that licenses, for example, voice telephony licenses, may only be issued to operators demonstrating a commitment to self-provide a minimum coverage of telecommunications infrastructure in the Member State itself. It is questionable whether these types of licensing requirements are in fact pro-competitive, and the European Commission has indicted that it would like to see general authorisations in their place.[12] Nevertheless, until the changes proposed by the 1999 Review come into effect, probably in 2003, such differentiated licences are allowed. The Interconnection Directive specifies that interconnection rates themselves may legitimately vary depending on the type of license an operator holds.[13]

Therefore, imposition of international interconnection could be seen as an unwarranted interference with the directed mandate of NRAs to decide for themselves under what terms and conditions licenses and therefore interconnection is to be granted. An expressed policy in favour of infrastructure provision would lose its force if operators in other Member States were not required to abide by the rules to obtain more favourable interconnection rates. Indeed, national operators might be at a disadvantage when compared to operators from other Member States, not required to obey domestic NRA regulations. This interpretation of the EU regulatory regime might result in the paradoxical (and wasteful) situation whereby domestic operators refiled domestic traffic as international in order to receive more favourable treatment. This would also violate the Treaty principle of subsidiarity whereby action is to be taken at the most appropriate (decentralised level).

D. World Trade and WTO Telecommunications Treaty Considerations

The WTO Telecommunications Treaty requires signatory states, including the EU as an entity and as individual Member States, to provide non-discriminatory interconnection regardless of the nationality of the applicant.[14] It could be argued that by allowing international interconnection of intra-EU traffic, the EU would open the door for applications for international interconnection from non-EU operators.

Even if international interconnection is not available directly for non-EU operators, however, it would be easy for non-EU operators to partner with a EU operator, route traffic from all over the world to the EU licensed operator and refile throughout the EU. This might severely hurt other EU operators without any assurance being received that EU operators could do the same in the coun-

---

[12] Communication from the Commission to the European Parliament, the Council, the Economic and Social Committee and the Committee of the Regions, Towards a new Framework for Electronic Communications infrastructure and associate services: The 1999 Communications Review, COM (1999) 539 §4.1 [hereinafter 1999 Telecommunications Review].

[13] Interconnection Directive, *supra* n. 1, art. 7(3).

[14] World Trade Organisation, General Agreement on Trade in Services, Annex on Telecommunications, §5(a).

tries where such traffic originates. Given the realities of the rapidly changing international telecommunications market, and regulatory actions taken by non-EU entities such as the US's FCC (the FCC's Benchmarks Order is a sterling example of neo-mercantilist policy), imposition of EU international interconnection might amount to unilateral European disarmament.

Europe could end up losing significant revenues from refiling or loss of accounting rates. Such loss would hurt consumers ultimately as operators move to recover lost revenues from domestic customers. At the same time, EU consumers would not receive a corresponding drop in international prices as third nations will likely not accept international interconnection and it may be more difficult to refile on other nations when the international interconnection loophole does not exist.

Perhaps because of the trade war considerations, the European Commission has not pushed this recommendation. There have been no decisions taken against Member States for failure to require incumbent operators to offer international interconnection. In spite of the lack of regulatory support, routing and termination of international traffic by means other than the accounting rates system is flourishing and growing. These alternatives have probably developed due to market and technological factors, but the European Commission's jawbone may have had an effect as well. The episode demonstrates the limitations of regulation. The market itself is more effective in lowering prices and increasing choice.

II. WHAT ARE "SPECIAL AND EXCLUSIVE RIGHTS?"

The concept or "special and exclusive rights" is often used in EU policy and legislation, particularly in telecommunications, but it is difficult to understand. The Treaty of Rome, Article 86, introduced the phrase and specifically allowed state monopolies, subject to competition law.

> "In the case of public undertakings and undertakings to which Member States grant special or exclusive rights, Member States shall neither enact nor maintain in force any measure contrary to the rules contained in this Treaty, in particular to those rules provided for in Article 12 and Articles 81 to 89."[15]

The Telecommunications Services Directive, issued in 1990, had the following definition:

> " 'special or exclusive rights' means the rights granted by a Member State or a public authority to one or more public or private bodies through any legal, regulatory or administrative instrument reserving them the right to provide a service or undertake an activity."[16]

---

[15] Consolidated Version Of The Treaty Establishing The European Community [1997] OJ C340/173–308 art. 86(1) [hereinafter EU Treaty].

[16] Commission Directive 90/388 of 28 June 1990 on competition in the markets for telecommunications services [1990] OJ L192/10 art. 1.1 [hereinafter Telecommunications Services Directive].

Thereafter, using its Article 86 powers, the European Commission was successful in regulating not only state-owned telecoms monopolies, but also entities having special or exclusive rights. The Full Competition Directive abolished all remaining telecoms monopolies as well as any remaining special or exclusive rights enjoyed by the incumbent telcos.[17]

Therefore, it would seem that special or exclusive rights would be a dead letter at this point, interesting from an historical point, or maybe if necessary to prove that Member States are not fulfilling their obligations to withdraw these rights. The Competition Directorate-General, however, was not through with issuing Article 86 directives in the telecommunications sector. Using its Article 86 power to unilaterally issue directives and citing Member State grants of special and exclusive rights, the Competition Directorate-General adopted a directive calling for legal separation of the telephone and cable television operations of dominant telcos.[18] As discussed in the previous chapter, the European Commission hoped the Amended CATV Directive would help promote the use of CATV networks for telecommunications services.

However laudable its aims, the European Commission was on shaky legal grounds in adopting this directive. The Directive's premise was that a Member State's historic grant of frequencies in mobile telephony or television broadcasting constituted continuing special or exclusive rights,[19] perhaps as a type of first mover advantage. Not only have special or exclusive rights been eliminated, but the European Commission acted in the field of mobile licences to ensure that any fees paid by new entrants was matched by incumbent mobile operators. Therefore, it is possible that the European Commission may issue more Article 86 directives in the future affecting telecommunications markets on the basis of a finding of special or exclusive rights in the past.

---

[17] Commission Directive 96/19 of 13 March 1996 amending Directive 90/388/EEC with regard to the implementation of full competition in telecommunications markets [1996] OJ L74/13 art. 1.2 [hereinafter Full Competition Directive].

[18] Commission Directive of 23 June 1999 amending Directive 90/388/EEC in order to ensure that telecommunications networks and cable TV networks owned by a single operator are separate legal entities [1999] OJ L175/39 [hereinafter Amended CATV Directive].

[19] *Ibid.*, recital 7. The recitals go on to note that many European incumbent telecoms operators also have existing special or exclusive rights for cable television networks, and the operative part of the Directive only reaches telcos who operate "a cable TV network established under special or exclusive right in the same geographic area." *Ibid.*, art. 1. The finding of special or exclusive rights in telecommunications operations was necessary because Competition Directorate-General only wanted to regulate cable television operations owned by dominant telcos, not all cable TV providers. Cable TV is usually provided under exclusive franchise in its service area, unarguably a grant of special or exclusive rights, and therefore subject to an Article 86 directive, but it was not the intent of the Directive to regulate all cable television operators. Hence the strain to find vestigial special or exclusive rights in the incumbent telcos, giving Competition Directorate-General jurisdiction. Perhaps the European Commission's Legal Services should have objected to the issuance of the Directive under such a stated basis.

A. Court Cases

There are two judgments of the ECJ concerning challenges brought by BT that involve consideration of the term special or exclusive rights. As noted above, the ONP Leased Lines Directive applied to all telecommunications organisations to which a Member State granted special or exclusive rights[20] for public networks or services. Member States were to notify the Commission of those telecommunications organisations to which special or exclusive rights were granted. By reference, the ONP Services Directive supplied the applicable definition of special and exclusive rights as:

> "the rights granted by a Member State or a public authority to one or more public or private bodies through any legal, regulatory or administrative instrument reserving them the right to provide a service or undertake an activity."[21]

BT contested the implementation of the Directive because "it does not enjoy special or exclusive rights within the meaning of the open networks directive and that it should not be subject to the obligations set out in the leased lines directive."[22]

The ECJ, in language similar to that employed in the recitals to the Amended CATV Directive, stated that:

> "the exclusive or special rights in question must generally be taken to be rights which are granted by the authorities of a Member State to an undertaking or a limited number of undertakings otherwise than according to objective, proportional and nondiscriminatory criteria, and which substantially affect the ability of other undertakings to provide or operate telecommunications networks or to provide telecommunications services in the same geographic area under substantially equivalent conditions."[23]

Regarding the requirement that Member States notify the names of favoured organisations, the Court took note of the fact that the UK government had submitted the name of BT, along with one hundred other telcos, as enjoying special or exclusive rights, and held that the notification while not binding would raise a presumption that BT in fact did hold special or exclusive rights.[24]

The ECJ held that the power to place telecommunications facilities, not being unique to BT, did not give the firm special or exclusive rights.[25] All telecoms

---

[20] Council Directive 92/44/EEC of 5 June 1992 on the application of open network provision to leased lines [1992] OJ L165/27 art. 7(1) [hereinafter Leased Lines Directive]. It is necessary to read the Directive in conjunction with Council Directive 90/387 of 28 June 1990 on the establishment of the internal market for telecommunications services through the implementation of open network provision [1990] OJ L192/1 [hereinafter ONP Services Directive].

[21] *Ibid.*, art 2.2.

[22] Case C–302/94 *The Queen* v. *Secretary of State for Trade and Industry, ex-parte British Telecommunications plc* [1996] ECR I–6417 para. 23.

[23] *Ibid.*, para. 34.

[24] *Ibid.*, para. 37.

[25] *Ibid.*, para. 41.

organisations possess this right under UK law. The same is true of the grant of a general license. In order to be "special or exclusive," the right must be such as to give the holder a "substantial advantage over their potential competitors."[26] However, the Court found that BT had been granted special or exclusive rights in that at the time of the judgment only BT and Mercury had licenses to operate international lines. This grant gave BT and Mercury "a substantial competitive advantage over other network operators and other providers of telecommunications services."[27] The Kingston Telephone Company, a small provider in the area of Hull (the only historic local provider in Britain other than BT), was also found to enjoy special or exclusive rights in that it had an exclusive right to operate a public network within its territory.

Unfortunately, the Court proceeded to broaden the scope of the Leased Lines Directive by finding that it applies not only to BT and Mercury, but also that the UK government was entitled to apply it to "only those 'telecommunications organisations' which are the principle operators of telecommunications lines in each of the geographic areas comprising its territory."[28] This implied that special or exclusive rights are synonymous with dominance. The two concepts are not the same. Totally private firms may be dominant and not enjoy special or exclusive rights. Conversely, firms with special rights may not be legally dominant.

Earlier case law on the meaning of special and exclusive rights is equally inconclusive. *Sacchi*[29] held that the granting of exclusive rights for radio and television transmission amounted to special or exclusive rights. A decision of the European Commission (*GEMA*[30]) declared that a music royalty society did not have special or exclusive rights as other collecting societies could benefit from the legislation in question also. In another case (*INNO*[31]), the ECJ considered that a Member State provision allowing manufacturers to engage in resale price maintenance (vertical price fixing) did not confer exclusive or special rights. In the *Telecommunications Services Directive Judgment*[32] the Advocate General submitted an opinion that exclusive rights are rights granted to one undertaking, while special rights are given to more than one, but a limited number of undertakings.

In the second telecommunications case, BT again challenged the applicability of a directive, this time the Procurement Directive, mandating that certain public utilities including incumbent telcos must follow procurement rules such as public bids, on similar grounds—that its monopoly position had been abol-

---

[26] Case C–302/94 *The Queen* v. *Secretary of State for Trade and Industry, ex-parte British Telecommunications plc* [1996] ECR I–6417 para. 41.

[27] *Ibid.*, para. 45.

[28] *Ibid.*, para. 57.

[29] Case 155/73 *Sacchi* [1974] ECR 409.

[30] *GEMA* [1971] OJ L134/15.

[31] Case 13/77 *INNO* v. *ATAB* [1977] ECR 2115.

[32] Joined Cases 271, 281 and 289/90 *Spain, Belgium, Italian Republic* v. *Commission* [1992] ECR I–5833 [hereinafter *Telecommunications Services Directive Judgment*].

ished.[33] At issue in this case was a reference to special and exclusive rights in the Procurement Directive.[34] The Directive also set up a specific exemption for telecommunications organisations in markets "where other entities are free to offer the same services in the same geographical area and under substantially the same conditions."[35] The Procurement Directive gave some guidance as to what may constitute special or exclusive rights, declaring that such rights may be found when:

> "for the purpose of constructing the networks or facilities referred to in paragraph 2, it may take advantage of a procedure for the expropriation or use of property or may place network equipment on, under or over the public highway."[36]

While the judgment turns more on the question of actual competition rather than the existence of special or exclusive rights, it is also worth examining on this general subject as there is a relationship between special or exclusive rights, dominance and the legal right to compete—this is particularly so when former state monopolies are involved.

The Advocate General was of the opinion that *de facto* dominance rather than *de jure* rights were key in determining whether BT faced competition.

> "First, it is by no means apparent from its actual wording that the provision in question is restricted to the obstacles resulting from statutory or regulatory provision. . . . Moreover . . . exclusion from the scope of the directive is subject to the condition that the activities of the entities in question should be '*directly exposed to competitive forces in markets to which entry is unrestricted.*' In short, it is certainly not sufficient for access to the market not to be excluded by law; there should also be genuine competition. The criteria mentioned in Article 8(1) of the directive must therefore be interpreted as meaning that they must be satisfied not only *de jure* but also *de facto.*"[37]

The Advocate General's insistence that the purpose behind the provision and the system as a whole should be examined and given effect is in line with the teleological (principle driven) approach to interpretation of European Community Law. The Advocate General recommended that exemptions be determined on a case-by-case basis by national authorities.

The Court's Judgment in the case noted the Procurement Directive article considering that special or exclusive rights are conferred by the privilege of placing utility facilities on public right of way. The Court also endorsed the position that exemptions must be considered on a case-by-case basis in order to determine whether "real competition" exists. According to the ECJ:

---

[33] Case C–392/93 *The Queen* v. *H. M. Treasury, ex-parte British Telecommunications plc* [1996] ECR I–1631 [hereinafter *British Telecom Procurement Judgment*].

[34] Council Directive 90/531/EEC of 17 September 1990 on the procurement procedures of entities operating in the water, energy, transport and telecommunications sectors [1990] OJ L297/1 art. 2(1)(b) [hereinafter Procurement Directive].

[35] *Ibid.*, art. 8(1)

[36] *Ibid.*, art. 2(3)(a).

[37] *British Telecommunications Procurement Judgment, supra* n. 33, Opinion of Advocate General para. 20.

"a decision to exclude certain services from the scope of the directive must be taken on an individual basis, having regard in particular to all their characteristics, the existence of alternative services, price factors, the dominance or otherwise of the contracting entity's position on the market and the existence of any legal constraints."[38]

Given BT's existing huge market share in the British telecoms market, the ECJ was certainly not willing to declare that BT was no longer dominant so as not to be subject to the requirements of the Procurement Directive.

There is an interesting post-script to this case, however. Even though BT was not successful in its court challenge, ultimately the European Commission took steps recognising the reality of competition in European telecommunications markets and correspondingly lifted the requirements of the Procurement Directive for every incumbent operator in Member States that had liberalised telecommunications markets.[39]

IV. THE EU'S TELECOMMUNICATIONS ACCESS NOTICE

An important policy statement of the European Commission regarding its views of European telecommunications markets and how competition law might apply in these markets is contained in the European Commission's 1998 Telecommunications Access Notice.[40] The Access Notice considered access as interconnection of networks and the ability to obtain leased lines, access to customer data or any other data, or facilities that may be necessary for a potential competitor to enter a telecommunications market.[41] If a potential service provider was refused access, there may be a remedy either through the established NRA, through national courts under national or EU competition law,[42] or by a complaint to the European Commission.[43] The tension between Member State regulation, supposed to come from independent[44] regulators, and the centralised European Commission regulation continues to be interesting to observe.

According to the Notice, the European Commission will "concentrate on notifications, complaints and [its] own-initiative proceedings having particular

---

[38] *British Telecommunications Procurement Judgment, supra* n. 33, Opinion of Advocate General para. 30.

[39] Communication from the Commission pursuant to Article 8 of Directive 93/38/EEC [1999] OJ C129/05 List of services regarded as excluded from the scope of Council Directive 93/38/EEC of 14 June 1993 coordinating the procurement procedures of entities operating in the water, energy, transport and telecommunications sectors pursuant to Article 8 thereof. <http://www.ispo.cec.be/infosoc/telecompolicy/en/en-10–5.doc>

[40] Notice on the Application of the Competition Rules to Access Agreements in the Telecommunications Sector, Framework, Relevant Markets and Principles, 31 March 1998 [1998] OJ C265/ 2 [hereinafter Access Notice] <http://europa.eu.int/smartapi/cgi/sga_doc?smartapi!celex-plus!prod!CELEXnumdoc&lg=en&numdoc=31998Y0822(01)>.

[41] *Ibid.*, para. 1.

[42] *Ibid.*, para. 11.

[43] *Ibid.*, para. 12.

[44] *Ibid.*

political, economic or legal significance."[45] The European Commission signaled its intention to set principles by taking formal decisions for a few notifications and otherwise acting via comfort letters.[46] The European Commission's assertion that access agreements notified to the NRAs might still need to be notified to the European Commission as well[47] is troubling from the standpoint of certainty and finality. Furthermore, the notification system itself may soon be modified or abolished. In the event of European Commission action, however, fines will not generally be levied for interconnection agreements notified to a NRA unless the European Commission determines that a serious breach of Article 81 or Article 82 has occurred,[48] in other words the usual grounds for imposition of fines.[49] If there are existing proceedings on a national or European level, the European Commission has indicated that it might refrain from pursuing an investigation for a period of six months after any proceedings have commenced,[50] as was the case in the fixed/mobile inquiry.[51] Interim measures, such as injunctions, may be taken by NRAs,[52] and if interim measures are not available for a complainant, the European Commission may accept an immediate complaint to safeguard competitors' rights.[53]

A. Relevant Markets

1. Product Markets

Consistent with Form A/B,[54] currently used to notify agreements under Article 81, the European Commission focuses on demand substitutability when considering what constitutes a relevant product market.[55] Form A/B generally defines the relevant product market as those products considered to be substitutes by the consumer.[56] The Access Notice discounts supply substitutability as a form of potential competition useful only for determining dominance; however, it retains the test of whether a concerted price rise of five to ten percent is sustainable.[57] This test in effect takes into account supply substitution, as a price rise

---

[45] *Ibid.*, para. 18.
[46] *Ibid.*
[47] *Ibid.*, paras. 19 and 38.
[48] *Ibid.*, para. 37.
[49] *Ibid.*
[50] *Ibid.*, para. 30.
[51] European Commission Press Release, "Commission concentrates on nine cases of mobile telephony prices" 27 July 1998, IP/98/707.
[52] Access Notice, *supra* n. 40, para. 32.
[53] *Ibid.*, para. 33.
[54] *Ibid.*, para. 43. For Form A/B, see [1985] OJ L 240/3–12.
[55] *Ibid.*, para. 40.
[56] *Ibid.*, para. 43, quoting Form A/B.
[57] *Ibid.*, para. 46.

will attract potential suppliers and prices will decrease as a result of their entry.[58]

The Access Notice identified two types of markets: telecommunications services, and a market of access to facilities necessary to provide telecommunications services, considered to be "information, physical network, etc."[59] The access to facilities market is stated to be most dependent on physical interconnection, allowing access to the termination points of end-users.[60] The effect of rapid technological change on product market definition is noted, and while alleged dominant operators might take comfort from this recognition, it might also lead to uncertainty as the European Commission reserves the right to determine the relevant product market on a case-by-case basis.[61] The earlier Telecommunications Competition Guidelines stressed the difficulty in determining relevant product markets in the sector.[62] The growth of an alternative infrastructure might also be expected to impact access market definition.[63]

While reasonable people usually take into consideration the factors outlined above, however, the Access Notice at this point takes a rather bizarre twist. It is effectively asserts that *telecommunications competition itself*—manifested in the form of access to the facilities necessary to compete—constitutes a separate market.[64] This raises the question of how competition in the "competition" market will be evaluated. By number of competitors? By market shares? By retail price levels and innovative service offerings? Indicators such as falling prices are traditionally seen as evidence of a competitive market. A telecoms incumbent, however, that lowers prices might still find itself accused of predatory conduct or engaging in a price squeeze, adding legal uncertainty to the usual commercial problems in pricing decisions.

2. Geographic Markets

The Access Notice returned to Form A/B for a definition of a relevant geographic market: an area in which competition conditions are sufficiently homogenous.[65] The effect of this definition may be national, given the European Commission's emphasis on terms of licenses or the existence of exclusive or special rights when determining relevant geographic markets.[66]

The reference to exclusive or special rights is puzzling, however, given that the Full Competition Directive required Member States to abolish all such rights

---

[58] *Ibid.*, para. 41.

[59] *Ibid.*, para. 45.

[60] *Ibid.*

[61] *Ibid.*, para. 47.

[62] Commission Guidelines on the Application of EC Competition Rules in the Telecommunications Sector [1991] OJ C233/2 paras. 26—27 [hereinafter Telecommunications Competition Guidelines].

[63] Access Notice, *supra*, n. 40, para. 53.

[64] *Ibid.*, para. 44.

[65] *Ibid.*, para. 54.

[66] *Ibid.*, para. 55.

for telecoms organisations.[67] Yet, even with Member States abolition of exclusive and special rights, the European Commission nonetheless indicated that the continued existence of "privileged access to facilities which cannot be duplicated, either for legal reasons or because it would cost too much" would also be considered when determining dominance.[68] Is "privileged access" a new category that the European Commission has created now that exclusive and special rights have disappeared? The emphasis on cost as a factor in determining privilege goes against the trend in competition policy of discounting capital cost as a barrier to entry. Given the vast sums of investment capital currently available in telecommunications markets, cost does not seem a legitimate barrier in the real world.

B. Access Principles

Part III of the Access Notice speaks to principles, specifically competition law principles considered in the context of telecommunications competition and regulation.[69] The European Commission stated that it would try to recognise and build on the principles included in the ONP harmonisation directives.[70] Universal service was recognised as possibly justifying non-application of competition rules under the principles of Article 82(2).[71] The accompanying reference to the telecommunication competition directives, effectively abolishing all special and exclusive rights, issued under the Commission's Article 86 authority, makes it difficult to envision an acceptable assertion of Article 86 monopoly rights by a Member State public enterprise in telecommunications.

Dominance, in the form of controlling access to facilities, will be monitored closely by the European Commission. Echoing the *British Telecom Procurement Judgment*,[72] the Access Notice stated that the fact that competition is legal will not automatically mean an entity is no longer dominant.[73] Market share in terms of turnover and comparative numbers of customers will be used to assist in determining whether a particular undertaking is dominant.[74] A fifty percent or greater market share may demonstrate dominance, but other factors, including the existence of alternative networks, will be considered when determining whether dominance exists.[75]

---

[67] Full Competition Directive, *supra* n. 17, art. 2.
[68] Access Notice, *supra* n. 40, para. 74.
[69] Access Notice, *supra* n. 40, para. 57.
[70] *Ibid.*, para. 58.
[71] *Ibid.*, para. 59.
[72] *supra* n. 33.
[73] *Ibid.*, para. 64.
[74] Access Notice, *supra* n. 40, paras. 70 and 72.
[75] *Ibid.*, para. 73.

1. *The* Tetra Pak *Case*

The European Commission also indicated that it would rely on the rationale of the *Tetra Pak*[76] judgment when determining dominance. *Tetra Pak* declared that the concept of dominance extends to markets where the firm is not dominant by finding "close links between the dominated and non-dominated market."[77] The finding of the ECJ that dominance can extend into a market where a firm is not dominant, so as to condemn conduct on the non-dominated market, was not sound, however. There was no proof that Tetra Pak was improperly leveraging its dominant position in one market to gain an advantage in another market. If there are anti-competitive effects in associated markets, the usual concepts of tying or anti-competitive leverage might be better applied than this amorphous concept of neighbouring markets. The *Tetra Pak* judgment thereore questioned *all* conduct by firms deemed dominant in a single market designed to exclude or eliminate competitors in any relevant market (at least where it is possible to claim associated links between the market in question and the market where the firm is dominant—in other words, all markets the dominant firm is involved with).

Competition law and policy, however, should encourage legitimate exclusionary conduct by competitors. The very nature of competition is to win in the market and thereby eliminate one's competitors.[78] Punishing legitimate competition can only lead to less competition and therefore higher prices for consumers, less technical innovation, and less choice. A more rational competition law policy is clearly in order. It is unfortunate that in its Access Notice the European Commission adopted the flawed reasoning of the *Tetra Pak* judgment with regard of finding dominance. Perhaps experience will demonstrate to the European Commission the folly of restricting competition by handicapping any competitors considered dominant in any markets arguably associated. If it is EU policy to subsidise inefficient firms, it would be more transparent to do so via state aids, than by punishing effective competitors. Under the neighbouring markets rationale, it is difficult to imagine traditional telcos ever escaping from the dominant label, no matter how much competition develops in specific markets such as business, international calls, mobile, or Internet provision.

2. *Market Power and Market Shares*

The Access Notice also called for a measurement of market power by considering the sales of a particular undertaking compared with the total sales of the party requesting access.[79] This will consistently tilt the legal scales in favor of

---

[76] Case C/333/94 *Tetra Pak International SA* v. *Commission* [1996] ECR I–5951.

[77] Access Notice, *supra* n. 40, para. 65.

[78] Valentine Korah, "Tetra Pak II—Lack of Reasoning in Court's Judgment", (1997) 2 *ECLR* 98, 101.

[79] Access Notice, *supra* n. 40, para. 72.

small providers. Calculation of these amounts will also require separating the functions of conveyance of telecommunications services and the provision of these services to end-users. While anti-competitive agreements could alone be sanctioned under Article 81, the Notice also asserts that when firms act together, possibly under interconnection agreements,[80] so that both exercised a monopoly over access to essential facilities, joint dominance could be found. If, for example, a traditional telephone company and a cable TV network provider were to together control the only existing effective means of accessing end-users, they might be considered as jointly dominant.[81]

Because of the current reality of availability of alternative infrastructure and service providers, the assumption of the Access Notice that dominance can be assumed for each geographic market is fundamentally flawed. As dense coverage of alternative infrastructure is currently available in some geographic markets, and will grow in all geographic markets in the future, a more flexible approach is in order (e.g., the City of London, the island of Manhattan, etc.). With telecommunications technology continuing its rapid development, the growth of commercially feasible alternatives should also continue, eroding further any credible assertions of dominance—that is the ability to act independently of the market. The Access Notice itself indicated that factors other than market share, including the existence of alternative networks would be considered when determining whether dominance exists in a telecoms market.[82]

3. Issues of Refusal to Deal

The Access Notice considered three types of refusal:[83]

(1) Where another operator (including the incumbent) already has access to provide the service in question. This is a discrimination problem, in the absence of an objective justification.[84]

(2) Where no operator has been given access to provide the service. This is a problem of essential facilities, and where capacity constraint is not a problem, then the ability to give an objective justification for refusal is doubtful.[85] Access to upstream network services may be of key importance.[86]

(3) There is a final category of refusal of access. That is where access is withdrawn. This will be analysed similarly to refusals to supply. "Withdrawal of access from an existing customer will usually be abusive."[87]

---

[80] *Ibid.*, para. 79.
[81] *Ibid.*, para. 80. See discussion in Chapter 10 regarding joint dominance.
[82] *Ibid.*, para. 63.
[83] Access Notice, *supra* n. 40, para. 84.
[84] *Ibid.*, para. 85.
[85] *Ibid.*, para. 87.
[86] *Ibid.*, para. 89.
[87] *Ibid.*, para. 100.

There also appears to be a forth type of "refusal." According to the Access Notice "a company may abuse its dominant position if by its actions it prevents the emergence of a new product or service".[88] Such a statement is particularly interesting, as it implies that if an operator does nothing and does not offer a new service itself, thereby preventing the benefits of the new service from reaching the market, the case for mandating access is strengthened. This is entirely consistent with principles of promoting consumer choice and technical progress. Indeed, Treaty Article 82 lists as a specific abuse of dominant position, "limiting production, markets or technical development to the prejudice of consumers."[89]

To analyse refusals of access, it is necessary to start with identifying relevant markets.[90] The European Commission's analysis of what circumstances justify mandating access deserves a close look:

(1) It must be shown that access is truly essential; that is the service would be either impossible of seriously uneconomic to provide without access.
(2) There must be sufficient available capacity.
(3) "[T]he facility owner fails to satisfy demand on an existing service or product market, blocks the emergence of a potential new service or product, or impedes competition on an existing or potential service or product market."[91]
(4) The requesting party must be willing to pay a reasonable price and abide by non-discriminatory terms.

There is no objective justification for refusing access such as technical difficulties. It is also stated that an acceptable justification for refusal includes "the need for a facility owner which has undertaken investment aimed at the introduction of a new product or service to have sufficient time and opportunity to use the facility in order to place that new product or service on the market."[92]

Therefore, a possible return on investment is recognised as a justification for failing to grant access, at least if the incumbent is out competing, rather than trying to deny consumers access to developing technologies. The European Commission is to be commended for this pro-competition and consumer welfare enhancing position.

C. Other Abuses

When determining where points of interconnection (POI) should be located, a point of particular interest is the European Commission's assertion that "com-

---

[88] Access Notice, *supra* n. 40, para. 90.
[89] EU Treaty, *supra* n. 15, art. 82(b).
[90] Access Notice, *supra* n. 40, para. 91.
[91] *Ibid.*, para. 91.c.
[92] *Ibid.*, para. 91.e.

petition rules require that the party requesting access must be granted access at the most suitable point for the requesting party, provided that this point is technically feasible for the access provider."[93] This may be consistent with language in the Interconnection Directive that all telecommunications organisations with "significant market power shall meet all reasonable requests for access to the network including access at points other than the network termination points offered to the majority of end-users."[94] The reference to "technically feasible" points of interconnection is interesting. This phrase is not found in the EU regulatory framework, but it is included in the US Telecommunications Act of 1996[95] as well as the WTO Telecoms Treaty Reference Paper.[96]

D. Excessive Pricing

The Access Notice asserts that charging excessive prices for access would be abusive.[97] However there is no guidance given as to what might be excessive. The existing EU regulatory framework requires that interconnection and other charges from telecoms operators with significant market power be cost-based. Is the Access Notice suggesting that access should be provided at less than cost if cost-based charges are excessive?

This may not be solely an academic question. Without complete tariff rebalancing, telecommunications operators may be providing some retail services below cost. Like the ill-defined notion of "affordable" discussed in chapter 15, *supra*, the concept of excessive is subjective. Even the Access Notice admits that there will be many elements to consider when weighing pricing. A preference was expressed for an approach comparing or "benchmarking" prices in other geographic areas or from markets considered to be open to competition to determine what is "fair."[98] This approach has been already been used for general (fixed-to-fixed) interconnection prices, as well as investigations into fixed-to-mobile prices and international accounting rates. Benchmarking, however, fails to consider either market conditions or unique costs in the relevant geographic market. It is micromanagement of the telecommunications industry and is not consistent with the EU principle of EU subsidiarity—Member States should have authority in appropriate areas. Furthermore, there is certainly nothing "fair" about prices or competition. One person's fair prices may be considered exploitative by another.

---

[93] *Ibid.*, para. 96.
[94] Interconnection Directive, *supra* n.1, art. 4(2).
[95] Telecommunications Act of 1996, Pub. LA. No. 104–104, 110 Stat. 56, (1996), §251(c)(2).
[96] World Trade Organisation, Reference Paper on Regulatory Principles, art. 2.2.
[97] Access Notice, *supra* n. 40, para. 105.
[98] *Ibid.*, para. 109.

E. Predatory Pricing

The Access Notice declared that a dominant provider pricing below average variable costs or average total costs would be abusive, stating that pricing too low might prevent the emergence of effective alternative infrastructures.[99] A preference is expressed to consider prices in relation to long term average incremental prices.[100] If the dominant provider prices infrastructure access too low, there would be no incentive for other sources to emerge. Potential competitive service providers would always select the low-cost infrastructure offered by the dominant provider.

F. Price Squeeze

The Access Notice's price squeeze formulation would require the dominant operator to charge competitors (including itself) a price for access to network infrastructure sufficiently below the retail price charged by the service subsidiary of the dominant operator so that competitors can enter the service market and make a profit, presumably by charging a price less than that of the dominant operator's service subsidiary.[101] The EU Commission should consider carefully the possible effects of a strictly enforced transfer pricing requirement.

G. Discrimination and Exclusivity

The Access Notice cited discrimination by dominant operators as an abuse in the absence of objective justifications.[102] Pricing discrimination is the most obvious form, particularly if done in exchange for a customer agreeing to exclusivity.[103] Differences between wholesale and resale prices, however, presumably including volume discounts, might not be discriminatory.[104] Discrimination could also exist in delays in installation or repairs, "technical access, routing, numbering, restrictions on network use . . . and use of customer network data."[105]

While EU regulatory legislation requires operators to enter access and interconnection agreements, the Access Notice perceives a danger that access or interconnection agreements might be used for anti-competitive purposes con-

---

[99] Access Notice, *supra* n. 40, para. 110.
[100] *Ibid.*, para. 115.
[101] *Ibid.*, para. 118.
[102] Access Notice, *supra* n. 40, para. 120.
[103] *Ibid.*, para. 122.
[104] *Ibid.*, para. 126.
[105] *Ibid.*, para. 125.

trary to Article 81 of the EU Treaty.[106] Exclusivity appears to be the European Commission's main concern, and will be prohibited unless objectively justified. Price coordination, market sharing, exclusion of third parties, and improper information exchanges are also noted as possible anti-competitive techniques.[107] In particular, confidential information should be shared among interconnecting parties only on a need-to-know basis, and then only with appropriate divisions of the companies.[108] Possible group boycotts were also mentioned as a concern.[109]

H. Permissible Prices

A telecommunications provider, deemed to be dominant, can therefore price only within a narrow range without violating competition law. Prices for essential facilities must mirror internal costs and be low enough for competitors to purchase these facilities and make a reasonable profit. Prices cannot be so high to lead as to excessive profits. Prices cannot be so low as to be considered as predatory. And finally, retail prices cannot be discriminatory—an alleged dominant provider may not price so as to meet the competition for customers. With all of these roadblocks to market pricing, perhaps providers should give up and ask the European Commission to set prices. The European Commission itself might find it impossible to meet all of these requirements, let alone run a business. Short of putting an army of competition lawyers and economists in charge of pricing policy, there is no sure way of pricing within the confines of the Access Notice so as to avoid the possibility of a competitor complaint or European Commission action.

I. The Access Notice and Market Realities

The Access Notice suggested that the physical structure of a telecommunications network (identified as a monopoly activity) can be separated from services provided by the network, at least for purposes of determining whether an operator should be considered dominant. In essence, the European Commission desires telecommunications organisations to split in two (at least in theory), with the operating organisation bearing provisioning costs (that is, the network), and the services organisation paying (again at least on paper) the same costs as competitors to access the network. This might be possible from an accounting standpoint (it would probably be very costly and speculative to divide costs in this way), but is it practical to separate a producer from its means of production? For products such as telecommunications services,

---

[106] *Ibid.*, paras. 131 and 136.
[107] *Ibid.*, para. 134.
[108] *Ibid.*, para.139.
[109] *Ibid.*, para. 143.

infrastructure itself might constitute part of the product. This principle is arguably consistent with the requirement of the first ONP Voice Telephony Directive that "[n]ational regulatory authorities shall ensure that telecommunications organizations adhere to the principle of non-discrimination when they make use of the fixed public telephone network for providing services which are or may also be supplied by other service providers."[110]

V. SHARED ACCESS: LEAPFROGGING TO THE NEXT GENERATION OF LOCAL LOOP UNBUNDLING

Although the Telecommunications Access Notice set the stage for entrants to claim access to unbundled local loops under European competition law, the EU regulatory framework itself was not much help in the area. Apart from interconnection, access to a limited number of telecoms facilities such as the purchase of leased lines, and special network access,[111] regulators in Member States were free to set their own policy as to whether to encourage provision of alternative infrastructure or to mandate local loop unbundling.

A. Legal and Regulatory Principles

Although the basic principle of the ONP policy was unbundling of telecoms network elements, ONP directives did not require full, physical unbundling of the local loop. The European Commission itself stated that:

> "Again, in the telecommunications sector, Community policy does not require a full unbundling of the local loop, or a structural separation of the associated infrastructure, from the provision of services carried over it. This does not exclude appropriate safeguards or requirements being introduced under competition rules. In reality, the issue of unbundling of the local end of transmission networks is complex and must be closely linked to the degree of overall competition in the market concerned; the availability of viable alternative distribution channels and the starting point for competition in the particular market. Some argue that unbundling may act against the consumer interest in the longer term by removing economic incentives for organisations to put their own wired or wireless networks in place."[112]

---

[110] Directive 95/62/EC of the European Parliament and of the Council of 13 December 1995 on the application of open network provision (ONP) to voice telephony [1995] OJ L321/6 art. 10(6) [hereinafter First ONP Voice Telephony Directive] <http://www.ispo.cec.be/infosoc/legreg/docs/9562ec.html>.

[111] Special network access is generally interpreted to mean enhanced service provision by competitors, but as more fully discussed below the term has been the subject of interesting interpretations. It was such an interpretation that led to the European Commission's recommendation on shared access.

[112] Green Paper on the Convergence of the Telecommunications, Media and Information Technology Sectors, and the Implications for Regulation, Towards an Information Society Approach, COM(97)623, IV.2.3.

Several Member States, notably the UK, adopted a policy similar to that suggested in the Advocate General's Opinion in the *Bronner*[113] case: that in the long run competition is best promoted by competitor independence from the dominant network provider. Currently there is a contrary trend towards the encouragement of immediate competitor entrance as suggested in the Access Notice and with national regulators mandating local loop unbundling. As of this writing, Austria, Denmark, Finland, Germany and The Netherlands require some form of local loop unbundling, and most of the remaining Member Sates are at least studying the issue or taking some steps towards requiring local loop unbundling.

As described below in chapter 18 on Mergers, the European Commission imposed local loop unbundling as a remedy in a proposed merger between two European incumbent telecoms operators.[114] The press release of the European Commission accompanying the *Telia/Telenor* merger decision noted the remedy of unbundling with favour and hinted that such a remedy might be used again, and not only with regard to merger cases. Nevertheless, the prospects for EU-wide unbundling appeared dim.

With the publication of the 1999 Telecommunications Review,[115] it was stated that EU unbundling, in the form of a directive, would have to wait until the proposed legislative agenda could be adopted, probably in 2003. The 1999 Telecommunications Review envisioned a new access and interconnection directive, probably including a requirement that dominant telcos, as well as those meeting the lower threshold of significant market power, provide access to unbundled local loops, with dominant providers having to provide loops at cost-oriented prices.[116]

1. Soft Law

The 1999 Telecommunications Review also called for greater application of soft law, however, by which was meant more use of informal guidelines and recommendations.[117] Because the EU legislative process can take so long, perhaps the European Commission felt it had no alternative but to rely on soft law to accomplish its goals. It might be better for the European Commission to use its Treaty Article 86 power to unilaterally issue directives in areas it feels to be critical, for example in the face of a real market breakdown. Although there might be

---

[113] Case D–7/97 *Oscar Bronner GmbH & Co. KG v. Mediaprint Zeitungs—und Zeitschriftenverlag GmbH & Co. KG and Others* Opinion of Advocate General Jacobs delivered on 28 May 1998 [1998] ECR I–8333.

[114] Case COMP/M.1439 *Telia/Telenor* [2000] OJ C 237/2000.

[115] Communication from the Commission to the European Parliament, the Council, the Economic and Social Committee and the Committee of the Regions, Towards a new Framework for Electronic Communications infrastructure and associate services: The 1999 Communications Review, COM (1999) 539, [hereinafter 1999 Telecommunications Review].

[116] *Ibid.*, §4.2.

[117] *Ibid.*, §3.3.2. Soft law in the EU framework is discussed in Chapter 10, *supra*.

political consequences from a new wave of Article 86 directives, the European Commission could achieve its objectives rapidly, with legal certainty, and with uniformity throughout the EU.

B. The European Commission's Unbundling Working Document

Whatever the virtues or vices of soft law, that is the device the European Commission is employing to unbundle local loops in Europe. The European Commission first issued a Working Document, designed to become a recommendation, calling for local loop unbundling, and stating that one form of unbundling, shared access, is already required under the existing EU regulatory framework.[118] The Commission's positions originated with the Telecommunications Review as well as the recent *eEurope* paper.[119] *eEurope* specifically called for Member States to require unbundling by the end of 2000[120] as a means of promoting "cheaper Internet access."

The Unbundling Working Document considered that unbundled "access to the local loop is a key element in any strategy to develop competition for local access."[121] Lack of local competition was an issue of concern driving the European Commission's Working Document proposals. If local telecoms competition were to develop effectively, this in turn would become an enabler of new services like broadband Internet access. User choice was seen as benefiting the market and helping speed deployment of broadband services, to meet consumer demand that incumbent operators were not meeting in the opinion of the Working Document.[122]

Distortions in long term infrastructure competition (that is disincentives for competitors to construct alternative infrastructure) were not seen as a danger if unbundled loops were "priced at a level that does not distort the 'make or buy' decision of an entrant."[123] Again we see the tendency of the European Commission to intervene in pricing decisions, but at least it is in the context of recognising that regulatory intervention in pricing matters can have market consequences. The consequences may be negative. This section of the Working Document does go on to state that the framework for unbundling, including prices should be according to "a standard of promoting economic efficiency, enabling wider competition and maximising consumer and user welfare."[124]

---

[118] Directorate-General Information Society Working Document Unbundled access to the local loop Brussels, 9 February 2000 INFSO A/1 [hereinafter Unbundling Working Document] <http://www.ispo.cec.be/infosoc/telecompolicy/en/ullwd10b.pdf>.

[119] "*eEurope* An Information Society For All", *Communication of a Commission Initiative for the Special European Council of Lisbon*, 23 and 24 March 2000 [hereinafter *eEurope*].

[120] *Ibid.*, §2. "By the end of 2000: Incumbents should offer unbundled local loops under non-discriminatory terms and conditions in order to allow all operators to provide innovative services."

[121] Unbundling Working Document, *supra* n. 118, §1.1

[122] *Ibid.*, §1.4.

[123] *Ibid.*

[124] *Ibid.*

The European Commission is to be commended for this policy statement. It is, however, debatable whether the suggested pricing controls lead to economic efficiency.

1. Three Unbundling Possibilities

The Working Document identified three possibilities of unbundling: full, shared access and bit stream.[125] The European Commission thought that these three are complementary—and all should be available.

a. Full Physical Unbundling

Full unbundling was not required under the EU regulatory framework at the time the Working Document was issued, but the European Commission supported Member States taking action to require full unbundling and "called on Member States to ensure that full unbundled local loops are available by the end of the year 2000.[126] The Working Document did not specify what action, if any, the European Commission might take if the Member States did not heed this call. Pricing issues for full unbundling, in particular the possibility of price squeezes, were noted.[127]

b. Shared Access

Shared access is the most interesting type of unbundling considered by the Working Document. "In this form of unbundling, the incumbent continues to provide telephone service, while the new entrant deliver[s] high speed data services over the same loop using its own high speed ADSL modems."[128] Shared access is the EU equivalent of line-sharing, required by the US FCC in late 1999.[129] Perhaps inspired by the FCC, The EU Commission rolled out its own version of line sharing in such a way as to leapfrog full unbundling requirements and require competitor access to local loops immediately throughout Europe.

Although the approach of the Working Document may be expeditious, the legal basis of mandatory shared access is not self-evident. The Working Document found a legal basis for shared access in the ONP Voice Telephony Directive. This directive requires telecoms providers having significant market power to grant competitors "special network access."[130] Although the meaning

---

[125] *Ibid.*, §2.

[126] *Ibid.*, §2.1.2

[127] *Ibid.*, §2.1.3.

[128] *Ibid.*, §2.2.1.

[129] Federal Communications Commission, In the Matters of Deployment of Wireline Services Offering Advanced Telecommunications Capability CC Docket No. 98–147 and Implementation of the Local Competition Provisions of the Telecommunications Act of 1996 CC Docket No. 96–98 Third Report And Order In CC Docket No. 98–147 Fourth Report And Order In CC Docket No. 96–98 <http://www.fcc.gov/Bureaus/Common_Carrier/Orders/1999/fcc99355.doc>.

[130] Directive 98/10/EC of the European Parliament and of the Council of 26 February 1998 on the application of open network provision (ONP) to voice telephony and on universal service for telecommunications in a competitive environment [1998] OJ L101/24 art. 16(7) [hereinafter ONP Voice Telephony Directive].

of the term "special network access" in the Directive had been the subject to debate (discussed in Chapter 11, *supra*), before the publication of the Working Document it had not been seriously considered that the term meant a form of local loop unbundling.

Assuming that the conclusion of the Working Document is correct and shared access is required by the Directive, there are still important issues to be considered. Some incumbents, notably Deutsche Telekom, are likely to object to providing shared access in that they are already required to or offer voluntarily full unbundled local loops. The argument will be made that competitors already have access to full loops, and therefore shared loops are not necessarily. Although this argument might work in the context of a competition law complaint, it does not respond to the assertion that shared access is required by the ONP Voice Telephony Directive. If shared access is required by the Directive, full unbundling is irrelevant. It is simply required, whatever other forms of unbundling are offered.

Other arguments may be anticipated from incumbent operators. Technical problems such as cross talk in cable runs where xDSL is present are sure to figure. Pricing issues will also be important. European incumbents are likely to raise the "access deficit" issue, alleging that their subscription prices do not cover the cost of providing service and therefore they should be able to charge substantially more than the subscription price for shared access. Indeed, once the hurdle of required shared access is overcome, pricing issues are likely to dominate the discussion.

The Working Document recognised that pricing was an important issue when considering shared access. Falling back on principles of non-discrimination, the Working Document recommended that transfer pricing be applied to shared access loops. "It would, therefore, be recommended that NRAs ensure that incumbents charge competitors a price for access to the high frequency spectrum of the local loop not higher than the one they charge themselves for their use of this high frequency spectrum for their own broadband access service."[131] This pricing position is consistent with the principles of the Telecommunications Access Notice. It is doubtful, however, that incumbents actually "charge" themselves anything for access to their own broadband frequencies. There is an element of justice in this pricing principle. If incumbents claim it is prohibitively expensive to give access to the broadband frequencies, or if they claim it is technically not feasible for competitors to use unbundled local loops to provide DSL services (arguments certain to be made by incumbents), regulators can reply, "how is it then possible for you, Mr. Incumbent, to provide DSL service at all and price it the way you do?"

This section of the Working Document went on to assert that the cost of shared access loops should be less than fully unbundled local loops or a basic voice subscription. The incumbent should be recovering its full costs from the

---

[131] Unbundling Working Document, *supra* n. 118, §2.2.3.

price of a basic voice subscription. The European Commission will likely respond to access deficit arguments by noting that incumbents may rebalance their tariffs, and that if there is a universal service problem, it should be dealt with through universal service support mechanisms, not by inflating costs borne by competitors.

c. Bit Stream (Wholesale) Unbundling

The final form of unbundling considered by the Working Document is bit stream access. In this form of unbundling, the incumbent owns and maintains equipment such as DSL modems (DSLAMs) in the local exchanges and gives competitors access at a point upstream in the network.[132] Although entrants have not been that interested in this type of service provision, if properly done by the incumbent it can offer advantages to entrants and to the market as a whole. Competitors can benefit from the ubiquitous network coverage of the incumbent operator. Likewise wholesale prices reflecting the incumbents' scale of operations should also be made available. The Working Document notes, however, that competitors would surrender control to the incumbent in a bit stream unbundling arrangement.[133] The Working Document asserted that incumbent operators were already obliged to give bit stream unbundling access under legal provisions forbidding dominant providers from engaging in discrimination.[134]

2. *Collocation*

Both full unbundling and shared access would carry with them a requirement of collocation, that is the ability of competitors to place equipment in the local exchanges/central offices of incumbents.[135] The Working Document claims that collocation is already "covered by" the Interconnection Directive,[136] which must certainly be a surprise to the Member States not requiring collocation. In fact, a majority of Member States did not require collocation at the time the Working Document was issued.

The European Commission, however, was implying more coverage under the Interconnection Directive than was present. Article 11 of the Interconnection Directive stated that Member States may encourage facility sharing, presumably including collocation. Specifically regarding collocation, however, the Directive stated that agreements between telcos "for collocation or facility sharing shall normally be a matter for commercial and technical agreement between the parties concerned."[137] Moreover, the Directive went on to prohibit Member States from imposing collocation without adequate public consultation.

---

[132] *Ibid.*, §2.3.1.
[133] *Ibid.*
[134] *Ibid.*, §2.3.2.
[135] *Ibid.*, §3.1.
[136] Interconnection Directive, *supra* n. 1, art. 11.
[137] *Ibid.*

Finally, contrary to the claim made by the European Commission in the Working Document, the Interconnection Directive most certainly does not authorise the European Commission to "specify that Member States, acting in accordance with Article 11 and Article 9 of the Interconnection Directive 97/33/EC, should take steps to ensure that third parties that are granted unbundled access to local loops are also able to collate equipment on the premises of the local loop operator."[138] The European Commission might have been on firmer ground if it had found a collocation requirement in the ONP Voice Telephony Directive's special network access requirement. It could be argued that shared access requirements would be meaningless without a place to put equipment. In that context, perhaps the Working Document's threat to specify collocation to the Member States makes more sense. The rest of the Working Document's collocation section deals with pricing and space issues, sure to be battlegrounds in the future.

C. Subsequent European Commission Unbundling Communication and Recommendation: Unbundling Comes to Europe at Last?

As promised in the Working Document, as well at the EU's March 2000 "dot com" summit held in Lisbon,[139] The European Commission moved quickly to upgrade its unbundling thoughts from the Working Document to a Recommendation.[140] At the same time, the European Commission issued a (slightly) more detailed Communication outlining local loop unbundling.[141]

1. The Unbundling Communication

Turning first to the Communication, it can be viewed as a refined version of the Working Document focusing on policy and technical ramifications of local loop unbundling. The Communication is up-front about the policy driving the move to impose unbundling requirements on European incumbents: "cheap internet services."[142] The way to cheap Internet access as well as to innovation in telecommunications markets is seen as happening through mandated unbundling.

---

[138] Unbundling Working Document, *supra* n. 118, §3.1.

[139] See Presidency Conclusions, Lisbon European Council, 23 and 24 March 2000, discussed *infra* in chapter 13.

[140] Commission Recommendation on Unbundled Access to the Local Loop Enabling the competitive provision of a full range of electronic services including broadband multimedia and high-speed Internet, Brussels, 26 April 2000, (2000) 1059 [hereinafter Local Loop Unbundling Recommendation] <http://www.ispo.cec.be/information_society/policy/telecom/localloop/pdf/c2000 1059_en. pdf>.

[141] Communication from the Commission, Unbundled Access to the Local loop: Enabling the competitive provision of a full range of electronic communication services including broadband multimedia and high-speed internet Brussels, 26.4.2000 COM(2000) 237 final [hereinafter Local Loop Unbundling Communication] <http://www.ispo.cec.be/information_society/policy/telecom/localloop/pdf/com2000_237en.pdf>.   [142] *Ibid.*, §1.1.

"Providing access to the local loop to all new entrants will increase the level of competition and technological innovation in the local access network, which in turn stimulate the competitive provision of a full range of telecommunication services from simple voice telephony to broadband services to the customer."[143]

The Communication relies heavily on the essential facilities doctrine to justify unbundling. Perhaps starting at the wrong point, the Communication states that incumbent operators have an unfair advantage in the market due to "the fact that operators rolled out their local access networks over significant periods of time protected by exclusive rights and were able to fund its investment costs through monopoly rents."[144] Whatever their source of funds and whatever rights enjoyed in the past, however, is irrelevant to whether access to a desired facility should be mandated by law today.

An explanation for the European Commission taking this as a legal starting point is found in the *Bronner* opinion. In that case that Advocate General opinion stated that the cost of constructing a desired facility might constitute an insurmountable barrier to entry particularly when the facility in question was constructed with public funds or under non-competitive conditions.[145] With elimination of special and exclusive rights and with privatisation of former state-owned telecoms monopolies, the fact that public funds were used to construct networks or that monopoly rents were one at one time extracted should not, standing alone, be enough to invoke the essential facilities doctrine. The European Commission may have to do more than baldly assert as it did in the Communication that "alternative local access infrastructures (cable-TV, wireless local loops, satellite, etc) cannot usually be constructed with the same ubiquity and competitive conditions within a reasonable time."[146] This may very well be the case, but in the event of a contested case, proof should be forthcoming.

The Communication finished the essential facilities test by asserting that as there are no "technical and commercial [*sic*] viable alternatives" to existing public telecommunications networks, "refusal to supply access by a dominant company holding such an infrastructure may . . . constitute an infringement of Article 82 of the Treaty."[147] Because of this legal basis and because of the bottleneck nature of the incumbent telco's local loops, the Communication considered that unbundling was necessary in the three complementary methods (full physical unbundling, shared access, and bit stream unbundling) presented in the Working Document. No alternatives such as wireless, CATV networks or energy (electricity) networks either alone or combined were seen as presenting a

---

[143] *Ibid.*

[144] *Ibid.*, §1.2.

[145] Case D–7/97 *Oscar Bronner GmbH & Co. KG* v. *Mediaprint Zeitungs—und Zeitschriftenverlag GmbH & Co. KG and Others* Opinion of Advocate General Jacobs delivered on 28 May 1998 [1998] ECR I–8333 para. 66 [hereinafter *Bronner*]. The opinion and judgment are examined in Chapter 10 *supra*.

[146] Local Loop Unbundling Communication, *supra* n. 141, §1.2.

[147] *Ibid.*

viable alternative to the existing PSTN, particularly for provision of broadband Internet access, a vote of confidence the DSL industry will certainly find encouraging.

While unbundling was presented as essential, the Communication recognised that loops should not be priced so as to "not distort the 'make or buy' decision of an entrant."[148] The European Commission accepted the theory that unbundling was a necessary step on the way to entrants building their own network infrastructure "by allowing entrants to test out the market before building their own infrastructure",[149] and therefore mandated unbundling would not decrease incentives for construction of alternative infrastructure. More on pricing later, but the Commission's stated policy is at least right, that the standard must be "promoting economic efficiency, enabling wider competition and maximising consumer and user welfare."[150] Whatever else comes of this unbundling exercise, at least it has caused the European Commission to take into account the fundamentals of competition policy. Progress has been made from the time of the publication of the Access Notice when even a footnote in favour of "competition, not competitors" was too much for the European Commission.

The Communication's short relevant market description is of interest. Various telecommunications services markets such as voice and broadband were noted.[151] Local loops themselves were seen as constituting "a new access market" that develops "as soon as access is given to this part of the incumbents' network."[152] Does this mean that if incumbents attempt to retain a local access monopoly by not giving competitors access, no relevant product market exists in local access? Such a reward for monopolistic behaviour cannot be the intention of the European Commission.

Regarding geographic markets, the Communication stated that local access markets would be national in scope, a position that is consistent with the *WorldCom/MCI*[153] and *Telia/Telenor*[154] merger decisions. A better definition, in light of existing and possible cross-border telecoms joint ventures and mergers would be to find that relevant geographic markets for local access are consistent with the geographic coverage offered by market participants. Given, however, the designation of national relevant geographic markets, the Communication found that it was not possible for any but incumbent telcos to effectively compete in the local access market. While construction and operation of alternative networks is possible, the Communication found that such alternatives were only being constructed in urban areas. Thus demand for national ubiquitous access networks was only fulfilled by incumbents; they are the only market participants.

---

[148] Local Loop Unbundling Communication, *supra* n. 141, §3.1.
[149] *Ibid.*
[150] *Ibid.*
[151] *Ibid.*, §3.2.
[152] *Ibid.*
[153] Case IV/M.1069 *WorldCom/MCI* [1999] OJ L116/1 paras. 58, 59, 80.
[154] Case COMP/M.1439 *Telia/Telenor* [2000] OJ C 237/2000 para. 119.

Perhaps the Communication should have stated that only incumbents actually provide ubiquitous national coverage. Even if possible, it is doubtful that entrants would want the burden and small revenue stream associated with serving certain low population density areas of nations. This is an advantage, but also a burden that incumbent operators have, closely linked to the historic public funding and monopoly rents the Communication objected to. Today, such coverage remains an incumbent burden, mandated by universal service requirements. No one will seriously contend that entrants would provide ubiquitous national coverage even if it would be feasible and in aggregate profitable to do so.

The Communication also cites the *Bronner* judgment for the proposition that incumbents must give access to their local loops because it is "economically unfeasible"[155] for entrants to build nationally ubiquitous alternative infrastructure. It is not, however, so clear that the *Bronner* judgment calls for this conclusion. The judgment paragraph cited by the Communication at this point actually states that "it does not appear that there are any technical, legal or even economic obstacles capable of making it impossible, or even unreasonably difficult, for any other . . .[competitor] to establish, alone or in cooperation with other . . .[competitors], its own nationwide . . ." alternative network.[156] By implication, the conclusion the Communication draws from this language is that if it can be demonstrated that it would be "unreasonably difficult" from an economic standpoint to build an alternative network, dominant providers must give access. First, the negative of the *Bronner* judgment language does not necessarily make the positive that the Communication assumed. It may be telling that the Court placed the modifying word "even" before the words "economic obstacles." For a full consideration of *Bronner's* impact, the Communication should also regard the impact of the next two Judgment paragraphs:

> "It should be emphasised in that respect that, in order to demonstrate that the creation of such a system is not a realistic potential alternative and that access to the existing system is therefore indispensable, it is not enough to argue that it is not economically viable by reason of the small circulation of the daily newspaper or newspapers to be distributed.
>
> For such access to be capable of being regarded as indispensable, it would be necessary at the very least to establish, as the Advocate General has pointed out at point 68 of his Opinion, that it is not economically viable to create a second home-delivery scheme for the distribution of daily newspapers with a circulation comparable to that of the daily newspapers distributed by the existing scheme."[157]

Therefore, the *Bronner* test is not whether it is economically feasible for competitors with a small market share to establish an alternative network, but whether it is impossible or unreasonable to establish such a network to serve a

---

[155] *Ibid.*
[156] Case C–7/97 *Oscar Bronner GmbH & Co. KG v. Meida Zeitungs—und Zeitschrifenverlag GmbH & Co. KG* [1998] ECR I–8333 para. 44 [hereinafter *Bronner* Judgment].
[157] *Ibid.*, paras. 45 and 46.

customer base such as possessed by the dominant operator. Contrary to what the Communication suggests, *Bronner* specifically held that it was *not* an abuse for a dominant operator to deny a competitor access to its network when the smaller competitor "by reason of its small . . .[size] is unable either alone or in cooperation with other . . . [competitors] to set up and operate its own . . .[network] in economically reasonable conditions. . ."[158]

While the authors of the Communication attempted to get around *Bronner* by asserting that alternative networks would be economically unfeasible on a nation-wide scale, *Bronner* requires requesting parties to demonstrate that that facilities would be economically unfeasible on a nation-wide basis, serving a similar number of customers as the current incumbent. As no incumbent telcos are dependent on state subsidies or cross-subsidising network operations out of monopoly rents from captive customers,[159] it will be hard for requesting entrants to show that they could not invest and operate a ubiquitous network profitably as incumbent operators are clearly able to do in the aggregate. It can hardly be claimed with a straight face that incumbent operators are exceptionally efficient.

Regarding the supposed unfairness of having a telecoms network originally built with public funds, as discussed in Chapter 10, *infra*, this discounts subsequent privatisation when investors reimbursed the state for its network construction. Investors bought the network. It is that simple. For European law to assert ex post facto that investors did not in fact buy the network, but must share it with all competitors at an internally non-discriminatory price, is a serious abrogation of contract and property rights. While the authors of the Communication should receive points for inventiveness and sticking to their purpose, *Bronner* does not support their assertion in the way alleged.[160]

It may well be that the Communication is correct that it is not economically feasible to duplicate the incumbents' networks on ubiquitous, nation-wide basis. As discussed in Chapter 9, *supra*, however, it does not automatically follow that entrants will then construct multiple ubiquitous, nation-wide terrestrial networks. Unbundling should, however, be considered as one of many pro-entry tools helping to stimulate sufficient new, alternative non-incumbent demand for facilities. This in turn should make additional facilities-based entry profitable.

The Communication is on firm ground when addressing the time problem in rolling out new networks. As EU policy makers view Internet access as an immediate priority, there is a corresponding need for immediate action to bring Internet access prices down in Europe. Unbundling is a tool to help accomplish that goal. In that respect, unbundling is essential after all.

---

[158] *Bronner* Judgment, para. 47.

[159] The failure of incumbents to rebalance tariffs and alleged "access deficits" may make a case that incumbents are operating networks at less than cost and may therefore be required to give access.

[160] *Bronner*'s inadequately discussed tying allegations may be useful in analysing requests for access to unbundled local loops.

Although the Communication did not specifically cite the Access Notice in this section, its treatment of incumbent failure to grant competitors access to local loops relied heavily on the Access Notice's analysis. The Communication considered that incumbent refusals might violate EU competition law as unjustified refusal to deal, discrimination or limitation of "production, markets, or technical development to the prejudice of consumers."[161] Perhaps the key statement in this area is the Communication's assertion that the "dominant operator would have to provide local loop access to all competitors on no less favourable conditions than those for its own downstream operation."[162] We shall see later how even the European Commission appears to be of two minds about this possible application of transfer pricing on incumbent operators. It is admitted that loops may only be required when there is sufficient capacity available and in the event that "there is no objective justification for refusing access."[163]

Pricing and conditions of access will of course be key in ensuring that local loop unbundling is no more than a paper commitment. The Communication flags potential problems in areas of delays (incumbents can delay provision of loops to entrants by reserving the xDSL market to themselves until well-established), discrimination (pricing issues and refusal of necessary operational support systems (OSS)) and abusive prices (as set forth in the Access Notice abusive prices may be excessive, predatory or not allow sufficient competitor margin (price squeezes)).[164]

Confirming the assertion of the Working Document, the Communication found an existing right to the shared access form of unbundling in the Voice Telephony Directive as well as the Interconnection Directive.[165] Full physical unbundling was stated not to be required under the existing EU regulatory framework. Bit stream unbundling was not specifically required either, but the Communication asserted that regulatory non-discrimination might cover the situation and require incumbents to provide this type of wholesale service in a similar fashion to that provided to its own subsidiary, if any.[166]

Unbundling without collocation being useless, the Communication would have national authorities require it, clarifying the implication of the Working Document that the current EU framework required collocation itself.[167] If incumbents plead that there is not adequate available space to accommodate competitor collocation (a very likely plea in spite of the fact that switch digitalisation has largely emptied local exchanges by dramatically shrinking the size of switches), the Communication calls for consideration of "virtual collocation." That is incumbents would be required to provide free transmission (and perhaps

---

[161] *Ibid.,* §4.1.
[162] *Ibid.*
[163] *Ibid.*
[164] *Ibid.,* §4.2.
[165] *Ibid.,* §5.2.
[166] *Ibid.,* §5.3.
[167] *Ibid.,* §5.5.

free collocation) to local exchanges where space does exist, certainly an incentive for incumbents not to invent space restrictions. The European Commission and/or national regulators might should consider requiring spot inspections as well to ensure that space limitations in fact exist when pled by incumbents. A healthy degree of scepticism is in order for these type of pleas.

Other policing duties are foreseen for national regulators, including an obligation to require that "pricing rules should ensure that the incumbent operator is able to cover its relevant costs plus a reasonable return;" and that "pricing of local loops should be compatible with the aim of fostering fair and sustainable competition, and providing efficient investment incentives in alternative local access network infrastructure"[168], the Communication asserting that such prices can be obtained by a system based on "current costs."[169] The Communication's recognition that the incumbent can recover its costs plus a reasonable profit is in line with the EU's interconnetion pricing principles, but does not seem to square with the Communication's earlier assertion that non-discriminatory internal transfer prices are to be used. Which is it, internal prices or prices with a reasonable profit? It may be that the Communication's apparently contradictory pricing principles reflect divisions within the European Commission.

2. The Unbundling Recommendation

The Unbundling Recommendation itself presents a few surprises, beginning with its format. Previous European Commission Recommendations were styled much like Commission communications or green papers. The Unbundling Recommendation looks like a directive, with recitals and formal operative articles. The only thing separating it from a European Commission directive issued under Treaty Article 86 is that in the place of ordering Member States to take certain actions ("Member States shall . . .") the Unbundling Recommendation couches its operative portions in the form of recommendations ("It is recommended that Member States . . ."). Perhaps this will be the format employed in all of the European Commission's future recommendations as it puts into effect its stated intention to rely more on soft law. Perhaps the innovative format was selected especially for this recommendation. It could be a not too subtle message to Member States and incumbent telcos. All it would take would be a change to "shall" and the European Commission could make its recommendation mandatory immediately under its Treaty Article 86 power.

The Recommendation's "recitals" note the Lisbon Summit's conclusions and the assumed link between unbundling and lower cost Internet provision.[170] The assumption of the Communication is repeated that entrants are unable to provide alternative infrastructure because the incumbents "rolled out their old

---

[168] *Bronner* Judgment, §6.
[169] *Ibid.*, fn. 18.
[170] Local Loop Unbundling Recommendation, *supra* note 140, recital 1.

copper local access networks over significant periods of time protected by exclusive rights and were able to fund its investment costs through monopoly rents."[171] The problem of incumbent delays in offering their own broadband services was noted.[172] Such delays are indeed unconscionable. Incumbents withhold new technologies to avoid "cannibalising" revenue from leased lines and such obsolete services as ISDN. Not only is this a blatant violation of EU competition law (giving the European Commission perfect justification to demand unbundling), it is also stupid from a business standpoint. If incumbents do not embrace and offer better and lower priced services, their competitors will. Market forces demand this.[173]

The Recitals also dealt with the tricky issue of universal service provision by noting that an incumbent operator will fulfil its universal service obligation to a particular end-user when that "customer decides to enter into a contractual agreement with a new entrant for exclusive provision of services by means of full unbundled local loop." The use of the phrase exclusive provision might need further explanation. Incumbents are sure to raise questions about what happens if an end-user orders a second (universal service) line then requests it to be unbundled for a competitor, about what happens if a competitor receives access to a shared access line and then the end-user cancels the remaining voice subscription with the incumbent, and so forth. Even if Member States adopt the Recommendation, there will be much to do regarding interpretation and implementation.

The operative part of the Recommendation is in line with the Working Document and the Communication. It is recommended that Member States mandate full physical unbundling of the local loop by 31 December 2000.[174] The positions of the European Commission regarding shared access (already required under the Voice Telephony Directive) and bit stream unbundling (already required for incumbents providing broadband services under the Treaty prohibition against discrimination) are reiterated.[175] More importantly, the principle of internal non-discrimination is to be imposed. Incumbents are to make new service roll-outs, access to local loops, availability of collocation space, as well as "provision of leased transmission capacity for access to collocation sites, ordering, provisioning, quality and maintenance procedures" available to requesting competitors "with the same conditions and time scales"[176] provided to themselves.

Despite this imposition of internal non-discrimination, including prices,[177] the Recommendation goes on to recommend that cost-oriented prices be used

---

[171] *Ibid.*, recital 6.

[172] *Ibid.*, recital 9.

[173] If these incumbent telcos had been incumbent transport providers at the start of the 20th Century, they doubtless would have fought against the introduction of the automobile in order to avoid cannibalising buggy whip revenues.

[174] *Ibid.*, art. 1.2. "Without prejudice to the application of Community competition rules . . .", a rather pointed reminder of the attitude of Competition Directorate-General regarding unbundling.

[175] *Ibid.*, art. 1.3.

[176] *Ibid.*, art. 1.4.

[177] *Ibid.*, art 1.7.

for lease of local loops,[178] presumably including a reasonable profit as called for in the Communication as well as in Recital 13 of the Recommendation itself. Current costs consisting of "the costs of building an efficient modern equivalent infrastructure and providing such a service today",[179] a type of long run incremental costing (LRIC) and resultant pricing is recommended to be used for unbundled local loop prices.

The Recommendation would change existing EU interconnection requirements. The Interconnection Directive requires incumbent operators to "meet all reasonable requests for access to the network including access at points other than the network termination points offered to the majority of end-users."[180] The Recommendation states that physical access (a type of interconnection) "should be provided to any feasible termination point"[181] of the local loop, language reminiscent of both the US Telecommunications Act of 1996 and the WTO Regulatory Reference Paper. In an attempt to head off inevitable incumbent attempts to restrict uses of unbundled local loops, the Recommendation would not allow any regulatory restrictions on entrant use of loops for DSL services, and any "network integrity" restrictions must be non-discriminatory and objectively justified in advance of any imposed restrictions.[182]

Incumbents are to make a reference unbundling offer, much like that currently required for interconnection, and ideally post it on the Internet.[183] An attached Annex gives a list of what the European Commission considered to be appropriate to include within the reference unbundling offer, including conditions and prices for shared access and full physical loops, collocation conditions and availability, OSS prices and conditions, and in short everything entrants might need to obtain and use full or shared loops.

3. The Proposed Unbundling Regulation

Perhaps it should not be surprising that the European Commission did not wait and study whether its unbundling recommendation was effective before taking further action. The European Council had endorsed the unbundling policy and Member States were not noticeably improving their glacial pace towards implementing unbundling. The UK stands out in that regard with Oftel endorsing a committee-laden process that would delay by at least eighteen months a requirement that BT actually offer unbundled loops.

When the European Commission unveiled its new proposed telecoms directives in July 2000, there was an additional piece of proposed legislation: a proposed unbundling regulation.[184] From the standpoint of the European

---

[178] *Ibid.*, arts. 1.6 and 1.8.   [179] *Ibid.*, fn. 15.
[180] Interconnection Directive, *supra* n. 1, art. 4.2.
[181] Local Loop Unbundling Recommendation, *supra* n. 140, art. 1.10.
[182] *Ibid.*, art. 1.11.   [183] *Ibid.*, art. 1.12.
[184] Proposal for a Regulation of the European Parliament and of the Council on Unbundled Access to the Local Loop Brussels, 12 July 2000 COM (2000) 394. <http://europa.eu.int/comm /information_society/policy/framework/pdf/com2000394_en.pdf>.

Commission, there were several advantages to a regulation over a directive. Directives can take a long time to pass the co-decision process involving the European Commission, Council and Parliament. After passage, there is a further delay while Member States enact the directive. Then there is a further possibility of inconsistent application and interpretation of the directive in different Member States. On the other hand, a regulation can be passed quickly, requiring unanimous approval of the European Council (which should be forthcoming if the Council lives up to its Lisbon declarations), and approval of the European Parliament. Once passed, the Regulation would be immediately effective directly throughout the EU. The proposal itself offered another rationale; national regulatory authorities wanted a stronger legal basis to require unbundling than a Commission recommendation.[185]

The proposed Regulation is similar to the Unbundling Recommendation. A departure from the unbundling rules envisioned by the 1999 Review is that the unbundling requirements (at cost-oriented prices) will apply to all operators with significant market power (SMP), not just to dominant operators.[186] There is also a difference with the Unbundling Recommendation in that the proposed Regulation would only require full physical unbundling and shared access. Bit stream unbundling is not specifically required. Given the European Commission's position that bit stream unbundling is already required under EU competition law, perhaps the European Commission did not see a specification of bit stream unbundling as necessary.

SMP providers would be required to "make available to third parties, by 31 December 2000 at the latest, unbundled access to the local loop".[187] This raises a question as to what is meant by "make available." Does this mean the loops must be ready for lease by competitors? Is this no more than a requirement to publish an offer (a requirement specifically imposed in article 3.2)? The matter is further muddied by the fact that the publication requirement is the same date (31 December) that the loops are to be made available. Certainly incumbents can do better than the foot dragging they have engaged in, but the European Commission should be more specific as to exactly what it expects the incumbents to provide and when. Again consistent with the Recommendation, internal non-discrimination would be required.

Collocation duties would be imposed on SMP operators as would a specific duty to "provide physical access for third parties to any technically feasible point of the copper local loop or sub-loop where the new entrant can collocate and connect its own network equipment and facilities".[188] This is a significant extension of unbundling duties and may prove useful to entrants. ADSL is distance and medium sensitive. If a local exchange is over three to five kilometres from an end-user, ADSL service provision becomes problematic. Putting DSL

---

[185] *Ibid.*, Explanatory Memorandum.
[186] *Ibid.*, arts. 1.1 and 4.1.
[187] *Ibid.*, art. 3.1.
[188] *Ibid.*, art. 3.2.

equipment closer to end-users than the local exchange may increase potential customers. Furthermore, as ADSL can only be provided over a copper loop, fibre links between the end-user and the local exchange could defeat service provision. Requiring sub-loop unbundling should reduce incentives for incumbent to place fibre solely to defeat competitor DSL provision.

Loop prices are to be such as will "foster fair and sustainable competition".[189] This is fleshed out in the Recitals to mean that regulators are to ensure that price squeezes do not occur.[190]

VI. CONCLUSION

Given the cumbersome nature of the EU legislative process, it is understandable that the European Commission is giving into the temptation to take the short cut of soft law to achieve its goals. The results may not be bad, but acting outside of normal channels can lead to even more cynicism about regulation. At a minimum, the European Commission should ensure that high level political support exists for its programme and that all industry participants, as well as users are given adequate opportunity to be heard regarding contemplated recommendations or guidelines. Recommendations should be followed up by hard law wherever possible. This appears to be what the European Commission has done with its proposed Unbundling Regulation. Now results should be judged.

---

[189] *Ibid.*, art. 4.1.
[190] *Ibid.*, recital 8.

13

The EU Approach to the Internet and Data Protection

I. INTRODUCTION

T HE INTERNET KNOWS no boundaries. This, like all clichés, has some truth behind it, but as an international phenomenon, it can also be said that the Internet is subject to an infinite number of regulators. Although the Internet has benefited from relatively light regulation, at least when compared with traditional telecommunications, this advantage may change as the presence and power of the Internet grows. With that in mind, it is useful to examine how EU institutions are approaching the Internet and privacy issues.

II. THE INFORMATION SOCIETY

In the early days of the Internet, US commentators and public policy officials used a transport metaphor to describe the Internet: the Information Superhighway.[1] EU policy discussions, however, typically employed a different term: the Information Society. The two different labels can be viewed as a metaphor itself of the differences between the US and the EU.

In broad terms, the EU views the Internet as a part of the overall information revolution or general growth of digital devices and applications in all aspects of business and personal life. This revolution is causing related changes in commercial transactions, employment, living conditions, and cultural relations: i.e., a fundamental "societal" change. These are all factors that the EU has a responsibility to consider under the basic tenets of the Treaty of Rome. While there is a recognition in EU institutions that the information revolution yields commercial benefits, EU officials, as well as many ordinary Europeans, wish to consider the effect of this revolution on society as a whole.

---

[1] There is some confusion, perhaps intentional on the part of politicians, between the Internet, which actually dates back to before 1969 and the "Information Superhighway," a term that first appeared in the US in the early 1990s. The Superhighway proponents had something other than the Internet in mind. It would have been constructed and operated by the US government, and most certainly was not the Internet, which had been in existence in various forms since before 1969. The FCC's *Computer Inquiry 1* Order was released in 1969, imposing the enhanced service provider exemption, and thereby effectively keeping the Internet and other data service provision free from regulation (long before Al Gore or Reed Hundt claimed to have respectively taken the initiative to create the Internet or decide that it would be unregulated). Statements by these two politicians, made as recently as 1999, demonstrate a continued belief in this US government run boondoggle.

This may help explain why Europe has not embraced the Internet as enthusiastically as the US. Of course, this is not the sole answer. In parts of Europe, such as the Nordic region, people are socially conscious while at the same time are great users of the Internet. The fact that flat rate dial up Internet access is much more prevalent in the US as opposed to Europe where usage based charges for basic telephone calls are the norm may also be part of the explanation. Whatever factors may be involved in differing levels of Internet penetration and usage between the US and the EU, the term "Information Society" is illustrative of the EU policy approach. Examination of some EU initiatives affecting the Internet show this policy in action.

III. THE INTERNET TELEPHONY NOTICE

In the time period before full liberalisation of telecommunications service in the EU on 1 January 1998, innovative operators tried to find ways to offer services that would compete with incumbent operators. As might be expected, incumbent operators also tried to maintain their monopolies for as long as possible. As discussed in Chapter 11, *supra*, the European Commission's progressive liberalisation programme first opened such areas as value added telecommunications services to competition. Member States could reserve basic voice telephony service as a monopoly until 1 January 1998, longer for certain "lesser developed" Member States.

During this pre-liberalisation period, questions arose about telecommunications services using the Internet: was this an area open for competition? Could incumbent operators claim that Internet telephony violated their remaining monopoly rights? Some nations, particularly developing nations, still try to prohibit Internet telephony. Beyond that was another question more fraught with policy implications, should Internet telephony, and therefore Internet provision itself, be regulated like the telephone industry? The European Commission attempted to address these questions in its Internet Telephony Notice[2] published in the early part of 1998. A notice is a statement of European Commission policy, no more. Nevertheless, it is important as a policy statement, giving guidance as to how the European Commission might decide on matters brought before it.

The European Commission's starting point was that all telecommunications services other than basic voice and public networks were considered competitive, even before the date of full liberalisation. In fact by the time the Internet Telephony Notice was published, even the remaining legal monopolies in basic voice and public networks had been abolished in most of the EU. The definition of "voice telephony" contained in several of the liberalisation directives was,

---

[2] Commission Notice concerning the Status of voice communications on Internet under community law and, in particular, pursuant to the Services Directive [1998] OJ C6/4 [hereinafter Internet Telephony Notice] <http://europa.eu.int/comm/competition/liberalization/legislation/voice_en.html>.

however, not a dead letter, as might be expected after full liberalisation had erased the possibility of incumbent operators continuing to operate as the sole provider of basic voice telephony. The Internet Telephony Notice quoted the Telecommunications Services Directive definition of voice telephony as follows:

". . . the commercial provision for the public of the direct transport and switching of speech in real-time between public switched termination points, enabling any user to use equipment connected to such a network termination point in order to communicate with another termination point."[3]

Accordingly, the Internet Telephony Notice asserted that *all* of the elements of basic voice telephony—(1) commercial service (primary focus of firm to be regulated is voice telephony); (2) switching; (3) real time provision; and (4) equipment connected to network termination points—must be present to consider a proposed telecommunications service as basic voice and therefore liable to be reserved for the dominant telecommunications provider by a Member State prior to the introduction of full telecommunications competition in January 1998.[4]

Pure Internet telephony, that is computer-to-computer, might not be considered switched, and therefore not meet this definition of basic voice. Such computer-to-computer telephony would also not meet the test of allowing the user to communicate with another termination point, defined as another point on the network and not another computer. The connection would take place in the Internet rather than at a switched network termination point.

Furthermore, it might be questionable whether the "real-time" requirement was met. The Notice considered that the then current state of Internet telephony involved significant time delays. It should be noted that Internet telephony technology has improved significantly, even by the time the Notice was published. There have been more improvements since, however, even with better quality, there will always be a slight, but perhaps imperceptible delay in speech. This is because of the way Internet telephony works. The bits of the telephone conversation enter a computer's RAM where a temporary recording is made before the bits are transferred out of RAM and converted to analogue speech. This is the same temporary recording that takes place whenever one views anything that is online, and it is this temporary recording that has caused some policy makers to consider that the mere act of viewing online materials might constitute copying. More fundamentally, packet switching involving sending bursts of packets through a network was never designed to handle two way voice communications. Packet switching is designed to allow for dropped packets; this matters little as long as all the data reaches the destination and can be

[3] Commission Directive of 28 June 1990 on competition in the markets for telecommunications services 90/388/EEC [1991] OJ L192/10, art. 1(1) [hereinafter Telecommunications Services Directive].

[4] Communication by the Commission to the European Parliament and the Council on the Status and Implementation of Directive 90/388/EEC on Competition in the Markets for Telecommunications Services, COM (95) 113 final 4 April 1995 at 14.

reassembled there. Voice conversations are different. Therefore, the quality of service or reliability of two way voice Internet services will not approach that of switched voice service for the foreseeable future.[5]

The European Commission did not find the last requirement of basic voice telephony either, that of a commercial service. The Notice stated that Internet telephony must be the main enterprise involved in a commercial offering, and it must hold itself out as such. At the time the Notice was published, there were relatively few Internet telephony providers so directed. The market has changed since then, and there are numerous Internet telephony providers in Europe.[6] Many of these providers are also focusing on PSTN to PSTN calling. This begins to look very much like basic voice telephony as defined by the European Commission. Indeed, the Notice itself stated that technical and commercial changes might cause it to re-examine its position in the future.

The consequences of categorising Internet telephony as a non-basic voice service went beyond the mere allowance of Internet telephony as an already liberalised service, especially as most EU Member States had full liberalisation in January 1998. Rather, as Internet telephony operators were not providing basic voice service, they did not have to comply with licensing requirements designed for voice telephony operators or contribute to any universal service fund. Although universal service funds and therefore fees turned out to be a dead letter in the EU (except for France) the intent of the European Commission was clearly to foster Internet telephony development by exempting it from certain regulatory burdens.

IV. DATA PROTECTION AND PRIVACY

A. Why Privacy Issues are so Important

A major issue regarding deployment of information technologies is the extent to which personal privacy may be compromised as a result. Indeed, the future of electronic commerce may ride on convincing consumers that their transactions are secure and private. It is also a concern of e-commerce providers that they stay within the bounds of the law, but can also make appropriate use of data gathered through their operations for marketing purposes. The EU has taken the world-wide lead in implementing a system designed to protect personal data from unwelcome use or dissemination. Privacy issues are also an area that may cause potential trade disputes between EU Member States and other countries, particularly the US, in the future. To date, the signs are encouraging that the EU

[5] See, e.g., Leslie Walker, "Your Desktop Yell-o-Phone", *The Washington Post*, 16 March 2000, at E01; Steve Rosenbush and Bruce Einhorn, "The Talking Internet", *Business Week*, 1 May 2000, ("Calls over the traditional system are completed on the first attempt 99.999 per cent of the time, and even if the power goes out, the network continues to work. The Internet, or people's connections to the Net, fail all the time—and if the power goes out, so does a phone link to the Net.")
[6] See, e.g., Stephen Baker, "Europe Swoons for Voice-on-the-Net", *Business Week*, 1 May 2000.

and the US are working together to find ways for the EU privacy requirements to be met even without binding US law in the area.[7]

With the advent of the Internet and the resultant explosion of communications involving personal data (especially through e-commerce activities), the need for European (and elsewhere for that matter) to deal with privacy in a coherent way grows exponentially each day. Indeed, as telecommunications competition and the number of providers increase, protecting consumers' privacy rights becomes a daunting challenge. The real challenge for policy makers, however, is how they should balance legitimate and important privacy considerations against the long-standing policy goals of ensuring secure and reliable telecommunications services to both industry and individuals.

B. The Telecommunications Data Protection Directive

There are currently two EU data protection directives. The most recently adopted is the Telecommunications Data Protection Directive.[8] As the requirements of the previously adopted EU Data Protection Directive were implemented, it become increasingly important to fill in the gaps in that directive regarding telecommunications related personal data. Although the Telecommunications Data Protection Directive is ostensibly directed at telephony, it also covers many data transfers related to the Internet and thus is worth examining in some detail.

The Telecommunications Data Protection Directive should be seen as an extension of and complementary to the EU Data Protection Directive.[9] Indeed,

---

[7] See generally, W.S. Blackmer, "Making the Web Less Sticky, Privacy and Consumer Protection in Electronic Commerce", (1999) 6 *Telecommunications & Space Law Journal* 179; K. Harvey, "Privacy and Cultural Geography in the Emerging Online World", (1999) 6 Telecommunications & Space Law Journal 233.

[8] Directive 97/66/EC of the European Parliament and of the Council of 15 December 1997 concerning the processing of personal data and the protection of privacy in the telecommunications sector, [1998] OJ L24/1 [hereinafter Telecommunications Data Protection Directive]. < http://www.ispo.cec.be/infosoc/telecompolicy/en/9766en.pdf>. When this directive was proposed, it contained a reference to ISDN in its title. Therefore, the proposal was often popularly called "the Proposed ISDN Directive." The Telecommunications Data Protection Directive concerns all types of telecommunications traffic and data; it is not restricted to ISDN, though the recitals to the Directive recognised that the growth of digital telecommunications services, including ISDN, increased the possibility of gathering sensitive information and correspondingly the need for a directive in this area. The Directive, as finally adopted, removed the specific reference to ISDN in its title. This was fortunate especially regarding popular understanding of the Directive, as it is not restricted to ISDN services. ISDN has never received mass market acceptance, however, telephone companies may have at last found a market for ISDN service as an Internet access service that is faster than PSTN dial-up access. This will likely be a narrow market window as broadband services such as DSL and cable modem service now making their presence felt on the market enable Internet access at speeds much faster than ISDN.

[9] Directive 95/46/EC of the European Parliament and of the Council of 24 October 1995 on the protection of individuals with regard to the processing of personal data and on the free movement of such data, [1995] OJ L281/31 [hereinafter EU Data Protection Directive] <http://158.169.50.95:10080/legal/en/dataprot/directiv/directiv.html>.

it is impossible to fully analyse the Telecommunications Data Protection Directive without reference to the EU Data Protection Directive[10] as some key terms are not defined in the former.

Telecommunications raises particular privacy concerns both for a standpoint of possible intrusion into one's life and also as a means of providing insight into one's habits, commercial transactions, and life in general. Due to these special considerations, the requirements of the EU Data Protection Directive needed to be particularised and complemented through a separate Telecommunications Data Protection Directive.[11] In addition, it was thought necessary to act via a harmonisation directive so that properly utilised telecommunications data and affected telecommunications equipment may move freely through the EU.[12] The Telecommunications Data Protection Directive may also be viewed as a fleshing out of earlier legislation recognising that Member States can take steps to protect the telecommunications data of end-users in the then-emerging competitive environment.[13]

1. Rights of "Natural" and "Legal" Persons

The first Article of the Telecommunications Data Protection Directive recognised a difference between the level of protection granted to natural persons and legal persons, that is businesses such as corporations.[14] As might be expected, natural persons were assumed to have a greater interest in the protection of privacy and receive a correspondingly higher degree of protection by the Directive. Indeed, it was specifically stated that the Directive should not be interpreted so as to expand the privacy rights of businesses beyond that required under the Data Protection Directive.[15] Nevertheless, the "legitimate interests"[16] of business telephone customers are to be protected, and business customers are included within the general definition of "subscriber"[17] qualifying for protection under the Directive.

The Telecommunications Data Protection Directive differentiated telecommunications subscribers and users, with the former (perhaps best considered as a bill payer) having contracts with a public telecoms service provider, and the later constituting any natural person who uses telecommunication services,[18]

---

[10] The following discussion will focus on the Telecommunications Data Protection Directive. When necessary, reference is made to the basic EU Data Protection Directive. All references to the EU Data Protection Directive are identified as such.

[11] Telecommunications Data Protection Directive, *supra* n. 8, art. 1.2.

[12] *Ibid.*, art. 1.1.

[13] Directive 97/33/EC of the European Parliament and of the Council of 30 June 1997 on interconnection in telecommunications ensuring universal service and interoperability through application of the principles on open network provision (ONP), art 10(d), [1997] OJ L199/32 [hereinafter Interconnection Directive].

[14] Telecommunications Data Protection Directive, *supra* n. 8, art. 1.1.

[15] *Ibid.*, recital 13.

[16] *Ibid.*, art. 1.2

[17] *Ibid.*, art 2(a).

[18] *Ibid.*, art 2(a)-(b).

presumably from any telephone. The definitions also repeat with slight variation the definitions of "public telecommunications network" and "telecommunications service" found in the European Commission's Telecommunications
Services Directive.[19] These are the only terms that are specifically defined; by
implication definitions from the EU Data Protection Directive must be used to
fill in the gaps.

2. State Actions

There was an important exception to the scope of the Telecommunications
Data Protection Directive set forth in Article One. That is an exception resulting from "activities concerning public security, defence, State security (including the economic well-being of the State when the activities relate to State
security matters) and the activities of the State in areas of criminal law."[20] In
other words, the State can still access telephone records, record numbers called
by a subscriber (a device capable of such recording is called a pen register; the
gathering of such information is now much easier through use of digital networks presenting calling and called line identification information) or intercept
telephone conversations themselves (a wiretap), presumably if properly
required by authorities in individual Member States. The reference to "economic well-being" is puzzling. Is this an endorsement of state sponsored economic espionage? If so, the EU allegations over the possibility that the US has
engaged in such spying seem a bit overblown.[21]

3. Personal Data and Digital Concerns

Article Three stated that the Telecommunications Data Protection Directive
applied to the processing of personal data in connection with the provision of
telecommunications services.[22] There was a vestigial reference to services provided "in particular via" ISDN and public digital mobile networks. The
Directive drafters had in mind the capabilities afforded by digital signalling
within telecommunication network operations.

---

[19] Telecommunications Services Directive, *supra* n.3.

[20] Telecommunications Data Protection Directive, *supra* n. 8, art. 1.3.

[21] European Parliament Working Document, An Appraisal of Technologies for Political Control,
6 January 1998 <http://www.aclu.org/echelonwatch/index.html> and <http://home.icdc.com/
~paulwolf/eu_stoa.htm>. *See* also Suzanne Daley, "An Electronic Spy Scare is Alarming Europe,"
New York Times, 24 Feb. 2000 <http://www.nytimes.com/library/tech/00/02/biztech/articles/
24spy.html>. While contending that European industry had little worth stealing, former CIA
Director James Woolsey nevertheless confirmed the existence of US industrial espionage and
claimed it was limited to ferreting out illegal activities like bribery by non-US companies. Duncan
Campbell, "Former CIA Director Says US Economic Spying Targets 'European Bribery' ", *Telepolis*,
12 March 2000, <http://www.heise.de/tp/deutsch/special/ech/6662/1.html>. A transcript of
Woolsey's remarks is posted at <http://cryptome.org/echelon-cia.htm>.

[22] *Ibid.*, art. 3.1.

The deployment of digital networks has facilitated use of signalling system seven (SS7), also sometimes designated as common channel signalling, and a corresponding growth of innovative and cost savings services by telecommunication operators. Simply put, SS7 works by sending an instantaneous signal when a number is dialled indicating the telephone number of the calling party (referred to as calling-line identification or CLI) as well as the intended destination of the call (connected line identification). This signal can go to a signalling control point or to the local exchange of the intended destination, indicated by geographic telephone numbers. An instantaneous check occurs whereby it can be determined whether the destination line is already engaged or otherwise unavailable. If the destination line is available, a message is sent back to the originating local exchange to put the call through. Until then the actual connection and call are not routed through the telecommunication network, saving connections in the network and correspondingly permitting greater network efficiency. SS7 makes available other service options that can be programmed by the telecoms operator or the end-user. For example, calls to a particular telephone number may by forwarded on a per-call or permanent basis to another number. When the SS7 signal is sent by the calling party, the destination local exchange returns a message that calls are forwarded to another location. The signal automatically routes to the new destination, and after receiving clearance, releases the call. This is only one example. Many other service options are possible: call waiting (in which the parties to a telephone conversation can receive a signal that another call is being made to their number, thereby giving the called party an option as to which call to take); three-way (or more) conference calling; voice mail; call back; and perhaps most importantly from a privacy standpoint, the ability of called parties to receive information about the calling party (sometimes referred to as caller identification or caller ID).

The Telecommunications Data Protection Directive recognised the special privacy concerns presented by the innovative services made possible by digital networks and SS7, and correspondingly placed burdens on digital network operators of requirements regarding presentation and restriction of calling and connected line identification, call tracing, and restrictions on automatic call forwarding.[23] These restrictions, represented by Directive articles eight, nine, and ten, could also apply to analogue exchanges, but only if such restrictions were technically possible and did "not require a disproportionate economic effort". It would be safe to assume that there would not be widespread deployment of the services in question in a network containing analogue exchanges.

Telecommunications service providers must take appropriate technical and organisational steps to protect the security of communications. Network providers may be required to make engineering changes to achieve an acceptable degree of security. Not every security measure is necessary; a balancing of the

---

[23] European Parliament Working Document, An Appraisal of Technologies for Political Control, 6 January 1998, art. 3.2.

costs of a particular measure and its expected result in meeting risks may be weighed. Service providers must notify subscribers of particular known security risks.[24]

4. Interceptions: Wiretapping and Recording

A security risk that comes immediately to mind is interception of communications. The Directive required Member States to "prohibit listening, tapping, storage; or other kinds of interception or surveillance or communications by others than users, without the consent of the users concerned, except when legally authorized".[25] Left unresolved by this list is the issue of user recording: may a user legally record conversations with another party without the other party's consent? Under US Federal Law, one party consent is acceptable,[26] but some individual US states have imposed a requirement that both parties to a telephone conversation consent to recording before it may be legally accomplished.[27] Given that the directive employs the plural "users" regarding consent to recording, it could be argued that the Directive required two party consent.

Another controversial area regarding interception and recording of telephone conversations is in the workplace. Employers may wish to monitor employee communications, including e-mail. This raises an interesting question about the scope of the Telecommunications Data Protection Directive; were e-mail communications included? Article five stated that "communications by means of a public telecommunications network and publicly available telecommunications services" should be protected from unauthorised interception.[28] "Communications" was not specifically defined, but e-mail can be accomplished via the public network and through publicly available telecommunication services. Interactive television and video on demand are noted as developing telecommunications technologies,[30] so perhaps e-mail should also be included within the definition of "communications." From a practical standpoint, e-mail is increasingly replacing fax as a communications choice. As with telephone monitoring, employer interception and use of employee e-mail raises privacy and labour law issues. Article 5.2 impliedly allows employer interception of employee communications (and indeed customer conversations as well) if such interception or recording is allowed under individual Member State law.[31]

---

[24] *Ibid.*, art. 4.

[25] *Ibid.*, art. 5.1

[26] Electronic Communications Privacy Act of 1986, 18 U.S.C. §2511(2)(d).

[27] It is the Maryland requirement of two party consent that is at issue in the prosecution of Linda Tripp for recording her telephone conversations with Monica Lewinsky.

[28] The Internet Telephony Notice, *supra* n. 2, however, opined that a communication accomplished on two computers does not utilise the public telecommunications network.

[30] Telecommunications Data Protection Directive, *supra* n. 8, recital 10.

[31] *Ibid.*, art. 5.2.

5. *Provider Processing of Telecoms Data—Consent*

The Telecommunications Data Protection Directive had a requirement that telecommunications network and service providers were to erase subscriber related traffic data upon completion of a call.[32] It was, however, recognised that this would make it impossible to bill for calls as well as for telecommunications providers to otherwise use call data legitimately. Therefore, the obligation to erase was made subject to an exception, lasting for the period during which bills may be challenged or payment sought by legal means (perhaps the statute of limitations for collection of debts), for the purpose of subscriber billing and interconnection payments.[33]

There was a further exception: the telecommunications provider may process call data for "the purpose of marketing its own telecommunications services " if the subscriber has given consent.[34] This is an issue that has been the subject of regulatory proceedings in the US before the FCC, and was mentioned in the US Telecommunications Act of 1996.[35]

The term "consent" is not defined in the Directive. By implication, the EU Data Protection Directive should be consulted to fill this gap, and supplies a definition as: "'the data subject's consent' shall mean any freely given specific and informed indication of his wishes by which the data subject signifies his agreement to personal data relating to him being processed."[36] The reference to "personal data" requires further examination, as the EU Data Protection Directive contains a specific definition for this term:

> " 'personal data' shall mean any information relating to an identified or identifiable natural person ('data subject'); an identifiable person is one who can be identified, directly or indirectly; in particular by reference to an identification number or to one or more factors specific to his physical, physiological, mental, economic, cultural or social identity."[37]

Arguably telecommunications call data would fall within this definition of personal data. There are certain types of personal data involving "racial or ethnic origin, political opinions, religious or philosophical beliefs; trade-union membership, and . . . health or sex life"[38] for which heightened protection was mandated by the EU Data Protection Directive, and for use of which "explicit consent" of the subject must be obtained before the data may be processed.[39] Presumably, call data would not fall under this more restrictive designation, and could be processed without the explicit consent of the subscriber. There was fur-

---

[32] Telecommunications Data Protection Directive, *supra* n. 8, recital 10, art. 6.
[33] *Ibid.*, art. 6.2.
[34] *Ibid.*, art. 6.3.
[35] 47 U.S.C. § 222.
[36] EU Data Protection Directive, *supra* n. 9, art. 2(h).
[37] *Ibid.*, art. 2(h).
[38] *Ibid.*, art. 8.1.
[39] *Ibid.*, art. 8.2(a).

ther guidance in the recitals of the Telecommunications Data Protection Directive.

> "[A]ny further processing which the provider of the publicly available telecommunications services may want to perform for the marketing of its own telecommunications services may only be allowed if the subscriber has agreed to this on the basis of accurate and full information given by the provider of the publicly available telecommunications services about the types of further processing he intends to perform."[40]

From this it may be concluded that telecoms providers have a duty to notify subscribers if they intend to process individual call data for sales or other promotional efforts in telecommunications service markets. The Telecommunications Data Protection Directive did not specify how subscribers were to be notified; a system such as bill inserts should be acceptable. Likewise, the Directive did not specify how subscribers were to signify agreement to the telecommunications provider processing the data for marketing purposes. Procedures already established under the EU Data Protection Directive and methods for determining agreement under the general law of individual Member States were to be consulted.

The Directive contained a further provision concerning "marketing processing" conducted by telecommunication providers. To the extent providers currently (on the date the Directive entered into effect in the Member State concerned) used subscriber calling data for marketing purposes, they might continue to do so.[41] Subscribers were to be informed of the processing (it was not specified whether the Member State or the provider is to perform the notification and by what means) and given an opportunity to object. "[I]f they do not express their dissent within a period to be determined by the Member State, they shall be deemed to have given their consent."[42] Presumably, new subscribers would be subject to the general consent provisions of Article 6.2.

Further safeguarding the processing of telecoms data was the requirement that access to such information be restricted to those with a need to know, that is personnel of telecommunications providers involved with billing, fraud detection, marketing, etc.[43] Authorities charged with settling billing or interconnection disputes might also access traffic data.[44]

6. Billing and Caller ID

The Telecommunications Data Protection Directive gave subscribers themselves the right to receive itemised bills; it was not specified to what level the

---

[40] Telecommunications Data Protection Directive, *supra* n. 8, recital 17.
[41] *Ibid.*, art 15.2.
[42] *Ibid.*, art 15.2.
[43] *Ibid.*, art. 6.4.
[44] *Ibid.*, art. 6.5.

itemisation should extend.[45] It was left for national authorities to decide if itemisations should include national (long distance) as well as local calls, and the level of detail for each call (date and time call was placed, called party number or name, length of call in minutes or seconds, etc). Conversely, subscribers wishing to preserve the verification advantages of itemisation, whilst still protecting their privacy, may benefit from national requirements that subscribers can receive itemisation without a full accounting of numbers called—the final digits of numbers may be removed. Likewise, alternatives allowing for anonymous payment were to be encouraged such as prepaid telephone cards or payment of monthly bills by credit card.

Telecommunications organisations are subject to certain requirements imposed on an EU level (universal service requirements), including a duty to publish directories listing names and telephone numbers of subscribers.[46] The Telecommunications Data Protection Directive expanded this duty to require that subscriber data furnished through directories or "through directory enquiry services should be limited to what is necessary to identify a particular subscriber, unless the subscriber has given his unambiguous consent to the publication of additional personal data."[47] Subscribers (here limited to natural persons[48]) were given the right to request omission from the directory, to request that the address be omitted, to request that one's name not be presented in such a way that it reveals the sex of the subscriber ("where this is applicable linguistically"[49]) or to indicate that listing information was not to be used for direct marketing purposes. Article 11.1 stated that the omission is to be given free of charge, but this is immediately contradicted by the terms of article 11.2 stating that operators may charge for the privilege of non-published numbers. The payment is to be limited to the amount necessary to reimburse the telecoms operator for the actual expenses involved in removing the subscribers' data from directory listings, and in any event the amount may not be such that subscribers would be discouraged from removing their data if they so choose.[50]

Calling-line identification (caller ID) presents many privacy challenges. On the one hand, caller ID can be seen as privacy enhancing, facilitating the ability of individuals to be left alone from the unwanted intrusion of undesired calls. Caller ID can be compared to a peephole in a door, allowing subscribers to "see" who is calling before deciding whether to "open the door" to a telephone con-

---

[45] Telecommunications Data Protection Directive, *supra* n. 8, recital 17, art. 7.1. An obligation to submit itemised bills was also imposed on telecoms organisations by Council Directive 95/62/EEC of 13 December 1995 on the application of open network provision (ONP) to voice telephony, art. 15 [1995] OJ L321/6.

[46] Directive 98/10/EC of the European Parliament and of the Council of 26 February 1998 on the application of open network provision (ONP) to voice telephony and on universal service for telecommunications in a competitive environment [1998] OJ L101/24 art. 6 [hereinafter ONP Voice Telephony Directive].

[47] Telecommunications Data Protection Directive, *supra* n. 5, art. 11.1.

[48] *Ibid.*, art. 11.3.

[49] *Ibid.*, art. 11.1.

[50] *Ibid.*, art. 11.2.

versation. Those who engage in obscene or harassing telephone calls may be less inclined to place these calls if there is a reasonable probability that their victims may easily identify them and turn them over to the police. On the other hand, callers may wish to preserve the right to make certain calls anonymously or without disclosing information that could be used to track down their location. Particular examples of legitimate anonymity include the identity of callers to crisis hot lines who might be reluctant to call if they felt their identity could be traced and callers from domestic violence shelters who might be fearful that their abusers would find them if the telephone number could be easily traced.

The Telecommunications Data Protection Directive attempted to balance these interests, allowing caller ID, but at the same time preserving the rights of those who wish to remain anonymous. Callers were to be given an option (free of charge) on a per-call basis to block presentation of caller ID information to the called party; a similar right was to be given on a per-line basis.[51] That is, a subscriber was to have the right to decide that caller ID information would never be presented when calls were made. Likewise, called parties wishing to assure potential callers of anonymity could request that caller ID information not be presented to their numbers.[52] In recognition of the desire not to be bothered by anonymous calls, subscribers were to be given the right and easy ability to reject calls when the calling party had eliminated caller ID information.[53] This could result in a battle of blockers when the caller blocks delivery of the caller ID information, and the called party blocks calls not containing caller ID from being completed. The obligation to allow for these types of blocking extends to calls between EU Member States.[54] There was a similar blocking right given regarding receipt of calls automatically forwarded by a third party. Such calls could be rejected by the recipient free of charge.[55]

There are some circumstances where caller ID type services will be always necessary. One is where a subscriber requests call tracing to eliminate or prosecute harassing calls. Another is automatically locating the source of emergency calls. Callers in need of medical attention or police assistance may be incapable of identifying themselves or their location. Caller ID information can automatically display identity and location information. The Directive allowed exceptions to the caller ID rules for both of these circumstances.[56] The Directive also called for the EU promotion of harmonisation of equipment standards, presumably for customer equipment such as caller ID boxes, so that terminal equipment meeting these common standards may be sold throughout the EU.[57]

---

[51] Telecommunications Data Protection Directive, *supra* n. 8, art. 8.1.
[52] *Ibid.*, art. 8.2.
[53] *Ibid.*, art. 8.3.
[54] *Ibid.*, art. 8.5.
[55] *Ibid.*, art. 10.
[56] *Ibid.*, art. 9.
[57] *Ibid.*, art. 13

7. Telemarketing: The Right to be Left Alone

The Telecommunications Data Protection Directive divided telemarketing, viewed as direct marketing via unsolicited calls, into two types: automated calling systems and all other types.[58] Automated calling was any method without human intervention, specifically including fax transmissions, and was only to be allowed to subscribers who consented to receive such calls prior to the actual marketing call. Commercial e-mail solicitations, popularly known as spam, were not specifically mentioned. It could be argued that spam was included within the Directive's restrictions as e-mail is often a substitute for fax, and indeed e-mail offers greater automation and wider distribution opportunities than fax at a fraction of the cost. Nevertheless, the Directive placed the restriction specifically on use of automatic calling machines or faxes and not e-mail. The omission of e-mail from this section could only mean that Member States were not under an obligation to place the restrictions on spam; presumably Member States could place similar restrictions if desired. Of course, having restrictions on paper is one thing and enforcement is another. E-mail, and indeed all telecommunications, are notorious disrespecters of international borders.

For other direct marketing calls, Member States were given a choice of whether to require marketers to receive prior consent, or if telephone subscribers can be required to take affirmative steps indicating they do not wish to receive such marketing calls.[59] The EU Data Protection Directive specifically established a right to object to the processing of personal data for purposes of direct marketing.[60]

The European Court of Justice (ECJ) examined the issue of regulation of telemarketing in the case of *Alpine Investments*.[61] The Netherlands prohibited certain financial investment providers from directly contacting potential investors via telephone (cold calling) or in person without first receiving written permission. The prohibition, extending to cold calling any destination in Europe from the Netherlands, was challenged as a violation of the Treaty of Rome's guarantee of the right to provide services. The ECJ held that the prohibition violated Treaty Article 49,[62] but the restrictions were acceptable as a measure necessary to preserve the integrity of the financial services market.[63] Given the ECJ's deference to EU directives, it is likely that the telemarketing restrictions in the Telecommunications Data Protection Directive will withstand judicial scrutiny.

---

[58] Telecommunications Data Protection Directive, *supra* n. 8, art. 8.1, art. 12.1–12.2.
[59] *Ibid.*, art. 12.2.
[60] EU Data Protection Directive, *supra* n. 9, art. 14.
[61] Case C–384/93 *Alpine Investments* [1995] ECR I–1141.
[62] *Ibid.*, para. 39.
[63] *Ibid.*, para. 49.

8. Administrative Details

The remainder of the Telecommunications Data Protection Directive is taken up with administrative matters such as confirming that Member States may take measures to protect national security and enforce criminal law[64] (presumably through use of wiretaps or examining subscriber calling records) and ensuring that the directive is consistent with provisions on judicial remedies and establishment of the Working Party on the Protection of Individuals with regard to the Processing of Personal Data provided for the EU Data Protection Directive.[65]

Technological development, particularly in the converging area of telecommunications and information technologies, offers many opportunities for economic development and individual freedom. At the same time, these technologies offer unprecedented avenues for unwelcome intrusions into private matters. It is to be hoped that the EU is striking the proper balance between bringing the benefits of the telecommunications revolution to the people while preserving their right to be left alone.

V. EU E-COMMERCE REGULATION

Data protection and privacy are key issues involved with e-commerce. E-commerce itself, using the Internet to buy, sell and trade goods and services among consumers and businesses, is closely connected with the current success and future possibilities of the Internet. It is in the area of e-commerce that full application of Information Society principles may be observed, specifically in the proposed e-commerce Directive.[66] As might be expected, many of the current provisions of this proposed Directive are controversial. Consumer groups favour some provisions that industry opposes and vice versa. Since the EU political system is conducive to compromise, the final result will likely be totally pleasing to no single interest, but neither be totally objectionable. The proposed Directive is the first attempt by the EU, and indeed the first attempt by any significant political body, to comprehensively address the unique issues raised by e-commerce.

The first part of the proposed e-commerce Directive, like every other directive, contains policy statements that are not of the same authority as the operative part of directives, but are useful in interpretation. The recitals in the proposed e-commerce Directive contain in one place many of the current tenets of the Information Society. As might be expected, homage is paid to the

---

[64] Telecommunications Data Protection Directive, *supra* n. 8, art. 14.1.

[65] *Ibid.*, art. 14.2–14.3.

[66] Commission of the European Communities, Amended proposal for a European Parliament and Council Directive on certain legal aspects of electronic commerce in the Internal Market, COM(1999)427 final [hereinafter proposed e-commerce Directive].

possibilities of greater employment, economic growth, and increased "competitiveness of European industry, provided everyone has access to the Internet."[67] Just how everyone is supposed to gain access to the Internet is not further spelled out, nor do the operative portions of the proposed Directive offer any concrete proposals to increase Internet penetration and use.

A problem in any legislation dealing with e-commerce is how to define it. The proposed e-commerce Directive refers to an earlier directive[68] defining "Information Society service" as "any service normally provided for remuneration, at a distance, by electronic means and at the individual request of a recipient of services."[69] From this definition, it is questionable whether selling of goods, say books, would be considered an Information Society service so as to be covered by the proposed Directive. Helpfully, the next recital states that Information Society services "can, in particular, consist of selling goods on line."[70]

A. Taxation

An important consideration involved with e-commerce matters is taxation. The US Congress declared a temporary moratorium on any new taxes targeted at e-commerce activities.[71] Governments dependent on sales tax revenues or value added taxes, and that includes all EU Member States, are nervous that e-commerce will erode their revenue collections. On the other hand, e-commerce providers may be faced with a multiplicity of different tax requirements and regimes that may be expensive to comply with, even beyond the cost of the actual tax owed. E-commerce consumers may also wish to avoid payment of sales taxes by ordering on line, certainly a factor in the success of e-commerce. Perhaps wisely, the drafters of the proposed e-commerce Directive sidestepped this controversy by declaring that taxation issues were to be excluded from the Directive.[72] The recital does note, however, the principle of taxation at the source. Presumably, this means that if a consumer in one Member State ordered goods from an e-commerce provider in another Member State, the VAT would be paid to the provider's Member State. It is doubtful whether Member States with high VATs will be pleased with this principle. E-commerce activities would tend to migrate to Member States with relatively low VATs.

---

[67] Commission of the European Communities, Amended proposal for a European Parliament and Council Directive on certain legal aspects of electronic commerce in the Internal Market, recital 2.

[68] Directive 98/48/EC of the European Parliament and of the Council of 20 July 1998 amending Directive 98/34/EC laying down a procedure for the provision of information in the field of technical standards and regulations [1998] OJ L 217/33.

[69] Proposed e-commerce Directive, *supra* n. 66, recital 2.c.

[70] *Ibid.*, recital 3.

[71] The Internet Tax Freedom Act, Title XI of P.L. 105–277, the Omnibus Appropriations Act of 1998.

[72] Proposed e-commerce Directive, *supra* n. 66, art. 22.1(a) and recital 18. E-commerce in the form of gambling activities is also specifically excluded from the scope of the Directive in Annex I.

B. Regulation and Freedom of Movement

The operative part of the proposed Directive establishes a principle of regulation at the source of the provision of the e-commerce activities.[73] Being subject to one Member State's regulation, such as complying with a general authorisaiton scheme and registering basic contact information, would create a presumption that the e-commerce provider is free to offer its goods or services throughout the EU. This is in accord with basic EU principles of freedom to provide services and freedom of movement of goods. Of course this principle is only effective for intra-EU e-commerce. It does not address or attempt to regulate e-commerce providers established outside the EU.

The Directive would require e-commerce providers to make available identity and contact information. This information is presumably necessary for receipt of consumer complaints.

The presumption of validity can be overcome and an intra-EU e-commerce provider's services banned from a Member State for a limited number of policy reasons. These include policies regarding of protection of minors, prohibition of hate crimes (this might include prohibition of delivery of racist material), protection of public health (this might keep out attempts to ship prescription drugs), public security, and consumer protection (potentially a very wide exception).[74] Any Member State intending to avail itself of these exemption rights would be required to first request the home Member State of the involved e-commerce provider to take action, and then if satisfactory relief is not forthcoming, the aggrieved Member State may itself take measures to restrict the e-commerce provider after first notifying the European Commission of its intentions. The proposed Directive does not spell out what steps the Member State could take. While it might be impossible for the Member State to block access to the web site of the objectionable e-commerce provider (though some nations such as Australia are attempting a national filtering system), presumably use of the Member State post office could be denied for shipment or customs enforcement could attempt to stop delivery.

C. Ban Spam!

Sure to be a popular item with e-mail users, the proposed Directive would take steps to control, at least in theory, "unsolicited commercial communications by electronic mail,"[75] or as it is more widely known, spam. All such commercial messages are to be labeled as such, and relevant provisions of the Data Protection Directives are to be honoured. In that regard, Member States can

---

[73] *Ibid.*, art. 3.
[74] *Ibid.*, art. 2.3(a)(i).
[75] *Ibid.*, art 7.

require that senders of such commercial e-mail consult and respect opt out lists maintained by Member States containing the names of those who do not wish to receive such communications. Of course regulation of intra-EU spam will do nothing to address the problem of non-EU originated spam, a product that the EU might have more trouble repelling than bananas or US beef.

D. e-contracts

Existing rules on contracts would be harmonised throughout the EU so as recognise the validity of electronic contracts.[76] If Member States wish to create exceptions, perhaps requiring certain contracts to be notarised for example, these rules would have to be notified to the European Commission. The principle for contract offer and acceptance is established that the consumer would signal acceptance of the e-commerce provider's offer by, for example, clicking on an icon. The provider would then electronically send a receipt (e-mail). A valid and enforceable contract would be established from the moment the consumer received this acceptance.[77] This represents a change from an earlier version of the proposed Directive whereby a contract was not valid until the consumer sent a further acknowledgement that the receipt was received. This elimination of one more exchange of e-mails should make e-contract formation a bit easier.

E. Limitation of Liability and Jurisdiction

Potential liability of e-commerce providers as well as transmitters of involved data is another key issue. The proposed Directive contains some good news for transmitters, if not the actual e-merchants. Operators whose service "consists of the transmission in a communications network of information" are to be insulated from liability other than injunctive relief.[78] Limitation of liability is also specifically envisioned for caching[79] (temporary storage of data by information service providers) and hosting[80] (storage of data for access by end-users) operations, provided the service provider does not have knowledge that illegal or harmful content is involved. Internet service providers (ISPs) sought limitation of liability such as is traditionally enjoyed by common carriers, and it is appropriate that they receive such protection. If an ISP or a telco was liable for the content of messages it delivered, without having the opportunity or even the right to inspect such messages, then the message senders would rapidly be put out of business. Insurance against damage claims would cost so much that the

---

[76] Proposed e-commerce Directive, *supra* n. 66, art. 22.1(a) and recital 18, art. 9.1.
[77] *Ibid.*, art. 11.1.
[78] *Ibid.*, art. 12.1.
[79] *Ibid.*, art. 13.
[80] *Ibid.*, art. 14.

service itself would become prohibitively expensive. In an industry such as telecommunications or Internet provision where the location and business of end-users are unknown, it would not be fair to subject service providers to potential claims from multiple jurisdictions. Furthermore, it would not be sound public policy to invite transmission service providers to monitor communications by raising the spectre of liability for contents. End-users probably do not want either government or service providers to keep track of what web sites they visit or the contents of their e-mails. The proposed Directive, while it would require Member States not to impose monitoring requirements on service providers, also recognises that service providers may legitimately be required to comply with judicial surveillance orders.[81]

Unfortunately, potential liability and jurisdiction issues are not so clearly resolved in favour of e-commerce providers. A continuing sticking point is whether e-commerce providers should be subject to claims only in their home market or wherever their customers are. E-commerce providers assert that subjecting their operations to multiple jurisdictions would cripple the industry. Consumer advocates want providers to be subject to claims wherever their customers are located. While it might be expensive for providers to comply with relevant law wherever their goods are delivered, not to mention the cost of hiring lawyers or otherwise addressing claims at these locations, it can also be argued that in effect the e-commerce providers agree to be subject to foreign jurisdictions when they accept customers from those jurisdictions and send their goods or services there.

As might be expected, the proposed e-commerce Directive attempts to steer a middle course between these concerns. Although jurisdiction for potential claims is not specifically covered in the proposed Directive, such claims would be subject to the tests laid out in the Distance Selling Directive.[82] Under the Distance Selling Directive, consumers may sue in their home courts if the goods or services in question were marketed with that "home" Member State in the mind of the provider. Contracts may not require consumers to waive any rights they might enjoy under the Distance Selling Directive, nor may the provider avoid the application of the Directive by choosing the law of a non-EU nation as governing the contract.[83]

The proposed e-commerce Directive, however, encourages alternative means of dispute resolution,[84] perhaps by electronic means. It also urges Member States to ensure that rapid and effective remedies are available through courts,[85] a prospect that may not cheer e-commerce providers.

---

[81] *Ibid.*, art. 15.

[82] *Ibid.*, recital 10, *citing* Directive 97/7/EC of the European Parliament and of the Council of May 1997 on the protection of consumers in respect of distance contracts [1997] OJ L144/19.

[83] Directive 97/7/EC of the European Parliament and of the Council of May 1997 on the protection of consumers in respect of distance contracts [1997] OJ L144/19.

[84] Proposed e-commerce Directive, *supra* n. 66, art.17.

[85] *Ibid.*, art. 18.

Like most EU actions, the proposed e-commerce Directive is a compromise. The EU should receive credit for at least attempting to address in a comprehensive, yet compact form, many of the legal issues raised by e-commerce. It is to be hoped that the final Directive will not retard market development, but will instead promote the interests of both providers and consumers and remain flexible enough for future relevance. Time will tell, and given the pace of Internet developments, not much time may be necessary.

VI. EUROPE: BLUEPRINT FOR THE FUTURE OF THE INFORMATION SOCIETY?

Market, technical and policy developments occur so rapidly in the Internet that it is difficult to draw a curtain over this subject. Perhaps a good place to stop would be with an EU policy document specifically looking towards the future of the Internet and appropriate policies to promote the Information Society.[86] As an agenda for what became the Lisbon "dot com" Summit, the EU issued a policy document in December 1999 containing distillation of the EU's Information Society policies. The *e*Europe document states that the EU's objectives regarding the Internet should be:

—"Bringing every citizen, home and school, every business and administration, into the digital age and online.
—Creating a digitally literate Europe, supported by an entrepreneurial culture ready to finance and develop new ideas.
—Ensuring the whole process is socially inclusive, builds consumer trust and strengthens social cohesion."[87]

These are noble goals, but it is questionable how much the EU or any other government can do to actually create the type of entrepreneurial culture needed to reach these objectives. Creativity cannot be mandated by a directive, no matter how carefully crafted.

While much of the *e*Europe Communication is little more than recitation of lofty education and employment goals, a section deals specifically with the link between "cheaper Internet access" and telecommunications.[88] Regulation itself in the form of excessive licensing requirements is cited as one of the causes of expensive Internet access. The potential of local loop unbundling in promoting local telecoms competition and therefore better Internet access is stressed, and the position of the European Commission as expressed in the 1999 Telecommunications Review[89] is noted.

---

[86] "eEurope: An Information Society For All". *Communications on a Commission Initiative for the Special European Council of Lisbon*, 23 and 24 March 2000 [hereinafter *e*Europe] http://europa.eu.int/comm/information_society/eeurope/pdf/com081299_en.pdf.

[87] *e*Europe, at 2.

[88] *e*Europe, at 8.

[89] Communication from the Commission to the European Parliament, the Council, the Economic and Social Committee and the Committee of the Regions, Towards a new Framework for Electronic

The *e*Europe Communication, however, while lauding the goals of the 1999 Telecommunications Review, found fault with the likely implementation process and schedule. As any new directives resulting form the 1999 Review process might be three or more years away, the drafters of the *e*Europe Communication proposed an acceleration of mandated local loop unbundling. This would require Member States to act themselves to mandate unbundling, as some were doing voluntarily. The *e*Europe drafters wanted the European Commission to recommend to the Member States that they require incumbents to unbundle their local loops and give competitors non-discriminatory access by the end of 2000. By that same time leased line prices should be significantly reduced and licensing requirements lightened.

The European Council endorsed *e*Europe policies in a subsequent European Council summit held in Lisbon in late March 2000. The leaders of the EU Member States agreed that the EU should set a goal *"to become the most competitive and dynamic knowledge-based economy in the world..."*[90] In order to achieve this goal, proper conditions for improvements in electronic commerce and more fundamentally, ubiquitous and affordable Internet access, would have to be met. Specifically recognising the role of telecommunications in Internet access, the Lisbon summit conclusions called on "the Member States, together with the Commission, to work towards introducing greater competition in local access networks before the end of 2000 and unbundling the local loop in order to help bring about a substantial reduction in the costs of using the Internet."[91] The European Council also stated that "[f]ully integrated and liberalised telecommunications markets should be completed by the end of 2001."[92]

Leaving aside the question of how the Council proposed to complete markets, the time guidelines are ambitious. Member States can of course work towards more opportunities for competitors to access end-users; that does not mean they will be successful or that local loops will actually be unbundled. Neither does it mean that all Member States will actually adopt meaningful unbundling or collocation rules anytime soon let alone by the end of 2000. Rules alone, even if they exist, are not enough for results. Incumbents can be quite effective in erecting roadblocks. Even with good faith efforts by incumbents, unbundling offers can take several months to finalise. This is in addition to any necessary technical and logistical arrangements that need to be made.

A final question, what enforcement tools does the EU have in mind for Member States that do not mandate unbundling by the deadline of end of 2000? As discussed in the preceding chapter, a recommendation of the European Commission regarding local loop unbundling was in fact issued in the spring of

Communications infrastructure and associate services: The 1999 Communications Review, COM (1999) 539 [hereinafter 1999 Telecommunications Review].

[90] Presidency Conclusions, Lisbon European Council, 23 and 224 March 2000 para. 5 <http://ue.eu.int/Newsroom/LoadDoc.cfm?MAX=1&DOC=!!!&BID=76&DID=60917&GRP=2379&LANG=1>.

[91] *Ibid.*, para. 11.

[92] *Ibid.*

2000.[93] It would be quite ambitious for local loop unbundling to be in place by the end of 2000, and this would require a great deal of assertiveness by European national regulatory authorities, and in effect acquiescence by the incumbent operators. Nevertheless, the combination of the European Commission and the European Council behind the fast unbundling policy shows that it is definitely on the way. Perhaps emboldened by the political endorsement of the European Council, the European Commission felt confident enough to propose an unbundling regulation to immediately resolve the unbundling issue on an EU wide basis.

VII. CONCLUSION

The Internet does not lend itself to the type of central planning sometimes associated with European governments. It should be recognised, however, that some primarily socialist states, such as the Nordic nations, have a high degree of Internet penetration. Therefore, a pure laissez faire approach is not necessary for Internet success. The European Commission's Internet Telephony Notice appeared to endorse a hands-off approach to new Internet services. On the other hand, the EU's Data Protection Directive is a more interventionist approach. The proposed e-commerce Directive attempts to steer a middle course. The *e*Europe Communication notes that Europe lags behind the US when it comes to Internet penetration and use, and the document suggests some steps that can be taken to close that gap. It will be interesting to observe whether these initiatives are effective in stimulating Internet use in Europe.

---

[93] Commission Recommendation on Unbundled Access to the Local Loop Enabling the competitive provision of a full range of electronic services including broadband multimedia and high-speed Internet 2000/417/EC (OJ L 156, 29 June 2000) [hereinafter Local Loop Unbundling Recommendation]

14

The EU's 1999 Telecommunications Review

I. INTRODUCTION

THE EUROPEAN COMMISSION was required[1] to review the state of telecommunications competition and regulation in Europe three years after the full competition framework had been put in place in 1996. That process started with the publication of the European Commission's Convergence Green Paper[2] in 1997.

II. THE CONVERGENCE GREEN PAPER

Not content with passage of the EU's telecoms regulatory framework and the advent of full competition in 1998, the European Commission opened a fresh debate in 1997 over the direction of the telecommunications industry and the role of regulation. The European Commission's Convergence Green Paper and resulting comments set the stage for the next generation of EU regulatory proposals.

A. Analytical Framework

Convergence is one of those overworked words that are in danger of losing all meaning. What the European Commission had in mind when it used the term "convergence" was the growth of digitalisation and computers, loosely referred to in EU institution documents as the Information Society. Convergence is to break down barriers between telecommunications, media and information

---

[1] Directive 97/33/EC of the European Parliament and of the Council of 30 June 1997 on Interconnection in Telecommunications with regard to ensuring universal service and interoperability through application of the principles of Open Network Provision (ONP) [1997] OJ L199/32, art. 22; Directive 98/10/EC of the European Parliament and of the Council of 26 February 1998 on the application of open network provision (ONP) to voice telephony and on universal service for telecommunications in a competitive environment [1998] OJ L101/24 recital 17.

[2] European Commission, Green Paper on the Convergence of the Telecommunications, Media and Information Technology Sectors, and the Implications For Regulation. Towards an Information Society Approach COM(97)623 [hereinafter Convergence Green Paper] <http://www.ispo.cec.be/convergencegp/97623.html>.

technology (IT) markets. This process can also be called platform independence, since similar content or services can be delivered through telecommunications (telephone wires), media (television), or computers. In the same way, end-user equipment such as telephones, televisions, and computers are no longer distinct; single devices can perform many functions. Telecommunications liberalisation has played a part in this revolution by helping to reduce prices, increase consumer choices and lead to technical progress, in the opinion of the European Commission. The emergence of new companies as well as mergers among existing participants has changed markets. Regulation, however, has not kept pace with these changes.

Politically, the Convergence Green Paper caused some difficulties for the European Commission as it suggested that television broadcasting might become subject to "convergence" regulation itself. The television industry jealously guards its privileged place and certainly does not want to be regulated like telecommunications.

The Green Paper noted barriers to continued progress in this convergence area, including competitor access to end-users, regulatory restrictions on use of infrastructure, prices for telecommunications services (still too high in the opinion of the European Commission), content (both in terms of availability and protection of intellectual property rights), and continued fragmentation of the EU market.[3] Focusing on regulation, the European Commission identified several potential barriers to progress, including regulatory uncertainty and multiple regulators, onerous licensing requirements, access to necessary infrastructure, allocation of scarce resources such as frequency rights, incompatible technical standards, inconsistent approaches to achieve policy objectives, and a general problem of lack of public confidence in matters like consumer and data protection.[4]

The growth of "convergence" markets since the publication of the Convergence Green Paper in 1997, perhaps best represented by the growth in the Internet and associated e-commerce activities, could demonstrate that the European Commission's fears about barriers were overblown. Nevertheless, it was wise to consider these issues before they caused problems in the market, particularly since it can take a great deal of time to change laws and regulation while Internet markets and developments occur rapidly. By the time a problem was actually detected, it might be too late to remedy it before lasting damage is done. Furthermore, although Europe has increased use of computers and the Internet since 1997, most of Europe, with the exception of the Nordic region, lags behind the US in this area.

After this overview of technological progress and market conditions, the Convergence Green Paper turned to an area that EU institutions and legislation can actually influence: regulatory implications and proposals for the future.

[3] Convergence Green Paper, chapter III.1.
[4] *Ibid.*, chapter III.2.

Although the Green Paper labels the convergence process as presenting "challenges" to the EU regulatory framework,[5] this is in reality a recognition that the regulatory framework does not meet the realities of today's telecommunications markets. The question is what, if any, regulation would be better? The European Commission's starting point, that "[r]egulation is not an end in itself"[6] is encouraging. Too often regulators exercise power for no other real reason than they can. While cases of regulators going out of business voluntarily are rare, however, the European Commission did voluntarily suspend public procurement rules for incumbent telecoms operators in markets that had become competitive.[7]

The European Commission goes on to list acceptable high level reasons for regulation including "efficiency, economic welfare, and the public and consumer interest."[8] Again, so far so good. Many regulatory documents, however, start out promising and end up proposing actions that are counter productive. Any replacement or modification of the current EU regulatory framework was to address various regulatory challenges. The role of market forces was recognised. Market based solutions are not automatically accepted in Europe with several socialist governments in place, but even socialists today (or "Third-Wayers" if they insist) admit the need for market solutions (related to this is whether items such as telecommunications networks should be considered as public or private property).

The Convergence Green Paper further noted the balance between regulation and competition law, regulatory consistency (very important in preserving proper business incentives), globalisation, and lastly regulatory structures to deal with these challenges. Indeed, the Convergence Green Paper recognised that regulation itself can be a barrier to the efficient functioning of the market.[9] It was suggested that regulation could be improved to remove barriers regarding: definitions, market entry and licensing, access to networks, conditional access systems (set top boxes), content, and frequencies, standards, and pricing. At this Green Paper stage, these regulatory problem areas were examined and alternatives discussed. Many of these alternatives were ambitious and probably not politically possible.

B. Back to Unbundling

Once again, there is a consideration of the issue of local loop unbundling. As explained in previous chapters, although local loop unbundling is not required

---

[5] *Ibid.*, chapter IV.1.

[6] *Ibid.*, chapter IV.1.

[7] Communication from the Commission pursuant to Article 8 of Directive 93/38/EEC [1999] OJ C129/05 List of services regarded as excluded from the scope of Council Directive 93/38/EEC of 14 June 1993 coordinating the procurement procedures of entities operating in the water, energy, transport and telecommunications sectors pursuant to Article 8 thereof.

[8] Convergence Green Paper, *supra* n. 2, chapter IV.1.

[9] *Ibid.*, chapter IV.2.

in the EU regulatory framework, it was possible to interpret some portions of the Interconnection Directive or the requirement of special network access as requiring full local loop unbundling. The Convergence Green Paper contained a statement of European Commission policy about local loop unbundling.

> "Again, in the telecommunications sector, Community policy does not require a full unbundling of the local loop, or a structural separation of the associated infrastructure, for the provision of services carried over it. This does not exclude appropriate safeguards or requirements being introduced under the competition rules. In reality, the issue of unbundling of the local end of transmission networks is complex and must be closely linked to the degree of overall competition in the market concerned, the availability of viable alternative distribution channels and the starting point for competition in the particular market. Some argue that unbundling may act against the consumer interest in the longer term by removing economic incentives for organisations to put their own wired or wireless networks in place."[10]

Given this policy statement, it is interesting that one of the few alternatives discussed in the Convergence Green Paper to actually make it to the next stage of being recommended in the 1999 Telecommunications Review, was for local loop unbundling (more on that below). The debate moved that far in two years.

C. Regulatory Solutions

To address these general regulatory problems, the Commission considered three broad alternatives: (1) build on current systems; (2) develop new regulation for new services; or (3) introduce a new regulatory model to cover all existing and new services.[11] The resulting recommendations of the 1999 Telecommunications Review did not fall squarely into any of these categories.

III. THE 1999 REVIEW

The central proposition of the EU Commission's 1999 Telecommunications Review[12] was a projected movement away from sector specific regulation and towards infusion of competition law principles in telecoms regulation. This can be seen as a step towards deregulation of the telecommunications industry. As in many such policy documents, the policies themselves sound good, but the details must be closely examined.

---

[10] Convergence Green Paper, *supra* n. 2, chap. IV.2.3.

[11] *Ibid.*, chap. V.2.

[12] Communication from the Commission to the European Parliament, the Council, the Economic and Social Committee and the Committee of the Regions, Towards a new Framework for Electronic Communications infrastructure and associate services: The 1999 Communications Review, COM (1999) 539 [hereinafter 1999 Telecommunications Review] <http://158.169.51.200/infosoc/telecompolicy/review99/review99en.pdf>.

A. Convergence and Policies

Building on the work and terminology of the Convergence Green Paper, the 1999 Review began by noting the trend towards convergence in the industry.[13] Specifically, there have been significant technical and market advances in the Internet, in the area of wireless communications, and in the general area of globalisation. Therefore, regulatory separation among convergent industries was itself obsolete, and a coherent and consistent regulatory regime was needed.

This raises the question of what a new regulatory framework should look like, beyond being coherent and consistent. The 1999 Review posited that a new regulatory framework should address the emerging shortcomings of the current framework. A primary target should be to reinforce competition, particularly at the local level. In recognition of the pace of change in the telecommunications industry, a new framework should cater for new, dynamic and largely unpredictable markets with many more players than are currently on the market. And perhaps most importantly, a new framework should clarify and simplify existing rules.

B. Legislative Simplification: A New Regulatory Framework

For example, the current EU telecommunications regulatory framework consists of over twenty directives, several of which have been repeatedly amended, as well as various guidelines, recommendations and communications. The 1999 Review recommends reducing the number of directives to six. Certainly this would simplify as well the task of lawyers, national regulators, and industry participants who must know and interpret the relevant telecommunications legislation. With a reduction in the number of directives, the policies of the European Commission would be come clearer, confusion and arguments with national regulators would decrease, and the resulting lessening of confusion would lead to greater business certainty.

The existing EU telecommunications regulatory framework would not disappear entirely, however. Neither would regulation of the telecommunications industry. The 1999 Review took the position that it was proper for regulation to address general interest objectives. Furthermore, regulation must remain, at least temporarily, to manage a transition of the market to becoming fully competitive—in effect, regulating to compete. This policy may not be as paradoxical as it sounds. The EU's 1999 Review stated a policy that there should only be regulation in portions of the market where it is needed, only to the extent it is needed, and should be withdrawn when no longer needed. It is hard to argue with this policy; its execution will be key. Further specified, the EU's regulatory

---

[13] *Ibid.*, §1.

policy will be to focus on the behaviour of incumbent operators and the rights of new entrants. Regulation is to be progressively reduced as markets become fully competitive.

The 1999 Review envisioned a new regulatory framework to address the emerging shortcomings of the current framework and to reinforce competition, particularly at the local level. It might be difficult to achieve this goal and still meet the 1999 Review's stated purpose of retaining flexibility in the face of dynamic markets and technologies as well as technological neutrality. An emphasis on local competition might over-regulate local network operators and not preserve the dynamism the 1999 Review sought. The cost of the regulatory burden, a cost ultimately paid by consumers, should be weighed against the expected benefits.

The European Commission's intention as stated in the 1999 Review to progressively reduce regulation, either through sunset provisions or forebearance, holds great promise of bringing the benefits of deregulation to Europe's telecommunications markets. The European Commission's general approach may be criticised in that it is difficult to decide when markets are fully competitive so as to justify deregulation. It would be best for there to be a harmonised approach on the European level so as to avoid fragmentation resulting from different Member State approaches. Furthermore, a mechanical market share test should be avoided. Market shares alone are not a proper test for whether a market is competitive. Rather, competitive opportunities should be the determinative factor.

Returning to the theme of convergence, the 1999 Review stated that any new regulatory framework should cover all communications infrastructure and associated services. This means that the framework would apply to telecommunications networks whether fixed or mobile, satellite networks, cable television networks, terrestrial broadcast networks, as well as all communications services using those networks. This is the principle of technological neutrality, a principle that will doubtless be enthusiastically welcomed by incumbent telecommunications operators, but not endorsed by other market players such as the mobile industry, Internet providers, and cable television network operators who until now had benefited from a lighter regulatory burden than the telecommunications industry.

C. New Directives

Regarding specific legislative proposals, the 1999 Review called for a new overall framework directive.[14] This would authorise and require sunset provisions in regulation as well as regulatory forebearance. Authorising regulators to forebear from regulation is sound policy, but one that regulators are loath to follow.

---

[14] 1999 Telecommunications Review, §3.3.1.

The US FCC was granted similar power under the 1996 Telecommunications Act to forebear from regulating in an area where it has authority, but one fails to notice wide-scale FCC abdications of authority. The 1999 Review's proposals attempted to address this shortcoming by: "requiring existing obligations to be lifted, either after a fixed period of time, or in accordance with pre-defined criteria once the underlying objective has been met."[15] Further guidance is not given in the 1999 Review; it will be interesting to observe how draft legislation will so ensure that regulators go against their basic instincts and understandable feelings of self-preservation by surrendering their regulatory control.

The 1999 Review's new framework directive would set forth high level telecommunications regulatory policy, provide definitions and authorise use of recommendations, best practice guides, codes of conduct and other complementary regulatory measures (soft law). In addition to this new framework directive, existing harmonisation directives would be replaced by four directives consisting of a licensing and authorisation directive, an access and interconnection directive, a universal service directive, and a telecommunications data protection directive. Although all these directives (and more) currently exist, the 1999 Review suggested that both the number and scope of regulatory directives should be reduced to what is necessary.

The current Licensing Directive[16] was seen by the 1999 Review as a success.[17] Nevertheless, different approaches and procedures for issuance of licences exist in EU Member States, and this could cause some problems that should be addressed.[18] Most Member States require licences for provision of voice telephony services. A minority, mainly Nordic countries, allow voice services to be provided under a general authorisation—in effect, no licence required. There are also wide variations in administrative procedures and costs required for licences. Germany was seen as a particularly high cost nation.

In order to remedy these defects, the 1999 Review proposed that general authorisations be used for all telecommunications network and service provision, with the exception of users of scarce resources such as radio spectrum or numbers. Of course, many telecommunications providers make use of numbering, but even for users of scarce resources, including radio frequencies, individual authorisations are to be used in the place of licences. Once again, in line with its convergence principle, the European Commission specifically noted that Internet provision may also be subject to general authorisation requirements, and assuming that the conditions outlined in the Internet Telephony Notice[19]

---

[15] *Ibid.*, §3.3.1.

[16] Directive 97/13//EC of the European Parliament and of the Council of 10 April 1997 on a common framework for general authorisations and individual licences in the field of telecommunications services [1997] OJ L117/15 [hereinafter Licensing Directive].

[17] 1999 Telecommunications Review, *supra* n. 12, §4.1.

[18] *Ibid.*, §4.1.1.

[19] Commission Notice concerning the Status of voice communications on Internet under community law and, in particular, pursuant to the Services Directive [1998] OJ C6/4 [hereinafter Internet Telephony Notice].

are met, providers of voice service over the Internet were to be treated like other voice telephony providers.[20] Technological and market developments in the field of Internet telephony make it increasingly likely that the service will meet the conditions of the Internet Telephony Notice.

The 1999 Review also considered that Member States should be restricted to charging authorisation fees that can be shown to relate to justified administrative expenses.[21] Even this "cost-based pricing" will be subject to benchmark comparisons among other Member States' authorisation fees in much the same way that the European Commission currently benchmarks incumbent interconnection fees.

1. Access and Interconnection

The furthest departure from the current directives is found in the 1999 Review's proposed access and interconnection directive. The 1999 Review recognised that a key policy consideration in the area of access is the need to maintain proper incentives for investment and innovation. In the past few years, the policy argument has boiled down to whether mandating access to certain network facilities, usually local loops, will hinder development of alternative local telecommunications network infrastructures. Should the policy goal be more loops or competitor access to existing loops?

Until recently, regulators in the EU seemed to be firmly in the "more loops" camp. OFTEL, the UK regulator, was noticeable in resisting calls to mandate unbundling of British Telecom's local loop.[22] The 1999 Review repeated the observation of the Convergence Green paper that full physical local loop unbundling is not required under the EU regulatory framework.[23] Unbundling requirements, however have been adopted in Denmark, Finland, Germany, The Netherlands, and Austria, and have been promised or studied in Italy, France, Sweden, Norway (not an EU Member State, but covered by the European Economic Area), and the UK.[24] In the immediate period before the 1999 Review was issued, the European Commission specifically applied local loop unbundling as a remedy in a proposed merger between two European incumbent telecommunications providers.[25]

Certainly there is an EU trend in favour of local loop unbundling. The perceived slow pace of local telecommunications competition in Europe has

---

[20] 1999 Telecommunications Review, *supra* n. 12, §4.1.5.

[21] *Ibid.*, §4.1.4.

[22] OFTEL has now required BT to make unbundled loops available by July 2001.

[23] "Community legislation does not explicitly require local loop unbundling", 1999 Telecommunications Review, *supra* n. 12, §4.2.3.

[24] *Ibid.*, §4.2.3.

[25] "The Commission considers that the availability of unbundled access to the local loop increases competition and that it could in addition speed up the introduction of high speed Internet access services." *Ibid.*, §4.2.3, *citing* Commission Decision on the Telia/Telenor merger (M.1439, 13.10.99 *not yet published*). The *Telia/Telenor* case is fully discussed below in Chapter 18.

increased calls for local loop unbundling, and the European Commission responded to these calls in the Review.

Mandated unbundling was viewed by the 1999 Review as a tool to assist competitors enter the market, and should be a transitory measure, lasting only until entrants should be capable of installing their own local infrastructure.[26] This is a sound view of the problem of competitor access to end-users. Entrants obviously need a way to access end-users. Although that access is possible through interconnection rights, entrants must still find a way of accessing "their" customers, and in a regulatory regime only allowing interconnection that access is only possible if the entrant constructs its own infrastructure, an expensive proposition, particularly for new entrants having no market share or recognition. Interconnection also leaves the incumbent in charge of many of the costs of the entrant. Ideally, regulation should take cognisance of the range of access opportunities entrants need in order to be able to effectively compete. Brand new entrants in telecommunications markets typically begin by setting up operations where end-users access their services through call-by call codes or pre-subscribing to select the entrant for usage calls while continuing to subscribe to basic telephone from the incumbent operator.

The EU regulatory framework currently requires that incumbent operators allow call-by-call and carrier pre-selection access to their subscription customers.[27] This type of end-user access gives an entrant market exposure, experience is dealing with billing and service matters, etc. The next step up might be that of reselling basic telephone service of another, usually from the incumbent provider. Although incumbent local providers in the US are required under the 1996 Telecommunications Act to provide such wholesale telephone service to competitors at a discount representing avoided costs, service resale is not part of the EU's regulatory framework, nor is it clearly mandated by regulation in any EU Member State with the exception of Denmark.[28] Although the 1999 Review did not specifically recommend mandated resale, it appeared to endorse this stepping stone approach to regulation creating conditions to promote entrance into the market and ultimately creation of genuine infrastructure choice by end-users.

Further experience and assets being added, entrants could then progress to the next stage, that of using unbundled local loops and co-locating their equipment in the central offices of the incumbent operators. Each stage requires more investment, more market commitment, and more experience. With the experience of actually running a local network, even a network mostly composed on

---

[26] *Ibid.*, §4.2.1.

[27] Directive 98/61/EC of the European Parliament and of the Council of 24 September 1998 amending Directive 97/33/EC with regard to operator number portability and carrier pre-selection [1998] OJ L268/37.

[28] Danish Act on Competitive Conditions and Interconnection in the Telecommunications Sector, Part 1(3)3, 4 December 1998.

local loops obtained from the incumbent operator, entrants are ready to begin construction and maintenance of their own loops.[29]

This portion of the 1999 Review did not spell out exactly what types of access should be mandated, but gave examples, including: local loops, mobile network infrastructures,[30] broadband networks, submarine networks, as well as ISP and content provider access to cable television networks (sometimes called open access).

The 1999 Review's recommendations did not appear final in this area, but basically a two (or three) tier approach was envisioned. While all access is to be primarily based on commercial negotiation, holders of significant market power (SMP)—presumed with a telecoms market share of at least twenty-five per cent—would be obligated to negotiate access to desired facilities.[31] An exception would be made for "small newly emerging markets", perhaps in order to reward the first movers in these markets. Presumably, operators with less than a twenty-five per cent market share would not be required to negotiate access to their end-users. It is possible to view every infrastructure based customer relationship as a type of bottleneck. The owner of the infrastructure controls access to connected customers as well regardless of whether the infrastructure provider has a small or large market share.

The 1999 Review would place a heavier burden on dominant providers, obliging them to grant all reasonable requests for access and to charge cost-oriented prices for such access. Normal EU competition law principles would be employed to determine dominance—that is with at least a fifty per cent market share dominance may be presumed, though many other factors weigh in a thorough dominance evaluation. Finally in this area, the 1999 Review proposes that regulatory intervention be available to resolve access disputes with either SMP or dominant operators.

The 1999 Review's approach was somewhat different regarding access to cable television networks. Current EU regulation requires legal separation between the telecommunications and cable television network operations of certain incumbent operators.[32] The 1999 Review did not recommend at this time mandating access at the EU level to cable television networks. The 1999 Review, however, considered that Member States may be justified in placing an

---

[29] 1999 Telecommunications Review, *supra* n. 12, §4.2.8 refers to the "transitory nature" of access to incumbent owned loops that entrants will likely require.

[30] An unresolved regulatory controversy in the EU involves claims by unlicensed operators to force interconnection with licensed mobile operators and otherwise use their mobile networks so as to become Mobile Virtual Network Operators. The 1999 Review summarised the controversy but did not take a position on it other than to note that it is an area of access dispute.

[31] 1999 Telecommunications Review, *supra* n. 12, §4.2.1. Although the Review does not specify what type of access request might trigger the negotiation obligation, access to local loops was implied.

[32] Commission Directive 1999/64/EC of 23 June 1999 amending Directive 90/388/EEC in order to ensure that telecommunications networks and cable TV networks owned by a single operator are separate legal entities [1999] OJ L175/39.

"obligation to negotiate access"[33] on cable television operators with significant market power for delivery of broadband services.

In what is sure to be one of the more controversial portions of the 1999 Review, it was recommended that mobile providers be required to at least offer call-by-call selection of competitive service providers.[34] Mobile operators are very concerned that any erosion of their rights of sole access to their end-users may interfere with their business opportunities and therefore their investments in very expensive frequency rights and mobile network infrastructure. The 1999 Review seemed to view this recommendation as a type of compromise. While recognising the business plans of mobile providers, a policy in favour of consumer choice and entrants' opportunities is also strong. Therefore, a requirement of SMP mobile operators opening themselves for call-by-call, but not carrier pre-selection competition, was not viewed by the 1999 Review as too burdensome on the highly lucrative mobile industry.

a. Access Pricing Issues

A key consideration in the most prevalent form of access, interconnection, is price. The 1999 Review noted with approval interconnection prices based on long run incremental cost methodology (LRAIC).[35] Although the existing EU Interconnection Directive requires that interconnection prices be cost-oriented, there is no mandated costing method. This gap had earlier been filled by the European Commission recommending that LRAIC be used,[36] in combination with best practices and benchmarking to ensure that interconnection prices are lowered and somewhat similar throughout Europe.

That said, the reality is that LRAIC interconnection prices are not employed throughout Europe, and the 1999 Review recognised that a proper pricing model, standing alone, is not enough to give access or interconnection prices that will properly promote competition. As markets become more competitive, the 1999 Review indicated that a pricing system based on retail prices minus (avoided costs) may be more appropriate. Cost-oriented pricing might yield prices for such items as unbundled loops that are near or even higher than the retail prices currently charged by incumbent operators for subscription and usage.

Suspect accounting practices by incumbents may be partially to blame. Incumbents may claim they suffer from an "access deficit," meaning they must provide subscription service at less than (the alleged) cost. To the extent this is a real problem, it is doubtless made worse by political pressure to keep basic telephone rates low, as well as the prevailing form of price cap regulation. The

---

[33] 1999 Telecommunications Review, *supra* n. 12, §4.2.1.

[34] *Ibid.*, §4.2.7.

[35] *Ibid.*, §4.2.8.

[36] Commission Recommendation 98/195/EC of 8 January 1998 on Interconnection in a liberalised telecommunications market [1998] OJ L73/42 and Commission Recommendation of 29 July 1998 amending Commission Recommendation 98/195/EC [1998] OJ L228/30.

1999 Review recommended that where cost-oriented prices for access would not yield a sufficient margin for competitors, that is a price squeeze, the remedy is price rebalancing. Retail prices would rise to a level where incumbent costs could be covered, and competitors could receive access with a sufficient margin to survive in the market. Both incumbents and entrants might welcome such a solution, but it remains to be seen whether national regulatory authorities will agree. It may be very difficult to sell the public on the benefits of competition if they see telephone bills increasing.

b. Access Summary

In summary, the 1999 Review proposed the following in the area of access and interconnection.[37]

—Specific EU legislation governing access and interconnection issues.
—Member State national regulatory agencies would deal with specific access issues, including the possibility of mandated resale according to conditions set out in EU legislation.
—SMP operators were to negotiate access on a commercial basis. Dominant operators were to grant reasonable access requests. There would be a possibility of national regulatory authority intervention in these negotiations.
—Interconnection was to continue to be provided on a cost-oriented basis, with a LRAIC costing-pricing model used for call termination on a dominant network. This includes a recognition that call origination, transit and termination are different markets.
—There will be an EU Commission recommendation to Member States on the technical and economic aspects of local loop unbundling.[38]
—In order to assist efficient access, standardisation of telecommunications infrastructures and services would be promoted.
—Call-by-call carrier selection should be made available to customers of mobile providers with SMP.

2. Universal Service

According to the 1999 Review, universal service policy should be limited to ensuring that a specified minimum quality telephone service is available throughout Europe at affordable prices.[39] The European Commission therefore considers that the current EU policies regarding universal service are basically functioning well. The 1999 Review did not think it wise to extend universal ser-

---

[37] 1999 Telecommunications Review, *supra* n. 12, §4.2.9.
[38] Issued in April 2000. Commission Recommendation on Unbundled Access to the Local Loop Enabling the competitive provision of a full range of electronic services including broadband multimedia and high-speed Internet, Brussels, 26 April 2000 C (2000) 1059 [hereinafter Local Loop Unbundling Recommendation].
[39] *Ibid.* §4.4.

vice to broadband networks. Neither should universal service funding or concepts be used in areas beyond the scope of ensuring minimum service at affordable prices.

To its credit, the European Commission in its 1999 Review recognised that universal service, and in particular universal service funds, are a real cost and a form of cross-subsidisation, and therefore should not be used unless necessary. Member States seem to be following the European Commission's thoughts, in that only one Member State (France) even has an universal service fund, though this is currently specifically authorised by the EU regulatory framework.[40] From this, the 1999 Review concluded that universal service has not been a real problem and that the current system should not be altered, though the 1999 Review mentioned the possibility of abolishing the authorisation of universal service funds, or conversely establishing "pay or play" schemes for universal service support.[41]

3. Numbering, Naming and Addressing

Number portability is a relatively new requirement in Europe.[42] Currently the EU regulatory framework requires operator portability—fixed line customers are to have the ability to keep their telephone numbers when switching providers. The 1999 Review recommended extending this requirement to mobile operators.[43] The new number portability requirements would only cover portability among mobile operators; there would not be a requirement of portability between fixed and mobile numbers. Although the 1999 Review indicated that the European Commission would like to see a centralised European number portability data base, it did not propose that such a data base be mandated.

This section of the 1999 Review also looked at Internet addressing and allocation, an area of contention between the US, with its historic monopoly over allocation of Internet addresses, and the EU. Although the European Commission noted its concerns, it did not propose regulation in this area, for now.

---

[40] Directive 97/33/EC of the European Parliament and of the3 Council of 30 June 1997 on Interconnection in Telecommunications with regard to ensuring universal service and interoperability through application of the principles of Open Network Provision (ONP) art. 5(1) [1997] OJ L199/32.

[41] The impact of universal service obligations on the "Telecoms Trade War" is discussed fully in chapter 15, *supra*.

[42] Directive 98/61/EC of the European Parliament and of the Council of 24 September 1998 amending Directive 97/33/EC with regard to operator number portability and carrier pre-selection [1998] OJ L268/37.

[43] 1999 Telecommunications Review, *supra* n. 12, §4.6.3.

C. Regulatory Structure and Standards

1. A Central European Regulator?

The 1999 Review concluded that Europe may not be ready for an overall European Regulatory Authority.[44] Nevertheless, the 1999 Review encouraged efforts to coordinate and harmonise regulatory conditions throughout the EU. As recognised in the 1999 Review, disparate regulatory approaches do not promote European integration or a single European telecommunications market. Developing European wide services may also be discouraged if national regulatory authorities are given too great a latitude to depart from harmonised regulation. This problem will only worsen as the EU grows in the future. Therefore, the 1999 Review stated that the European Commission should promote regulatory harmonisation throughout the EU, preventing discrimination based on the attitude of a particular national regulatory authority.

Along these lines, the 1999 Review desired that the regulatory principles enunciated by the European Commission should be adopted as policy by all European national regulatory authorities. While a single super European regulatory authority would undoubtedly promote a single approach to regulation and hence a single European telecommunications market, the 1999 Review considered that it might be prohibitively expensive to establish and staff such a new regulator.

A central European regulator might also be too remote from actual industry participants and customers that would be affected by its exercise of power. As the EU grows in size, it becomes more conscious of the principle of subsidiarity, that decisions should be taken and power exercised as close as possible to those affected by such decisions. An EU telecommunications regulator might also duplicate the work of existing national regulatory authorities, leading to further inefficiencies and inconsistencies in the system. There is not the political will or available resources for the EU to take over complete jurisdiction of telecommunications regulation from the Member States.

Taking these factors into consideration, the 1999 Review steered a middle course, calling for an expanded role for the existing EU Communications Committee (COCOM) and High Level Communications Group (HLCG). COCOM would have advisory and regulatory roles in that it would provide input to European Commission Decisions on such matters as allegations of violations of EU regulation or competition law. The HLCG would advise the European Commission on standards, the issuance of guidelines on market definitions, and monitor national regulatory activities. This signalled intention to issue more guidelines and recommendations demonstrates the European Commission's desire for a more flexible approach to regulation as well to be

---

[44] 1999 Telecommunications Review, *supra* n. 12, §§2.5 and 4.8.1.

able to react quickly and decisively outside the normal legislative process, a desire for the ability to impose "soft law" in the industry.[45]

2. *The Future of EU Soft Law*

The European Commission's intention to rely more in the future on soft law may in reality be no more than a recognition of current practice. Nevertheless, caution should be employed in this area. While soft law has an advantage in giving regulatory flexibility, it can also lead to a great deal of uncertainty and therefore interfere with business decisions and commercial practices. Furthermore, it is outside of the normal political process for adoption of law, including regulations. There is a risk that adoption of soft law may not adequately take into account concerns of industry participants, consumers or other affected parties.

Reliance on soft law can also raise issues of transparency and accountability. The situation is made worse by the European Commission's reliance on outside studies and "expert" consultants as a basis for many of its recommendations or other soft law documents. Some of the selected consultants may lack independence. While the European Commission's staffing and resource limitations are evident, outsiders with possible interests in the outcome of European Commission policy should not be allowed undue influence. If the European Commission wishes to use the expedient of soft law, it should also make needed reforms to ensure that consultants or law firms employed by the European Commission do not benefit from the soft law they in effect are responsible for.

On the other hand, the policy behind promotion of soft law, the increased importance of competition law as telecommunications becomes deregulated, is to be applauded. Competition law regulation would be less expensive for the European Commission, Member States and certainly industry, allowing consumers to benefit in turn from lower prices, greater choice, and more technical and market innovation. Substitution of competition law for sector specific regulation would be non-discriminatory, as it would begin to treat telecommunications like other industries—a treatment richly deserved when and if convergence becomes real. The IT industry, comprising computer hardware and software as well as the Internet, has benefited tremendously from not carrying the burden of sector specific regulation. For the most part, competition in the IT industry is only regulated by competition law itself. Competition law would also alleviate the problem of regulatory capture. Competition law enforcement officials as well as courts will not have an interests in pleasing their "clients" on an on-going basis.

While the goal of competition law substitution should be supported, care should also be taken that the net effect is not merely the addition of another layer of regulation or additional regulatory categories, without any corresponding regulatory relief. This is a danger with the 1999 Review's recommended two-tier

---

[45] *Ibid.*, §3.3.2.

approach of retaining significant market power (SMP) classification and regulatory duties, while creating a new regulatory category based on dominance.[46]

The two-tier approach will perpetuate confusion over the SMP title. The concept of "market power" is a term from competition law that connotes dominance. The telecommunications harmonisation directives' presumption of "significant market power" with only a twenty-five per cent market share flies in the face of judgments from the European Court of Justice (ECJ) that it is not proper to presume (or even find) dominance with only a twenty-five per cent market share. A presumption of dominance with at least a fifty per cent market share, while more in accord with ECJ judgments, may also lead to confusion between competition law and regulatory law, and not allow for the full market consideration demanded by competition law.

In that regard, if dominance categories are to be employed, it should only be with full market examinations, and any such determination should be made by qualified experts (competition law enforcement officials) and not by Member State national regulatory authorities. National regulatory authorities are usually not qualified or equipped for market evaluations, and may have a tendency to mechanically impose market share tests, without considering factors such as ease of entry. Therefore, the European Commission should be wary of devolving too much authority to national regulatory authorities, particularly as the industry moves towards competition law enforcement and away from regulation. Definite sunset provisions regarding powers of national regulatory authorities would be helpful in ensuring that regulation for the sake of regulation alone does not continue when no longer needed.

IV. CONCLUSION: THE DEATH OF REGULATION?

In conclusion, the approach of the 1999 Review should be considered as a step in the right direction. A test of its effectiveness may be how fast, if ever, it puts regulators out of business.

---

[46] 1999 Telecommunications Review, *supra* n. 12, §4.2.

PART IV

CASE STUDIES IN REGULATORY CYNICISM

15

Case Study: Comparing the US and EU Approaches to Universal Service

A s a general proposition, universal service is certainly a worthy social goal and a very important public policy. However, the United States and Europe have taken remarkably different approaches to this issue. In the former case, because the Clinton/Gore Administration has turned universal service into a centrepiece of their political agenda, current US universal service programs are actually entry deterring and harmful to consumer welfare.[1] In contrast, Europe has recognised the significant harms to consumer welfare that a subsidy-laden universal service program can cause, and has taken a far more restrictive and constructive approach to this important issue. More importantly, however, given this difference in approach, universal service is nonetheless a festering issue in the growing telecoms trade war.

II. THE US APPROACH

A. Statutory Requirements

Under the US Communications Act of 1934, US citizens are entitled to some notion of "universal service"—*i.e.*, the notion that "all the people of the United States, without discrimination on the basis of race, color, religion, national origin, or sex," should have, "so far as possible" access to a "rapid, efficient, Nation-wide, and world-wide wire and radio communication service with adequate facilities at reasonable charges."[2] This is certainly a worthy social goal. At

---

[1] In fact, former FCC Chairman Reed Hundt admits repeatedly (and proudly) in his self-titled book *So You Want a Revolution* (Yale University Press, 2000) that he repeatedly met clandestinely with Clinton/Gore officials in the Executive Branch to advance the Administration's Schools and Libraries agenda. Apparently Mr. Hundt has a different interpretation of the WTO's regulatory "transparency" requirement—i.e., actions that are so transparent that nobody needs to know about it at the time. See also Daniel J. Silver, "Dialing Up a Whole New World", *Wall Street Journal, 25 April 2000*, ("Whatever the virtue of his pro-market decisions, Mr. Hundt's own partisanship is disturbing. Heads of executive agencies are expected to act, in part, in deference to the White House. The problem is, the FCC is an independent agency, answerable not to the president but to Congress. Does that make a difference? It should. It didn't to Reed Hundt.")

[2] See Communications Act Section 1, 47 U.S.C. § 151.

the insistence of the Clinton/Gore Administration, however, the 1996 Telecoms Act has politicised universal service obligations to such a degree that it actually has an adverse effect on market performance.

Specifically, under the US Telecoms Act, telecommunications firms are required to provide "universal service" to, among other entities, rural health care providers, educational providers and libraries. (See 47 U.S.C. § 254.) "Universal Service," however, is defined as the FCC's subjective notion of "an evolving level of telecommunications services" which:

(1) "are essential to education, public health or safety";
(2) "have through the operation of market choices by customers, been subscribed to by a substantial majority of residential customers";
(3) "are being deployed in public telecommunications networks by telecommunications carriers"; and
(4) "are consistent with the public interest, convenience and necessity."[3]

Unlike most other rate prescription statutes—where rates typically must only be "just and reasonable"[4]—the rates for universal service must be "just, reasonable and affordable."[5] According to the statute, "affordable" appears to mean rates that are "*less than* the amounts charged for similar services to other parties . . . that the [FCC] . . . and the States . . . determine is appropriate and necessary to ensure affordable access to and use of such services by such entities."[6] Thus, under this mandate, regulation will continue to be an important factor that can affect firms' conduct, because even if there is a "competitive" price, that competitive price has no meaning if it is not "affordable."

B. Analytical Problems

As a general notion, if (a) regulation and competition are supposed to be substitutes, not complements; and (b) the whole purpose of the 1996 Act was ostensibly to promote competition and lead to deregulation,[7] then it does seem a bit paradoxical that Congress rationally believed that society could have *both* "competitive" markets yet, at the same time, required firms (1) to guarantee that everyone will receive reliable service, and moreover (2) to ensure that particular

---

[3] See 47 U.S.C. § 254(c)(1).
[4] See full discussion in chapter 7.
[5] See 47 U.S.C. § 254(b)(1).
[6] Emphasis added. See 47 U.S.C. § 254(h)(1)(B). Moreover, the FCC has a substantial challenge ahead to ensure that "affordable" prices do not result in confiscatory rates.
[7] See *Janet Reno et al.* v. *American Civil Liberties Union*, 117 S. Ct. 2329, 2337–38 (1997) (Telecommunications Act of 1996 was "an unusually important legislative enactment" because its "primary purpose was to reduce regulation and . . . to promote competition in the local telephone service market, the multichannel video market, and the market for over-the-air broadcasting").

sectors of society will enjoy not only "reliable" service but also some sort of *subsidised* service as well.[8]

Yet, as if implementing Congress's apparent schizophrenic policy objectives wasn't difficult enough, the FCC inadvertently made matters far worse by deliberately politicising the universal service program to advance improperly the Clinton/Gore Administration's schools and libraries program.[9] In fact, the FCC actually hindered and delayed new advanced telecommunications services to

---

[8] See Thomas G. Krattenmaker, "The Telecommunications Act of 1996", (1996) 49 *Fed. Comm. L.J.* 1, 41–43 ("[u]niversal service, as defined in the new Act, and competitive markets cannot coexist, where the goods produced have many substitutes or where the technology is dynamic." Accordingly, argues Krattenmaker, *"it is both bad competition policy and bad regulatory policy to think that one can achieve properly functioning telecommunications markets while a regulator sees to it that these same markets generate subsidised pro-societal benefits"*)(emphasis supplied.); "What Hath Congress Wrought? Reorienting Economic Analysis After the 1996 Act", *Antitrust* (American Bar Association, 1997) 32, 34 and citations therein; see also Harold Demsetz, "Barriers to Entry", (1982) 72 *Am. Econ. Rev.* 37–47; William J. Baumol et al., *Contestable Markets and the Theory of Industry Structure* (1988) 362; Easterbrook, full reference required here, at 15–16 ("[P]eople demand laws just as they demand automobiles, and some people demand more effectively than others. Laws that benefit the people in common are hard to enact because no one can obtain very much of the benefit of lobbying for or preserving such laws." As such, because "cohesive groups can get more for themselves by restricting competition and appropriating rents than by seeking rules that enhance the welfare of all . . . we should expect regulatory programs and other statutes to benefit the regulated group. . . ." Accordingly, these groups "need not 'capture' the programs, because they owned them all along. The burgeoning evidence showing that regulatory programs increase prices for consumers and profits for producers supports this understanding." (emphasis supplied and citations omitted)); see also George Stigler, "The Theory of Economic Regulation", (1971) 2 *Bell J. Econ. & Mgmt. Sci.* 2–21. The FCC should also be aware that its current universal service program is great consternation abroad as well. See David Molony, "EC and U.S. to Clash Over Universal Service Funds", *Communications Week International* 6 April 1998.

[9] Another classic example of this improper politicisation occurred just as this book went to press. First, President Clinton, after visiting briefly the Navajo Indian reservation in New Mexico and Arizona, announced at a computer trade show that because nearly 80 per cent of the homes on that reservations do not have telephones, the rest of us will pay a "few pennies more" each month for long-distance service, with the proceeds going to the installation of telephones in 300,000 I\Indian homes. See Ann Compton, abcNEWS.com, 18 April 2000. At the same time, FCC Chairman Kennard and other democrat FCC Commissioner Gloria Tristani (both of whom had accompanied President Clinton on his trip) issued a public statement that they "joined President Clinton" and announced a plan to provide local phone service for $1 a month in Indian country which, in their words, fulfils "a promise to make sure no corner of America is left behind." (Emphasis in original.) To pay for this plan, the Universal Service fund would be increased by 0.4 per cent that, in the FCC's estimation, would only cost $17 million dollars. Kennard and Tristani's actions were immediately criticised by Republican FCC Commissioner Michael Powell, who stated that he was "sincerely troubled by what appears to be the unabashed politicization of Commission business." Commissioner Powell went on to write that he further strongly objected:

> to the Chairman carefully orchestrating Commission business to play on the political stage in support of White House activities. In particular, I am disturbed when the Commission's professional staff is unwittingly employed in support of such an endeavour. Such action puts at risk the independence and integrity of the FCC and its career staff by purposely joining our authority and agenda with that of the Administration. We are now credibly subject to the criticism that our decisions are not the product of an independent evaluation of what is in the public interest, but are instead a bow to what is in the political interest.

As such, Commissioner Powell concluded that he "sincerely hope[d] that this matter is not just the first in a series of activities designed to build a legacy and promote political outcomes in this election year. If so, the FCC institution that remains after the principal actors have exited stage left will be badly tarnished."

schools, libraries, hospitals and rural areas, because not only does a mandatory universal service requirement—and, in particular, the mandatory requirement that *all* "providers of interstate telecommunications" that offer such telecommunications "to others for a fee" must contribute substantial sums of their *gross* revenues to the universal service fund[10]—impose a significant dead weight efficiency loss on consumer welfare,[11] but, in more practical terms, such a policy also acts as a *major* barrier to entry for new firms. This regulatory barrier to entry is simply exacerbated by the fact that, with one exception discussed *infra*, neither the FCC nor the courts have yet to apply these definitions to any individual cases, hence it is unclear who or what will ultimately be called on to contribute to the fund and how much they will owe. Thus, not only would "typical" providers of interstate telecommunications be required to contribute to the fund (*e.g.*, common carriers and private line operators of telephone or wireless companies) but, more importantly, firms that just *incidentally* may be in telecommunications could be required to contribute. These types of firms could range anywhere from a utility that simply seeks to lease dark fibre to a CLEC, to a Seven-Eleven convenience store that sells phone cards. In addition, because the universal payments are characterised, as of the time of this writing, as "contributions," these "contributions" may not be deducted on a contributing firm's tax return.[12] Accordingly, if a new entrant (or even an existing firm) perceives that the costs imposed by the 1996 Act's mandatory universal service obligations and payments may actually exceed[13] the initial profits it hopes to receive, then entry (or a continued presence in the market) will not be economical and will not occur.[14] The net result of such politicisation is the sad fact that the greatest impediment to true universal service has been the FCC's own policies—and not

---

[10] See Federal-State Joint Board on Universal Service, CC Docket No. 96–45, Report & Order, FCC 97–157 (rel. May 8, 1997) at ¶¶ 794–96.

[11] See Hausman, "Taxation by Telecommunications Reputation" in Tax Policy and the Economy (1998).

[12] What is particularly disturbing about this scenario is the fact that this exact type of non-price competition is one of the major reasons why it is highly unlikely that long-distance carriers can successfully engage in some sort of tacit collusion under current market conditions.

[13] Perhaps if Congress is really so concerned about wiring the schools, a direct tax credit may be a better way to go—i.e., we eliminate the "middle man" and carriers can get direct positive public-relations benefits from the whole endeavour. This approach might even encourage entry! As the empirical evidence unfortunately shows, a multi-billion dollar fund creates just too many incentives for nefarious behaviour. See, e.g., James K. Glassman, "Gore's Internet Fiasco", *Washington Post*, 2 June 1998 at A13.

[14] See Scott Cleland, "Subsidy Reform—Big Skunk at the Competition Picnic?" *Telecom Watch* (Wash. Research Group, 1997) ("FCC's subsidy reform of universal service and access charges will prove to be a larger impediment to the development of local competition than most appreciate."); Robert J. Samuelson, "Telephone Straddle", *Washington Post*, 14 May 1997 at A21 (while Universal Service's "educational benefits may be phantom . . . the higher overall phone rates needed to pay for them aren't"; moreover, while the "subsidies for the poor may be justified[, t]he rural subsidy isn't. *If people prefer to live in rural Montana, they should enjoy the pleasures and bear the costs.*" (emphasis supplied)).

any action by the market—that act as substantial barriers to entry and dead weight loss to society.[15]

Even more appalling is that entrants do not know how much they will owe to the fund until "bills" are sent out. The FCC revises the USF contribution factors every six months, and those factors are calculated to cover expected costs. Providers are then required to pay that percentage of their revenue from the *prior year*. The result is that a provider can only guess how much of the revenues it generates today will be taxed next year, because today no one can accurately estimate what next year's USF expenses will be. Imagine that you are a telecommunications provider and you are attempting to put together your balance sheet (particular, your accrued liabilities account) for a US Securities and Exchange Commission filing—how do you explain to your auditor your justification for reserving 2 per cent, 4 per cent or even 6 per cent of your gross interstate telecommunications revenues for possible taxation next year? This retroactive taxation is unconscionable, and the resulting uncertainty serves only to decrease the changes that a firm will enter the telecommunications industry, as opposed to other industries where changes in tax rates only apply prospectively.

More importantly, however, is that the FCC apparently believes erroneously that all entrepreneurial firms have some sort of "captured" ratebase just like an established firm, such that they can ensure a constant stream of contributions to the USF. The problem with the FCC's assumption is that entrepreneurial firms, by definition, do not have a steady or guaranteed revenue stream. It is therefore wholly inappropriate for the FCC to talk about taxing gross revenues when entrepreneurial firms are attempting to assuage their venture capital investors by producing positive net revenues—an exercise which is essential to continued survival in the first instance. The FCC further exacerbates this already difficult entrepreneurial challenge by imposing additional universal service charges that actually force entrepreneurs' prices to rise—and, *a fortiori*, become less attractive and competitive to established firms' products and services—than they would otherwise be.

Finally, perhaps the most egregious analytical assumption on the part of the Clinton/Gore Administration is the deliberate blurring of the discrete concepts of "low income" verses "low volume" customers. Indeed, just because someone lives in a rural area does not per se mean that they have a low income; nor does it mean that someone who has a high income necessarily is a high-volume user. (For example, Howard Hughes was a billionaire, Howard Hughes was also a hermit. Thus, Howard Hughes might have been a low-volume user, but he certainly was not a low-income user.) Until this basic concept is understood and accounted for in universal service policies, many USO initiatives will continue to harm, rather than promote, overall consumer welfare.[16]

[15] See Jerry Hausman, *supra* n. 11 (calculating that the efficiency loss to society of policy to raise $2.25 billion per year to fund an Internet subsidy to schools and libraries to be approximately $1.25 per dollar raised, or a total of approximately $2.36 billion per year (in addition to the $2.25 billion per year of tax revenue)); Robert J. Samuelson, *supra* n. 14.

[16] See, e.g., John C. Panzar and Steven S. Wildman, "Network Competition and the Provision of Universal Service", (1995) 4 *Industrial and Corporate Change* 711.

C. The "Stevens Report"

The one instance where the FCC did provide some clarity on the issue was in its report to Congress on Universal Service (*aka* the "Stevens Report").[17] In the Stevens Report, the FCC decided that it would consider imposing access charge and universal service contributions (albeit on a case-by-case basis) on Internet telephony (IP) providers, which, if adopted in practice, would eviscerate nearly fifteen years of past precedent.[18] At the time of the original *Computer II* inquiry, more enlightened forward-looking FCC staff realised that technological developments may reach a point where enhanced services may truly be a close substitute for traditional, switched-voice services. Rather than attempting to regulate these developments, the FCC decided to let this process begin. Yet—low and behold—just when technology finally has caught-up and IP telephony (complete with the concurrent construction of new state-of-the art networks) is now starting to exert desired downward pressure (both domestically and especially internationally) on the need for universal service and access charges, the FCC has set the stage to pull a regulatory "bait and switch." Specifically, the FCC is now improperly attempting to claim that it is *reducing* the amount each industry participant may contribute overall *yet, at the same time, the FCC is actually increasing the number of people who must contribute to the fund!* Accordingly, the FCC has done nothing more than surreptitiously ensure that the overall amount in the universal service fund arguably will stay the same by deterring competition and denying consumers access to the additional choices and lower prices they deserve and expect. Thus, no one should really be surprised when incumbents immediately attempted to do what the FCC stated that they now were apparently entitled to do (*i.e.*, impose access charges on IP providers).[19]

D. Universal Service as a Self-Defeating Exercise

What is particularly sad about this whole process is that entry can solve many of the universal service problems the FCC is so concerned about. To wit, why do you see Apple Computer give equipment to schools and libraries? Are they really so altruistic? Of course not. Because the US computer market is conducive to competitive rivalry (*i.e.*, low barriers to entry, low switching costs, *etc.*), Apple has the incentive to subsidise schools and libraries voluntarily in order to help build brand loyalty in a viciously competitive market. In other words, given this structure and firms' conduct in this structure, the US computer market is

---

[17] *In re Federal-State Joint Board on Universal Service*, Report to Congress, FCC 98–67 (rel. April 10, 1998).

[18] *Ibid.*, at ¶¶ 83–93.

[19] See "Official Says FCC Hasn't Ruled on IP Telephony Access Charges", *TRDaily* 8 Sept. 1998.

demonstrating good economic performance by producing declining costs, technological innovation and, most importantly, the societal benefits politicians want to see.

Notwithstanding the above, with the increasing politicisation and cynicism creeping into the policy-making process, it seems unlikely that any politician will have the political courage to express confidence in the economics of entry verses the immediate political gain of the current program. Indeed, now that the proverbial "pork" from the US Universal Service Fund has started to flow, no politician on either side of the aisle is going to tell their constituents that children, libraries and hospitals are not going to receive "free computers" and access to the "Information Society." So long as anything related to the "Internet" continues to be a hot-button populist issue with US politicians, therefore the US telecommunications industry (and by extension US consumers) will also continue to pay for the yellow-brick toll road that will lead our children over the bridge to the twenty-first century—even if it takes backroom deals and regulatory coercion to accomplish this goal.[21]

III. THE EU'S APPROACH

To the European Commission's credit, they have taken a far more constructive approach to universal service than their American counterparts. In fact what is so surprising is that it was a majority of the European Union Member States (many of which have long and well-documented histories of socialist-type public welfare policies), and not the United States (allegedly the paragon of a successful capitalist, democratic society), that recognised that trying to reconcile these diametrically opposed goals would be a fool's errand. As such, the European Commission has specifically refused to permit Member States to use universal service to subsidise Internet access to the schools.[22]

[21] See Scott Cleland, "The 'Real Story' Behind the FCC's Subsidy Reform Decision?", *Telecom Bulletin*, 9 May 1997 (Wash. Research Group) ("[O]nly 'escape route' possible from the 'political trap' of appearing to be increasing the nation's telephone rate burden to pay for new school subsidies" was for the FCC to enter into a "last minute 'deal' with AT&T," which, in "return for public promises from AT&T to pass on any access charge reductions to basic consumers for the first time in years, the FCC would decrease the local telcos' price caps by an additional $750 million." This "'deal,' combined with a slower phase-in of the new universal service fund, enabled the FCC to defensively claim 'offsetting savings' for both long distance and local customers to pay for the $3 billion in new subsidies."); "Furchtgott-Roth Tells LECs To 'Stand Up' to FCC on Universal Service", *Comm. Daily*, 5 Mar. 1998, at 3, 4 (reporting that a packed ballroom audience erupted in applause and jumped to their feet when Commissioner Furchtgott-Roth "sharply criticised fellow commissioners for what he declared was 'secret deal' made with AT&T and MCI to conceal actual costs for USF and access reform charges: 'I will never support negotiations in secret without public notice and comment.' [In addition, Furchtgott-Roth, i]n strongest criticism, questioned increase in administrative expenses for Universal Service Administrative Corp. (USAC) to $4.4 million from $2.7 million—65 per cent—in latest quarter: 'That's $18,000 per day in additional expenses.' ").

[22] See "EU's Bangemann Says Only France, Italy Adopt Universal Service Telecom Funding", *AFX News*, 25 Feb. 1998, available in WL ALLNEWSPLUS Database (indicating EC does not "intend to allow money raised from universal-service funding to be used to fund internet in schools";

Given its traditions of state intervention and consumer protection, the EU policies regarding universal service may come as a surprise. The policy can be summarised as a requirement that a minimum quality telephone service be available at affordable prices. While much might lurk behind this policy, the EU Commission has not attempted to meet any other policy goals through its universal service legislation. Frankly, this is an area where the EU beats the US hands down. The EU approach has been consistent ever since it started seriously examining universal service issues in 1996.[23]

In Europe, incumbent operators, like incumbents everywhere, resisted competition and used universal service as a justification. With the EU Commission's gradualist approach to liberalisation, basic voice service was not subject to competition in the first wave of liberalisation, the European Court of Justice did not accept the incumbent argument that competition would so weaken them as to interfere with their universal service obligations.[24] By the time full telecoms competition arrived in 1998, the ability of the (soon to be former) legal monopolies to meet the universal service obligations was no longer a real issue. Nevertheless, the EU regulatory framework made provisions as to how Member States might legitimately require universal service obligations and if necessary fund these obligations.

The Interconnection Directive specifically allowed Member States to establish a fund to support universal service.[25] The provisions establishing the funding mechanism contains a short and useful definition of universal service obligations: "the provision of a network and service throughout a specified geographical area, including—where required—averaged prices in that geographical area for the provision of that service."[26] Universal service cost would be the difference between the cost of fulfilling a Member State's universal service obligation and "operating without the universal service obligation." That is, an affected telecommunications operator can in theory access a universal service fund even if operating at a net profit. What sort of elements can be recovered?

rather, while this Internet access to the schools should be encouraged, it should appropriately "be paid out of education budgets."); see also Spiwak, "The Search for Meaningful Definitions", full reference required here (outlining massive economic costs to consumer welfare by current universal service policies).

[23] Communication To The European Parliament, The Council, the Economic and Social Committee and the Committee of the Regions, Universal Service For Telecommunications In The Perspective of a Fully Liberalised Environment: An Essential Element of the Information Society, COM(96)73, 14/3/96.

[24] Case 202/88 *France* v. *Commission* [1991] ECR I–1223 and Joined Cases 271, 281 & 289 *Spain, Belgium, Italian Republic* v. *Commission* [1992] ECR I–5833.

[25] Directive 97/33/EC of the European Parliament and of the Council of 30 June 1997 on Interconnection in Telecommunications With Regard to Ensuring Universal Service and Interoperability Through Application of the Principles of Open Network Provision (ONP) [1997] OJ L199/32 art. 5 [hereinafter Interconnection Directive]. The use of the term "universal service" in the title is interesting as a relatively small portion of the Interconnection Directive actually deals with universal service issues, as universal service is usually considered. It may be that the Directive's policy of "any-to-any" communications and resultant imposition of interconnection duties, noticeably on significant market power providers, is itself a universal service duty.

[26] *Ibid.*, Annex III.

Beyond build out and provision required for rural or special needs customers, specific items mentioned are the cost of providing emergency numbers, pay telephones in certain (presumably low-density) areas, and supplying special equipment or services to the disabled. The Directive Annex states that in calculating any such costs, a forward-looking cost basis should be used. If a Member State determines that complying with the universal service obligation is "unfair" for its designated universal service operator (almost certainly the incumbent telco), it may establish a fund to share the net cost of these obligations that all operators of public networks and providers of public telecommunications services may be required to pay into.[27] When making these types of calculations, the Member State is to take into account not only costs associated with the universal service obligation, but also "the market benefit if any" an operator possessing an ubiquitous network enjoys.

Many European incumbent operators complain that they suffer from an "access deficit." That is, it costs the operator more to provide (usually basic subscription) service to its customers than it receives in revenue from these services. This leads the incumbents to usually suggest as a remedy that it be allowed to charge high prices for interconnection or other forms of access in order to remedy this deficit. There are several things wrong with this analysis. First, it ignores the obvious benefit of operating a ubiquitous telecommunications network, a benefit the Interconnection Directive recognised and a benefit that has become more noticeable since the economic theory of network externalities has become more prominent. Second, the access deficit analysis ignores usage revenues that are associated with subscriptions; even in the presence of carrier selection, incumbent operators will gain a significant amount of usage charges. If flat-rate pricing became the norm in Europe, this could change. Third, if an access deficit does in fact exist, the remedy is either to rebalance end-user charges, specifically allowed by the EU regulatory framework, or to recover from an universal service fund. Rebalancing end-user prices by charging more might stimulate competition by making the local access market more attractive, however, it will be difficult to sell the public on the benefits of competition when they see telephone bills increase.

As it happened, the universal service funds have not been much of an issue in the EU. Only one Member State, France, has even taken the step of establishing a universal service support fund.[28]

The EU's universal service policy was further established in the ONP Voice Telephony Directive.[29] Universal service was presented as a "defined minimum

---

[27] *Ibid.*, art. 5.

[28] Communication from the Commission to the European Parliament, the Council, the Economic and Social Committee and the Committee of the Regions, Towards a new Framework for Electronic Communications infrastructure and associate services: The 1999 Communications Review, COM (1999) 539 §4.4 [hereinafter 1999 Telecommunications Review].

[29] Directive 98/10/EC of the European Parliament and of the Council of 26 February 1998 on the application of open network provision (ONP) to voice telephony and on universal service for telecommunications in a competitive environment [1998] OJ L101/24 [hereinafter ONP Voice

set of services of specified quality which is available to all users independent of their geographical location and in the light of specific national conditions, at an affordable price."[30] This raises several questions concerning what is meant by a minimum set, geographical location, and affordable prices. The Directive provided some guidance in answering these questions, but first it required all Member States to ensure that the defined set of universal services are made available to all users in their territory,[31] and authorises Member States to designate fixed line operators so their entire territory is covered.[32] By geographical areas, the Directive signals that it has rural areas in mind, usually seen as expensive to serve because of the great distances between users as well as the often rugged terrain. Regarding users, the Directive meant that it should include those with special needs such as the disabled or elderly. In order to ensure that these groups receive services at affordable prices, prices that likely bear little relation to the cost of providing the service, Member States are authorised to engage in price controls through geographic averaging or price caps "until such time as competition provides effective price control."[33] While competition should be effective in holding down telephone prices in high density areas or for highly sought after customers, it is very doubtful that competition will result in uniform prices throughout a nation so as to fulfill the geographic uniformity requirement. Indeed it is most unlikely that market forces would result in uniform prices; even with vigorous competition in all geographic areas of a nation, prices would seek a level above costs, and as costs vary so would prices. Therefore, if "effective price control" means uniform prices (apparently one of the goals of the EU's universal service policy), competition will never give this. Price controls would have to remain in place. Incumbents could then rightly complain that they were left with only the undesirable, universal service customers. This issue should be revisited by policy makers as actual competition in telecoms markets grows. If low or uniform prices are desired for rural or special needs customers, perhaps a more rational means such as direct revenue support or types of "telecoms vouchers" should be provided rather than distorting the market through artificial averaging requirements. The ONP Voice Telephony Directive refers to the universal service funding mechanism established by the Interconnection Directive, but does not expand the wording or requirements as set forth in the Interconnection Directive.[34]

Telephony Directive]. This Directive contains provisions the obligations of telecoms operators with significant market power (SMP) towards their own end users as well as to other, competitive, providers. For the purposes of this discussion, the relations between the operator and its end users will be emphasised, however, the obligations of SMP providers to competitors can also be considered under this Directive as falling under universal service obligations. These duties include the obligation to offer "special network access" (art.16), the definition of this term and the duties it carries are still very much in dispute.

[30] *Ibid.*, art. 2(f).
[31] *Ibid.*, art. 3.1.
[32] *Ibid.*, art. 5.1.
[33] *Ibid.*, art. 3.1.
[34] *Ibid.*, art. 4.

Another potential problem lies with the concept of "affordability", which, as outlined *supra* is by its nature a subjective principle. What is affordable for one is beyond the means of another. This may be true even for those with identical incomes. Some may desire a particular product or service more than another with identical resources to spend. Unfortunately, the Directive does not offer any further guidance on the issue of affordability.

Most of the rest of the universal service provisions of the ONP Voice Telephony Directive was taken up with descriptions of what services were necessary to constitute the minimum necessary so as be an universal service. The list begins with directories.[35] All subscribers who do not notify the universal service operator that they do not wish to be listed shall have their telephone numbers published, and the operator is under an obligation to provide these listings on "fair, cost oriented and non-discriminatory" terms to requesting parties. This provision should end any arguments about the copyrightability of directory listings (likely to vary from Member State to Member State) as well as the rights of producers of alternative directories to obtain access to the listing information under competition law principles. Member States must also ensure that an adequate number of public pay telephones are available (even though with the growth in penetration of mobile telephones, pay telephones are rapidly becoming an anachronism) and free access to emergency numbers (the number 112 is specified as the European emergency number).

The Directive goes as far as specifying some aspects of the business relationship between the universal service provider and its customers—all its customers, not just the "universal" ones. Contracts are to be provided,[36] quite an undertaking for firms with millions of customers most of which until now did not have a written contract with their service provider. The existence of contracts, however, does not absolve the operators from continuing to publish detailed tariffs containing standard terms and conditions, including technical information such as network interfaces, presumably needed by competitors.[37] This highlights the dual nature of the Directive's universal service requirements, both to end-users as well as to competitors. Tariffs are to be cost oriented, even for end-user prices for fixed network access and usage.[38] Affected operators must maintain a level of quality of service for both end-users and competitors using its network.[39] National regulatory authorities were to monitor quality of service and take appropriate action to ensure that quality meets minimum levels. End-users were to receive itemised bills

---

[35] *Ibid.*, art. 6.

[36] *Ibid.*, art. 10.

[37] ONP Voice Telephony Directive, art. 11.

[38] *Ibid.*, art 17.2. The Directive mandated a cost accounting system to verify the cost-oriented nature of prices and included general items that may be properly considered such as direct and common costs. *Ibid.*, art 18. The Directive, however did not specify what cost accounting method, indicating that methods such as historic costs or forward looking costs were proper. The Directive also gave no guidance as to how much profit may be realised before the prices lose their cost-oriented nature.

[39] *Ibid.*, arts. 12 and 13.1.

on request.[40] Europe does not have history of provision of itemised billing, perhaps privacy is a partial explanation. Some individuals may wish to keep their calling destinations a secret, even from other family members.

The Directive even spoke to procedures that must be used to terminate customers for non-payment of bills.[41] The deadbeat customer is to be warned before termination, and even then unless "fraud, persistent late payment or non-payment" can be shown, termination is to be "confined to the service concerned." Presumably, if subscription charges are paid but not usage charges, the subscription could not be cancelled, at least until it amounted to a persistent problem. Likewise, if the end-user did not pay for international or value added calls (such as sex lines), the appropriate and proportional remedy would be to block access to those services only. Operators doubtless resent this tampering with their service cut-off bill collection weapon.

An important, but not very well understood section of the Directive concerns "special network access."[42] The term was not spelled out in the definitions section of the Directive. The Interconnection Directive had a similar requirement that significant market power providers "shall meet all reasonable request for access to the network including access at points other than the network termination points offered to the majority of end-users."[43] The ONP Voice Telephony Directive required national regulatory authorities to:

> "ensure that organisations with significant market power in the provision of fixed public telephone networks deal with reasonable requests from organisations providing telecommunications for access to the fixed public telephone network at network termination points other than the commonly provided network termination points"[44]

This loose language has given rise to a great deal of speculation as to what exactly special network access is. The recitals accompanying the Directive gave no guidance. It is possible to read into this term mandatory resale of basic telephony or local loop unbundling, as some commentators or national regulatory authorities have attempted to do. The European Commission itself had been remarkably silent on the subject until its Local Loop Unbundling Working Document was issued.[45]

The EU's universal service policy may be viewed as paternalistic, attempting to protect consumers and manage how telephone services are to be offered to them. That, however, is what universal service is all about. Furthermore, the realisation that even this form of universal service regulation may be obviated by competitive developments is significant. The EU attempts to mandate no

---

[40] *Ibid.*, art. 14.1.
[41] *Ibid.*, art. 21.
[42] *Ibid.*, art 16.
[43] Interconnection Directive, *supra* n. 23, art. 4.2.
[44] ONP Voice Telephony Directive, *supra* n. 27, art. 16.
[45] Directorate-General Information Society Working Document Unbundled access to the local loop Brussels, 9 February 2000 INFSO A/1. The Working Document is discussed above in Chapter 12.

more than what is necessary to ensure a minimum quality of service is available to its citizens at affordable prices. The policy is not confused with other goals such as wiring the schools or paving the information superhighway. However laudable these goals are, they are not universal service, and forcing operators to finance these policies in the name of universal service distorts the market, penalising some participants and subsidising others. Thankfully, the EU has not fallen into that trap. It is to be hoped that it continues this wise policy.[46]

IV. INTERNATIONAL IMPLICATIONS OF US DOMESTIC USF POLICIES

One of the cornerstones of the WTO Reference Paper is the provision that:

> "Any Member has the right to define the kind of universal service obligation it wishes to maintain. Such obligations will not be regarded as anti-competitive *per se*, provided they are administered in a transparent, non-discriminatory and competitively neutral manner and are not more burdensome than necessary for the kind of universal service defined by the Member."[47]

As such, US and European international telecoms policies also materially affect universal service initiatives world-wide because many countries (developed or developing)—who may not have a domestic access charge regime—use revenues from settlement rate outpayments to pay for domestic universal service programs.

Naturally, this reality conflicts directly with the United States' efforts to set unilaterally settlement rate benchmarks. Indeed, as explained in greater detail in chapter 7, the FCC in its *Benchmarks Order*, takes great pains to argue that it must reduce the tremendous outflow of settlement rate payments and bring them in line with some ill-defined notion of "costs." Yet, on the same time, the US courts have upheld the FCC's actions to permit *domestic* access charges to be above costs to account and pay for additional infrastructure investment and universal service obligations.[48] In other words, a *lawful* cross-subsidisation. Indeed, according to the Eighth US Circuit Court of Appeals, access charges (the US domestic version of settlement rates) imposed on long-distance providers that include LECs' universal service costs are not "above-cost" "*since universal service contributions are a real cost of doing business.*"[49] Yet, if the logic of the

---

[46] The 1999 Telecommunications Review indicates that the European Commission is pleased with its universal service policy and does not recommend any changes except perhaps allowance of "play or pay" schemes whereby market participants could be required to support universal service either by paying into a fund (remembering that only France currently has such a fund) or by actually providing universal type services itself. 1999 Telecommunications Review, *supra* n. 26, §4.4.

[47] See Regulatory Reference Paper at ¶ 3.

[48] Setting rates that account for both costs and non-cost factors is perfectly legal under U.S. law and accepted economic theory so long as the end collection rates continue to fall within the "zone of reasonableness" and produce neither "confiscatory" rates nor "creamy returns."

[49] *Southwestern Bell Telephone* v. *FCC*, 153 F.3d 523, 554 (8th Cir. 1998) (emphasis added).

Eighth Circuit is followed, then current settlement rates are similarly not "above-cost," since international settlement rates are also simply "a real cost of doing business."

Thus, at bottom, it seems somewhat hypocritical that the FCC can set US *domestic* access charges to account for universal service and infrastructure, yet at the same time argue that foreign countries (who may not have a domestic access charge regime) should be *prohibited* from using their traditional funding mechanism for these services—international settlement rate revenue. Stated another way, in the FCC's view, the US' regulatory regime is somehow a *lawful* cross-subsidisation of universal service and infrastructure deployment under the WTO, but the rest of the international telecoms community's efforts are an *unlawful* cross-subsidisation of the very same policy objectives.[50] Accordingly, it would seem that if a non-US country can produce an accurate cost study which shows both: the actual costs of terminating a call and legitimate *non-cost factors* (*i.e.*, infrastructure build-out and USO obligations), then it is clear that the FCC's policies violate the WTO and deprive consumers in other countries (especially those in developing countries) from the benefits of the Information Society.

As demonstrated *passim*, the rest of the international community has been— to state it politely—extremely dismayed and chagrined with the FCC's unilat- eral neo-mercantile actions. Thus, in response to the FCC's unilateral actions, on November 6, 1998, the international community—via the Focus Group to ITU-T Study Group 3—submitted a "Final Report" regarding "Accounting Rate Principles for International Telephone Service."[51] This International Telecommunication Union (ITU) Report, quite deliberately, took a very differ- ent approach to settlement rate reductions than the FCC's improper and arbi- trary attempt to do so unilaterally. In the ITU's own terse words:

> "The figures attained by applying the Focus Group's methodology contrast markedly with those that would be necessary if the FCC's "Benchmark" methodology were applied. The FCC methodology makes no allowance for dependence on net settlement payments. In almost all cases the average rate of reduction necessary under the FCC's methodology is steeper than even the worst case under the Focus Group methodology. In particular, for low-income countries, the FCC's necessary rate of reduction would be between 22 and 28 per cent per year. For middle income countries, the necessary rate of reduction is between 31 and 38 per cent per year, while high income countries would need to achieve a reduction equivalent to a 50 per cent cut in one year during the remaining three months of 1998. Application of the FCC methodology would be particularly disadvantageous to small island states especially for those such as [the] Cayman Islands, New Caledonia or British Virgin Islands that are categorised as being high income and which currently have settlement rates of around 0.3 SDR per minute. In order to comply with the FCC benchmark for the upper middle income group, they would be required to cut their settlement rate to 0.112 SDR within three months. This

---

[50] The fact that the FCC "magnanimously" agreed to permit developing nations up to four years to meet its benchmarks does not mitigate this hypocrisy.

[51] This Final Report takes the formal form of a new draft Annex E to ITU-T Recommendation D.140 and is available at <http://www.itu.int/intset/focus/index.html>.

represents an annualised rate of reduction in excess of 95 per cent! Overall, if the Focus Group methodology is applied, the average rates of reduction that would need to be applied by a typical (median) country / territory are around 6 per cent per year (between 1999 and 2004) for an LDC or a low teledensity country with a high dependence on net settlements ranges, 7 per cent for small island states (between 1999 and 2001) and around 16 per cent per year (between 1999 and 2001) for other countries. On the other hand, if the FCC methodology is applied (for different target year-ends between 1998 and 2002) the average necessary rate of reduction would be some 34 per cent year. The FCC methodology implies a rate of reduction which is at least twice as fast as that required by the Focus Group methodology and, in some cases, is up to five times faster."[52]

Thus, in marked contrast to the FCC's "exacting" draconian unilateral actions in which rates are prescribed arbitrarily, the ITU believes the better way to obtain a "smoother transition path" is through "bilateral negotiations" using a wide variety of tools including, but not limited to:

(1) Staged reductions negotiated on the basis of volume-based settlement rates;

(2) Staged reductions negotiated in absolute amounts (e.g., going down by 0.1 SDR per year, rather than by the same per centage each year (i.e., the per centage reduction in the early years is less dramatic than in the later years);

(3) Negotiating an agreement under which the accounting revenue could be split in a manner which deviates from 50/50 by a few per centage points—e.g., asymmetric arrangements could be triggered if the net settlement payment were to fall by more than a certain amount in any given year (According to the ITU, this type of asymmetric arrangement could be negotiated in advance, at any time during the transition period, but applied retrospectively);[53] and

---

[52] See Methodological Note on Transition Paths to Cost-Orientation, Revision 1 of Contribution from the ITU Secretariat, 9 Nov. 1998 (visited Nov. 16, 1998) <http://www.itu.int/intset/focus/ transition_path%20rev1.pdf>.

[53] In the ITU's view, applying asymmetric arrangements during the transition to cost orientation may be appropriate because such mechanisms may both: (a) achieve a faster rate of reduction in the total accounting rate; and (b) stimulate increases in the volume of traffic. Moreover, as briefly alluded to above, the ITU would find it perfectly acceptable for an asymmetric arrangement to be based on a prior agreement but applied retrospectively in the event of a sudden fall in the net settlement payment in order to "cushion the impact of the changing international telecommunications environment on those countries/territories which are considered the most vulnerable." *Ibid*.

Finally, in addition to these proposed areas where asymmetric arrangements could be applied, the ITU also acknowledged that regulators "in high teledensity countries may, on a voluntary basis, offer cost-oriented call termination at cost-oriented rates without requiring reciprocal treatment." *Ibid*. The ITU provided two reasons to support allowing the possibility for this non-reciprocal treatment: First, the ITU recognised that because "many countries have made commitments under the WTO agreements relating to basic telecommunications to apply principles such as non-discrimination, national treatment and most-favoured nation (MFN) status to market access, these same principles could, in theory, also be applied to the termination of international traffic." *Ibid*. While the ITU conceded that this interpretation is "not explicitly covered by the existing WTO agreements,"

(4) Extending the transition period by mutual agreement.[54]

Again, the ITU reiterated that:

"These are only examples of the sort of the arrangement that could be made to smoothen the transition period, for instance by making revenue stabilisation measures to assist the Administration/ROA which is the net recipient. The final report is not intended to be prescriptive. The *exact form that a 'smoother transition path' could take is better left to bilateral negotiations.*"[55]

Given its actions and policies to date, however, it is highly doubtful that the United States would react positively if, for example, a country hypothetically defined its internal version of universal service as "a wireline phone to every family unit with installation and usage charges not to exceed those in the United States, ninety per cent funded by international carriers in the settlement-of-account process based on their volume of calls terminating in US territory," even though such a universal service program would seem to meet all the criteria of the WTO Reference Paper.

Notwithstanding the above, the FCC's actions indicate that the Clinton/Gore Administration consistently believes that it must also find some way to impose its universal service charade on the international telecommunications community as well.[56] That is, so long as foreign carriers must pay access charges to ter-

this interpretation might be made explicit by "new WTO agreements concluded during the lifetime of the transition period (i.e., before 2001 or 2004)." *Ibid.* As the ITU further recognised, however, implementation "would imply moving away from the bilateral regime of the ITU towards a multilateral accord," and it is "likely that such arrangements would be based on interconnection agreements rather than on settlement rates." *Ibid.* Second, the ITU argued that "a non-reciprocal commitment to call-termination at cost-oriented rates could be offered in order to enhance Universal Access to telecommunications among the Least Developed Countries and other countries/territories with low teledensity" because, in general terms, "these countries/territories produce very little outgoing international traffic." *Ibid.* Therefore, "the possible loss to the higher teledensity economy in offering this favourable treatment is likely to be minimal." *Ibid.* Indeed, argued the ITU, "if the cost savings achieved by the low teledensity country are passed on to its consumers in terms of lower collection charges, then the net result could be a lower net settlement payable by the high teledensity country." *Ibid.*

[54] *Ibid.*

[55] *Ibid.*, (emphasis added).

[56] See, for example, *Benchmarks Order, supra* n. 315, paras. 148, 171, where the FCC recognised that the "Reference Paper on Procompetitive Regulatory Principles negotiated as part of the WTO Basic Telecom Agreement states that universal service obligations must be 'administered in a transparent, non-discriminatory and competitively neutral manner.'" *Ibid.*, para. 148. Further, the FCC noted that, "[h]idden subsidies such as those contained in settlement rates and subsidies borne disproportionately by one service, or in the case of settlement rates, by consumers from net payer countries, are not consistent with these principles and cannot be sustained in a competitive global market. We also disagree with those commenters that compare the hidden subsidies in settlement rates to domestic universal service policies in the United States, which rely on explicit and transparent funding mechanisms. Universal service in the U.S. market is based on and uses end user telecommunications revenues in the United States, not settlements revenues paid by foreign carriers". *Ibid.*, (citation omitted).

Of course, given FCC officials' flagrant denials that these fees even exist at all, this regulatory deception really should not be too surprising. See, e.g., Mike Mills, "AT&T Imposing Fee on Residential Users", *Washington Post*, 6 May 1998, at C11 (reporting that AT&T has begun to impose a fee on residential customers to pay for FCC's universal service program. In a bald-faced

minate a call in the United States, these foreign carriers—and *a fortiori* their customers—must pay into the US universal service fund whether they like it or
not.[57]

Fortunately, however, the international community is not so naïve as the FCC
apparently believes. As the ITU recently pointed out:

"[I]f the international accounting rate system were ever intended to provide a mechanism for transferring funds from high teledensity countries to low teledensity ones,
then it is a singularly inefficient mechanism for doing so. Indeed, high cost countries,
which usually have a low teledensity, are cross-subsidising low cost countries in that
the accounting rate system, as it currently works, is based on revenue-sharing rather
than underlying costs. Thus, because the accounting rate is invariably split 50/50, the
high cost country (which has a lower mark-up over its real cost base) gains less
from the transaction than the lower cost country (which has a higher mark-up).
Thus a settlements system which is actually cost-oriented should be more effective in
transferring funds between countries to meet differing needs because the underlying
cost differences would be reflected in asymmetric rates for call termination."[58]

So long as the FCC continues to strain its own credibility—as well as the
Administration's overall reputation—abroad, the FCC simply continues to
deprive both US consumers and businesses of the very benefits that these policies were supposed to achieve originally.[59]

Fortunately, however, the Fifth US Circuit Court of Appeals was able to apply
some restraint on the FCC's attempts to foist its USO obligations on the rest of
the international telecoms community. *In Texas Office of Public Utility Counsel*

lie, however, FCC officials complained that AT&T and other carriers should be absorbing the
charges themselves, and were never ordered by the FCC to pass them on to consumers. "'This is not
a federal charge. This is a charge that AT&T is creating on its own,' said the FCC's Chief of Staff,
John Nakahata." *Ibid.* Such a claim is really quite incredulous, given the fact that former FCC
Chairman Reed Hundt tried actively to "keep the fees from appearing as new line items on consumers' bills. Long-distance companies declined that request, but in a deal with [Hundt,] AT&T
said it would refrain [temporarily] from charging the fees to consumers who pay undiscounted rates
for long-distance service.").

[57] See David Molony, *supra* n. 8, at 1, 30 (reporting that Diane Cornell, then-chief of the telecoms
division of the FCC's international bureau, argued that foreign carriers should pay their fair share
to use U.S. local networks because an "'international carrier benefits from being able to terminate a
call to rural areas or low-income subscribers'" in the United States. The article further reported,
however, that the international telecoms community found this official U.S. response to be specious
at best. Quoting, among other anonymous sources, a leading Washington, D.C. telecommunications analyst, the article questioned why, given the scale and scope of the U.S. domestic telecommunications network, "'[e]very call from the poorest African nation is paying for an ISDN link to
Ted Turner's ranch.'").

[58] Methodological Note on Universal Service Obligations, Note by the ITU Secretariat, Oct. 9,
1998 (visited Nov. 16, 1998) <http://www.iut.int/intset/focus/usos3.doc>.

[59] See also Spiwak, "The Search for Meaningful Definitions", supra n. 22, at 19–21 (explaining
ill-effects of Administration's "neo-mercantile policies"). Unfortunately, the U.S. continues to
attempt to perpetuate (unsuccessfully) this charade even at the time of this writing. See, e.g.,
Remarks of Vice President Al Gore Before the ITU Plenipotentiary Conference in Minneapolis, calling for a "Digital Declaration of Interdependence" because "our children and our world are waiting." (Oct. 12, 1998). If this indeed is the case then, as discussed *supra*, the current universal service
program is clearly "taxation without representation."

v. *FCC*,[60] several parties appealed the FCC's universal service support mechanism and methodology. Among those parties was COMSAT, a small interstate carrier specialising in providing international telephone service, which challenged the FCC's decision to define the universal service base to include the international revenues of interstate carriers. According to COMSAT, because it derives such a small portion of its revenues from interstate service that it would end up with universal payment obligations exceeding its interstate revenues, it argued that this bizarre outcome violates Communication Act section 254(d)'s requirement that all universal service contributions be "equitable and non-discriminatory" and the FCC's own principle of competitive neutrality. At the very least, moreover, COMSAT argued that this result showed that the FCC's actions were arbitrary and capricious.[61] The FCC, as usual, fell back on its failsafe argument that under US administrative law, a regulatory agency has great discretion to balance the competing concerns set forth in § 254(b), which include the need for sufficient revenues to support universal service.

The court, however, disagreed with the FCC. The court found that "[w]hile the statute allows the FCC a considerable amount of discretion, however, that discretion is not absolute" and that the "heavy inequity the rule places on COMSAT and similarly situated carriers cannot simply be dismissed by the agency as a consequence of its administrative discretion."[62] In particular, the court found that the FCC's interpretation of "equitable and non-discriminatory"—which improperly allowed it to impose prohibitive costs on carriers such as COMSAT—is "arbitrary and capricious and "manifestly contrary" to the statute, because COMSAT and carriers like it will contribute more in universal service payments than they will generate from interstate service. Additionally, the court also found that the FCC's interpretation is "discriminatory," because the agency concedes that its rule damages some international carriers like COMSAT more than it harms others, and that the agency had offered no reasonable explanation of how this outcome—which would require companies such as COMSAT to incur a loss to participate in interstate service—satisfied the Telecoms Act's "equitable and non-discriminatory" language. As such, the court reversed and remanded the FCC's order further consideration.[63]

V. CONCLUSION

In sum, although universal service is indeed a worthy social goal, it nonetheless unfortunately appears that politicians (especially in the United States) are using children as ad hominem "regulatory human shields" to defend and excuse flawed (and indeed self defeating) economic policies.[64]

---

[60] 183 F.3d 393 (5th Cir. 1999).   [61] 183 F.3d at 433.
[62] 183 F.3d at 434.   [63] *Ibid.*, at 434–435.
[64] See e.g., June 1998 Statement of FCC Chairman William E. Kennard ("America's *children*, especially low income and rural *children*, need access to today's technology if they are to compete

Stated another way, if someone criticises these entry-deterring policies in any way, then the full wrath of government rains furiously down upon them in a McCarthy-like fashion branding them an enemy of children everywhere. As both of us are parents of young children we find such attacks unconscionable and offensive. As such, perhaps Whittaker Chambers expressed it the best:

> "When you understand what you see, you will no longer be children. You will know that life is pain, that each of us hangs always upon the cross of himself. And when you know this is true of every man, woman and child on earth, you will be wiser".[65]

in tomorrow's workforce . . . ending this effort is not in the best interest of the American public".); 12 June 1998 Statement of Vice President Al Gore ("I will fight to reject efforts by those who would turn out the lights on our *children* by pulling the plug on the E-rate . . . My commitment to preparing our *children* for the 21st century will not end until every *child* in every classroom and library in America can tap into the Internet . . . we will fight to protect our *children's* future and oppose any effort by Congress to eliminate or delay the goal of expanding the educational horizons of our *children*", emphasis supplied). Moreover, according to Al Gore, access to the Internet and bridging the "Digital Divide" is a "fundamental civil right". In saying this Mr Gore has turned universal service into another hot-button racial issue and has despicably played the race card from the bottom of the deck. See Remarks by Vice President Al Gore at Morgan State University (15 Feb. 2000).

[65] Whittaker Chambers, *Witness, A Letter to my Children* (Washington, Heritage, 1986).

16

Case Study: FCC's International Spectrum Policies

This chapter seeks to address a very simple and direct question: If the community of nations has made a collective decision that a vibrant global commercial satellite market is in the public interest, then why is the United States, via the Federal Communications Commission, threatening to kill this industry (including America's own significant private space industry[1]) by enacting poorly conceived—and indeed socially irresponsible—international spectrum policies which include erecting naked barriers to entry, threatening to open up yet another front in the growing "telecoms trade war" and introducing yet another example of the growing regulatory cynicism in Washington.[2]

In this case, the root of the problem stems from the FCC's ill-conceived notion that new entrants into international satellite markets should be forced to pay spectrum relocation fees just as new entrants had to pay in the US domestic PCS context.[3] Such a "cookie-cutter" approach to spectrum management is *per se* arbitrary and capricious, however, because what is good for the US domestic wireless industry is **not** *a fortiori* good for the international commercial satellite

---

[1] Indeed, United States Deputy Secretary of Commerce Robert L. Mallet warned recently that the when it comes to maintaining American leadership in the commercial space industry, it is very possible for ill-formed policies to appear to win a battle yet, in reality, "lose the war." As such, Mallet warned that America public policies must "anticipate the direction space, business and the world are taking so we in the US can benefit." In particular, argued Mallet: "We cannot let innovations pioneered by Americans be captured by the corporations of Europe, the Pacific Rim or anywhere else. We must stand up for what we believe, for if we can fight for our vision of the future, it will be a spectacular launch for the US into the 21st century." Robert L. Mallet, "Viewpoint", *Aviation Week & Space Technology* 19 April 1999 at 74. See also *In the Matter of Inquiry Concerning the Deployment of Advanced Telecommunications Capability to All Americans in a Reasonable and Timely Fashion, and Possible Steps to Accelerate Such Deployment Pursuant to Section 706 of the Telecommunications Act of 1996*, FCC 99–5 (rel. Feb. 2, 1999) at ¶ 39 (hereinafter Section 706 Report) (FCC found specifically that since 1993, over $20 billion has been invested in the space industry, of which much has gone into the broadband satellite telecommunications sector and that satellite infrastructure revenues for the time period 1997–2001 are estimated at $277 billion).

[2] See "Business and Regulatory: FCC on the Defensive Over EU Satellite Concerns", *Communications Week International*, 25 August 2000.

[3] See in re Matter of Amendment of Section 2.106 of the Commission's Rules to Allocate Spectrum at 2 Ghz for Use by the Mobile-Satellite Service, Second Report & Order and Second Memorandum and Order, FCC 00-233 (rel. July 3, 2000).

industry as well.[4] While it is true that there are certain valuable lessons that can be learned from the US domestic experience and applied onto the international market, because the domestic and international markets (as the FCC often readily admits) have very different structural economic characteristics, these markets therefore do not warrant homogeneous regulatory treatment either. As such, the FCC's policies harm—rather than promote—consumer welfare because they *inter alia*: (a) erect—rather than eliminate—barriers to entry and deter competition; (b) fail to reflect the international context in which spectrum use occurs; (c) increase—rather than reduce—transaction costs to make entry prohibitive; and (d) deter—rather than accelerate—expansion of competitive advanced broadband services to rural and poor areas (whether domestic or abroad).

To illustrate this point, this Chapter examines first why policy-makers have long-held that a rivalrous private commercial satellite industry is in the public interest. Among other reasons, this Chapter shows policy makers believe strongly that a rivalrous satellite industry can act as a potent weapon in the ongoing battle to promote competition in retail telecoms markets. More importantly, however, this Chapter shows that—consistent with public statements from the FCC itself—a rivalrous satellite industry could be among the best technologies to provide consumers who live in poor and rural areas with truly "affordable" advanced telecommunications products and services.

Next, this chapter examines exactly what economic preconditions are required for a workable global satellite industry. In particular, this Chapter examines briefly what economic factors come into play when a new firm is contemplating whether to enter a market, and how regulatory policies affect significantly this entry decision.

Third, because the international satellite industry is so wholly dependent on access to spectrum, this chapter examines briefly how regulators should formulate policies that achieve the most efficient and pro-competitive use of this scarce resource. To facilitate this analysis, this Chapter outlines briefly five discrete public policy objectives and then shows how the FCC ignored each of these objectives when formulating its international spectrum policies. Instead, the only thing the FCC's arbitrary "cookie-cutter" approach to international spectrum management achieves is the unjust enrichment of spectrum incumbents in violation of both US and international law.

Finally, this chapter demonstrates how the FCC's flawed international spectrum policies will adversely effect consumer welfare far beyond the narrow confines of the global satellite industry. In particular, this Chapter demonstrates that by imposing unilaterally spectrum relocation fees on new entrants, the US government continues to demonstrate to the international community that

---

[4] Such an approach is especially odd in light of the FCC's long-standing policies imposing different regulatory regimes on domestic and international services in light of clearly different economic structural characteristics of these respective markets.

America believes that its commitments in the WTO and ITU are not worth the paper they are written upon. Rather than affirmatively promote competition and free trade, the FCC's actions instead create improperly a strong incentive to *close* markets in direct violation of the letter and the spirit of the February 1997 WTO Treaty on Basic Telecoms Services. As mentioned in the **Foreword**[?] to this book, Federal Reserve Chairman Alan Greenspan warned that such an "essentially adversarial" approach will do nothing but harm overall consumer welfare. More importantly, however, by taxing new entry into the global satellite market, the FCC is in effect taxing the Internet. In doing so, the FCC is once again depriving consumers in poor, rural and other high-cost areas not only in the US but *world-wide* of the very advanced broadband services promised to them so prolifically by the Telecommunications Act of 1996 and the WTO Telecoms Treaty.

Finally, this chapter demonstrates how the FCC's flawed international spectrum policies will adversely affect consumer welfare far beyond the narrow confines of the global satellite industry.

II. WHY A VIBRANT PRIVATE COMMERCIAL SATELLITE INDUSTRY IS IN THE
PUBLIC INTEREST

As demonstrated in great detail in chapter 3, it is widely recognised among scholars that the "public interest" standard is, at bottom, a consumer welfare-maximisation standard.[5] As such, regulatory agencies subject to this standard should be concerned about solving two basic economic problems: (1) assuring that the regulated firms under their jurisdiction do not engage in anticompetitive behaviour or charge captive ratepayers monopoly prices; and (2), where practical, formulating regulatory paradigms designed to improve overall market performance in both the short-run and especially, given the huge sunk costs inherent to the telecommunications industry, the long-run.[6] This emphasis on improving market

[5] Lawrence J. Spiwak, "Antitrust, the "Public Interest" and Competition Policy: The Search for Meaningful Definitions in a Sea of Analytical Rhetoric", *Antitrust Report* (Matthew Bender, 1997); Gregory L. Rosston and Jeffrey S. Steinberg, "Using Market-Based Spectrum Policy to Promote the Public Interest", (1997) 50 *Fed. Com. L.J.* 87.

[6] Spiwak, *supra*, n. 3. It should be noted, however, that the FCC's challenge is made more complex because telecommunications is clearly an industry characterised by rapid change and innovation. This challenge is now exacerbated with the passage of the Telecommunications Act of 1996; see also *Turner Broadcasting System Inc.* v. *FCC*, 117 S. Ct. 1174, 1189 (1997) (regulatory schemes concerning telecommunications have "special significance" because of the "inherent complexity and assessments about the likely interaction of industries undergoing rapid economic and technological change"); *Denver Area Educational Telecommunications Consortium Inc.* v. *FCC*, 116 S. Ct. 2374, 2385 (1996) (Court is "aware . . . of the changes taking place in the law, the technology, and the industrial structure, related to telecommunications, see, e.g., Telecommunications Act of 1996 . . ."); *Columbia Broadcasting Inc* v. *Democratic National Committee*, 412 U.S. 94, 102, 93 S. Ct. 2080, 2086 (1973) ("The problems of regulation are rendered more difficult because the . . . industry is dynamic in terms of technological change"); *FCC* v. *Pottsville Broadcasting Co.*, 309 U.S. 134, 138 (1940) ("Communications Act is not designed primarily as a new code for the adjustment of conflicting private rights through adjudication. Rather it expresses a desire on the part of Congress to

performance is key, because as market performance improves and competition takes hold, consumers will receive the benefits of both static (declining prices) and dynamic (increased innovation) economic efficiencies or, preferably, both. Moreover, as market performance improves and competition takes hold, consumers will enjoy other societal benefits such as the long-term growth of real income per person and greater employment opportunities.[7] Most importantly, however, is that if a market is performing well, *then the need for stringent "public-utility"-type government regulation should be unnecessary.*[8]

To date, the challenge of promoting competition for local telecommunications service (especially in the United States) has proved to be a difficult process. For this reason, Congress and the FCC have long-found that the public interest is well-served by a vigorous and vibrant private commercial satellite industry that can provide an alternative to the incumbents' monopoly control of local loop plant and, as such, have traditionally promoted aggressively American leadership in space. One only needs to look back to the FCC's original "Open-Skies" policies of the 1970s and 1980s to see how the FCC would take no second to achieve this goal—even if it meant contravening (correctly) the specific findings of the US Department of Justice.[9] Moreover, the FCC's ostensible belief in the public interest benefits received from vigorous private competition in the international satellite industry continues directly through to this day.[10]

Most significantly, however, is that the FCC has repeatedly found that a vibrant commercial international satellite industry is among the best hopes of

---

maintain, through appropriate administrative control, a grip on the dynamic aspects" of the telecommunications industry).

[7] See F.M. Scherer & David Ross, *Industrial Market Structure And Economic Performance* (3rd ed., publisher, 1990) at 4–5.

[8] See Walter Adams, "Public Policy in a Free Enterprise Economy", in Walter Adams (ed.) *The Structure of American Industry* (7th ed., publisher, 1986) (primary purpose of economic public policy paradigms should be to "perpetuate and preserve, in spite of possible cost, a system of governance for a competitive, free enterprise economy" where "power is decentralized; . . . newcomers with new products and new techniques have a genuine opportunity to introduce themselves and their ideas; . . . [and] the 'unseen hand' of competition instead of the heavy hand of the state performs the basic regulatory function on behalf of society").

[9] See, e.g., *United States* v. *FCC*, 652 F.2d 72 (D.C. Cir. 1980) (*en banc*).

[10] See, e.g., *In re Establishment of Policies and Service Rules for the Mobile Satellite Service in the 2 GHz Band*, Notice of Proposed Rulemaking, FCC 99–50 (rel. March 25, 1999) at ¶ 95 (hereinafter "March 1999 NPRM"); see also Rosston & Steinberg *supra* n. 3 at 113: "United States consumers and producers can also potentially benefit from the development of worldwide seamless networks. Roaming agreements that permit customers of personal wireless services to make and receive phone calls easily while away from their home nations, and agreements that facilitate free circulation of communications equipment between nations, such as mutual recognition agreements for the type approval of terminals, can contribute to the development of such networks. In addition, policies that promote use of the same spectrum for the same services around the world may facilitate the development of global systems and seamless networks by eliminating the need for equipment that can operate on multiple frequency bands, as well as for protocols to convert international communications from one frequency to another. Furthermore, consistency in spectrum allocations among different countries may produce economies of scale for equipment manufacturers, thereby reducing prices for consumers."

achieving truly "affordable" universal service and advanced broadband deployment to poor and rural areas in America. In the FCC's own words:

"Satellites are an excellent technology for delivering both basic and advanced telecommunication services to unserved, rural, insular or economically isolated areas, including Native American communities, Alaska, Hawaii, and Puerto Rico, and US territories and possessions such as communities within the US Virgin Islands, Guam and American Samoa.[11] Satellites may offer a cost advantage over wireline access alternatives in remote areas where a limited population may not provide the economies of scale to support the deployment of wireline or terrestrial wireless networks. The basic build-out required to obtain satellite service is for earth stations to transmit and receive satellite signals.[12] The Commission is committed to encouraging delivery of telecommunications services, including satellite services, to unserved and high-cost communities and seeking to develop cost-effective incentives for such services. Once authorized, many of the 2 GHz MSS systems will be capable of providing voice and data communications to these communities."[13]

In fact, FCC Chairman William E. Kennard himself conceded recently that:

"It may well be that the answer, particularly in rural markets, lies in wireless and satellite technologies. It is therefore imperative that we continue to maximize the amount of spectrum available for broadband uses. In short, we must use all the tools we have to accelerate deployment of advanced telecommunications throughout America."[14]

In light of the above, therefore, responsible public policies must continue to promote, rather than prohibit, new entry into the global satellite industry.

III. THE ECONOMICS OF ENTRY

Having therefore determined that a vibrant commercial satellite industry is in the public interest, the next question to ask is what does it take to create a market structure that is conducive to entry and vigorous rivalry?

As explained in Chapter 2, the telecoms industry in general—and certainly the global satellite industry in particular—is an extremely capital and time intensive business. As further explained in Chapter 2, under basic economic theory, however, *entry will occur only if firms perceive that entry will be profitable.*

---

[11] See *Federal-State Joint Board on Universal Service*, CC Docket No. 96–45, Second Recommended Decision, FCC 98–7, at ¶ 55 (rel. November 25, 1998).

[12] In fact, the FCC noted specifically that American Mobile Satellite Corporation, a GSO MSS licensee, is providing service to a police force in the Navajo Nation and to the remote community of Tortilla Flat, Arizona, and that General Communications, Inc., an earth station operator, provides voice and private line services to fifty rural Alaskan Bush communities. See March 1999 NPRM, *supra* n. 9 at 44, n. 216.

[13] March 1999 NPRM, *supra* n. 9 at ¶ 95.

[14] Separate Statement of FCC Chairman William E. Kennard in the Commission's Section 706 Report, *supra* n. 1.

A. Common Examples of Entry Costs for the Global Satellite Industry

Exogenous entry costs are those substantial costs which new entrants must incur, usually up-front, a great deal of which will be irrecoverable (*i.e.*, sunk) if exit is required. Exogenous entry costs for the global satellite industry, to state it mildly, are *very* high.[15] Not only do global satellite providers face the same exogenous entry costs as any other would-be provider of telecommunications and information services must face (*e.g.*, marketing for, and the retention of, new consumers, investment in new plant, capitalisation, *etc.*[16]), but the majority of global satellite providers' initial physical plant (*i.e.*, satellites) must be hurled hundreds of miles into outer-space on top of a rocket than can (and often does) explode.[17] Moreover, as FCC Commissioner Susan Ness has recognised, the planning stages to a satellite launch alone can take five years or longer.[18] Yet, if regulatory policies promote rather than deter entry—notwithstanding the Iridium and ICO bankruptcies of 1999—entrepreneurs are still willing to undertake these risks and enter the market because they still expect post-entry profits to be greater than zero.[19]

---

[15] The operational and financial importance of capital intensity, sunk costs and investment irreversibility for satellite systems is compounded by the fact that non-geostationary satellite systems, in particular, are not easily divisible into different discrete geographic market units—unlike a terrestrial radio point to point or broadcast system. While satellite systems can be designed to address a single country or location within a larger area, doing so sacrifices the very economic advantages that make satellite systems attractive. Satellite systems lack much of the scalability—build a small part, then add another and another—of terrestrial systems. They are not as easily adaptable to future market or technological change as terrestrial systems. Adding or subtracting capacity or changing design or service capability is difficult and costly even in the few instances in which doing so is even possible. For example, Section 706 Report at ¶ 39 (satellite infrastructure revenues for the time period 1997–2001 are estimated at $277 billion.); [insert Iridium problems here.] Iridium spent upwards of $5 billion for satellite construction and utterly failed. The satellites in the Iridium constellation will probably be intentionally crashed. Although Iridium's multiple problems (Iridium is a case-study in how not to launch a service and run a company) cannot be blamed on regulatory intervention, Iridium demonstrates the necessary high investment cost in the industry and real risk of spectacular failure.(see, e.g., Theresa Foley, "Iridium Faces Launch Delays", *Comm. Wk. Int'l,* 3 Feb. 1997) and ICO is spending upwards of $3 billion to construct 12 satellites in California (Theresa Foley, "ICO Faces Uphill Struggle for U.S. Licenses", *Comm. Wk. Int'l,* 4 May 1998.

[16] FCC's Section 706 Report found specifically that some estimates reveal that approximately $65 billion in financing will be required over the next five years to fund the next generation of satellites, including broadband satellite systems. See *supra* n. 1 at ¶ 39.

[17] See, e.g., Theresa Foley, "Iridium and Globalstar hit by Delays", *Comm. Wk. Int'l,* 21 Sept. 1998 (reporting that 12 of Globalstar's satellites were destroyed in a Russian-Ukrainian Rocket Failure); Theresa Foley, "Iridium Faces Launch Delays", *supra* n. 13 (reporting that Iridium had "no idea" when the Delta rocket, which will launch 43 or more of its 66 satellites, will be cleared to resume launches after "spectacular" failure that destroyed a military satellite.)

[18] See Separate Statement of FCC Commissioner Susan Ness in FCC's Section 706 Proceeding, *supra* n. 1.

[19] Theresa Foley, "Special Report: Satellite Funding—Star Attractions", *Comm. Wk. Int'l,* 16 August 1999 (reporting that "[i]nvestment in satellite projects is looking healthier than ever—despite major setbacks in the global mobile services market" and that the satellite industry is set to attract record new investment of $5 billion in 1999, higher than the $4.2 billion raised in 1998 for satellites from public debt and equity markets"); but *cf.* "Space Cadet, LEX", *Financial Times,*

B. How Regulation Effects Entry Into the Global Satellite Industry

Endogenous entry costs are those sunk costs that a new entrant must incur that are induced directly by incumbents or by regulation.[20] If these costs are so great as to make post-entry profit less than zero, then entry simply will not occur. Since regulation can be such a significant source of entry costs, however, one should not be surprised to find incumbent firms using regulation (and litigation in the courts) as an entry deterrent.[21] Indeed, so long as the incumbent protects more profits than it spends on deterrence, the incumbent will find entry deterrence to be profitable undertaking.[22] These costs are more than just financial, however. Given the incredibly dynamic nature of telecoms markets, regulatory delay is an equally effective mechanism for quashing prospective competitive entry.[23]

For any industry that relies primarily on spectrum, there are three primary types of endogenous entry costs: (a) auctions; (b) spectrum fees; and (c) relocation costs. As explained *infra*, while one regulator certainly has the power to make endogenous entry costs so high as to be unprofitable in a single domestic

---

18 August 1999 at 18 ("The only silver lining [of Iridium's bankruptcy] is the damage all this is inflicting on Iridium's rivals. The market it is now targeting does not look like one that can support a number of satellite systems.")

[20] To wit Business Week Magazine proclaimed 1999 as the "Year of the Regulator" for telecoms, *Business Week Magazine*, 11 January 1999 at 98.

[21] See, e.g., Mark Leibovich, "A Digital Capital Emerges on the Potomac" *Washington Post*, 6 Dec. 1998 where it was reported that: "Regulation can make or break any of these [MSS] companies. Which is why [Iridium's general counsel Thomas] Tuttle's attorneys specialize in using the regulatory process to gain a competitive advantage. After Tuttle's meeting, he walks down the hall to another group of regulatory attorneys. They discuss ways of stopping rival ICO Global Communications from getting regulatory clearance for its planned satellite system. . . . [Tuttle] leaves the meeting grinning, pleased that his team is proficient in both regulatory hardball and gentle diplomacy."

[22] See Ford. One real-world example of a endogenous sunk cost is the cost of physical collocation in an ILEC central office. That space can, because of regulation, only be used to provide telecommunications services—once procured, the CLEC cannot readily convert collocation space to a condo or a youth education center. ILECs know this, and rationally price collocation in a manner akin to an "entry tax." Sadly, these construction costs are lightly and ineffectually regulated (if at all) and oftentimes are in excess of $100,000 for each central office. With that type of entry tax, it is not surprising that there has been little entry into smaller or rural central offices. In California, for example, acquiring a customer requires the entrant to make a one-time, nonrefundable payment to the incumbent of about $400. Acquiring 1,000 customers, a trivial 0.01 percent market share in California, would cost the entrant $400,000 in nonrefundable payments to the incumbent. Perhaps even more problematic are the high nonrecurring charges for co-location space in the incumbent's central office. These payments, nonrefundable on exit of the industry, are in most states hundreds of thousands of dollars. In New York, for example, 100 square feet of co-location space can require a nonrefundable payment of around $1 million. Even in the less densely populated Southern states, nonrecurring charges for co-location space can exceed $300,000. With a 10 percent market share in an average central office, a payment of this size costs the entrant roughly $5 per customer per month. *Ibid.*

[23] The need for spectrum is especially acute for the non-geostationary systems that have constellations of satellites that move relative to the earth. Although these systems are capable of providing services anywhere in the world, in order for entry to be profitable, these constellations need adequate spectrum in which to operate. See Rosston and Steinberg, *supra* n. 3 at 113.

context, endogenous entry costs can be particularly prohibitive in the international satellite context given the multiple levels of regulatory clearance required for entry.

IV. INTERNATIONAL SPECTRUM POLICY: HOW DO WE MAXIMISE THE PUBLIC INTEREST?

A. Regulators Must Formulate Policies that Promote Competition and Reduce Entry Barriers in Light of the Special Conditions of the International Satellite Industry

As mentioned *supra*, the "public interest" standard is a consumer welfare-maximisation standard. To achieve this end, The United States' Congress has made clear that the United States shall maintain control over spectrum within the nation's jurisdiction, and that a license to use spectrum shall not constitute ownership of that spectrum.[24] Accordingly, as Gregory Rosston and Jeffrey Steinberg contend:

> "[T]he public interest is best served by ensuring that the American people receive the maximum benefit from the spectrum resource. Therefore, the Commission's spectrum policy should advance the goal of ensuring that the full benefit of the spectrum resource accrues to the public and the goal of achieving the most beneficial uses of spectrum."[25]

As such, having first decided that (a) a vibrant commercial satellite industry is in the public interest; but also realising that (b) entry is expensive and will only occur if it is perceived to be profitable, the next step in the analysis must be to identify the specific public policy decisions society needs make in order to achieve this goal. Rosston and Steinberg proposed an excellent set of policy guidelines for international spectrum management. These proposals include, *inter alia*, the notions that:

(1) "Promotion of competition should . . . be a principle consideration" and, as such, the FCC should "strive to reduce barriers to entry";[26]
(2) The FCC's "spectrum policy decisions should reflect the international context in which spectrum usage occurs. Radio waves do not stop at national borders. Therefore, domestic policies must take into account the

---

[24] See Communications Act Section 301, 47 U.S.C. § 301, which provides specifically that: "It is the purpose of this Act, among other things, to maintain the control of the United States over all channels of radio transmission; and to provide for the use of such channels, but not the ownership thereof, by persons for limited periods of time, under licenses granted by Federal authority, and no such license shall be construed to create any right, beyond the terms, conditions, and periods of the license."

[25] See Rosston and Steinberg, *supra* n. 4 at 91.

[26] *Ibid.*, at 97.

spectrum policies of other nations. The United States' spectrum policies should, among other things, support global systems and seamless international networks, in both satellite and terrestrial operations, where such systems promote the public interest";[27]

(3) Because non-geostationary satellite constellations need adequate spectrum in which to operate in order to be profitable, the FCC "need[s] to develop spectrum policies for the entry of foreign-owned satellite systems into the United States";[28]

(4) The FCC "should pursue policies that facilitate the development of world-wide seamless networks without precluding other uses and technologies. This end can be achieved by promoting policies that *reduce the transaction costs, both in the United States and abroad, of participating in worldwide seamless networks.* Specifically, the United States should support spectrum allocations in the International Telecommunication Union, domestically, and in other countries that would allow the same equipment to operate worldwide but would allow other uses as well";[29] and finally

(5) "[G]lobal spectrum policies, like global wireline telecommunications policies, should seek to extend connectivity to citizens around the world. Intergovernmental satellite organizations such as INTELSAT and Inmarsat have been instrumental in bringing communications to the developing world and ensuring that all nations are interconnected to the global public switched network. As private nongeostationary and geostationary satellite systems are licensed, and the natures of INTELSAT and Inmarsat change, it is important that the United States' and global policy support expansion of competitive communications in developing nations."[30]

As shown below, however, the FCC ignored every single one of these maxims when it formulated its international spectrum policies post-WTO by requiring new entrants to pay spectrum-clearing fees. In particular, by imposing spectrum clearing fees on new entrants, the FCC's policies, *inter alia*: (a) erect—rather than eliminate—barriers to entry and deter competition; (b) fail to reflect the international context in which spectrum use occurs; (c) increase—rather than reduce—transaction costs to make entry prohibitive; and (d) deter—rather than accelerate—expansion of competitive advanced broadband services to rural and poor areas (whether domestic or abroad). The FCC's international spectrum policies therefore do more to harm, rather than to promote, overall consumer welfare.

---

[27] *Ibid.*, at 112; see also Douglas W. Webbink, *Frequency Spectrum Deregulation Alternatives*, (FCC OPP Working Paper No. 2, October 1980) at 39 ("In any case, as long as U.S. spectrum users abide by international regulations, foreign countries should not be concerned how U.S. users are selected, or who the specific users are.")

[28] Rosston and Steinberg, *supra* n. 4 at 113.

[29] Rosston and Steinberg, *supra* n. 4 at 114 (emphasis supplied).

[30] *Ibid.*, at 114–115.

B. Why the FCC's Current Approach is both Inappropriate and Anticompetitive

Over the last several years there has been a significant amount of work supporting the notion that the most efficient way to allocate domestic spectrum is to bestow some sort of "property right" to the license.[31] While this notion of a "property right" falls clearly short of a "fee simple absolute,"[32] given the huge sums firms pay to use the spectrum (either via auctions, user-fees or relocation costs), there is a clearly an expectation of use and renewal for this spectrum—a "leasehold" if you will.[33] Douglas Webbink, the current Chief Economist of the FCC's International Bureau, described this notion close to twenty years ago as an "economic" property right because a "legal" property right is *expressly prohibited* under Section 301 of the Communications Act of 1934.[34]

The FCC was able to use successfully this notion of spectrum "property rights" when it auctioned off spectrum for US domestic PCS services in the early 1990's.[35] While this analytical "fiction" may make sense in the *domestic* context, however, this notion of "property rights" (economic or legal) simply has *no meaning* when one views spectrum from either a *cross-border* (international) or *outer-space* perspective: First, as Rosston and Steinberg explained *supra*, spectrum emissions respect neither national geographic boundaries nor altitude ceilings. Second, and more importantly, it is legally (and indeed metaphysically) impossible to grant a property right over matter which is clearly not under your jurisdiction or control in the first instance. It is for this very reason therefore that spectrum for international satellite service is allocated on a *global* basis by international consensus through the International Telecommunication Union (ITU) process.[36]

---

[31] See generally, John W. Berresford, *The Future of the FCC, Promote Competition, Then Turn Out the Lights?* (Economic Strategy Institute, 1997).

[32] Indeed former FCC Chairman Reed Hundt constantly sought to impose content requirements on broadcasters because, in his view, "in exchange for use of the public's airwaves, the Communications Act requires broadcasters to serve the "public interest, convenience and necessity." See, e.g., Chairman Reed E. Hundt, Federal Communications Commission, Speech to the Annenberg Public Policy Center's 2nd Annual Conference on Children And Television Washington, D.C., "Getting Better All The Time" (June 9, 1997) (http://www.fcc.gov/Speeches/Hundt/spreh731.html); Chairman Reed E. Hundt, Federal Communications Commission, Speech To The Center For Media Education's Press Conference On The New Children's Television Act Rules, Washington, D.C. "Kids TV: The Impossible Has Become Inevitable" (September 18, 1997)(http://www.fcc.gov/Speeches/Hundt/spreh731.html).

[33] Other commentors have analogised status to a "right of use" such as a "mineral right" (see Glenn Harland Reynolds, "International Space Law: Into the Twenty-First Century", 25 *Vand. J. Transnat'l L.* 225, 235) another commentator has described this bizarre process as "not establishing property rights, but merely reallocating them with prices." (see Dean Lueck, "The Rule of First Possession and the Design of the Law", (1995) 38 *J.L. Econ.* 393, 421).

[34] Webbink, *supra* n. 25 at 8–9; Communications Act Section 301, *supra* n. 22.

[35] See Rosston & Steinberg, *supra* n. 3 at n. 19 and citations therein.

[36] For a good primer of how the ITU process works, see generally, Jannat C. Thompson, "Space for Rent: The International Telecommunications Union, Space Law, and Orbit/Spectrum Leasing", (1996) 62 *J. Air L. & Com.* 279.

Notwithstanding the above, however, the FCC decided (in the face of significant political pressure) to apply the domestic PCS model—although the FCC denies specifically doing so—onto the international satellite market as well.[37] In so doing, the FCC risks making the transaction costs associated with the global satellite industry so exorbitant as to make entry prohibitive.[38] That is to say, while spectrum clearing costs may be "manageable" when you are dealing with a single country (*i.e.*, the US's experience with PCS in the domestic context), these transaction costs are going to be multiplied exponentially as new entrants are forced to pay clearing costs to every single indigenous operator on the planet with whom they cannot share spectrum.[39] As US-based Teledesic LLC explained emphatically to the FCC recently:

> "In addressing this issue, the Commission should be sensitive to the effects its decision will have outside the United States. It has been noted that political considerations may induce [foreign] regulatory authorities to adopt relocation rules that are more generous to incumbents than what economic efficiency would dictate, in order to attract the support (or diminish the opposition) of politically powerful incumbent operators. But

[37] Indeed, although the FCC in a recent docket (*In re Matter of Amendment of Section 2.106 of the Commission's Rules to Allocate Spectrum at 2 GHz for Use by the Mobile-Satellite Service*, Memorandum Opinion and Third Notice of Proposed Rulemaking, FCC 98–309, 13 FCC Rcd 23,949 (1998) (hereinafter "Third NPRM") stated specifically that it did not base its relocation policy for MSS service on its PCS proceeding but instead on its Emerging Technology Proceeding (¶ 22), just three paragraphs later the FCC concedes explicitly that "all new PCS licenses [in the 1850–1990 Mhz band] were subject to the relocation rules of the Emerging Technology Proceeding." (¶ 25); see also *In re Matter of Amendment of Section 2.106 of the Commission's Rules to Allocate Spectrum at 2 GHz for Use by the Mobile-Satellite Service*, First Report and Further Notice of Proposed Rulemaking, FCC 97–93, 12 FCC Rcd 7388 (1997) at ¶ 42 ("We will provide for MSS sharing with, and any relocation of, FS incumbents in accordance with the policies in our Emerging Technology Proceeding.")

Moreover, procrastination or outright ignoring deliberately this issue won't make it go away either. See, e.g., Third NPRM at ¶ 16, noting that the FCC has yet examine specifically whether its Emerging Technology policies should be applied to international satellite services. To her credit, FCC Commissioner Susan Ness wrote separately in a separate statement to "highlight" the fact that because there are "unique regulatory challenges facing international satellite systems globally. . . ." she specifically "encouraged the Commission generally to consider the effect of our spectrum management policies have on international satellite systems seeking to be licensed and begin offering services globally as one of a host of issues that we will explore in the upcoming spectrum management en banc." This did not occur, however. What makes this statement truly embarrassing, however, is the fact that the European Commission observed publicly that "such a statement implies a tacit recognition that the FCC has not yet given proper consideration to the impact that the FCC spectrum management policies have at [the] international level." See 3 March 1999 Reply Comments by the European Commission to the FCC's Third NPRM at ¶ 8.

[38] See, e.g., Sheridan Nye, "ICO Faces $2 Billion Bill as US Rejects EC Complaints", *Comm. Wk. Int'l*, 2 Dec. 1997 (Reporting that Sir Leon Brittan, then-European Commission Vice President and trade commissioner, warned the U.S. that the FCC's policies of forcing new entrants to pay spectrum relocation fees might provoke copy-cat actions in other countries in which case other MSS operators, "including the U.S.' own Iridium and Globalstar MSS operators, could find themselves facing similar charges in other overseas markets") (emphasis supplied.)

[39] To wit, assume *arguendo* that you want to mail a letter from the United States to Japan. It is affordable currently because you only have to pay one postage rate to the originating country. Yet, if you were required suddenly to pay a postage tariff for every single country through which the letter must pass over or through to reach the end destination during transit, then the cost of mailing this letter has suddenly become cost prohibitive.

the Commission must attend to the likelihood that regulators outside the US will require at least as much from the US-dominated satellite industry as the FCC requires. Because the FCC's rules may be replicated around the world, giving FS operators a windfall here in the US could ultimately result in a huge and unjustified transfer payment from US satellite companies to non-US terrestrial operators. *This would be an extremely expensive way to placate one domestic interest group.*"[40]

Pardon the pun, therefore, but it doesn't take a rocket scientist to figure out that when endogenous entry cost—costs that are out of your control but are in complete control of regulators—exceed any conceivable profit margin, entrepreneurial entry simply will *not* occur. Prohibiting entry is the *sine qua non* of anticompetitive conduct and contravenes the core letter and spirit of both the 1996 Act and the WTO. Thus, if the FCC's policies are not revised quickly, then the only parties left standing may be government-controlled enterprises—the very result the US has been attempting vigorously to eliminate since the notion of private commercial space exploration was first entertained.

Finally, what is particularly egregious about the FCC's arbitrary and anticompetitive policy is that the FCC *admits openly* that holding incumbent users harmless is a more important public policy objective than promoting new entry into the global satellite industry. To wit, in the FCC's Third Notice, when the FCC was confronted with the fact that entry simply may not occur if new satellite entrants are forced to pay clearing costs to every single indigenous operator with whom they cannot share spectrum, the FCC nonetheless deliberately "decline[d] to deviate" from its established Enhanced Services policy because "*incumbents arguably could be directly, adversely impacted by such a decision.*"[41] This statement is truly incredulous and such a naked admission of regulatory capture has no place in the public dialectic.[42] More importantly, however, by telling spectrum incumbents that it is perfectly acceptable to "stay until you are paid to move," the FCC has unjustly enriched these incumbents by granting them *de facto* property rights in spectrum which is a clear violation of both US and international law![43]

---

[40] Teledesic's November 19, 1999 Comments in *In re Redesignation of the 17.7–19.7 GHz Frequency Band*, IB Docket No. 98–172 at 18, n. 39 (emphasis supplied).

[41] Third NPRM, supra n. 37 at ¶ 16 (emphasis supplied).

[42] *SBC Communications* v. FCC, 56 F.3d 1484, 1491 (D.C. Cir. 1995)(regulator is "not at liberty to subordinate the public interest to the interest of equalizing competition among competitors")(citing *Hawaiian Telephone* v. FCC, 498 F.2d 771 (D.C. Cir. 1974)); *W.U. Telephone Co.* v. FCC, 665 F.2d 1112, 1122 (D.C. Cir.1981) ("equalization of competition is not itself a sufficient basis for Commission action")). See also Frank Easterbrook, "The Court and the Economic System", (1984) 98 *Harv. L. Rev.* 4, 15–16.

[43] Indeed, these U.S. policies potentially violate at least two provisions of the WTO. First, Under Article VI, Section 4 of the GATTs, the FCC's policies are neither "(a) based on objective and transparent criteria, such as competence and the ability to supply the service" nor "(b) not more burdensome than necessary to ensure the quality of the service. . . ." Similarly, U.S. policies appear to violate ¶ 4 of the Reference Paper, which provides that "Any procedures for the allocation and use of scarce resources, including frequencies, numbers and rights of way, will be carried out in an objective, timely, transparent and non-discriminatory manner."

V. HOW THE FCC'S INTERNATIONAL SPECTRUM POLICIES ALSO EXACERBATES
A GROWING "TELECOMS TRADE WAR" THAT IS DANGEROUSLY CLOSE TO
SPIRALING OUT OF HAND

While it is it bad enough that the FCC's flawed "cookie-cutter" approach to international spectrum could harm materially or even destroy outright the commercial satellite industry, policy-makers must also understand that these poorly-conceived policies will have dire ramifications far beyond the industry itself as they add further fuel to the current telecoms trade war.

A. The FCC's Actions Close Markets and Call into Question America's International Credibility

1. *International Trade Concerns*

Forcing unilaterally new satellite entrants to pay spectrum-clearing costs to every single indigenous operator with whom they cannot share spectrum is precisely the kind of "essentially adversarial" tactic Chairman Greenspan warned specifically about. See *supra* Chapter 1. Indeed, from an international trade perspective, the FCC's old-standby argument that it is not asserting jurisdiction over international spectrum but only using its authority under the Communications Act of 1934 "to impose on FCC licensees conditions and obligations consistent with the public interest, convenience and necessity" is the very epitome of such an "essentially adversarial" approach.[44] The FCC must recognise that in *any* international context—where it must deal with multiple *co-sovereign* nations—what is good for the goose also will be good for the gander. In other words, if the US is free to unilaterally impose regulation (spectrum clearing fees, whatever), *then every other* signatory to either the WTO or the ITU may *a fortiori* do so as well! Thus, as explained in more detail *infra*, even though a US court has upheld the FCC's unilateral "first among equals" approach for IMTS service[45] it still doesn't mean that it is good policy in the first instance.[46]

This growing "telecoms trade war" must be reigned in. Doesn't the FCC realise that it is once again "shooting itself in the foot" by inviting a "feeding frenzy" against US firms in this case? Surely the last thing the anyone wants to see the FCC achieve is to place US firms in the difficult position of inadvertent

---

[44] Third NPRM, *supra* n. 37 at ¶16.

[45] See *Cable & Wireless* v. *FCC*, 166 F.3d 1224 (D.C. Cir, 1999). The court reached its flawed decision by totally misunderstanding the facts and economics of the case, however, by throwing into question established U.S. competition and ratemaking law and, most embarrassing of all, misquoting repeatedly the ITU treaty.

[46] This reality is nothing unexpected. Even the EU specifically warned the FCC that its approach can have significant impacts on the licensing of MSS and other global services in other countries and that the EU is "particularly concerned" about the "negative precedent" the FCC policies could set in other countries. EU Reply Comments to Third NPRM, *supra* n. 37 at ¶ 8.

pawns in a telecoms trade war when they seek to enter foreign markets. Yet, until the FCC revises its current policies, the FCC's "essentially adversarial" policies not only make such retaliation possible, it makes retaliation *inevitable* as well.

In the specific case of the international satellite industry, as both Chairman Greenspan and Teledesic pointed out *supra*, retaliation probably means inevitable naked attempts by foreign to extract supra-competitive spectrum clearing fees from US firms when they seek to enter foreign markets. Indeed, if the US can unilaterally impose spectrum-licensing fees (*i.e.*, endogenous entry costs), then what is to stop Belgium, England, Togo or Upper Uzbekistan from doing so as well? Moreover, while these above-cost fees will be designed ostensibly for spectrum clearing purposes, it will be quite clear to all involved that these above-cost fees are, in sad reality, reciprocal measures designed to retaliate specifically against the US and its business community. As such, if these above-cost relocation fees are likely to occur, then why open US firms up to such an easy shakedown?

2. Effect on US International Commitments in the WTO

The notions of international comity and respect for treaty obligations are at the heart of public international law jurisprudence.[47] Yet, as shown below, because the FCC believes that it may impose unilaterally spectrum relocation costs on new satellite entrants, the US government continues to demonstrate to the international community that America believes that its commitments in the WTO are not to be taken seriously.

Indeed, the US played a significant role in bringing consensus for this landmark agreement and, as noted *passim*, promised proudly that it would lead by example. Yet, what example has the US really set for the community of nations? Apparently, not a very exemplary one.[48] Now, by believing erroneously that it may unilaterally "impose a relocation compensation condition on the US-licensed space segments", the US once again enacts policies that in reality improperly close—rather than appropriately open—American markets. If American markets are closed, however, then other sovereign nations are invited to erect similar barriers to entry. When this "domino-effect" occurs, the US moves the international telecommunications market in the wrong direction and in direct contravention of the fundamental marketing-opening principles of the WTO and the GATT. As such, unless and until the FCC revises its policies, the

---

[47] See, e.g., Article 38 of the Charter of the International Court of Justice, which provides that the Court shall apply: "(a) international conventions, whether general or particular, establishing rules expressly recognized by the contesting states; (b) international custom, as evidence of a general practice of accepted law; (c) the general principles of law recognized by civilized nations; [and] (d) subject to the provisions of Article 59 [of the Court's charter], judicial decisions and the teachings of the most highly qualified publicists of the various nations, as subsidiary means for the determinations of the rules of law."

[48] See *supra*.

US may well find itself before a WTO dispute panel for such anticompetitive and market-closing conduct.[49]

B. By Taxing Entry, the FCC *a fortiori* Taxes the Internet and Deprives Consumers Who Live in Poor and Rural Areas of Advanced Broadband Telecommunications Service

One of the thorniest issues confronting public policy-makers today is how to achieve truly competitive and deregulated markets yet at the same time ensure that all of their citizens receive "affordable" access to advanced telecommunications products and services.[50] As demonstrated above, exogenous (x) and endogenous (e) entry costs are extremely high, and the necessity to overcome these costs is a major reason for the slow pace of local loop competition to date. What often tips the scales against entry into rural and poor areas is the fact that post-entry profit is likely to be extremely low at the outset, thus virtually assuring that entry will be, by definition, a losing venture. Yet, the nature of global satellite service can actually alter this equation in *favor* of entry to these poor and rural areas because global satellite operators, with their huge economies of scale and ubiquitous scope, have excellent spillover effects—*i.e.*, it is far easier for them to enter these markets than for any other firm.

If these statements are indeed true, then what exactly is the problem here? The FCC must realise that its poorly-conceived international spectrum policies are actually yet another *self-defeating exercise* in the quest to bring true "affordable" advanced telecommunications products and services for all Americans. Once again, it does not take a rocket-scientist to figure out the simple fact that no consumer—whether they live in New York City or in the Alaskan tundra— is going to receive the benefit of affordable global satellite services *if entry does not occur in the first instance!* Thus, by charging unilaterally an "entry fee", the FCC has effectively "taxed" the Internet itself out of the hands of the very consumers who need advanced broadband services most.[51] Such a result is clearly

---

[49] See, e.g., EU Reply Comments to Third NPRM, *supra* n. 37 at ¶ 10: "The EC would like to reaffirm that it will remain attentive to the treatment given to European-based satellite systems in the U.S. The EC will be particularly attentive to any behaviour which is contrary to the spirit or letter of the commitments undertaken by the U.S. within the WTO agreement on basic telecommunications services" (emphasis supplied); see also European Commission Report on United States Barriers to Trade and Investment (July 2000) at 57–9 <http://europa.eu.int/comm/trade/pdf/US_bt2000.pdf>.

[50] See, e.g., Communications Act Section 254, 47 U.S.C.§ 254; OFTEL Consultation Document, *Universal Telecommunication Services* (July 1999).

[51] *Cf.* Jerry Hausman, "Taxation by Telecommunications Regulation", in *Tax Policy and the Economy* (1998). Moreover, by unreasonably deterring the deployment of MSS service, the FCC is also impeding the ability of international humanitarian or disaster relief operations such as the International Red Cross from doing their job effectively. See Mohammed Harbi, "Perspective: Humanitarian Solution to Hardware Constraints", *Comm. Wk. Int'l*, 29 June 1998, noting that "[n]ew kinds of systems, such as . . . emerging new handheld global Personal Communications Services (GMPCS) networks such as Iridium or Globalstar, have the added advantage of remaining

the exact opposite of the ostensible goals expressed by both Congress and the Clinton Administration.

More importantly, however, the FCC's unilateral policies encourage other countries to impose a similar entry "tax" on the Internet. By crippling the US global satellite industry, therefore, the FCC effectively helps to remove the "G" from the "GII" or "Global Information Infrastructure" and to return improperly the Internet back to an "NII or "*National* Information Infrastructure." This too is in direct contrast to both Congress' and the Clinton Administration's public statements that it wants to promote vigorous international e-commerce.

Finally, such anticompetitive policies have more than just economic implications, for they raise broader societal implications as well. The most obvious effect is that the FCC's policies help deprive people living in developing countries of access to advanced telecommunications products and services, thus helping to retard the economic development of those very countries who need it most.[52] What is more sad from a US policy perspective, however, is that the FCC's policies also *a fortiori* help to deprive these same people of access to the most effective medium to learn about core American cultural values such as democracy, individual liberty, free speech, and the benefits of a free-market economy.

VI. CONCLUSION

If the FCC is truly serious about promoting tangible competition and de-regulation, then the FCC must recognise the inevitable consequences of its policies and take responsibilities for its actions. Remember, for the last twenty years, the industry has invested billions of dollars based upon policy makers' public statements that a commercial international satellite industry is in the public interest. Crippling international commercial efforts to privatise space now by changing horses from pro-entry to anti-entry mid-stream—without any rational explanation—is simply unconscionable. As such, the international community cannot condone the FCC's capricious efforts to abrogate its public interest mandate to maximise consumer welfare by promulgating economically flawed policies that deter, rather than promote, new facilities-based entry and, more importantly, again exacerbate a growing telecoms trade war that is dangerously close to spiraling out of hand.

operation even when local phone networks have been knocked out." However, the author also explains that it "might come as a great surprise that despite the acknowledged importance of telecoms equipment in emergency relief, many disaster victims do not currently benefit from this vital resource. The reason? Simply put, and regrettably, bureaucratic red tape. . . ."

[52] Indeed, such actions are particularly hypocritical given the fact that current FCC Chairman William E. Kennard has made the promotion of telecoms investment in developing countries a focal point of his administration. See, e.g., Keynote Speech of William E. Kennard, Chairman Federal Communications Commission before the Annual General Meeting Telecommunications Regulators Association of Southern Africa (TRASA) August 11, 1999 Gaborone, Botswana "Unleashing The Potential: Telecommunications Development in Southern Africa" (http://www.fcc.gov/Speeches/Kennard/spwek927.html).

17

Case Study: International Submarine Cable Landing Petitions

ONE WOULD THINK that something innocuous like undersea cable landing petitions could never create a firestorm between major trading partners. Indeed, if some one were going to spend the huge amount of effort to lay a cable through shark-invested waters, one would think that government would try to expedite, rather than hinder this process. As shown below, however, this has not been the view of the FCC over the last several years.

II. WHY IS SUBMARINE CABLE CAPACITY SO IMPORTANT?

Undersea cable service is the primary medium for international telecoms traffic and, as such, the performance of this market segment is an important component of the performance of the overall international telecoms market for several reasons.

First, without undersea cable, the enormous growth of international data communications—driven principally by the accelerating growth of Internet traffic—would be substantially constrained. (The adoption of the WTO agreement has only begun to spur greater growth in international communications.)

Second, undersea cable is increasingly the most efficient medium for many telecoms services because new technologies have reduced submarine cable unit costs dramatically in the last few years. Five years ago, a 15-gigabit per second (Gbps) cable, such as the transatlantic TAT–12/13, was the state of the art. The new TAT–14, which is scheduled to go into service by the end of 2000, will have a capacity of 640 Gbps. There are now plans for cables with a capacity twice as great as that of the TAT–14, that is, 1.2 terabits per second.

Finally, satellite service is not a full substitute for undersea cable service. Although satellite service is a good medium for data transfer and an excellent medium for broadcasting, it is a poor medium for two-way voice applications. Voice communications are particularly intolerant of the delays inherent in geostationary satellite communications and, unlike cables, satellites and earth stations are vulnerable to sunspot activity and hurricanes. Moreover, a modern submarine cable offers much greater capacity than a satellite, and at a much lower unit cost.

If a foreign carrier wants to land an undersea cable onto another country's shores, then this carrier must generally obtain landing rights approval. In the case of the United States these situations are governed by the Cable Landing License Act, which gives the President of the United States broad discretion to grant, withhold, condition or revoke cable landing licenses if the President determines:

> "after due notice and hearing that such action will assist in securing rights for the landing or operation of cables in foreign countries, or in maintaining the rights or interests of the United States or of its citizens in foreign countries, or will promote the security of the United States, or may grant such license upon such terms as shall be necessary to assure just and reasonable rates and service in the operation and use of cables so licensed."[1]

By Executive Order, the FCC has been delegated the responsibility for issuing cable landing licenses. This delegated authority is subject to the proviso, however, that "no such license shall be granted or revoked by the Commission except after obtaining approval of the Secretary of State and such advice from any executive department or establishment of the Government as the Commission may deem necessary."[2] As demonstrated below, however, the FCC of late has used this authority to engage in more of the same type of aggressive mercantilism that has characterised FCC policy of late, causing FCC Commissioner Harold Furchtgott-Roth to note publicly that "this whole [cable landing application] process is subject to abusive, clandestine arm-twisting."[3]

IV. ECO AND SUBMARINE CABLE LANDING RIGHTS: THE TLD AND
C&W ECO CASES

Even though there is no "public interest" standard contained in the Cable Landing License Act, prior to the enactment of the WTO Basic Agreement, the FCC decided to apply its *ECO* test to these situations as well.[4] For example, in *Telefonica Larga Distancia de Puerto Rico, Inc.* (TLD),[5] the FCC denied TLD's applications to acquire ownership interests in the COLUMBUS II Cable System (COLUMBUS II)—a common carrier cable—and for Section 214 authority to provide service to Spain on COLUMBUS II. Specifically, TLD, "which [was] affiliated with Telefonica de España, [applied] to have ownership interests as a

---

[1] 47 U.S.C. § 35 (1998).
[2] Exec. Order No. 10,530, 19 Fed. Reg. 2709, 2711 (1954).
[3] Concurring Statement, Japan-US petition (FULL CITE)
[4] See chapter 6 *supra*.
[5] *Telefonica Larga Distancia de Puerto Rico, Inc., Memorandum Opinion and Order*, 12 F.C.C.R. 5173, 8 Comm. Reg. (P & F) 64 (1997) [hereinafter Telefonica Memorandum Opinion and Order].

licensee in a submarine cable landing in both the United States and its home market, Spain. The ownership interests consist of three minimum investment units ('MIUs') from the United States to Spain to be jointly owned with Telefonica de España."[6] Yet, because, in the FCC's opinion:

"US carriers [were] denied effective competitive opportunities to have ownership interests in cable facilities landing in Spain and to operate as facilities-based international service providers in Spain,"[7]

the FCC denied TLD's application.

In defence of its actions, the FCC stated that its actions were fully in accord with the co-ordinated positions of the US State Department, the Department of Defence, the National Telecommunications & Information Administration, and the Office of US Trade Representative, and that it was also legally required to "consider whether granting a license will assist in securing the rights for US companies to land or operate cables in foreign countries."[8] Moreover, even though the FCC conceded that it did not address its market entry rules for applications under the Cable Landing License Act in its *ECO Order*—and, in particular, that its analysis as it applies to applications under the Cable Landing License Act "is similar but not identical to" its analysis under Sections 214 and 310(b)(4) of the Act—this *Order* gave it:

"the opportunity to explain [its] historical approach to those types of applications, and how it relates to the effective competitive opportunities analysis adopted in the *Foreign Carrier Entry Order*."[9]

Once again, the FCC defined market power as "the ability of the carrier to act anticompetitively against unaffiliated US carriers through the control of bottleneck services or facilities on the foreign end."[10] Thus, because the FCC found that:

"US carriers [were] forbidden from having ownership interests in the Spanish end of international submarine cable systems . . . Telefonica de España, through its control of TLD, [would] have ownership interests at both ends of the cable with monopoly control at the Spanish end."[11]

Because, in the FCC's view, there would be no:

"equivalent rights . . . for US carriers to have ownership interests in submarine cables in Spain, . . . the Spanish market . . . [did] not pass the first prong of its analysis that looks at the legal, or *de jure*, ability of US carriers to have ownership interests in submarine cables landing in Spain."[12]

---

[6] *Ibid.* para. 31. "A MIU is the minimum unit of investment for ownership in *COLUMBUS II*. Each MIU contained 30 64 Kbit/s voice paths." *Ibid.* n.41.

[7] *Ibid.*, para. 2.

[8] *Ibid.*, para. 25 (citation omitted).

[9] *Ibid.*, para. 26.

[10] *Ibid.*, para. 28.

[11] *Ibid.*, para. 32 (citation omitted).

[12] *Ibid.*

Moreover, despite the fact that the FCC found TLD's ownership in COLUM-BUS II

> "would yield significant economic benefits to Puerto Rican consumers that would outweigh [its] concerns about the lack of effective competitive opportunities for US carriers to have ownership and operation rights in the Spanish market,"

there were no countervailing reasons for it to grant this application.[13]

Not content to apply its *ECO* test exclusively to landing applications from common carrier undersea cables, the FCC announced that it would also apply its *ECO* test to cable landing license applications from private (i.e., non-common carrier) submarine cables as well. As a test case for this new policy shift, the FCC decided to use an application by Cable & Wireless (C&W) to land a private undersea cable between the United Kingdom and the United States.[14] C&W responded, however, that its application was not subject to an *ECO* analysis because the FCC previously determined in the *Foreign Carrier Entry Report and Order* that the *ECO* analysis did not apply to "domestic interexchange services, enhanced services, separate satellite systems and other non-common carrier facilities."[15]

Citing its previous decision in the *Telefonica Memorandum Opinion and Order*, the FCC rejected C&W's argument.[16] Yet, while the FCC recognised that C&W, unlike TLD, was requesting authority to land and operate a non-common carrier cable, the FCC nonetheless concluded that it should conduct an *ECO* analysis in this situation because the same principles "apply regardless of whether a carrier seeks to own and operate a cable system on a common carrier or non-common carrier basis because all submarine cable applications are subject to the provisions of the Cable Landing License Act."[17] As such, the FCC looked to see whether C&W could exercise market power—that is, whether C&W had the ability " 'to act anticompetitively against unaffiliated US carriers through the control of bottleneck services or facilities on the foreign end.' "[18]

---

[13] Telefonica Memorandum Opinion and Order, para. 33. In a related part of this Order, the FCC—for reasons similar to those provided to support a denial of TLD's cable landing petition—also denied TLD's Section 214 application to provide IMTS service between the United States and Spain. Notwithstanding Spain's failure of the FCC's ECO test, the FCC added that a denial was also warranted in this case due to the FCC's concerns about Telefonica de España's high accounting rates for traffic between the United States and Spain. In the FCC's view, not only were these rates much higher than other European countries' rates, but Telefonica de España's affiliates' rates to the United States were also "quite high." As such, the FCC reminded the industry that while it declined to make cost-based accounting rates a precondition to entry in the *Foreign Carrier Entry Report and Order*, it would consider the presence of cost-based accounting rates as part of its overall public interest analysis. In the FCC's view, therefore, the above-cost accounting rate of Telefonica de España was simply another negative factor in its overall public interest analysis. *Ibid.*, para. 39.

[14] See Cable & Wireless, PLC., Application for a License to Land and Operate in the U.S. a Private Submarine Fiber Optic Cable Extending Between the U.S. and the U.K., *Cable Landing License*, 12 F.C.C.R. 8516, 8 Comm. Reg. (P & F) 712 (1997).

[15] *Ibid.*, para. 19 (citing *ECO Order*, *supra* n. 56).

[16] *Ibid.*, para. 22.

[17] *Ibid.*, para. 25 (citation omitted).

[18] *Ibid.*, para. 26 (citation omitted).

Upon review, the FCC found that at the time of this *Order*, there was a "wide availability of circuits between the United States and the United Kingdom."[19] Moreover, the FCC found that the government of the United Kingdom had just "issued licenses to forty-five new entrants, including a number of US carriers, to provide UK facilities-based service."[20] Because no further authorisation was needed to land cables in the United Kingdom under the terms of these licenses, the FCC also expected that "new entrants [would] take advantage of this liberalization to construct and operate new cable facilities in competition with BT and Mercury."[21] Accordingly, the FCC concluded that C&W did not have market power in the United Kingdom, and, as such, it did not have to "reach the issue of whether the United Kingdom affords US carriers effective competitive opportunities to land and operate cable systems in the United Kingdom."[22]

v. THE JAPAN/US INCIDENT

A. Background

The first major test of the FCC's adjudication of a cable landing petition post-WTO came when the Japan/US Cable Network applied for permission to expand its existing cable from Japan to the US. There, the FCC—after eight long months—reluctantly granted the cable-landing petition filed by the Japan-US Cable Network (JUS) consortium. What makes this case so remarkable, however, is that it represents a textbook example of regulatory cynicism and the improper exploitation of the proverbial "revolving door" between the public and private sector.

Specifically, in what should have been a routine proceeding, on January 4, 1999, Global Crossing (hereinafter "GC") filed a petition with the FCC to defer action on JUS' November 17, 1998 petition to land a new undersea cable between Japan and the United States pursuant to the Cable Landing Act[23] and Section 1.767 of the FCC's Rules.[24] Out of nowhere, subsea cable builder Global Crossing Ltd. (and a direct competitor of the Japan-US Network) asked the Federal Communications Commission to "defer" consideration of the JUS petition in order to consider whether undersea cable consortia still served the "public interest" in a post-WTO world. [25]

Rather than set forth anything substantive, however, Global Crossing hired a bevy of high-priced former Clinton/Gore Administration officials as lobbyists—including Anne Bingaman, the former Assistant Attorney General for Antitrust

---

[19] *Ibid.*, para. 16 (citation omitted).
[20] *Ibid.*, para. 34.
[21] *Ibid.*
[22] *Ibid.*
[23] 47 U.S.C. §§ 34–39 (1994).
[24] 47 C.F.R. § 1.767.
[25] FCC Case 99–167.

for the US Department of Justice,[26] Peter Cowhey, the former Chief of the FCC's International Bureau, and Greg Simon, former domestic policy adviser to Vice President Gore—to argue its case. After reviewing the voluminous record in this proceeding however, it is apparent that GC was not attempting to reduce legitimate and indeed significant entry barriers in the Japanese domestic market (of which there are many) but to instead make itself better off—via manipulation of the regulatory process by Administration cronies—at the expense of its rivals. By introducing such a naked level of cynicism into the process, the Global Crossing crew actually has made it more difficult for other people with legitimate and well-reasoned claims to seek WTO relief from the real structural problems confronting the Japanese markets (sort of a regulatory version of the "boy who cried wolf").

B. GC's Arguments to the FCC

As stated above, new entry into the undersea cable industry is a very pro-competitive development and should be encouraged actively. On the surface, GC attempted to have the FCC believe that action is necessary in this case to mitigate the generic harms created by "club" cable consortia in the post-WTO world. Rather than submit constructive ways to move the process forward, GC simply raised pedantic "big is bad" arguments in an unlawful attempt to have the FCC improperly "subordinate the public interest to the interest of 'equalizing competition among competitors.' "[27]

The first thing GC's lobbyists argued for was to have the FCC engage in naked horizontal market division. Why? Because although GC had tremendous success in the Atlantic but not in the Pacific, GC decided apparently that there must be wrong with the underlying structure of the market in that region. Frustrated by its lack of success, therefore, its lobbyists essentially asked the FCC to engage in the worst form of central planning—*i.e.*, GC wanted the FCC to force the Consortium to assign GC its existing customers (*i.e.*, GC's "Fair Marketing Period" proposal) and, moreover, to have the Consortium give GC the facilities with which it can provide service to these customers as well (*i.e.*, GC's divestiture proposal). *Such cynicism cannot be condoned.* It is black-letter competition law that horizontal market division among competitors is *per se* illegal.

The next thing GC's lobbyists argued for was for the FCC to establish, as a condition of the license for JUS, a "fair marketing period" to commence on the date that the license is granted. According to GC, a "fair marketing period" is necessary to ensure that potential customers of JUS have an opportunity to

---

[26] See Matt Kelly, Associated Press, 12 November 1999, (reporting that GC paid Anne Bingaman more than (US) $2.5 million to lobby the FCC, the White House Counsel of Economic Advisors and other federal officials.)

[27] See *supra* n. 22.

negotiate the lowest price under conditions that "their decisions are not influenced by a massive aggregation of market power on both ends of the JUS cable."[28] GC was wrong.

As a general proposition, it is perfectly legitimate for government to intervene (either by regulation or antitrust) and abrogate a private contract if the economic costs imposed by integration contract outweigh the efficiencies created by the contract.[29] As discussed in Chapter 3, this situation often referred to as a "policy relevant barrier to entry" and is the very root of the FCC's program access policies[30] and the "public interest" exception to the *Mobile-Sierra* doctrine.[31] As explained in more detail in Chapter 8, for this reason, the FCC's "Fresh Look" authority is *not* unfettered.[32]

As Judge Bork once explained:

> "Although the legal standard for changing contract rates (they must be 'unlawful') differs from the standard for changing other contract provisions (they must disserve 'the public interest'), in fact the two standards are not very different. Before changing rates, the Commission must make a finding that they are 'unlawful' according to the terms of the governing statute, which typically requires a finding that existing rates are unjust, unreasonable, unduly discriminatory, or preferential. . . . *But as the Supreme Court recognized in Sierra, complaints about existing rates do not concern the Commission unless the problems raised are sufficiently serious to 'adversely affect the public interest'.*"[33]

For this reason, Judge Bork held that the FCC was not justified in abrogating a settlement agreement that established compromise rates for leasing special access facilities and set specific procedures for changing those rates in the future.[34]

GC's claim failed this test, however. As demonstrated above, merely expensive exogenous entry costs—*i.e.*, costs that *all* new firms must bear as a condition of entry—are *not* sufficient to constitute a public policy-relevant barrier to

---

[28] GC 22 April 1999 *ex parte* at 2–3.

[29] See, e.g., *Cable & Wireless* v. *FCC*, 166 F.3d 1224, 1231–32 (D.C. Cir. 1999). Indeed, exclusive distribution contracts have long provided fertile grounds for protracted antitrust litigation. See James Olson & Lawrence J. Spiwak, "Can Short-Term Limits on Strategic Vertical Restraints Improve Long-Term Cable Industry Market Performance?" (1994) 13 *Cardozo Arts & Ent. L.J.* 283.

[30] See Cable Report Appendix H.

[31] See *United Gas Co.* v. *Mobile Gas Corp.*, 350 U.S. 332, 339–343 (1956); *FPC* v. *Sierra Pacific Power Co.*, 350 U.S. 348, 353–55 (1956). Under the *Mobile-Sierra* doctrine, an administrative agency has the power to prescribe a change in contract rates when it finds them to be unlawful, and to modify other provisions of private contracts when necessary to serve the public interest. See also *Cable & Wireless* v. *FCC*, 166 F.3d 1224, 1231–32 (D.C. Cir. 1999).

[32] *Papago Tribal Authority* v. *FERC*, 723 F.2d 950, 954 (D.C. Cir. 1983), *cert. denied*, 467 U.S. 1241 (1984); but *cf.*, *Northeast Utilities Service Company* v. *FERC*, 55 F.3d 686 (1st Cir. 1995) ("We do not think that *Papago*, read in context, means that the 'public interest' standard is practically insurmountable in all circumstances. It all depends on whose ox is gored and how the public interest is affected.").

[33] See *Western Union Tel. Co.* v. *FCC*, 815 F.2d 1495, 1501–02 at 1501 n.2 (D.C. Cir. 1987) (citations omitted and emphasis supplied).

[34] *Ibid.*, at 1501–02.

entry and therefore warrant government remediation. Indeed, they are far from it. Quite to the contrary, new entrants to the IMTS market chose deliberately JUS over GC's PC-1 cable not because of any coercion but because it was the *most efficient* business option at this time.[35] Perhaps Viatel—*an existing Global Crossing customer in the Atlantic on GC's AC-1 cable*—stated it best: "Global Crossing should reassess its own pricing structure instead of (a) manufacturing alleged anticompetitive conspiracy theories to explain why . . . others have chosen to participate and purchase capacity from JUS and (b) seeking Commission intervention and assistance from marketplace realities."[36]

Moreover, let's return to the macro-policy question posited at the beginning of this Chapter: Even assuming *arguendo* that the JUS cable consortium does constitute a policy-relevant barrier to entry, *would granting GC's request for a "Fresh Look" and "Fair Marketing Period" do anything to change the entry conditions of the domestic Japanese market?* Like it or not, the answer to this question is clearly no.

Although the FCC has the lawful authority to abrogate private contracts when the public interest warrants, the FCC must be especially judicious in using this authority in the international context. International ventures by definition involve a high degree of risk, and the parties' belief that a contract will not be abrogated or challenged goes a long way towards mitigating that risk.[37] Accordingly, should the FCC use unilaterally its proverbial "silver bullet" in a case such as this which clearly does not rise to the level of a policy-relevant barrier to entry, then the FCC has in fact made entry far more difficult for all US firms—telecoms or otherwise—to do business abroad.

Moreover, even assuming *arguendo* that some sort of "fair marketing period" was warranted in which the FCC would allocate customers and facilities to specific competitors, GC's proposal contained so many analytical flaws that it is impossible to discern a rational plan of action.

To begin, GC's lobbyists essentially reinvented the concept of "market power" to fit their regulatory objectives. According to GC, a "submarine cable cannot be 'owned' by a consortium of carriers which together have 'market power' on both ends of the cable." Rather than use any form of accepted economic literature or competition law precedent to define market power (i.e., some sort of ability to raise price or restrict output), however, GC's lobbyists redefined "market power" to "mean, with respect to either end of a cable, carriers

---

[35] See PSINet Reply at 5 ("JUS network is just plain cheaper"); Qwest Reply at 4–5 ("Qwest considered all available alternatives, including purchase of capacity from Global Crossing, but found that participation in JUS was economically more attractive. Among other factors, Qwest concluded that the *governance structure* of the JUS Consortium would give Qwest an opportunity to participate in decisions affecting the network—*a benefit that Global Crossing did not offer for carriers obtaining capacity on PC–1.*" (Emphasis supplied); SBCI Reply at 4, 6 (SBCI chose deliberately JUS cable over GC's cable because JUS permits SBCI to self-provision its capacity needs on the trans-Pacific route.")

[36] Viatel Reply at 4–5.

[37] See, e.g., Oliver E. Williamson, *The Economic Institutions of Capitalism* (1985).

with a combined market share of more than 50 per cent of the *active half circuits* on a particular end of a cable, as of the time that the carriers enter [sic] into the Construction and Maintenance Agreement" (emphasis supplied.)

As a preliminary matter, as discussed in great detail in Part I of this book, "market power" cannot be "defined" by a picking a number out of a hat, because market shares simply define the structure of the market. Market power falls more accurately under conduct, because the concept of "market power" represents the ability of one or more firms to engage in some form of strategic anticompetitive conduct—i.e., the ability to raise prices or restrict output. For this reason, both US antitrust courts and the FCC have long-recognised that market share alone is not sufficient to confer market power.[38] This is why, in the context of telecommunications, the analysis must always move beyond mere market shares and toward the evaluation of the elasticities of supply and demand and, in particular, the presence (or lack) of barriers to entry.[39]

Second, GC's lobbyists also proposed a rather bizarre market definition within which the FCC was supposed to measure the aforementioned market shares—i.e., GC did not define the relevant market as termination access but rather on the ownership of the cable itself (IRUs). Thus, GC's definition of market power did not inquire as to whether the Consortium members actually have market power in US or Japanese termination markets (which was the *sine qua non* of its claim against the Consortium) but rather on whether the Consortium has market power over its own cable! This flawed reasoning is the analytical equivalent of arguing that Hostess has market power over its own brand of Wonder Bread.

More significantly, GC forgot that it should be careful for what it wished for. To wit, as noted above, GC's lobbyists' proposed definition of market power did not focus on termination markets, but rather on ownership of the cable itself. If this argument is taken to its (il)logical conclusion, however, because GC owns the private cable equivalent of IRUs on both ends of its own cable (indeed, it owns the full circuit), then GC would by its own definition also have "market

---

[38] See, e.g., *United States v. Baker Hughes Inc.*, 908 F.2d 981, 986 (D.C. Cir. 1990) (Thomas, J.) (market share statistics "misleading" in a "volatile and shifting" market); *Southern Pac. Communications Co. v. AT&T*, 740 F.2d 980, 1000 (D.C. Cir. 1984), cert. denied, 470 U.S. 1005 (1985) (When a "predominant market share may merely be the result of regulation, and regulatory control may preclude the exercise of market power . . . in such cases market share should be at most a point of departure in determining whether market power exists."); *Metro Mobile CTS Inc. v. NewVector Communications Inc.*, 892 F.2d 62, 63 (9th Cir. 1989) ("Reliance on statistical market share in cases involving regulated industries is at best a tricky enterprise and is downright folly where . . . the predominant market share is the result of regulation"); see also *In re Motion of AT&T Corp. to Be Reclassified as a Non-Dominant Carrier*, FCC 95–427, 11 FCC Rcd 3271 (rel. Oct. 23, 1995) at ¶ 32 n.90 and citations therein.

[39] See generally Duncan Cameron & Mark Glick, "Market Share and Market Power in Merger and Monopolization Cases", (1996) 17 *Managerial & Decision Econ.* 193 (legal precedent requiring courts to draw inferences about market power based primarily or exclusively on market shares and/or market concentration can often be misleading; the only alternative to such bright-line rules is to utilise modern economic tools to undertake more extensive competitive analyses).

power" and therefore should also be subject appropriately to some form of dominant carrier regulation.

GC did provide one exception to its proposed solution, however: Although GC would have the FCC prohibit a consortium from "owning" a cable where that consortium has "market power" on both ends of the cable, in GC's view, it "would, however, be permissible to have an ownership consortium with 'market power' on *one end* of the cable." (Emphasis supplied.) As such, perhaps a review of the salient facts of this case are in order to determine whether the Consortium in this case has market power at only one end of the cable.

First, let's look at the Japanese market. Admittedly, while conditions in the Japanese market are certainly not great, there are some small signs of improvement. There are at least four carriers for domestic long-distance service in Japan and at least three carriers for IMTS service.[40] Moreover, Japan has agreed to implement the WTO Regulatory Reference Paper in full, and also has agreed recently to make significant improvements in its telecoms deregulation efforts.[41]

To wit, Japan has committed to specific new measures to more effectively introduce competition into its $130 billion telecommunications sector by:

—ensuring that interconnection rates—the rates charged competitors of NTT to access the majority of Japanese customers—are set below retail rates;

—defining measures that will assure NTT DoCoMo's (cellular service provider) interconnection rates are more fairly priced by being purely based on costs;

—authorising interconnection "clearing-house" for new entrants in the Japanese market which will dramatically speed market entry;

—liberalising the use of flexible network arrangements, thus allowing businesses to build out their networks more rapidly and efficiently;

—improving methods to ensure that new entrants have fair and non-discriminatory access to international cable landing stations, controlled by KDD (which holds sixty per cent market share of the international telephony market);

—introducing number portability and dialling parity as early as FY 2000;

—opening-up Cable TV to one hundred per cent foreign investment (and clearly restricting NTT from using its control of fiber optic cable reaching residential customers to distort competition in the cable TV/telephony market);

—proposing new regulations by mid-year to facilitate use of electrical wiring systems for communications purposes; and

—resolving rights-of-way issues.[42]

---

[40] See, e.g., Cowhey affidavit at 4–6.

[41] See reference to be completed.

[42] See "United States Welcomes Progress Under U.S.-Japan Enhanced Deregulation Initiative", 3 May 1999, http://www.ustr.gov/releases/1999/05/99–42.html; "Fact Sheet, Second Joint Status Report under the U.S.-Japan Enhanced Initiative on Deregulation and Competition Policy", 3 May

What is even more encouraging is the fact that the Japanese government has agreed to take further steps to ensure true transparency in the Japanese regulatory system. These pro-competitive steps will now include:

—the creation of formal Public Comment Procedures for Formulating, Amending or Repealing Regulations (a cornerstone of the US regulatory system for more than 50 years);
—the advancement of legislation to establish an Information Disclosure Act;
—reducing the standard processing period for the issuance of licenses, permits and approvals; and
—providing for the use of the Overall Greatest Value Methodology (OGVM) by local governments as a method of determining the successful bidder in local government procurement.[43]

Finally, as an additional pro-competitive prophylactic measure, Japan has agreed to revise and improve significantly its competition law enforcement regime. Among other steps, Japan will be:

—launching proactive steps under competition policy advocacy by creating a model Antimonopoly Act Compliance Program for private firms;
—using various means, including public hearings, to actively expand public involvement and address deregulation and competition policy issues;
—reviewing business entry regulations and "supply/demand adjustment" regulations and, where appropriate, proposing the removal of such regulations;
—reviewing competition-restricting regulations on the central and local government level and, in appropriate cases, propose abolishing or revising such regulations;
—actively filing criminal accusations with the Prosecutor's Office in anti-cartel cases; and

---

1999, http://www.ustr.gov/releases/1999/05/fact.html. Specifically, USTR reports that the Government of Japan surveyed the existing circumstance on the procedures to use available properties (such as land and facility) for laying of cables, and released the results of the study on 25 December 1998. In line with the results of the study, the government published the results of its research of the measures for improvement taken by the entities concerned on 26 March 1999. Second, the Government of Japan will receive complaints with regard to laying of cables, look into the matters needed within the scope of available cooperation from related entities and then reply to the complaint of applicants in the form of appropriately compiled results. The cases will be regarded as references for the consideration of further improvement in the review during FY 1999. However, USTR also stated that it would be necessary to conduct further study in the future, considering how the proposed measures will work and listening to a broad range of views. In FY 1999, a review will be conducted with participation of the Ministries concerned. Finally, USTR reports that in FY 1999, the Government of Japan will continue to make efforts to facilitate laying of cables by telecommunications carriers and cable television operators. In this connection, the review group will closely monitor implementation of the measures for improvement, evaluate their effectiveness in improving access to rights-of-way, consider complaints, opinions and questions from domestic and foreign entities, and review the need for other means of improving access to rights-of-way. *Ibid.*

[43] *Ibid.*

—amending its Bidding Instructions to make clear that firms bidding on public works contracts cannot consult with competitors about prices.[44]

As such, it reasonable to conclude that the conditions in the Japanese markets should improve as this process moves forward.

Finally, as also discussed *passim,* the FCC, as an additional backstop measure, has imposed unilaterally stringent competitive safeguards to mitigate any potential residual anticompetitive distortion in the US market.

Now let's look at the US end of the cable. As explained in Chapters 4 and 9, local termination/origination markets are far from competitive, nor is there any real expectation that these markets will be become vigorously competitive anytime soon.[45] What is crucial always to keep in mind, however, is the simple fact that US local markets are not dominated by members of the Consortium but are instead controlled overwhelmingly by incumbent LECs who clearly charge extremely "high" access charges (notwithstanding the fact that the 8th Circuit held that these are not "above cost" because they are a "real cost of doing business").[46] Thus, it would be extremely difficult, if not outright impossible, for the Consortium members to collude in order to control some sort of ephemeral "homogenous" US termination market—again, the *sine qua non* of GC's claim of market power against the Consortium.[47]

Moreover, GC once again forgot that it lives in the proverbial "glass house." At the time of this case, GC had just announced that it intended to merge with US West—a BOC with dominant, if not outright monopoly, control of access lines in fourteen states. Although this deal fell apart, GC eventually bought Frontier, an incumbent LEC in New York. Under any scenario, however, GC adopted a US entry strategy that was not predicated upon new facilities-based entry but instead primarily upon *merger* with the dominant incumbent. As such, it seems a bit incredible that on one hand GC asked the FCC to attack collaterally Japanese WTO commitments and subsequent bilateral commitments because entry is just too "expensive" yet with a straight face have its merger partner argue vehemently the exact opposite position domestically. Again, the "D" in "domestic" does not stand for "different."

As explained in earlier chapters, the US IMTS market, however, is quite rivalrous.[48] Indeed, the FCC has found repeatedly using the accepted definition of

---

[44] "United States Welcomes Progress Under U.S.-Japan Enhanced Deregulation Initiative", 3 May 1999.

[45] See George Ford, "Flow-Through and Competition in the International Message Telephone Service Market" (unpublished, 1994), on file with the International Journal of Applied Economics; see also *Business Week* 11 January 1999 (According to SBC CEO Ed Whitacre: "We can sit here and get picked on" . . . "or get bigger and have more clout.")

[46] *Southwestern Bell Tel. Co. v. FCC,* 153 F.3d 523, 554 (8th Cir. 1998).

[47] One member of the consortium, SBCI-Pacific Networks, is an affiliate of SBC under Section 272 of the 1996 Act. However, SBCI owns only four per cent of the Consortium and, as a new entrant, has neither market share nor international transportation facilities. See SBCI-Pacific Reply Comments at 2.

[48] See Ford, *supra* n. 45. (Finding strong evidence that IMTS prices are closely related to settlement costs and that these prices fully reflect differences in settlement costs. Moreover, paper also finds that the estimated relationship between prices and settlement costs indicates, under certain

market power (e.g., "ability to raise costs profitably above competitive levels for a sufficient period of time"), that US-origination markets are, in fact, workably competitive.[49] Thus, if the Consortium members lack market power on the US end, then—under GC's very own proposal—there should be no competitive problem and therefore no reason to deny JUS' petition.

Finally, and perhaps most egregiously, was the fact that GC's lobbyists (who, given their previously high-ranking policies positions inside the Clinton/Gore Administration, should have known better) deliberately ignored the presence of Japan's offer in the WTO and the fact that these very WTO regulatory commitments explicitly prevented, rather than facilitated, JUS' purported ability to somehow raise their costs. In a similar vein, GC's lobbyists also conveniently ignored the fact that Japan and the United States Trade Representative had just reached an additional understanding about many of the exact issues GC erroneously claimed the FCC has the authority to remedy.

But, perhaps most cynical and specious of all was that GC's lobbyists arguments also ignored deliberately the FCC's own residual prophylactic "Competitive Safeguards"—*i.e.*, the FCC's unilateral benchmark condition and "No Special Concessions Rule"—*safeguards that the FCC put into place precisely because they did not trust the efficacy or commitments of foreign regulators*. What makes the regulatory cynicism in this case so deliciously exquisite, however, was *the hypocritical fact these unilateral safeguards that were promulgated under the watch of the very high-powered Washington DC lobbyists that Global Crossing hired to argue the exact opposite view*. Publicly insulting the Japanese government—an equal, *co-sovereign* entity—by arguing *post-hoc* that both their WTO commitments and these new additional market-opening commitments are now unacceptable is precisely the kind of "essentially adversarial" tactic Chairman Greenspan warned specifically about.[50]

C. The FCC's Decision

On 8 July 1999, after over eight long months, the FCC finally (and begrudgingly) granted JUS's landing petition.[50a] However, although the FCC—to its credit—

---

assumptions, that the IMTS industry is very competitive. Thus, Ford concludes that the "IMTS industry is far more competitive than Cournot, and very close to perfect competition" which, according to Ford, is at "at odds with the economic advocacy of incumbent monopolists in both the U.S. and abroad."); see also James Alleman, Gary Madden and Scott J. Savage, "Dominant Carrier Market Power in US International Telephone Markets", presented at IFCF Conference, Denver Colorado (June 1999); R. Carter Hill and T. Randolph Beard, "A Statistical Analysis of the Flow-Through of Reductions in Switched Access Charges to Residential Long Distance Rates" 24 May 1999.

[49] See, e.g., *AT&T Int'l Non-Dom* at ¶ 40 (market power defined as the "power to control prices or exclude competition"); see also *Foreign Participation Order* at ¶ 144 (market power defined as a "carrier's ability to raise price by restricting it output of services.")

[50] See Chapter 1.

[50a] In *re AT&T et al., Joint Application for a License to Land and Operate a Submarine Cable Network Between the United States and Japan*, FCC R&D, FCC No. 99–167 (rel. 9 July 2000).

did eventually grant the JUS petition, the outstanding question that remains is at exactly what cost?

On one hand, the FCC required JUS to amend "voluntarily" its private organisational contracts as a pre-condition of approval. As FCC Commissioner Harold Furchtgott-Roth—who did not take part in the FCC's decision—wrote disdainfully: "(T)he applicants were 'persuaded' (under threat of application denial or further delay) in order to satisfy the desires of regulators (and the applicants' competitors) . . . The lesson appears to be that if the FCC can't get what it wants directly, it's easy to employ an unlawful delegation of power to achieve the same result."

Moreover, the FCC stated that it would institute a proceeding to investigate whether undersea cable consortia "may slow the growth of competition in international telecommunications" and, if so, whether the efficiency benefits of undersea cable consortia offset those anticompetitive effects. Reading between the lines, the FCC is saying that if the dominant firm in a foreign market is also a member of a cable consortium serving that market, then the consortium, *a fortiori*, has the ability to control all traffic in that market, incoming and outgoing. By that logic, a U. S. firm that is not a member of the consortium cannot enter the foreign market; thus, U. S. regulatory intervention is required. That overly-broad conclusion simply is wrong.

First, any notion that undersea cable consortium are somehow "*per se* anti-competitive" just doesn't hold water under current market conditions. To wit, the FCC has found repeatedly that supply or undersea capacity is elastic (albeit with temporary shortages). Similarly, several recent studies show that the IMTS market is workably competitive[51] and, moreover, the non-IMTS market (data) has been competitive for years.

Given this information, why would a firm nonetheless choose to join a cable consortium rather than purchase capacity on the open market? There may be *multiple* reasons why smaller companies may want to join a cable consortium simply because it is more *efficient*—i.e., it reduces transaction costs—to do so. For example, membership in a cable consortium might simply be *cheaper*; membership might provide better restoration rights or management rights; and, in today's fast paced world, membership might provide faster time to market than could be obtained through other means. Finally, risk sharing is perfectly appropriate to serve aggregated demand, especially as many participants are new entrants and have a small market share of international traffic (IMTS or data).

Second, the FCC's purported rationale for its inquiry is that foreign firms in telecoms consortia control "key inputs" of production similarly makes no sense. Just what inputs does the FCC have in mind? In the JUS case, the FCC was sympathetic to GC's argument for American regulatory intervention in a foreign destination market, simply because certain inputs—for example, back-haul

---

[51] Ford, *supra* n. 45; Alleman, Madden & Savage *supra* n. 48.

capacity (facilities for transferring traffic from a cable landing to a distribution point), rights of way, and real estate—are "*too expensive.*"

Like it or not, telecoms is an expensive business because it requires expensive inputs. The FCC should not confuse the normal costs of entering a market with incumbent- or regulation-imposed costs that require governmental intervention (*e.g.*, exorbitant one-time charges for collocating in an incumbent's local exchange/central office or cable-landing stations, hidden "universal service" fees, high access and interconnection charges). The inability of a potential entrant into the undersea cable market to afford the price of admission is not a cause for intervention.[52]

There *are* regulation- and incumbent- imposed entry costs in foreign markets. Should the FCC assert extra-territorial jurisdiction to deal with such costs? Again, the answer is no. Like it or not, through the WTO agreement a majority of America's trading partners made specific commitments about the openness of their telecoms markets—and the United States accepted those commitments.[53] Moreover, through those commitments, there already exists currently a comprehensive regulatory regime designed specifically to handle the exact concerns the FCC is ostensibly concerned about. If another WTO Member State, as an equal, *co-sovereign* entity, fulfills its WTO regulatory commitments, then potential "vertical" harms in the US market (*e.g.*, "price-squeeze type" conduct, raising rivals' costs, predation) go away—*even if entry into the foreign market proves slow in coming.*[54] Moreover, even assuming *arguendo* that the WTO Member State's government is incapable of promulgating effective domestic regulation, the US may not also ignore the "Competitive Safeguards" required by the FCC's *Foreign Participation Order*—*i.e.*, the FCC's unilateral imposition of the Benchmark Condition and the FCC's "No Special Concessions" rule—*safeguards which are designed specifically to handle this situation and to act as further prophylactic measures primarily because the FCC did not trust fully foreign regulators' incentive or ability to implement a sufficient regulatory framework.*[55]

---

[52] See, e.g., "WebCel asks U.S. Appeals Court to Halt LMDS Auction", *Communications Daily*, 18 Feb. 1998 (Reporting that D.C. Circuit Court of Appeals rejected wireless start-up's petition to stay FCC's spectrum auction due to lack of adequate financing, especially as the FCC already had stayed previously auction for three months due to peitioner's request that it needed more time to seek additional capital.)

[53] In fact, in the specific case of Japan, Japan's commitments are pretty good. These commitments include market access and national treatment for all services, with a twenty per cent limit on foreign investment in KDD and NTT. Moreover, Japan has agreed to adopt the Regulatory Reference Paper in full. See Laura B.Sherman, " 'Wildly Enthusiastic' About the First Multilateral Agreement on Trade in Telecommunications Services", (1998) 51 *Fed. Com. L.J.* 61, 106. The Japanese Ministry recently has demonstrated its resolve to be impartial and independent by just announcing that it would not interfere in a bidding war between NTT and KDD for IDC, Japan's second largest provider of international phone service. See Junko Fujita, "Japan's Telecoms Ministry Won't Meddle in Bids for IDC", *Bloomberg News*, 4 June 1999.

[54] *Cf.* Doug Galbi, Former Chief Economist, FCC Int'l Bureau, *Model-Based Price Standards for Terminating International Traffic* (FCC Staff Paper, Room Document No. 10, OECD Ad Hoc Meeting on International Telecommunications Charging Practices and Procedures, 17 Sept. 1997) (proposing a model that any country can use to compute economically relevant price standards for termination by its international correspondents).

In fact, given this comprehensive regulatory regime of checks and backstops, the FCC no longer takes an in depth look at conditions in the foreign end as a pre-condition of entry as it used to do in its *Effective Competitive Opportunities Order*.[56] More importantly, because of these regulatory prophylactics, the FCC also adopted a "rebuttable presumption that such competitive concerns are not raised by applications to land and operate submarine cables from WTO Members. . . ."[57] Indeed, the FCC stated specifically (despite substantial international objection) that it would only deny entry to a WTO Member country in the *"very rare circumstances"* if "other public interest factors" (*i.e.*, the general significance of the proposed entry to the promotion of competition in the US communications market, the presence of cost-based accounting rates, and any national security, law enforcement, foreign policy and trade policy concerns brought to its attention by the Executive Branch) warrant.[58]

Accordingly, if the US government needs a reason to intervene, then the questions therefore become quite straightforward: First, is the WTO Member State living up to its WTO commitments? If the answer is yes, then the inquiry is over. If the answer is no, however, then the appropriate remedy is *not* to ask the FCC to resolve a trade dispute but for aggrieved American firms to petition USTR under Section 1377 of the US Trade Act to bring a claim against the violating Member State in the WTO.[59] The FCC is an *independent* regulatory body and is not part of the Executive Branch where those trade responsibilities appropriately lay.

Second, if a Member State has not lived up to its WTO commitments and relief is slow in coming from the WTO, then we must ask if the FCC's safeguards are ineffective or superfluous. If they are not, then the inquiry in this proceeding is again at an end. If the answer is yes, then the FCC is obligated legally to remove its own superfluous regulation as part of the FCC's biennial regulatory review process.[60] Certainly, it is highly doubtful that GC's lobbyists would wish to initiate such an outcome.

Accordingly, if the FCC wants to act, it is unclear what it should do. One option is to deny a foreign entity's request for a US cable landing, which the FCC

---

[55] See generally Rules and Policies on Foreign Participation in the U.S. Telecomm. Market, *Report and Order on Reconsideration*, 12 F.C.C.R. 23,891, 10 Comm. Reg. (P & F) 750 (1997) [hereinafter *Foreign Participation Order*] at ¶ 145–149.

[56] *Foreign Participation Order* at ¶ 69.

[57] *Ibid.*, at ¶ 50.

[58] *Ibid.*, at ¶ 50, 65. Moreover, given the substantial criticism received by the FCC that it was inappropriately stepping beyond its mandate, the FCC was also quick to emphasise that it would only "make an independent decision on applications to be considered and [would] evaluate concerns raised by the Executive Branch agencies in light of all the issues raised (and comments in response) in the context of a particular application." *Ibid.*, ¶ 66. The FCC was equally quick to point out, however, that it expected "that the Executive Branch [would] advise [it] of concerns relating to national security, law enforcement, foreign policy, and trade concerns only in very rare circumstances, [and that those concerns] . . . must be communicated in writing and [would] be part of the public file in the relevant proceeding." *Ibid.*, at ¶ 50 (citation omitted).

[59] Omnibus Trade & Competitiveness Act of 1988, 19 U.S.C. § 3106.

[60] See Communications Act Section 11, 47 U.S.C. § 161.

has done before. But if an entity says it is willing to risk a significant amount of capital to lay a cable on our shores to meet an ever-expanding demand, you might expect the FCC to accelerate the approval process rather than engage in regulatory shenanigans. But you would be wrong. As noted above, FCC Commissioner Harold Furchtgott-Roth noted that "this whole process is subject to abusive, clandestine arm-twisting."

A second option is for the FCC to use its delegated authority under the Cable Landing Act to grant a license only "upon such terms as shall be necessary to assure just and reasonable rates and service." But, as explained earlier in this Chapter, the FCC already has travelled (unsuccessfully) down that route with its unilateral "competitive safeguards"—much to the dismay and consternation of America's trading partners.

Finally, we have the troubling third option advocated by the aforementioned former Clinton/Gore administration officials that the FCC should initiate a "fair marketing period," during which the US government would abrogate private submarine consortia contracts and assign customers among specific competitors.

That approach has several fundamental problems. First and most obviously, it is simply the worst form of central planning and should not be condoned. Regulators should not be able to assign customers to specific competitors; instead, consumers should be permitted to choose among competitive suppliers based upon price and quality considerations. As stated above, such a proposal amounts to nothing less than an attempt at government-mandated horizontal market division, which US courts as far back as *Addyston Pipe* (1899) have held to be a *per se* violation of antitrust law. Moreover, the institution of a so-called fair marketing period would violate not only the FCC's prime directive but also black-letter case law that forbids it to "subordinate the public interest to the interest of 'equalizing competition among competitors.' "

As also noted above, such a proposal would take the FCC's authority under the *Mobile-Sierra* doctrine onto uncharted and dangerous ground. Under *Mobile-Sierra*, government may abrogate a private contract if the contract is contrary to the "public interest" (*e.g.*, the economic costs imposed by the contract out-weigh the efficiencies created by the contract). Before government may exercise its authority, however, it must cross a threshold that courts have held to be "practically insurmountable."

Although the Clinton/Gore Administration has succeeded in eroding *the Mobile-Sierra* Doctrine to permit government to abrogate private contracts on its whim,[61] it is still nonetheless doubtful that the abrogation of international cable consortia agreements could meet even this watered-down test. International ventures are inherently risky, and the mitigation of risks through joint ventures has been standard industry practice for sixty years. The parties to joint ventures must have confidence that their contracts will not be abrogated or

---

[61] See Chapter 8 *supra*.

challenged in either domestic or (especially) foreign courts. FCC intervention to abrogate contracts in the undersea cable market—where there is no policy-relevant barrier to entry—would undermine the sanctity of private contracts and make it far more difficult for all U. S. firms—telecoms or otherwise—to do business abroad.

D. The Aftermath: The EU's Studied Reaction

As might be expected the rest of the telecoms world watched the FCC proceedings with interest. Much of the world's international telecommunication needs are met via undersea cables and the importance of this transmission medium is growing as both capacity and need for capacity grows. Although the EU has not directly taken any action that corresponds to what the FCC has done, it did commission a Study examining submarine cable landing rights.[62] The policy behind the study is clear: the EU should promote submarine cable provision and lighten regulatory burdens on submarine cable operators. The development of alternative providers of submarine cables is viewed favourably by the Study, and access to traditional consortia cables is no longer seen as essential.[63]

What the Study did think was necessary was clarification of rights of landing and interconnection. It is not enough to actually plan, finance and even lay submarine cables, there must be rights to land and interconnect submarine cables so as to actually transmit telecommunications traffic. This is where difficulties may arise and where the Study concluded EU action may be needed. Interestingly, the Study noted that zoning and envoronmental rules may be more of a burden on potential landers than actual telecommunications licenses,[64] though "excessive fees" may also be charged for landing rights.[65]

Most of the Study was taken up with examining rights of interconnection once cables have actually reached the beach. Starting with the beach, the first point of potential interconnection is with landing facilities and "cable headends"[66] usually owned and operated by incumbent operators. The Study concluded that interconnection between landed submarine cables and cable headends is required under the existing EU Interconnection Directive,[67]

---

[62] Hogan & Hartson L.L.P., *Study on Submarine Cable Landing Rights and Existing Practices for the Provision of Transmission Capacity on International Routes*, Report to the Commission of the European Communities August 1999 [hereinafter EU Submarine Cable Study] <http://www.ispo.cec.be/infosoc/telecompolicy/en/subcables.pdf>. Such studies are not to be considered as official EU positions, however, many EU recommendations or directives start as studies or reports performed by non-EU entities, but paid for by the EU.

[63] *Ibid.*, at 10, 11

[64] *Ibid.*, at v.

[65] *Ibid.*, at vi.

[66] *Ibid.*, at 20.

[67] Directive 97/33/EC of the European Parliament and of the Council of 30 June 1997 on Interconnection in Telecommunications With Regard to Ensuring Universal Service and Interoperability Through Application of the Principles of Open Network Provision (ONP) [1997] OJ L199/32 [hereinafter Interconnection Directive].

since "[s]ubmarine cable heads are part of the 'public telecommunications network' ".[68] The interconnection provisions of the WTO Telecoms Treaty are noted as well.[69] Therefore, potential submarine cable operators should be able to interconnect with national PSTN operators in the EU.

Assuming interconnection can be ensured, there may still be a problem of delivering traffic from the point of interconnection (here the cable headend) to either an end-user or a subsequent POP of the operator. The Study, much like the EU Commission's international interconnection proposal (discussed in Chapter 13, *supra*), concluded that backhaul should be available to competitors; the Study found a right to backhaul under the existing EU leased lines Directive.[70]

Even with the arguable application of existing EU directives to submarine cable interconnection and (land-based) transmission, the Study also considered that there may exist other avenues of remedy for alternative submarine cable operators as set forth in the EU Commission's Telecommunications Access Notice.[71] The Study invited aggrieved operators to consider competition law complaints based on violation of the essential facilities doctrine or on grounds of unlawful discrimination.[72]

Finally, considering the specific Global Crossing compliant to the FCC, the Study stated that:

> "Given the seriousness of GCL's [Global Crossing] allegations, European regulators should monitor the progress of this proceeding and assess independently its implications. The Community also must be vigilant to ensure that actions taken in this US-Japan context do not affect adversely the interests of European industry, either in the club cables or with respect to smaller enterprises taking service or buying IRUs on cables."[73]

Other than monitoring, it is unclear what the EU can do about possible FCC action. While the Study noted the possible effects of FCC actions on "European industry" in general, it would also have been appropriate for the author of the study to add that FCC action could also affect the future of international telecommunications. Can the EU do anything in response? Comments with the FCC can be filed or diplomatic channels tried. These routes may not be very helpful. The temptation may to be retaliate in kind if the EU is displeased with FCC action, thus spiraling trade tension higher. Perhaps this would be a good case to bring to the WTO, creating precedent for what national regulators can and cannot do in the international telecommunications infrastructure area.

---

[68] EU Submarine Cable Study, *supra*, n. 62, at 20.

[69] *Ibid.*, at 13.

[70] *Ibid.*, at 5.

[71] *Ibid.*, at 26. The Access Notice (Notice on the Application of the Competition Rules to Access Agreements in the Telecommunications Sector, Framework, Relevant Markets and Principles, 31 March 1998 [1998] OJ C265/ 2 [hereinafter Access Notice]) is discussed in Chapter 12, above.

[72] *Ibid.*, at 27.

[73] *Ibid.*, at 31.

V. CONCLUSION

So where do we go from here? If the US government really favours creating a global information infrastructure, it simply makes no sense to erect barriers to entry into the primary market for international voice and data communications. The FCC-instigated telecoms trade war is dangerously close to getting out of hand. Although this is getting both tiresome and frustrating, it seems that we must again remind the Federal Communications Commission that trade and public utility regulation do not mix. Indeed, given America's already tenuous credibility in the international community, the FCC's inept Machiavellian manoeuvres can only goad other nations to retaliatory acts that will make it more difficult for US firms to do business abroad (contrary to the Clinton/Gore Administration's ostensible goals) and, more importantly, will harm US consumers. Accordingly, the FCC must take care to ensure that its efforts do not turn out to be a self-defeating exercise. Whether they want to or not, it is the regulator's responsibility to do everything in their power to lawfully promote, and not hinder, construction of new cable capacity.

18

Case Study: International Mergers and Global Alliances

I. INTRODUCTION

OVER THE LAST several years, there have been several attempts to re-concentrate the international telecoms industry. Given the rise of mercantilism in international telecoms policies, however, meaningful analysis of the competitive effects (pro and con) of these transactions was often over looked in favour of using these proceedings to advance nationalistic trade agendas.[1] When this improper politicisation occurred, numerous deals—such as BT's investment in MCI, the Global One Alliance between Sprint, Deutsche Telekom and France Télécom, and the Telia/Telenor merger—simply could not remain viable, regardless of whether these proposed deals ever raised legitimate competitive concerns, or moreover, even ever made business sense.

---

[1] See e.g., "Review and Outlook: Washington Calling" *Wall Street Journal* 6 July 2000, criticising a collation of US Senators led by Senator Fritz Holling objection to a rumoured acquisition of US long distance operator Sprint by German Government-controlled Deutsche Telekom on "national security" grounds. (In fact, Hollings went so far as to attach language to a spending bill that would prohibit the FCC from spending any funds processing the application of a firm indirectly owned by a foreign government that is seeking to buy a US telecommunications company.) According to me Journal, they "hope this doesn't mean they're concerned about Gerhard Schroeder's German government using a backdoor key to break into the Clinton White House's mysterious email system through Sprint's network". Suffice it to say, the European Union was not pleased with this mercantile action, noting that such a law violate's the US' commitment in the WTO and would cast doubt on future trade negotiations between the US and EU, Mark Wigfield, "Telecom Foreign Ownership Ban Violates WTO Agreement" *Dow Jones Newswires*, 21 July 2000.

Moreover as highlighted in chapter 1 *supra*, these mercantile trade wars are not limited to telecoms exclusively. Take the 1997 merger between Boeing and McDonnell Douglas. This case involved the commercial airframe industry, which was already highly concentrated and is clearly characterised by the presence of huge sunk costs, high barriers to entry, and very inelastic supply and demand. Yet, the deal nonetheless virtually sailed through the FTC without any major problems. How did this happen? Easy: trade concerns. In other words, antitrust and other government officials apparently believed that it is wholly acceptable to further reconcentrate the US airframe industry because the newly merged company will be in a stronger position to beat up the French and their European allies (aka Airbus Industrie). For this reason, the US and the EU came to the brink of an all-out trade war, each openly (and completely inappropriately) using their respective antitrust enforcement agencies as foot soldiers. See, e.g., Steven Pearlstein & Anne Swordson, "US Gets Tough to Ensure Boeing, McDonnell Merger: Retaliation Plan in Works as Europe Threatens", *Washington Post*, 17 July 1997, at D1.By doing so, once again antitrust was improperly used to benefit competitors, not competition. See Catherine Yang, "Commentary: When Protectionism Wears Camouflage", *Business Week*, 2 June 1997, at 60. (US and EU's antitrust actions in this case acted as "a stalking horse for economic nationalism. When that happens, the first casualty is competition").

With the rapid pace of telecommunications industry consolidation, competition enforcement officials and regulators are faced with both a difficult challenge and an opportunity. The challenge is to ensure that the wave of mergers do not distort telecommunications markets. The opportunity is that conditions can be attached to mergers—in effect regulatory conditions that officials may have desired to impose—but lacked the opportunity to do so directly under current law until the merger came before them. Although this regulation or legislation through merger review is outside of usual procedures, enforcement officials and regulators are engaging in such practices nevertheless.

Accordingly, for good or ill, regulatory trends may be observed by examining conditions placed on recent telecommunications mergers. Merger review should not be a substitute for developing a cohesive regulatory framework however. Such an ad hoc approach will lead to even greater disparities in regulation, perhaps rewarding those telcos who do not merge with fewer regulatory burdens. On the other hand, enforcement officials have an obligation to ensure that reconcentration does not lead to new monopolies arising phoenix-like from the ashes of the old before telecoms competition has even had a chance to truly assert itself.

There are several arguments floating around Brussels and Washington to convince regulators and competition law enforcement officials that the recent reconcentration trend will not lead to poor long-term telecommunications market performance. Most common of these arguments is one of the most over-used defences in competition law jurisprudence—i.e., consolidation (rather than contractual arrangements) will permit the merging parties to maximise economies of scale and scope, and therefore generate (and, of course, guarentee that they will pass on these) substantial savings to consumers.

But will it really? On one hand, fewer dominant players controlling monopoly plants cannot be good for consumers. On the other hand, there have also been a number of new players in the telecommunications industry, firms offering new products and services, often in niche markets. Some of these new telcos are driven by new technologies or markets. Some are taking advantage of opportunities created by regulators, such as local loop unbundling. Some of the new companies are creations of other mergers. For every merger, there is usually an acquiring and acquired company, a winning and losing team. The loser management team will for the most part move on to other opportunities, this is only part of the efficiencies that ostensibly drive mergers (this is politer than saying many mergers result in mass layoffs). Many of these managers are too talented and young to simply count the value of their redundancy package. Several new telcos such as Level 3 and Qwest were staffed thus, and doubtless this trend will continue. Therefore, rather than industry consolidation into fewer firms, a trend of talent recycling into new companies may be observed, a healthy trend that contradicts the conventional wisdom. Accordingly, there is no "one size fits" all answer to industry concentration. Regardless of whether telecommunications providers end up numbering five or fifteen hundred, telco mergers continue at a furious pace, therefore, effective and meaningful merger review must be an important part of regulation today.

A. EU Merger Review

1. Legislative Background

EU legislation requires that mergers (concentrations) meeting certain criteria must be notified to the European Commission for approval.[2] Qualifying mergers are those where the parties involved have an annual combined worldwide turnover of at least 2.5 billion Euros and at least two of the companies involved have more than 100 million Euros annual turnover in the EU, unless such European turnover is concentrated in one EU Member State. An advantage for merging companies of falling under the Merger Regulation is that it provides a one-stop shop. That is, mergers reviewed by the EU Commission are not required to be notified in any of the individual Member States. The Merger Regulation calls for a fast review procedure. A qualifying merger is to be notified to the Commission within seven days of the merger agreement. This starts a 30-day review period, known as Phase One, with the possibility of extension to 6 weeks if a settlement is under consideration.

The European Commission is to appraise mergers to establish "whether or not they are compatible with the common market."[3] There follows a list of factors to be considered including the need to maintain and develop effective competition, the structure of all markets concerned, actual or potential competition present in these markets, and the market position of the involved companies. The market position would cover market shares and includes the companies' economic and financial power. Other factors the European Commission is required to consider are alternatives available to suppliers and users, access to markets and barriers to entry, supply and demand trends, and the development of technical and economic progress.

This last factor, the development of technical and economic progress, touches on a key EU policy as expressed in Treaty Article 81(3), concerning anti-competitive agreements. This Treaty provision allows anti-competitive agreements to be exempted from prohibition if it can be demonstrated that the agreement "contributes to improving the production or distribution of goods or to promoting technical progress, while allowing consumers a fair share of the resulting benefit."[4]

---

[2] Council Regulation (EEC) No 4064/89 of 21 December 1989 on the control of concentrations between undertakings, [1989] OJ L 395/1, [1989] OJ L 257/13, with amendments introduced by Council Regulation (EC) No 1310/97 of 30 June 1997, [1997] OJ L180/1, [hereinafter EU Merger Regulation] <http://europa.eu.int/eur_lex/en/lif/dat/1989/en_389R4064.html>.

[3] *Ibid.*, art. 2.

[4] Consolidated Version of the Treaty Establishing The European Community, [1997] OJ C340/173–308, art. 81(3), [hereinafter EU Treaty].

The importance of technical and economic progress is emphasised throughout EU policy documents, legislation and judgements. It must always be borne in mind that the EU is first and foremost an economic organisation. "Compatibility with the common market" is a vague standard of review, but fortunately the Merger Regulation provides more concrete guidance.

> "A concentration which does not create or strengthen a dominant position as a result of which effective competition would be significantly impeded in the common market or in a substantial part of it shall be declared compatible with the common market."[5]

The common market refers to the borders of the EU, while a "substantial part of it" can be considered as no more than a single Member State. Therefore, if it can be shown that a proposed merger would create or strengthen a dominant position in at least one Member State, it is to be prohibited or modified so as to remove the danger of dominance.

2. Procedural Process: Stage One Review

In its Phase One investigation, the European Commission, represented by the Merger Task Force, a special division of the Competition Directorate-General, conducts an initial review of a proposed merger. In reality, the Merger Task Force relies heavily on third-party comments, either supplied voluntarily or through the submission of requests for information to competitors, suppliers and customers of the merging parties.[6]

At the end of the Phase One review period, the European Commission may clear the merger, attach conditions (known as undertakings) to the merger, or decide to open a more in-depth investigation. Specifically, Merger Regulation Article 6(1)(c) provides that if the merger "raises serious doubts as to its compatibility with the common market, [the Merger Task Force] shall decide to initiate proceedings."[7] That is, when the Merger Task Force reaches a preliminary finding that a proposed merger would create or strengthen a dominant position, it will conduct a Phase Two investigation, lasting for up to an additional four months.

3. Procedural Process: The Phase Two Investigation

During the Phase Two investigation, the Merger Task Force will submit further requests for information and accept third-party comments (possibly including consultations with economists and other experts provided by third parties), and if the Merger Task Force remains convinced that the competitive situation would be altered by the proposed merger, it proceeds with a Statement of Objections outlining the problems seen with the proposed merger. The

---

[5] Merger Regulation, *supra* n. 2, art. 2(2)
[6] *Ibid.*, art. 11.
[7] Merger Regulation, *supra* n. 2, art 6(1)(c).

Statement of Objections functions as a kind of draft decision, and is commonly circulated within the European Commission, as well as being circulated to the merging parties and intervening third parties.

At this point, the Phase Two investigation takes on more of an aspect of an adversarial nature, with the merging parties on one side arrayed against the Merger Task Force supported by intervening third parties on the other. While any third party, including suppliers, consumers, workers or their representatives, that may be affected by the proposed merger has standing to comment on and intervene with the Merger Task Force, in practice competitors of the merging parties are most likely to commit the substantial resources necessary for an effective intervention. The Merger Task Force may hold an oral hearing to which the merging parties, intervening third parties, and representatives of the Member States (usually competition enforcement officials) are invited. Under the competition enforcement co-operation treaty between the EU and the USA, officials of the US Department of Justice may (with permission of the merging parties) share in the investigation of the Merger Task Force and attend hearings as observers. During this hearing, the Merger Task Force in effect tests its Statement of Objections, presenting its case and allowing the European Commission to consider the arguments of the merging parties as well as the intervening third parties.

If it is felt that a good case remains, the Merger Task Force will draft and circulate a Draft Decision for the European Commission, usually largely based on its Statement of Objections. The Merger Regulation prescribes that before a decision is finalised, it is to be submitted to Member State representatives, organised into an Advisory Committee. The European Commission must "take the utmost account of the opinion" of the Advisory Committee.[8] The entire European Commission is then to vote on the final decision, which is announced via a press release, as publication in all of the official languages of the EU may take several months.

In the final step of the process, the European Court of Justice (ECJ) may review merger decisions, in the same way that it may review all European Commission decisions. In practice, however, as judicial review is very slow, any ECJ judgment would come too late to provide any real relief to the merging parties.

4. Procedural Process: Settlement Negotiations

While the mandated procedure of a Phase Two investigation goes forward, the merging parties will usually conduct settlement discussions with the Merger Task Force. The parties will typically offer to divest certain enterprises or make other commitments satisfying the Merger Task Force's concerns about the creation or strengthening of a dominant position. If the Merger Task Force is

---

[8] *Ibid.*, art. 19(6).

prepared to accept such a settlement offer, it will submit (market test) the offer to the intervening third parties for their reaction. In practice, most mergers that make it to Phase Two are settled in this manner. The European Commission totally bans relatively few mergers, but has shown increased interventionist tendencies lately.

B. US Merger Framework

1. *The Role of the US Antitrust Enforcement Agencies*

a. Statutory Authority

The US Department of Justice (DOJ) and Federal Trade Commission (FTC) are the agencies responsible for enforcing US antitrust laws. With specific regard to mergers and joint ventures, they seek to enforce Section 7 of the Clayton Act, which prohibits a firm from acquiring stock and assets "in any line of commerce in any section of the country the effect of [which] may be substantially to lessen competition, or to tend to create a monopoly."[9]

US competition law enforcement authorities can also use the Sherman Act to review "every contract, combination . . . or conspiracy, in restraint of trade," and to examine claims of monopolisation (single firm conduct) in trade of commerce "among the several States, or with foreign nations."[10] Similarly, Section 2 of the Sherman Act prohibits monopolisation, attempts to monopolise, and conspiracies to monopolise "any part of trade or commerce among the several States or with foreign nations."[11]

In 1982, Congress refined this language by enacting the Foreign Trade Antitrust Improvements Act of 1992 (FTAIA), [12] which amended both the Sherman Act and Section 5 of the FTC Act.[13]

Under this statute, the FTAIA eliminates US antitrust jurisdiction over "conduct involving trade or commerce (other than import trade or import commerce) with foreign nations" *unless:*

(1) such conduct has a direct, substantial, and reasonably foreseeable effect—
   (a) on trade or commerce which is not trade or commerce with foreign nations, or on import trade or import commerce with foreign nations; or

---

[9] 15 U.S.C.A. § 18.

[10] 15 U.S.C. § 1.

[11] 15 U.S.C. 2.

[12] Pub. L. No. 97–290, 96 Stat. 1246 (1982), codified at 15 U.S.C. § 6a (1988).

[13] Section 5 of the Federal Trade Commission Act ("FTC Act") declares unlawful "unfair methods of competition in or affecting commerce, and unfair or deceptive acts or practices in or affecting commerce." 15 U.S.C. § 45 (1988 & Supp. 1993).

(b) on export trade or export commerce with foreign nations, of a person engaged in such trade or commerce in the United States; and

(2) such effect gives rise to a claim under the provisions of sections 1 to 7 of this title shall apply to such conduct only for injury to export business in the United States.

However, this statute goes on to state that if "Sections 1 to 7 of this title apply to such conduct only because of the operation of paragraph (1)(B), then sections 1 to 7 of this title shall apply to such conduct only for injury to *export business* in the United States." (Emphasis supplied.)

With regard to *import* commerce (*i.e.*, imports of products into the US directly), the US Supreme Court in *Hartford Fire Insurance* v. *California* held that the Sherman Act applies to foreign conduct "that was meant to produce and did in fact produce some substantial effect in the United States."[14] Thus, *Hartford* appears to require both *intent* and *demonstrable harm*.

b. Issues of Comity

Under the 1995 Joint Department of Justice/Federal Trade Commission Antitrust Enforcement Guidelines for International Operations,[15] both the DOJ and the FTC must consider international comity when enforcing the US antitrust laws. Comity reflects the broad concept of respect among co-equal sovereign nations and plays a role in determining the recognition which one nation allows within its territory to the legislative, executive or judicial acts of another nation.[16] Thus, in determining whether to assert jurisdiction to investigate or bring an action, or to seek particular remedies in a given case, each Agency must take into account whether significant interests of any foreign sovereign would be affected.[17] However, it is also important to note that a comity inquiry is not reserved exclusively for antitrust enforcement agencies. Rather, in disputes between private parties, many courts are willing to undertake a comity analysis.[18]

In performing a comity analysis, the DOJ and the FTC must take into account all relevant factors. Among others, these factors may include: (1) the relative significance to the alleged violation of conduct within the United States, as compared to conduct abroad; (2) the nationality of the persons involved in or affected by the conduct; (3) the presence or absence of a purpose to affect US consumers, markets, or exporters; (4) the relative significance and foreseeability of the effects of the conduct on the United States as compared to the effects abroad; (5) the existence of reasonable expectations that would be furthered or

---

[14] 113 S.Ct. 2891, 2909 (1993).

[15] http://www.usdoj.gov/atr/public/guidelines/internat.txt

[16] Through concepts such as positive comity, one country's authorities may ask another country to take measures that address possible harm to competition in the requesting country's market.

[17] See International Guidelines at § 3.2 and n. 73, noting that both the DOJ and the FTC have agreed to consider the legitimate interests of other nations in accordance with the recommendations of the Organisation for Economic Co-operation and Development (OECD) and various other bilateral agreements.

[18] See, e.g., *Timberlane Lumber Co.* v. *Bank of America*, 549 F.2d 597 (9th Cir. 1976).

defeated by the action; (6) the degree of conflict with foreign law or articulated foreign economic policies; (7) the extent to which the enforcement activities of another country with respect to the same persons, including remedies resulting from those activities, may be affected; and (8) the effectiveness of foreign enforcement as compared to US enforcement action.[19]

According to the *International Guidelines*, the relative weight that each factor should be given depends on the facts and circumstances of each case. If there is, in fact, a "conflict in law" between two countries—*e.g*, a foreign nation permits price fixing and cartels; the US does not—then the Agencies are supposed to ask first what laws or policies of the arguably interested foreign jurisdictions are implicated by the conduct in question. However, there are often many situations where there may be no actual conflict between the antitrust enforcement interests of the US and the laws or policies of a foreign sovereign. This is increasingly true as more countries adopt antitrust or competition laws that are compatible with those of the US. In these cases, the anticompetitive conduct in question may also be prohibited under the pertinent foreign laws, and thus the possible conflict would relate to enforcement practices or remedy. If the laws or policies of a foreign nation are neutral, it is again possible for the parties in question to comply with the US prohibition without violating foreign law.[20]

However, the *International Guidelines* also require the DOJ and FTC to take full account of comity factors beyond whether there is a conflict with foreign law. In deciding whether or not to challenge an alleged antitrust violation, the Agencies would, as part of a comity analysis, consider whether one country

---

[19] The first six of these factors are based on previous Department Guidelines. The seventh and eighth factors are derived from considerations in the US-EC Antitrust Cooperation Agreement. *Ibid.*, at nn. 74 & 46. See Agreement Relating to Mutual Cooperation Regarding Restrictive Business Practices, June 23, 1976, U.S. Federal Republic of Germany, 27 U.S.T. 1956, T.I.S. No. 8291, reprinted in 4 Trade Reg. Rep. (CCH) P 13,501; Agreement Between the Government of the United States of America and the Government of Australia Relating to Cooperation on Antitrust Matters, June 29, 1982, US- Australia, T.I.A.S. No. 10365, reprinted in 4 Trade Reg. Rep. (CCH) P 13,502; and Memorandum of Understanding as to Notification, Consultation, and Cooperation with Respect to the Application of National Antitrust Laws, March 9, 1984, U.S.-Canada, reprinted in 4 Trade Reg. Rep. (CCH) P 13,503. The Agencies also signed a similar agreement with the Commission of the European Communities in 1991. See also Agreement Between the Government of the United States of America and the Commission of the European Communities Regarding the Application of Their Competition Laws, Sept. 23, 1991, 30 I.L.M. 1491 (Nov. 1991), reprinted in 4 Trade Reg. Rep. (CCH) P 13,504. However, on August 9, 1994, the European Court of Justice (ECJ) ruled that the conclusion of the Agreement did not comply with institutional requirements of the law of the EU. Under the ECJ's judgment, action by the EU Council of Ministers is necessary for this type of agreement. See Case C–327/91 *France* v. *Commission* [1994] ECR I–364. Council approval was forthcoming. Agreement between the Government of the United States of America and the Commission of the European Communities regarding the application of their competition laws [1995] OJ L 95/47–50 <http://europa.eu.int/comm/dg04/interna/95145b.htm>. See also 95/145/EC, ECSC Decision of the Council and the Commission of 10 April 1995 concerning the conclusion of the Agreement between the European Communities and the Government of the United States of America regarding the application of their competition laws [1995] OJ L 95/45; and Agreement between the European Communities and the Government of the United States of America on the application of positive comity principles in the enforcement of their competition laws [1998] OJ L 173/28.

[20] International Guidelines at § 3.2.

encourages a certain course of conduct, leaves parties free to choose among different strategies, or prohibits some of those strategies. In addition, the Agencies must take into account the effect of their enforcement activities on related enforcement activities of a foreign antitrust authority. For example, the Agencies must consider whether their activities would interfere with or reinforce the objectives of the foreign proceeding, including any remedies contemplated or obtained by the foreign antitrust authority.[21]

Moreover, the DOJ and FTC must also consider whether the objectives sought to be obtained by the assertion of US law would be achieved in a particular instance by foreign enforcement. In lieu of bringing an enforcement action, the Agencies may consult with interested foreign sovereigns through appropriate diplomatic channels to attempt to eliminate anticompetitive effects in the US. In cases where the US decides to prosecute an antitrust action, however, such a decision would represent a determination by the Executive Branch that the importance of antitrust enforcement outweighs any relevant foreign policy concerns.[22]

c. Practice and Procedure

US competition law authorities' approach towards mergers differ from the FCC's review of mergers in that they serve in a *prosecutorial* role and bring actions on a case-by-case basis. To facilitate their objective, Congress bestowed certain powers on them, such as the Hart-Scott-Rodino confidentiality and subpoena provisions, so that they can seek an injunction of a proposed merger "before the eggs are scrambled" if they think the transaction substantially lessens competition. However, because the DOJ, and not the defendant, has the burden to demonstrate to a judge and jury (or, in the case of the FTC, the full Federal Trade Commission) either that a specific transaction would substantially lessen competition under current market conditions or that one or more parties have engaged or attempted to engage in anticompetitive conduct, these agencies typically view economic analysis through a "static" model. That is to say, their determinations generally utilise narrow market definitions and short time periods because they assume that the quantity of inputs is fixed and the state of technology is given and unchanging.[23]

2. The Role of Administrative Agencies Responsible for Economic Regulation

a. Statutory Authority

The FCC reviews telecoms mergers, acquisitions and joint ventures under a

---

[21] *Ibid.*

[22] *Ibid.*

[23] Notwithstanding the above, however, antitrust enforcement agencies often cannot overcome the temptation to become pseudo-regulators. See *ibid.*, at 33; This trend appears to have increased exponentially over the last several years, as the various antitrust enforcement agencies on several occasions simply have ordered the defendants to obey applicable FCC regulation(s).

variety of statutes. The FCC is required to review telecommunication industry mergers, acquisitions and joint ventures under several different statutes. As explained above in Chapter 9, these provisions include:

—*Communications Act Section 310(d), § 47 U.S.C. 310(d)*. Under this statute, no construction permit or station license may be transferred, assigned or disposed of in any manner, "voluntarily or involuntarily, directly or directly, *or by transfer or control of any corporation holding such license or permit*" to any person "except upon application to the Commission and upon finding by the Commission that the public interest, convenience and necessity will be served thereby."

—*Communications Act Section 310(b)(4), 47 U.S.C. § 310(b)(4)*. Under this statute, no broadcast or common carrier license may be controlled, directly or indirectly, by a foreign entity if the FCC finds that "the public interest will be served by the refusal or revocation of such license."

—*Communications Act Section 214, 47 U.S.C. § 214*. Under section 214, no common carrier shall acquire any line "unless and until there shall first have been obtained from the Commission a certificate that the present or future public convenience and necessity require or will require" the operation of the line.

—*Communications Act Section 221(a), 47 U.S.C. § 221(a)*. Under section 221(a), if the FCC finds that a "proposed consolidation, acquisition, or [acquisition of] control" of "telephone companies" "will be of advantage to the persons to whom service is to be rendered and in the public interest, it shall certify to that effect; and thereupon any Act or Acts of Congress making the proposed transaction unlawful shall not apply."[24] The statute expressly preserves any state jurisdiction over mergers.[25]

—*Communications Act Section 314, 47 U.S.C. § 314*. Section 314 of the Communications Act forbids anticompetitive acquisitions of certain international carriers. No reported court or FCC decision has interpreted this statute in more than a cursory way, or has found a violation of it.

—*Clayton Act Section 11, 15 U.S.C. § 21*. Under this provision, the FCC is vested with the authority to enforce section 7 of the Clayton Act over common

---

[24] The section has various other requirements: the telephone companies must apply for the antitrust exemption; and the FCC must give notice to the Governor and state Commission of each affected state, must accept comments, and must hold a public hearing in certain circumstances.

The FCC has held the "public hearing" requirement to be satisfied by its notice and comment procedures. *Pacific Northwest Bell Tel. Co., Memorandum Opinion and Order* (ENF 85–52), 1986 WL 292012 (¶¶ 5–9) (Com. Car. Bur. 1986) (hereinafter "PNB"), reconsideration granted in part and denied in part, 2 F.C.C. Rcd. 2019 (Com. Car. Bur. 1987). This is consistent with numerous holdings that "hearing" means an opportunity for interested persons to make their views known. Except in the rare case where witnesses' factual perceptions are in dispute (such as "who had the green light?"), a "hearing" need not be a "trial-type" evidentiary hearing. *United States v. Florida East Coast Railway Co.*, 410 U.S. 224, 243–46 (1973); *The Bell Telephone Co. of Pennsylvania v. FCC*, 503 F.2d 1250, 1266 (3d Cir. 1974), *cert. denied*, 422 U.S. 1026 (1976). Only statutes that require a "hearing on the record" confer the right to the latter kind of hearing. See *United States v. Florida East Coast Railway Co.*, 410 U.S. 224 (1973).

[25] It states: "Nothing in this subsection shall be construed as in any way limiting or restricting the powers of the several States to control and regulate telephone companies."

carriers.[26] If the FCC elects to use its section 7 authority, it must issue an administrative complaint alleging a violation of section 7 of the Clayton Act, and set the matter for hearing.[27] However, unlike the mandatory requirements of sections 214 and 310 above, the FCC's section 7 authority is discretionary. Moreover, The FCC has only "limited" experience under Section 11.[28]

Under both Title II and Title III of the Communications Act, the FCC may attach such terms and conditions as in its judgment the public convenience and necessity may require. [29]

b. Practice and Procedure

As explained in chapter 3, in contrast to the antitrust enforcement agencies, administrative agencies such as the FCC serve as independent *regulatory* bodies. In other words, interested parties must first seek their approval before they may engage in a jurisdictional activity. In contrast to the DOJ and FTC procedure, therefore, the burden rests with the moving parties—and not with the regulatory agencies—to show that a particular transaction meets the relevant statutory criteria.

Notwithstanding this procedural difference, because regulators serve as both investigators and adjudicators, regulatory agencies are bound by the US Administrative Procedures Act. As such, these agencies must examine, *inter alia*, all of the relevant facts, and must make clear the "basic data and the 'whys and wherefores' of [their] conclusions."[30] Moreover, these regulatory agencies must take great care to ensure procedural due process for all parties in a proceeding.

---

[26] Section 7 of the Clayton Act prohibits a firm from acquiring stock and assets "in any line of commerce in any section of the country the effect of [which] may be substantially to lessen competition, or to tend to create a monopoly." 15 U.S.C.A. § 18.

[27] The language of Section 11 and cases involving the enforcement activities of other agencies suggest that the FCC must await an agreement between the parties (though not the consummation of the agreement) before bringing an administrative complaint. See *FTC* v. *Dean Foods Co.*, 384 U.S. 597, 605 (1965); *United States* v. *Manufacturers Hanover Trust Co.*, 240 F. Supp. 867 (S.D.N.Y. 1965). However, the FCC may seek a preliminary injunction from the Court of Appeals under the All Writs Act to prevent consummation of the agreement pending prosecution of the administrative proceeding. *FTC* v. *Dean Foods Co.*, 384 U.S. at 605. (Court of Appeals has jurisdiction to issue a preliminary injunction preventing consummation of an agreement upon a showing that effective remedial action post-consummation would be virtually impossible, rendering enforcement of final divestiture decree futile).

[28] See H.R. Rep. No. 580, 86th Cong., 1st Sess. 20 (1959), cited in *United States* v. *FCC*, 652 F.2d 72, 85 n.65 (D.C. Cir. 1980) (*en banc*). Thus, as discussed below, while the FCC's Clayton Act authority is often alluded to in FCC orders involving industry transactions, the FCC typically acts either under Section 310 or 214 of the Communications Act. Accordingly, we are unaware of any recent case where the FCC actually brought a Clayton Act administrative complaint. See, e.g., In re Applications of NYNEX and Bell Atlantic for Consent to Transfer Control, Memorandum Opinion and Order, FCC 97–286 (rel. Aug. 14, 1997) at ¶ 29; In re Applications of Ameritech and SBC Communications for Consent to Transfer Control, Memorandum Opinion and Order, FCC 99–279 (rel. Oct. 8, 1999) at ¶ 53.

[29] See 47 U.S.C. §§ 214(c), 316.

[30] See, e.g., *City of Holyoke Gas & Electric Dept.* v. *FERC*, 954 F.2d 740, 743 (D.C. Cir. 1992) ("Since it is already doing the relevant calculation, it is a small matter to abide by the injunction of the arithmetic teacher: Show your work! For the Commission to do less deprives the [consumer] of a rational explanation of its decision.").

If an agency fails in any or all of these responsibilities, a reviewing court may reverse and remand the agency's decision as arbitrary and capricious.[31]

As noted *passim* regulatory agencies are, at bottom, concerned about solving two basic economic problems: (1) assuring that the regulated firms under their jurisdiction do not engage in anti-competitive behaviour or charge captive ratepayers monopoly prices; and (2), where practical, formulating regulatory paradigms designed to improve overall market performance in both the short-run and especially, given the huge sunk costs inherent to the telecommunications and electric utility industries, the long-run.[32] Given this daunting and difficult task, US courts generally hold that the powers of regulatory agencies responsible for economic regulation are significantly *broader* than those of the antitrust enforcement agencies, because they are "entrusted with the responsibility to determine when and to what extent the public interest would be served by competition in the industry."[33]

---

[31] *City of Holyoke Gas & Electric Dept.* v. FERC, 954 F.2d 740, 743 (D.C. Cir. 1992) .

[32] It should be noted, however, that the FCC's challenge is made more complex because telecommunications is clearly an industry characterised by rapid change and innovation. This challenge is now exacerbated with the passage of the Telecommunications Act of 1996. See also *Turner Broadcasting System Inc.,* v. *FCC,* 117 S. Ct. 1174, 1189 (1997) (regulatory schemes concerning telecommunications have "special significance" because of the "inherent complexity and assessments about the likely interaction of industries undergoing rapid economic and technological change"); *Denver Area Educational Telecommunications Consortium, Inc.* v. *FCC,* 116 S. Ct. 2374, 2385 (1996) (Court is "aware . . . of the changes taking place in the law, the technology, and the industrial structure, related to telecommunications, see, e.g., Telecommunications Act of 1996."); *Columbia Broadcasting Inc* v. *Democratic National Committee,* 412 U.S. 94, 102, 93 S. Ct. 2080, 2086 (1973) ("The problems of regulation are rendered more difficult because the . . . industry is dynamic in terms of technological change"); *FCC* v. *Pottsville Broadcasting Co.,* 309 U.S. 134, 138 (1940) ("Communications Act is not designed primarily as a new code for the adjustment of conflicting private rights through adjudication. Rather it expresses a desire on the part of Congress to maintain, through appropriate administrative control, a grip on the dynamic aspects" of the telecommunications industry).

[33] *FCC* v. *RCA Communications Inc.,* 346 U.S. 86, 93–95 (1953); *Northeast Utils. Serv. Co.* v. *FERC,* 993 F.2d 937, 947–48 (1st Cir. 1993) (public interest standard does not require agencies "to analyse proposed mergers under the same standards that the [DOJ] . . . must apply" because administrative agency is not required to "serve as an enforcer of antitrust policy in conjunction" with the DOJ or FTC; thus, while agency "must include antitrust considerations in its public interest calculations . . . it is not bound to use antitrust principles when they may be inconsistent with the [agency's] regulatory goals"). See also *National Broadcasting Co.* v. *United States,* 319 U.S. 190, 219 (1943) (Congress, through the Communications Act, "gave the Commission not niggardly but expansive powers."); *Craig O. McCaw,* Memorandum Opinion & Order, 9 FCC Rcd. 5836 (1994) at ¶ 7, aff'd, *SBC Communications* v. *FCC,* 56 F.3d 1484 (D.C. Cir. 1995) (FCC's "jurisdiction under the Communications Act gives us much more flexibility and more precise enforcement tools that the typical court has").

III. INDIVIDUAL EXAMPLES

A. The Global One Alliance

1. *The EU's Approach*

In their desire to serve multi-national corporations (MNCs), as well as to for defensive purposes, large telecommunications companies began to form a series of global alliances in the mid-1990s. Although the business record of these alliances has been spectacularly unsuccessful, their formation and especially their review by regulatory agencies is important and interesting, giving a window on regulatory thinking during this time and clues for future direction.

The most important of these alliances, from a European perspective, involved Deutsche Telekom (DT), France Télécom (FT), and Sprint, in what became known as Global One.[34] As Global One was not a full merger, the European Commission reviewed it under the standards of Treaty Article 81, instead of the EU Merger Regulation.

The European Commission found that the relevant product market was "the provision of non-reserved telecommunications services to corporate users both Europe-wide and nationally."[35] When considering the term, "non-reserved," it is important to remember that in 1996, when the case was decided, not all telecommunications services were open to competition. Member States could still "reserve" basic voice telephony and public network operations for monopoly providers. By non-reserved services, generally value added services or telephony services to closed user groups (CUGs) were meant. Obviously, as holders of monopoly rights in their home countries until 1998, neither DT nor FT wanted to accelerate the date of full telecommunications competition.

Two relevant product markets were found within the general category of non-reserved services: "customized packages of corporate telecommunications services"[36] and "packet-switched data communications services."[37] The European Commission found the first relevant product market for "customized packages of corporate telecommunications services" to be more specifically composed of "mainly liberalized voice services including voice communication between members of a closed group of users (virtual private network (VPN) services), high-speed data services and outsourced telecommunications services."[38] The European Commission accepted that there was a large demand for such enhanced services with close customer support among large corporate users. Moreover, the European Commission defined three relevant geographic markets for "customized packages of corporate telecommunications services":

---

[34] Case IV/35.337 *Atlas* [1996] OJ L239/23.
[35] *Ibid.*, para. 4.
[36] *Ibid.*, para. 5.
[37] *Ibid.*, para. 8.
[38] *Ibid.*, para. 5.

global, cross-border regional, and national.[39] The European Commission drew this distinction mainly because the required telecommunications infrastructure was provided on these geographical bases.

The other relevant product market, that of packet-switched data services, the European Commission considered to be a type of closed network, here for transmission of X.25 protocol data. Geographic markets for "packet–switched data communications services" were also considered to exist on global, cross-border regional, and national levels. The Internet did not enter into the European Commission's Decision, or apparently into the business plan for Global One.

As Global One was a new joint venture, the European Commission considered current market shares of DT and FT to assess the competitive impact of the proposed joint venture,[40] finding, not surprisingly, that while their market shares were relatively low in the EU as a whole, in their home countries the market shares were high in the relevant product markets, reaching over 75 per cent for data services in France and Germany.

In addition to divestiture requirements that included the sale of FT's data transfer subsidiary, the parties agreed to conditions of non-discrimination vis-à-vis competitors. The parties would be required to supply infrastructure such as leased lines to Global One only on terms that would be available to competitors.[41] The European Commission held that as the parties were "indispensable suppliers of building blocks",[42] non-discrimination was essential, particularly regarding domestic and international leased lines. Likewise, the European Commission held that the proposed alliance was:

> "not to be granted more favourable treatment than third parties in connection with other reserved facilities and services and with such facilities and services *which remain an essential facility after full and effective liberalization* of telecommunications infrastructure and services in France and Germany."[43]

The reference to essential facilities in the preceding paragraph is important in that the European Commission was instrumental in promoting the adoption of the essential facilities doctrine into European competition law. The non-discrimination undertaking was to apply to any "reserved and/or essential services, which would enable it [Global One] to offer services which competition providers are prevented from offering."[44] The non-discrimination commitment was also to extend to necessary technical and commercial information.

The European Commission was not satisfied with the contractual undertakings of the parties regarding non-discrimination, however, and, as such, it imposed other "behavioural constraints"[45] as well—notably, a change in

---

[39] Case IV/35.337 *Atlas* [1996] OJ L239/23, para. 12.
[40] *Ibid.*, para 16.
[41] *Ibid.*, para. 21.
[42] *Ibid.*, para.28.
[43] *Ibid.*, (emphasis supplied).
[44] *Ibid.*, para. 28.
[45] *Ibid.*, para. 29.

telecommunications regulation law in Germany and France. Stated another way, as the price for approval of the Global One joint venture, the European Commission extorted a commitment from the French and German governments to liberalise their telecommunications markets before the date then required by the EU regulatory framework.

"In letters sent to the Commission, the French and German governments have undertaken to take the necessary steps to effectively allow the use of alternative infrastructure for the provision of liberalized telecommunications services by 1 July 1996 and to liberalize the voice telephony service and all telecommunications infrastructure fully and effectively by 1 January 1998. The availability of alternative telecommunications infrastructure in Germany and France renders competitors of ATLAS [Global One] independent of DT and FT's infrastructure for the purposes of creating trunk network infrastructure to provide liberalised services."[46]

The European Commission's Full Competition Directive subsequently adopted these dates for all Member States without derogations.[47] For political reasons, the European Commission probably would not have been able to issue this Directive with the date of 1 July 1996 for infrastructure liberalisation, if it had not obtained the support of France and Germany through its strong-arm tactics. France and Germany were further required to ensure separation of their regulatory and operative (government operation of FT and DT) functions, non-discriminatory access, and to prevent cross-subsidies.[48] The French and German governments were also required to licence at least two non-incumbent operators for "the construction or ownership, and control, of telecommunications infrastructure."[49] British Telecommunications (BT) subsequently initiated judicial proceedings to revoke the approval of the Global One joint venture on the basis that the German government failed to issue the required licences.

Although the European Commission's Decision was thorough, it may be faulted for imposing a remedy that was not clearly related to market changes caused by the proposed joint venture. The European Commission appeared eager to take advantage of the Global One deal to get what it wanted anyway from France and Germany. On the other hand, if the alleged advantages of Global One had actually materialised, perhaps the European Commission's actions would have been warranted. If Global One is viewed as the first stage of a potential merger of FT and DT, the European Commission was probably right in sending a warning that significant regulatory concessions would be on tap. It has been hard enough to competitors to break into the French and German markets. A full merger of two incumbent operators in adjacent countries would result in a very strong market position and offer advantages that might be

---

[46] *Ibid.*, para. 31.
[47] Commission Directive 96/19 of 13 March 1996 amending Directive 90/388/EEC with regard to the implementation of full competition in telecommunications markets [1996] OJ L74/13, [hereinafter Full Competition Directive].
[48] *Global One* Decision, *supra* n. 34, para. 31.
[49] *Ibid.*, para 78, art 2.

impossible for entrants to overcome, particularly without significant regulatory changes. the European Commission would have a chance to examine such a case in the proposed Telia-Telenor merger, discussed below.

2. The FCC's Approach

The FCC decided to grant, subject to certain conditions, Sprint's requests for rulings that a proposed alien ownership in Sprint by FT and DT of up to 28 per cent was "not on balance inconsistent" with Section 310(b)(4) of the Communications Act, and that the proposed transaction was "not on balance inconsistent" with the public interest. [50] The FCC also found that "10 per cent equity investments each by France Telecom (FT) and Deutsche Telekom (DT) in Sprint [did] not result in a transfer of control of Sprint to FT and DT and thus [did] not require prior Commission approval under Section 310(d) of the Act." [51] As explained more fully below, while the FCC was concerned that France and Germany did not offer effective competitive opportunities for US carriers, the FCC nonetheless granted the petition because the FCC found that: (a) the proposed transaction would create pro-competitive benefits; and (b) "the French and German governments [were] committed to full competition, . . . in which US companies [would] be allowed to participate." [52]

What is particularly significant (and humorous) about this *Order*, however, is the FCC's apparent inability to decide whether it should apply its "Effective Competitive Opportunities Test or "*ECO*" test in this situation. [53] At first, the FCC decided to apply the *ECO* test to the proposed transaction simply because of the size of the carriers involved. [54] Yet, several paragraphs later, the FCC changed its mind and decided that an *ECO* analysis was unwarranted in this case because it had already reached "the ultimate conclusion . . . that, on balance, the public interest weighs in favour of granting Sprint's petition." [55] Notwithstanding this statement, however, commenters had convinced the FCC that the proposed transaction created "*ECO*-type" competitive concerns, and the FCC stated that it would address these concerns in this proceeding nonetheless—*independent* of the *ECO* analysis. [56]

In particular, the FCC shared the commenters' fundamental concerns "about the potential for anticompetitive behaviour by FT and DT on the US-France and US-Germany routes." [57] The FCC again pointed out that:

---

[50] Sprint Corp., Petition for Declaratory Ruling Concerning Section 310(b)(4) and (d) of the Communications Act, *Declaratory Ruling and Order*, 11 F.C.C.R. 1850, 2 Comm. Reg. (P & F) 409 (1996) [hereinafter *Sprint Declaratory Ruling and Order*] at para. 1.

[51] *Ibid.*

[52] *Ibid.*, para. 3.

[53] For a full discussion of the FCC's ECO test, see chapter 6 above.

[54] *Ibid.*, para. 39.

[55] *Ibid.*, para. 49.

[56] *Ibid.*, para. 51.

[57] *Ibid.*, para. 55.

"FT and DT [were] monopoly providers of French and German international facilities-based services, [they controlled] the local termination points in those countries, and [they controlled] the national long distance networks to which interconnection is essential for the distribution of international traffic."[58]

As such, the FCC reasoned that although prior to the "proposed transaction, FT and DT had no incentive to discriminate in favor of Sprint, the Joint Venture or any of their competitors over others," after the transaction FT and DT would "each [have] a substantial financial stake in the success of Sprint and the Joint Venture and [would], therefore, give each an incentive to engage in anticompetitive strategies to maximize the return on their investment."[59] As such, the FCC concluded that

"[a]bsent effective conditions, such strategic behavior could yield Sprint more customers, calls and revenues, and ultimately higher returns, than would otherwise be the case."[60]

Notwithstanding the above, however, the FCC found several strong countervailing reasons to grant the petition. First, the FCC believed that the recent

[58] *Ibid.* One other interesting aspect in this case is that the FCC specifically rejected Sprint's claims that FT and DT had no more leveraging power than BT did in the *BT/MCI* proceeding. For example, the Commission pointed out that Sprint overlooked the fact that, in the United Kingdom, there was *de jure* competition in nearly every market segment (in that BT faced competition to some extent at all levels), and, unlike in France and Germany, US carriers had a choice of carriers to haul their traffic. The FCC also found that as of the time of this Order, there was an effective regulatory authority that is independent of BT, which employed fair and transparent procedures while there were no such independent regulatory authorities with fair and transparent procedures in France or Germany. *Ibid.*, para. 58. Finally, the Commission rejected Sprint's arguments that EU regulatory prohibitions on discriminatory conduct by FT and DT were sufficient to protect competition, particularly in the US market for "global, seamless services." *Ibid.*, para. 60.

[59] *Ibid.*, para. 56. According to the FCC, potential discrimination could take a number of forms, such as: (1) routing calls to Sprint and the Joint Venture in proportions greater than those justified under [its] proportionate return policy; (2) otherwise manipulating the calculations and settlements payments to wrongfully favour Sprint and the Joint Venture; (3) routing high-profit calls to Sprint and the Joint Venture, and leaving the rest to their competitors; (4) undercharging Sprint and the Joint Venture and/or overcharging their competitors for use of the same essential facilities in France or Germany; (5) leaking to Sprint and the Joint Venture the confidential information that FT or DT receives from Sprint's and the Joint Venture's competitors; (6) giving Sprint and the Joint Venture advance notice of network changes and other information that Sprint, the Joint Venture and their competitors will need to know; or (7) either as an agent or through an affiliated third party, selling the services of Sprint or the Joint Venture in ways that use FT's and DT's home market power. *Ibid.*, (citation omitted).

[60] *Ibid.*, para. 57. In the end, the FCC imposed the following five conditions: first, the Commission classified Sprint as a dominant carrier (without price cap regulation, however) for the provision of US international services on the US-France and US-Germany routes. Second, the Commission prohibited Sprint from operating additional circuits "on the U.S.-France and U.S.-Germany routes until France and Germany . . . liberalized two important markets: alternative infrastructure for already liberalized services (which include most non-public voice services) and basic switched voice resale." *Ibid.*, para. 4. Third, the Commission required Sprint to comply with non-discrimination and reporting requirements. Fourth, the Commission held that the proposed transaction would serve the public interest only if Sprint obtained a written commitment from FT to lower the accounting rate between the United States and France to the same range as the US-UK and US-Germany accounting rates. *Ibid.*

liberalisation efforts by the French and German governments were an important first step toward effective facilities and services competition.[61] Moreover, the FCC noted that the European Union established 1 January 1998,

"as the date by which most Member States, including France and Germany, must fully open their telecommunications markets by liberalizing existing monopolies for public voice telephony services and transmission facilities."[62]

Second, the FCC found that the proposed transaction would result in significant pro-competitive benefits—primarily by permitting Sprint to use the substantial sum of new investment capital to upgrade its existing infrastructure—in a variety of relevant product markets, including domestic interexchange services, terrestrial commercial mobile radio services (CMRS), US international services, and the nascent market for global seamless services.[63] While the FCC reasoned that:

"capital investment is not, by itself, necessarily procompetitive or efficient, the competitive forces in [these markets should] drive Sprint to devote the investment to making itself a stronger competitor in the ways it describ[ed]."[64]

As such, the FCC believed that:

"Sprint's strengthening of itself as a competitor against its larger rivals, AT&T and MCI, should yield procompetitive benefits for consumers. . . . [B]y permitting Sprint to expand and upgrade its existing network, undertake additional research and develop new applications and services, the capital should ultimately benefit consumers through lower prices and more service choices."[65]

---

[61] *Ibid.*, paras. 63–73.

[62] *Ibid.*, para. 74.

[63] *Ibid.*, para. 88. The FCC recognized that at the time of the *BT/MCI* decision, there were no established global seamless service providers. At the time of Sprint's petition, there were several such providers in this market, such as AT&T's partnerships (through Worldpartners and Uniworld), and the BT/MCI alliance (Concert). As such, the FCC held that the "Joint Venture between Sprint, FT and DT would add another significant competitor to this market" and would yield significant competitive benefits for US customers. *Ibid.*, para. 86. Specifically, the FCC reasoned that "[t]he establishment of a new, viable competitor in this area should result in more competitive options for U.S. customers, particularly in terms of pricing and variety of services available for large scale, high-end customers such as multinational corporations." *Ibid.*, para. 87. In addition, the FCC believed that the Joint Venture would "offer a number of efficiencies for Sprint, such as greater economies of scale, easier entry into new markets and the sharing of risks. Given that several strong competitors already exist[ed] in this market," the FCC therefore concluded that "the procompetitive effects of the Sprint/FT/DT transaction outweigh[ed] any possible anticompetitive results in this market." *Ibid.*

[64] *Ibid.*, para. 80 (citations omitted).

[65] *Ibid.*, (citation omitted).

B. *BT/MCI*

The case of BT/MCI is long and complex. The story begins with BT's desire to make an equity stake in MCI. In the next chapter of the story, BT attempts to acquire outright MCI. Like so many case studies highlighted in this book, however, once again regulators could not keep their attention on comparative issues and instead yielded once again to introducing trade concerns into the analysis. Each chapter of the saga is outlined briefly below.

1. *The EU's Approach*

a. Joint Venture Approval

The European Commission reviewed the first BT/MCI case under its Treaty Article 81 authority.[66] That is, the European Commission did not find that the joint venture was sufficiently "concentrative" for the Merger Regulation to apply, and therefore it was reviewed as a "co-operative" joint venture. The European Commission's review focused on the restrictions of competition brought about by the joint venture weighed against its pro-competitive effects, a type of rule of reason analysis as set forth in Treaty Article 81(3).[67] The parties also had to wait longer for a decision as the time deadlines of the Merger Regulation did not apply.

The European Commission identified the product market in question as being "global products," further subdivided into six different categories: data services, value added services, traveller services, intelligent network services, other services such as integrated network services and global outsourcing.[68] Given the exclusive focus on the joint venture on global services, it is not surprising that a global relevant geographic market was found.[69] The European Commission's description of competitors is interesting and rather quaint, as most of the listed companies have failed or been absorbed.[70] Even though the Decision is only a few years old, the errors in market predictions are striking. Indeed, the whole

---

[66] Case IV/34.857 *BT/MCI (I)* [1994] OJ L223/36.

[67] "The provisions of paragraph 1 may, however, be declared inapplicable in the case of:

—any agreement or category of agreements between undertakings;

—any decision or category of decisions by associations of undertakings;

—any concerted practice or category of concerted practices, which contributes to improving the production or distribution of goods or to promoting technical or economic progress, while allowing consumers a fair share of the resulting benefit, and which does not:

(a) impose on the undertakings concerned restrictions which are not indispensable to the attainment of these objectives;

(b) afford such undertakings the possibility of eliminating competition in respect of a substantial part of the products in question." EU Treaty, *supra* n. 4, art 81(3).

[68] *BT/MCI (I)*, *supra* n. 66, para. 6.

[69] *Ibid.*, para. 15.

[70] *Ibid.*, paras. 17 and 56. The list includes AT&T Worldsource, Unisource, Eunectom, STET, DEC, Geis, Sprint International, IBM, and CompuServe.

concept of global alliances to address global customers has been an unbroken chain of failures, most recently exemplified by Iridium. Conspicuous in its absence from the European Commission's analysis is any mention of the Internet.

The European Commission identified concerns it had received from an unnamed third party regarding the potential anticompetitive effects of the BT/MCI joint venture. These focused on BT's "control of local access facilities in the United Kingdom" and the commentator's desire to see requirements placed on BRT/MCI top forbid discrimination and cross-subsidistion.[71] The European Commission was not impressed, finding that current regulatory safeguards in both the US and the UK were adequate to protect competitors ("existing regulation to which BT and/or MCI are subjected in their respective countries prevents such cross-subsidization and/or discrimination from taking place."[72]) There follows a short recitation of the provisions of the US Communications Act of 1934 and the UK Telecommunication Act of 1984 forbidding such practices. Unlike the FCC, the European Commission did not find it necessary to engage in a lengthy examination of regulatory reality. Perhaps this was a reflection of the relative inexperience, at this date, of the European Commission in examining telecoms joint ventures and mergers. The European Commission did note that in the event BT/MCI engaged in unlawful discrimination or cross-subsidisation enforcement action could be taken on the European level.[73]

Under the structure of an Article 81 review, the European Commission must first determine whether there were restrictions on competition so as to fall under Article 81 (easily met in this case), and then to determine whether the conditions for an exemption under Article 81(3) were present. The European Commission accepted the parties' reasoning as to what was driving the joint venture. BT asserted that that the joint venture was part of its plan "to become a leading global provider of international value-added and enhanced telecommunications services in the world," while MCI wanted "to maintain its competitive position in the Americas, in particular against AT&T," for which purpose a global reach was necessary.[74] The European Commission found the requisite benefits to the market in that BT, and hence European customers, would gain access to "MCI technology, which is said to be one of the most credible and user friendly in the world."[75] Accepting BT/MCI's claims about their planned "seamless" network with state of the art capabilities, the European Commission reasoned that large European corporations, expected to be BT/MCI's customers, would greatly benefit from having access to this network.[76] Such a network itself might be a

---

[71] *BT/MCI (I)*, *supra* n. 66, para. 33.
[72] *Ibid.*, para. 57.
[73] *Ibid.*
[74] *Ibid.*, para. 51.
[75] *Ibid.*, para 53.
[76] *Ibid.*

type of competitive advantage, and European industry would be enabled "to better withstand global competition from other corporations operating from parts of the world where technological advance in telecommunications is becoming common-place."[77] BT/MCI did a much better job in selling the European Commission on the values of its services than it ever did in the real market. As such the European Commission concluded that the joint venture was so pro-competitive as to meet the exemption test of Article 81(3).

2. The Completed (and Dead) BT/MCI Merger

The European Commission's analysis of the proposed full merger of BT and MCI[78] was conducted under the EU Merger Regulation.[79] Perhaps because of that, or because of the European Commission's greater experience in telecoms matters, *BT/MCI (II)* is more thorough and sophisticated in its analysis than *BT/MCI (I)*.

Regarding relevant product markets, the European Commission noted that the parties contended that there was no overlap in the proposed merger other than in the relevant product markets of audioconferencing and the product markets covered by the Concert joint venture.[80] The European Commission added that both parties were involved in their own domestic markets ("domestic public switched voice services, enhanced value added services, private leased lines"[81] and also provision of international telecommunications to their domestic customers) and international voice telephony services (international direct dialled calls (IDD) and international private leased circuits (IPLC)).[82] The international voice telephony market was further divided, from the consumers' view, into relevant geographic markets of specific country pairs.[83] This seems logical as a firm's strength in infrastructure between country A and B is irrelevant to an end-user calling from county C to D.

The European Commission also mentioned the possibility of re-routing or "hubbing" traffic so as to avoid direct routing between countries. In the above terms, a telephone call originating in country A might reach country B by routing through, or "transiting" county C or D. Despite that fact that the practice of re-routing or "refiling" had already become prevalent by the time of the *BT/MCI (II)* Decision, the European Commission stated that re-routing:

> "does not appear to be a viable commercial possibility at present, since under the existing system of accounting rates and proportionate return it would be more expensive than using direct routes."[84]

---

[77] *Ibid.*
[78] Case IV/M.856 *BT/MCI (II)* [1997] OJ L336/1.
[79] EU Merger Regulation, *supra* n. 2.
[80] *BT/MCI (II)*, *supra* n. 78, para. 10.
[81] *Ibid.*, para. 11.
[82] *Ibid.*, paras 13–15.
[83] *Ibid.*, para. 19.
[84] *Ibid.*

This leads one to conclude that the European Commission did not understand the arbitrage opportunities presented by the inequality in accounting rates and international traffic patterns. Refiling was already rampant at the time of this decision, though in theory forbidden by International Telecommunication Union Rules and Regulations. The European Commission subdivided the country-pair international markets even further, by originating and terminating portions of a call, but the (then flourishing) call-back market was noted as confusing the nature of originating and terminating markets.[85]

With the country-pair relevant market definition, the European Commission found that the parties would have a high market share on the UK-US route. The problem in this area was made more worrisome to the European Commission by the fact that "BT still also enjoys a very strong position in the domestic [UK] markets."[86] BT's strength in the international voice telephony market, represented specifically by the UK-US route, was likely to remain for some time since BT's market power "is underpinned by its current control of the local loop in the United Kingdom."[87] The European Commission thus linked control over the local loop, representing a control over access to end-users, with a downstream market, here dominance in international voice telephony. In the event, the European Commission did nothing about BT's dominance in the local loop. Instead, the European Commission chose to trumpet the "progressive move of many national regulatory regimes towards full liberalization of their telecoms markets."[88] The UK government had recently issued "45 new international facilities licences", and the FCC had issued an order through which:

> "US carriers will be permitted to negotiate alternative settlement payment arrangements that deviate from the accounting rate regime with foreign correspondents in countries which satisfy the 'effective competitive opportunities' test (ECO) adopted by the FCC, or in any case where the US carrier can demonstrate that the deviation from the existing regime will promote market-oriented pricing and competition, while precluding abuse of market power by the foreign correspondent."[89]

Thus, far from stoking the flames of a trade war with the US, the European Commission appears to be saluting the efforts of the FCC, efforts that ironically had the effect as well as probable intent to harm non-US carriers. To say the European Commission was naïve in its understanding is an understatement. The Decision continued its Panglossian praises:

> "As a result of these regulatory developments, the option now exists for an international carrier licensed in both the United States and the United Kingdom of providing telephony services between these two countries on an end-to-end basis, by terminating the call at the foreign end of its own international facilities and getting

---

[85] *Ibid.*
[86] *BT/MCI (II)*, *supra* n. 78, para. 25.
[87] *Ibid.*, para. 26.
[88] *Ibid.*, para. 32.
[89] *Ibid.*

direct access to the unbundled functions of the domestic network of the foreign country, as well as whatever facilities of its own it has established there."[90]

Even as a possibility, this statement was false. The UK did not require BT to provide unbundled local loops so there was no possibility of complete end-to-end routing involving the UK by BT's competitors. Only BT could originate or terminate calls to the vast bulk of UK end-users. In theory, it may have been possible for BT's competitors to build their own local loops to end-users, but competition law should deal with market realities, especially when end-to-end competition is notably lacking. Even in the US where local loop unbundling was a legal possibility, not many loops had actually been sold by this date, as demonstrated by the fact that none of the US regional Bell companies (RBOCs) had met the test to enter the US long distance market (including origination and termination of international traffic) at this date. The *BT/MCI (II)* Decision itself immediately backtracked from this absurd assertion, noting that "entry of new operators"[91] was key for competition in international voice telephony, and in that regard, "access to transatlantic cable capacity, as well as domestic interconnection with transatlantic cable capacity and local loop termination at either end"[92] were all important in assessing the proposed merger.

Some intervenors demanded that at least equal access (sometimes called carrier pre-selection) be made available in the UK as a condition for approval of the BT/MCI merger.[93] The European Commission decided that it did not need to consider this as a possible remedy, since if there were problems in the UK with equal access, they existed before, and the European Commission concluded that the merger would not change the situation in any way. With no change there can be no remedy through merger review.

Such a conclusion ignores how the addition of MCI would give BT increased end-to-end connectivity, however. On the UK-US route, BT would have the UK locked up for origination and termination of calls. MCI could give transmission (backhaul) throughout the US, with points of presence (POPs) in every US region, and established customer relations with a good portion of US end-users. No established carrier or potential entrant could hope to match that advantage. Indeed, perhaps reflecting a split within the European Commission Merger Task Force Team examining the proposed merger, the Decision noted that:

"By bringing together BT's and MCI's cable capacity on the UK-US route, the merger would provide the parties with the possibility of 'self-corresponding', that is to say, they could carry their transatlantic traffic over end-to-end connections owned entirely

[90] *Ibid.*, para. 33.
[91] *Ibid.*, para 36.
[92] *Ibid.*
[93] *Ibid.*, para. 37. Despite the requirements of the EU's Number Portability Directive (Directive 98/61/EC of the European Parliament and of the Council amending Directive 97/33/EC with regard to operator number portability and carrier pre-selection, [1998] OJ L268/37) regarding carrier pre-selection, as of this writing the UK has still not adopted effective carrier pre-selection. BT claims that its switches are not up to the task without expensive routing mechanisms.

by them. The merged entity would therefore be able to internalize settlement payments for all of the traffic which BT and MCI currently send each other on a correspondent basis . . ."[94]

The European Commission also flagged a danger that BT/MCI would be in a dominant position for end-to end connectivity on the UK-US route, but fingered transatlantic cable capacity as the real culprit rather than end-user access.

"Given BT's and MCI's combined position on the UK-US cable capacity and BT's position in the generation of outbound traffic from the United Kingdom, the merged entity would be in a position to prevent other incumbents from providing end-to-end services for a significant volume of traffic."[95]

The European Commission believed that existing rules against discrimination by BT were sufficient to guard against any abuse of a dominant position in the area of end-user access or competitor access to bottleneck facilities.[96] UK regulation required BT to provide interconnection at long-run incremental prices,[97] and Oftel would monitor BT's backhaul prices.[98] The standard the European Commission is to apply, however, is not whether a dominant provider can be stopped from abuse by existing law or regulation. Rather, the European Commission is to judge whether a proposed concentration would create or strengthen a dominant position.[99] We shall see below how the European Commission, perhaps educated as to the realities of the market, was much more amenable to a regulatory remedy in the *Telia/Telenor* Decision.

The European Commission did find a problem with availability of capacity on transatlantic cables, and the parties agreed to sell the overlap in the transatlantic cable capacity.[100] Furthermore, BT agreed to sell its audioconferencing business, Darome, in the UK to prevent overlap with Concert's audioconfernecing business. The European Commission's stated concerns about the merged entity's end-to-end capabilities were well founded, however, its remedy, divestiture of overlapping transatlantic cable capacity, did not address the problem. It is relatively easy to enter the market for international cable capacity, more cables are coming on line rapidly with even more planned. Perhaps the European Commission should have directly addressed originating and terminating access, areas where entry is difficult and unlikely, especially over the short term.

---

[94] *Ibid.*, para 58.
[95] BT/MCI (II), *supra* n. 78, para. 60.
[96] *Ibid.*, para. 55.
[97] *Ibid.*, para. 56.
[98] *Ibid.*, para. 57.
[99] Case T–102/96 *Gencor* v. *Commission* [1999] ECR II–753, paras. 94, 106, 154.
[100] BT/MCI (II), *supra* n. 78, para. 76.

3. *The FCC's Approach*

a. *BT/MCI I*[101] and *BT/MCI II*[102]

BT/MCI I and *II* marked the first time that the FCC was forced to deal with a substantial investment by a dominant foreign firm into one of the largest telecommunications firms in the United States. In an apparent effort to avoid a lengthy regulatory approval process, MCI and BT filed a petition for declaratory ruling that: (1) the terms and conditions of BT's investment in MCI did not result in a transfer of control of MCI to BT, and, accordingly, prior FCC approval was not required pursuant to Section 310(d) of the Act; and (2) BT's proposed 20 per cent ownership interest, even when aggregated with existing non-BT foreign investment for a total of up to 28 per cent foreign investment, was consistent with and permissible under Section 310(b)(4) of the Communications Act.[103]

Resolution of both questions was expeditious. In the former case, the FCC found that because, under the deal as then-structured, BT would not be able to exercise control over MCI, the transaction did "not constitute a transfer of control and, therefore, did not require Commission approval under § 310(d) prior to consummation of the transaction."[104] Similarly, the FCC found no public interest reason under Section 310(b)(4) to deny the petition because the proposed investment did:

> "not raise the traditional concerns present in a Section 310(b)(4) analysis as [there was] only the potential 3 per cent fluctuation in alien ownership beyond the 25 per cent statutory benchmark due to the widely-held nature of [MCI's] stock."[105]

Yet, despite the fact that the FCC "granted" the BT/MCI petition, the FCC announced that because of other:

---

[101] MCI Comm. Corp. & British Telecomm. PLC, *Declaratory Ruling and Order*, 9 F.C.C.R. 3960, 75 Rad. Reg. 2d (P & F) 1024 (1994) [hereinafter BT/MCI I Order].

[102] MCI Comm. Corp. & British Telecomm. PLC, *Declaratory Ruling*, 10 F.C.C.R. 8697 (1995) [hereinafter BT/MCI II].

[103] In *BT/MCI II*, MCI petitioned the FCC to declare that an increase in the foreign ownership of MCI's capital stock from 28 to 35 per cent would be consistent with the public interest under Section 310(b)(4) and would not constitute a transfer of control under Section 310(d). The FCC granted the petition, finding that the increase in foreign ownership of MCI would come from passive investors— each of which would own less than one per cent of MCI stock. These new owners would have neither the incentive nor the ability to control MCI. Moreover, the FCC found that BT's ownership in MCI was not expected to change as a result of the proposed increase in MCI's foreign ownership, and, in any event, MCI continued to be bound by the requirements of the previous *BT/MCI I Order* outlined above. *Ibid.*, para. 9.

[104] *BT/MCI I Order*, *supra* n. 101, para. 18; see also *ibid.*, paras. 10–17.

[105] *Ibid.*, paras. 19–23. The FCC was also comforted by the fact that the transaction involved "a dominant U.S. presence among MCI's officers, directors and shareholders." *Ibid.*, para. 22. As such, the FCC stated that it would view "the possible 3 per cent fluctuation in non-BT alien ownership beyond the statutory benchmark . . . in light of the presence of 80 per cent U.S. directors and 100 per cent U.S. officers in MCI, in addition to the 100 per cent U.S. officers and directors in MCI's Title III licensee subsidiaries." *Ibid.*

"public interest concerns . . . regarding the effect that the BT and MCI alliance may
have on competition in the telecommunications market as a result of the potential for
either discrimination or other anticompetitive conduct,"

it would, nonetheless, conduct a *post hoc* in-depth review of the likely competitive effects of the investment.[106] For example, the FCC believed that, post-
merger, "BT could leverage its dominant position in both the UK international
and local exchange markets to favor MCI . . . to the disadvantage of competing
US International carriers."[107] According to the FCC, this:

"favorable treatment could manifest itself in a variety of ways, such as preferential
pricing or the provision of technical network information in advance of such disclosure to other US carriers."[108]

To wit, at the time of the proposed merger, BT controlled ninety-seven per cent
of the local termination points and had the most fully developed long-distance
network to which interconnection is essential for the distribution of international traffic in the United Kingdom.[109]

On the US end, the FCC found that "MCI [was] the second largest interexchange carrier and international service provider in the market and, as such,
maintained a significant US customer base."[110] As such, the FCC reasoned that

"BT's 20 per cent interest in such a major US carrier, coupled with its participation on
MCI's Board of Directors, [might] provide BT with the incentive both to discriminate
in favor of MCI and to influence the corporate decision-making process of MCI."[111]

"Thus, in spite of the fact that MCI and BT [were] not 'affiliated' within the meaning
of [the FCC's] rules, [the FCC] believe[d] that these factors create[d] additional incentives for BT to favor MCI, directly or indirectly."[112]

The curious thing about this conclusion, however, is that despite the potential incentives for strategic behaviour mentioned above, the FCC nonetheless
concluded that dominant carrier regulation was not necessary for MCI.[113] The
FCC reached this conclusion for two reasons: (1) "the safeguards imposed in the
order [were] sufficient to ensure that the parties do not engage in anticompetitive activities" (basically *de minimis* reporting requirements); and (2) MCI's
agreement to a "no special concessions" provision.[114] For example, the FCC
found that:

[106] *BT/MCI I Order*, para. 29.
[107] *Ibid.*, para. 30.
[108] *Ibid.*
[109] *BT/MCI I Order*, *supra* n. 101, para. 36.
[110] *Ibid.*
[111] *Ibid.*
[112] *Ibid.*
[113] *Ibid.*, para. 37.
[114] *Ibid.*, (citation omitted). Indeed, the FCC specifically found that "nothing in the record indicate[d] that there [was] any need for several key provisions of dominant carrier regulation, such as
filing of tariffs on 45-days notice, requirement of cost support justification, and prior Section 214
authorization for circuit additions. [According to the FCC,] these restrictions would be needlessly
burdensome in this context." *Ibid.*, n.69.

"the amendment of MCI's international Section 214 certificates to include a "no special concessions" obligation would preclude MCI from accepting from BT, or from any other foreign carrier or administration, preferential or exclusive operating agreements or marketing arrangements for the provision of basic telecommunications services, including the introduction and provision of new basic services."[115]

Similarly, the FCC found that MCI's amended certificates would:

"preclude it from accepting from BT any distribution or interconnection arrangements, including pricing, technical specifications, functional capabilities, or other quality and operational characteristics, such as provisioning and maintenance times, at rates or on terms and conditions that are not available on a nondiscriminatory basis to all competing US carriers."[116]

The FCC also rejected arguments that BT and MCI could use their relationship to manipulate traffic streams or accounting rates, again repeating its belief that *"existing Commission policy with respect to these matters effectively limits the parties' ability to engage in such anticompetitive conduct."*[117]
Finally, the FCC made two other significant findings in this case that it would be forced to ignore deliberately two years later in *BT/MCI III*—*that is, that BT's failure to enter independently would not make a significant competitive impact in either the US domestic market or the market for US-originated traffic on the US-UK route.*[118] Indeed, based on specific findings that even though BT had previously demonstrated an active interest in (and made two unsuccessful attempts to enter) the US market, and, absent this transaction, BT might have elected to enter the US telecommunications market on its own, the FCC found that even if BT were viewed as a potential entrant, there did not appear to be any anticompetitive effect if BT did not enter.[119] Indeed, the FCC noted that, at the time of this *Order*, there were "several hundred carriers, both facilities- and resale-based, competing in the US interexchange market" and, as such,

"the loss of the incremental competition that might [have been] provided by BT's independent entry into the US telecommunications market . . . appear[ed] to be of little competitive significance."[120]

Similarly, because at the time of this *Order* there were "approximately 10 international facilities-based carriers and hundreds of international resellers providing US-UK telecommunications services," the FCC again "conclude[d] that the number of existing and potential competitors indicate[d]" that BT's failure to

---

[115] *Ibid.*, para. 37.
[116] *Ibid.*, (citation omitted).
[117] *Ibid.*, para. 38 (emphasis added).
[118] *Ibid.*, para. 50. Subsequent to this *Order*, the FCC granted BT's US affiliate a Section 214 application, subject to certain reporting requirements, to provide US-originated IMTS service. See BT North America, Inc., *Order and Certification*, 9 F.C.C.R. 6851, 76 Rad. Reg. 2d (P & F) 920 (1994).
[119] *BT/MCI I Order, supra* n. 101, para. 49.
[120] *Ibid.*
[121] *Ibid.*, para. 50 (citation omitted).

enter independently would "not significantly lessen potential competition in the provision of US-UK telecommunications services."[121]

4. Timing, Politics and Manoeuvring

When BT tried to purchase all of MCI two years later, however, this case became yet another causality of the Telecoms Trade War. Indeed, because of the extremely political nature of this case (i.e., the British were invading) and the fact that this case would be the first test to see exactly how strongly committed the United States was to the (then) just-concluded WTO Telecoms Accord, a tremendous amount of politics and manoeuvring was taking place in Washington to influence the decision-making process. However, it appeared that any inquiry about whether the merger may actually lead to a potential reduction of output or increase in price was not high on the priority list.

For example, because the ink on the WTO Telecoms Treaty was not yet totally dry, the US was trying to see how far it could unilaterally stretch the edge of the envelope to assuage nationalistic constituencies before it had to pay attention to international comity concerns. At the same time, however, because the 1996 Act sparked a worldwide trend in telecommunications industry reconcentration (of which the *BT/MCI III Order* was a part), the FCC was under substantial pressure to explain what steps it planned to take in order to ensure that the old Bell System was not reconstituted. Finally, and certainly not least on the FCC's collective mind, because the Eighth Circuit Court of Appeals struck down the FCC's interconnection rules, the FCC was under substantial political pressure to make it look like they were doing something to "enhance competition."

Yet, while all this bickering was going on, everyone seemed to forget that the merger agreement was conditioned on FCC action by date certain.[122] In order to complete the negotiations and not have a multi-billion dollar deal fall through because of regulatory delay, the FCC issued a very cryptic press release stating that it had approved the merger, with conditions, over *one month* before it released a final, written order.[123]

5. The BT/MCI III Order

On September 24, 1997, well over one month after the FCC purportedly adopted its *Order* and issued its cryptic press release, the FCC finally released its final *Order* in the *BT/MCI III Order*.[124] For purpose of its analysis, the FCC

---

[122] See BT/MCI Merger Agreement Article VI (Conditions Precedent), Section 6.1(d) ("If then legally required, an FCC Order shall have been obtained, which has not been revoked or stayed as of the Closing Date."). The Merger of MCI Comm. Corp. and British Telecomm. PLC, *Memorandum Opinion and Order*, 12 F.C.C.R. 15,351, paras. 298–303, 9 Comm. Reg. (P & F) 657 (1997) [hereinafter *BT/MCI III Order*].

[123] "International Action FCC Approves MCI/British Telecom Merger Subject to Certain Conditions", Rep. No. IN 97–25, 1997 FCC LEXIS 4489, 21 Aug. 1997.

[124] *BT/MCI III Order*, *supra* n. 123.

identified "three relevant *end-user markets* that [were] likely to be affected by the merger of BT and MCI: (1) US local exchange and exchange access service; (2) US-UK outbound international service; and (3) global seamless services."[125] In addition, the FCC identified "six relevant *input markets*: (1) international transport between the United States and United Kingdom; (2) UK cable landing station access; (3) UK backhaul; (4) UK intercity transport; (5) UK local terminating access services; and (6) UK local originating access services."[126]

The FCC provided two very legitimate reasons for considering input markets in the context of this case:

"First, if as a result of the merger, the merged parties have increased market power over an input, they might be able to raise the price of that input, either unilaterally or through coordinated interaction, which could harm consumers to the extent that, in the absence of regulation in the end-user market, the increased input price would be passed on in the form of higher end-user prices. Second, if as a result of the merger, the merged parties possessed market power over an essential input and, at the same time, competed in the downstream, competitive, end-user market, the merged company conceivably could injure competition by discriminating against unaffiliated producers of the end-user service. Because BT control[led] numerous inputs in the United Kingdom that other carriers need in order to provide US-UK outbound international service and global seamless services, [the FCC reasoned that] these input markets [were] accordingly relevant in assessing the competitive effects of the merger of BT and MCI."[127]

Turning to the merits of the case, the FCC found it unlikely that the merger would "have any [horizontal] anti-competitive effects on any of the three relevant end-user markets."[128] In fact, the FCC actually found that the merger would have pro-competitive benefits in two of the three relevant markets—"the market for US local exchange and exchange access services and the market for global seamless services."[129] The FCC similarly concluded that it was unlikely that the merger would have any horizontal anticompetitive effects in four out of the five input markets. The only reservation the FCC had was toward the merger's affect on the market for international transport between the United States and the United Kingdom. The FCC found that, at the time of this *Order*, there was a short-term capacity constraint that the merged company could use to its strategic advantage to the detriment of competition as a whole. Until this short-term constraint was ameliorated, therefore, the FCC suggested, and the applicants "voluntarily" proposed, certain commitments to mitigate the FCC's concerns.[130]

---

[125] *Ibid.*, para. 52; see also *ibid.*, paras. 53–57.
[126] *Ibid.*, para. 52; see also *ibid.*, paras. 58–60.
[127] *Ibid.*, para. 58.
[128] *Ibid.*, para. 132.
[129] *Ibid.*; see also *ibid.*, paras. 126–31.
[130] *See ibid.* paras. 133–52. Specifically, BT/MCI committed to:

(1) offer UK international facilities licensees a total of 147 whole circuits, for sale on an IRU basis to new entrants; (2) allow certain UK international facilities licensees that are currently taking eastern end half-circuit international private leased circuits (IPLCs) for international simple resale to convert the IPLCs into IRUs; (3) sell to US correspondents or their UK affiliates, upon request, eastern end matched half-circuits owned by

The FCC next looked to see if the applicants, post-merger, would be able to use their position in any of the input markets to create successfully any vertical anti-competitive effects in any of the relevant end-user markets. In the FCC's opinion, because of the voluntary commitments offered by BT, it was unlikely that the merged entity could use its position in the international transport on the US-UK market to affect adversely the performance of any of the end-user markets.[131] The FCC also concluded that, given demonstrable entry and effective regulation by OFTEL, it was unlikely that the merged company could use its positions in the UK cable landing station access,[132] UK backhaul,[133] UK intercity transport,[134] and UK terminating access services[135] markets. The FCC was, however, very concerned about the merged entity's ability to use its position in the UK originating access services market to affect anti-competitively the three end-user markets.[136] Unfortunately, it appears that these concerns are related more to the British government's refusal to adopt a regulatory regime identical to one adopted in the United States, rather than any particular harm specifically created by the merger. As such, even though the FCC conceded that BT faced "increasing competition in this market,"[137] and that:

> "UK originating access services [were] subject to many of same regulatory constraints as those described for terminating access services (*e.g.*, price caps and various license conditions regarding non-discriminatory behavior),"

the FCC again had little reservation in publicly criticising another sovereign government.[138] To wit,

> "[o]ther UK regulatory policies, however, undermine these constraints and allow BT to leverage its market power over originating access market [*sic*] into the markets for end-user services that depend on originating access (e.g., UK domestic and international services)."[139]

> "[T]hese policies include the decision not to require BT to provide equal access to other long distance carriers, to provide unbundled local network elements to other carriers, and to resell local service at wholesale prices. Alternatives to BT's local network may grow in time and eventually constrain BT's control of originating access services, but they do not significantly do so at this time. *In fact, the absence of equal access, unbundled local exchange network elements, and resale in the United*

BT and currently used for the provision of IMTS or international private line services between BT and the US correspondents; and (4) offer to convert such international private lines leases into IRUs in such a manner that international simple resellers that become UK international facilities licensees will be in the same financial position as if their international private line leases had been scheduled to terminate on the date on which the conversion takes place.

Ibid., para. 136 (citations omitted).
[131] See *ibid.*, paras. 164–65. [132] See *BT/MCI III Order, supra* n. 123, paras. 166–69.
[133] See *ibid.*, paras. 170–71.
[134] See *ibid.*, paras. 172–74.
[135] See *ibid.*, paras. 178–80.
[136] *Ibid.*, para. 181.
[137] *Ibid.*
[138] *Ibid.*, para. 182.
[139] *Ibid.*

Kingdom appears to create the conditions by which BT's market power over UK domestic and international services will be perpetuated."[140]

Both

"BT/MCI and the UK Government respond[ed] that there [wa]s no need to require BT to implement equal access in order to ensure effective competition in the provision of UK outbound calls to the United States."[141]

In their view:

"the different regimes in the United States and the United Kingdom [were] due to differences in the development of the telecommunications markets and competition in the respective countries. More specifically, the UK Government state[d] that its industrial policy of encouraging facilities-based competition would be undermined by the introduction of equal access."[142]

The FCC ignored and rejected outright these comity arguments. In the FCC's opinion, "[b]y not providing equal access to long distance carriers," BT was engaging—with the help of Her Majesty's Government—"in a form of non-price discrimination which allow[ed] it to leverage power over the local exchange to enhance its control over the UK long distance and international markets."[143] To prove this point, the FCC proudly pointed out that equal access was an essential requirement for the development of competitive intercity and international markets.[144] Yet, because the United Kingdom refused to implement an equal access policy (even though this policy was intended to, and succeeded in, "foster the development of alternative facilities-based local infrastructure"), the FCC maintained that this "deliberate omission allowed BT to minimize its loss of intercity and international market share."[145] In this case, however, because the European Union was making its own plans to implement an equal access requirement for Member States by 1 January 2000, the FCC conditioned its:

"grant of this license transfer upon MCI's non-acceptance of BT traffic originated in the United Kingdom to the extent BT is found to be in non-compliance with UK regulations implementing the European Union's equal access requirements."[146]

The FCC was equally dismayed with the UK's choice not to require incumbent LECs (i.e., BT) to provide unbundled local exchange network elements and

---

[140] *Ibid.*, (emphasis added).

[141] *Ibid.*, para. 186.

[142] *Ibid.*, (citations omitted).

[143] *Ibid.*, para. 187.

[144] *Ibid.*

[145] *Ibid.*, para. 188. But *cf.* Maev Sullivan, "Why USTR is too Quick to Cry Foul" Communications Week International, 22 May 2000 (commenting that the USTR's decision to criticise Europe for failing to accelerate its unbundling programmes was unfair, because "Europe has, at the United States' insistence, concentrated on implementing equal access on carrier pre-selection" which, given technological improvements, "will probably be as useful as an ashtray on a motorbike by the time it is running smoothly because unbundling and DSL will have overtaken it, and voice will doubtless be thrown in for free by dot.com trillionaires").

[146] *Ibid.*, para. 294; see also *ibid.*, paras. 190–91.

resale as US ILECs are required to do under the Telecommunications Act of 1996.[147] Once again, the UK Government disagreed that " 'lineside' unbundling was necessary or appropriate in the United Kingdom." In its view,

> "the cost advantages of lineside unbundling would be small in the United Kingdom because prices are in line with costs, interconnection charges are to be based on long-run incremental costs, and access deficit charges have been abolished. The UK Government also claimed that making BT unbundle its local exchange network elements would be unlikely to promote local competition but would instead jeopardize the development of facilities-based local competition now underway."[148]

And, once again, the FCC ignored and rejected outright these comity arguments.[149] Yet, the FCC found that other factors were present—in particular, the recently concluded WTO Telecoms Treaty and ongoing EU regulatory initiatives—to mitigate its concerns.[150]

Finally, even though the WTO Agreement was signed just over seven months prior to this *Order*, because the FCC had yet to adopt final rules that implemented the WTO Basic Telecom Agreement, it stated that it was obligated to examine BT's entry as a foreign carrier into the US market under its *ECO* test.[151] Because the FCC had previously found that BT did possess market power in its home market, but that the UK market nonetheless provided US carriers with effective competitive opportunities, the FCC decided to regulate the merged entity as a dominant carrier.[152] On its own motion, however:

> "[the FCC] waive[d] the application of [its then]-current dominant carrier requirements to MCI pending the effective date of any new rules [it might] adopt in the *Foreign Participation* proceeding."[153]

Instead, because the FCC believed that:

> "it would be unduly burdensome, and therefore not in the public interest, to require MCI at this time to comply with [its then-]current dominant carrier regulations which may be modified in a few months,"

the FCC simply required MCI to continue to comply with the safeguards it imposed on MCI in *BT/MCI I* until it adopted final dominant carrier regulations.[154]

---

[147] *Ibid.*, para. 192.

[148] *Ibid.*, para. 194.

[149] *Ibid.*, para. 195.

[150] *BT/MCI III Order, supra* n. 123, paras. 197–98.

[151] *Ibid.*, para. 214.

[152] BT North America, Inc., *Order and Authorization*, 13 F.C.C.R. 5992 (1997).

[153] *BT/MCI III Order, supra* n. 123, para. 286.

[154] *Ibid.*, para. 287. In a small gesture of international comity, however, the Commission recognized "OFTEL's active role in the United Kingdom in protecting against abuse of market power by BT." *Ibid.* para. 288. This gesture completed, the FCC went on to state that "[it did] not believe that OFTEL's regulation of BT alone [was] sufficient to justify regulating MCI as non-dominant on the U.S.-U.K. route. [In the FCC's view,] [u]naffiliated U.S. competitors of BT/MCI who must rely on BT in order to terminate traffic in the United Kingdom should be able to rely on [its] enforcement process to address complaints of discrimination." *Ibid.*, para. 288.

6. The Fallout

In the end, all the effort—both public and private sector—that was put into resolving this case, was for naught. After MCI announced that it lost over $800 million in its efforts to enter the US local market, (not surprising given the FCC's almost total failure post-1996 Act to promote affirmatively new facilities-based entry for local service), coupled with all of the events chronicled above, BT was looking for an excuse to get out of the deal. As fate would have it, Bernie Ebbers of WorldCom gave BT that excuse by counter-offering $34.5 billion (and, coincidentally, providing BT with a $1.2 billion profit on their original investment made in *BT/MCI I*).[155]

Yet, regardless of whether BT had decided to go ahead with its acquisition of MCI, the adverse precedent created by the FCC's embarrassing conduct in the *BT/MCI III Order*—in particular, the stringency of "voluntary commitments" the FCC imposed and the appalling breach of international comity—makes neither investment in US companies an attractive opportunity for foreign firms nor does it help grease the skids for US firms to make investments abroad.[156] Moreover, the analytical hypocrisy of this case is truly astounding, as it is quite unclear why the FCC found it necessary to impose *more* regulation on the parties in *BT/MCI III* than it imposed in *BT/MCI I* (even though the FCC proceeded to waive these additional regulatory constraints), *when competitive conditions both in the UK domestic market and along the US-UK route for IMTS service demonstrably and substantially improved since BT/MCI I.*[157] Of course, considering the fact that the Chairman of the FCC during this period stated publicly that if the FCC approves the various mergers pending before it, it is actually possible to have *more* competition with *three* RBOCs—down from the original seven—we really should not be so surprised.[158]

---

[155] See Peter Elstrom et al., "The New World Order", *Business Wk.*, 13 Oct. 1997, at 26.

[156] See, e.g., Guy de Jonquieres, "Rules for the Regulators", *Financial Times*, 2 Mar. 1998, at 21 (While the "US, in particular, is a frequent advocate of global rules—where they suit its own interests . . . it has [, however,] been repeatedly tripped up by its own demands" in cases like its dispute with the Japanese in the WTO about film and its dispute with Mexico about how inadequate regulation is blocking US companies' access to Mexico's telecommunications markets.); Mark Clough, "Caught Out on Film", *Financial Times*, 20 Jan. 1998, at 13 ("The US cannot credibly criticize [WTO] panel decisions that refrain from findings on restrictive business practices when such practices are not within its jurisdiction.").

[157] Indeed, just three months after the FCC issued its *BT/MCI III Order*, the European Commission issued a public report finding that "[e]ffective local loop competition currently only takes place in three Member States"—one of which is the United Kingdom. See Commission Communication Concerning the Review Under Competition Rules of the Joint Provision of Telecommunications and Cable TV Networks by a Single Operator and the Abolition of Restrictions on the Provision of Cable TV Capacity over Telecommunications Networks, [1998] OJ C 71/4, 7; see also Guatam Naik, "Telecom Deregulation in Britain Delivered a Nice Surprise: Jobs", *Wall Street Journal*, 5 Mar. 1998, at A1.

[158] See Jared Sandberg & Steven Lipin, "Bell Atlantic and GTE Boards Approve Plans for a Merger", *Wall Street Journal*, 28 July 1998, at A3 (According to Mr. Hundt, the spate of recent consolidations (in particular, AT&T/TCI, Ameritech/SBC, and Bell Atlantic/GTE) "would mean a triumvirate of telecom giants is likely to emerge, resulting in more competition.") (emphasis added).

The indignities of this case did not end here, however. Shortly after this regulatory debacle concluded, the final epitaph to this regulatory passion play came when AT&T announced that it planed to enter a $10 billion joint venture with British Telecom that will, of course, "enable BT and AT&T to deliver in a unique and powerful way the seamless global services [its] customers need and want."[159] What was particularly interesting/humorous about this proposed joint venture with BT, however, is that AT&T was one of the most vociferous opponents of the proposed BT/MCI deal and was the primary motivating force behind the FCC's decision to insert that fiery, neo-mercantilist rhetoric in the BT/MCI Order referenced above. In other words, "what's changed?" Yet, because what is good for the goose must also be good for the gander, when the FCC approved this deal, the FCC took another swipe at OFTEL, noting that only because OFTEL has instituted a Consultation Document on unbundling did the FCC "declin[e] to impose any unbundling requirement on BT in this proceeding."[160]

C. MCI/WorldCom

The MCI/WorldCom merger highlighted several of the major analytical issues facing telecom practitioners today. For example, the case demonstrates the international nature of the telecommunications industry and how telecoms companies must deal with multiple multi-jurisdictional legal and regulatory regimes. Second, MCI/WorldCom is noteworthy as it was the first major merger decision in which regulators and competition law authorities had to deal squarely with issues concerning the internet. Specifically there were fears that if the merger had proceeded as planned, then the new entry would have been able to dominate the market for Internet backbones. From a business perspective alone, the merger is emblematic of the pace of consolidation in the telecommunications industry. The result indicates how similar mergers may fare before enforcement bodies.

Finally, the MCI/WorldCom case was among the first case to free policymakers to explore directly the economic concept of "network externalities" in the telecoms industry. Although some may consider network externalities to be a novel economic theory and not sufficiently supported to be applied in such a case, it is certainly being argued for more frequently, for example in the US government's case against Microsoft alleging monopolisation from its computer operating system.

---

[159] See Associated Press, "British Telecom, AT&T Form Alliance", 27 July 1998 filed 10:07 am EDT.
[160] *In the Matter of AT&T Corp., British Telecommunications, plc, et al.* For Grant of Section 214 Authority, Modification of Authorizations and Assignment of Licenses in Connection With the Proposed Joint Venture Between AT&T Corp.and British Telecommunications, plc, Memorandum Opinion And Order, FCC 99–313, (rel. 29 October 1999) at ¶ 99.

1. Business Background

As noted in the previous Section British Telecom bought an interest in MCI and entered into a joint venture with MCI known as Concert.[161] The focus of Concert was to market advanced business telecommunications services to large multinational corporations. Subsequently, British Telecom negotiated an agreement to obtain a controlling interest in MCI. The merger was approved by the EU Commission in the spring of 1997. Before the merger could be finalised, by the summer of 1997, BT stockholders began to express reservation about the price offered for MCI. MCI had suffered losses as a result of its (unsuccessful) effort to break into the local telephone service market in the United States. WorldCom, sensing an opportunity, offered a higher price to MCI shareholders, higher than the original BT offer. The higher WorldCom bid, totalling [US]$ 34.5 billion, prevailed.

The merger was notified to the United States Department of Justice under the provisions of the Hart-Scott-Rodino Act. The FCC also reviewed the merger under its public interest standard for transfer of the relevant licences. The parties notified the merger to the EU Commission in November 1997.

Soon after the merger was notified, it became obvious that the review would focus on the parties' position in the Internet market, particularly in the area of Internet backbones. MFS, with whom WorldCom (then known as LDDS WorldCom, a long distance reseller based in Jackson, Mississippi) merged in 1996, had earlier acquired UUNet, a leading Internet Service Provider (ISP), as well as provider of Internet backbones. By the fall of 1997, WorldCom bought or controlled ISP operations and Internet infrastructure of UUNet, ANS, CNS, GridNet, Brooks Fiber (Verio), as well as the Internet infrastructure of AOL and CompuServe Network Services. In addition, WorldCom controlled Internet network access points known as Metropolitan Access Exchanges, consisting in the United States of MAE-East, MAE-West, MAE-Dallas, MAE-Los Angeles, and MAE-Chicago. MCI itself had extensive ISP and Internet backbone operations. It was alleged that together MCI and WorldCom would have controlled 50 per cent to 60 per cent of the Internet backbone market.

2. Technical Background

In order to help readers understand the various issues raised by the proposed MCI WorldCom merger, some background information about how the Internet functions, particularly regarding traffic exchange, would be useful at this point.

Residential Access—An end-user or surfer, typically accesses the Internet through a PC using a dial-up connection and a modem. Larger users such as businesses may have a dedicated connection to the Internet. Residential users typically in effect make a telephone call to their ISP. The ISP in turn routes the

---

[161] *BT/MCI (I)*, *supra* n. 66, and *BT/MCI (II)*, *supra* n. 78.

packet from the end-user (perhaps consisting of an e-mail message or a request to view Internet content) on to its destination. In order to route these packets and deliver content back to its customers, an ISP needs to interconnect with Internet backbones serving other ISPs or Internet sites on which the desired content is located.

Internet interconnection at the level of the large dedicated Internet backbones is different from exchanges of ordinary voice telephone traffic (expressed as public switched telephone network, or PSTN traffic). PSTN interconnection is closely regulated at local and national level and governed by treaty and long-standing arrangements at the international level. As much Internet traffic is international in nature, at least for Internet users outside of the United States, a comparison between international PSTN exchanges and Internet traffic is helpful in understanding how Internet routing occurs and ultimately the concerns raised by the MCI WorldCom merger.

International PSTN traffic is usually exchanged under a system set up under treaty and regulations of the International Telecommunication Union (ITU), though in practice the ITU lacks any enforcement power. The calling end-user places an international call through a carrier, who in turn sends the call to the destination country, where a terminating carrier delivers the call to its destination. The originating carrier bills the calling party and keeps the revenue from the call. The originating carrier is also to keep a record of calls placed to carriers in different countries. Periodically, international carriers submit records to a clearinghouse that calculates net results.

For example, carrier X in one country might have sent one thousand more minutes of traffic to carrier Y in another country than carrier Y sent to carrier X. Therefore, carrier X would owe carrier Y a fee for terminating those one thousand minutes. The principle is that carriers pay to terminate traffic. This system, sometimes called the settlement rate or accounting rate system, is breaking down due to technological and commercial alternatives, but it is still the prevalent method for international PSTN traffic exchanges. Internet traffic exchanges are not covered by the ITU Treaty and are treated differently from PSTN exchanges. Whereas in PSTN exchanges the basic principle is that the sending carrier pays to terminate, in Internet exchanges the principle is that the receiving party, perhaps expressed as the party requesting Internet content should pay.

Part of the explanation for this difference is the technical difference between PSTN circuit based network architecture and Internet architecture. Internet routing relies on packet transmission, and network engineers see sending packets as a burden. Excessive demands for packets can clog the network. This means that Internet network administrators must be able to justify honouring requests to send packets. In the early days of the Internet, this was not a problem; not much Internet traffic existed, and the network operations were subsidised by government or academia. Traffic exchanges were free, known as peering, and often occurred at network access points such as the MAEs named above.

When commercialisation of the Internet grew, so did pressure to justify routing arrangements. Operators of the Internet backbones began to refuse peering requests from smaller Internet backbone operators and ISPs that did not have the ability or the customer base to send an equivalent amount of traffic to the larger backbone operator. The larger backbone operator would still send Internet content to the smaller backbone and its customers, however, the larger backbone operators felt justified in charging for this interconnection and unbalanced traffic arrangement. Although technically the same as peering, this paid arrangement is known as transit, and is provided on a commercial basis by those whose strong bargaining position enables them to extract paid interconnection from smaller operators. There is no accounting of traffic and no payment of net amounts as occurs with PSTN exchanges. It is a "winner takes all" arrangement. As a rule transit is only provided to the customer and its direct customers, the larger backbone will not route traffic through to operators its transit customers peer or link for free with.

3. The EU Decision

a. Background

Jurisdictional Issues—Because of the fast procedure mandated by the Merger Regulation, the EU reached a decision[162] before either the US Department of Justice of the FCC could act. In effect, this meant that the EU decided the case, and there was some criticism raised in the US about how the European Commission adjucated on a case involving two US (i.e. non-jurisdictional) companies, notable from FCC Commissioner Furchtgott-Roth. It should be borne in mind that this case arose in the wake of the Boeing and McDonnell Douglas merger, a case where the EU Commission insisted on restrictions and which strained relations between the US and the EU.

The EU Decision found that the MCI WorldCom merger did fall under the merger regulation, despite the grumbling about jurisdiction. The required turnover thresholds were met, and the condition of "a Community dimension" was present.[163] EU jurisdiction should not be surprising. The European Commission as well as the ECJ have largely adopted the US' effects doctrine for jurisdiction in competition law matters. Laying aside the jurisdiction granted by meeting the turnover thresholds, there is no doubt that Internet users and Internet backbone customers in Europe would have been affected by the merger. Much of the Internet content viewed by end-users in Europe originates in the US, and therefore European operators, ISPs and ultimately end-users must interconnect with Internet backbones in the US.

Relevant Product Market—As with most merger cases, definition of the relevant product markets was very important. In general in merger cases, notifying

---

[162] Case IV/M.1069 WorldCom/MCI [1999] OJ L116/1 <http://europa.eu.int/smartapi/cgi/sga_doc?smartapi!celexplus!prod!CELEXnumdoc+Ig=EN+numdoc=31999D0287>.

[163] *Ibid.*, para. 10.

parties wish to draw the relevant product and geographic markets as broadly as possible, thereby reducing their market shares. Enforcement officials favour narrower market definitions for the same reason. Most of the defined relevant product markets such as long distance or international PSTN did not raise concerns. At issue in the MCI case was how to evaluate competition for Internet-related services.

On one hand, MCI WorldCom argued for a general data communication service market, with all data traffic including, but not limited to, Internet traffic counted.[164] Market shares could be determined by gross data traffic revenue. Even granting that the Internet was special, MCI WorldCom consistently argued that the Internet was one network, open to all, and in fact deriving its value from its openness and ease of transmission.

The European Commission did not agree with MCI's argument, but accepted the position of intervening third parties that the Internet should be considered as a series of markets.[165] These markets were related and dependent on each other. Each market could be considered a link in a chain, each link being necessary for Internet communications to function. Moving from the end-user, the first relevant market would be access by the end user to an ISP accomplished via public telecommunications network infrastructure or other means of access such as dedicated lines or cable access. The relevant geographic market at this stage is defined according to the extent of the local operator's network coverage.[166] Moving one step upstream, the next market would consist of Internet access services or ISPs, again usually provided on a regional or national geographic basis.[167] The next step up, and where the problem was found to exist, was a market for Internet backbones. The European Commission, however, defined the market even more narrowly and found the relevant product market to consist of top level Internet networks able to provide universal Internet connectivity. As the connectivity must be universal, the relevant geographic market was global in scope.[168] The plurality of Internet networks, even within the same product market should be stressed. It was this plurality that set the basis for the economic argument of network effects, that Internet traffic would tend to migrate to the largest proprietary Internet backbone, giving its holder (MCI WorldCom) an insurmountable dominant position.

The question of what is meant by top level networks must be considered. This is not a term that is used in the telecommunications or Internet industries, at least before this decision. A term that was used was Tier One backbones, consisting at the time of this decision of WorldCom, MCI, Sprint, and GTE/BBN.[169] The European Commission considered that a relevant product

---

[164] *Ibid.*, para. 13.
[165] *Ibid.*, para. 16.
[166] Case IV/M.1069 WorldCom/MCI [1999] OJ L116/1, paras. 58,59, 80.
[167] *Ibid.*, paras. 60, 81.
[168] *Ibid.*, paras. 62–65, 82.
[169] *Ibid.*, para. 102.

market composed of only the Tier One providers would be too narrow. Logically, the European Commission felt that it should properly include all Internet backbone providers having peering arrangements, and therefore free interconnection, with all four of the Tier One providers.

While it is true that the top level network providers would similarly not have to pay for routing of Internet traffic. The European Commission's analysis neglects the bargaining strength of the Tier One providers. Downstream customers, ISPs and smaller backbone providers, will need to select at least one top level provider and buy transit service to be able to obtain universal Internet connectivity. Buying transit from a smaller top level network would give universal connectivity, but it would not necessarily give a direct connection to the backbones where a large amount of desirable content resides. MCI and WorldCom together had a large per centage of the most popular web sites exclusively connected to their backbones.[170] A top-level network can peer with a Tier One provider, but it must go through an interconnection point, and, therefore a router hop to accomplish this connectivity. Buying transit from a Tier One provider means that fewer router hops are necessary and the packets are correspondingly delivered faster to end-users. Tier One backbones are able to retain their status as desirable peers through a combination of large transmission facilities and desirable content. Big pipes alone cannot grant peering or top level status. Peering is given to providers able to offer equivalent demanded traffic flows. The Internet backbone able to command free peering for all of their traffic acquire this status though a combination of appropriate network infrastructure and a customer base bringing with it desirable traffic flows.[171]

The European Commission was on firm ground in accepting the slightly broader product market definition of top level networks. Under the hypothetical monopolist test, if all top level networks were to raise their prices by 5 per cent to 10 per cent for downstream operators to purchase transit, the customers would have no alternative but to pay the price increase. Only by buying transit from a provider having full coverage, guaranteed only by having peering rights with all four of the Tier One providers, could an ISP guarantee coverage to its own customers. It would be practically impossible for smaller backbones to construct their own peering system so as to avoid the Tier One backbones.[172]

Market Share Analysis—A selection of a relevant product was one step. The European Commission next faced the task of measuring market shares. MCI WorldCom suggested that revenues for all Internet access be used. Their share of total estimated Internet access revenues would give a market share to the combined entity of less than 20 per cent.[173] The European Commission did not consider that this was a proper method to determine market shares. Some sort

---

[170] *Ibid.*, para. 93.
[171] *Ibid.*, para. 134.
[172] *Ibid.*, para. 75.
[173] *Ibid.*, para. 88.

of count of traffic volumes was necessary, but there were no readily available statistics to use.

The European Commission finally employed a complicated ratio analysis designed to weigh traffic flowing out, in and between Internet backbones.[174] Using this market share methodology, if the Tier One provider relevant product market definition had been accepted, then the combined operations of MCI WorldCom would have had a market share of between seventy-five per cent and eighty-five per cent.[175] With the broader top-level product market definition, MCI WorldCom would have still have had over a fifty per cent market share. Such a market share calls for a presumption of dominance under EU law. The significance of the projected market share is increased by considering that MCI WorldCom's share would have been much larger than the next largest competitor.[176]

Given the above, the European Commission found that the new entity could behave independently of its competitors and customers, setting prices and contract terms as it wished, free from the constraints of the marketplace. This dominance and market independence would affect consumers in Europe as much as consumers anywhere in the world. ISPs in Europe might pay more in price for Internet connectivity or receive unfavourable contract terms and this cost would be passed on to European end-users. Entry by new competitors offsetting MCI WorldCom's advantage was unlikely due to the MCI WorldCom's achievement of a critical mass for acting independently of competitors, an advantage that would grow in the future.

b. Network Effects

The European Commission based its analysis of MCI WorldCom's advantages on the economic theory of network effects, sometimes called network externalities.[177] In a nutshell, this theory maintains that the value of a network is exponentially related to the number of users attached to it. That is, a product or service that can be defined as networked, perhaps because of user standards, becomes more valuable as the number of users increases. As users increase, a tipping point may be reached after which the product or service in question will come to dominate the market.[178]

The principle of network effects dictate that larger Internet backbones have an advantage. ISPs want to connect to the largest Internet backbone network having the most popular Internet content. A direct connection to the backbone

---

[174] *Ibid.*, para. 109.

[175] *Ibid.*, para. 110.

[176] *Ibid.*, para. 117.

[177] Case IV/M.1069 WorldCom/MCI [1999] OJ L116/1, para. 126.

[178] As explained in Chapter 2, examples of network products and network externalities include differing formats for video players (VHS versus Betamax), and computer operating systems (DOS/Windows versus Macintosh, UNIX. OS/2, etc.). In the cases of VHS and DOS it is argued that the winning format prevailed not because of its technical merit, but because its proponents succeeded in attracting a critical mass of users. Future purchasers were left with no real option, as the desire was paramount to be compatible with the existing base of installed users.

having the most popular content results in the fastest access for the ISPs' end-customers.[179]

A dominant Internet backbone could re-enforce its position by selective pricing or degrading connection points to other backbones.[180] A dominant provider could unilaterally terminate free peering arrangements and charge for Internet interconnection. In fact, the European Commission noted that WorldCom's Internet subsidiary UUNet had already attempted to alter existing peering arrangements in 1997.[181] By moving rivals to paid interconnection, the dominant provider would benefit from competitors and influence their costs of production.[182]

In sum, the European Commission concluded that there was an unacceptable risk that if MCI and WorldCom were allowed to combine their Internet operations, the new company would be able to corner the market for Internet transmission. The remedy was that the potential overlap between the companies' Internet operations was to be eliminated. MCI WorldCom negotiated with the European Commission and reached agreement that MCI's Internet operations would be sold.[183] Cable & Wireless, a European company, bought the MCI operations for $1.75 billion. The divestiture was to include not only the physical network infrastructure, but also associated personnel to operate the network and the MCI Internet customer contracts. The European Commission took pains to ensure that the combination of physical infrastructure and traffic, the hallmarks of power in the market, were transferred. Cable & Wireless, however, has complained bitterly and sued MCI WorldCom alleging that the divestiture did not occur as the Commission ordered.

4. US Department of Justice Action

Acting pursuant to the agreement on co-operation between EU and US competition authorities,[184] the US Department of Justice Antitrust Division co-operated closely with their European counterparts during the course of the EU notification proceedings. In theory, the investigations were conducted independently, but with the parties' consent, the agencies shared information and held joint meetings. It is doubtful that the EU would have settled the case without

---

[179] *Ibid.*, para. 127.

[180] *Ibid.*, paras. 118, 121.

[181] *Ibid.*, para. 117.

[182] *Ibid.*, para. 123.

[183] *Ibid.*, para. 136.

[184] Agreement between the Government of the United States of America and the Commission of the European Communities regarding the application of their competition laws [1995] OJ L95/47–50. See also 95/145/EC, ECSC Decision of the Council and the Commission of 10 April 1995 concerning the conclusion of the Agreement between the European Communities and the Government of the United States of America regarding the application of their competition laws [1995] OJ L95/45; and Agreement between the European Communities and the Government of the United States of America on the application of positive comity principles in the enforcement of their competition laws [1998] OJ L173/28.

WorldCom receiving assurances that the Department of Justice would approve and not seek further or even inconsistent remedies. Regardless, the Department of Justice publicly announced that the MCI Internet divestiture resolved any competitive concerns that may have existed with the merger.[185]

5. FCC Review

Matters were not so cut and dried with the FCC. While the extensive FCC opinion[186] included a review of all markets that would be affected by the merger, as might be expected, the most interesting portion dealt with the Internet.

Since the FCC has continuing regulatory duties as well as responsibility for reviewing certain mergers, it was natural that consideration of Internet backbone interconnection would lead in turn to consideration of whether the FCC should regulate this area. There is a perception that a reason for the Internet's spectacular growth is due to its (supposed) unregulated status. Such a statement is not entirely true.[186a] Quite to the contrary, although the FCC have imposed "price" regulation on the recent Internet industry, as discussed in great detail in chapter 2, the fact that the FCC imposed stringent *conduct* of *structural regulation* (e.g., standard interfaces) is one of the primary reasons the Internet flourishes so much today. Given the rapid "politicisation" of the Internet however, certainly the FCC is deluged with protests whenever it takes or considers any action that might be considered as a move to regulate the Internet.[186b]

At the outset, the FCC was quick to point out that by its review of the proposed merger, it was in no way seeking to regulate the Internet.[187] Nevertheless, the Order proceeded to review how the Internet functions and focused on the interconnection of the Internet backbones, much as the EU Commission's Decision had done. The FCC also reached the same conclusion as the EU Commission that the proposed fusion of MCI and WorldCom's Internet backbones would have created a problem because of the size of the resulting operation would significantly outweigh that of its rivals.

---

[185] "Justice Department Clears WorldCom/MCI Merger After MCI Agrees To Sell Its Internet Business Largest Divestiture of Company in Merger History", US Department of Justice Press Release 15 July 1998, 98–329, <http://www.usdoj.gov/atr/public/press_releases/1998/1829.htm>.

[186] FCC 98–225, CC Docket No. 97–211, *In the Matter of Application of WorldCom Inc. and MCI Communications Corporation for Transfer of Control of MCI Communications Corporation to WorldCom Inc.*, Memorandum Opinion And Order, 14 September 1998, [hereinafter FCC MCI WorldCom Order], <http://www.fcc.gov/Bureaus/Common_Carrier/Orders/1998/fcc98225.txt>.

[186a] But *c.f.*, Michael Kinde, *The Digital Handshake*, Federal Communications Commission Office of Plans and Policy Working Paper No. 32 (Sept. 2000) and Jason Oxman, *The FCC and the Unregulation of the Internet*, Federal Communications Commission Office of Plans and Policy Working Paper No. 31 (July 1999), both of which seek to revise history by claiming that the growth of the Internet is due to the total absence of FCC regulatory intervention.

[186b] See generally, Phil Spector and P.S. Campbell, "FCC Regulation of the Internet: Fact or Fiction?" (1999) 6 *Telecommunications and Space Law Journal* 281 (arguing that despite FCC Chairman Kennard's promise that "as long as I am Chairman of the FCC, we will not regulate the Internet", the FCC have intervened significantly into the mechanisms and networks upon which the Internet flows).

[187] FCC MCI WorldCom Order, para. 142.

In an apparent endorsement of the theory of network externalities, the FCC noted the contention "that the benefits Applicants [MCI WorldCom] derived from interconnecting with rivals would have been far less than the benefits rivals derived from interconnecting with Applicants."[188] Likewise the FCC listed possible anti-competitive effects that included raising rivals' costs and degrading the quality of interconnection.[189]

Turning to possible remedies, the FCC was confronted with a fait accompli; the European Commission and the US Department of Justice had already accepted the MCI Internet divestiture as adequate. After reviewing the divestiture terms, the FCC concurred.

The problem of Internet backbone interconnection terms and conditions remained, however. Some commentators requested the FCC to take action and mandate when free peering or paid transit would be appropriate. The FCC declined to do so, at that time, holding that a merger review was not the proper vehicle for such a wide-ranging review, but indicated that it would continue to monitor the situation and might take action in the future.[190] In fact, the FCC subsequently declined to exercise jurisdiction in this area.

FCC Commissioner Furchtgott-Roth filed a separate statement concurring in the result of the merger review, but expressing reservations about several aspects of the case, including the length of time the FCC takes to review mergers, the standards the FCC employs, and in particular the role the EU played in the case. Commissioner Furchtgott-Roth has repeatedly voiced concern that the FCC takes too long to review mergers. He here added that the FCC's delay enable[d] a foreign agency, the EU, to take effective control of its decision. Commissioner Furchtgott-Roth concurred with the FCC's Order and the proposed Internet divestiture, but questioned whether the required divestiture of MCI's Internet operations "is either economically or legally necessary.[191]

While the Commissioner contended that divestiture may not have been proper because entry into the Internet business was easy, his real problem with the divestiture requirement appeared to be that it was first mandated by the EU Commission. In his view, the EU had no business exercising jurisdiction over MCI and WorldCom and their "business activities in the United States."[192] However, given the FCC's mercantile actions of the last eight years, the merits (good or bad) of the Commissioner's concerns now fall on deaf ears.

To be fair, the Commissioner wrote that the EU is closely allied with the US, and it is unlikely that the EU would have required the Internet divestiture without the tacit approval of US officials or "had there been the slightest likelihood of dissatisfaction from the United States."[193] This is not evident. The Commissioner should not be so quick to assume that the EU Commission sought

---

[188] *Ibid.*, para. 149. [189] *Ibid.*, para. 149.
[190] *Ibid.*, para. 155.
[191] *Ibid.*, Statement of Commissioner Furchtgott-Roth, at 3.
[192] *Ibid.*, at 5. There was a ringing recitation of US efforts against foreign domination going back to the Barbary Pirates.
[193] *Ibid.*, at 6.

permission from the US. Given the loud and public trade quarrels over bananas, hormone treated beef, and the Boeing/McDonnell Douglas merger, it is very likely that the EU and the US would have come to loggerheads over the MCI WorldCom merger if a fortuitous meeting of the minds had not occurred among EU and US enforcement officials. There was an evident sense of relief that the EU Commission, the US DOJ and ultimately the FCC reached the same conclusion in the case. Commissioner Furchtgott-Roth was right that it would have been an awful mess if the responsible bodies had reached different results or demanded inconsistent remedies.

As such, even though the United States and the European Union do have a close relationship, perhaps the Commissioner is right in calling for "better and more expeditious ways to review international mergers."[194] This better way, however, does not consist of attempting to seal national jurisdictional boundaries in the face of international realities, like the Internet. The US has aggressively exported its jurisdictional reach. It should come as no surprise when other jurisdictions attempt to do the same, particularly in an area like the Internet where US domination is so acutely felt. Perhaps a better way would be for the WTO or other international body to assume jurisdiction in mergers affecting international commerce. The US, however, has resisted attempts to extend the WTO's jurisdiction into competition law matters.

6. *The Lessons of the MCI* WorldCom *case*

A general lesson of the case is how effective enforcement officials from different nations can be when they work in harmony. Whatever differences the EU Commission and the US Department of Justice may have had over the case remained hidden. International politics and foreigner-bashing did not cloud the review in either the US or the EU. A second lesson was the growing importance of the Internet. Regulators were confronted with the question of whether concepts such as interconnection and its associate requirements applied to Internet traffic. Resolution of this problem might take some time. It remains to be seen whether national and WTO interconnection requirements apply to Internet traffic. Differences between PSTN traffic exchanges and Internet traffic were highlighted. The ability to deliver desired traffic is key to power in the Internet backbone market. This is very different from the old world of international traffic exchanges governed by treaty and large consortia. Finally, of note is the acceptance of the economic theory of network effects, a theory that is particularly useful in high technology industries often dependent on (possibly incompatible) standards.

---

[194] *Ibid.*, Statement of Commissioner Furchtgott-Roth, at 7.

D. The Telia/Telenor Merger

1. Background

After at least one aborted effort, Telia, the Swedish incumbent telecommunications operator, and Telenor, the Norwegian incumbent telecommunications operator, announced a merger in January 1999. The parties' joint press release portrayed the merger as an effort to create an entity large enough to compete throughout Europe and the world. The new "Nordic Giant" or "Scandinavian Flagship," both phrases used in the companies' publicity, would have been Europe's sixth largest telecommunications company. The EU Commission's review of this proposed merger, the conditions the EU placed on approval, and the ultimate demise of the merger before it could even be implemented are illustrative of current legal and business reality in Europe.

The turnover thresholds for application of the EU's Merger Regulation were met. Norway is not an EU Member State, but as a member of the European Free Trade Area (EFTA) is subject to many identical laws and Treaty provisions. The proposed merger received careful attention by the European Commission, perhaps especially due to the fact that it was announced at the same time that Deutsche Telekom was attempting to merge with Telecom Italia. Any action of the European Commission regarding the first full merger of incumbent operators would be seen as a precedent for future mergers.

Telia and Telenor finally formally notified the proposed merger to the EU Commission in April 1999.[195] After a preliminary review, the EU Commission decided to initiate a Phase Two investigation, a finding that the merger as proposed would have created or strengthened a dominant position.

2. Analysis

The European Commission found that both Telia and Telenor were dominant in their home telecommunications markets[196] and that the proposed merger would have simply reinforced their dominance. As Sweden and Norway are adjacent countries, their operations including their telecommunications network infrastructure could effectively combine into one operation and one network, greatly increasing its size. This would mean a larger network and business footprint, accordingly larger than the operations of its competitors.[197]

Although not a part of the European Commission's Decision, it should also be taken into account that both companies were state-owned and would remain that way as the merger agreement stated that a majority of the shares in the new company would be owned by the Swedish and Norwegian states for a least

---

[195] Case COMP/M.1439 *Telia/Telenor* [2000] OJ C 237/2000 <http://europa.eu.int/comm/competition/mergers/cases/decisions/m1439.pdf>.

[196] *Ibid.*, para.130.

[197] *Ibid.*, paras. 130, 155.

sixteen years, an extremely long time in the telecommunications industry. While state-ownership is still common in Europe and in recognised under the EU Treaty[198] it is not conducive to regulatory independence as required under the EU telecoms regulatory framework directives. The regulator of a state-owned company may have conflicting loyalties between accomplishing its regulatory duties and protecting the state's investment. This conflict may be made worse by political pressure to protect the "good" jobs provided by incumbent telecoms operators.

In addition, the regulatory framework in Sweden and Norway was more incumbent friendly than in the rest of the Nordic countries: Denmark and Finland. At the time the proposed Telia/Telenor merger was under review, both Denmark and Finland required incumbent operators to provide competitors access to unbundled local loops while Sweden and Norway did not.[199] The effect of this was that Telia/Telenor could maintain their dominant position in their home territory safe from competition while taking advantage of the more entrant favourable regimes available in neighbouring countries.

This situation was comparable to dumping. While the European Commission was not this blunt in its Decision, the reality was that compared to other Nordic countries, the regulators in Sweden and Norway were weak and not really independent. The European Commission did state that potential future regulatory oversight by the national regulatory authorities in Sweden and Norway was insufficient to address the creation or strengthening of a dominant position that would have resulted from the merger as originally proposed.[200]

The European Commission also considered concerns about the proposed merger's effects on television broadcasting markets. The parties would have been completely vertically integrated in television markets, controlling end-user access through cable TV networks, content production, and control of satellite transponder operations.[201]

In telecommunications, concerns involved the loss of potential and actual competition. The parties were the most likely entrants into each other's markets.[202] Due to geographic proximity, similarity of language and cultural, and historic ties, Telia and Telenor were the most likely candidates to enter and succeed in the other company's territory. Because of these factors and the regulatory environment in their home countries as opposed to that of Finland and Denmark, the resulting company was also likely to dominate telecommunications markets throughout the Nordic region. The blow to competition was not only theoretical. Both parties were already present and competing in each other's home market.[203] While divestiture might have enabled others to step

---

[198] EU Treaty, *supra* n. 4, arts. 85 and 295.
[199] *Telia/Telenor*, *supra* n. 200, para. 131.
[200] *Ibid.*, para. 137.
[201] *Telia/Telenor*, *supra* n. 200, para. 265.
[202] *Ibid.*, paras 148–154.
[203] *Ibid.*, paras. 138, 139.

into the parties' competitive shoes, no other potential competitor was as well positioned to take on Telia and Telenor.[204] Indeed, the merger between these two parties was no accident. It provided unique benefits to the parties by combining their adjacent networks and at the same time eliminating their most potent threat.

The parties would also eliminate or internalise costs that used to be paid to the other. This effect is clearly expressed in the example of exchanges of international traffic between the parties. Before the merger, the parties would pay international accounting rates to each other, the same as for any other exchange of international voice traffic. After the merger, all international traffic exchanges between Telia and Telenor, that is the bulk of the international voice traffic between Sweden and Norway, would be terminated on a cost free basis, an advantage no competitor would be able to match. Furthermore, Telia and Telenor would be able to extend their origination and termination advantage throughout the Nordic region. They would control a dominant share of local loops in Sweden and Norway through the PSTN and cable TV networks they operate. In the rest of the Nordic region, they could obtain access to local loops at terms mandated by the national regulators.

No competitor could match this advantage the merged entity would possess to provide end-to-end access throughout the Nordic region. The merged entity alone could provide attractive bundled telecommunications services, in particular those involving broadband services, throughout the Nordic region.[205] The European Commission considered that this internalisation effect would lead to the creation or strengthening of a dominant position.[206]

With the elimination of potential and actual competition, other entrants would be harmed by the elimination of the moderating influence each party exercised on the other in the market.[207] Before the merger, if either Telia or Telenor attempted to raise termination prices, expressed perhaps as either international accounting rates or interconnection, the party so raising termination prices ran an unacceptable risk that the other party would retaliate against it. All competitors thereby benefited from the moderating influence the parties exercised on each other. After the merger this moderating influence would be gone. The merging parties would not fear retaliation by incumbents from other Nordic countries as the more vigilant regulators in those countries would not allow such retaliation.

In summation, the differences before and after the merger are as follows. Pre-merger, Telia and Telenor are separate entities; post merger, they become a single entity. Pre-merger, they are dependent on each other for termination; post-merger, they no longer charge each other for termination. Pre-merger, they therefore have an incentive not to harm each other and to keep termination

---

[204] *Ibid.*, paras. 140–147.
[205] *Ibid.*, para. 160.
[206] *Ibid.*, para. 157.
[207] *Ibid.*, para. 165.

prices reasonable; post-merger, they have an incentive to increase prices and eliminate competitors.

3. Proposed Remedies

The solution to the competitive problem caused by the proposed merger was to mandate better access to end-users for competitors in the parties' home markets. If there were effective access to end-users, the merged entity would not be able to use its strengthened dominance to exclude competitors. Attempts to raise interconnection prices could be countered by competitor use of unbundled local loops or other forms of end-user access such as mandated wholesale of voice service by the incumbent operator. Local loop unbundling was necessary because "access to the local loop on competitive terms is an important if not an essential requirement for many telecommunication markets, in particular for broadband services."[208] Therefore, the European Commission decided that effective end-user access must be available upon completion of the merger.

4. Approval Conditions

Following its customary procedure, the EU Commission issued a press release[209] announcing its decision. The release noted that this was "a complicated case" and "the first case under the EU Merger Regulation which involves the merger of two incumbent European Union telecom operators."[210] Besides elimination of the overlaps in the companies' operations in Sweden, Norway and Ireland, the parties committed to divest their cable TV networks in Sweden and Norway as well as to agree to local loop unbundling in both countries. The EU Commission stated that these measures would ensure competitors access to end-users "and that the merged entity will not be the only company having such access across those two countries, and the Nordic region."[211]

The cable TV divestiture served a dual purpose. This would break the parties' complete vertical integration in the television markets. It would also provide an alternative network for delivery of telecommunications services. The EU has promoted the idea of use of cable TV infrastructure as second network for telephone traffic. Two directives were issued in support of this policy, one authorising the use of alternative networks, like cable TV networks, for telecommunications services, other than basic voice, before the 1998 liberalisation,[212] and the other requiring some European incumbent providers to struc-

---

[208] *Ibid.*, para. 150.

[209] Commission clears merger between Telia (Sweden) and Telenor (Norway) with substantial conditions, 13 October 1999, IP/99/746 <http://europa.eu.int/rapid/start/cgi/guesten.ksh?p_action. gettxt=gt&doc=IP/99/746|0|RAPID&lg=EN>.   [210] *Ibid.*

[211] Commission clears merger between Telia (Sweden) and Telenor (Norway) with substantial conditions, 13 October 1999, IP/99/746.

[212] Commission Directive 95/51/EC amending Directive 90/388/EEC with regard to the abolition of the restrictions on the use of cable television networks for the provision of already liberalised telecommunications services [1995] OJ L256/49.

turally separate their telephone and cable TV operations.[213] The practicality of using cable TV networks for telephone calls is questionable. Coaxial cables, however, have proved a successful medium for broadband Internet access. Substantial investment would still be necessary to prepare a cable TV network for provision of cable modem Internet access service.

Local loop unbundling was a new policy and remedy for the EU Commission. The current EU regulatory framework does not require physical local loop unbundling. A regulatory remedy and commitment such as unbundling is unusual for the EU Commission, but not without precedent as the EU Commission conditioned approval of the Global One joint venture on regulatory commitments by the French and German governments to liberalise telecommunications network operations. It was the changed competitive situation represented by the Telia Telenor merger that justified the EU Commission in insisting that the parties agree to unbundling. Furthermore, the EU Commission intended its decision as a signal that similar remedies would be sought in the future. Competition Commissioner Monti was quoted as stating that this "is unlikely to be the last time that we will require cable TV network divestiture and/or local loop unbundling to resolve competition issues." Notably absent from this statement is any qualification that such remedies would be limited to merger cases.

5. *Postscript to Telia/Telenor: the Death of the Nordic Giant*

The postscript to the EU Commission's decision is anti-climatic. By the end of 1999, the parties decided not to consummate the merger. The immediate cause was a dispute over whether the headquarters for the new entity's mobile unit would be located in Sweden or Norway. Moreover, given the huge amount of human capita invested, the dissolution of this deal almost brought down the Norwegian government.

It is impossible to state whether pressures caused by the required divestitures, including valuation and splits of proceeds from the cable TV operations, as well as the unpalatability of unbundling their networks contributed to the new company's demise, before it could even be born. Certainly the strain of the merger review and the associated negotiations did nothing to improve the parties' regard for each other. The companies had proceeded to divest some of the overlapping entities, but had not yet divested their cable TV networks nor had they implemented the unbundling requirement. Those provisions were therefore of no immediate impact. With the merger's end before it could be implemented, the parties would not be required to follow through on the approval conditions. Nevertheless, the Telia/Telenor Decision will set the stage for future regulatory developments in Sweden and Norway and stand as an important precedent for EU merger review and competition law.

---

[213] Commission Directive of 23 June 1999 amending Directive 90/388/EEC in order to ensure that telecommunications networks and cable TV networks owned by a single operator are separate legal entities [1999] OJ L175/39.

IV. CONCLUSION

As demonstrated by this chapter, merger review is important in today's telecoms markets because of its effects on business and consumers, as well as from the analytical standpoint. Merger review provides an excellent vantage point to observe the interplay of competition and regulatory principles. It also shows the tactics and casualties of the Telecoms Trade War. As regulators have gained experience in review of the blizzard of telecoms mergers, it is be hoped that they have also grown wiser in the ways of the market and what are appropriate conditions to impose on mergers. On the other hand, regulators may have only grown more cynical, viewing mergers as an opportunity for back door regulation, to accomplish what they could not by normal methods.

PART V

CONCLUSION

19

O Shame! Where is Thy Blush?

A. War by other means

ALTHOUGH REGULATORS LIKE to trumpet that we are in the midst of a telecommunications revolution (led of course by regulators), as we attempted to show in this book, the truth is somewhat different. Thanks to regulatory cynicism, the gains wrought through technological innovation and market advances are imperiled. Rather than a revolution, we are experiencing war. Domestically, it is a civil war between groups of competitors struggling to capture regulators and therefore benefit themselves at the expense of other competitors. Internationally, it is an old-fashioned trade war, and the promise of the WTO Telecoms Treaty is becoming a cruel farce, as governments, doing the bidding of interested providers, rattle sabres of complaints. Lost in all this sound and fury are the interests of those for whom the game is ostensibly played: *the consumer*. Responsible regulators and enforcement officials therefore should face up to some simple truths: competition is not a zero sum game and trade wars—telecoms or otherwise—harm consumer welfare.

B. Neo-Mercantilism and Neo-Competition

The basic truth of the incompatibility of competition law and trade policy is grounded in the fact that the two policies promote different goals. The goal of competition law and regulation is to promote the overall competitive process. That is, competition policy should lead to lower prices (static efficiencies) and more innovation and technological advancement (dynamic efficiencies) in the market. Trade policy usually has different goals in mind, to express it mildly. Trade policy seeks to promote the interests of favoured firms, usually domestic, in repelling non-favoured (foreign) firms from domestic markets while, at the same time, assist domestic firms to enter foreign markets. While both jobs are completely legitimate roles for government to undertake (and, in fact, many of their respective goals may not even be in conflict with each other), it must be understood that trade policy has no place in sound regulatory decision-making.

Moreover, while having a coherent trade and regulatory policies is always good idea, neither trade nor regulatory policy should espouse the discredited notion of mercantilism. Although lip service is still paid to free trade principles (hence the cynicism of observers and regulators themselves), and most developed nations have committed themselves to the WTO Treaties, including the WTO Telecoms Treaty, the promise of the WTO is nonetheless deteriorating into nothing more that a forum to score points against foreign governments and promote the mercantilist interests of domestic firms—the exact opposite of the WTO principle. For this reason, leading financial experts and economists such as Alan Greenspan in the US have warned publicly of the economic consequences of continuing down the mercantilist path.

This cynicism is not exclusive to international telecommunications either. On the domestic front, firms also seek to persuade regulators to promote their interests above that of other firms: a type of intra-jurisdictional mercantilism. Given the importance of international traffic exchanges in today's telecommunications markets, the clearest expression of which is the Internet, it may not even be possible to separate domestic from international competition, trade and regulatory policy. Thus, we see not only the predominance of neo-mercantilism, but neo-competition as well.

Regulators are guilty of shirking their duty to regulate so as to promote competition. Instead, they are regulating so as to promote competitors, to ensure that the market pie is sliced in a fair way. It is almost too elementary to repeat, but regulators should seek to grow a larger pie, not slice the existing pie so finely that all the proper interests get their fair share (with a healthy helping for pet regulatory projects like wiring schools). Ironically, the emphasis on "fair, competition-like outcomes" accompanied by the benevolent use of "market-friendly regulation" is restricting industry growth. Allowed to develop without counter-productive regulatory burdens, the telecommunications industry "pie" would grow so that providers, most importantly consumers, and even politicians and their regulatory servants could achieve their dreams. That's one of the wonderful things about market forces: the ability to fulfil desires.

Regulators have forgotten that economic regulation is a substitute for, and not a complement to, competitive rivalry. As such, regulation should only be used (as a substitute for market forces) where necessary, and regulators should consider carefully what the effect of their policies will be. Regulation should be tailored to mitigate specific anticompetitive harms or to remove "public policy-relevant" barriers to entry, and should not be imposed just because regulators have the power and ability to do so. Regulation is an expensive and inefficient form of wealth allocation. Competition is an efficient form of allocation.

As we also explain, today's regulatory policy is expressed as a "transition to competition"—i.e., when markets have been sufficiently nurtured by regulators they may be ready for competition forces, rather like children being raised by loving parents being made ready to venture into the world alone—but nonetheless fails to articulate a coherent view of long-term industry structure. This absence of analytical cohesion begs questions of what is this transition to? What will the telecommunications industry look like? These are hard question with significant societal implications and, therefore, cannot be approached with a cavalier or cynical attitude.

Ideally, regulatory policy should not pick winners and losers. Rather, regulation should seek to promote entry in telecommunications markets. The test of regulatory efficacy should be whether policies are promoting entry. The goal must be independent entry, not artificially subsidised. The moment the subsidy, be it from other operators, taxation or consumers, disappears, the beneficiary of the subsidy will likely disappear with it.

Perhaps because the EU started later than the US did, the EU did not repeat many of the mistakes made by the US. The EU does not seem to be as influenced by trade war considerations either, at this point. The EU policies of the Single Market and the Information Society appear more important than naked mercantilism. EU policy makers are more concerned about US dominance through the Internet than worrying about allocating rents to favoured competitors. This might explain why the EU is now taking action to mandate local loop unbundling and seem open to trying anything else that may, in the opinion of regulators, lead to greater Internet use. This air of desperation, however, can lead to poor policies. The EU's embrace of the essential facilities doctrine as the basis for telecommunications regulation is troublesome. The essential facilities doctrine is a tool of competition law enforcement that should be used only as a last resort. When access through the essential facilities principle is coupled with EU concepts of non-discriminatory (internal) pricing and joint dominance, reasonable incentives for creation of alternative networks may be harmed. Similarly, the EU's move towards "light-handed regulation"—absent other alternative steps to reduce barriers to entry or to mitigate strategic anticompetitive conduct—is also troubling.

II. WHAT WILL WORK?

Many portions of telecommunications market are functioning extremely well, and correspondingly there is no need for further regulation. For those areas that are functioning poorly (e.g., local access), it is the responsibility of policy-makers to find constructive ways to improve this performance. Regulation should only occur if economic costs of intervention do not outweigh competitive benefits. As such, policy-makers must be on constant guard to mitigate only those "policy-relevant barriers to entry" discussed *passim*.

A. Local Markets

The one portion of the telecommunications market that is seen as a continued and difficult problem is local telecommunications, sometimes expressed as the local or end-user access market. What can be done about this market, assuming regulation has anything beneficial to offer? As stated above, the goal must be promotion of entry. This is not to say subsidised or artificial entry. Mere promotion of a perpetual resale of existing telecommunications infrastructure will not work. The real problem is that dominant firms control access to the monopoly local plant. The problem can be solved by entry of new alternative rival suppliers. We need and want vigorous price and non-price competition; elastic supply and demand; low switching costs; low barriers to entry. Regulators must keep this in mind when considering restructuring of the industry.

Why restructure? Two words: real competition. Sometimes, regulators use this phrase to mean a certain number of competitors being present in a market or a certain division of market shares. Real competition does not mean a mathematical tallying of incumbent lost market share. This is counter-productive and will likely lead to a situation where consumers subsidise competitors; in effect consumers will pay more for the privilege of receiving poor service from a large number of "competitors," hardly the best method to sell the general public on the benefits of competition. They may long for the good old monopoly days. Competition will not be promoted just by hurting incumbents. It bears repeating in order to remember that the policy must be to protect competition, not competitors.

Market definitions may be difficult in telecommunications. Likewise market share tests should not be used mechanically. For example, it is relatively easy to enter the "long distance" market in the US and the EU. Therefore, high market shares alone are not determinative of market power.

Regulators must realise and act on the axiom that competition is not a zero sum game. Promoting entry and expansion rather than splitting the market will give the best results. What will promote sustainable entry into the local access market? The creation and use of alternative means of access would be very helpful. We need more loops, not a perpetual resale of existing plant. The best solution would be for alternative, non-incumbent distribution companies to prosper—selling loops on a wholesale to retail providers. However, regulatory burdens make it less likely that alternatives will be built. Regulatory policy should therefore borrow from medicine and take as its first principle: "do no harm."

The reality, however, is that much of today's regulation does much harm. There are exceptions, such as the EU's recognition that the licensing process itself is a barrier to entry and should be changed to a general authorisation, with fees as low as possible. The EU is also to be commended for its universal service policy, placing as light a burden as possible on the market to meet universal service concerns. The result is that only one EU Member State even has a universal service support fund. Contrast this with the US where due to wilful confusion of universal service objectives and the availability of a ready source of revenue (that at least does not have to be called a tax, even though it is), telecommunications markets are burdened with a deadweight loss that must ultimately be paid by consumers and that acts as a detriment to entry.

Other fees are extracted from market participants, notably for rights to use spectrum. We examined how spectrum allocation procedures for satellites can burden the industry and be a trade barrier. Auctions for mobile telephone licenses can also be a problem, demonstrated historically by the large sums of money raised in the US from auctioning PCS rights. Doubtless US government officials congratulated themselves at the time over the money raised, money that was theirs without the political difficulties associated with raising taxes. It probably never occurred to them that these high fees would be a drag on the industry; they probably do not realise still that these fees may be a major reason digital mobile telephony has not been very successful in the US.

Once again, a contrast with Europe is illustrative. Instead of a patchwork of conflicting standards, spotty coverage and complex roaming arrangements, the GSM industry offers near ubiquitous coverage, easy roaming, declining prices, and increasing innovation. The EU leads the US in mobile penetration and usage. Until now, auctions have not been universally used in Europe to distribute mobile spectrum rights. The high sums bid in the UK for rights to supply third generation mobile service demonstrates that those days may be over. The European mobile industry, and certainly consumers, will suffer as a result. There is no such thing as a free lunch, and the auction fees will be paid through slower development and higher prices.

B. International Markets

The pernicious effects of the current trend in regulatory cynicism are clearest in the area of international traffic exchanges. Unfortunately, the US is leading the way in increasing tensions in this area—in fact, the leading US export in telecommunications regulation may be the reality of its cynical neo-mercantilist policy—because trade promotion has become of naked paramount concern to the FCC. The FCC's actions showed that it really did not trust the WTO commitments of other nations and would continue to act in furtherance of US trade policy. The Benchmarks Order and the resultant judicial decision is really an embarrassing case for the US. The incident demonstrates ignorance of how international traffic exchanges occur, the ITU process, and principles of international comity.

So far the EU has not retaliated in kind. Trade concerns are influencing the EU, however, as demonstrated by its abortive effort to promote international interconnection for intra-EU international traffic. Removing intra-EU traffic from the settlements rate regime would have opened the door for non-EU nations, in particular US based carriers, to plead the WTO Telecoms Treaty as mandating similar treatment for all international traffic, treatment that the US would certainly find a way to avoid giving foreigners. Thus we see the paradoxical effect of the WTO Telecoms Treaty: a jurisdiction afraid to take liberalising steps because of trade war concerns. This result is the responsibility of the neo-mercantilist policies of the US.

The FCC action in the area of submarine cable landing rights is also cynical in nature and detrimental to the interests of consumers. Rather than promoting growth of available facilities, the FCC was responsive to competitor attempts to restrict market entry and divide customers among competitors. Allocating customers or forbidding customers from selecting certain providers (what the EU did in the MCI WorldCom merger decision) is the rankest market interference. An EU study did not recommend that the EU take the same approach that the FCC did regarding submarine cables, but there is apparently a lot of confusion over the FCC action throughout the world.

Even though unilateral lowering of trade barriers is economically advantageous for the nations brave enough to so act, it goes against human nature (and political reality) to expect targets of US trade imperialism not to retaliate. The prognosis, therefore, is not good. There are, however, some encouraging signs. Though the record of reviewing mergers is mixed, progress has been made in sophistication of review and imposing appropriate remedies. There is still a tendency, particularly in the US, to extract remedies unrelated to changed market conditions caused by mergers. As opposed to some mergers, such as in the aerospace industry, the plethora of recent telecoms mergers have not led to any major international public rows.

III.   AND FINALLY

Although we have attempted to shine the light of truth on today's telecommunications regulatory process and the dangers inherent in many of the current practices, it was never our intention to be unduly harsh or destructive. Rather, it is because we care about the state of telecommunications markets that we are obligated to remind regulators of their obligations to serve the interests of consumers, not a few well-connected firms and their political protectors. So in parting, we urge regulators and enforcement officials to act so as to promote consumer welfare, to eschew cynicism, and to drop the weapons of the telecoms trade war before it is to late. We say to regulators, as Hamlet entreated his mother:

"O, throw away the worser part of it, And live the purer with the other half."

Appendix: The FCC's Competitive Carrier Paradigm

W E DECIDED TO dedicate this Annex to a brief examination of the major cases of the FCC's *Competitive Carrier* Paradigm because, in our view, it represents the epitome of what a well-reasoned, analytically coherent, and narrowly-tailored regulatory initiative should be.[1] Indeed, it represents the very best of what good government should be.

That is to say, prior to the break-up of the old AT&T monopoly, forward-looking people at the FCC believed that, with the appropriate regulatory framework, it was actually possible to have competition for long-distance service on the trunk-side of the switch.[2] Such a "radical" view was considered economic heresy at the time, especially since your home phone was actually considered an integral part of the overall public switched telephone network. (For those that remember, this is why the old Bell system telephones were actually hard-wired into the network, and the only choice of colour was basic black.) Indeed, there are legions of tales about how AT&T's lobbyists would visit the FCC, pick-up the telephone receiver for emphasis, and say with a straight face that it the FCC decided to proceed with its actions, there would be no dial tone. (If ever there was a case of political pressure, this tactic was probably it.)

Despite such pessimism, however, the FCC's then-bold actions actually *worked*. Why? Because the FCC set forth a clear vision of long-term industry structure, and never deviated from this framework.

II. BOLD BEGINNINGS

The *Competitive Carrier* process started actually in 1980 (pre-MFJ), when the FCC completely re-thought the way it regulates the domestic, long-distance service industry. In order to promote competition for long-distance service, the FCC devised a regulatory scheme designed, in part, to spur new entry into the

---

[1] Indeed, all of the various orders related to this paradigm would fill far too many notebooks and, moreover, this topic has been covered extensively in other journals. See, e.g., Scott M. Schoenwald, "Regulating Competition in the Interexchange Market: The Dominant/Nondominant Carrier Approach and the Evolution of Forbearance", (1997) 49 *Fed. Comm. L.J.* 367.

[2] See, e.g., Nina Cornell, Peter Greenhalgh & Daniel Kelley, *Social Objectives and Competition in Common Carrier Communications: Incompatible or Inseparable?*, (Federal Communications Commission OPP Working Paper No. 1, 1980).

marketplace. The mechanism derived was the dominant/non-dominant regulatory scheme.[3] Under this process, if the FCC determined that a common carrier was "non-dominant," the regulatory requirements imposed on that non-dominant carrier would be substantially reduced—if not outright eliminated. Such "streamlined" regulation included, but was not limited to: (a) a presumption that the rates charged by a non-dominant carrier would be *per se* just and reasonable; and (b) reduced notice periods for non-dominant carrier tariff filings.[4]

As we show below, what is particularly significant about the FCC's approach is that the FCC deliberately did not first define the relevant markets for telecommunications services or consider whether these markets were competitive and regulate them accordingly. In other words, rather than apply the mechanistic, "competition law by the numbers" in favour with so many policymakers and practitioners today, the FCC did their homework and returned to economic principles to solve the problem. (After all, one cannot ignore the laws of economics just as one cannot ignore the laws of gravity.)

III. THE FIRST STEPS

In its *First Report & Order*,[5] the FCC defined a dominant carrier to be any carrier that "possesses market power."[6] According to the FCC,

"Market power refers to the control a firm can exercise in setting the price of its output. A firm with market power is able to engage in conduct that may be anticompetitive or otherwise inconsistent with the public interest. This may entail setting price above competitive costs in order to earn supranormal profits, or setting price below competitive costs to forestall entry by new competitors or to eliminate existing competitors. In contrast, a competitive firm, lacking market power, must take the market price as given, because if it raises price it will face an unacceptable loss of business, and

---

[3] See *Policy & Rules Concerning Rates for Competitive Common Carrier Services and Facilities Authorisations Therefore*, CC Docket No. 79–252 ("*Competitive Carrier Proceeding*"), Notice of Inquiry and Proposed Rulemaking, 77 FCC 2d 308 (1979); *First Report & Order*, 85 FCC 2d 1 (1980); Further Notice of Proposed Rulemaking, 84 FCC 2d 445 (1981), *Second Report & Order*, 91 FCC 2d 59 (1982); recon. 93 FCC 2d 54 (1983); Second Further Notice of Proposed Rulemaking, FCC 82–187, released 21 April 1982; Third Further Notice of Proposed Rulemaking, Mimeo No. 3347, released June 14, 1983, 48 Fed. Reg. 28,292 (June 21, 1983); *Third Report & Order*, Mimeo No. 46,791, released October 6, 1983; 48 Fed. Reg. 46,791 (Oct. 6, 1983); *Fourth Report & Order*, 95 FCC 2d 554 (1983); Fourth Further Notice of Proposed Rulemaking, 96 FCC 2d 1191 (1984); *Fifth Report & Order*, 98 FCC 2d 1191 (1984); *Sixth Report & Order*, 99 FCC 2d 1020 (1985), rev'd, MCI v. FCC, 765 F.2d 1186 (D.C. Cir. 1985).

[4] An important complement to the FCC's Competitive Carrier paradigm was its its 1980 MTS/WATS resale decision, see, e.g., Resale and Shared Use of Common Carrier Domestic Public Switched Network Servs., *Report and Order*, 83 F.C.C.2d 167, 48 Rad. Reg. 2d (P & F) 1067 (1980), which helped new entrants, inter alia, to appear to consumers that they had a nationwide, facilities-based presence until their networks could be completed.

[5] *In re Policy and Rules Concerning Rates for Competitive Common Carrier Services and Facilities Authorisations Therefor*, Docket No. 79–252, 85 FCC 2d 1 (1980).

[6] See also 47 C.F.R. § 61.3(o)("dominant carrier" is defined as any "carrier found by the Commission to have market power (i.e., power to control prices)").

if it lowers price it will face unrecoverable monetary losses in an attempt to supply the market demand at that price."[7]

The FCC believed that in order to determine whether a firm can exercise market power, the appropriate starting point should be an examination of whether there are any "clearly identifiable market features." According to the FCC, such features could include "the number and size distribution of competing firms, the nature of barriers to entry, and the availability of reasonably substitutable services."[8]

In the *First Report & Order*, however, the FCC particularly focused on whether or not a carrier controlled "bottleneck facilities." The FCC defined control of bottleneck facilities as whenever

"a firm or group of firms has sufficient command over some essential commodity or facility in its industry or trade to be able to impede new entrants. Thus, bottleneck control describes the structural characteristics of a market that new entrants must either be allowed to share the bottleneck facility or fail."[9]

According to the FCC, control of bottleneck facilities was "prima facia evidence of market power requiring detailed regulatory scrutiny."[10]

At the time of the *First Report & Order*, the MFJ did not exist. Thus, the FCC found that "AT&T, including its 23 associated telephone companies and its Long Lines Department, dominates the telephone market by any method of classification."[11] The FCC gave three general reasons to support its conclusion.

First, the FCC found that AT&T at that time controlled access to over 80 per cent of the nation's telephones. Because many of AT&T's competitors required access to that network if they were to succeed, the FCC reasoned that AT&T possessed control of bottleneck facilities. Thus, under the standard articulated above, the FCC concluded that AT&T must be treated as a dominant carrier.[12]

Second, the FCC reasoned that AT&T had market power in long distance telephone service given its "overwhelming share of the MTS[13] and WATS[14] market." According to the FCC, the growing demand for long-distance telephone service and the current difficulties of entering this market on a large scale with alternative distribution facilities conferred substantial market power on AT&T. Thus, according to the FCC, because there was "a very real possibility" that the report of AT&T's long-run profit maximising behaviour, in the absence of regulation, would be to increase price above cost for long distance service,

---

[7] *First Report & Order* at ¶ 56.

[8] *Ibid.*, at ¶ 57.

[9] *Ibid.*, at ¶ 59.

[10] *Ibid.*, at ¶ 58.

[11] *Ibid.*, at ¶ 62.

[12] *Ibid.*

[13] "MTS" stands for "Message Telecommunications Service," which is AT&T's name for standard, switched telephone service.

[14] "WATS" stands for "Wide Area Telecommunications Service." This service is basically discounted toll service provided by all long-distance and local phone companies.

continued application of the FCC's "full panoply" of traditional regulations to AT&T's long distance telephone service was warranted.[15]

Third, the FCC found that AT&T has market power in the private line service market. According to the FCC, AT&T's revenues from private line services in 1978 amounted to over $ 2 billion, while the revenues of the specialised common carriers were about $ 153 million. While the FCC stated that a precise determination of AT&T's market share in private line was not possible, the FCC nonetheless concluded that AT&T was dominant in virtually every private line service market where other common carriers also competed.[16]

IV. REFINEMENTS TO THE PARADIGM

After AT&T was forced to divest its local loop facilities under the MFJ, the FCC decided to adapt its initial analysis to the changed conditions of the market. After all, even though AT&T was forced to divest itself of its local loop plant, AT&T—as the dominant player in the market in the long-distance market—nonetheless retained the ability to raise prices and restrict output.

For this reason, in the FCC's *Fourth Report & Order*[17] the FCC elaborated on its market power paradigm for long-distance service. In this order, the FCC outlined both the Areeda & Turner approach and the Landes & Posner approach for analysing the presence of market power. Under the Areeda & Turner approach, market power is defined as "the ability to raise prices by restricting output." That is to say, in a competitive market, a firm finds it unprofitable to restrict output; if it did, some of its potential buyers simply would turn to alternative suppliers that stand ready to sell to them at the competitive price. A decision by a firm lacking market power to restrict output does not significantly lessen output in the market, and thus does not raise prices in the market. In contrast, a firm possessing market power may find it profitable to restrict its output to a level below what it would supply in a competitive market. Without sufficient close alternative suppliers, enough of its potential buyers will pay a supracompetitive price for the smaller output that the firm's total profits will rise. In this case, the firm has the ability to restrict market output, raise market prices, and impair consumer welfare.[18]

Under the Landes & Posner approach, the definition of market power focuses on the ability to raise and maintain price above the competitive level without driving away so many customers as to make the increase unprofitable. For purposes of this test, the competitive price is based on opportunity cost, not historical cost. That is to say, in some markets, a firm earns "economic rents" because it possesses

---

[15] *First Report & Order* at ¶ 63.

[16] *Ibid.,* at ¶ 64.

[17] In re Policy & Rules Concerning Rates for Competitive Common Carrier Services and Facilities Authorisations Therefor, 95 FCC 2d 554 (Released November 2, 1983).

[18] *Ibid.,* at ¶ 7 (citations omitted).

a scarce resource obtained at less than its current market value (opportunity cost). Its average cost of production, based on historical cost, may be lower than that of other firms in the market because of scarce resources. But, explained the FCC, these rents should not be confused with profits attributable to market power. According to the FCC, the difference is that monopoly profits generally result from artificially decreased market output while economic rents do not. Thus, cautioned the FCC, the supracompetitive-price approach to defining market power must be applied precisely so that economic rents are distinguished from monopoly profits, *i.e.*, so that price reflects opportunity rather than historical costs.[19]

With this introduction, the FCC then attempted to define the relevant product and geographic markets. According to the FCC, the three different types of interstate domestic interexchange services—MTS/WATS, private line and public switched record—are actually in the same product market because they are close demand and/or supply substitutes. Thus, the FCC held that for purposes of assessing the competitive checks on the prices charged by *non-dominant* carriers, all interstate, domestic, interexchange services comprise a single relevant product market with no relevant submarkets.[20] As for the geographic market, the FCC concluded that there is a national market for interstate, domestic, interexchange telecommunications because of the supply substitutability and low entry barriers.[21]

Notwithstanding the above, however, the FCC specifically stated that it would not consider in this proceeding the appropriateness of applying this market definition in assessing the market power of AT&T.[22]

---

[19] *Ibid.*, at ¶ 8 (citations omitted).

[20] *Ibid.*, at ¶ 14.

[21] *Ibid.*, at ¶ 26.

[22] What is particularly interesting to note is the fact that on the same day which the FCC adopted its *Fourth Report & Order*, the FCC issued an notice of inquiry (NOI) to determine "the appropriate long-run regulation of AT&T's basic interstate services under the policies of the Communications Act of 1934 and the statutory obligations of the Commission." *In re Long Run Regulation of AT&T's Basic Domestic Interstate Services*, 95 FCC 2d 510 (1987) at ¶ 1. In this NOI, the FCC sought comments on, inter alia, the level of AT&T's then-current market power. The FCC suggested that interested parties use, as a starting point, the market definitions outlined in the *Fourth Report & Order, supra, ibid.*, at ¶ 53.

Turning to more substantive points, the FCC also recognised that the actual or readily-available capacity of AT&T's competitors in the relevant market, and not just their actual sales, poses a check on AT&T's ability to restrict output and thereby raise market prices. However the FCC recognised that while domestic, interstate resellers (i.e. non-facilities based competitors) can also provide a check on AT&T, the strength of this rivalry depends on AT&T's rate structure. *Ibid.*, at ¶¶ 54–55.

Moreover, the FCC found that another factor relevant to the analysis of AT&T's market power is the entry and expansion of its competitors. That is to say, the FCC recognised that in an unregulated market, the success of new rivals and a firm's falling market share can suggest that an existing firm lacks market power or that its market power is declining. This is because new rivals can increase market output and check the ability of a firm to restrict its output and thereby raise market prices. However, the FCC also recognised that the absence of entry does not show that an existing firm possesses market power, because existing firms may be charging competitive prices because of competition among themselves or the threat of potential entry, and thereby make entry unattractive. *Ibid.* at ¶ 56.

Finally, the FCC recognised that persistent supracompetitive profits can indicate that an unregulated firm possess market power. According to the FCC, evaluation of a firm's profits as supracompetitive

V. STREAMLINING OF BUSINESS SERVICES

The next step in this gradual process was for the FCC to "streamline" its regulation of AT&T's business long-distance services.[23] As support for this action, the FCC specifically found that AT&T's competitors "have enough readily available supply capacity to constrain AT&T's market behaviour and inhibit it from charging excessive rates."[24] Moreover, the FCC rejected the argument that AT&T enjoys market power simply by virtue of "its size, superior resources, financial strength, and technical capabilities." According to the FCC,

> "The issue is not whether AT&T has advantages, but, if so, why, and whether any such advantages are so great as to preclude the effective functioning of a competitive market. An incumbent firm in virtually any market will have certain advantages, scale economies, established relationships with suppliers, ready access to capital, etc. Such advantages do not, however, mean that these markets are not competitive, nor do they mean that it is appropriate for government regulators to deny the incumbent efficiencies its size confers in order to make it easier for others to compete. Indeed, the competitive process itself is largely about trying to develop one's own advantages, and all firms need not be equal in all respects for this process to work."[25]

In fact, the FCC recognised that AT&T may, in certain respects, be disadvantaged by its size, because, for example, it may be more difficult for AT&T to address the individualised needs of some customers or to respond quickly to market-place changes.[26]

Finally, the FCC found that because the business long-distance telephone market was competitive, continued stringent regulation on AT&T actually

must reflect the riskiness of the firm's activities and its ability to earn economic rents. However, the FCC pointed out that the absence of such profits does not indicate the lack of power, because while the firm may be engaging in strategic behaviour or simply not earning the profits that its market position would seem to make possible, the firm may be able to earn supracompetitive profits in the future. Moreover, the FCC recognised that regulation of AT&T has constrained its overall rate of return though at times AT&T has earned less than its authorised rate of return. Thus, the FCC stated that the fact that in the past AT&T has earned persistent supracompetitive profits is not empirical evidence that AT&T would be powerless under less stringent regulation. However, the FCC further recognised that future evidence that AT&T is earning persistent high profits may indicate that the prevailing regulation and certain options involving further relaxation of regulatory compliance may be "undesirable." *Ibid.*, at ¶ 57.

However, despite this NOI, nothing ever became of the inquiry. On 11 January 1990, the FCC released an order terminating the NOI. The FCC supported its actions by reasoning that such an NOI was unnecessary because of the "fundamental changes in the telecommunications industry," such as the MFJ, "the wide-spread deployment of equal access for AT&T's competitors, the installation of sophisticated nation-wide fibre optic networks by MCI . . . and Sprint . . . , as well as other companies, and continued decreases in AT&T's share of the interstate long distance telephone market." January at ¶ 3.

[23] *In re Competition in the Interstate Interexchange Market place*, 6 FCC Rcd 5889 (1991)(IXC Rulemaking Order).

[24] IXC Rulemaking Order at ¶ 48.

[25] *Ibid.*, at ¶ 60.

[26] *Ibid.*, at 5891, n.100.

imposed "indirect costs on consumers by distorting the competitive process." For example, the FCC found that stringent regulation denies AT&T the full pricing flexibility needed to react to market conditions and customer demands and thus diminishes AT&T's ability to compete as a full-fledged competitor. Second, the FCC found that by creating regulatory delays and uncertainty, stringent regulation reduces the value of AT&T's service offerings. Third, the FCC found that affording AT&T's competitors substantial advanced notice of AT&T's price and service changes fosters a "reactive market, rather than a proactive one," and thus reduces the incentives for AT&T's competitors to "stay on their competitive toes." Finally, the FCC found that by negating, in whole or in part, AT&T's ability to take advantage, as its competitors can, of being a "first-mover" in the market, lessens AT&T's incentive to initiate pro-consumer price and service changes.[27]

VI. REVISION OF AT&T'S PRICE CAPS

Next, the FCC revised the price cap rules for AT&T.[28] In this order, the FCC removed AT&T's commercial services from price cap regulation,[29] because it found that there are enough competitive alternatives to AT&T's commercial long-distance service to constrain AT&T's exercise of monopoly power for these services.[30] To support this decision, the FCC held, *inter alia*, that several factors would prevent the largest interexchange carriers from engaging in oligopolistic co-ordination resulting in prices above competitive levels. For example, the FCC held that because the networks of the interexchange carriers have significant capacity, the cost of serving additional traffic is very low and, conversely, the cost savings associated with a traffic reduction are also "quite low." Thus, concluded the FCC, these carriers have a great incentive to protect their substantial investment in these facilities by keeping their prices low to attract and keep customers. Moreover, the FCC also found that the possibility of oligopolistic co-ordination to raise prices is limited by the demonstrated willingness and ability of commercial long distance customers to move among various commercial long distance services offered by the numerous interexchange carriers.[31]

---

[27] *Ibid.*, at ¶ 80.

[28] *In re Revisions to Price Cap Rules for AT&T Corp., Report & Order*, FCC Docket No. 95–18 (rel. 12 January 1995).

[29] However, the FCC did not remove either analogue private line or 800 directory assistance prom price cap regulation in this order.

[30] 12 January Order at ¶ 26.

[31] *Ibid.*, at ¶ 26.

VII. THE LIGHT AT THE END OF THE TUNNEL

Finally, after fifteen long years, the market for domestic long distance service was sufficiently rivalrous as to warrant the de-regulation of AT&T and to reclassify it as a non-dominant carrier.[32] De-regulating the last remnant of "Ma Bell" did not come easy, however.

For example, many parties argued that AT&T had market power simply by virtue of having a 60 per cent market share. Upon review, however, the FCC found that while AT&T did have a very large market share, AT&T nonetheless faced a very elastic demand curve, in which consumers were very likely to switch carriers in the event of a price increase or unsatisfactory service. The FCC further found that AT&T no longer controlled any bottleneck facilities, and supply was highly elastic both in terms of excess capacity and the number of competing firms. The FCC also found strong evidence of nonprice competition in the form of frequent-flyer points or tie-ins with other products.

Given such a market structure, the FCC found that it would be difficult for AT&T to successfully engage in strategic anticompetitive conduct. As such, the FCC decided to remove the asymmetrical regulation previously imposed on AT&T, realizing that the economic harms created by asymmetrical dominant carrier regulation outweighed the public interest benefits the dominant carrier regulation was originally intended to achieve.

This is not to say that politics did not affect the outcome of the proceeding in any way. Quite to the contrary, despite overwhelming economic evidence and legal authority to support this decision,[33] as mentioned *passim*, Reed Hundt nonetheless extracted a [US] $100 million "voluntary" commitment to wire the schools of America, as well as significant protections for "low volume" and "low income" users.[34]

VIII. CONCLUSION

The success of the FCC's *Competitive Carrier* paradigm is undeniable. To give readers some idea of this success, at the time of this writing, not only do many

---

[32] *In re Motion of AT&T Corp. to Be Reclassified as a Non-Dominant Carrier*, FCC 95–427, 11 FCC Rcd 3271 (rel. Oct. 23, 1995).

[33] See Jerry Duvall et al., "Market Performance in the Long Distance Telecommunications Industry: The AT&T Non-Dominance Petition", Paper presented to the 2nd Annual Conference of Consortium for Research on Telecommunications Policy, Evanston, Ill., 11 May 1996 <http://www.phoenix-center.org/library/longlist.doc>.

[34] "Statement of Reed Hundt in Response to AT&T's Pledge of $150 Million to Help Put the Nation's Schools on the Information Superhighway", 1995 FCC LEXIS 7113, 31 Oct. 1995 ("We at the FCC hope that AT&T's gift" mysteriously made concurrent with the FCC's decision to declare AT&T as a non-dominant carrier for domestic service "of free internet access and voice-mail to all the children of America will catalyze a nationwide public/private partnership to network all classrooms as the President and Vice President have challenged".)

discount plans offer rates as low as (US) $0.07/minute, but consumers also benefit from the on-going non-price competition (e.g., frequent flyer miles, cash to transfer carriers, etc.)

Accordingly, the FCC's *Competitive Carrier* Paradigm is perhaps the greatest example of what a well-conceived and narrowly-tailored regulatory policy can do to maximise consumer welfare successfully. As such, policy-makers now attempting to liberalise and restructure their own markets should read this material carefully and take it to heart, for many useful lessons can be gleaned there from. As the old adage goes, those who do not learn from history are doomed to repeat it.

Index